Cases and Materials on the Law of International Organizations

In less than 100 years, international organizations have evolved from curiosities into keystones of international law. What began long ago as an unremarkable effort to coordinate a limited number of technical issues has grown into a global, multilevel, blended governing project with diverse competences in most fields of human endeavor and interests.

Law graduates who enter the field of international law, as well as political science, international relations, and diplomacy, are increasingly expected to have a strong knowledge of the law of international organizations. Beyond knowledge, graduates are also expected to be able to solve new emerging legal problems confronting organizations.

This book introduces students to the law of international organizations through the careful study of the most recent cases and other materials from the International Court of Justice, United Nations Security Council and General Assembly, World Trade Organization, international criminal tribunals, European Union, European Court of Human Rights, International Labour Organization, various domestic courts and arbitral panels, and other bodies. In doing so, it undertakes a critical examination of legal rights and duties, exposing the fundamental questions that arise when addressing a range of issues within an organization. In order to provide the best foundation, the textbook focuses on several key topics: the law of treaties, creation of organizations, membership, powers of organizations, legal effects of their acts, organs, immunities, and responsibility.

This book is best suited for students who are studying international organizations and who have already had one or more courses on international and/or European law.

William Worster is a Senior Lecturer at The Hague University of Applied Sciences, where he specializes in international law, international migration law, and the law of international organizations.

Cases and Materials on the Law of International Organizations

William Worster

First published 2021
by Routledge
2 Park Square, Milton Park, Abingdon, Oxon OX14 4RN

and by Routledge
52 Vanderbilt Avenue, New York, NY 10017

Routledge is an imprint of the Taylor & Francis Group, an informa business

© 2021 William Worster

The right of William Worster to be identified as author of this work has been asserted by him in accordance with sections 77 and 78 of the Copyright, Designs and Patents Act 1988.

All rights reserved. No part of this book may be reprinted or reproduced or utilized in any form or by any electronic, mechanical, or other means, now known or hereafter invented, including photocopying and recording, or in any information storage or retrieval system, without permission in writing from the publishers.

Trademark notice: Product or corporate names may be trademarks or registered trademarks, and are used only for identification and explanation without intent to infringe.

British Library Cataloguing in Publication Data
A catalogue record for this book is available from the British Library

Library of Congress Cataloging-in-Publication Data
Names: Worster, William Thomas, author.
Title: Cases and materials on the law of international organizations / William Thomas Worster.
Description: Abingdon, Oxon ; New York, NY : Routledge, 2020. | Includes bibliographical references and index. | Identifiers: LCCN 2020014963 | ISBN 9781138056640 (hardback) | ISBN 9781138056664 (paperback) | ISBN 9781315165189 (ebook)
Subjects: LCSH: International agencies—Law and legislation. | LCGFT: Casebooks (Law)
Classification: LCC KZ4850 .W67 2020 | DDC 341.2—dc23
LC record available at https://lccn.loc.gov/2020014963

ISBN: 978-1-138-05664-0 (hbk)
ISBN: 978-1-138-05666-4 (pbk)
ISBN: 978-1-315-16518-9 (ebk)

Typeset in Sabon
by Swales & Willis, Exeter, Devon, UK

For Vanessa, who has endless patience.

Contents

List of cases and materials	xi
List of abbreviations	xxv

1 Introduction to international organizations — 1

- 1.1 Introduction to international organizations — 1
- 1.2 Definition of an international organization — 2
- 1.3 International organizations as a field of study — 6
- 1.4 Overview of this textbook — 7

2 Law of treaties — 10

- 2.1 Treaties regarding international organizations — 10
- 2.2 Special rules in the law of treaties applying to international organizations — 12
  - 2.2.1 Treaties adopted within an international organization — 13
  - 2.2.2 Adherence to treaties — 17
  - 2.2.3 Reservations to treaties — 19
  - 2.2.4 Invalidity of treaties — 20
  - 2.2.5 Interpretation of treaties — 29

3 Creation and dissolution — 34

- 3.1 Creation of an international organization — 34
  - 3.1.1 International legal personality — 34
    - 3.1.1.1 Identifying international legal personality — 35
    - 3.1.1.2 Objective and relative international legal personality — 48
  - 3.1.2 Agreement under international law by subjects of international law — 54
  - 3.1.3 Meaningful independence — 56
  - 3.1.4 Certain objectives — 66
- 3.2 Dissolution of an international organization — 68

4 Membership — 76

- 4.1 Types of members — 76
- 4.2 Qualification for membership — 80
    - 4.2.1 Statehood — 80
    - 4.2.2 Other substantive requirements — 89
    - 4.2.3 Assessing qualifications — 95
    - 4.2.4 Procedural law of the decision on qualification — 99
    - 4.2.5 Succession to membership — 108
    - 4.2.6 Representation and credentials — 124
- 4.3 Suspension or termination of membership — 127
    - 4.3.1 Extinction of the state — 127
    - 4.3.2 Suspension of membership — 127
    - 4.3.3 Termination of membership — 128

5 Powers — 131

- 5.1 Sources of powers — 131
    - 5.1.1 Express attribution of powers — 136
    - 5.1.2 Implied powers — 141
    - 5.1.3 Inherent powers — 171
    - 5.1.4 Balance of powers with member states — 176
    - 5.1.5 Other limitations on powers — 184
- 5.2 Issues of ultra vires acts — 187

6 Legal effects of acts — 195

- 6.1 Basis for legal effect — 195
- 6.2 Legal value of the act — 208
    - 6.2.1 Binding legal effect — 213
        - 6.2.1.1 United Nations Security Council — 213
        - 6.2.1.2 United Nations General Assembly — 227
        - 6.2.1.3 International Court of Justice — 234
    - 6.2.2 Non-binding legal effect — 239

7 Organs — 254

- 7.1 Definition of organs — 254
- 7.2 "Family" structure — 255
    - 7.2.1 Principal organs — 264
        - 7.2.1.1 Limited competences — 265
        - 7.2.1.2 Institutional balance — 268
        - 7.2.1.3 Judicial review — 276
    - 7.2.2 Subsidiary organs — 280
        - 7.2.2.1 Independence — 281
        - 7.2.2.2 Judicial review of a principal organ — 286
- 7.3 Function of the organ — 303

8	**Privileges and immunities**	**308**
	8.1 Legal basis for privileges and immunities	*308*
	8.1.1 Jurisdiction	*308*
	8.1.2 Privileges and immunities	*309*
	8.2 Justification for privileges and immunities of international organizations	*309*
	8.2.1 Functional necessity for independence	*309*
	8.2.2 Limitations of the functional theory	*322*
	8.3 Privileges and immunities enjoyed by different actors	*331*
	8.3.1 International organizations	*332*
	8.3.2 State representatives	*338*
	8.3.3 Employees of international organizations	*340*
	8.3.4 Experts on mission	*351*
	8.3.5 Waiver	*368*
9	**Responsibility**	**369**
	9.1 Responsibility in international law	*369*
	9.1.1 Possibility for responsibility	*369*
	9.1.2 General and special rules of responsibility	*371*
	9.2 General rules on responsibility of international organizations	*372*
	9.2.1 Existence of a binding international obligation	*373*
	9.2.2 Attribution of an internationally wrongful act	*377*
	9.2.2.1 Internationally wrongful act	*377*
	9.2.2.2 Attribution of the act	*379*
	9.2.3 Other modes of responsibility	*420*
	9.2.4 Circumstances precluding wrongfulness	*420*
	9.2.5 Consequences of responsibility	*421*
	9.3 Subsidiary responsibility for member states	*421*
10	**Conclusion**	**439**
	Index	*444*

Cases and materials

[A] et al. and the Association of Citizens Mothers of Srebrenica v. State of the Netherlands (Ministry of General Affairs) and the United Nations, Case No. 295247/HA ZA 07-2973; LJN: BD6796, Judgment, 160 International Law Reports 558 (Rechtbank 's-Gravenhage (District Court in the Hague), Civil Law Section, Netherlands, 10 July 2008) 377–379

Mahmoud Abbas, President of the State of Palestine, Letter to the Registrar of the International Criminal Court, Declaration accepting the Jurisdiction of the International Criminal Court (31 December 2014) 83

Accordance with International Law of the Unilateral Declaration of Independence by the Provisional Institutions of Self-Government of Kosovo, Advisory Opinion, 2010 ICJ Reps. 403 (International Court of Justice, 22 July 2010) 377

African Union Constitutive Act, 11 July 2000, 2158 UNTS 37733 .... 128n28

Agreement between the World Health Organization and the Pan American Sanitary [Health] Organization concerning the integration of the Pan American Sanitary Organization with the World Health Organization, 24 May 1949, 32 UNTS 387 411

Agreement between the European Union and the Federal Republic of Yugoslavia on the activities of the European Union Monitoring Mission (EUMM) in the Federal Republic of Yugoslavia, Official Journal of the European Communities [Union] L 125/2 (5 May 2001) 40n4

Agreement for the Establishment of the Global Crop Diversity Trust, 4 October 2004, FAO Treaty Doc. No. 34 40

Agreement for the Establishment of the Joint Vienna Institute, 27, 29 July, 10, 19 August 1994, 2029 UNTS 391, BGBl. III (No. 95) (12 August 2004), as amended 1 May 2003 .... 55n13

Agreement regarding the Headquarters of the Organization of the Petroleum Exporting Countries, 18 February 1974, Austria-OPEC, 2098 UNTS 416 ..... 53n10

C. F. Amerasinghe, Principles of the Institutional Law of International Organizations (Cambridge University Press, second revised edition, 2005) 2–3

Appeal Relating to the Jurisdiction of the ICAO [International Civil Aviation Organization] Council (India v. Pakistan) Judgment, 1972 ICJ Reps. 46 (International Court of Justice, 18 August 1972) 188n16

Applicability of Article VI, Section 22, of the Convention on the Privileges and Immunities of the United Nations ["Mazilu case"], Advisory Opinion, 1989 ICJ Reps. 177 (International Court of Justice, 15 December 1989) 362n25, 381n23

Application for Review of Judgment No. 273, Advisory Opinion, 1982 ICJ Reps. 325 (International Court of Justice, 20 July 1982) 170

Application for Revision of the Judgment of 11 July 1996 in the Case Concerning Application of the Convention on the Prevention and Punishment of the Crime of Genocide (Bosnia and Herzegovina v. Yugoslavia), Preliminary Objections, Judgment, 2003 ICJ Reps. 7 (International Court of Justice, 3 February 2003) 111–112, 113

Application of the Interim Accord of 13 September 1995 (The Former Yugoslav Republic of Macedonia v Greece), Judgment, 2011 ICJ Reps. 644 (International Court of Justice, 5 December 2011) 104–108

Arab Monetary Fund v. Hashim and others (No. 3), [1991] UKHL J0221-1, [1991] 2 AC 114, [1991] 2 WLR 729 (House of Lords, United Kingdom, 21 February 1991) 54

Articles of Agreement of the International Bank for Reconstruction and Development, 22 July 1944, 2 UNTS 134 as amended 338n15, 430

Austria E GmbH v. European Patent Organization, Judgment, 7 Ob 627/91, (1992) 47 Österreichische Juristenzeitung 661 (Supreme Court [OGH], Austria, 11 June 1992) 338n13

Bagosora, Ntabakuze & Nsengiyumva v. Prosecutor, Case No. ICTR-98-41-A, Decision on Aloys Ntabakuze's Motion for Injunctions, Against the Government of Rwanda Regarding the Arrest and Investigation of Lead 362–367

Convention for the Protection of Human Rights and Fundamental Freedoms ["European Convention on Human Rights"], 4 November 1950, 213 UNTS 221 165–166

Counsel Peter Erlinder (International Criminal Tribunal for Rwanda, Appeals Chamber, 6 October 2010) 362–367

Bank Bumiputra Malaysia Bhd. v. International Tin Council and Another, [1987] 2 Malaya Law Journal 732; 80 International Law Reports 24 (High Court, Malaysia, 13 January 1987) 320–322

Behrami and Behrami v France, Application No. 71412/01, Saramati v France, Germany and Norway, Application No. 78166/01, Decision as to the Admissibility (European Court of Human Rights (Grand Chamber), 2 May 2007) 383–390, 399, 430

Bosphorus Hava Yollari Turizm ve Ticaret Anonim Şirketi v. Ireland, Application No. 45036/98, Judgment (European Court of Human Rights (Grand Chamber), 30 June 2005) 401–402

Bosphorus Hava Yollari Turizm ve Ticaret AS v. Ireland, Application No. 45036/98, Decision as to the Admissibility, (European Court of Human Rights (Fourth Section), 13 September 2001) 402n32

Branno v Ministry of War, 1954-I Giurisprudenza Italiana 1, 904; 22 International Law Reports 756 (Court of Cassation (United Chambers), Italy, 14 June 1954) 311–312, 315

Broadbent, et al v. Organization of American States, et al, 628 F. 2d 27 (1980); 63 International Law Reports 337 (Court of Appeals, District of Columbia, United States, 8 January 1980) 332–338

In re B[ustani] (OPCW), Judgment No. 2232 (International Labour Organisation Administrative Tribunal, 16 July 2003) 57–63, 303

Case 9/56, Meroni & Co., Industrie Metallurgiche, S.p.A v. High Authority of the European Coal and Steel Community, Judgment (Court of Justice of the European Communities [Union], 13 June 1958) 268

Case 6/60, Jean-E. Humblet v. Belgian State, Judgment (Court of Justice of the European Communities [Union], 16 December 1960) 351n24

Case 25/60, De Bruyn v. European Parliamentary Assembly [Parliament], Judgment (Court of Justice of the European Communities [Union] (First Chamber), 1 March 1962) 331n9

Case C-22/70, Commission of the European Communities v Council of the European Communities [*In re* European Road Transport Agreement (ERTA)], Judgment (Court of Justice of the European Communities [Union], 31 March 1971) 18, 40, 48, 159–162, 163

Case 50/76, Amsterdam Bulb BV and Producktschap voor Siergewassen (Ornamental Plant Authority), Judgment (Court of Justice of the European Communities [Union], 2 February 1977) 403–407

Case 45/86, Commission of the European Communities v Council of the European Communities [*In re* Generalised Tariff Preferences] (Court of Justice of the European Communities [Union], 26 March 1987) 191–192

Case 85/86, Commission of the European Communities v Board of Governors of the European Investment Bank (EIB) (Court of Justice of the European Communities [Union], 3 March 1988) 346–351

Case C-159/90, Society for the Protection of Unborn Children [SPUC] Ireland Ltd v Grogan et al., Judgment (Court of Justice of the European Communities [Union], 4 October 1991) 176–180, 184

Case C-327/91, French Republic v. Commission of the European Communities, Judgment (Court of Justice of the European Communities [Union], 9 August 1994) 265–268, 276, 374, 438n64

Case C-376/98, Federal Republic of Germany v European Parliament and Council of the European Union [*In re* "Tobacco Directive"], Judgment (Court of Justice of the European Communities [Union], 5 October 2000) 136–141, 188, 276

Joined cases C-402/05 and C-415/05 P, Kadi and Al Barakaat International Foundation v Council and Commission of the European Union, Judgment (Court of Justice of the European Communities [Union] (Grand Chamber), 3 September 2008) 22–28, 31, 376, 400

Case C-205/06, Commission of the European Communities v Republic of Austria [*In re* bilateral agreements with third countries], Judgment (Court of Justice of the European Communities [Union] (Grand Chamber), 3 March 2009) 180–184

Case C-135/08, Rottman v Freistaat Bayern, Judgment (Court of Justice of the European Union (Grand Chamber), 2 March 2010) 30n23

Case Concerning Application of the Convention on the Prevention and Punishment of the Crime of Genocide, (Bosnia and Herzegovina v. Yugoslavia (Serbia and Montenegro)), Further Requests for the Indication of Provisional Measures, Order, 1993 ICJ Reps. 325 (International Court of Justice, 13 September 1993) 184–187, 375, 376

Case Concerning Application of the Convention on the Prevention and Punishment of the Crime of Genocide, (Bosnia and Herzegovina v Yugoslavia [Serbia and Montenegro]), Preliminary Objections, Judgment, 1996 ICJ Reps. 595 (International Court of Justice, 11 July 1996)...110n15

Case Concerning Application of the Convention on the Prevention and Punishment of the Crime of Genocide, (Bosnia and Herzegovina v. Serbia and Montenegro), Judgment, 2007 ICJ Reps. 43 (International Court of Justice, 26 February 2007) 119–121

Case Concerning Avena and Other Mexican Nationals (Mexico v United States), Judgment, 2004 ICJ Reps. 12 (International Court of Justice, 31 March 2004) ..202

Case Concerning East Timor (Portugal v Australia), Judgment, 1995 ICJ Reps. 90 (International Court of Justice, 30 June 1995) 212–213

Case Concerning Legality of Use of Force, (Yugoslavia [Serbia and Montenegro] v Belgium), Request for the Indication of Provisional Measures, Order, 1999 ICJ Reps. 124 (International Court of Justice, 2 June 1999) 110n16, 112

Case Concerning Legality of Use of Force, (Serbia and Montenegro v. Belgium), Preliminary Objections, Judgment, 2004 ICJ Reps. 279 (International Court of Justice, 15 December 2004) 113–118

CASES AND MATERIALS   xv

Case Concerning Military and Paramilitary Activities in and against Nicaragua, (Nicaragua v United States), Merits, Judgment, 1986 ICJ Reps. 14 (International Court of Justice, 27 June 1986) 231n12, 250–253

Case Concerning Questions of Interpretation and Application of the 1971 Montreal Convention Arising from the Aerial Incident at Lockerbie, (Libya v United Kingdom), Preliminary Objections, Judgment, 1988 ICJ Reps. 9 (International Court of Justice, 27 February 1998) 225–226, 277–280

Certain Expenses of the United Nations (Article 17, Paragraph 2, of the Charter), Advisory Opinion, 1962 ICJ Reps. 151 (International Court of Justice, 20 July 1962) 151–159, 188n15, 248, 269–275, 382

Charter of Fundamental Rights of the European Union, 7 December 2000, Official Journal of the European Communities [Union] C 364/1 (18 December 2000) 165

Charter of the Organization of American States, 30 April 1948, 119 UNTS 3 .... 182n27

Charter of the United Nations, 24 October 1945, 1 UNTS XVI 11, 18, 20, 29, 35–36, 38, 39, 67–68, 76–77, 95, 100, 124, 128, 130, 147, 159, 208, 209, 213, 229, 231, 244, 269, 275, 280

Chemidlin v. International Bureau of Weights and Measures, Gazette du Palais (16 October 1945), 12 International Law Reports 281 (Tribunal Civil of Versailles, France, 27 July 1945) 331n10

Competence of the General Assembly for the Admission of a State to the United Nations ["Second Admissions Case"], Advisory Opinion, 1950 ICJ Reps. 4 (International Court of Justice, 3 March 1950) 32, 100–103, 227n10, 269

Competence of the International Labour Organization in Regard to International Regulation of the Conditions of Labour of Persons Employed in Agriculture, Advisory Opinion, 1922 PCIJ (Ser. B) No. 2 (Permanent Court of International Justice, 12 August 1922) 132–133

Competence of the International Labour Organization to Regulate, Incidentally, the Personal Work of the Employer, Advisory Opinion, 1926 PCIJ (Ser. B) No. 13 (Permanent Court of International Justice, 23 June 1926) 148n3

Conditions of Admission of a State to Membership in the United Nations (Article 4 of the Charter) ["First Admissions Case"], Advisory Opinion, 1948 ICJ Reps. 57 (International Court of Justice, 28 May 1948) ..95–99, 134–135, 231n11, 304–306

Constitution of the Maritime Safety Committee of the Inter-Governmental Maritime Consultative Organization, Advisory Opinion, 1960 ICJ Reps. 150 (International Court of Justice, 8 June 1960) 192–194

Convention (I) for the Amelioration of the Condition of the Wounded and Sick in Armed Forces in the Field, 12 August 1949, 75 UNTS 31 .... 18n12

Convention of the World Meteorological Organization, 11 October 1946, WMO-No. 15, 77 UNTS 143, as amended 209–210

Convention on International Civil Aviation ["Chicago Convention"], 7 December 1944, 15 UNTS 102, ICAO Doc. 7300/9 .... 209, 226–227

Convention on International Trade in Endangered Species of Wild Fauna and Flora, 3 March 1973, 993 UNTS 243 .... 41n8

Convention on the Prevention of Marine Pollution by Dumping of Wastes and Other Matter, 29 December 1972, 1046 UNTS 120 .... 41n8

Convention on the Prohibition of the Development, Production, Stockpiling and Use of Chemical Weapons and on their Destruction ["Chemical Weapons Convention"], 27 September 2005, 1974 UNTS 45 211

Cooperatieve Producentenorganisatie van de Nederlandse Kokkelvisserij U.A. v. The Netherlands, Application No. 13645/05, Decision as to the Admissibility (European Court of Human Rights (Third Section), 20 January 2009) 403

Council of Europe, Parliamentary Assembly, Report on the enlargement of the Council Europe, Document 6975, Rapporteur: Reddemann (13 December 1993) 90–91

Council of Europe, Parliamentary Assembly, Opinion on the enlargement of the Council of Europe, Document 7148, Rapporteur: Atkinson (13 September 1994) 91–93

Council of Europe, Parliamentary Assembly, Recommendation 1247 (1994) on the enlargement of the Council of Europe, Document 7103 (4 October 1994) 93–94

Council Decision 2006/526/EC of 17 July 2006 on relations between the European Community on the one hand, and Greenland and the Kingdom of Denmark on the other, Official Journal of the European Union L 208/28 (29 July 2006) 129n30

Council Decision 2011/297/CFSP of 23 May 2011 amending Joint Action 2001/555/CFSP on the establishment of a European Union Satellite Centre, Official Journal of the European Union L 136/62 (24 May 2011) 69n16

Cristiani v Italian Latin-American Institute, Case No 5819/1985, 1986 Rivista di diritto internazionale 146, 87 International Law Reports 20 (Court of Cassation (plenary session), Italy, 25 November 1985) 313–315

Curran v City of New York, et al., 77 NYS 2d 206, 14 International Law Reports 154 (Supreme Court (Special Term) of Queen's County, New York, United States, 29 December 1947) 344–346

Dalfino v. Governing Council of European Schools and European School of Brussels I, 1982 RACE 1544, 108 International Law Reports 638 (Conseil d'Etat, Belgium, 17 November 1982) 331n11

Denmark and the Treaty on European Union["Edinburgh Agreement"], 11-12 December 1992, Official Journal of the European Communities [Union] C 348/1 (31 December 1992)...20n17

Designation of the Workers' Delegate for the Netherlands at the Third Session of the International Labour Conference, Advisory Opinion, 1922 PCIJ (Ser. B) No. 1 (Permanent Court of International Justice, 31 July 1922) 126n24

Difference Relating to Immunity from Legal Process of a Special Rapporteur of the Commission on Human Rights ["Cumaraswamy case"], Advisory Opinion, 1999 ICJ Reps. 62 (International Court of Justice, 29 April 1999) 352–361, 367, 381n23

Economic Community of West African States [ECOWAS] v BCCI [Bank of Credit and Commerce International], 1993 Clunet 353, 113 International Law Reports 473 (Court of Appeal of Paris (First Chamber), France, 13 January 1993) 48–51, 52–53

Effect of Awards of Compensation Made by the United Nations Administrative Tribunal, Advisory Opinion, 1954 ICJ Reps. 47 (International Court of Justice, 13 July 1954) 148–150, 163, 232–233, 280–281, 282–285, 303, 307, 330, 331

European Communities – Protection of Trademarks and Geographical Indications for Agricultural Products and Foodstuffs, WTO Case No. WT/DS174/1/Add.1, Request for Consultations by the United States, Addendum (World Trade Organization, 10 April 2003) 407–408

European Communities – Protection of Trademarks and Geographical Indications for Agricultural Products and Foodstuffs, WTO Case No. WT/DS174/R, Report of the Panel (World Trade Organization, 15 March 2005) 408–411

European Communities – Regime for the Importation, Sale and Distribution of Bananas ["EC-Bananas III"], WTO Case. WT/DS27/AB/R, Report of the Appellate Body (World Trade Organization, 9 September 1997) 126

Evangelical Church (Augburg and Helvitic Confessions) in Austria v. Grezda, 6 Ob 302/63, 38 International Law Reports 453 (Supreme Court, Austria, 27 February 1964) 351n23

Exchange of Greek and Turkish Populations (Lausanne Convention VI, January 30th, 1923, Article 2) (Greece v Turkey), Advisory Opinion, 1925 PCIJ (Ser. B) No. 10 (Permanent Court of International Justice, 21 February 1925) 40

Food and Agriculture Organization v. INPDAI [Istituto Nazionale di Previdenza per I Dirigenti di Aziende Industrialia (Italy)], Case No. 5399, 1983 Rivista di diritto internazionale 187, 87 International Law Reports 1 (Court of Cassation (plenary session), Italy, 18 October 1982) 315–320

H.v.d.P. v The Netherlands, Communication 217/1986, Decision on Admissibility, UN Doc. A/42/40 (Human Rights Committee, 28 August 1987) ... 64–65, 421–422

International Civil Aviation Organization [ICAO] v. Tripal Systems Pty Ltd et al., CLOUT Case No. 182 (Superior Court of Quebec, Canada, 9 September 1994) 331n8

International Criminal Court, Office of the Prosecutor, Situation in Palestine (3 April 2012) 81–82

International Institute of Refrigeration v. Elkaim, 77 International Law Reports 498 (Court of Appeal of Paris, France, 7 February 1984) (Cour de Cassation, France, 8 November 1988) 338n14

International Labour Organization, Declaration on Fundamental Principles and Rights at Work, Adopted by the International Labour Conference at its Eighty-sixth Session, Geneva, 18 June 1998, Annex 16–17

International Law Commission, Sub-Committee on State Responsibility, Summary record of the second meeting (Monday, 7 January 1963, at 3 p.m.), II Yearbook of the International Law Commission 229 (1963), UN Doc. A/CN.4/SER.A/1963/ADD.1, Annex I, Report by Mr. Roberto Ago (16 January 1963), UN Doc. A/CN.4/152, Appendix I 370

International Law Commission, II(2) Yearbook of the International Law Commission (2001) 2, 3–4, 10n2, 17n8, 21n19, 370n4, 372n7, 373n8, 375n15, 380n20, 381n24, 382n26, 412n36, 422n59

International Law Commission, Draft articles on the responsibility of international organizations, II(2) Yearbook of the International Law Commission (2011), UN Doc. A/CN.4/SER.A/2011/Add.1 (Part 2) 20–21, 254–255, 369–371, 372, 373, 375–376, 377, 379–383, 412, 419, 420n38–42, 420n44–57, 422, 430, 431

International Status of South West Africa, Advisory Opinion, 1950 ICJ Reps. 128 (International Court of Justice, 1 July 1950) 69–74, 213, 227, 231, 240

Interpretation of the Agreement of 25 March 1951 Between the WHO and Egypt, Advisory Opinion, 1980 ICJ Reps. 73 (International Court of Justice, 20 December 1980) 244–247, 374, 374n10

Interpretation of the Greco-Turkish Agreement of December 1st, 1926 (Final Protocol, Article IV), Advisory Opinion, 1928 PCIJ (Ser. B) No. 16 (Permanent Court of International Justice, 28 August 1928) 148n3

Iran-US Claims Tribunal v A.S., 18 Netherlands Yearbook of International Law 357 (1987) (Supreme Court [Hooge Raad], Netherlands, 20 December 1985) 54–55

J.H. Rayner (Mincing Lane) Ltd v Department of Trade and Industry and Others, and related appeals, Maclaine Watson & Co Ltd v Department of Trade and Industry, Maclaine Watson & Co Ltd v International Tin Council, Decision on Appeal, [1989] UKHL J1026-1, [1990] 2 AC 418, [1989] 3 WLR 969 (House of Lords, United Kingdom, 26 October 1989) 423–430, 431, 437

Judgment No. 2867 of the Administrative Tribunal of the International Labour Organization upon a Complaint Filed against the International Fund for Agricultural Development [IFAD], Advisory Opinion, 2012 ICJ Reps. 10 (International Court of Justice, 1 February 2012) 42–47

Jurisdiction of the European Commission of the Danube Between Galatz and Braila, Advisory Opinion, 1927 PCIJ (Ser. B) No. 14 (Permanent Court of International Justice, 8 December 1927) 40, 148n3

Karl M. v. Provincial Revenue Office for Vienna, Case No. Zl. 1509/69, 71 International Law Reports 573 (Administrative Court, Austria, 20 November 1970) 351n24

Ali Kashan, Minister of Justice, Palestinian National Authority, Letter to the Registrar of the International Criminal Court, Declaration accepting the Jurisdiction of the International Criminal Court (21 January 2009) 81

Klarsfeld v. Office Franco-Allemand pour la Jeunesse, 1969 (II) Juris-Classeur Périodique 15725, 72 International Law Reports 191 (Court of Appeal of Paris (21st Chamber), France, 18 June 1968) 331n10

Vojislav Koštunica, President of the FR Yugoslavia, Letter to the UN Secretary-General, United Nations Doc. A/55/528-S/2000/1043 (27 October 2000) 111n17

LaGrand Case (Germany v United States), Jurisdiction and Admissibility, Judgment, 2001 ICJ Reps. 466 (International Court of Justice, 27 June 2001) 234–239

Legal Consequences for States of the Continued Presence of South Africa in Namibia (South West Africa) Notwithstanding Security Council Resolution 276 (1970), Advisory Opinion, 1971 ICJ Reps. 16 (International Court of Justice, 21 June 1971) 213–221, 227, 240

Legal Consequences of the Construction of a Wall in the Occupied Palestinian Territory, Advisory Opinion, 2004 ICJ Reps. 136 (International Court of Justice, 9 July 2004) 221–225, 232n13

Legality of the Threat or Use of Nuclear Weapons [on request of the UN General Assembly], Advisory Opinion, 1996 ICJ Reps. 226 (International Court of Justice, 8 July 1996) 259–264

Legality of the Use by a State of Nuclear Weapons in Armed Conflict [on request of the World Health Organization], Advisory Opinion, 1996 ICJ Reps. 66 (International Court of Justice, 8 July 1996) 12–13, 39n2, 256–258

Marrakesh Agreement Establishing the World Trade Organization, 14 April 1994, 1867 UNTS 4, 154 .... 18n13

[Mbodina Iribi] v. Staatssecretaris van Veiligheid en Justitie [Secretary of State of Security and Justice], Ruling 201310217/1/V1 (ECLI:NL:RVS:2014:2427) (Supreme Court [Raad van Staat], Netherlands, 27 June 2014) 376n17

Medellín v Texas, Case No. 06-984, Judgment, 552 US 491 (2008) (Supreme Court, United States, 25 March 2008) 202–208

Mininni v Bari Institute of the International Centre for Advanced Mediterranean Agronomic Studies, 1981 Rivista di diritto internazionale 685, 78 International Law Reports 112 (Tribunal of Bari (Labor Chamber), Italy, 20 June 1981) ..338n14

Mukeshimana-Ngulinzira and Others v. Belgium and Others, RG Nos. 04/4807/A and 07/15547/A, Judgment (Court of First Instance of Brussels, Belgium, 8 December 2010) 400

Negotiated Relationship Agreement between the International Criminal Court and the United Nations, ICC Resolution ICC-ASP/3/Res.1, ICC Doc. ICC-ASP/3/Res.1 (7 September 2004) 19n14

Nissan v Attorney-General, [1969] UKHL 3, [1970] AC 179 (House of Lords, UK, 11 February 1969) 400

Patricia O'Brien, UN Legal Counsel and Under-Secretary-General for Legal Affairs, Note to Alain Le Roy, UN Under-Secretary-General for Peacekeeping Operations, MONUC – draft policy on conditionality of support to the FARDC (12 October 2009) 420n23

Opinion 2/94 [*In re* competence of the Community to accede to the European Convention for the Protection of Human Rights and Fundamental Freedoms (ECHR)] (Court of Justice of the European Communities [Union], 28 March 1996).. 163–165

Opinion 2/00, [*In re* accession to the Cartagena Protocol on Biosafety] (Court of Justice of the European Communities [Union], 6 December 2001)............. 188–191

People of New York v Dominique Strauss-Kahn, Indictment No. 02526/2011, Recommendation for Dismissal (Supreme Court, New York, 22 August 2011) 341n19

Re Pisani Balestra Di Mottola, 1971 Rivista di diritto internazionale 691, 71 International Law Reports 571 (Court of Cassation (Criminal), Italy, 10 July 1969)........ 339–340

Porru v. Food and Agriculture Organization, Case No. 4961, Judgment, 1969 UN Juridical Yearbook 238; 72 International Law Reports 191 (Rome Court of First Instance (Labour Section), Italy, 25 June 1969) 310–311, 312, 315

Prosecutor v Haradinaj et al., Case No. IT-04-84-AR65.1, Decision on Ramush Haradinaj's Modified Provisional Release (International Criminal Tribunal for the former Yugoslavia, Appeals Chamber, 10 March 2006) 281n15

Prosecutor v Lubanga Dyilo, Situation in the Democratic Republic of the Congo, Case No.: ICC-01/04-01/06, Redacted Decision on the request by DRC-D01-WWWW-0019 for special protective measures relating to his asylum application (International Criminal Court, Trial Chamber, 5 August 2011) 376n17

Prosecutor v Nikolic´, Case No. IT-94-2-PT, Decision of Defence Motion Challenging the Exercise of Jurisdiction by the Tribunal (International Criminal Tribunal for the former Yugoslavia, Trial Chamber II, 9 October 2002) 412–419

Prosecutor v. Tadic´ a/k/a "Dule," Case No. IT-94-1, Decision on the Defence Motion for Interlocutory Appeal on Jurisdiction (International Criminal Tribunal for the former Yugoslavia, Appeals Chamber, 2 October 1995) 286–302, 307

Prosecutor v Tadic´, Case No. IT-94-1-A-R77, Judgment on Allegations of Contempt against prior counsel, Milan Vujin (International Criminal Tribunal for the Former Yugoslavia, Appeals Chamber, 31 January 2000) 172–175

R (on the application of Al-Jedda) v Secretary of State for Defence, Judgment, [2007] UKHL 58, [2008] 1 AC 332, [2008] 2 WLR 31 (House of Lords, United Kingdom, 12 December 2007) 391–399

Registrar of the International Criminal Court, Letter to Mahmoud Abbas, President of the State of Palestine, Ref. 2015/IOR/3496/HvH (7 January 2015) 83

Railway Traffic between Lithuania and Poland (Railway Sector Landwarów-Kaisiadorys), Advisory Opinion, 1931 PCIJ (Ser. A/B) No. 42 (Permanent Court of International Justice, 15 October 1931) 195–202, 248n14

Reineccius et al. v Bank for International Settlements, Partial Award on the Lawfulness of the Recall of privately Held Shares on 8 January 2001 (Arbitration Tribunal under the Permanent Court of Arbitration, 22 November 2002) 55n14

Reparation for Injuries Suffered in the Service of the United Nations, Advisory Opinion, 1949 ICJ Reps. 174 (International Court of Justice, 11 April 1949) 33, 35–38, 39, 41, 48, 52, 66–67, 141–148, 151, 159, 162, 163, 167–170, 225, 369, 380–381, 440

Reservations to the Convention on Genocide, Advisory Opinion, 1951 ICJ Reps 15, 25 (International Court of Justice, 1951) 374n11

Rome Statute of the International Criminal Court, 17 July 1998, 2187 UNTS 90 .... 18, 82, 210

Rotterdam Convention on Prior Informed Consent, 10 September 1998, 2244 UNTS 337 .... 41n8

Henry G. Schermers & Niels M. Blokker, International Institutional Law (Martinus Nijhoff, fourth revised edition, 2003) 2

Shearson Lehman Brothers Inc. and Another v Maclaine Watson & Co. Ltd and Another (No. 2), [1988] 1 WLR 16, 77 International Law Reports 107 (High Court, Queen's Bench Division, England, 29 June 1987) 338n17

Situation in the State of Palestine, No. ICC-01/18, Prosecution request pursuant to article 19(3) for a ruling on the Court's territorial jurisdiction in Palestine (International Criminal Court, Pre-Trial Chamber I, 20 December 2019) 83–88

South West Africa Cases(Ethiopia v. South Africa, Liberia v. South Africa), Second Phase [Merits], Judgment, 1966 ICJ Reps. 6 (International Court of Justice, 18 July 1966) 227–229, 240, 248–249

Teixera v. Secretary-General of the United Nations, Judgment No. 230 (United Nations Administrative Tribunal, 14 October 1977) 330n7

Treaty Between the Republic of Tajikistan, the Kyrgyz Republic, the Republic of Kazakhstan and the Ismaili Imamat for the Establishment of the University of Central Asia, Aug. 28–31, 2000, 2159 UNTS 161 ....55n14

Treaty Establishing the European Coal and Steel Community ["Treaty of Paris"], 18 April 1951, 261 UNTS 140 208

Treaty Establishing the European Economic Community ["Treaty of Rome"], 25 March 1957, 298 UNTS 11 438

Treaty of Amsterdam amending the Treaty on European Union, the Treaties establishing the European Communities and certain related acts, 2 October 1997, Official Journal of the European Communities [Union] C 340/1 (10 November 1997)..39

Treaty of Lisbon amending the Treaty on European Union and the Treaty Establishing the European Community, 13 December 2007 Official Journal of the European Union C 306/1 (17 December 2007) 39, 40, 165

Treaty of Nice amending the Treaty on European Union, the Treaties establishing the European Communities and certain related acts, 26 February 2001, Official Journal of the European Communities C 80/1 (10 March 2001) 28

Treaty of the Functioning of the European Union (consolidated version), Official Journal of the European Union C 326/47 (26 October 2012)..................... 208–209

Treaty on European Union (consolidated version), Official Journal of the European Union C 115/13 (9 May 2008)............................... 128n26, 165, 166, 184, 268, 276

Treaty on European Union ["Maastricht Treaty"], 7 February 1992 , Official Journal of the European Communities C 191/1 (29 July 1992)......................................39

United Nations, Office of Legal Affairs, Memorandum of the UN Office of Legal Affairs, 15 June 1972, 1972 UN Juridical Yearbook 153 ....18n10

United Nations, Office of Legal Counsel, Legal Opinion No. 15, Questions regarding the scale of assessment for Belarus and Ukraine, 1992 United Nations Juridical Yearbook 435 .... 77–79, 124

United Nations Educational, Scientific and Cultural Organization [UNESCO] (Constitution) Case, 16 International Law Reports 331 (Special Arbitral Tribunal, 19 September 1949) 135

United Nations Framework Convention on Climate Change [UNFCCC], 21 March 1994, 1771 UNTS 107..41n8

United Nations General Assembly Resolution 95(I) (11 December 1946) Affirmation of the Principles of International Law recognized by the Charter of the Nurnberg Tribunal..248

United Nations General Assembly Resolution 260 (III)(A) (9 December 1948) Prevention and punishment of the crime of genocide (Adoption of the Convention on the Prevention and Punishment of the Crime of Genocide)......................................13

United Nations General Assembly Resolution 2758 (XXVI) (25 October 1971) Restoration of the lawful rights of the People's Republic of China in the United Nations 125

United Nations General Assembly Resolution 47/1 (22 September 1992) Recommendation of the Security Council of 19 September 1992 ....109n14

United Nations General Assembly Resolution 55/12 (1 November 2000) Admission of the Federal Republic of Yugoslavia to membership in the United Nations 111n19

United Nations General Assembly, Report of the Secretary-General, Financing of the United Nations Protection Force, the United Nations Confidence Restoration Operation in Croatia, the United Nations Preventive Deployment Force and the United Nations Peace Forces Headquarters, UN Doc. A/51/389 (20 September 1996) 370n3

United Nations Secretariat, Depositary Notification, Rome Statute of the International Criminal Court, Rome 17 July 1998, Reference: C.N.13.2015. TREATIES-XVIII.10, State of Palestine: Accession (6 January 2015) 82

United Nations Security Council Resolution 82 (25 June 1950) [Complaint of aggression upon the Republic of Korea] 212

United Nations Security Council Resolution 713 (25 September 1991) [Socialist Federal Republic of Yugoslavia] 109n12

United Nations Security Council Resolution 757 (30 May 1992) [Bosnia and Herzegovina] 109n13

United Nations Security Council Resolution 777 (19 September 1992) [Federal Republic of Yugoslavia] 111

United Nations Security Council Resolution 1326 (31 October 2000) [Admission of new members] 111n18

United Nations Security Council Resolution 1973 (17 March 2011) [Libya] 229–230, 231

United Nations Security Council, Provisional verbatim record of the 2046th meeting held at Headquarters, New York, on Friday, 31 January 1992, at 10:30 a.m., UN Doc. S/PV.3046 (31 January 1992) 109, 122–123

United States v. Gereschi, 1978 Rivista di diritto internazionale 573, (1978–9) 4 Italian Yearbook of International Law 173, 77 International Law Reports 598 (Court of Cassation (Joint Session), Italy, 14 October 1977) 331n9

Vienna Convention on Consular Relations, 24 April 1963, 596 UNTS 261 ....202n1

Vienna Convention on the Law of Treaties, 23 May 1969, 1155 UNTS 331 .... 4, 10, 12, 15, 17, 20, 30–31, 32–33, 48, 74–75, 134, 136, 374, 440

Vienna Convention on the Law of Treaties between States and International Organizations or between International Organizations, 21 March 1986 (not yet in force), International Law Commission, II(2) Yearbook of the International Law Commission 17, 23 (1982) 4, 10–11, 17

Voting Procedure on Questions Relating to Reports and Petitions Concerning the Territory of South-West Africa, Advisory Opinion, 1955 ICJ Reps. 67 (International Court of Justice, 7 July 1955) 240–244, 247

Waite & Kennedy v. Germany, Application No. 26083/94, Judgment (European Court of Human Rights (Grand Chamber), 18 February 1999) 21n20, 323–330

Westland Helicopters Ltd and Arab Organization for Industrialization, et al., ICC Case No. 3879/AS, Interim Award Regarding Jurisdiction ("Compétence") of the Arbitral Tribunal, 80 International Law Reports 595, 600 (International Chamber of Commerce, Court of Arbitration, Arbitral Tribunal, 5 March 1984) 21–22, 431–437

World Health Organization, Constitution of the World Health Organization, Adopted by the International Health Conference, New York, 22 July 1946, 2 Official Records of the World Health Organization 100, As amended at the Twenty-sixth, Twenty-ninth, Thirty-ninth and Fifty-first World Health Assemblies, Resolutions WHA26.37, WHA29.38, WHA39.6 and WHA51.23 14

World Health Organization, Resolution WHA58.3 Revision of the International Health Regulations, World Health Organization, Fifty-eighth World Health Assembly, Geneva, 16–25 May 2005, Resolutions and Decisions, Annex (2005) WHO Doc. WHA58/2005/REC/1 15

World Health Organization and Verstuyft v. Aquino and Others, 69 Official Gazette 1914, 48 Supreme Court Reps. Annotated 242, 52 International Law Reports 389 (Supreme Court, Philippines, 29 November 1972) 341–344

Boris N. Yeltsin, President of the Russian Federation, Letter to the UN Secretary-General (24 December 1991), IAEA Doc. INFCIRC/397 (9 January 1992) Attachment 2 121–122

Juan Ysmael & Co. Inc. v. Government of the Republic of Indonesia, [1955] AC 72, [1954] 3 WLR 531, 21 International Law Reports 95 (Judicial Committee of the Privy Council, 7 October 1954) 338n16

Abbreviations

AOI	Arab Organization for Industrialization
ASP	Assembly of States Parties
AU	African Union
CONEFO	Conference of the New Emerging Forces
COP	Conference of Parties
CSP	Conference of States Parties
EC	European Community
ECHR	European Convention on Human Rights
ECOWAS	Economic Community of West African States
EEC	European Economic Community
EPO	European Patent Office
EU	European Union
FAO	UN Food and Agriculture Organization
FARDC	Armed Forces of the Democratic Republic of the Congo
FR Yugoslavia	Federal Republic of Yugoslavia
FYROM	Former Yugoslav Republic of Macedonia
GATT 1947	General Agreement on Tariffs and Trade of 1947
GAVI	Global Alliance for Vaccines and Immunization
Global Fund	Global Fund to Fight AIDS, Tuberculosis and Malaria
IAEA	International Atomic Energy Agency
ICAO	International Civil Aviation Organization
ICC	International Criminal Court
ICJ	International Court of Justice
ICRC	International Committee of the Red Cross
ICTR	International Criminal Tribunal for Rwanda
ICTY	International Criminal Tribunal for the former Yugoslavia
IFAD	International Fund for Agricultural Development
ILC	International Law Commission
ILO	International Labour Organization
ILOAT	International Labour Organization Administrative Tribunal
IMCO	Inter-Governmental Maritime Consultative Organization
ITU	International Telephone (now Telecommunications) Union
KFO	Kosovo Force

MONUC	United Nations Organization Mission in the Democratic Republic of the Congo
NATO	North Atlantic Treaty Organization
NGO	non-governmental organization
OPCW	Organization for the Prohibition of Chemical Weapons
OPEC	Organization of Petroleum Exporting Countries
OSCE	Organization for Security and Co-operation in Europe
PAHO	Pan American Health Organization
PCIJ	Permanent Court of International Justice
PLO	Palestinian Liberation Organization
SFOR	Stabilization Force in Bosnia and Herzegovina
SFR Yugoslavia	Socialist Federal Republic of Yugoslavia
SHAPE	Supreme Headquarters Allied Powers Europe
UAE	United Arab Emirates
UK	United Kingdom
UN	United Nations
UNAMIR	United Nations Assistance Mission for Rwanda
UNAT	United Nations Administrative Tribunal
UNCCD	United Nations Convention to Combat Desertification
UNEP	United Nations Environment Programme
UNESCO	United Nations Educational, Scientific and Cultural Organization
UNFICYP	United Nations Peacekeeping Force in Cyprus
UNGA	United Nations General Assembly
UNIDO	United Nations Industrial Development Organization
UNMIK	United Nations Interim Administration Mission in Kosovo
UNOLA	United Nation Office of Legal Affairs
UNRWA	United Nations Relief and Works Agency for Palestine Refugees in the Near East
UNSC	United Nations Security Council
UNSG	United Nations Secretary-General
UNWTO	World Tourism Organization
UPU	Universal Postal Union
US	United States of America
WHO	World Health Organization
WIPO	World Intellectual Property Organizations
WMO	World Meteorological Organization
WTO	World Trade Organization

CHAPTER 1

Introduction to International Organizations

1.1 INTRODUCTION TO INTERNATIONAL ORGANIZATIONS

In less than 100 years, international organizations have evolved from curiosities into keystones of international law. What began long ago as an unremarkable effort to coordinate a limited number of technical issues has grown into a global, multi-level, blended governing project with diverse competences in most fields of human endeavor and interests, including nuclear weapons, migration, weather activity, telecommunications, languages, rivers, intellectual property, criminal activity, tuberculosis, bananas and coffee, and so on. In New York, Brussels, Geneva, The Hague, Vienna, Nairobi, and cities throughout the world, thousands of international civil servants and experts go to work every day, each attempting to make one small contribution in the larger web of organizations. This decentralized, fragmented, and sometimes overlapping governance project is, in principle, focused on the goal of addressing international challenges efficiently, effectively and peacefully, without the resort to competitive violence that has characterized the human condition for most of our history. To a degree, this goal has largely been achieved, although admittedly large-scale violence does still happen all too frequently, and many organizations still struggle with a legacy of embedded political and coercive power differentials.

The emergence of international organizations has been both rapid and incremental. It is rapid in the sense of the sheer number of organizations constituted since the creation of the United Nations (UN). It is incremental in the sense that each organization is created to solve a discrete problem, often with little regard to the other organizations already operating, and yet may experience significant mission creep as the nature of the problem, and the organization's relationship with its member states, evolve over time. There was no real "constitutional moment" in international law, so this rapid and incremental development applied to an international legal community with deeply entrenched differences in power and role. Now, international organizations operate as some of the most important actors in international law, though the legacy of their growth raises a wide range of questions about their nature, powers, governance, responsibility and overall relationship to the states that created them.

1.2 DEFINITION OF AN INTERNATIONAL ORGANIZATION

A preliminary issue is to establish the scope of this textbook by defining international organizations. For students who have already studied international law, they will recall the difficulties in defining a state, in order to determine whether a given entity qualifies as a state. International organizations are not so different. The challenge is to determine from what source a definition would come.

In its project on international organization responsibility, the International Law Commission (ILC) looked to customary international law for a definition of an organization. The ILC, based on the research of the Special Rapporteur, Giorgio Gaja, concluded:

**International Law Commission,
Draft articles on the responsibility of international organizations
II(2) Yearbook of the International Law Commission (2011)
UN Doc. A/CN.4/SER.A/2011/Add.1 (Part 2)**[1]

Article 2 Use of terms

For the purposes of the present draft articles,
(a) "international organization" means an organization established by a treaty or other instrument governed by international law and possessing its own international legal personality. International organizations may include as members, in addition to States, other entities;

Other authors have disagreed on these elements. For example, Niels Blokker offers the following definition:

**Henry G. Schermers & Niels M. Blokker
International Institutional Law
(Brill/Martinus Nijhoff, fourth revised edition, 2003)**

§33 In this study, international organizations are defined as forms of cooperation founded on an international agreement usually creating a new legal person having at least one organ with a will of its own, established under international law

Yet another author, C.F. Amerasinghe, suggests his own distinct definition:

---

1 From the Yearbook of the International Law Commission, by the International Law Commission © 2011 United Nations. Reprinted with the permission of the United Nations.

C.F. Amerasinghe,
Principles of the Institutional Law of International Organizations
(Cambridge University Press, second revised edition, 2005)[2]

[p. 10] ... Suffice it to identify the basic characteristics which distinguish the public international organization from other organizations, particularly private international organizations. These are: (i) establishment by some kind of international agreement among states; (ii) possession of what may be called a constitution; (iii) possession of organs separate from its members; (iv) establishment under international law; and (v) generally but not always an exclusive membership of states or governments, but at any rate predominant membership of states or governments.

Notes

- What are the elements in each definition? Compare and contrast with the elements in the competing definitions.
- What are the significances of the differences?
- How do we explain these differences? What are the authors looking for?
- Is it problematic if there are multiple definitions? Does that outcome undermine the coherence of international law of organizations? Consider a situation where an organization qualifies as such under one definition, but not under another definition? What would such an organization look like?

Notwithstanding the differences in the definitions, these divergences may not be as problematic as they might appear. In the ILC study, the Special Rapporteur also included the following observation in the commentary to the draft articles:

International Law Commission,
Draft articles on the responsibility of international organizations
II(2) Yearbook of the International Law Commission (2011)
UN Doc. A/CN.4/SER.A/2011/Add.1 (Part 2)[3]

Article 2 Use of terms

Commentary
(1) The definition of "international organization" given in article 2, subparagraph (a), is considered as appropriate for the purposes of the present draft articles and is not intended as a definition for all purposes. It outlines certain common characteristics of the international organizations to which the following articles apply. The same characteristics may be

---

2 Reproduced with permission of The Licensor through PLSclear.
3 From the Yearbook of the International Law Commission, by the International Law Commission © 2011 United Nations. Reprinted with the permission of the United Nations.

relevant for purposes other than the international responsibility of international organizations.

(2) The fact that an international organization does not possess one or more of the characteristics set forth in article 2, subparagraph (a), and thus is not within the definition for the purposes of the present articles, does not imply that certain principles and rules stated in the following articles do not apply also to that organization.

(3) Starting with the 1969 Vienna Convention, [footnote omitted] several codification conventions have succinctly defined the term "international organization" as "intergovernmental organization". [footnote omitted] In each case, the definition was given only for the purposes of the relevant convention and not for all purposes. The text of some of these codification conventions added some further elements to the definition: for instance, the 1986 Vienna Convention only applies to those intergovernmental organizations that have the capacity to conclude treaties. [footnote omitted] No additional element would be required in the case of international responsibility apart from possessing an obligation under international law. However, the adoption of a different definition is preferable for several reasons. First, it is questionable whether by defining an international organization as an intergovernmental organization one provides much information: it is not even clear whether the term "intergovernmental organization" refers to the constituent instrument or to actual membership. Second, the term "intergovernmental" is in any case inappropriate to a certain extent, because several important international organizations have been established with the participation also of State organs other than Governments. Third, an increasing number of international organizations include among their members entities other than States as well as States; the term "intergovernmental organization" might be thought to exclude these organizations, although with regard to international responsibility it is difficult to see why one should reach solutions that differ from those applying to organizations of which only States are members.

Notes

- What does the Special Rapporteur mean by this article? Are the ILC articles governing international organizations or not? Are any organizations excepted? If so, what rules govern them?
- The Special Rapporteur refers to "purposes." What is the purpose of the draft articles he wrote? What would be other purposes? How would different purposes necessitate different definitions? Is not the point of creating international organizations to have objective entities that can accomplish certain objectives?
- This textbook uses the term "international organizations." The Special Rapporteur distinguishes this term from "inter-governmental organizations." Why?

What significance does this have for the study of organizations? Would this textbook be different if it focused on inter-governmental organizations?
- Does this commentary mean that we cannot study international organizations as a coherent topic? Are all organizations so different that they share no commonalities? If they do share commonalities, what would those areas be?

Strangely enough, no one knows how many international organizations exist. There are some obvious ones, such as the United Nations and European Union (EU). Then there are ones that students of international law may learn about, such as the World Trade Organization (WTO), International Criminal Court (ICC), International Atomic Energy Agency (IAEA), North Atlantic Treaty Organization (NATO), and various UN agencies, but the bulk of organizations are not present in the front of most people's minds, even if they might be critical to the world we have today. These organizations include the World Health Organization (WHO), Organization of Petroleum Exporting Countries (OPEC), or International Labour Organization (ILO). Very few people may think of the World Meteorological Organization (WMO) or World Intellectual Property Organization (WIPO), and even fewer may know of the World Tourism Organization (UNWTO), the Rhine Commission, the *Organisation internationale de la Francophonie*, or the International Coffee Union. There are surely more international organizations than there are states in the world, but the vast numbers of them are smaller, relatively technical bodies that do not dominate the front pages of newspapers.

A secondary reason for not knowing the number of organizations is the problem of the definition above. Some restrictive definitions of international organizations might limit the scope of consideration to only the UN family of organizations, while other, more liberal definitions would include the International Olympics Committee and the International Committee of the Red Cross (ICRC). Most authorities consider the first international organization, which still exists, to be the *Administration général de navigation du Rhine*, founded in 1804. Other older organizations are the International Telephone (now Telecommunications) Union (ITU) and Universal Postal Union (UPU). Whether these entities are the oldest organizations depends, in turn, on the definition. This textbook does not take a definitive view on the definition, other than to suggest a possible working one, but would prefer to leave it to the reader to formulate a definition of his or her own making. The result is that the student of international organizations law must begin the study of organizations already in a state of inquiry about the scope of the study itself, its definition, and how many organizations are even included.

This textbook proposes the following working definition of international organizations for the purposes of this study: an international legal person established by agreement under international law between subjects of international law with a degree of meaningful independence of judgment and action from its members to accomplish certain limited objectives. Students will note that this definition overlaps in many important ways with the definitions reproduced above, but it also excludes certain topics, such as the need to have organs, and it brings in a revised element, the notion of meaningful independence, rather than "will of its own." Students are invited to critique this definition and find its shortcomings; however, this is the definition that will be applied in the remainder of chapter, and the book as a whole. We will revisit this definition in the chapter on the creation of a new international organization.

1.3 INTERNATIONAL ORGANIZATIONS AS A FIELD OF STUDY

A very natural question to ask at this point is whether it is even possible to study the law of international organizations as a coherent course. Many law schools, even those specializing in international law, often do not even offer a course on international organizations. To some degree this can be mitigated in various other substantive courses where there may be some overlap. A course in international trade might feature the WTO, a course in international criminal law will probably discuss the ICC, a course in European law must include the EU, and virtually any course in general international law must certainly cover the United Nations. However, these courses will likely address these organizations from the perspective of substantive law, so a course covering the WTO, ICC, or EU would most likely focus on the WTO agreements, crimes under the Rome Statute of the ICC, or EU internal market rules, rather than discussing those organizations as institutions governed by law. It would be comparable to studying a state's constitution with an almost exclusive focus on the individual rights enumerated within the constitution, and largely omitting discussion of the legal issues involved in governance, such as federalism and the balance of powers. A large part of this lack of courses on international organizations is based on the view that organizations are not a study unto themselves, but rather merely a phenomenon emerging from treaties and international relations.

If we do attempt to study organizations as such, one must wonder whether it is possible, given their variety. If every organization was founded for a particular purpose, with its own rules and powers, and operates within a framework of stronger and weaker states, then surely every organization is a political actor. As such, when it operates in an international relations environment, surely it is also looking for leverage, advantage, and opportunities for cooperation in order to advance its interests. Of course this is true, just as it is true for states. But all states have a constitution and a legal order, and operate within an international legal system that establishes reasonably foreseeable expectations on behavior. Just like states, every international organization has a constitutional framework and an internal order for governance, and just like states, international organizations also operate within the same international legal system. Within that system, however, organizations may or may not have similar powers and lawmaking abilities as states. Of course, not all organizations enjoy UN Security Council Chapter VII powers, mandatory dispute settlement, or direct effect in domestic legal orders, among many other powers and competences.

While the precise answers to these questions from international law may vary from organization to organization, the law has developed common principles and rules to produce these answers. For example, when we try to determine whether an organization has a particular power granted to it by states, there is a common analytical methodology for approaching this question, even though it will produce an answer specific to that organization. In addition, virtually all organizations have some common challenges. Every organization has staff with human resources management issues. Every organization has a headquarters building located in some state with the challenge of agreeing on immunities and operating fees with the host state. Every organization has member states that create the organization, fund the organization, and want to exercise oversight. Every organization needs to have rules of procedure for making decisions. Every organization may, intentionally or accidentally, violate international law and need to be held to account. In fact, organizations are quite consistent in how they approach questions of budgeting, membership, interpretation of their constitutive instrument, application of the principal–subsidiary organ structure, the special nature of judicial organs, and many other areas where a fairly consistent corpus of international law has emerged. However, where organizations have differences, we can take a comparative approach. Students may find that through a comparative approach, they see consistency in the framework for analyzing the existence of powers or the legal effect of acts. Thus, in the view of this author, it is not correct to simply throw up our hands and say that all international organizations are different. The perspective of this textbook is that, even if all international organizations have some differences, we can still study the law of international organizations as a coherent topic. After all, all states have differences too, and we can clearly study both international law and comparative constitutional law.

1.4 OVERVIEW OF THIS TEXTBOOK

In Chapter 2, the textbook will begin the study of international organizations by revisiting the law of treaties and considering the ways in which that law might be modified in the case of organizations. This discussion is foundational for the chapters that follow because international organizations are constituted by treaties, and treaties form their constitutive instrument, a kind of quasi-constitutional framework. Without a firm basis in the law of treaties, we will struggle to interpret and apply the constitutive instruments.

In Chapter 3, we consider the life cycle of an organization from its creation to its dissolution. We will revisit the definition of international organizations and examine the various legal elements that need to be present. This study will include issues of objective and relative international legal personality and the legal structuring of independence and dependence of the organization on the member states. Turning to dissolution, it will also consider the rules for ending an organization and the succession to its rights and obligations.

Chapter 4 will examine the issue of membership in greater detail. Students will study how states qualify for membership either as original members or members joining later, and the substantive and procedural rules for joining. We will also consider succession to membership when states dissolve and the rules on appointing agents to represent the state's interests at the organization. Lastly, the chapter will discuss the various grounds for suspending or terminating membership.

Chapter 5 moves from these structural issues to the substantive question of powers. Every organization is created to accomplish certain objectives. In so doing, it is given powers by the member states. This chapter analyzes the methodology for assessing which powers an organization enjoys and how those powers are held in tension with the sovereignty of the member states. It will also discuss the legal rules for determining when an organization has acted beyond its powers and the remedies for *ultra vires* acts.

Chapter 6 follows Chapter 5's study of powers by considering the legal effects of the organization's acts. These two chapters go hand-in-hand. We first need to know whether an organization has a power, and whether it has acted within its powers, and then we need to know what legal rights and obligations are created by that act. Legal effect is divided into binding acts and non-binding acts. In order to determine which category applies, we need to study the law on assigning legal force. Even if this analysis leads to an act being non-binding, we also need know the significance, within the legal system, of a non-binding act.

Chapter 7 returns to quasi-constitutional structural issues. This chapter focuses on the organs of international organizations. The first consideration is how the organization is organized internally. While it may act with binding or non-binding effect, from an internal perspective it is also critical to know which organ acts and how it relates to the other organs. In addition, different organs may be created with different nature and characteristics. These considerations will condition the ability of the organ to act, and will have implications for its exercise of powers on behalf of the organization as a whole.

Chapters 8 and 9 turn to the external relations of the organization with other actors in international law. Chapter 8 considers the privileges and immunities that international organizations and their agents enjoy. Unless students undertake employment with an international organization, Chapter 8 may be most relevant to students when they interact professionally with an organization and its agents. This chapter will break down the field of immunities into those enjoyed by a variety of different persons, and then assess the legal rules on determining which individuals and acts are protected.

Chapter 9 addresses the issues of the responsibility of international organizations. Whether they are immune or not, whether they have acted outside their powers or not, organizations can violate international law. However, organizations are already accountable to their members, and in some ways are dependent on their members, so the question in this chapter focuses on identifying which rules of international law apply to organizations, distinguishing those actions where the organization and the member states are responsible, and enforcing international law against organizations.

Chapter 10 concludes the textbook with reflections on the study and some of the preliminary questions raised in this chapter.

There are potentially more chapters that could have been added: for example, this book will not address financing of international organizations, voting rules within each organ, international engagement in dispute resolution, or staff employment regulations. Instead, this book concentrates on the fundamental issues in the law of international organizations, on which many of the other issues rest. For example, without a critical understanding of the complex relationship between member states and the organization, it is quite difficult to understand the obligation to finance an organization. The objective of this book is to examine fewer topics, though fundamental topics, and in more depth.

The book will adopt the following educational approach. It will present a series of extracts from original cases or other materials. Each extract will be followed by a series of question notes for discussion or individual consideration. These questions may not have easy answers, or any clear answer at all. They may allude to issues beyond the reading excerpt or link to other issues of international law. They are not intended to serve as a series of questions that, if you can concisely answer them in 25 words or less, will guarantee that you will pass any exam or get a job at an international organization. Instead, the goal of the question notes is to trigger students to read the text carefully and critically, and reflect on the material deeply within the context of the study of international law. They will alternate between looking at the reading excerpt from a very narrow focus to a wide focus. For each reading excerpt, there are far more possible questions, and these are only the beginning of possible avenues of critique. It is anticipated that through this approach, students will become accustomed to reading texts to uncover underlying rules and assumptions, and linking recurring issues across the entire study of international organizations, and international law.

CHAPTER 2

Law of treaties

2.1 TREATIES REGARDING INTERNATIONAL ORGANIZATIONS

In beginning the study of international organizations law, we must first consider the ways in which the law of treaties applies for organizations. Students of international law already know that treaties have their own set of laws that govern their adoption, application, and termination. For those who are encountering this topic for the first time, it is important to note that international law governing treaties has evolved over centuries under customary international law and was codified in the Vienna Convention on the Law of Treaties of 1969 ("Vienna Convention").[1] This treaty eventually entered into force when enough states became party to it, and it is now the most important foundational framework for applying the law of treaties. However, this treaty only applies to treaties between states. Shortly after it entered into force, study and negotiations began for another treaty on the law of treaties, but this time applicable to international organizations. This latter treaty, the Vienna Convention on the Law of Treaties between States and International Organizations or between International Organizations ("Vienna Convention for International Organizations") was adopted in 1986, but has not yet entered into force as of the time of writing this textbook.[2] Nonetheless, the Vienna Convention for International Organizations was also intended to be the codification of many decades of customary international law practice, so the Convention, despite the fact that it has not itself entered into force, remains as a very good statement of customary international law. It also largely tracks similar rules in the original Vienna Convention. For this reason, this textbook will largely follow and make reference to the Vienna Convention when discussing the applicable rules.

The need for a separate Vienna Convention already shows that the law of treaties applies slightly differently for international organizations than it does for states. One of the most significant differences is that international organizations are constituted by treaties, although there are a number of other significant differences beyond that. This chapter will proceed through the various rules in the law of treaties, highlighting variances and other important considerations when a treaty concerns an international

---

[1] Vienna Convention on the Law of Treaties, 23 May 1969, 1155 UNTS 331.
[2] Vienna Convention on the Law of Treaties between States and International Organizations or between International Organizations, 21 March 1986, not yet in force, International Law Commission, II(2) Yearbook of the International Law Commission 17, 23 (1982).

organization. The chapter will largely assume that students have encountered the Vienna Convention before. Those students who have not studied the Vienna Convention before may wish to complete some supplementary studying when any of the topics below become unclear.

One initial observation is that sometimes an international organization is charged with treaty depositary duties.[3] A depositary is an entity that archives the official, original treaty text, along with all adherence instruments such as signatures, ratifications, declarations, and reservations. It also issues certified copies upon request. Traditionally, states performed this function, but more recently depositary practice has largely shifted to international organizations. For example, the Council of Europe, International Civil Aviation Organization, International Maritime Organization, International Labour Organization, Organization of American States, and several other organizations register treaties and maintain a treaty series. These organizations usually only hold and register treaties that were negotiated within the relevant organization. The UN is special in this regard. The UN will register any treaty where at least one party is a UN member. Also, the UN Charter provides that:

**Charter of the United Nations
24 October 1945
1 UNTS 16[4]**

Chapter XVI Miscellaneous Provisions
Article 102

1. Every treaty and every international agreement entered into by any Member of the United Nations after the present Charter comes into force shall as soon as possible be registered with the Secretariat and published by it.
2. No party to any such treaty or international agreement which has not been registered in accordance with the provisions of paragraph 1 of this Article may invoke that treaty or agreement before any organ of the United Nations.

This provision means that UN members are obliged to register their treaties with the UN Secretary-General if they want the treaty to have any relevance for UN considerations. One final comment is that depositaries, including the UN, do not take a view on the legal status of instruments submitted to them. It is tempting to interpret registration by the UN or another international organization as an endorsement that the agreement qualifies as a treaty and produces legal effects, but this is not the case.

This chapter will now examine some of the most important ways the law of treaties applies when it concerns international organizations. This chapter will not

---

3 *See* Vienna Convention, articles 76–77.
4 From the United Nations Treaty Series, by the United Nations © 1945 United Nations. Reprinted with the permission of the United Nations.

examine all of the law on treaties generally, which would constitute its own textbook. Where students may be not be familiar with the law of treaties, they are advised to consult the Vienna Convention as the primary text.

2.2 SPECIAL RULES IN THE LAW OF TREATIES APPLYING TO INTERNATIONAL ORGANIZATIONS

The first overarching consideration when it comes to the law of treaties is whether treaties concerning international organizations are of a significantly different character than those concerning other matters. At this point, it will be helpful to distinguish between types of treaties. First, we have treaties between states or between international organizations, or a mixture of the two, that create obligations. Second, we have treaties also between subjects of international law, but that create international organizations. The Vienna Convention takes the view that it applies to both equally:

**Vienna Convention on the Law of Treaties
23 May 1969
1155 UNTS 331**[5]

Article 5
Treaties constituting international organizations and
treaties adopted within an international organization

The present Convention applies to any treaty which is the constituent instrument of an international organization and to any treaty adopted within an international organization without prejudice to any relevant rules of the organization.

However, the International Court of Justice (ICJ) has observed the following:

**Legality of the Use by a State of Nuclear Weapons in Armed Conflict
[on request of the World Health Organization]
Advisory Opinion
1996 ICJ Reps. 66
International Court of Justice, 8 July 1996**

... the constituent instruments of international organizations are also treaties of a particular type ... conventional and at the same time institutional; the very nature of the organization created, the objectives which have been

---

5   From the United Nations Treaty Series, by the United Nations © 1969 United Nations. Reprinted with the permission of the United Nations.

assigned to it by its founders, the imperatives associated with the effective performance of its functions, as well as its own practice, are all elements which may deserve special attention when the time comes to interpret those constituent treaties.

Notes

- What is the view in the Vienna Convention on treaties that are constitutive instruments? What is the view in the *Nuclear Weapons (WHO)* opinion?
- Is the ICJ view limited to only treaty interpretation? Or is the reasoning more extensive?
- Does the ICJ opinion mean that constitutive instruments are no longer treaties and are not governed by the Vienna Convention?
- Can we say that the Vienna Convention views constitutive instruments as mere treaties, and the ICJ views them as quasi-constitutions? Or is that too simplistic? Is there a way to view constitutive instruments as both at the same time? What results would differ depending on which perspective was emphasized in a given case?
- Perhaps instead we can view constitutive instruments from an "internal" or "external" viewpoint. The internal perspective would be constitutional and would focus on internal organization and governance, and the external perspective would focus on rights and obligations among international actors. Does this view clarify or confuse the question? Are there internal questions that would be better addressed through an external viewpoint? And vice versa?

2.2.1 Treaties adopted within an international organization

Treaties on a range of matters are adopted in various contexts. The classic paradigm is the representatives of two states sitting across a table negotiating on a document, and then signing and ratifying it. This image is actually very unusual, and most treaties are bureaucratic exchanges of letters reaching agreements on a range of mundane matters. The classic image only really applies to cases of treaties with significant political gravity, and even then, the vast majority of negotiations are concluded through extensive formal and informal means.

One context that cannot be overlooked is that these negotiations can take place within the framework of discussions at an international organization. Rather than set up an international conference specifically for the one treaty, states often take advantage of the continuous operation of international organizations and the infrastructure they offer. At the end of negotiations, the parties can adopt the agreement in the final act of a conference, but in some cases the agreement could be adopted as a resolution of the relevant organization's organ. For example, the Genocide Convention was adopted as UN General Assembly Resolution 260 (III) of 9 December 1948. However, as the UN General Assembly does not have law-making powers, the resolution merely served to adopt the final text and then open the document to adherence by states. If no states or an insufficient number of states adhered, then the treaty would never enter into force.

Some international organizations do, however, have limited law-making powers. This issue will be discussed in more detail in Chapter 5 on the powers of international organizations, but in this section it is only important to note that, for those organizations, the adoption of a treaty text might make the treaty binding from the moment of adoption, without the need for subsequent signature, ratification, or accession. For example, consider the following provision from the Constitution of the World Health Organization:

**Constitution of the World Health Organization
Adopted by the International Health Conference, New York, 22 July 1946
2 Official Records of the World Health Organization 100
as amended at the Twenty-sixth, Twenty-ninth, Thirty-ninth and
Fifty-first World Health Assemblies,
Resolutions WHA26.37, WHA29.38, WHA39.6 and WHA51.23[6]**

Article 21

The Health Assembly shall have authority to adopt regulations concerning:

(*a*) sanitary and quarantine requirements and other procedures designed to prevent the international spread of disease;
(*b*) nomenclatures with respect to diseases, causes of death and public health practices;
(*c*) standards with respect to diagnostic procedures for international use;
(*d*) standards with respect to the safety, purity and potency of biological, pharmaceutical and similar products moving in international commerce;
(*e*) advertising and labelling of biological, pharmaceutical and similar products moving in international commerce.

Article 22

Regulations adopted pursuant to Article 21 shall come into force for all Members after due notice has been given of their adoption by the Health Assembly except for such Members as may notify the Director-General of rejection or reservations within the period stated in the notice.

---

6 Reprinted from Official Records of the World Health Organization, Vol. 2, World Health Organization, Constitution, p. 100 © 1946 World Health Organization, *available at* http://apps.who.int/gb/bd/PDF/bd47/EN/constitution-en.pdf?ua=1.

Resolution WHA58.3 Revision of the International Health Regulations
World Health Organization,
Fifty-eighth World Health Assembly, Geneva, 16-25 May 2005,
Resolutions and Decisions, Annex (2005) WHO Doc. WHA58/2005/REC/1[7]

The Fifty-eighth World Health Assembly,

Having considered the draft revised International Health Regulations;

Having regard to articles 2(k), 21(a) and 22 of the Constitution of WHO

Recalling references to the need for revising and updating the International Health Regulations in resolutions WHA48.7 on revision and updating of the International Health Regulations, WHA54.14 on global health security: epidemic alert and response, WHA55.16 on global public health response to natural occurrence, accidental release or deliberate use of biological and chemical agents or radionuclear material that affect health, WHA56.28 on revision of the International Health Regulations, and WHA56.29 on severe acute respiratory syndrome (SARS), with a view to responding to the need to ensure global public health;

...

1. ADOPTS the revised International Health Regulations attached to this resolution, to be referred to as the "International Health Regulations (2005)";
2. CALLS UPON Member States and the Director-General to implement fully the International Health Regulations (2005), in accordance with the purpose and scope set out in Article 2 and the principles embodied in Article 3;

Notes

- What is the mechanism for adhering to treaties negotiated at the WHO? What are the limits on this practice?
- Does this practice violate the Vienna Convention rules on adherence to treaties being based on expressing state consent? What does the Vienna Convention require in order for states to be bound to a treaty? Specifically, the Vienna Convention, article 11, states that "The consent of a State to be bound by a treaty may be expressed by signature, exchange of instruments constituting a treaty, ratification, acceptance, approval or accession, or by any other means if so agreed."

---

7 Reprinted from International Health Regulations, 3d ed., World Health Organization, p. 3 © 2005 World Health Organization, *available at* http://apps.who.int/iris/bitstream/10665/246107/1/9789241580496-eng.pdf?ua=1.

In addition, the ILO International Labour Conference determined that some of the treaties adopted within its framework were so fundamental that all states, whether they have adhered to those treaties or not, must be bound. Since the International Labour Conference includes participation of all the states parties, a declaration on this point was adopted, and now those fundamental treaties do indeed bind all member states, regardless of their adherence through the usual procedure:

Declaration on Fundamental Principles and Rights at Work Adopted by the International Labour Conference [of the International Labour Organization] at its Eighty-sixth session, Geneva, 18 June 1998, Annex

The International Labour Conference,

1. Recalls:
   (a) that in freely joining the ILO, all Members have endorsed the principles and rights set out in its Constitution and in the Declaration of Philadelphia, and have undertaken to work towards attaining the overall objectives of the Organization to the best of their resources and fully in line with their specific circumstances;
   (b) that these principles and rights have been expressed and developed in the form of specific rights and obligations in Conventions recognized as fundamental both inside and outside the Organization.
2. Declares that all Members, even if they have not ratified the Conventions in question, have an obligation arising from the very fact of membership in the Organization to respect, to promote and to realize, in good faith and in accordance with the Constitution, the principles concerning the fundamental rights which are the subject of those Conventions, namely:
   (a) freedom of association and the effective recognition of the right to collective bargaining;
   (b) the elimination of all forms of forced or compulsory labour;
   (c) the effective abolition of child labour; and
   (d) the elimination of discrimination in respect of employment and occupation.

Annex (Revised)
Follow-up to the Declaration

I. Overall purpose

1. The aim of the follow-up described below is to encourage the efforts made by the Members of the Organization to promote the fundamental principles and rights enshrined in the Constitution of the ILO and the Declaration of Philadelphia and reaffirmed in this Declaration

....

3. The two aspects of this follow-up, described below, are based on existing procedures: the annual follow-up concerning non-ratified fundamental Conventions will entail merely some adaptation of the present modalities of application of article 19, paragraph 5(e), of the Constitution; and the Global Report on the effect given to the promotion of the fundamental principles and rights at work that will serve to inform the recurrent discussion at the Conference on the needs of the Members, the ILO action undertaken, and the results achieved in the promotion of the fundamental principles and rights at work.

Notes

- How is this mechanism different from the WHO practice above? What is the basis for this practice, and what are the limits?
- Following from the analysis in the context of the WHO, does the practice of the ILO violate the Vienna Convention rules on adherence to treaties?

2.2.2 Adherence to treaties

In Section 2.2.1, we already began discussion on the topic of adherence to a treaty concerning international organizations. For states negotiating and adopting a treaty within the context of an international organization, it is possible for the treaty to enter into effect upon a decision of the competent organ. But the key question, in addition to state consent, was whether the organ was competent. This question can be settled by consulting the organization's constitutive instrument to see if this power was provided. For more on this question of powers, you may wish to consult Chapter 5 in this book on powers.

Similarly, when an international organization wishes to adhere to a treaty, it will also be constrained by its limited powers. The Vienna Convention for International Organizations provides the following:

Vienna Convention on the Law of Treaties between States and International Organizations or between International Organizations, 21 March 1986 (not yet in force) International Law Commission, II(2) Yearbook of the International Law Commission 17, 23 (1982)[8]

Article 6 Capacity of international organizations to conclude treaties

The capacity of an international organization to conclude treaties is governed by the rules of that organization.

---

8 From the Yearbook of the International Law Commission, by the International Law Commission © 1982 United Nations. Reprinted with the permission of the United Nations.

States have adopted rather inconsistent practice specifying rules for international organizations on concluding treaties. Some constitutive instruments envision that the organization would enter into an agreement or agreements with a state or states. For example, the Rome Statute of the International Criminal Court, article 3(2), contemplates a headquarters agreement between the ICC and The Netherlands.[9] However many organizations do not include specific terms in the constitutive instrument limiting treaty-making capacity. For example, the UN Charter does not authorize the organization to enter into a headquarters agreement with the United States of America (US). In these cases, the competent organ may authorize the organization to enter into a treaty. Where the competent organ has not authorized the organization, it can be difficult to establish the scope of the organization's treaty-making capacity. Certainly, issues of headquarters and immunities would always be implied for any organization, though more reaching agreements might need stronger justification. One of the most important considerations would be the general competence that the member states have delegated to an organization, and whether that competence necessarily entails reaching international agreements. On this basis, even if the UN wished to adhere to, for example, the Geneva Conventions concerning conduct in armed conflict, and the Conventions permitted the UN to participate, the UN Office of Legal Affairs has taken the position that the UN would not be able to participate because it does not have the requisite powers.[10]

One difficulty, however, will be matters where the member states and organization share competence. In Chapter 5 on the powers of an organization, this question will be explored in more detail, for example in *Case C-22/70, Commission v Council [ERTA]*,[11] where the court had to determine whether the European Community (EC, now European Union) could participate in the European Road Transport Agreement (ERTA) when both the European Community and the Member States had competences over laws pertaining to road transport regulations.

Of course, the other issue is whether the treaty in question permits adherence of subjects of international law aside from states. For example, the Geneva Conventions are only open to "Powers,"[12] whereas the WTO Agreement is open to the "European Communities" [Union].[13]

---

9   Rome Statute of the International Criminal Court, 17 July 1998, 2187 UNTS 90, article 3(2). International Criminal Court, *available at* www.icc-cpi.int/resource-library/Documents/RS-Eng.pdf.
10 *See* Memorandum of the UN Office of Legal Affairs, 15 June 1972, 1972 UN Juridical Yearbook 153.
11 *See* Case C-22/70, Commission of the European Communities v Council of the European Communities [*In re* European Road Transport Agreement (ERTA)], Judgment (Court of Justice of the European Communities [Union], 31 March 1971).
12 *See e.g.* Convention (I) for the Amelioration of the Condition of the Wounded and Sick in Armed Forces in the Field, 12 August 1949, 75 UNTS 31, articles 56, 60.
13 *See* Marrakesh Agreement Establishing the World Trade Organization, 14 April 1994, 1867 UNTS 4, 154 (WTO Agreement), article XIV(1).

Treaties can also be adopted between international organizations exclusively, again, providing the relevant organizations have the necessary capacity. An example is the working agreement between the ICC and UN.[14]

The final type of treaty is one between states and/or international organizations, but creating yet another new international organization. When another state wishes to join such a treaty later, it is not merely a process of simple treaty accession, but a generally more complex procedure provided in the treaty for newly admitted members. For some organizations, this admission procedure can be non-burdensome and straightforward, but for others, it can involve quite a demanding negotiation process. Consider that, while the accession of Kyrgyzstan to the WTO took just under three years, the negotiations over Russia's accession took almost two decades and involved almost 90 separate bilateral agreements on particular trade issues. The question of admission to membership will be discussed in more detail in Chapter 4 on membership. For the purposes of the law of treaties, it suffices to be aware that joining an international organization is a far more involved process than mere accession to a treaty.

2.2.3 Reservations to treaties

Under the law of treaties, states may be free to enter reservations when they adhere to treaties, provided the reservation is not forbidden by the treaty, does not violate the object and purpose of the treaty, or otherwise violate peremptory norms of international law (*jus cogens* norms). A similar rule applies when international organizations wish to adhere to treaties where reservations are permitted.

Treaties creating international organizations largely follow the same rule, although it is more unusual for reservations to be permitted.[15] In 1953, the then USSR attempted to join the ILO with a reservation, but the attempt was rejected by the Director-General because reservations were not permitted. The USSR joined the following year without its reservation.

Reservations should be distinguished from declarations, which are policy statements, not intended to modify any legal provision in the treaty. India communicated a "condition" when it adhered to the Inter-Governmental Maritime Consultative Organization in 1959. The condition was discussed in the UN General Assembly, and it concluded that this communication was a non-binding declaration of policy, so it did not amount to a reservation, and India could maintain it.[16]

Reservations should also be distinguished from "opt-outs," which are agreements, especially true of the EU, where the Member States negotiate and permit one or more states to have certain exemptions or modified terms under the treaty. These

---

14 *See* Negotiated Relationship Agreement between the International Criminal Court and the United Nations, ICC Resolution ICC-ASP/3/Res.1, ICC Doc. ICC-ASP/3/Res.1 (7 September 2004).
15 *See e.g.* WTO Agreement, article XVI(5) ("No reservations may be made in respect of any provision of this Agreement").
16 *See* 1959 UN Yearbook 407–8.

agreements are not unilateral like reservations or declarations, and form part of the negotiated arrangement.[17]

When states enter reservations pertaining to an organization's constitutive instrument, and are permitted by the constitutive instrument, the reservation must also be permitted by the organization itself:

Vienna Convention on the Law of Treaties
23 May 1969
1155 UNTS 331[18]

Article 20
Acceptance of and objection to reservations

3. When a treaty is a constituent instrument of an international organization and unless it otherwise provides, a reservation requires the acceptance of the competent organ of that organization.

A reservation could be rejected by the other states parties and/or the organization for a number of reasons. Those reasons could include that the reservation is prohibited by the treaty or violates certain fundamental, peremptory norms of international law (*jus cogens* norms). Reservations might be rejected because the other states and/or organization simply do not agree with the exception. Another basis for rejecting a reservation is that it is invalid because it defeats the object and purpose of the treaty. While some of these bases for rejecting reservations are, in principle, objective, whether a reservation violates one of the conditions is an assessment made by the other states parties and the organization, as a part of membership accession. For this reason, there still is scope for interpretation and application of these exceptions. For example when Austria joined the United Nations, it included an official declaration of the state's neutrality, which could suggest that Austria was not in a position to fully discharge its obligations under the UN Charter. Nonetheless, the declaration was accepted as such, and Austria was admitted to the UN.

2.2.4 Invalidity of treaties

One issue is whether the creation of an international organization could itself be an unlawful act. The Draft Articles on the Responsibility of International Organizations,

---

17 *See e.g.* Denmark and the Treaty on European Union, ("Edinburgh Agreement"), Official Journal EU C 348, 1 (31 December 1992) ("Against this background, the European Council has agreed on the following set of arrangements, which are fully compatible with the Treaty, are designed to meet Danish concerns, and therefore apply exclusively to Denmark and not to other existing or acceding Member States …"). http://eur-lex.europa.eu, © European Union, 1998–2020.
18 From the United Nations Treaty Series, by the United Nations © 1969 United Nations. Reprinted with the permission of the United Nations.

in Article 28, International responsibility in case of provision of competence to an international organization, has concluded that:[19]

1. A State member of an international organization incurs international responsibility if it circumvents one of its international obligations by providing the organization with competence in relation to that obligation, and the organization commits an act that, if committed by that State, would have constituted a breach of that obligation.
2. Paragraph 1 applies whether or not the act in question is internationally wrongful for the international organization.

The European Court of Human Rights[20] has similarly found that:

> Where States establish international organizations in order to pursue or strengthen their cooperation in certain fields of activities ... It would be incompatible with the purpose and object of the Convention, however, if the Contracting States were thereby absolved from their responsibility under the Convention in relation to the field of activity covered by such attribution.

These views suggest that the creation of an organization would be effective *de jure*, even if the states creating the organization violated the law in creating it. The issues in these excerpts above are really focused on the responsibility of the state for trying to evade its international obligations or failing to be diligent in its oversight of the organization it created.

This question might change its character if the violation was a norm of *jus cogens* character. In addition to conventional (treaty) law, customary international law, and general principles of law, some rules of international law are raised to the level of being *jus cogens* norms, meaning they express rules that are non-derogable. Under the law of treaties, some treaties are rendered invalid *ab initio* by the nature of the obligations they create, if they violate norms of *jus cogens*. The problem in the case of international organizations from the perspective of the law of treaties is that the constitutive instrument creates a new person with independence from its members. It is difficult to imagine that a new international legal person operating *de facto* could be held invalid *de jure* because its very purpose or objectives violate norms of *jus cogens*. For example, in the *Westland Helicopters*

---

19 International Law Commission, Draft articles on the responsibility of international organizations, II(2) Yearbook of the International Law Commission (2011), UN Doc. A/CN.4/SER.A/2011/Add.1 (Part 2). From the Yearbook of the International Law Commission, by the International Law Commission © 2011 United Nations. Reprinted with the permission of the United Nations.
20 Waite and Kennedy v. Germany, Application No. 26083/94, Judgment (European Court of Human Rights (Grand Chamber), 18 February 1999). © Council of Europe.

Ltd arbitration,[21] the arbitral tribunal observed that the "'Arab Organization for Industrialization' ... was [formed for] the development of an arms industry for the benefit of the four States." Of course, this objective in itself is not a *jus cogens* violation, but it does show that international organizations might be founded for objectives not in keeping with our usual expectations of peace and justice. One would have to imagine an organization created expressly for a purpose that in itself was a clear *jus cogens* violation for there to be an issue of the organization's nullity. For example, an organization created specifically in order to engage in slavery or torture, or perpetrate genocide.

A related question concerns situations where an organization is not expressly created to violate *jus cogens* norms, but it later undertakes measures that could be violations. In Chapter 5 on powers and Chapter 9 on responsibility, we will consider whether a *jus cogens* violation by an international organization would amount to a question of an *ultra vires* exercise of power or a question of responsibility. In this section, the question is whether the law of treaties, with its specific terms on *jus cogens* norms, has any role to play. Consider the following case:

Joined Cases C-402/05 P and C-145/05 P
Kadi and Al Barakat International Foundation v. Council and Commission of the European Union
Judgment
Court of Justice of the European Communities [Union] (Grand Chamber), 3 September 2008[22]

By their appeals, Mr Kadi (C-402/05 P) and Al Barakaat International Foundation ("Al Barakaat") (C-415/05 P) seek to have set aside the judgments of the Court of First Instance of the European Communities of 21 September 2005 in Case T-315/01 *Kadi* v *Council and Commission* [2005] ECR II-3649 ("*Kadi*") and Case T-306/01 *Yusuf and Al Barakaat International Foundation* v *Council and Commission* [2005] ECR II-3533 ("*Yusuf and Al Barakaat*") (together, "the judgments under appeal").

...

Legal context

3   Under Article 1(1) and (3) of the Charter of the United Nations, signed at San Francisco (United States of America) on 26 June 1945, the purposes of the United Nations are inter alia "[t]o maintain international peace and security" and "[t]o achieve international cooperation in solving international problems of an economic, social, cultural, or humanitarian character, and in promoting and encouraging respect

---

21 Westland Helicopters Ltd and Arab Organization for Industrialization, et al., ICC Case No. 3879/AS, Interim Award Regarding Jurisdiction, 80 International Law Reports 595 & 600 (International Chamber of Commerce, Court of Arbitration, Arbitral Tribunal, 5 March 1984) © Sir E. Lauterpacht, published by Cambridge University Press. Reproduced with permission of The Licensor through PLSclear.

22 http://eur-lex.europa.eu, © European Union, 1998–2020.

for human rights and for fundamental freedoms for all without distinction as to race, sex, language, or religion".

...

13 On 15 October 1999 the Security Council adopted Resolution 1267 (1999), in which it, inter alia, condemned the fact that Afghan territory continued to be used for the sheltering and training of terrorists and planning of terrorist acts, reaffirmed its conviction that the suppression of international terrorism was essential for the maintenance of international peace and security and deplored the fact that the Taliban continued to provide safe haven to Usama bin Laden and to allow him and others associated with him to operate a network of terrorist training camps from territory held by the Taliban and to use Afghanistan as a base from which to sponsor international terrorist operations.

14 In the second paragraph of the resolution the Security Council demanded that the Taliban should without further delay turn Usama bin Laden over to appropriate authorities in a country where he has been indicted, or to appropriate authorities in a country where he will be arrested and effectively brought to justice. In order to ensure compliance with that demand, paragraph 4(b) of Resolution 1267 (1999) provides that all the States must, in particular, "freeze funds and other financial resources, including funds derived or generated from property owned or controlled directly or indirectly by the Taliban, or by any undertaking owned or controlled by the Taliban, as designated by the Committee established by paragraph 6 below, and ensure that neither they nor any other funds or financial resources so designated are made available, by their nationals or by any persons within their territory, to or for the benefit of the Taliban or any undertaking owned or controlled, directly or indirectly, by the Taliban, except as may be authorised by the Committee on a case-by-case basis on the grounds of humanitarian need".

15 In paragraph 6 of Resolution 1267 (1999), the Security Council decided to establish, in accordance with rule 28 of its provisional rules of procedure, a committee of the Security Council composed of all its members ("the Sanctions Committee"), responsible in particular for ensuring that the States implement the measures imposed by paragraph 4, designating the funds or other financial resources referred to in paragraph 4 and considering requests for exemptions from the measures imposed by paragraph 4.

16 Taking the view that action by the Community was necessary in order to implement Resolution 1267 (1999), on 15 November 1999 the Council adopted Common Position 1999/727/CFSP concerning restrictive measures against the Taliban (OJ 1999 L 294, p. 1).

...

31 On 17 October and 9 November 2001 the Sanctions Committee published two new additions to its summary list, including in particular the names of the following entity and person:

– Al-Qadi, Yasin (A.K.A. Kadi, Shaykh Yassin Abdullah; A.K.A. Kahdi, Yasin) ..., and

– Barakaat International Foundation ...

32 By Commission Regulation (EC) No 2062/2001 of 19 October 2001 ..., Mr Kadi's name was added, with others, to Annex I.

33 By Commission Regulation (EC) No 2199/2001 of 12 November 2001 ..., the name Al Barakaat was added, with others, to Annex I.

...

46 By applications lodged at the Registry of the Court of First Instance, Mr Kadi and Al Barakaat both brought actions seeking annulment of Regulation No 467/2001, the former seeking annulment also of Regulation No 2062/2001 and the latter annulment also of Regulation No 2199/2001, in so far as those measures concern them. During the proceedings before the Court of First Instance, the appellants amended their claims and pleas in law, so as to refer thenceforth to the contested regulation, in so far as that measure concerns them.

...

73 As regards, last, the pleas alleging, in both cases, breach of the applicants' fundamental rights, the Court of First Instance considered it appropriate to consider, in the first place, the relationship between the international legal order under the United Nations and the domestic or Community legal order, and also the extent to which the exercise by the Community and its Member States of their powers is bound by resolutions of the Security Council adopted under Chapter VII of the Charter of the United Nations. This consideration would effectively determine the scope of the review of lawfulness, particularly having regard to fundamental rights, which that court must carry out in respect of the Community acts giving effect to such resolutions. It is only if it should find that they fall within the scope of its judicial review and that they are capable of leading to annulment of the contested regulation that the Court of First Instance would have to rule on those alleged breaches (*Kadi*, paragraphs 178 to 180, and *Yusuf and Al Barakaat*, paragraphs 228 to 230).

74 Examining first the relationship between the international legal order under the United Nations and the domestic legal orders or the Community legal order, the Court of First Instance ruled that, from the standpoint of international law, the Member States, as Members of the United Nations, are bound to respect the principle of the primacy of their obligations "under the Charter" of the United Nations, enshrined in Article 103 thereof, which means, in particular, that the obligation, laid down in Article 25 of the Charter, to carry out the decisions of the Security Council prevails over any other obligation they may have entered into under an international agreement (*Kadi*, paragraphs 181 to 184, and *Yusuf and Al Barakaat*, paragraphs 231 to 234).

75 According to the Court of First Instance, that obligation of the Member States to respect the principle of the primacy of obligations undertaken by virtue of the Charter of the United Nations is not affected by the EC Treaty, for it is an obligation arising from an agreement concluded before the Treaty, and so falling within the scope of Article 307 EC. What is more, Article 297 EC is intended to ensure that that principle is observed (*Kadi*, paragraphs 185 to 188, and *Yusuf and Al Barakaat*, paragraphs 235 to 238).

76 The Court of First Instance concluded that resolutions adopted by the Security Council under Chapter VII of

the Charter of the United Nations are binding on all the Member States of the Community which must therefore, in that capacity, take all measures necessary to ensure that those resolutions are put into effect and may, and indeed must, leave unapplied any provision of Community law, whether a provision of primary law or a general principle of Community law, that raises any impediment to the proper performance of their obligations under that Charter (*Kadi*, paragraphs 189 and 190, and *Yusuf and Al Barakaat*, paragraphs 239 and 240).

77 However, according to the Court of First Instance, the mandatory nature of those resolutions stemming from an obligation under international law does not bind the Community, for the latter is not, as such, directly bound by the Charter of the United Nations, not being a Member of the United Nations, or an addressee of the resolutions of the Security Council, or the successor to the rights and obligations of the Member States for the purposes of public international law (*Kadi*, paragraph 192, and *Yusuf and Al Barakaat*, paragraph 242).

78 Nevertheless, that mandatory force binds the Community by virtue of Community law (*Kadi*, paragraph 193, and *Yusuf and Al Barakaat*, paragraph 243).

79 In that regard, the Court of First Instance referring, by analogy, to Joined Cases 21/72 to 24/72 *International Fruit Company and Others* [1972] ECR 1219, paragraph 18, in particular, held that, in so far as under the EC Treaty the Community has assumed powers previously exercised by Member States in the area governed by the Charter of the United Nations, the provisions of that Charter have the effect of binding the Community (*Kadi*, paragraph 203, and *Yusuf and Al Barakaat*, paragraph 253).

80 In the following paragraph in those judgments, the Court of First Instance concluded, first, that the Community may not infringe the obligations imposed on its Member States by the Charter of the United Nations or impede their performance and, second, that in the exercise of its powers it is bound, by the very Treaty by which it was established, to adopt all the measures necessary to enable its Member States to fulfil those obligations.

81 Being thus called upon, in the second place, to determine the scope of the review of legality, especially in the light of fundamental rights, that it must carry out concerning Community measures giving effect to resolutions of the Security Council, such as the contested regulation, the Court of First Instance first recalled, in *Kadi*, paragraph 209, and *Yusuf and Al Barakaat*, paragraph 260, that, according to case-law, the European Community is based on the rule of law, inasmuch as neither its Member States nor its institutions can avoid review of the question whether their acts are in conformity with the basic constitutional charter, the EC Treaty, which established a complete system of legal remedies and procedures designed to enable the Court of Justice to review the legality of acts of the institutions.

82 In *Kadi*, paragraph 212, and *Yusuf and Al Barakaat*, paragraph 263, the Court of First Instance considered, however, that the question arising in the cases before it was whether there exist any structural limits, imposed by general international law or by the EC Treaty itself, on that judicial review.

83 In that connection the Court of First Instance recalled, in *Kadi*, paragraph 213, and *Yusuf and Al Barakaat*, paragraph 264, that the contested regulation, adopted in the light of Common Position 2002/402, constitutes the implementation at Community level of the obligation placed on the Member States of the Community, as Members of the United Nations, to give effect, if appropriate by means of a Community act, to the sanctions against Usama bin Laden, members of the Al-Qaeda network and the Taliban and other associated individuals, groups, undertakings and entities, which have been decided and later strengthened by several resolutions of the Security Council adopted under Chapter VII of the Charter of the United Nations.

84 In that situation, the Community acted, according to the Court of First Instance, under circumscribed powers leaving it no autonomous discretion in their exercise, so that it could, in particular, neither directly alter the content of the resolutions at issue nor set up any mechanism capable of giving rise to such alteration (*Kadi*, paragraph 214, and *Yusuf and Al Barakaat*, paragraph 265).

85 The Court of First Instance inferred therefrom that the applicants' challenging of the internal lawfulness of the contested regulation implied that the Court of First Instance should undertake a review, direct or indirect, of the lawfulness of the resolutions put into effect by that regulation in the light of fundamental rights as protected by the Community legal order (*Kadi*, paragraphs 215 and 216, and *Yusuf and Al Barakaat*, paragraphs 266 and 267).

...

87 In *Kadi*, paragraph 226, and *Yusuf and Al Barakaat*, paragraph 277, the Court of First Instance found that it was, none the less, empowered to check, indirectly, the lawfulness of the resolutions of the Security Council in question with regard to jus cogens, understood as a body of higher rules of public international law binding on all subjects of international law, including the bodies of the United Nations, and from which no derogation is possible.

88 In paragraphs 227 to 231 of *Kadi*, drawn up in terms identical to those of paragraphs 278 to 282 of *Yusuf and Al Barakaat*, the Court of First Instance held as follows:

> "227 In this connection, it must be noted that the Vienna Convention on the Law of Treaties, which consolidates the customary international law and Article 5 of which provides that it is to apply 'to any treaty which is the constituent instrument of an international organisation and to any treaty adopted within an international organisation', provides in Article 53 for a treaty to be void if it conflicts with a peremptory norm of general international law (jus cogens), defined as 'a norm accepted and recognised by the international community of States as a whole as a norm from which no derogation is permitted and which can be modified only by a subsequent norm of general international law having the same character'. Similarly, Article 64 of the Vienna Convention provides that: 'If a new peremptory norm of general international law emerges, any existing treaty which is in conflict with that norm becomes void and terminates'.

228 Furthermore, the Charter of the United Nations itself presupposes the existence of mandatory principles of international law, in particular, the protection of the fundamental rights of the human person. In the preamble to the Charter, the peoples of the United Nations declared themselves determined to 'reaffirm faith in fundamental human rights, in the dignity and worth of the human person'. In addition, it is apparent from Chapter I of the Charter, headed 'Purposes and Principles', that one of the purposes of the United Nations is to encourage respect for human rights and for fundamental freedoms.

229 Those principles are binding on the Members of the United Nations as well as on its bodies. Thus, under Article 24(2) of the Charter of the United Nations, the Security Council, in discharging its duties under its primary responsibility for the maintenance of international peace and security, is to act 'in accordance with the Purposes and Principles of the United Nations'. The Security Council's powers of sanction in the exercise of that responsibility must therefore be wielded in compliance with international law, particularly with the purposes and principles of the United Nations.

230 International law thus permits the inference that there exists one limit to the principle that resolutions of the Security Council have binding effect: namely, that they must observe the fundamental peremptory provisions of jus cogens. If they fail to do so, however improbable that may be, they would bind neither the Member States of the United Nations nor, in consequence, the Community.

231 The indirect judicial review carried out by the Court in connection with an action for annulment of a Community act adopted, where no discretion whatsoever may be exercised, with a view to putting into effect a resolution of the Security Council may therefore, highly exceptionally, extend to determining whether the superior rules of international law falling within the ambit of jus cogens have been observed, in particular, the mandatory provisions concerning the universal protection of human rights, from which neither the Member States nor the bodies of the United Nations may derogate because they constitute 'intransgressible principles of international customary law' (Advisory Opinion of the International Court of Justice of 8 July 1996, The Legality of the Threat or Use of Nuclear Weapons, Reports 1996, p. 226, paragraph 79; see also, to that effect, Advocate General Jacobs's Opinion in Case C-84/95 *Bosphorus* [1996] ECR I-3953, paragraph 65)."

...

91 In *Kadi*, paragraphs 239 and 240, and *Yusuf and Al Barakaat*, paragraphs 290 and 291, the Court of First Instance held that the exemptions to and derogations from the obligation to freeze funds provided for in the contested regulation as a result of its amendment by Regulation No 561/2003, itself putting into effect Resolution 1452 (2002), show that it is neither the purpose nor the effect of that measure to submit the persons entered in the summary list to inhuman or degrading treatment.

92 In *Kadi*, paragraphs 243 to 251, and *Yusuf and Al Barakaat*, paragraphs

294 to 302, the Court of First Instance held, in addition, that the freezing of funds did not constitute an arbitrary, inappropriate or disproportionate interference with the right to private property of the persons concerned and could not, therefore, be regarded as contrary to jus cogens, having regard to the following facts:

...

326 It follows from the foregoing that the Community judicature must, in accordance with the powers conferred on it by the EC Treaty, ensure the review, in principle the full review, of the lawfulness of all Community acts in the light of the fundamental rights forming an integral part of the general principles of Community law, including review of Community measures which, like the contested regulation, are designed to give effect to the resolutions adopted by the Security Council under Chapter VII of the Charter of the United Nations.

327 The Court of First Instance erred in law, therefore, when it held, in paragraphs 212 to 231 of *Kadi* and 263 to 282 of *Yusuf and Al Barakaat*, that it followed from the principles governing the relationship between the international legal order under the United Nations and the Community legal order that the contested regulation, since it is designed to give effect to a resolution adopted by the Security Council under Chapter VII of the Charter of the United Nations affording no latitude in that respect, must enjoy immunity from jurisdiction so far as concerns its internal lawfulness save with regard to its compatibility with the norms of jus cogens.

...

369 The contested regulation, in so far as it concerns Mr Kadi, was adopted without furnishing any guarantee enabling him to put his case to the competent authorities, in a situation in which the restriction of his property rights must be regarded as significant, having regard to the general application and actual continuation of the freezing measures affecting him.

370 It must therefore be held that, in the circumstances of the case, the imposition of the restrictive measures laid down by the contested regulation in respect of Mr Kadi, by including him in the list contained in Annex I to that regulation, constitutes an unjustified restriction of his right to property.

371 The plea raised by Mr Kadi that his fundamental right to respect for property has been infringed is therefore well founded.

372 It follows from all the foregoing that the contested regulation, so far as it concerns the appellants, must be annulled.

Notes

- Before getting into the substance of the case, first consider which court is this? What is its jurisdiction? What is the measure being challenged? Is it a Security Council resolution, or is it an EU regulation? What is the legal effect of that measure; what does it oblige its addressee to do?

- Are there *jus cogens* norms at issue? Which ones are they? And how does the court identify whether they rise to that character? Does the measure actually violate *jus cogens*? In what way?
- What is the court's view on the role of the Vienna Convention regarding *jus cogens* norms? What are the precise legal effects when a measure violates *jus cogens*? Is the measure invalidated and/or does it cease to have legal effect? Is the actor held responsible? Does it constrain the actor's powers? Does it impact the constitutive instrument, and if so, what is the scope of that impact?
- Based on your answers to the above questions, which organization has violated a norm of *jus cogens* character, if any? Does the court declare that the UN or EU has violated *jus cogens*? What would be the correct result from such an action?
- Is the court really applying the correct result? Is the court considering the rule prohibiting *jus cogens* treaty terms as a rule of treaty (or a treaty provision) validity, or a question of the interpretation of a treaty provision? Or the interpretation of an international organization's act?

Another way in which treaties can be rendered invalid is when one party commits a material breach of the treaty. Contrasted with the situation discussed above, which would invalidate the treaty *ab initio*, in this case we are discussing a later event that would invalidate the treaty as from the moment of the event. This outcome is highly unusual, and most treaty violations are not going to rise to the level of such significance as to be material breaches. Again in the case of international organizations, it may be that this threshold of materiality is understood to be even higher. We would have to imagine a violation of a constitutive instrument that was of such gravity as to abolish the organization. But if the organization still has several other member states, and if it has meaningful independence from the members, then it is difficult to think of a scenario in which a material breach would lead to the dissolution of the organization. Consider, for example, that the United Nations continues to exist notwithstanding that some of its members have used military force against each other in a clear violation of one of the fundamental rules in the UN Charter. Rather than looking to the rules on material breach when there are fundamental violations, it is better to look at the rules in the constitutive instrument on expulsion of members or perhaps on dissolution of the organization. Both of these topics will be addressed in later chapters.

2.2.5 Interpretation of treaties

The last issue for the law of treaties concerning international organizations that we will deal with in this textbook is the interpretation of treaties. The member states, as authors of the constitutive instrument and in their role exercising oversight of the organization, are the primary interpreters of that instrument. However, because an organization has meaningful independence and the constitutive instrument functions as a quasi-constitution, the organization may also interpret it itself. This interpretive function may be exercised by all of the organs of the organization, including subsidiary organs. They will all have a role in determining whether they are acting within the scope of the constitutive instrument. Some organizations may assign particular significance to the interpretations by one organ above the others, generally a judicial organ. This is not always the case, and it needs to be very clear from the instrument and the governing structure that this is intended. For example, the Court of Justice of the EU has a decisive role within that organization, although the International Court of Justice does not have a similar role in the UN. This relationship between organs will be discussed in more detail in Chapter 7 on organs. For the purposes of this chapter, it suffices to take note that in many of the cases in this textbook, an organization is interpreting its own constitutive instrument. This act of interpretation may have implications for the relationships between organs, the relationship between the organization and its member states, and possibly the relationship between those actors and individuals where individuals may benefit directly from the constitutive instrument. For example, the Court of Justice of the EU can render binding judgments on the meaning of the EU treaties concerning the status of EU citizenship and its rights for individuals.[23]

In interpreting the constitutive instrument, the organization applies the Vienna Convention. The rules on interpretation in the Vienna Convention for International Organizations are identical to the rules in the Vienna Convention, so we will only work with the latter convention. The Vienna Convention provides the following "general rule of interpretation":

Vienna Convention on the Law of Treaties
23 May 1969
1155 UNTS 331[24]

Article 31
General rule of interpretation

1. A treaty shall be interpreted in good faith in accordance with the ordinary meaning to be given to the terms of the treaty in their context and in the light of its object and purpose.

2. The context for the purpose of the interpretation of a treaty shall comprise, in addition to the text, including its preamble and annexes:
    a. Any agreement relating to the treaty which was made between all the parties in connexion with the conclusion of the treaty;

---

23 *See e.g.* Case C-135/08, Rottman v Freistaat Bayern, Judgment, paras. 1–2 (Court of Justice of the European Union (Grand Chamber), 2 March 2010) ("The reference for a preliminary ruling concerns the interpretation of the provisions of the EC Treaty relating to citizenship of the European Union. The reference was made in connection with proceedings between Dr. Rottmann and the Freistaat Bayern, concerning the latter's withdrawal of the naturalisation of the applicant in the main proceedings").
24 From the United Nations Treaty Series, by the United Nations © 1969 United Nations. Reprinted with the permission of the United Nations.

b. Any instrument which was made by one or more parties in connexion with the conclusion of the treaty and accepted by the other parties as an instrument related to the treaty.
3. There shall be taken into account, together with the context:
   a. Any subsequent agreement between the parties regarding the interpretation of the treaty or the application of its provisions;
   b. Any subsequent practice in the application of the treaty which establishes the agreement of the parties regarding its interpretation;
   c. Any relevant rules of international law applicable in the relations between the parties.
4. A special meaning shall be given to a term if it is established that the parties so intended.

Article 32
Supplementary means of interpretation

Recourse may be had to supplementary means of interpretation, including the preparatory work of the treaty and the circumstances of its conclusion, in order to confirm the meaning resulting from the application of article 31, or to determine the meaning when the interpretation according to article 31:
   a. Leaves the meaning ambiguous or obscure; or
   b. Leads to a result which is manifestly absurd or unreasonable.

This methodology is both helpful and frustrating at the same time. On the one hand, it is helpful to prescribe a way to think about treaties, yet on the other hand, there is so much room for disagreement over these terms that we do have to wonder about their value. The rule also seems to be assuming that the interpreter would apply normal concepts of scientific logic and grammar, but also seems to be missing established doctrines of interpretation such as *ejusdem generis* or *favor rei*. In addition, where is the approach to using *jus cogens* as an interpretive tool that we saw in the *Kadi* case above? Interestingly enough, the Vienna Convention contains both the interpretation methodology and one of the first statements of the effect of *jus cogens* obligations on treaties, yet *jus cogens* is completely absent from the interpretation methodology. Perhaps its absence here makes us reconsider the EU Court of Justice's approach in *Kadi*?

Nonetheless, even before the Vienna Convention entered into force, international organizations were already applying a methodology much like that above, based on customary international law:

Competence of the General Assembly for the Admission of a State to the United Nations
["Second Admissions Case"]
Advisory Opinion
1950 ICJ Reps. 4
International Court of Justice, 3 March 1950

The Court considers it necessary to say that the first duty of a tribunal which is called upon to interpret and apply the provisions of a treaty, is to endeavour to give effect to them in their natural and ordinary meaning in the context in which they occur. If the relevant words in their natural and ordinary meaning make sense in their context, that is an end of the matter. If, on the other hand, the words in their natural and ordinary meaning are ambiguous or lead to an unreasonable result, then, and then only, must the Court, by resort to other methods of interpretation, seek to ascertain what the parties really did mean when they used these words. As the Permanent Court said in the case concerning the Polish Postal Service in Danzig (P.C.I.J., Series B, No. 11, p. 39):

> "It is a cardinal principle of interpretation that words must be interpreted in the sense which they would normally have in their context, unless such interpretation would lead to something unreasonable or absurd."

When the Court can give effect to a provision of a treaty by giving to the words used in it their natural and ordinary meaning, it may not interpret the words by seeking to give them some other meaning. In the present case the Court finds no difficulty in ascertaining the natural and ordinary meaning of the words in question and no difficulty in giving effect to them. Some of the written statements submitted to the Court have invited it to investigate the travaux preparatoires of the Charter. Having regard, however, to the considerations above stated, the Court is of the opinion that it is not permissible, in this case, to resort to travaux preparatoires.

The conclusions to which the Court is led by the text of Article 4, paragraph 2, are fully confirmed by the structure of the Charter, and particularly by the relations established by it between the General Assembly and the Security Council.

Notes

- To what degree does the court follow the Vienna Convention methodology, recognizing of course that the Vienna Convention was not yet in force at the time of the opinion? If the court had to articulate its own general rule of interpretation, what would that be? What is the place of the text and ambiguous result in the court's methodology?
- Notwithstanding the above question, is there any way to argue that the court's methodology in this excerpt is actually in compliance with the Vienna Convention? If a court was interpreting a treaty after the entry into force of the Vienna

Convention, and it encountered text, whose ordinary meaning was quite clear, surely it would apply that meaning, wouldn't it? How can we reconcile that approach with the methodology in the Vienna Convention?

In the next chapter on the creation of international organizations, we will study the *Reparation for Injuries Suffered in the Service of the United Nations* case in more detail, but at this point, we only want to be alert to the interpretive methodology that the court applies in the following excerpt:

Reparation for Injuries Suffered in the Service of the United Nations
Advisory Opinion
1949 ICJ Reps. 174
International Court of Justice, 11 April 1949

To answer this question, which is not settled by the actual terms of the Charter, we must consider what characteristics it was intended thereby to give to the Organization.

...

In the opinion of the Court, the Organization was intended to exercise and enjoy, and is in fact exercising and enjoying, functions and rights which can only be explained on the basis of the possession of a large measure of international personality and the capacity to operate upon an international plane. ... It must be acknowledged that its Members, by entrusting certain functions to it, with the attendant duties and responsibilities, have clothed it with the competence required to enable those functions to be effectively discharged.

Notes

- Review the Vienna Convention methodology. How is it structured? Does it prescribe steps of interpretation? Is there a clear hierarchy of considerations? Does it not offer any suggestions about what "ordinary meaning," "context," and "object and purpose" mean?
- What interpretive technique does the text above suggest? Is it focused on text, context, or object and purpose? If it is focused on text, then which parts of the text are considered? Is that the ordinary meaning? If it is focused on context, how does the court define context? If it is focused on object and purpose, how does the court identify and appreciate the object and purpose of the UN Charter?

CHAPTER 3

Creation and dissolution

3.1 CREATION OF AN INTERNATIONAL ORGANIZATION

This chapter will explore the life cycle of international organizations, from birth to death. Along the way, we will apply the definition of an international organization in order to know whether one has been created. We will also need to examine the concept of international legal personality and its acquisition. At the end of the chapter, we will consider the winding up and termination of an organization, including the issue of succession to its international rights and obligations.

Ultimately, the decision to create an international organization to accomplish some objective is a purely political one. States must determine that, for the sake of best discharging its role, an organization is needed, and that the organization needs a particular infrastructure, staffing and status. The decision to dissolve an organization is similarly political. However, both of these choices are somewhat constrained by legal issues. If an organization is created, then it will have the capacity to hold international rights and obligations, its officials will benefit from immunity, and its acts may carry legal effect. If an organization is dissolved, all legal rights and obligations created with it may be jeopardy.

In Chapter 1, we considered whether there was a consistent definition of international organizations, and in this chapter, we will use the definition that was developed in the first chapter to identify the elements that must be met in order to create and international organization. Recall that, in this book, the elements are: (1) international legal person (2) created by an agreement under international law (3) between subjects of international law (4) with a degree of meaningful independence from its members (5) to accomplish certain objectives. If these criteria have been met, then we will view the situation as the creation of a new international organization.

3.1.1 International legal personality

The first element of the definition is that the entity has international legal personality.

Legal personality is essentially the status of being capable of holding rights and obligations in a legal system. However, the status of personality is distinct from the rights and obligations an entity holds. What is less clear is whether rights and obligations flow from the status of personality, or whether personality is a status that comes from the receipt of rights and obligations. In domestic legal systems, a human is a natural person, and hence a legal person with capacity for rights and obligations. Corporations are legal persons, and hence are also capable of holding rights and duties. Other entities in domestic law are not legal persons, such as plants and animals.

One critical difference between natural and legal persons is whether they are real or not. That statement might sound like a deeply philosophical one, but how we conceive of legal persons has a critical influence on how we interpret the law and apply it to them. On the one hand, legal persons, such as corporations, are created by people and continue to exist with the participation of people. They cannot take any action without that action being imagined, planned, and implemented by people. Without managers, employees, and customers, they cease to exist in any true sense. Imagine if the articles of incorporation of a company were misplaced and everyone forgot that it existed. In essence, it would no longer exist. Natural persons clearly exist in a physical form that cannot be denied, even if we misplace their birth certificate. In this sense, legal persons do not exist other than in our imagination. On the other hand, legal persons also certainly do exist, because they create, control, and manage huge workforces and sums of money, in some cases larger than the populations or budgets of some states. In this contrary sense, legal persons definitely exist.

These same considerations apply within the international legal system. States are clearly international legal persons, often considered "organic" persons, in that their personality arises from the natural historical process. In that way, states in international law resemble humans in the domestic legal system. International organizations, however, are more akin to corporations, in that they are created, deriving their personality from a constitutive act. In the earlier years of international law, it was unclear whether the UN and other organizations had personality or not. The issue was whether international law, as a legal system, entertained the notion of persons who were not states.

3.1.1.1 Identifying international legal personality

The next case, *Reparation for Injuries Suffered in the Service of the United Nations* (*Reparations* case), is one of the most significant cases, perhaps *the* most significant, in the area of international legal personality. The UN had authorized a representative to travel to Israel, which was not a member state of the UN at the time, to oversee peace discussions. During that visit, the representative was killed by a terrorist group. The UN demanded compensation, i.e. "reparations," for the injuries suffered by this person when the state failed to protect him. However, there were several obstacles for the UN to have a legal basis to claim reparations. Firstly, it was unclear whether the UN had any international legal personality to make claim in its own name, or whether such a claim should be made by the state of nationality of the deceased. Perhaps surprisingly, the UN Charter does not mention whether the UN has international legal personality. For this reason, the question was submitted to the International Court of Justice for an advisory opinion:

Reparation for Injuries Suffered in the Service of the United Nations
Advisory Opinion
1949 ICJ Reps. 174
International Court of Justice, 11 April 1949

[p. 174]
On December 3rd, 1948, the General Assembly of the United Nations adopted the following Resolution:

> "Whereas the series of tragic events which have lately befallen agents of the United Nations engaged in the performance of their duties raises, with greater urgency than ever, the question of the arrangements to be made by the United Nations with a view to ensuring to its agents the fullest Measure of protection in the future and ensuring that reparation be made for the injuries suffered; and
>
> Whereas it is highly desirable that the Secretary-General should be able to act without question as efficaciously as possible with a view to obtaining any reparation due; therefore
>
> The General Assembly
>
> Decides to submit the following legal questions to the International Court of Justice for an advisory opinion:
>
> '1. In the event of an agent of the United Nations in the performance of his duties suffering injury in circumstances involving the responsibility of a State, has the United Nations, as an Organization, the capacity to bring an international claim against the responsible de jure or de facto government with a view to obtaining the reparation due in respect of the damage caused (a) to the United Nations, (h) to the victim or to persons entitled through him?
>
> II. In the event of an affirmative reply on point 1 (b), how is action by the United Nations to be reconciled with such rights as may be possessed by the State of which the victim is a national?'
>
> Instructs the Secretary-General, after the Court has given its opinion, to prepare proposals in the light of that opinion, and to submit them to the General Assembly at its next regular session."

...
[p. 176]
...

"In the event of an agent of the United Nations in the performance of his duties suffering injury in circumstances involving the responsibility of a State, has the United Nations, as an Organization, the capacity, to bring an international claim against [p. 177] the responsible de jure or de facto government with a view to obtaining the reparation due in respect of the damage caused (a) to the United Nations, (b) to the victim or to persons entitled through him?"

* * *

...
[p. 178]
...

To answer this question, which is not settled by the actual terms of the Charter, we must consider what characteristics it was intended thereby to give to the Organization.

The subjects of law in any legal system are not necessarily identical in their nature or in the extent of their rights, and their nature depends upon the needs of the community. Throughout its history, the development of international law has been influenced by the requirements of international life, and the progressive increase in the collective activities of States has already given rise to instances of action upon the international plane by certain entities which are not States. This development culminated in the establishment in June 1945 of an international organization whose purposes and principles are specified in the Charter of the United Nations. But to achieve these ends the attribution of international personality is indispensable.

The Charter has not been content to make the Organization created by it merely a centre "for harmonizing the actions of nations in the attainment of these common ends" (Article 1, para. 3). It has equipped that centre with organs, and has given it special tasks. It has defined the position of the Members in relation to the Organization by requiring them to give it every assistance in any action undertaken by it (Article 2, para. 5), and to accept and carry out the decisions of the Security Council; by authorizing the General Assembly to make recommendations to the Members; [p. 179] by giving the Organization legal capacity and privileges and immunities in the territory of each of its Members; and by providing for the conclusion of agreements between the Organization and its Members. Practice – in particular the conclusion of conventions to which the Organization is a party – has confirmed this character of the Organization, which occupies a position in certain respects in detachment from its Members, and which is under a duty to remind them, if need be, of certain obligations. It must be added that the Organization is a political body, charged with political tasks of an important character, and covering a wide field namely, the maintenance of international peace and security, the development of friendly relations among nations, and the achievement of international co-operation in the solution of problems of an economic, social, cultural or humanitarian character (Article 1); and in dealing with its Members it employs political means. The "Convention on the Privileges and Immunities of the United Nations" of 1946 creates rights and duties between each of the signatories and the Organization (see, in particular, Section 35). It is difficult to see how such a convention could operate except upon the international plane and as between parties possessing international personality.

In the opinion of the Court, the Organization was intended to exercise and enjoy, and is in fact exercising and enjoying, functions and rights which can only be explained on the basis of the possession of a large measure of international personality and the capacity to operate upon an international plane. It is at present the supreme type of international organization, and it could not carry out the intentions of its founders if it was devoid of international personality. It must be acknowledged that its Members, by entrusting certain functions to it, with the attendant duties and responsibilities, have clothed it with the competence required to enable those functions to be effectively discharged.

Accordingly, the Court has come to the conclusion that the Organization is an international person. That is not the same thing as saying that it is a State, which it certainly is not, or that its legal personality and rights and duties are the same as those of a State. Still less is it the same thing as saying that it is "a super-State", whatever that expression may mean. It does not even imply that all its rights and duties must be upon the international plane, any more than all the rights and duties of a State must be upon that plane. What it does mean is that it is a subject of international law and capable of possessing international rights and duties, and that it has capacity to maintain its rights by bringing international claims. ...

Notes

- Why does the court start with the characteristics that were intended to be given to the UN? Is that a legal test for personality? Or the evaluation of evidence satisfying some other test?
- Among the various matters that the court considered in its assessment of rights and obligations is that under the UN Charter, the UN enjoys "in the territory of each of its Members such legal capacity as may be necessary for the exercise of its functions and the fulfillment of its purposes" and "such privileges and immunities as are necessary for the fulfillment of its purposes."[1] On this basis, the UN likely has legal personality under the domestic law of each state to enter into contracts, bring legal actions, and so on. Any further legal rights, obligations, or status must be granted because they are necessary for the fulfillment of the UN's purposes. Does international legal personality fulfill the UN's purposes? Could the UN operate an as "unincorporated" entity?
- The court states that the subjects of a legal system can be different from each other. Is this true? How do natural and legal persons in domestic legal systems differ from each other? What rights and obligations do they enjoy, distinct from the other? You might consider whether a corporation can be held responsible for a crime, or whether it has constitutional rights, and whether a natural person can enjoy limited liability.
- The question above was one of the differences between classes of persons, such as natural persons and corporations, or states and organizations. But are there not differences in rights and obligations between persons of the same class? Not all states enjoy Most-Favored-Nation trading status with other states. Only a few states sit as permanent members of the UN Security Council. Some organizations have coercive powers, and others have only advisory powers. Do these distinctions among members of the same class undermine the argument above?
- The court notes that the differences among legal persons are based on the "needs of the community." Is this the test for legal personality? Or the test for which rights and obligations organizations hold? And which community is at issue? Who participates in this community? What are its nature and contours? Consider whether a domestic community is the relevant actor for determining the

---

1 UN Charter, articles 104, 105.

rights and obligations of a person under domestic law, and then transfer that question to the international plane.
- The court also notes that the UN is "certainly" not a state. Why is that the case? While it sounds nonsensical, is there any argument that the UN is a kind of state? The court also concludes that the UN is not a "'super-State', whatever that expression may mean." What would that expression mean? Would the EU qualify as a super-state? Or is the EU just another international organization? Would certain ancient entities, such as the Holy Roman Empire, qualify as super-states? Why does the court feel the need to even mention this possibility? The answer to this last question may not be in the text above, so you will need to speculate.

In the end, the court concluded that the UN has international legal personality. The approach the court took was, in simplified form, to begin with the understanding that, as a derived legal person, international legal personality must be granted to the organization by states.[2] In order to determine whether this grant has been made, the court first considered whether personality was granted expressly in the UN Charter. It was not. Second, the court examined whether international legal personality was granted by implication. The approach for this question is to determine whether international legal personality is necessary for the purposes, rights, and obligations of the entity, as provided in its constitutive instrument. In addition, this test for necessity looks at the subsequent practice of the organization and how it is treated by the international community. The court did not, at least explicitly, adopt the view that any organization created by international action inherently has international legal personality. This approach of looking for express or implied grant, and being informed by subsequent practice, continues to be used, for example, delegations from the EU to non-member states and organizations are generally accredited and provided with diplomatic rank and status, even in the absence of a formal statement of recognition. In addition, the express/implied/subsequent practice approach will return when we examine the question of the powers of an international organization.

A surprisingly large number of international organizations do not have an express grant of personality in their constitutive instrument, meaning we may need to take a *Reparations* analytical approach with all of them. The European Union was not expressly granted international legal personality until fairly recently in the Lisbon Treaty amendment. Previously, the European Union, as established in the Maastricht Treaty of 1992, was an umbrella entity covering the European Economic Community, the European Coal and Steel Community, and Euratom (sometimes collectively termed the "European Communities"). Each of those entities benefited from an express grant of legal personality, though the Union did not. The Amsterdam Treaty of 1997 and the Nice Treaty of 2001 amended the constitution of these entities, but did not change this awkward structure. This anomaly explains why the European Union became a

---

2 *Also see* Legality of the Use by a State of Nuclear Weapons in Armed Conflict [on request of the WHO], Advisory Opinion, 1996 ICJ Reports 66, paragraph 25 (International Court of Justice, 8 July 1996).

member of the World Trade Organization as the "European Communities," though it does not completely explain why the EU is still a member with that designation. However, even before the Lisbon Treaty, the EU had already begun entering into treaties as if it had international legal personality itself.[3] The situation was finally resolved in the Lisbon Treaty, where the EU's international legal personality was confirmed.

That being said, some other organizations benefit from an express grant of personality. For example, the largely unknown Global Crop Diversity Trust acquired international legal personality in this way.[4] Of course, this is the most helpful practice in establishing a grant of personality.

One difficulty, however, is that it still remains unclear whether personality is the status that provides the basis for holding international rights and obligations, or whether having international rights and obligations establishes capacity and thus personality. Perhaps this distinction is really just a question of evidence contrasted with a legal test. In the *Exchange of Greek and Turkish Population* case[5] and *European Commission on the Danube* case,[6] the court appeared to apply an approach of presuming that organizations had personality unless it was established that they did not. But this approach may not be entirely satisfactory because it essentially evades the question of the basis for personality and rights. In Chapter 5 on powers, we will examine in more detail *Case 22/70, Commission v. Council [ERTA]*,[7] but one small portion of that case is relevant here. The court observed that "Article 210 [of the Treaty Establishing the European Economic Community, 25 March 1957 [now renamed the Treaty on the Functioning of the European Union] provides that 'The Community shall have legal personality.'" The court then continued, to deduce that:

> This provision ... means that in its external relations the Community enjoys the capacity to establish contractual links with third countries over the whole field of objectives [in the Treaty]. Such authority arises not only from an express conferment by the Treaty ... but may equally flow from other provisions of the Treaty ...

---

3 *See e.g.* Agreement concluded between the EU and Yugoslavia concerning the activities of the EU Monitoring Mission in Yugoslavia, Official Journal of the European Union L 125/1 (2001).

4 *See* Agreement for the Establishment of the Global Crop Diversity Trust, 4 October 2004, FAO Treaty Doc. No. 34 (entered into force 21 October 2004) ("the Parties to this Agreement ... have agreed to establish the Global Crop Diversity Trust as an international fund with its own international legal personality ...").

5 *See* Exchange of Greek and Turkish Populations (Lausanne Convention VI, January 30th, 1923, Article 2) (Greece v Turkey), Advisory Opinion, 1925 PCIJ (Ser. B) No. 10 (Permanent Court of International Justice, 21 February 1925)

6 *See* Jurisdiction of the European Commission of the Danube Between Galatz and Braila, Advisory Opinion, 1927 PCIJ (Ser. B) No. 14 (Permanent Court of International Justice, 8 December 1927).

7 *See* Case C-22/70, Commission of the European Communities v Council of the European Communities [*In re* ERTA], Judgment (Court of Justice of the European Communities [Union], 31 March 1971).

Thus, the capacity for powers of the European Economic Community, now European Union, follows from the grant of international legal personality.

One question raised in the notes for the *Reparations* case above is whether the UN could operate without international legal personality. Some organizations are created explicitly without international legal personality. One increasingly common approach in international governance is to adopt a treaty and create a treaty body that facilitates, manages, monitors, and reports on compliance by states with the treaty. These bodies are often simply "secretariats" staffed with a small number of civil servants, sometimes as few as four or five, under a head of the office. A recent example is the Secretariat of the Arms Trade Treaty, but there are others monitoring the operation of arms control, environmental, and other treaties. The treaty body usually operates under the oversight of a "Conference of Parties," "Conference of States Parties," "Assembly of States Parties," or an entity with similar name, usually abbreviated COP, CSP, or ASP, respectively. Certainly an ASP could oversee the operation of a proper international organization, such as the case with the ASP that oversees the International Criminal Court. However, many treaty bodies have only a COP and a secretariat. Making matters even more complicated, a treaty body does not usually have a budget for a distinct headquarters, nor does it need one with such a small staff. General practice is for such a secretariat to be housed within the headquarters building of another international organization. For example, the Arms Trade Treaty Secretariat is housed on the second floor of the World Meteorological Organization headquarters in Geneva.[8] In addition, again for the sake of efficiency, the international organization hosting the treaty body might even manage human resources, budgeting, financial control, and other matters for the treaty body. In essence, a civil servant might go to work every day to an international organization headquarters, be paid by the organization, comply with human resources and management of that organization, and even benefit from visa and benefits support from the organization, yet be formally employed by the treaty body secretariat. In such cases, we must wonder whether this treaty body secretariat is an international organization or not.

Consider the following case, where a civil servant disputed the application of her terms of employment. Often organizations delegate these kinds of disputes to the International Labour Organization Administrative Tribunal (ILOAT) for convenience, but others resolve it through an internal dispute settlement

---

8 *Also see* United Nations Framework Convention on Climate Change (UNFCCC), 21 March 1994, 1771 UNTS 107 (UNFCCC Secretariat within the United Nations Secretariat); Convention on International Trade in Endangered Species of Wild Fauna and Flora, 3 March 1973, 993 UNTS 243 (Secretariat housed within the UN Environment Programme (UNEP) Secretariat); Convention on the Prevention of Marine Pollution by Dumping of Wastes and Other Matter, 29 December 1972, 1046 UNTS 120 (Secretariat housed within the International Maritime Organization (IMO) Secretariat); Rotterdam Convention on Prior Informed Consent, 10 September 1998, 2244 UNTS 337 (Secretariat housed jointly within the UNEP and Food and Agriculture Organization Secretariats).

mechanism. Following a decision by the ILOAT, staff may appeal to the International Court of Justice in the form of an advisory opinion. The following case went to the ICJ:

Judgment No. 2867 of the Administrative Tribunal of the International Labour Organization upon a Complaint Filed against the International Fund for Agricultural Development [IFAD]
Advisory Opinion
2012 ICJ Reps. 10
International Court of Justice, 1 February 2012

IV. Merits

49. The request for an advisory opinion from the Court concerns the validity of the judgment given by the ILOAT [International Labour Organization Administrative Tribunal] relating to Ms Saez García's contract of employment. …

50. In December 2005, a decision was made not to renew Ms Saez García's contract of employment as from March 2006 on the alleged basis that her post was being abolished. She challenged that decision by filing an appeal with the Joint Appeals Board of the Fund …. On 13 December 2007 the JAB unanimously recommended that Ms Saez García be reinstated and that she be awarded a payment of lost salaries, allowances and entitlements. …

51 The Fund contends, as it did before the Tribunal, that Ms Saez García was a staff member of the Global Mechanism [Global Mechanism of the United Nations Convention to Combat Desertification in Those Countries Experiencing Serious Drought and/or Desertification, Particularly in Africa] and not of IFAD and that her employment status has to be assessed in the context of the arrangement for the housing of the Global Mechanism made between the Fund and the COP [Conference of the Parties of the United Nations Convention to Combat Desertification in Those Countries Experiencing Serious Drought and/or Desertification, Particularly in Africa].

…

52. Part III of the UNCCD [United Nations Convention to Combat Desertification in Those Countries Experiencing Serious Drought and/or Desertification, Particularly in Africa], which came into force in 1996, is entitled "Action Programmes, Scientific and Technical Co-operation and Supporting Measures" … Under Article 21, paragraph 4, a "Global Mechanism" is established "[i]n order to increase the effectiveness and efficiency of existing financial mechanisms". … It is to function under the authority and guidance of the COP and to be accountable to it. Under paragraph 5, the COP was to identify, at its first ordinary session, an organization to house the Global Mechanism. Paragraph 6 provides this elaboration: the COP was to make appropriate arrangements with the housing organization "for the administrative operations of such Mechanism, drawing to the extent possible on existing budgetary and human resources". …

53. Part IV of the Convention, entitled "Institutions", follows immediately the provisions of Article 21 which have

just been discussed. It provides for the establishment of the COP, a Permanent Secretariat ... and a Committee on Science and Technology as a subsidiary body of the COP (Arts. 22, 23 and 24). The Conference's powers include the power to establish subsidiary bodies, to approve a programme and a budget, and to make arrangements, at its first session, for a Permanent Secretariat (Art. 22, paras. 2 *(c)* and *(g)*, and Art. 23, para. 3). The Permanent Secretariat's functions include: to enter, under the guidance of the Conference of the Parties, into such administrative and contractual arrangements as may be required for the effective discharge of its functions (Art. 23, para. 2 *(e)*).

54. So far as the arrangement for the housing of the Global Mechanism is concerned, the COP, at its first session, held in 1997, decided to select IFAD for that purpose. In 1999 the Conference and the Fund signed a "Memorandum of Understanding ... regarding the Modalities and Administrative Operations of the Global Mechanism" (hereinafter the "MOU"). The MOU provides, under Section II A, that "[w]hile the Global Mechanism will have a separate identity within the Fund, it will be an organic part of the structure of the Fund directly under the President of the Fund". It also provides, under Section II D, that the Managing Director of the Global Mechanism shall be nominated by the Administrator of the United Nations Development Programme and appointed by the President of the Fund and that, in discharging his or her responsibilities, the Managing Director shall report directly to the President of IFAD. Under paragraph (1) of Section III A, headed "Relationship of the Global Mechanism to the Conference", the Global Mechanism functions under the authority of the COP and is fully accountable to it. Under paragraph (2) of the same section, the chain of accountability runs directly from the Managing Director to the President of the Fund to the COP, and the Managing Director submits reports to the COP on behalf of the President of the Fund. Under Section III A, paragraph (4), the Global Mechanism's work programme and budget, including proposed staffing, are prepared by the Managing Director, reviewed and approved by the Fund's President and forwarded to the Executive Secretary of the Convention for consideration in the preparation of the budget estimates of the Convention. Under Section II B, the resources of the Global Mechanism are held by the Fund in various accounts. Under Section IV B, the Managing Director, on behalf of the President, submits reports on the Global Mechanism's activities to each ordinary session of the COP. The Fund and Convention Secretariat are to co-operate in various ways. The final substantive provision of the MOU, Section VI, entitled "Administrative Infrastructure", provides that the Global Mechanism shall be located at the headquarters of the Fund in Rome where it "shall enjoy full access to all of the administrative infrastructure available to the Fund offices, including appropriate office space, as well as personnel, financial, communications and information management services". The terms of that provision reflect those of paragraph 6 of Article 21 of the UNCCD set out above (see paragraph 52 above).

55. For its Permanent Secretariat, the COP made an arrangement with the United Nations. The General Assembly approved the institutional linkage between

the Secretariat of the Convention and the United Nations in accordance with the offer made by the Secretary-General and accepted by the COP (General Assembly resolution 52/198 of 18 December 1997 and COP decision No. 3/COP.1). Under the arrangement, the Secretariat functions under the authority of the Secretary-General as chief administrative officer of the organization (UN doc. A/52/549 of 11 November 1997, para. 25). While institutionally linked to the United Nations, the Secretariat is not fully integrated in the work programme and management structure of any particular department or programme (*ibid.*, para. 26; COP decision No. 3/COP.1 and General Assembly resolution 52/198 of 18 December 1997, eighth preambular paragraph).

56. The General Assembly also noted that the COP had decided to accept the offer of the Government of Germany to host the Convention Secretariat in Bonn (General Assembly resolution 52/198 of 18 December 1997, para. 3). In 1998, the Secretariat of the Convention, the Government of the Federal Republic of Germany and the United Nations concluded an Agreement concerning the Headquarters of the Convention's Permanent Secretariat (*UNTS*, Vol. 2029, p. 316). Under the Agreement, the Convention Secretariat possesses, in the host country, the legal capacity to contract, to acquire and dispose of movable and immovable property, and to institute legal proceedings (*ibid.*, Art. 4; see also Arts. 3 and 4 of the Agreement between the United Nations and the Federal Republic of Germany relating to the Headquarters of the United Nations Volunteers Programme, 10 November 1995 (*UNTS*, Vol. 1895, p. 103), which is applicable, *mutatis mutandis*, to the Permanent Secretariat).

57. The Court observes that, under Part IV of the Convention entitled "Institutions", the COP and the Permanent Secretariat are expressly established as such. These institutions are given the following powers : in the case of the COP, it is given the power to "make appropriate arrangements" to house the Global Mechanism, to "undertake necessary arrangements" for the financing of its subsidiary bodies and to "make arrangements" for the functioning of the Permanent Secretariat (Arts. 21 (6), 22 (2) *(g)* and 23 (3), respectively); in the case of the Permanent Secretariat, it is given the general power "to enter, under the guidance of the Conference of the Parties, into such administrative and contractual arrangements as may be required for the effective discharge of its functions" (Art. 23 (2) *(e)*).

As the above account indicates, both have exercised those powers. By contrast, the Global Mechanism is not included in Part IV of the Convention. It is not given any express powers of contracting or entering into any agreement by the Convention nor by a headquarters agreement such as that relating to the Permanent Secretariat. Moreover, the record before the Court does not include any instances of it entering into contracts or agreements. IFAD, on 14 May 2010, during the period when the first round of written statements was being prepared, wrote to the Managing Director of the Global Mechanism seeking information on that matter in the following terms:

> "In order to help us prepare our submission to the ICJ, IFAD kindly requests that your Office supply a comprehensive list of all agreements and legal documents signed between

the Global Mechanism and other entities, including international organizations and private entities. We intend to provide this list as part of our submission to the ICJ in order to show that the GM is recognized as having the capacity to enter into agreements." (UN doc. ICCD/COP(10)/INF.3 of 11 August 2011, p. 30.)

The written statement of IFAD submitted five months later includes no such list.

58. The position of the Global Mechanism may also be contrasted with that of IFAD, its housing body. The Agreement establishing IFAD expressly provides that "[t]he Fund shall possess international legal personality" (Art. 10, Sec. 1). Its privileges and immunities are defined by reference to the Convention on the Privileges and the Immunities of the Specialized Agencies of 21 November 1947 (Art. 10, Sec. 2, of the Agreement establishing IFAD). Under Article II, Section 3, of that Convention, specialized agencies subject to it, which include IFAD, are given the express capacity to contract, to acquire and dispose of movable and immovable property, and to institute legal proceedings in those States, including Italy, which are parties to the Convention.

59. The Court recalls a point made by the Fund in its response to a question put by a Member of the Court to IFAD – and through it to Ms Saez García. According to the Fund, should the Court decline to provide an advisory opinion, it would forsake the opportunity to "assist the international community by clarifying how the rules concerning the ILOAT's jurisdiction should operate in respect of entities hosted by international organizations". The Fund contends that this phenomenon of "hosting" arrangements is "one of the most significant developments since the adoption of Article XII of the ILOAT Statute in 1946".

60. The Court is aware that there exists a range of hosting arrangements between international organizations which are concluded for a variety of reasons. Each arrangement is distinct and has different characteristics. There are hosting arrangements between two entities having separate legal personalities, and there are others concluded for the benefit of an entity without legal personality. An example of the former is the arrangement between the World Intellectual Property Organization – as the hosting organization – and the International Union for the Protection of New Varieties of Plants – as the hosted organization – which has legal personality under Article 24, paragraph 1, of its constituent instrument, the International Convention for the Protection of New Varieties of Plants of 2 December 1961.

61. By contrast, with regard to the Global Mechanism, the Court notes that the Convention directs the COP to identify an organization to house it and to make appropriate arrangements with such an organization for its administrative operations. It was for this reason that a Memorandum of Understanding was concluded between the COP and IFAD in 1999 as described in paragraph 54 above. Neither the Convention nor the MOU expressly confer legal personality on the Global Mechanism or otherwise endow it with the capacity to enter into legal arrangements. Further, in light of the different instruments setting up IFAD, the COP, the Global Mechanism and the Permanent Secretariat, and of the practice included in the record before the Court, the Global Mechanism had no

power and has not purported to exercise any power to enter into contracts, agreements or "arrangements", internationally or nationally.

...

66. Before the Tribunal, the Fund contended that its acceptance of the jurisdiction of the ILOAT did not extend to entities that are hosted by it pursuant to international agreements. It maintained that the Global Mechanism was not an organ of the Fund, and that, even if the Fund administered the Global Mechanism, this did not make the Complainant a staff member of the Fund; nor did it make the actions of the Managing Director of the Global Mechanism attributable to the Fund. According to the Fund, despite the fact that the staff regulations, rules and policies of IFAD were applied to the Complainant, she was not a staff member of the Fund. Conversely, the Complainant submitted that she was a staff member of IFAD throughout the relevant period until her separation on 15 March 2006, and that her letters of appointment and renewal of contract all offered her an appointment with the Fund.

67. In its Judgment No. 2867 of 3 February 2010, the Tribunal rejected the jurisdictional objections made by the Fund and declared itself competent to entertain all the pleas set out in the complaint submitted by Ms Saez García. After examining the Fund's argument that the Tribunal did not have jurisdiction because the Fund and the Global Mechanism had separate legal identities, the Tribunal observed that:

> "The fact that the Global Mechanism is an integral part of the Convention and is accountable to the Conference does not necessitate the conclusion that it has its own legal identity ....
Nor does the stipulation in the MOU that the Global Mechanism is to have a 'separate identity' indicate that it has a separate legal identity, or more precisely for present purposes, that it has separate legal personality." (Judgment No. 2867, p. 11, para. 6)

The Tribunal then referred to the provisions of the MOU, and stated that:

> "[I]t is clear that the words 'an organic part of the structure of the Fund' indicate that the Global Mechanism is to be assimilated to the various administrative units of the Fund for all administrative purposes. The effect of this is that administrative decisions taken by the Managing Director in relation to staff in the Global Mechanism are, in law, decisions of the Fund." (Judgment No. 2867, p. 12, para. 7)

Following this analysis, the Tribunal concluded as follows:

> "Given that the personnel of the Global Mechanism are staff members of the Fund and that the decisions of the Managing Director relating to them are, in law, decisions of the Fund, adverse administrative decisions affecting them are subject to internal review and appeal in the same way and on the same grounds as are decisions relating to other staff members of the Fund. So too, they may be the subject of a complaint to this Tribunal in the same way and on the same grounds as decisions relating to other staff members." (Ibid., p. 14, para. 11)

68. It is this confirmation by the Tribunal of its "competence to hear" the complaint filed by Ms Saez García that is challenged by the Executive Board of the Fund, under Article XII of the Annex to the Statute of the ILOAT and is the object

of the first question put to the Court as reproduced in paragraph 63 above. To answer this question, the Court has to consider whether the Tribunal had the competence to hear the complaint submitted by Ms Saez García in accordance with Article II, paragraph 5, of its Statute. According to this provision, for the Tribunal to exercise its jurisdiction it is necessary that there should be a complaint alleging non-observance of the "terms of appointment of officials" of an organization that has accepted its jurisdiction or "of provisions of the Staff Regulations" of such an organization. It follows from this that the Tribunal could hear the complaint only if the complainant was an official of an organization that has recognized the jurisdiction of the Tribunal, and if the complaint related to the non-observance of the terms of appointment of such an official or the provisions of the staff regulations of the organization. The first set of conditions has to be examined with reference to the competence *ratione personae* of the Tribunal, while the second has to be considered within the context of its competence *ratione materiae*.

...

76. The Court observes that a contract of employment entered into between an individual and an international organization is a source of rights and duties for the parties to it. In this context, the Court notes that the offer of appointment accepted by Ms Saez García on 17 March 2000 was made on behalf of the Fund by the Director of its Personnel Division, and that the subsequent renewals of this contract were signed by personnel officers of the same Division of the Fund. ... It follows from this that an employment relationship, based on the above-mentioned contractual and statutory elements, was established between Ms Saez García and the Fund. This relationship qualified her as a staff member of the Fund. The fact that she was assigned to perform functions related to the mandate of the Global Mechanism does not mean that she could not be a staff member of the Fund. The one does not exclude the other.

...

95. The Court, therefore, finds, in response to the first question put to it by IFAD, that the ILOAT was competent to hear the complaint introduced against IFAD, in accordance with Article II of its Statute, in view of the fact that Ms Saez García was a staff member of the Fund, and her appointment was governed by the provisions of the staff regulations and rules of the Fund.

Notes

- What is the structure and interrelationships of all of these entities? You may want to prepare a small chart to keep track. What is IFAD? The UNCCD? The COP? The Secretariat? The Global Mechanism? Then, what are the relationships between all of these actors? What reports to what? What manages what?
- Does the Global Mechanism have international legal personality? Does the Secretariat? Does IFAD? What do the various agreements provide, expressly or impliedly? Also, in line with the discussions above, what kind of rights and obligations do these actors have? The ICJ refers to some of these actors as "institutions." What significance does this term have? The ICJ also refers to the term

"separate identity." What is its significance? And how is that different from being an "institution," if at all?
- What rights and obligations does the ICJ believe follow from the assessment of personality? Is this approach similar to or distinct from the approach that the ICJ took in the *Reparations* case or that the EU Court of Justice took in *Case 22/70, Commission v Council [ETRA]*? If the Global Mechanism had legal personality, then what will be the consequence? Could it submit to the jurisdiction of the ILOAT?
- In the end, who was the employer? What facts seem critical to that assessment? Does the fact that the Global Mechanism might or might not have personality play a role in identifying which entity employed this civil servant?
- Why do you think the parties to agreements creating treaty bodies with a COP and Secretariat choose not to give the operation international legal personality? What are the advantages and disadvantages of this choice, both legally and politically?

3.1.1.2 Objective and relative international legal personality

However, even if an entity has international legal personality, it might not have that personality in relation to a state that was not member of the organization. Consider in the *Judgment No. 2867* case above that the Secretariat had legal personality in Germany, pursuant to its Headquarters Agreement with that state, to take certain actions, such as enter into contracts or sell property. It might not have had that same degree of personality in other domestic legal orders, or under international law. If we transfer that same idea to the international plane, then international organizations might only have personality in their relations with their member states. Constitutive instruments of international organizations are treaties, and treaties are only binding on the parties to them. The Vienna Convention on the Law of Treaties expressly provides that treaties cannot create rights or obligations for non-parties without their consent, i.e. the *pacta tertiis* rule. Consider the following case:

Economic Community of West African States [ECOWAS] v BCCI [Bank of Credit and Commerce International]
1993 Clunet 353, 113 International Law Reports
473 Court of Appeal of Paris (First Chamber), France, 13 January 1993[9]

An appeal has been lodged before this Court by the Economic Community of West African States ("ECOWAS") and the Cooperation, Compensation and Development Fund of that Community ("the Fund") against a judgment rendered on 4 December 1991 by the *Tribunal de commerce* of Paris. ... The *Tribunal de commerce* ... rejected a claim for (the value in francs of the principal sums of) US $6,346,849.63 and UK £2,308,441.84, corresponding to the

---

[9] © Sir E. Lauterpacht, published by Cambridge University Press. Reproduced with permission of The Licensor through PLSclear.

amounts of their respective deposits at the agency in Paris of the Bank of Credit and Commerce International, which is now in judicial liquidation.

...

The Economic Community of West African States was established between sixteen States by a treaty signed on 28 May 1975 in Lagos (Nigeria) for the purpose of promoting cooperation and development in all fields of economic activity as well as social and cultural affairs, with the aim of raising the standard of living of the peoples of those States, increasing and maintaining economic stability, strengthening relations between the Member States and contributing to the progress and development of the African continent.

...

ECOWAS and the Fund opened accounts at the subsidiary in France of the foreign bank BCCI. The credit balances on the accounts were respectively US $6,346,849.63 and UK £2,308,441.84. On 4 July 1991, acting pursuant to Article 44 of the Law of 24 January 1984, the Banking Commission appointed a provisional administrator for BCCI who, on the following day, closed its counters and on 18 July 1991 issued a statement that payments would no longer be made.

By a judgment of 23 July 1991 the *Tribunal de commerce* of Paris opened proceedings for judicial recovery in relation to BCCI Overseas in France, provisionally fixing 4 July as the date when payments ceased to be effective. On 23 July 1992, the *Tribunal de commerce* of Paris converted the administration under court supervision into winding-up by court decision.

Invoking the immunities, exemptions and privileges arising from their international statute, ECOWAS and the Fund instituted proceedings against BCCI, its administrator, its court-appointed administrator and the representative of its creditors, for payment of the above-mentioned sums before the *Tribunal de commerce* of Paris, which had rendered the judgment under appeal.

In the judgment under appeal, the *Tribunal de commerce* held that since France was not a party to the Treaty establishing ECOWAS or to the Protocol concerning the Fund, it was not appropriate either to stay proceedings or to declare that the immunities, privileges and exemptions provided for by that Treaty could be relied upon in France under municipal law, in particular against the Law of 25 January 1985 concerning recovery and the winding-up of companies by court decision. ...

In support of their appeal, ECOWAS and the Fund state:

– They are public international bodies with independent legal personality on the territory of the Member States whose "objective international personality" is binding upon third States;

– Consequently they enjoy absolute jurisdictional immunity, which they have not waived since such waiver can only occur in the forms and according to the procedures laid down by their statutes, which is not the case here ....

– As international organizations, they enjoy immunity from execution which prevents their funds from being seized by private creditors so that the Banking Commission and the judicial administrator were not entitled to freeze their deposits without first examining whether they were allocated for the foreign activities of the organization or, on the contrary, provided support for sovereign activities (*actes de puissance publique*);

...

– No other exception, whether based on *force majeure*, the fact that the Law of 25 January 1985 is a matter of public policy, good faith or the absence of discrimination between nationals and foreigners, can limit the principle that rules of international law are of general and binding application.

The appellants therefore request the Court to quash the judgment under appeal, to recognize the existence of immunities, exemptions and privileges attached to their international status and to order BCCI and its legal representatives to pay the above-mentioned sums with interest at the legal rate from the date of the issuing of the writ in the proceedings at first instance.

In submitting that the judgment under appeal should be confirmed, the respondents argue:

– The provisions of the Agreement establishing ECOWAS and the Protocol relating to the Fund concern privileges and immunities which cannot be invoked before the French courts;

...

– Even accepting that it exists and may be relied upon against a national court, the immunity from execution invoked by the appellants is merely a plea in bar which cannot prevent the application of a rule of private law governing commercial relations between individuals to the benefit of international organizations occupying the procedural position of the claimants.

...

Grounds of the judgment

At the date when payments ceased to be made by BCCI Overseas, a procedure for judicial settlement having been opened on 23 July 1991, the accounts of ECOWAS and the Fund held at the bank were in credit in the amounts of US $6,346,849.63 and UK £2,308,441.84 respectively.

According to Article 33 of the Law of 25 January 1985 concerning recovery and the judicial winding-up of companies, a decision opening the procedure for judicial recovery carries with it an absolute prohibition on the payment of any debt arising prior to the date of that decision. Furthermore, according to Article 47, such a decision suspends or prohibits any judicial proceedings seeking in particular the payment of a sum of money to creditors whose rights have arisen prior to that decision.

ECOWAS and the Fund nevertheless issued a writ on 12 August 1991 against BCCI and its legal representatives for payment of the above-mentioned sums considering that their status as international organizations included the immunities, exemptions and privileges, arising from the Treaty and Protocol establishing them, which could be invoked in France and prevented reliance against them upon any provisions of municipal law having the effect of bringing about the sequestration or attachment of the funds in dispute.

In particular, ECOWAS and the Fund seek to rely upon the international personality which they enjoy in order to invoke the benefit in France of jurisdictional immunity and immunity from execution.

[This Court considers] that such immunities can only be lawfully invoked in France by those international organizations if they result from either an international agreement to which France is a party or from a customary rule.

France is a member of neither ECOWAS nor the Fund and it has not been alleged that it has ever concluded any agreement with either body which would confer such immunity upon them on its territory.

Proof of the existence of an international custom which would constitute an exception to the basic principle concerning the relative effect of treaties has not been produced.

It therefore follows that the appellants cannot base any appeal on jurisdictional immunity which, in any case, they have expressly and necessarily waived by instituting proceedings in France for payment against BCCI

....

Consequently, and for these reasons alone, the judgment under appeal must be confirmed ....

Notes

- How does this case come before the Paris Court of Appeal? Why would this international organization bring legal action against a bank? Does the court find it significant that this lawsuit was initiated by the organization, rather than the bank?
- International organizations commonly open bank accounts in various countries. Not being a state, they do not have any central bank or treasury office, so, much like corporations, they need a private bank account for their operations. Especially if the organization operates in many states, then it might need multiple bank accounts spread out across many states. To what degree is this practice necessary for international organizations? Consider how an organization could pay staff salaries without a bank account. Does the case give any indication why ECOWAS opened this bank account? Is that relevant for this case?
- How did ECOWAS manage to open a bank account with BCCI when the French State does not appear to recognize its international legal personality? Was BCCI aware of the particular nature of ECOWAS? Should it make any difference whether BCCI was aware of that fact?
- If the French State will not consider ECOWAS an international legal person, then what does it consider ECOWAS to be? Does it assimilate it to a domestic or international non-governmental organization (NGO) or corporation? What will be the consequence of that decision for the ability of ECOWAS to enter into contracts, compared to enjoying immunity? Or does France regard ECOWAS as being a non-entity? In that case, would not the French court dismiss this case for lack of standing?

A similar question was also raised in the *Reparations* case, because the UN wished to bring a claim against Israel and that state was not a member of the UN at the time. Keeping *ECOWAS v BCCI* in mind, consider this passage from the *Reparations* case:

Reparation for Injuries Suffered in the Service of the United Nations
Advisory Opinion
1949 ICJ Reps. 174
International Court of Justice, 11 April 1949

The question remains whether the Organization has "the capacity to bring an international claim against the responsible de jure or de facto government with a view to obtaining the reparation due in respect of the damage caused (a) to the United Nations, (b) to the victim or to persons entitled through him" when the defendant State is not a member of the Organization.

In considering this aspect of Question 1 (a) and (b), it is necessary to keep in mind the reasons which have led the Court to give an affirmative answer to it when the defendant State is a Member of the Organization. It has now been established that the Organization has capacity to bring claims on the international [p. 185] plane, and that it possesses a right of functional protection in respect of its agents. Here again the Court is authorized to assume that the damage suffered involves the responsibility of a State, and it is not called upon to express an opinion upon the various ways in which that responsibility might be engaged. Accordingly the question is whether the Organization has capacity to bring a claim against the defendant State to recover reparation in respect of that damage or whether, on the contrary, the defendant State, not being a member, is justified in raising the objection that the Organization lacks the capacity to bring an international claim. On this point, the Court's opinion is that fifty States, representing the vast majority of the members of the international community, had the power, in conformity with international law, to bring into being an entity possessing objective international personality, and not merely personality recognized by them alone, together with capacity to bring international claims.

Accordingly, the Court arrives at the conclusion that ail affirmative answer should be given to Question 1 (a) and (b) whether or not the defendant State is a Member of the United Nations.

Notes

- How do we reconcile *ECOWAS v BCCI* with the *Reparations* case? Is the distinction based on the kind of lawsuit or on the nature of the organization? *ECOWAS v BCCI* was a case about bankruptcy and liquidation, whereas *Reparations* was about maintaining a claim on the international plane. Why should the distinction between those two kinds of actions be significant?
- Perhaps an alternative distinction is the nature of the two organizations. How does the ICJ view the UN compared to the French court's view of ECOWAS? Is

the UN somehow special? You might want to revisit the excerpts from the *Reparations* case at the beginning of this chapter, where the ICJ described the role of the UN in the international community. Does the court view the UN as having a particularly significant role, even compared to other international organizations? How would such a special appreciation be expressed or assessed? It could be that the language on the special role of the UN was only used because there were so few international organizations in the world at that time.

- Maybe the distinction pertains to the way in which the two organizations were created? Could we say that, while the UN was created under general international law, that ECOWAS was created under a particular international law? That argument may be difficult to sustain because they were both created by treaties, and, at least at the beginning, the United Nations did not have universal membership. ECOWAS also does not have universal membership, though it is a major international organization with a significant footprint in the world. That being said, ECOWAS only aspires to be a regional organization. Does that make a difference? Keep in mind, of course, that the EU is also a regional organization. Could we imagine the EU receiving the same treatment that ECOWAS did in a non-state party?
- Following from all of this discussion, how would you distinguish an organization with objective legal personality, such as the UN, from organizations with a relative legal personality, such as ECOWAS?

There are some solutions for international organizations to have their international legal personality acknowledged in non-state parties. The first possibility would be for a non-state party to simply, expressly, recognize the international organization as having international legal personality. For example, OPEC, the Organization of Petroleum Exporting Countries, maintains its headquarters in Austria, which is not a member of the organization. In the headquarters agreement between OPEC and Austria, "[t]he Government recognizes the juridical personality of OPEC."[10] Switzerland adopted a similar practice when it was still not a member of the United Nations, yet hosted the UN Office in Geneva at the *Palais des Nations*, the former headquarters building of the League of Nations. In the alternative, a state could impliedly recognize the international legal personality of an organization, such as when the United States accepts and accredits the mission and diplomats from the European Union.

The second possibility for an international organization to enjoy legal personality in a non-state party would be through the application of the state's domestic law that identifies and governs legal personality, in effect, its private international law. Some states that have adopted highly monist legal orders will give effect within the domestic legal system to an organization created under international law, more or less automatically. This was the approach the Supreme Court of The Netherlands

---

10 Agreement regarding the Headquarters of the Organization of the Petroleum Exporting Countries, 18 February 1974, Austria-OPEC, 2098 UNTS 416, article 7.

took when it had to decide whether the Iran-US Claims Tribunal based in The Hague had legal immunity.[11] In a more dualist legal system, it might be possible to establish that comity under domestic law recognizes the personality of entities that enjoy personality in other domestic legal systems. In the *Arab Monetary Fund v. Hashim* case, the United Kingdom (UK) House of Lords held that:

> when the AMF [Arab Monetary Fund] Agreement was registered in the UAE [United Arab Emirates] by means of Federal Decree No. 35, that registration conferred on the international organization legal [personality] and thus created a corporate body which the English courts can and should recognize.[12]

3.1.2 Agreement under international law by subjects of international law

The second element of the definition is an agreement under international law. Typically, international organizations are created by a treaty. Sometimes an organization is created as part of a larger treaty. For example, the International Labour Organization was created in the Versailles peace treaty ending World War I. In other cases, the organization might be created by a UN General Assembly Resolution, such as the case with the United Nations Industrial Development Organization (UNIDO), United Nations Environment Programme (UNEP) and the United Nations Relief and Works Agency for Palestine Refugees in the Near East (UNRWA). Or it could be created by a Memorandum of Understanding or comparable legal instrument with unclear legal value. For example, OPEC was created by a resolution of a conference of governments on petroleum export. The Nordic Council was created through the joint legislative action of the parliaments of the Nordic states, following an informal international agreement to adopt this legislation. A few organizations are even created by passive, implied agreements, such as the development of a *de facto* international trade organization following the adoption of the General Agreement on Tariffs and Trade, but before the formal creation of the World Trade Organization.

The agreement under international law must also be adopted by subjects of international law. We speak about subjects of international law rather than states because international legal persons, other than states, can constitute and become members of international organizations. First, international organizations can create another international organization. It is rather unusual, however, for an international organization to do so. The World Trade Organization is a striking exception

---

11 Iran-US Claims Tribunal v A.S., 18 Netherlands Yearbook of International Law 357 (1987) (Supreme Court [*Hooge Raad*], Netherlands, 20 December 1985).
12 Arab Monetary Fund v. Hashim and others (No. 3), [1991] UKHL J0221-1, [1991] 2 AC 114, [1991] 2 WLR 729 (House of Lords, United Kingdom, 21 February 1991) (*as per* Templeman, L., 731). Contains Parliamentary information licensed under the Open Parliament Licence v3.0.

where the EU is a member. When international organizations do create or join international organizations, they are usually joined by states. This author knows of no international organization solely created by other international organizations. Even the Joint Vienna Institute which was created by the Bank for International Settlements, European Bank for Reconstruction and Development, International Bank for Reconstruction and Development, International Monetary Fund, and Organization for Economic Cooperation and Development included Austria as the sole state member.[13]

Second, other subjects of international law, such as the Holy See, can become members of international organizations. The Holy See is a member of the Universal Postal Union and the International Atomic Energy Agency, as well as being a party to the International Wheat Agreement and the Grains Trade Convention that both have treaty bodies, rather than formal international organizations. Instead of the Holy See, the Vatican City State is a member of the International Telecommunications Union. It is not entirely clear why the decision was made in some cases to become party through the statehood of the Vatican or through the alternative original legal personality of the Holy See, but the practice of this subject of international law is quite unique and limited.

The only requirement on the number of subjects participating is that there are at least two. So, for example, the treaty between Belgium and The Netherlands creating the *Nederlandse Taalunie* (Dutch Language Union) would qualify as creating an international organization. In addition, the mere participation of one or more entities that are not subjects of international law does not appear to undermine the status of an international organization, provided there are at least two subjects of international law party to the agreement. An example of this practice is the constitution of the Bank for International Settlements which was adopted by several states, plus the participation of banks.[14]

A few very unusual cases have occurred over the years where an entity was established, not by subjects of international law, but has later been elevated to the international plane. In some cases, this elevation is more practical than legally substantive, as is the case with Greenpeace or Doctors Without Borders, which are clearly not international organizations, though they operate globally. However, in other cases, the elevation has substantive legal consequences. The primary entity falling under this rule is the International Committee of the Red Cross (ICRC). A Swiss NGO,

---

13 Agreement for the Establishment of the Joint Vienna Institute, BGBl. III (No. 95) (12 August 2004), Article XVI, *as amended* 1 May 2003.
14 *See e.g.* Reineccius et al. v Bank for International Settlements, Partial Award on the Lawfulness of the Recall of privately Held Shares on 8 January 2001 (Arbitration Tribunal under the Permanent Court of Arbitration, 22 November 2002). *Also see* Treaty Between the Republic of Tajikistan, the Kyrgyz Republic, the Republic of Kazakhstan and the Ismaili Imamat for the Establishment of the University of Central Asia, 28–31 August 2000, 2159 UNTS 161.

founded by individuals well before the modern practice of international organizations coalesced, the organization operates worldwide and has a special role as a relief agency under the Geneva Conventions. In time, Switzerland decided to treat the ICRC as if it was an international organization, even entering into a Headquarters Agreement with it and respecting its inviolability, and other states have followed suit. The UN has also granted the ICRC observer status. Before the International Criminal Tribunal for the former Yugoslavia, the ICRC was successful in blocking court testimony from one of its agents on the grounds that it was an international entity with quasi-sovereign privileges. A small number of other private NGOs are also slowly being elevated into international organizations, such as the International Olympics Committee, the World Anti-Doping Agency, the Global Fund to Fight AIDS, Tuberculosis and Malaria (Global Fund), the Global Alliance for Vaccines and Immunization (GAVI), and the International Air Transport Agency, though none of these has yet attained the unique position of the ICRC.

3.1.3 Meaningful independence

The next element of the definition in this textbook is a degree of meaningful independence of the organization from its members. This independence has several layers and can manifest itself in differing ways, but the primary question is whether the organization can make decisions and take actions separate from the will of any single state or group of states. Its actions must be taken in the best interest of all of the states parties.

This situation does not mean that the organization is unaccountable. Every organization falls under the oversight of its members and must answer to them, but it must answer to the entire membership as a whole. The distinction is that, aside from any rules in the constitutive instrument modifying this understanding, the organization should not be a proxy for one state or a small group of powerful states. The organization must serve its purpose, and thus the entire membership, and be accountable to the entire membership.

Thus, the question of meaningful independence is one of a balance between the entire membership establishing objectives, and the organization taking the most effective steps to realize those objectives; of the entire membership monitoring and correcting the direction of the organization, and the organization taking global leadership in the best interest of all the members. A glaring example of this tension is the International Criminal Court, which operates under the oversight and governance of its ASP, yet its prosecutor might very well be independently investigating the very governmental officials monitoring the organization at the same time. The challenge for the ICC ASP is to ensure that the organization does not violate its mandate, yet at the same time preserves enough independence that it can effectively bring individuals to justice.

A relatively easier case of independence is to examine the international civil servants who staff international organizations. Certainly, the UN Secretary-General operates with a degree of independence. The judges on the International Court of

Justice are similarly highly protected. But consider the following case concerning the termination of the Director-General of the Organization for the Prohibition of Chemical Weapons (OPCW):

In re B[ustani] (OPCW), Judgment No. 2232
International Labour Organization Administrative Tribunal, 16 July 2003

A. The complainant [José Bustani], a Brazilian national born in 1945, is a former Director-General of the OPCW.

He was appointed, for a period of four years, as Director-General on 13 May 1997 by the Conference of the States Parties upon recommendation of the Executive Council. On 19 May 2000, one year before the end of his term, the Conference of the States Parties decided, again upon a recommendation of the Executive Council, to renew his contract for a further four years.

On 21 March 2002, at the 28th Session of the Executive Council, a no-confidence motion, calling for the complainant to resign as Director-General, was introduced by a State Party (the United States of America). The motion failed. A special session of the Conference of the States Parties was subsequently called for by the same State Party and at its meeting of 22 April 2002 the Conference adopted a decision to terminate the appointment of the Director-General effective immediately. That is the impugned decision.

...

D. In his rejoinder the complainant presses his pleas regarding receivability and the competence of the Tribunal. He argues that he is indeed an "official" of the OPCW; this is clear from the terms of the Headquarters Agreement between the Organisation and the Kingdom of the Netherlands according to which "[o]fficials of the OPCW" means the Director-General and all members of the staff of the Technical Secretariat. In addition, his contract of employment makes it clear that he was to receive his benefits and entitlements in accordance with the Staff Regulations and Interim Staff Rules. Consequently, the Tribunal is competent to hear his complaint, just like that of any other staff member of the OPCW. He contends that decisions regarding the appointment of a director-general are "administrative" despite being taken by the Conference of the States Parties, a political organ, because these are taken in its capacity as an appointing authority.

...

CONSIDERATIONS

1. Under the terms of Article VIII, paragraph 4, of the Convention establishing the OPCW, the organs of the Organisation are "the Conference of the States Parties, the Executive Council, and the Technical Secretariat". According to paragraph 41 of that same Article:

> "The Technical Secretariat shall comprise a Director-General, who shall be its head and chief administrative officer, inspectors and such scientific, technical and other personnel as may be required."

Paragraph 43 reads as follows:

> "The Director-General shall be appointed by the Conference upon the recommendation of the Executive Council for a term of four years,

renewable for one further term, but not thereafter."

2. Pursuant to those provisions and to paragraph 21(d) of Article VIII, which provides that the Conference of the States Parties shall "[a]ppoint the Director-General of the Technical Secretariat", the Conference appointed the complainant as Director-General for a four-year term by a decision of 13 May 1997. It decided on 19 May 2000 to renew that appointment for another four-year term, which began on 13 May 2001 and was due to end on 12 May 2005. By that same decision, the Conference authorised its Chairman to sign a contract with the Director-General, incorporating terms and conditions already stipulated in an Executive Council decision of 30 January 1998. On 23 February 2001 an exchange of letters between the Chairman of the Conference and the Director-General formalised the renewal of the latter's term.

3. The Organisation points out in its submissions that at the time when the renewal was decided certain Member States already had reservations as to the Director-General's management style, and that they had accepted the renewal of his term only in the absence of an alternative candidate and in the hope that he would improve his performance, but this hope did not materialise.

These "reservations" did not prevent the complainant from obtaining a unanimous vote "by acclamation". Nevertheless, the Director-General's management was subsequently called into question and in March 2002 a Member State, namely the United States of America, which is a major contributor to the funding of the Organisation, submitted a no-confidence motion to the Executive Council ... by a majority of 48 votes in favour, with 7 against and 43 abstentions (2 States Parties being absent), the Conference took the decision to terminate the complainant's appointment with immediate effect. The majority of the Conference thereby intended to underline its determination "to work for the preservation and effective functioning of the Organization and the Convention, which [were] put in jeopardy by the lack of confidence in the present Director-General of the Technical Secretariat".

4. Having thus been removed from office, the complainant filed a complaint on 19 July 2002 asking the Tribunal to set aside the decision to terminate his appointment and to order the Organisation to pay him damages in respect of the material and moral injury which it has caused him.

5. The Organisation replies that the Tribunal lacks jurisdiction to hear his case and raises several objections to receivability.

6. On the issue of jurisdiction the Organisation recalls that, by a letter of the Director-General dated 2 July 1997, it has accepted the Tribunal's jurisdiction to hear complaints concerning non-observance of the terms of appointment of staff members, and of such provisions of the Staff Regulations as are applicable. The relevant Staff Regulations provide:

"Regulation 11.1:

Staff members have the right of appeal against any administrative decision alleging non-observance of the terms of appointment, including relevant Staff Regulations and Rules, and against disciplinary action.

Regulation 11.3

Arrangements shall be made for the hearing by the Administrative Tribunal of the International Labour Organisation of appeals by staff members against the administrative decisions referred to in Staff Regulation 11.1. These arrangements shall fully respect the Annex on the Protection of Confidential Information of the Convention and the OPCW Policy on Confidentiality."

According to the defendant, the complainant was not a "staff member" within the meaning of those provisions, and the decision he impugns is not an administrative decision, but a political decision taken in a political context by the highest legislative and political body of the Organisation. The complainant asserts, on the contrary, that the Tribunal's jurisdiction is determined by Article II, paragraph 5, of its Statute, which provides as follows:

"The Tribunal shall also be competent to hear complaints alleging non-observance, in substance or in form, of the terms of appointment of officials and of provisions of the Staff Regulations of any other international organization meeting the standards set out in the Annex hereto which has addressed to the Director-General a declaration recognizing, in accordance with its Constitution or internal administrative rules, the jurisdiction of the Tribunal for this purpose, as well as its Rules of Procedure, and which is approved by the Governing Body."

The complainant argues that he was indeed an "official" of the Organisation, appealing against a breach of his contractual rights. He asserts that his complaint can be heard by the Tribunal since the defendant has recognised its jurisdiction.

7. The first issue to be resolved is that of whether the complainant is an "official" within the meaning of the Statute of the Tribunal, and a "staff member" for the purposes of the Organisation's submission to the Tribunal's jurisdiction. There is no doubt that the complainant was an "official" within the meaning of the Statute of the Tribunal. In his capacity as head of the Technical Secretariat he was in fact the foremost "official" of the Organisation. Indeed, the Headquarters Agreement between the Organisation and the Kingdom of the Netherlands specifically defines "officials" of the OPCW as including "the Director-General and all members of the staff of the Technical Secretariat of the OPCW, except those who are locally recruited and remunerated on an hourly basis". Although, as the defendant rightly points out, the terms of the Headquarters Agreement have no effect on the Tribunal's jurisdiction, the fact remains that at the time when that Agreement was signed, the word "officials", in standard usage, was considered by the Organisation to include the Director-General. The Tribunal must hold that, in accordance with the provisions of its Statute, its jurisdiction does, in principle, extend to disputes concerning that "official".

8. However, that jurisdiction must not be excluded either by the Organisation's submission to the Tribunal's jurisdiction or by its own statutory provisions. In this connection, the submission to jurisdiction refers to "complaints alleging non-observance, in substance or in form, of the terms of the appointment of staff" and the relevant provisions of the

Organisation's Staff Regulations confer a right of appeal on "staff members". The defendant argues that this category excludes the Director-General on the following grounds: Staff Regulation 1.2 expressly provides that staff members are subject to the authority of the Director-General and responsible to him in the exercise of their functions, whilst the Staff Rules – established by him – apply to "staff members appointed by the Director-General", as provided by Staff Rule 0.0.1, which would exclude the Director-General himself. The Tribunal cannot accept that view: the Director-General, as head of the Technical Secretariat, is appointed by decision of the competent authority which establishes his conditions of remuneration and defines the benefits to which he, like other senior-ranking staff members of the Technical Secretariat, is entitled pursuant to the Organisation's Staff Regulations and Interim Staff Rules. Moreover, Article VIII, paragraph 46, of the Chemical Weapons Convention provides that:

> "In the performance of their duties, the Director-General, the inspectors and the other members of the staff shall not seek or receive instructions from any Government or from any other source external to the Organization. They shall refrain from any action that might reflect on their positions as international officers responsible only to the Conference and the Executive Council."

Thus, the Director-General, like other staff members, is clearly deemed to have the status of an international civil servant. Consequently, the Director-General must be regarded as a staff member both for the purposes of the Organisation's submission to the Tribunal's jurisdiction and Staff Rule 11.3.01(a).

...

10. Thus, the Tribunal's jurisdiction *ratione personae* is established. But what of its jurisdiction *ratione materiae*? The defendant contests it, arguing that the decision impugned before the Tribunal is not an administrative decision, but essentially a political one. Staff Regulations 11.1 and 11.3 provide that staff members are entitled to challenge "administrative decisions" contravening the terms of their appointment. The Organisation refers to Judgment 209, in which the Tribunal held that it lacked jurisdiction to rule on the legality of a resolution adopted by the Plenipotentiary Conference of the International Telecommunication Union, the Union's "legislative organ". That ruling is clearly not applicable to the present case: a decision terminating the appointment of an international civil servant prior to the expiry of his/her term of office is an administrative decision, even if it is based on political considerations. The fact that it emanates from the Organisation's highest decision-making body cannot exempt it from the necessary review applying to all individual decisions which are alleged to be in breach of the terms of an appointment or contract, or of statutory provisions.

11. The defendant raises several objections to receivability. It considers that the complaint is irreceivable *ratione personae*, because the former Director-General does not have *locus standi* to bring his case before the Tribunal, and also *ratione materiae*, in that the impugned decision is not an administrative decision of the kind which may be referred to the Tribunal. Furthermore, it argues, the

applicable statutory provisions stipulate that before a dispute can be referred to the Tribunal, it must first be examined by the Appeals Council, which is competent to hear appeals by staff members against administrative decisions concerning them, and this procedure was plainly inconceivable in the case of an appeal by the former Director-General.

12. The first two objections to receivability have been sufficiently addressed in the foregoing discussion on the Tribunal's jurisdiction: the complainant was an international civil servant who was entitled to appeal to the Tribunal against a decision to terminate his appointment. That decision must be viewed as an administrative decision, even though it was taken by the Conference of the States Parties.

13. The third objection to receivability raises a more delicate issue. Staff Rule 11.3.01(a) provides that staff members can appeal to the Tribunal against administrative decisions and disciplinary actions taken after reference to the Appeals Council, which implies that the provisions governing the composition and procedural rules of the Appeals Council must also be taken into account. In the present case, that procedure was not and clearly could not have been followed. Indeed, it is hard to imagine how the Director-General, stripped of his functions, could have appealed to the Appeals Council established under his own authority, against a decision of the Conference of the States Parties, with a view to obtaining a final decision by the new Director-General. The defendant rightly submits that this procedure is entirely inappropriate, which the complainant accepts. However, the fact that these rules are unsuitable cannot have the effect of depriving an international civil servant of the right to have his complaint examined by a judicial body. An appeal to the Appeals Council was inconceivable, and the impugned decision was clearly a final decision – within the meaning of Article VII of the Tribunal's Statute – that only the Conference of the States Parties itself could have quashed, which could not be envisaged under the circumstances. In that situation, a direct appeal to the Tribunal – which Staff Rule 11.3.01(b) in fact permits – was clearly the only remedy available to the complainant. The complaint must therefore be considered receivable.

14. On the merits, the complainant puts forward several grounds for setting aside the impugned decision: he argues that the decision was taken following a flawed procedure, because the convening of the Special Session of the Conference of the States Parties contravened the Conference's Rules of Procedure; that it was taken by a noncompetent authority and lacks both a valid legal basis and sufficient motivation; that it violated his contractual rights; and that it amounted to misuse of authority, having been taken under pressure from one of the States Parties, the United States of America, which had threatened to withhold its financial contributions to the Organisation were the Director-General to remain in office.

15. At the insistent request of the United States, the Conference of the States Parties felt bound to terminate the complainant's appointment, despite the fact that it had been renewed by acclamation less than two years prior to the no-confidence motion presented to the Executive Council in circumstances which are described under A above. The

evidence on file and the applicable texts indicate that although the convening of the Special Session of the Conference of the States Parties was procedurally correct, and although the Conference does indeed have a broad competence, under Article VIII, paragraphs 19 and 21, of the Convention, to examine all problems lying within the scope of the Convention, "including those relating to the powers and functions of the Executive Council and the Technical Secretariat", and to appoint the Director-General, the reasons put forward in announcing what can only be described as the dismissal of the Director-General were extremely vague. Admittedly, the Permanent Representative of the United States to the OPCW had informed the Director-General, on 28 February 2002, of his Government's criticisms regarding the Director-General's management, and had asked him to resign. The "concerns" entertained by the United States were expressed in a paper published on 1 April 2002 by the US Department of State, and some of its grievances were highlighted by the US Permanent Representative in his statement to the Special Session of the Conference of the States Parties: poor financial management, abdication of transparency, destruction of staff morale, negligence and, in general, betrayal of the trust placed in him by the States Parties. It was on the basis of those charges, to which the complainant responded, that the Conference took its decision, and it may be assumed that the majority of its Members intended to endorse those views by voting in favour of the impugned decision, having been convened for a special session at the urgent request of the United States. However, the decision itself merely indicates that the Conference is determined "to work for the preservation and effective functioning of the Organization and the Convention, which are put in jeopardy by the lack of confidence in the present Director-General of the Technical Secretariat". Thus, the motion that was voted on was a genuine no-confidence motion, with no other basis than the threat which the complainant's conduct and management posed to the Organisation.

16. In accordance with the established case law of all international administrative tribunals, the Tribunal reaffirms that the independence of international civil servants is an essential guarantee, not only for the civil servants themselves, but also for the proper functioning of international organisations. In the case of heads of organisations, that independence is protected, *inter alia*, by the fact that they are appointed for a limited term of office. To concede that the authority in which the power of appointment is vested – in this case the Conference of the States Parties of the Organisation – may terminate that appointment in its unfettered discretion, would constitute an unacceptable violation of the principles on which international organisations' activities are founded (and which are in fact recalled in Article VIII of the Convention, in paragraphs 46 and 47), by rendering officials vulnerable to pressures and to political change. The possibility that a measure of the kind taken against the complainant may, exceptionally, be justified in cases of grave misconduct cannot be excluded, but such a measure, being punitive in nature, could only be taken in full compliance with the principle of due process, following a procedure enabling the individual concerned to defend his or her case effectively before an independent and impartial body. In this instance,

the complainant had no procedural guarantee, and given the circumstances of his case, he has good grounds for asserting that the premature termination of his appointment violated the terms of his contract of employment and contravened the general principles of the law of the international civil service.

17. Consequently, the impugned decision must be set aside and the complainant's further pleas need not be examined by the Tribunal. The complainant, who does not seek reinstatement, is entitled to compensation in respect of the injury caused by his unlawful dismissal. The Tribunal considers that his material injury may be properly assessed by determining the amount he would have received in salaries and emoluments (excluding representation allowance) between the date of his dismissal and 12 May 2005, subject to the deduction of any sums paid to him in connection with the cessation of his functions. As regards compensation for the moral injury undoubtedly suffered by the complainant, the Tribunal shall award him 50,000 euros in moral damages, which he shall be free to dispose of as he sees fit.

18. Since he succeeds, the complainant is entitled to an award of costs, which the Tribunal sets at 5,000 euros.

Notes

- Who was the employee who was wrongfully dismissed? What was his position, title, and function? Is he an official of the organization, or does he play a different role? What significance does this have for the case?
- What is the procedure for his appointment and removal? What person or organ makes decisions on those questions? And what considerations can they take into account when they reach decisions? How would we characterize the nature of that person or organ making this employment decision? And how should the nature of the act be characterized?
- The OPCW is arguing that the decision to dismiss the Director-General was a political decision, not an administrative one. Is this a relevant distinction?
- What are the legal arguments in favor of and against his dismissal? Are there any suggestions that the political decisions were improperly made, for example due to undue influence? If they were, does that issue have any meaning for a political body?
- Officials of international organizations are sometimes caught in an unusual tension. On the one hand they may be expected to be visionary leaders, but on the other hand the states parties may want to exercise considerable control over them. What kind of independence did this official have? Does an official's position, title, and function suggest the degree of independence the person should enjoy? What does this case say about the independence granted to international civil servants?

Setting aside the question of individual international civil servants, it may be more difficult to see the independence of organs that are member driven. Does the UN Security Council have a degree of independence from the member states of the UN? And from the member states that sit on the Security Council? While each state that is a member of the Security Council could take its own independent view on whether the use of force was appropriate in a given situation, at the Security Council those states must reach a consensus that the use of force is appropriate. In discussing, moderating, and amending views, and reaching compromises, the decision coming out of the Security Council could be uniquely different from that held by any one of the states independently.

Consider the case of *HvdP v The Netherlands*, before the Human Rights Committee. In this matter, an employee of the European Patent Office (EPO), located in Berlin, complained that he had been ill-treated by the office in violation of his human rights:

H.v.d.P. v The Netherlands, Communication 217/1986
Decision on Admissibility
UN Doc. A/42/40, at 185
Human Rights Committee, 28 August 1987[15]

2.1 The author, who was an industrial engineer in the Netherlands, is now employed as a substantive patent examiner at the European Patent Office (EPO) in Munich, Germany. He states that in January, 1980 he applied for a post as examiner in EPO. He was offered the post at the AI, step 2 level and he accepted it. Only after he had been several months with the organization, and had had the opportunity to compare his credentials and experience with that of his peers, did he realize that he had apparently been appointed at a discriminatorily low level and he felt that the preponderance of citizens of the Federal Republic of Germany in the higher grades was the result of the discriminatory practices of the organization. He thus lodged an appeal on the basis of denial of equal treatment, both within the Co-ordinated Organizations (North Atlantic Treaty Organization, Council of Europe, European Space Agency, etc.) and within EPO itself, claiming that he should have been appointed at the A2 level in 1980. His appeal was rejected on 19 January 1982 by the President of EPO as ill-founded. He then appealed to the Internal Appeals Committee, which on 6 December 1982 submitted its report rejecting the author's appeal and concluding that "no breach of the Service Regulations or of any rule of general law affecting international civil servants has been established". In reaching its decision, the Internal Appeals Committee relied heavily on the judicial precedents of the Administrative Tribunal of the International Labour Organisation.

...

2.3 The author then turned to the Human Rights Committee, which he considers competent to consider the case, since five States parties (France, Italy, Luxembourg, the Netherlands and Sweden) to the European Patent Convention are also parties to the Optional Protocol to the International Covenant on Civil

---

15 From UN Document A/42/40, by the Human Rights Committee © 1987 United Nations. Reprinted with the permission of the United Nations.

and Political Rights. He argues that "pursuant to article 25 (c), every citizen shall have access, on general terms of equality, to public service in his country. EPO, though a public body common to the Contracting States, constitutes a body exercising Dutch public authority". The appeal to the President of EPO and the opinion given by the Internal Appeals Committee, the author argues, do not constitute an effective remedy within the meaning of article 2 of the Covenant against violations of article 25 (c) of the Covenant. Moreover, "the Internal Appeals Committee is a travesty of competence, independence and impartiality as required by article 14 of the Covenant. IAC declines to adjudicate on the basis of public international law invoked by the applicant, i.e. law which the Contracting States undertook solemnly to observe".

...

3.2 The Human Rights Committee observes in this connection that it can only receive and consider communications in respect of claims that come under the jurisdiction of a State party to the Covenant. The author's grievances, however, concern the recruitment policies of an international organization, which cannot, in any way, be construed as coming within the jurisdiction of the Netherlands or of any other State party to the International Covenant on Civil and Political Rights and the Optional Protocol thereto. Accordingly, the author has no claim under the Optional Protocol.

4. The Human Rights Committee therefore decides:

The communication is inadmissible.

Notes

- The employee brought an action against The Netherlands. Is he complaining that he was badly treated by The Netherlands? Or by the European Patent Office? Or by the member states overseeing the EPO?
- What does the committee mean by "jurisdiction" in this case? Prescriptive, adjudicatory or enforcement jurisdiction? Or something else? We know that the state can have jurisdiction, but is it possible for an international organization to have jurisdiction in this sense?
- What degree of independence does the organization have? Although it operates in the territory of Germany, what kind of oversight does Germany have? And although it is constituted by several states, including The Netherlands, what kind of oversight does The Netherlands have?
- What kinds of steps could Germany or The Netherlands take to ensure that human rights are protected within the European Patent Office's governance and administered management? What body exercises governance oversight above the European Patent Office? Could the states have brought up the issue of this employee in political discussions over the EPO? Should these states have threatened to withhold funding of the organization until the employee received the correct treatment?
- Consider the policy implications of a single state holding up the work of the organization on the basis of particular concerns. What if those concerns were

mala fides? Should the EPO be independent of this kind of micromanagement? This concern might be even more acute in the case of the state that hosts the organization playing a disproportionate role. What kinds of concerns should justify state intervention in the operation of an international organization? How would we determine which concerns are valid and which are not?
- Or would be better to avoid the question of whether concerns are valid or not, and instead solve this question procedurally? For example, we could say that the concerns of any state or states could not influence the independence of the organization, unless by the unanimous or majority decision of the member states of the organization. Consider whether your view would be different if The Netherlands or Germany were able to convince the states parties of the EPO to alter its constitutive instrument and protect employees' human rights. Would that still constitute inefficient micromanagement, or would it rather amount to proper accountability?

International organizations are, after all, justified by being more efficient ways to organize international relations. If it was just as easy to manage transnational patent harmonization through the decentralized coordination of states, then there would be no added benefit in creating the EPO. Instead, it is far more effective to manage many issues through an organization rather than through the *ad hoc* bilateral relations between states. However, in order to do this, organizations need some freedom from states in order to operate in the benefit of all the states. This freedom entails the ability to make choices within its mandate.

3.1.4 Certain objectives

The final element of the definition in this book is that an organization must have some goal. Lawyers, political scientists, social scientists, and even anthropologists have attempted to identify the reason for having states. It could be a way to manage violence more efficiently, or coordinate water use or grain production, but, in the end, states are organic persons and do not need to justify their reason for existing. They simply exist. International organizations, however, are created deliberately for certain purposes, and those objectives play a strong role in how we apply the law to them. It guides our understanding of their nature, powers, immunities, and a whole range of other considerations:

**Reparation for Injuries Suffered in the Service of the United Nations
Advisory Opinion
1949 ICJ Reps. 174
International Court of Justice, 11 April 1949**

The Charter has not been content to make the Organization created by it merely a centre "for harmonizing the actions of nations in the attainment of these common ends" (Article 1, para. 3). It has equipped that centre with organs, and has given it special tasks. It has defined the position of the Members in relation to the Organization by requiring them to give it every assistance in any action undertaken by it (Article 2, para. 5), and to accept and carry out the decisions of the Security Council; by authorizing the General Assembly to make recommendations to the Members; [p. 179] by giving the Organization legal capacity and privileges and immunities in the territory of each of its Members; and by providing for the conclusion of agreements between the Organization and its Members. Practice – in particular the conclusion of conventions to which the Organization is a party – has confirmed this character of the Organization, which occupies a position in certain respects in detachment from its Members, and which is under a duty to remind them, if need be, of certain obligations. It must be added that the Organization is a political body, charged with political tasks of an important character, and covering a wide field namely, the maintenance of international peace and security, the development of friendly relations among nations, and the achievement of international co-operation in the solution of problems of an economic, social, cultural or humanitarian character (Article 1); and in dealing with its Members it employs political means. The "Convention on the Privileges and Immunities of the United Nations" of 1946 creates rights and duties between each of the signatories and the Organization (see, in particular, Section 35). It is difficult to see how such a convention could operate except upon the international plane and as between parties possessing international personality.

In the opinion of the Court, the Organization was intended to exercise and enjoy, and is in fact exercising and enjoying, functions and rights which can only be explained on the basis of the possession of a large measure of international personality and the capacity to operate upon an international plane. It is at present the supreme type of international organization, and it could not carry out the intentions of its founders if it was devoid of international personality. It must be acknowledged that its Members, by entrusting certain functions to it, with the attendant duties and responsibilities, have clothed it with the competence required to enable those functions to be effectively discharged.

Notes

- What is the purpose of the United Nations? Some people might argue that it is entirely useless, and presumably has no purpose. The court cites the Charter for the notion that it is more than simply a harmonization body. Certainly, it does appear to often serve as an office for any and all international issues. But it is also charged with some specific tasks. Perhaps it is best described as promoting international peace? But then how would that purpose be any different from the EU or almost any other international organization?
- Recall from the discussion above that the court in the *Reparations* case was trying to answer the question of whether the UN had international legal personality. Based on the purposes of the organization, the court concludes that it could

not imagine that international legal personality was refused, because it would be necessary for those purposes. Considering the purposes identified in answers to the previous question, does it really stand to reason that those purposes necessitated personality?
- If we were to remove one or several of the purposes of the United Nations, what impact would that have? Is there some point at which the loss of purposes results in the loss of personality? What if the UN was simply a large, empty building in New York where any states could argue about anything? Would it still be an international organization? Surely an international organization must do something? Despite the occasional complaints that the UN does nothing, if it truly did nothing, would it not be dissolved and wound down by its membership? Keep this question in mind in the next section on dissolution of international organizations.

3.2 DISSOLUTION OF AN INTERNATIONAL ORGANIZATION

All things must end, and international organizations are no different. The general practice is that organizations may be dissolved when they are no longer useful. For example, the Warsaw Pact was dissolved in 1991 when the various communist regimes in Eastern Europe came to an end.

Only rarely does the constitutive instrument include any terms on dissolution, although some may provide for a limited lifetime, such as many commodity organizations, or that the organization will terminate if enough members leave, as is the case with the European Space Agency. In a few cases, the constitutive instruments grant the plenary organ the power to dissolve the organization by vote. This is the case with the World Bank and other financial organizations. In fact, one of the most prominent dissolutions of international organizations, the ending of the League of Nations, was effected by the decision of its Assembly on 18 April 1946. However, the usual method of dissolution is for the member states to reach an international agreement terminating the organization. In unusual cases, an organization, such as the East African Community, may wither to such an extent that it ceases all activity without ever being formally abolished.

While organizations are generally dissolved when they are no longer useful, this is often in the context of the creation of a new international organization that will take over some of the prior organization's tasks, and, it is hoped, be more effective. For example the International Institute of Agriculture was dissolved in favor of the creation of the Food and Agriculture Organization, and the International Refugee Organization was abolished and transferred its duties to the Office of the UN High Commissioner for Refugees.

Generally, the terms on succession are provided either in the constitutive instrument of the new organization or in a protocol agreement. For example, the Council of the European Union agreed that the European Union Satellite Centre would assume the residual tasks of the Western European Union when that organization had ceased most of its activities and relevance.[16] In the case of the League of Nations, the members of the League adopted a "Common Plan" with the new United Nations on 12 February 1946 for the succession to property, archives (including deposited treaties), assets, and personnel (including pensions). What was more problematic was the political operations of the League. In cases such as this one, the intended result might be that those functions are terminated by implication.

The International Court of Justice had to deal with just this question because South Africa argued that the UN did not expressly assume responsibility under the trusteeship system for the old League of Nations mandates regime. Therefore, the mandate governance obligations regarding the territory of South West Africa (Namibia) had lapsed and South Africa was free to return to the prior, colonial, governance system:

International Status of South West Africa
Advisory Opinion
1950 ICJ Reps. 128
International Court of Justice, 1 July 1950

[p. 128]
The request for an opinion begins with a general question as follows:

"What is the international status of the Territory of South-West Africa and what are the international obligations of the Union of South Africa arising therefrom?"

...

[p. 131]
The Territory of South-West-Africa was one of the German overseas possessions in respect of which Germany, by Article 119 of the Treaty of Versailles, renounced all her rights and titles in favour of the Principal Allied and Associated Powers. When a decision was to be taken with regard to the future of these possessions as well as of other territories which, as a consequence of the war of 1914–1918, had ceased to be under the sovereignty of the States which formerly governed them, and which were inhabited by peoples not yet able to assume a full measure of self-government, two principles were considered to be of paramount importance: the principle of non-annexation and the principle that the well-being and development of such peoples form "a sacred trust of civilization".

With a view to giving practical effect to these principles, an international régime, the Mandates System, was created by Article 22 of the Covenant of the League of Nations. A "tutelage" was to be established for these peoples, and this tutelage was to be entrusted to certain advanced nations and exercised by them "as mandatories on behalf of the League".

[p. 132]
Accordingly, the Principal Allied and Associated Powers agreed that a Mandate for the Territory of South-West Africa should be conferred upon His Britannic Majesty to be exercised on his

---

16 See Council Decision 2011/297/CFSP of 23 May 2011 *amending* Joint Action 2001/555/CFSP on the establishment of a European Union Satellite Centre.

behalf by the Government of the Union of South Africa and proposed the terms of this Mandate. His Britannic Majesty, for and on behalf of the Government of the Union of South Africa, agreed to accept the Mandate and undertook to exercise it on behalf of the League of Nations in accordance with the proposed terms. On December 17th, 1920, the Council of the League of Nations, confirming the Mandate, defined its terms.

In accordance with these terms, the Union of South Africa (the "Mandatory") was to have full power of administration and legislation over the Territory as an integral portion of the Union and could apply the laws of the Union to the Territory subject to such local modifications as circumstances might require. On the other hand, the Mandatory was to observe a number of obligations, and the Council of the League was to supervise the administration and see to it that these obligations were fulfilled.

The terms of this Mandate, as well as the provisions of Article 22 of the Covenant and the principles embodied therein, show that the creation of this new international institution did not involve any cession of territory or transfer of sovereignty to the Union of South Africa. The Union Government was to exercise an international function of administration on behalf of the League, with the object of promoting the well-being and development of the inhabitants.

It is now contended on behalf of the Union Government that this Mandate has lapsed, because the League has ceased to exist. This contention is based on a misconception of the legal situation created by Article 22 of the Covenant and by the Mandate itself. The League was not, as alleged by that Government, a "mandator" in the sense in which this term is. used in the national law of certain States. It had only assumed an international function of supervision and control. The "Mandate" had only the name in common with the several notions of mandate in national law. The object of the Mandate regulated by international rules far exceeded that of contractual relations regulated by national law. The Mandate was created, in the interest of the inhabitants of the territory, and of humanity in general, as an international institution with an international object – a sacred trust of civilization. It is therefore not possible to draw any conclusion by analogy from the notions of mandate in national law or from any other legal conception of that law. The international rules regulating the Mandate constituted an international status for the Territory recognized by all the Members of the League of Nations, including the Union of South Africa.

[p. 133]
The essentially international character of the functions which had been entrusted to the Union of South Africa appears particularly from the fact that by Article 22 of the Covenant and Article 6 of the Mandate the exercise of these functions was subjected to the supervision of the Council of the League of Nations and to the obligation to present annual reports to it; it also appears from the fact that any Member of the League of Nations could, according to Article 7 of the Mandate, submit to the Permanent Court of International Justice any dispute with the Union Government relating to the interpretation or the application of the provisions of the Mandate.

The authority which the Union Government exercises over the Territory is based on the Mandate. If the Mandate lapsed, as the Union Government contends, the latter's authority would equally have lapsed. To retain the rights derived from the Mandate and to deny the obligations thereunder could not be justified.

These international obligations, assumed by the Union of South Africa, were of two kinds. One kind was directly related to the administration of the Territory, and corresponded to the sacred trust of civilization referred to in Article 22 of the Covenant. The other related to the machinery for implementation, and was closely linked to the supervision and control of the League. It corresponded to the "securities for the performance of this trust" referred to in the same article.

The first-mentioned group of obligations are defined in Article 22 of the Covenant and in Articles 2 to 5 of the Mandate. The Union undertook the general obligation to promote to the utmost the material and moral well-being and the social progress of the inhabitants. It assumed particular obligations relating to slave trade, forced labour, traffic in arms and ammunition, intoxicating spirits and beverages, military training and establishments, as well as obligations relating to freedom of conscience and free exercise of worship, including special obligations with regard to missionaries.

These obligations represent the very essence of the sacred trust of civilization. Their raison d'être and original object remain. Since their fulfilment did not depend on the existence of the League of Nations, they could not be brought to an end merely because this supervisory organ ceased to exist. Nor could the right of the population to have the Territory administered in accordance with these rules depend thereon.

This view is confirmed by Article 80, paragraph 1, of the Charter, which maintains the rights of States and peoples and the terms of existing international instruments until the territories in question are placed under the Trusteeship System. It is true that this provi-[p. 134]sion only says that nothing in Chapter XII shall be construed to alter the rights of States or peoples or the terms of existing international instruments. But –as far as mandated territories are concerned, to which paragraph 2 of this article refers – this provision presupposes that the rights of States and peoples shall not lapse automatically on the dissolution of the League of Nations. It obviously was the intention to safeguard the rights of States and peoples under all circumstances and in all respects, until each territory should be placed under the Trusteeship System.

This view results, moreover from the Resolution of the League of Nations of April 18th, 1946, which said:

> "Recalling that Article 22 of the Covenant applies to certain territories placed under Mandate the principle that the well-being and development of peoples not yet able to stand alone in the strenuous conditions of the modern world form a sacred trust of civilization:
>
> ...
>
> 3. Recognizes that, on the termination of the League's existence, its functions with respect to the mandated territories will come to an end, but notes that Chapters XI, XII and XIII of the Charter of the United Nations embody principles corresponding to

those declared in Article 22 of the Covenant of the League;

4. Takes note of the expressed intentions of the Members of the League now administering territories under Mandate to continue to administer them for the well-being and development of the peoples concerned in accordance with the obligations contained in the respective Mandates, until other arrangements have been agreed between the United Nations and the respective mandatory Powers."

As will be seen from this resolution, the Assembly said that the League's functions with respect to mandated territories would come to an end; it did not say that the Mandates themselves came to an end. In confining itself to this statement, and in taking note, on the other hand, of the expressed intentions of the mandatory Powers to continue to administer the mandated territories in accordance with their respective Mandates, until other arrangements had been agreed upon between the United Nations and those Powers, the Assembly manifested its understanding that the Mandates were to continue in existence until "other arrangements" were established.

A similar view has on various occasions been expressed by the Union of South Africa. In declarations made to the League of Nations, as well as to the United Nations, the Union Government has acknowledged that its obligations under the Mandate continued [p. 135] after the disappearance of the League. In a declaration made on April 9th, 1946, in the Assembly of the League of Nations, the representative of the Union Government, after having declared his Government's intention to seek international recognition for the Territory of South-West Africa as an integral part of the Union, stated: "In the meantime, the Union will continue to administer the Territory scrupulously in accordance with the obligations of the Mandate for the advancement and promotion of the interests of the inhabitants as she has done during the past six years when meetings of the Mandates Commission could not be held." After having said that, the disappearance of the Mandates Commission and of the League Council would "necessarily preclude complete compliance with the letter of the Mandate", he added: "The Union Government will nevertheless regard the dissolution of the League as in no way diminishing its obligations under the Mandate, which it will continue to discharge with the full and proper appreciation of its responsibilities until such time as other arrangements are agreed upon concerning the future status of the Territory."

In a memorandum submitted on October 17th, 1946, by the South-African Legation in Washington to the Secretary-General of the United Nations, expression was given to a similar view. Though the League had at that time disappeared, the Union Government continued to refer to its responsibility under the Mandate. It stated: "This responsibility of the Union Government as Mandatory is necessarily inalienable." On November 4th, 1946, the Prime Minister of the Union, in a statement to the Fourth Committee of the United Nations General Assembly, repeated the declaration which the representative of the Union had made previously to the League of Nations.

In a letter of July 23rd, 1947, to the Secretary-General of the United Nations, the

Legation of the Union referred to a resolution of the Union Parliament in which it was declared "that the Government should continue to render reports to the United Nations Organization as it has done heretofore under the Mandate". It was further stated in that letter: "In the circumstances the Union Government have no alternative but to maintain the status quo and to continue to administer the Territory in the spirit of the existing Mandate."

These declarations constitute recognition by the Union Government of the continuance of its obligations under the Mandate and not a mere indication of the future conduct of that Government. Interpretations placed upon legal instruments by the parties to them, though not conclusive as to their meaning, have considerable [p. 136] probative value when they contain recognition by a party of its own obligations under an instrument. In this case the declarations of the Union of South Africa support the conclusions already reached by the Court.

...

For the above reasons, the Court has arrived at the conclusion that the General Assembly of the United Nations is legally qualified to exercise the supervisory functions previously exercised by the League of Nations with regard to the administration of the Territory, and that the Union of South Africa is under an obligation to submit to supervision and control of the General Assembly and to render annual reports to it.

...

On April 9th, 1946, before the Assembly of the League of Nations, the Union representative declared that "it is the intention of the Union Government, at the forthcoming session of the United Nations General Assembly in New York, to formulate its case for according South-West Africa a status under which it would be internationally recognized as an integral part of the Union".

In accordance with these declarations, the Union Government, by letter of August 12th, 1946, from its Legation in Washington, requested that the question of the desirability of the territorial, integration in, and the annexation to, the Union of South Africa of the mandated Territory of South-West Africa, be included in the Agenda of the General Assembly. In a subsequent letter of October 9th, 1946, it was requested that the text of the item to be included in the Agenda be amended as follows: "Statement by the Government of the Union of South Africa on the outcome of their consultations with the peoples of South-West Africa as to the future status of the mandated Territory, and implementation to be given to the wishes thus expressed."

...
[p. 142]
...

By thus submitting the question of the future international status of the Territory to the "judgment" of the General Assembly as the "competent international organ", the Union Government recognized the competence of the General Assembly in the matter.

[p. 143]
The General Assembly, on the other hand, affirmed its competence by Resolution 65 (1) of December 14th, 1946. It noted with satisfaction that the step

taken by the Union showed the recognition of the interest and concern of the United Nations in the matter. It expressed the desire "that agreement between the United Nations and the Union of South Africa may hereafter be reached regarding the future status of the Mandated Territory of South-West Africa", and concluded: "The General Assembly, therefore, is unable to accede to the incorporation of the Territory of South-West Africa in the Union of South Africa."

Following the adoption of this resolution, the Union Government decided not to proceed with the incorporation of the Territory, but to maintain the status quo. The General Assembly took note of this decision in its Resolution 141 (II) of November 1st, 1947.

On the basis of these considerations, the Court concludes that competence to determine and modify the international status of South-West Africa rests with the Union of South Africa acting with the consent of the United Nations.

Notes

- What was the mandate system? What was the history and intention behind it? And how does that compare to the trusteeship system?
- Who granted the mandate? What was the nature of this grant? Was it some kind of legal authority that was given by another state, a group of states, or an international organization? Was it an agreement between a state in military occupation of some territory and one of those actors? What was the role of the indigenous population?
- What was the content of the mandate? What rights and obligations did South Africa accrue because it held a mandate? Did it have sovereignty over the territory or jurisdiction, or rights of administration? Did it include rights to use the territory? Would it have held those rights without the mandate?
- What rights did the League of Nations have in connection with the mandate? Could it oversee and monitor the operation of the mandate? Could it intervene or even revoke the mandate in case of maladministration?
- Was this mandate tied to the League of Nations, and did it depend on it? If the League of Nations had dissolved without a successor, would the mandate have necessarily terminated? Or was the mandate more like a human rights treaty with an additional protocol creating a treaty monitoring body? In those cases, the obligations would continue, even if the treaty monitoring body was ever abolished.
- Note that the Vienna Convention on the Law of Treaties, art. 70 provides that:
    1. Unless the treaty otherwise provides or the parties otherwise agree, the termination of a treaty under its provisions or in accordance with the present Convention:
        (a) Releases the parties from any obligation further to perform the treaty;
        (b) Does not affect any right, obligation or legal situation of the parties created through the execution of the treaty prior to its termination.

2. If a State denounces or withdraws from a multilateral treaty, paragraph 1 applies in the relations between that State and each of the other parties to the treaty from the date when such denunciation or withdrawal takes effect.

Does this provision impact your view on the effect of dissolving the League? The Vienna Convention article ensures what outcome? Why is this provision necessary or useful? How is that utility informative by way of analogy in the *International Status of South West Africa* case?

- What was the substance of the understanding between the League of Nations and United Nations on succession to the mandate system? How does the court understand what these two organizations intended? Or is it South Africa's interactions with the United Nations that provide us with terms for succession? Did South Africa assume any obligations following the dissolution of the League?

CHAPTER 4

Membership

4.1 TYPES OF MEMBERS

A major recurring theme in the law of international organizations is the relationship between the organization and its members, so this chapter will address questions of membership. It will begin by looking at the various types of members.

The first type of member is the "original" member. This category identifies between members that were present for the initial negotiations over the creation of the organization and then became members at the moment of creation. These members would be distinct from members that join the organization later. The UN Charter takes note of this distinction between these two categories:

Charter of the United Nations
24 October 1945
1 UNTS 16[1]

Chapter II Membership
Article 3.

The original Members of the United Nations shall be the states which, having participated in the United Nations Conference on International Organization at San Francisco, or having previously signed the Declaration by United Nations of 1 January 1942, sign the present Charter and ratify it in accordance with Article 110.

Article 4.

1. Membership in the United Nations is open to all other peace-loving states which accept the obligations contained in the present Charter and, in the judgment of the Organization, are able and willing to carry out these obligations.

---

1 From the United Nations Treaty Series, by the United Nations © 1945 United Nations. Reprinted with the permission of the United Nations.

While the UN Charter makes this distinction, it is not completely clear whether this distinction has any significance. Certainly, it has some political significance, because these are the states that agreed on the purposes, powers, and structure of the organization; members that subsequently join clearly have no say in these issues. Legally speaking, perhaps the only significance of being an original member is that it is only the views of those states, expressed at the time of negotiating the creation of the organization, that are taken into consideration for interpreting the original meaning of the constitutive instrument.

In addition, original members do not necessarily need to satisfy the membership criteria that are applied to states that join the organization later. When the states of Belarus and Ukraine became independent following the dissolution of the Soviet Union, one question was whether these newly independent states had to apply for admission to the UN as new members. The other states that emerged from the Soviet Union applied individually for admission on their own merits. However, one unusual aspect of the UN is that Belarus and Ukraine had been members of the UN from its founding, even though they were both constituent members of the Soviet Union, in a unique political compromise. In determining what their financial contributions to the UN should be, the UN Office of Legal Counsel had to determine whether they were original members or new members:

United Nations, Office of Legal Counsel
Legal Opinion No. 15
Questions regarding the scale of assessment for Belarus and Ukraine
1992 United Nations Juridical Yearbook 435[2]

1. Are Belarus and Ukraine "new Member States" or are they in terms of Article 3 of the Charter of the United Nations the original Members of the United Nations, participating in its activities since its inception?

The participation of the then Byelorussian Soviet Socialist Republic and Ukrainian Soviet Socialist Republic at the San Francisco Conference, and eventually in the Organization as original Members, was the subject of an agreement reached among the sponsoring Powers at Yalta in 1945. Pursuant to that agreement, the second plenary session of the San Francisco Conference on 27 April 1945 resolved that "the Ukrainian Soviet Socialist Republic and the Byelorussian Soviet Socialist Republic be invited to be initial Members in the proposed international organization". At the end of the San Francisco Conference, both countries signed the Charter and subsequently deposited their instruments of ratification. Since then, they have never been expelled from the Organization or readmitted to it. The recent constitutional changes, the change in the relationship between them and the former USSR or changes in their official

---

2 From the United Nations Office of Legal Counsel Legal Opinion Number 15 (1992), by the United Nations © 1992 United Nations. Reprinted with the permission of the United Nations.

designations did not and could not somehow transform them automatically into new Members of the Organization. There is no procedure for that, either in the Charter or in any other document. Belarus (the new name of the Byelorussian SSR) and Ukraine are, and remain, consequently "original Members" of the United Nations within the purview of Article 3 of the Charter and they are correctly listed as Members since 1945 in the official records of the Organization. [footnote omitted]

2. Is the scale of assessment adopted by consensus for the period of 1992, 1993 and 1994 as contained in General Assembly resolution 46/221 A of 21 December 1991 valid for Belarus and Ukraine?

Paragraph 1 of General Assembly resolution 46/221 A provides for a scale of assessments for the contributions of Member States to the regular budget of the United Nations for 1992, 1993 and 1994, unless a new scale is approved earlier

4. Are the recommendations of the Committee on Contributions aimed at reviewing and drastically increasing the rate of assessment of Belarus and Ukraine in the middle of a three-year assessment period consistent with the provision of resolution 46/221 and rule 160 of the rules of procedure of the General Assembly?

The report of the Committee on Contributions includes a chapter entitled "Assessment of new Member States". [footnote omitted] The chapter begins with a statement that: "The Committee considered the assessment of new Member States in the context of paragraph 1 of General Assembly resolution 46/221 A and rule 160 of the rules of procedure of the General Assembly." Further on in the chapter, the Committee reviewed the manner in which the rates of assessment of Belarus and Ukraine had been determined since 1946. It then concluded:

> "In view of the unique manner in which the rates of assessment for Belarus and Ukraine were determined in the context of the former Union of Soviet Socialist Republics and because of the special relationship Which existed among the 15 republics of the former Union of Soviet Socialist Republics during the base period of the scale of assessments, the Committee decided to include Belarus and Ukraine in its considerations as well." [footnote omitted]

...

As to the change in the relations that existed between Belarus, as well as Ukraine, and the former Soviet Union, paragraph 36 of the report of the Committee on Contributions seems to imply that in the view of the Committee that change is a fundamental change of circumstances which justifies the treatment of the two States as new Member States, be it in itself or taken together with the "unique" method by which their rates of assessment were determined. Nothing, however, in rule 160 would give a basis for such reasoning. Rule 160 speaks of new Member States without any specifications or qualifying additions. This seems to indicate that the term has to be understood in the same sense as elsewhere in the rules of procedure of the General Assembly, i.e., as meaning States newly admitted as Members through the procedure laid down in Article 4 of the Charter, chapter XIV of the rules of procedure of the General Assembly and the relevant provisions of the provisional rules of procedure of the Security Council.

Nor does anything in resolution 46/221 point to the admissibility of treating previously assessed Members of the Organization belatedly as new Member States, either generally, or in the particular case of Belarus and Ukraine. In this regard, it should be noted that the resolution was adopted only on 20 December 1991, when the process of change was well established both in Belarus and in Ukraine.

Finally, there is no precedent case in which a Member State has been treated in the context of assessment as a new Member other than in connection with its first assessment following its admission to the United Nations. I arrive, therefore, at the conclusion that the treatment of Belarus and Ukraine as new Member States, as recommended by the Committee on Contributions, is not consistent with resolution 46/221 and rule 160.

Notes

- Why were Belarus and Ukraine members even though the Soviet Union was also a member? Is this justifiable? This question will be discussed even more detail in Section 4.2 on qualifying for membership.
- In the view of the Office of Legal Counsel, what is the significance of the distinction between the original members and those that join later? What consequence does that have for Belarus and Ukraine?
- Why is the dissolution of the Soviet Union, which is an extinction and fragmentation of one of the original members of the UN, not considered a fundamental change of circumstances?

In addition to this distinction between original members and those that join later, some organizations also offer other categories of membership, such as associate members. For instance, the International Maritime Organization has three associate members: the Faroe Islands, Hong Kong, and Macau. Associate members usually have a clear distinction of status in the constitutive instrument because, even though they are members, they may have different powers or authority than other members. The usual scenario is that associate members may fully participate, but cannot vote or formally participate in forming consensus.

This question of categories of membership can also be distinguished from the rights that different members have within the organization. Usually the practice of international organizations is that all states have equal voting rights, but this is not always the case. A pretty obvious example is the UN Security Council, where five states (China, France, Russia, the UK, and the US) not only have permanent seats on the Council, but also have the right to veto any substantive decision of the Council. This is not a right that is held by any other state that is a member of the United Nations, even if that state is elected to temporary membership on the Council.

Keep in mind that these distinctions between categories of members, if they are made at all, are quite a different matter from a state or other entity participating in the organization as an observer. Most organizations permit certain entities to observe, and even partially participate, despite not being members. This is usually a practice that is understood to be impliedly permitted by the constitutive instrument, so, for example, the UN Charter does not even mention the term "observer." In this way, Switzerland was represented at the UN even though it was not a member during most of the UN's existence. Other prominent observers at the UN have included the Holy See and the Palestine Liberation Organization (PLO). The latter has recently shifted the nature of its presence from being represented as the PLO to the State of Palestine. Both Palestine and the Holy See have significant rights of participation, including the right to circulate documents, even though they are not members. Formal observation is also extended to certain other non-state organizations, for example other international organizations such as the EU, and prominent non-governmental organizations such as the International Committee of the Red Cross.

4.2 QUALIFICATION FOR MEMBERSHIP

Setting aside the somewhat special situation of original members, this section will discuss what criteria need to be satisfied in order for a new member to join an existing international organization.

4.2.1 Statehood

The first, most obvious, criterion is that the new member must be a state. However, this rule is not absolute. The major exception to this rule is that, in some cases, international organizations can create and join other international organizations. For example, the EU is a member of the World Trade Organization. We can recall that international organizations have international legal personality and the competence to enter into treaties. This does not mean that every constitutive instrument will permit international organizations to join as members. In the case of the WTO, the agreements establishing the organization specifically provided that organizations such as the EU could join. Without this provision, organizations of that nature could not become members.

In addition to the specific provision for international organizations to join as members, the requirement that a new member be a state also needs to be understood in the context of the organization and its constitutive instrument. Some treaties creating organizations will only permit states that are members of the United Nations or one of its specialized agencies to become a member, but other treaties do not necessarily impose the same limitation. One example of this practice is the relationship between Palestine and the International Criminal Court (ICC). Consider the following sequence of communications:

Ali Kashan, Minister of Justice,
Palestinian National Authority
Letter to the Registrar of the International Criminal Court
Declaration accepting the Jurisdiction of the International Criminal Court
21 January 2009[3]

In conformity with Article 12, paragraph 3 of the Statute of the International Criminal Court, the Government of Palestine hereby recognizes the jurisdiction of the court for the purpose of identifying, prosecuting and judging the authors and accomplices of acts committed on the territory of Palestine since 1 July 2002.

International Criminal Court, Office of the Prosecutor
Situation in Palestine
3 April 2012[4]

1. On 22 January 2009, pursuant to article 12(3) of the Rome Statute, Ali Khashan acting as Minister of Justice of the Government of Palestine lodged a declaration accepting the exercise of jurisdiction by the International Criminal Court for "acts committed on the territory of Palestine since 1 July 2002." [footnote omitted]

2. In accordance with article 15 of the Rome Statute, the Office of the Prosecutor initiated a preliminary examination in order to determine whether there is a reasonable basis to proceed with an investigation. ...

3. The first stage in any preliminary examination is to determine whether the preconditions to the exercise of jurisdiction under article 12 of the Rome Statute are met.

...

5. The issue that arises, therefore, is who defines what is a "State" for the purpose of article 12 of the Statute? In accordance with article 125, the Rome Statute is open to accession by "all States", and any State seeking to become a Party to the Statute must deposit an instrument of accession with the Secretary-General of the United Nations. In instances where it is controversial or unclear whether an applicant constitutes a "State", it is the practice of the Secretary-General to follow or seek the General Assembly's directives on the matter. This is reflected in General Assembly resolutions which provide indications of whether an applicant is a "State". [footnote omitted] Thus, competence for determining the term "State" within the meaning of article 12 rests, in the first instance, with the United Nations Secretary General who, in case of doubt, will defer to the guidance of General Assembly. The

---

3 International Criminal Court, *available at* www.icc-cpi.int/NR/rdonlyres/74EEE201-0FED-4481-95D4-C8071087102C/279777/20090122PalestinianDeclaration2.pdf.
4 International Criminal Court, *available at* https://legal-tools.org/doc/f5d6d7/pdf.

Assembly of States Parties of the Rome Statute could also in due course decide to address the matter in accordance with article 112(2 (g) of the Statute.

6. In interpreting and applying article 12 of the Rome Statute, the Office has assessed that it is for the relevant bodies at the United Nations or the Assembly of States Parties to make the legal determination whether Palestine qualifies as a State for the purpose of acceding to the Rome Statute and thereby enabling the exercise of jurisdiction by the Court under article 12(1). The Rome Statute provides no authority for the Office of the Prosecutor to adopt a method to define the term "State" under article 12(3) which would be at variance with that established for the purpose of article 12(1).

7. The Office has been informed that Palestine has been recognised as a State in bilateral relations by more than 130 governments and by certain international organisations, including United Nation bodies. However, the current status granted to Palestine by the United Nations General Assembly is that of "observer", not as a "Non-member State". The Office understands that on 23 September 2011, Palestine submitted an application for admission to the United Nations as a Member State in accordance with article 4(2) of the United Nations Charter, but the Security Council has not yet made a recommendation in this regard. While this process has no direct link with the declaration lodged by Palestine, it informs the current legal status of Palestine for the interpretation and application of article 12.

8. The Office could in the future consider allegations of crimes committed in Palestine, should competent organs of the United Nations or eventually the Assembly of States Parties resolve the legal issue relevant to an assessment of article 12 or should the Security Council, in accordance with article 13(b), make a referral providing jurisdiction.

**UN Secretariat
Depositary Notification,
Rome Statute of the International Criminal Court, Rome, 17 July 1998
Reference: C.N.13.2015.TREATIES-XVIII.10
State of Palestine: Accession
6 January 2015**[5]

The Secretary-General of the United Nations, acting in his capacity as depositary, communicates the following:

The above action was effected on 2 January 2015.

The Statute will enter into force for the State of Palestine on 1 April 2015 in accordance with its article 126 (2) …

---

5   From UN Document C.N.13.2015.TREATIES-XVIII.10, by the United Nations © 2015 United Nations. Reprinted with the permission of the United Nations.

Mahmoud Abbas, President of the State of Palestine
Letter to the Registrar of the International Criminal Court
Declaration accepting the Jurisdiction of the International Criminal Court
31 December 2014[6]

In conformity with Article 12, paragraph 3, of the Rome Statute of the International Criminal Court, ... The Government of the State of Palestine hereby recognizes the jurisdiction of the Court for the purpose of identifying, prosecuting and judging authors and accomplices of crimes within the jurisdiction of the Court committed in the occupied Palestinian territory, including East Jerusalem, since 13 June 2014.

Registrar of the International Criminal Court
Letter to Mahmoud Abbas, President of the State of Palestine
Ref. 2015/IOR/3496/HvH
7 January 2015[7]

Excellency,

I hereby confirm receipt, on 1 January 2015, of your 31 December 2014 "Declaration Accepting the Jurisdiction of the International Criminal Court" ...

I hereby accept the declaration and I have transmitted it to the Prosecutor for her consideration. This acceptance is without prejudice to any prosecutorial or judicial determinations on this matter.

Situation in the State of Palestine, No. ICC-01/18
Prosecution request pursuant to article 19(3)
for a ruling on the Court's territorial jurisdiction in Palestine
International Criminal Court, Pre-Trial Chamber I, 22 January 2020[8]

B. Palestine is a "State" for the purpose of article 12(2)(a) of the Rome Statute

93. The Prosecution has conducted a preliminary examination into the situation of Palestine. After a thorough analysis, the Prosecutor is satisfied that there is a reasonable basis to initiate an investigation into the situation in Palestine pursuant to article 53(1) of the Statute. [footnote omitted]

94. On the basis of the available information, there is a reasonable basis to believe that war crimes were committed in the context of the 2014 hostilities in Gaza. [footnote omitted] In particular, there is a reasonable basis to believe that

---

6 International Criminal Court, *available at* www.icc-cpi.int/iccdocs/PIDS/press/Palestine_A_12-3.pdf.
7 International Criminal Court, *available at* www.icc-cpi.int/iccdocs/PIDS/press/150107-Registrar-Letter-to-HE-President-Abbas-regarding-Palestine-Art-12-3--Declaration.pdf.
8 International Criminal Court, *available at* www.icc-cpi.int/CourtRecords/CR2020_00161.PDF.

members of the Israel Defense Forces ("IDF") committed the war crimes of: intentionally launching disproportionate attacks in relation to at least three incidents which the Office has focussed on (article 8(2)(b)(iv)); wilful killing and wilfully causing serious injury to body or health (articles 8(2)(a)(i) and 8(2)(a)(iii), or article 8(2)(c)(i)); and intentionally directing an attack against objects or persons using the distinctive emblems of the Geneva Conventions (article 8(2)(b)(xxiv), or 8(2)(e)(ii)). In addition, there is a reasonable basis to believe that members of *Hamas* and Palestinian armed groups ("PAGs") committed the war crimes of: intentionally directing attacks against civilians and civilian objects (articles 8(2)(b)(i)–(ii), or 8(2)(e)(i)); using protected persons as shields (article 8(2)(b)(xxiii)); wilfully depriving protected persons of the rights of fair and regular trial (articles 8(2)(a)(vi) or 8(2)(c)(iv)) and wilful killing (articles 8(2)(a)(i), or 8(2)(c)(i)); and torture or inhuman treatment (article 8(2)(a)(ii), or 8(2)(c)(i)) and/or outrages upon personal dignity (articles 8(2)(b)(xxi), or 8(2)(c)(ii)). …

95. In addition, there is a reasonable basis to believe that in the context of Israel's occupation of the West Bank, including East Jerusalem, members of the Israeli authorities have committed war crimes under article 8(2)(b)(viii) in relation, *inter alia*, to the transfer of Israeli civilians into the West Bank since 13 June 2014. The Prosecution has further concluded that the potential case(s) that would likely arise from an investigation of these alleged crimes would be admissible pursuant to article 17(1)(a)–(d) of the Statute.

…

101. Further, the Prosecution considers that Palestine is the "State on the territory of which the conduct in question occurred" (under article 12(2)(a)) because of its status as an ICC State Party. Once an entity has become a State Party, the Rome Statute does not require the Prosecutor to conduct a new assessment regarding its statehood to trigger the Court's jurisdiction. Alternatively, if the Chamber disagrees and finds it necessary to conduct such assessment, the Prosecution submits that Palestine is also a "State" for the purposes of the Rome Statute under relevant principles and rules of international law.

…

1. The Prosecution's primary position: Palestine is a "State" for the purpose of article 12(2)(a) because of its status as an ICC State Party

103. The Prosecution considers that a "State" for the purposes of articles 12(1) and 125(3) should also be considered a "State" under article 12(2) of the Statute. Following the deposit of its instrument of accession with the UN Secretary-General pursuant to article 125(3), Palestine qualified as a "State on the territory of which the conduct in question occurred" for the purposes of article 12(2)(a) of the Rome Statute. This means that once a State becomes party to the Statute, the ICC is automatically entitled to exercise jurisdiction over article 5 crimes committed on its territory. No additional consent or separate assessment is needed.

104. This flows from the statutory scheme, whereby a State that becomes a Party to the Statute pursuant to article 125(3) "thereby accepts the jurisdiction of the Court" in accordance with article

12(1). Article 12(2) in turn specifies the bases on which the Court may exercise its jurisdiction as a consequence of a State being a Party to the Statute under article 12(1), or having lodged a declaration in accordance with article 12(3).

105. There is no indication that the term "State" in article 12(2) should be interpreted in a different way from that term in article 12(1). [footnote omitted] Likewise, in the ICC context it would contradict the principle of effectiveness to permit an entity to agree to the terms of the Rome Statute and thereby join the Court, to then later negate the natural consequence of its membership – the exercise of the Court's jurisdiction in accordance with the Statute.

106. This position accords with the Prosecutor's previously announced practice in relation to this situation, and is consistent with the Court's practice. [footnote omitted] Moreover, since its accession to the Statute, the Assembly of States Parties ("ASP") has not treated Palestine any differently from any other State Party. There is no reason why the Court should do so now.

(a) Article 125 regulates accession by States to the Rome Statute

107. Unlike some treaties and organisations, [footnote omitted] the Rome Statute does not specify the requirements that an entity must satisfy to become a State Party. Accordingly, article 12(1)350 must be read with article 125(3), which affords membership to "all States" depositing instruments of accession with the Secretary-General:

> This Statute shall be open to accession by *all States*. Instruments of accession shall be deposited with the Secretary-General of the United Nations. [footnote omitted]

108. Article 125(3) reflects the adoption of the "all States" formula for determining party status, that is, a State's competence to join the Rome Statute. This formula has a special meaning and requires the UN Secretary-General to follow a certain procedure to ascertain whether an entity may become a party to a treaty deposited with him/her. As the UN's Office of Legal Affairs ("OLA") has explained in its Summary of Practice of the Secretary-General as Depositary of Multilateral Treaties: [footnote omitted]

...

> He would not wish to determine, on his own initiative, the highly political and controversial question of whether or not the areas whose status was unclear were States. Such a determination, he believed, would fall outside his competence. He therefore stated that when the "any State" or "all States" formula was adopted, *he would be able to implement it only if the General Assembly provided him with the complete list of the States coming within the formula* ...

110. For the purposes of the Rome Statute, the necessary effect of article 125(3) and the "all States" formula is to condition accession to the Statute on "unequivocal indications from the [UN General] Assembly that it considers a particular entity to be a State". [footnote omitted] If such indications exist, the Secretary-General will receive the instrument of accession and the State will become a Party to the Statute thus accepting the jurisdiction of the Court within the terms of article 12(1).

111. In adopting the "all States" formula, the Statute does not prescribe criteria for the Court (or its organs) to determine "the highly political and controversial question" [footnote omitted] of whether certain entities are States under international law. Rather, the institutional design of the Rome Statute links this question to determinations made outside the Statute's framework, namely the UN General Assembly, given the depository functions of the UN Secretary-General. ...

(b) Article 12(2) should be interpreted consistently with article 12(1) and article 125(3)

112. Once a State becomes a Party to the Statute, the Court may exercise its jurisdiction on the territory of a State Party and/or over its nationals pursuant to article 12(2). [footnote omitted] This is because a "State" for the purposes of articles 12(1) and 125(3) is also a "State" under article 12(2) of the Statute. Therefore, after depositing its instrument of accession with the UN Secretary-General, a State becomes Party to the Statute, and the Court may exercise its jurisdiction pursuant to article 12(2) provided the requirements under article 53(1) (to open an investigation) are met.

113. Against this position, it has been argued that the term "State" should be defined in the Rome Statute in accordance with its ordinary meaning and general rules of international law governing Statehood. It has been posited that this was the drafters' intention. [footnote omitted] This approach would require that *after* a State has joined the Court but *before* the Court exercises its jurisdiction over it, the Court should necessarily determine whether that State Party is also a sovereign State under international law. This would require the Court to assess whether a State Party meets the criteria under article 1 of the Montevideo Convention, which is the most accepted formulation of statehood criteria in international law. [footnote omitted]

114. Yet, the Rome Statute does not require a State Party to fulfil additional criteria for the Court to be able to exercise jurisdiction over its territory or its nationals. Nor does it require the Court to conduct a separate assessment of the status of a State Party before it can exercise its jurisdiction under article 12. If the exercise of the Court's jurisdiction were to be restricted with respect to certain States, then logically any such limitation would have to have been introduced upon the *admission* of such States. This has been practice in certain conventions and international organisations where membership is limited to certain States [footnote omitted] or States fulfilling certain criteria. [footnote omitted] It would appear contrary to the principle of effectiveness and good faith [footnote omitted] to allow an entity to join the ICC but then to deny the rights and obligations of accession – *i.e.* the Court's exercise of jurisdiction for crimes committed on its territory or by its nationals, whether prompted by the State Party or otherwise.

...

118. Moreover, this approach would not prevent the Court from defining "State" differently in other areas of the Statute to the extent needed. [footnote omitted] Specifically, although the Court should follow the General Assembly practice and resolutions on whether an entity is permitted to become a State

Party (in accordance with the Secretary-General depository functions under article 12.5(3)), such determinations would be without prejudice to the Court's own judicial functions in interpreting and applying the term "State" in other parts of Statute, such as in the contextual element of war crimes, [footnote omitted] for the crime of aggression, [footnote omitted] or for complementarity purposes. The International Criminal Tribunal for the Former Yugoslavia (ICTY), for example, initially broadly defined "State" in its Rules of Procedure and Evidence to include non-recognised State-like entities such as the Republic Srpska, [footnote omitted] while ICTY Chambers have applied the Montevideo criteria to define "State" in the contextual element of war crimes. [footnote omitted] In assessing complementarity in the *Georgia* Article 15 Decision, the Majority of Pre-Trial Chamber I appeared to consider domestic proceedings conducted by States under public international law. The Majority found that "any proceedings undertaken by the *de facto* authorities of South Ossetia are not capable of meeting the requirements of article 17 of the Statute, due to South Ossetia not being a recognized State". [footnote omitted] ...

(c) This position is consistent with previous practice

121. The Prosecution has already taken this position. On 3 April 2012 the Prosecution (after seeking the views of interested parties and considering the Secretary-General's Depositary Summary Practice) rejected Palestine's first declaration under article 12(3) because Palestine only had "observer" status within the UN and therefore would not ordinarily be capable of acceding to or otherwise accepting the exercise of jurisdiction by the Court under the "all States" formula. [footnote omitted] However, on 16 January 2015 after receiving Palestine's second declaration under article 12(3), the Prosecution reopened its preliminary examination into the situation in Palestine. [footnote omitted] By this time, Palestine had become a UN "non-member observer State". [footnote omitted] In both instances, the Prosecution interpreted the term "State" in article 12(3) consistently with article 12(1) and article 12.5(3). The Prosecution sees no reason to define the term "State" in article 12(2) differently now.

...

123. Further, Palestine's accession to the Statute is consistent with the approach taken by the Court towards other "atypical" entities. For example, the Cook Islands, a self-governing entity in free association with New Zealand, which is not widely regarded as an independent State [footnote omitted] and which is not a UN member State or a UN non-member observer State, acceded to the Statute on 18 July 2008 without controversy. In that case, the Secretary-General permitted the Cook Islands to join treaties with the "all States" formula after he "felt that the question of the status, as a State, ... had been duly decided in the affirmative by the World Health Assembly, whose membership [accepted in 1984] was fully representative of the international community". [footnote omitted] The Secretary-General considered that due to "its subsequent admittance to other specialized agencies [...] without any specifications or limitations, [...] the Cook Islands could henceforth be included in the "all States" formula, were it to wish to participate in treaties

deposited with the Secretary-General". [footnote omitted]

...

2. The Prosecution's alternative position: Palestine may be considered a "State" for the purposes of the Rome Statute under relevant principles and rules of international law

136. The Prosecution considers Palestine to be a State for purposes of article 12(2) because it is a State Party in accordance to article 125(3). At this stage, for the Court to exercise its jurisdiction, it need not conduct a separate assessment of Palestine's statehood under international law. Nonetheless, if the Chamber were to consider it necessary to determine whether Palestine is a "State" in light of the relevant principles and rules of international law, [footnote omitted] the Prosecution submits that Palestine is also a "State" for the purposes of the Rome Statute. [footnote omitted]

137. Statehood has generally been considered to depend on the fulfilment of the four criteria under article 1 of the 1933 Montevideo Convention (the so-called "Montevideo criteria") coupled with international recognition. However, the Montevideo criteria have been less stringently applied in cases where circumstances so warrant. This would include the recognition of a right to self-determination of peoples within a territory, and importantly, an inability to fulfil all of the criteria because of acts deemed to be illegal or invalid under international law. Moreover, international recognition of statehood has remained a valid consideration and in some cases has been determinative.

138. Palestine has a population and a demonstrated capacity to conduct itself in the international scene. [footnote omitted] Further, the Occupied Palestinian Territory has long been recognised as the territory where the Palestinian people are entitled to exercise their right to self-determination and to an independent and sovereign State. [footnote omitted] While Palestine – upon its own acknowledgement [footnote omitted] – may not have full authority over the entirety of the Territory, this is not determinative for the Court's purposes. Significantly, there appear to be several reasons why a case-specific application of the Montevideo criteria to Palestine is warranted. *First*, the internationally recognised right to self-determination of the Palestinian people in the Occupied Palestinian Territory. *Second*, the detrimental impact of the ongoing breaches of international law on Palestine's effective authority over the Occupied Palestinian Territory and on the realisation of the right of self-determination of its people. Finally, the bilateral recognition of Palestine afforded by at least 138 States.

Notes

- On what basis did Palestine assert its capacity to join the International Criminal Court? Is this a justifiable argument? Be attentive to the question of whether Palestine was joining the court as a member or accepting the court's jurisdiction over its territory and nationals. What is the distinction?

- On what basis did the prosecutor react negatively? Does the prosecutor have the authority to question this act by Palestine? Would that authority be different if it was a question of joining the court versus accepting the court's jurisdiction? What is the prosecutor's initial reasoning for why Palestine does not have this capacity?
- What changes took place between 2012 and 2015? Perhaps it is interesting to know that during that time Palestine joined the United Nations Educational, Scientific and Cultural Organization (UNESCO). How would that act have any relevance for the International Criminal Court? How do we explain the prosecutor's change of position?
- Can the question of whether Palestine is a state be answered differently in relation to the International Criminal Court, UNESCO, and the UN? What about the WTO and the EU? If there is any distinction, what explains this distinction?

In fact, the determination of whether an entity is a state or not for purposes of membership does appear to have some relativity. We have already observed the case of the original members of Belarus and Ukraine, but it is also important to take note of the UN membership of India and the Philippines, both of which joined the UN before they were formally independent states. In the case of Namibia, it joined the Food and Agriculture Organization and International Labour Organization before it was an independent state. In an unusual case, though not strictly about membership, the princely state of Hyderabad was permitted to address the UN Security Council as a state when India became independent from the UK and Hyderabad sought to reassert its pre-colonial sovereignty, which India promptly suppressed militarily. And lastly, even within the membership of an international organization, some members might not recognize other members as states; the most notorious example is the refusal of Iran, Pakistan, Saudi Arabia, and the United Arab Emirates to recognize the State of Israel, despite all of those entities being members of the UN.

In this context, and again remembering the example of Belarus and Ukraine, perhaps it is interesting to observe that China is a member of the World Trade Organization, and yet so is the Republic of China (commonly called "Taiwan"), using the name "Chinese Taipei." Recall that it is official state policy of both of these entities that there is only one China. To add even more confusion, Hong Kong is also a separate member of the WTO. And this situation is not entirely unique, because the European Union is a member of the WTO (under the older designation "European Communities"), yet the various Member States of the EU are also members in their own right.

4.2.2 Other substantive requirements

Beyond qualifying as a state or other entity that the constitutive instrument would permit to be a member, there may be additional substantive requirements in order to join an international organization.

One requirement is particularly important for organizations that do not aspire for universal membership, but limit their membership for certain purposes or have a regional role. For example, members of the African Union must be states in Africa, members of the *Organisation internationale de la Francophonie* must be Francophone states, and members of OPEC must be petroleum exporting states. Of course, even within these categories, assessing the qualifications can sometimes be difficult. Consider, for example, the discussion over whether states are part of Europe for purposes of membership in the Council of Europe:

**Council of Europe, Parliamentary Assembly
Report on the enlargement of the Council Europe, Document 6975
Rapporteur: Reddemann
13 December 1993**[9]

Summary
Time has come for the Council of Europe to set limits to its enlargement.

As the boundaries of Europe have not yet been comprehensively defined under international law, the Council of Europe should, in principle, base itself on the generally accepted geographical limits of Europe.

Only states whose territory lies wholly or partly in Europe, and whose culture is closely linked with European culture should be able to request membership of the organisation.

II. Explanatory memorandum by Mr REDDEMANN

1. The Rapporteur considers that the information report on the enlargement of the Council of Europe (Doc. 6629) which was debated by the Assembly in Budapest on 30 June 1992, still provides a valid basis for discussion on the limits of the organisation. It should be remembered that Appendices I, II and III to this report respectively contain the conclusions of the Bureau of the Assembly, the Committee on Relations with European Non-Member Countries and the Committee on Legal Affairs and Human Rights on the enlargement of the Council of Europe.

2. As regards the geographical limits of Europe, the Rapporteur accepts those adopted by European geographers and set out in most of European encyclopedias, such as the Encyclopaedia Britannica (1984 edition) which reads:

"As to the territorial limits of Europe, while these seem clear on its three seaward flanks, they have been uncertain and hence much debated on the east, where the continent merges, without sundering physical limits, with parts of western Asia. Even to the north and west, many island groups – Svalbard (Spitsbergen), the British Isles, the Faeroes, Iceland, and the Madeira and Canary islands – that are European by culture are included in the continent, although Greenland is conventionally allocated to North America. Further, the Mediterranean coast lands of northern Africa and southwest Asia also exhibit some European physical and cultural affinities, and Turkey and Cyprus, while geologically Asian, possess elements of European culture and may, perhaps, be regarded as parts of Europe.

---

9 © Council of Europe.

Eastward limits, now adopted by European (including Soviet) geographers, assign the Caucasus to Asia and are taken to run southward along the eastern foot of the Urals, and then across the Mugodzhar Hills (Mugodzharskiye Gory), along the Emba River (Vaike Emajogi), and along the northern shore of the Caspian Sea. West of the Caspian, the European limit follows the Kumo-Manych Depression (Kumo-Manychskaya Vpadina) and the Kerch Strait (Kerchensky Proliv) to the Black Sea."

Council of Europe, Parliamentary Assembly
Opinion on the enlargement of the Council of Europe, Document 7148
Rapporteur: Atkinson
13 September 1994[10]

1. During the Parliamentary Assembly's January 1994 part-session, Mr Reddemann presented an initial report on the enlargement of the Council of Europe (Doc. 6975), which ruled out the possibility of the three Transcaucasian republics, Armenia, Azerbaijan and Georgia, becoming full members of the Council of Europe.

Many members of the Assembly disagreed with this position during the debate and the issue was referred for report to the Political Affairs Committee and for opinion to the Committee on Legal Affairs and Human Rights and the Committee on Relations with European Non-Member Countries.

2. In its second report on the issue (Doc. 7103), the Political Affairs Committee stated that "in view of their cultural links with Europe, Armenia, Azerbaijan and Georgia would have the possibility of applying for membership provided they clearly indicate their will to be considered as part of Europe". I welcome this development as it is in keeping with the conclusions of the Bureau of the Assembly as approved on 22 April 1992 and the opinion of the members of the Committee on Relations with European Non-Member Countries who on 18 March 1994 approved the following contribution which, in my capacity as Rapporteur, I have had forwarded to Mr Reddemann:

3. The draft recommendation suggests that, according to the generally accepted geographical limits of Europe, the Caucasus is part of Asia. To support this assertion the explanatory memorandum only quotes the 1984 edition of the Encyclopedia Britannica.

4. Thus, the aspirations of Georgia, Armenia and Azerbaijan to become full members of the Council of Europe, would be rejected without any consultation as to their interpretation of location and, more importantly, without considering the political implications of denying these countries all the positive influences of full membership.

5. This approach is unworthy of the Parliamentary Assembly. The Committee on Relations with European Non-Member Countries urges the Political Affairs Committee to take account of the following considerations.

---

10 © Council of Europe.

The Encyclopedia Britannica

6. This is not a European encyclopedia. It has been published in the United States since 1922, and has been based in Chicago since the 1940s. The Britannica definition of Europe is that of Soviet geographers which is arbitrary and is suspiciously close to the borders of long-standing Russian and Cossack settlement.

Other encyclopedias

7. Those that are genuinely European, such as the British Everyman and the French Larousse; both say that the eastern boundary of Europe is formed by the Caucasus mountains which are composed of the Greater Caucasus and the Lesser Caucasus. If the Lesser Caucasus mountains are taken to be the edge of Europe then the whole of Georgia and Azerbaijan and part of Armenia would be on the European side. The rest of Armenia is adjacent to Turkey which, of course, is a member.

The clearest geographical definition

8. This can surely be obtained by looking at a map. If the Ural mountains are accepted as the eastern boundary of Europe, then logic suggests that the Ural river which flows into the Caspian Sea extends this natural boundary southwards. Thus the Caucasus, being west of the Caspian Sea, is European.

The CSCE definition of Europe

9. For the purposes of the Conventional Forces in Europe (CFE) Treaty it was agreed that the area of application of the treaty in the case of the (former) USSR "includes all territory lying west of the Ural river and the Caspian Sea", a description which clearly includes the three Caucasian states.

It is surely desirable to coincide the Council of Europe's definition of Europe with that of the CSCE.

The United Nations definition of Europe

10. All three Caucasian republics are members of the Eastern European Group in the United Nations, not the Asian Group.

It would surely make little sense if the Council of Europe definition of Europe did not coincide with that of the United Nations.

Historical and cultural dimensions

11. Historically, the Transcaucasus has been the meeting point and sometimes the battleground between the three major regional powers: Russia, Turkey and Persia (Iran) of which the first two are and remain primarily European.

12. The history of both Georgia and Armenia is traced back directly to the adoption of Christianity early in the fourth century AD. The Georgian nationality is distinguished by an Ibero-Caucasus language and script. Both countries have retained their direct links with "Christendom" which is almost synonymous with Europe and the associated traditions of art, architecture and music.

13. Azerbaijan is more difficult to link with European history and culture until it was conquered by the Russians early in the nineteenth century. However, the fact that there are no natural boundaries separating the Azeris from the Georgians and the Armenians suggest a strong case for including the entire Caucasus region in Europe.

The political case

14. To exclude the Caucasian republics from the potential benefits of Council of

Europe membership would be illogical, unjust and lacking in foresight. They are small states that do not naturally belong to any other regional association. Their larger Turkish neighbour to the south has already fully been accepted as a member and is also an applicant for European Union membership. Their even larger neighbour to the north, the Russian Federation, is regarded as a European state as far as the Urals which are well to the east of the Caucasus.

15. The Council of Europe should be encouraged that the three Caucasian republics are willing to follow the path of western parliamentary democracy and to implement our standards of human rights and minority rights. This would do much to counter those ethnic tensions which are causing the current conflicts.

16. To exclude them permanently from full membership of European institutions would be to leave them isolated and without alternative links. Such a vacuum would, once again, encourage the regional powers to intervene. Indeed, they already are. That is a future which is neither in the interests of the Caucasus, nor of Europe. It can be avoided by wholeheartedly encouraging the three countries to become full members of the Council of Europe.

Conclusion

17. I cannot but welcome the fact that the Rapporteur of the Political Affairs Committee has taken account of the arguments set out above. I therefore wholeheartedly endorse the provisions of the draft recommendation contained in Doc. 7103.

18. However, with regard to Mr Reddemann's explanatory memorandum, I believe that there is a need for clarification of the last sentence: "In any case, the Rapporteur considers that no difference must be made between [these states] in this respect". Although no difference should, in fact, be made as regards their belonging to Europe, it should be quite clear that the applications by Armenia, Azerbaijan and Georgia for special guest status and any subsequent applications on their part for membership of the Council of Europe will have to be examined on the basis of each country's respective merits and of the progress it has made on the road to democracy, respect for human rights and the establishment of the rule of law.

Council of Europe, Parliamentary Assembly
Recommendation 1247 (1994) on the enlargement of the Council of Europe, Document 7103
4 October 1994

1. The Council of Europe is an Organisation of sovereign states striving to achieve close co-operation on the basis of democratic constitutions and the European Convention on Human Rights. It is in Europe's interest that its basic values and ideas on human rights permeate neighbouring cultures, but without seeking in any way to question, let alone destroy, those cultures.

2. Membership of the Council of Europe is in principle open only to states whose national territory lies wholly or partly in Europe and whose culture is

closely linked with the European culture. However, traditional and cultural links and adherence to the fundamental values of the Council of Europe might justify a suitable co-operation with other states neighbouring the "geographical" boundaries.

3. The boundaries of Europe have not yet been comprehensively defined under international law. The Council of Europe therefore should, in principle, base itself on the generally accepted geographical limits of Europe.

4. Accordingly, within their internationally recognised borders, all member states of the Council of Europe are European: Austria, Belgium, Bulgaria, Cyprus, Czech Republic, Denmark, Estonia, Finland, France, Germany, Greece, Hungary, Iceland, Ireland, Italy, Liechtenstein, Lithuania, Luxembourg, Malta, Netherlands, Norway, Poland, Portugal, Romania, San Marino, Slovakia, Slovenia, Spain, Sweden, Switzerland, Turkey and the United Kingdom.

5. The states whose legislative assemblies enjoy special guest status with the Parliamentary Assembly of the Council of Europe are also considered European, as defined in paragraph 3 above. These states are: Albania, Belarus, Bosnia-Herzegovina, Croatia, Latvia, The Former Yugoslav Republic of Macedonia, Moldova, Russia and Ukraine.

6. The possibility of membership is open to the republics of the former Socialist Federal Republic of Yugoslavia – Montenegro and Serbia – which currently have no formal status with the Council of Europe because of their responsibility for the crisis and the United Nations sanctions against them.

7. The possibility of membership is also open to the Principality of Andorra.

8. In view of their cultural links with Europe, Armenia, Azerbaijan and Georgia would have the possibility of applying for membership provided they clearly indicate their will to be considered as part of Europe. However, a new iron curtain should not be drawn behind these states as this would run the risk of preventing the spread of the Council of Europe's basic values to other countries. Neighbouring countries of "geographical" Europe should, if they so wish, be viewed as possible candidates for suitable co-operation.

9. Countries bordering directly on Council of Europe member states should be able to enjoy privileged relations with the Parliamentary Assembly, if they so wish. This applies in particular to the states on the eastern and southern shores of the Mediterranean.

10. Even after internationally recognised declarations of sovereignty, any non-European parts of member states which break away from the latter should only be able to apply to participate as observers in the Parliamentary Assembly's work.

11. Delegations to the Parliamentary Assembly should comprise a minimum of two and a maximum of eighteen members.

12. The Assembly therefore recommends that the Committee of Ministers define the limits of the enlargement of the Council of Europe taking into account the above-mentioned principles.

Notes

- Which states were proposed for membership in the Council of Europe? What are the criteria for membership that are at issue in the above discussions? Without knowing anything about the discussions above, what would your expectation be whether those states were qualified? On what would you base that assessment?
- What were the criteria that were proposed by the Rapporteur? And why was this criticized? What was the underlying motivation for the critique? Do you have a sense that the criticism actually began with an expectation that certain states would be admitted and that the criteria should be crafted to fit those states?
- What does this discussion tell us about the role of politics in the legal criteria for membership? One view could be that the admission of members is pure politics and that legal rules are irrelevant. Another view would be that legal rules are critical and play an apolitical role in membership decisions. The truth is in between. How would you explain the interrelationship of law and politics in membership decisions?

4.2.3 Assessing qualifications

Recall from the section above that the UN Charter establishes the following requirements for membership: "Membership in the United Nations is open to all other peace-loving states which accept the obligations contained in the present Charter and, in the judgment of the Organization, are able and willing to carry out these obligations." In the early days of the UN, there was some question whether micro-states, such as Liechtenstein or Monaco, had the capacity to carry out the obligations of UN membership. Those issues have largely been resolved in favor of the micro-states, and both Liechtenstein and Monaco are now members of the UN. But this decision raises the question of whether there are any political requirements for membership, in addition to the legal requirements presented in the Charter:

**Conditions of Admission of a State to Membership in the United Nations
(Article 4 of the Charter)
["First Admissions Case"]
Advisory Opinion
1958 ICJ Reps. 57
International Court of Justice, 28 May 1948**

[p. 61]

The question put is in effect confined to the following point only: are the conditions stated in paragraph 1 of Article 4 exhaustive in character in the sense that an affirmative reply would lead to the conclusion that a Member is not legally entitled to make admission dependent on conditions not expressly provided for in that Article, while a negative reply would, on the contrary, authorize a Member to make admission dependent also on other conditions.

* * *

Understood in this light, the question, in its two parts, is and can only be a purely legal one. To determine the meaning of a treaty provision–to determine, as in this case, the character (exhaustive or otherwise) of the conditions for admission stated therein–is a problem of interpretation and consequently a legal question.

It has nevertheless been contended that the question put must be regarded as a political one and that, for this reason, it falls outside the jurisdiction of the Court. The Court cannot attribute a political character to a request which, framed in abstract terms, invites it to undertake an essentially judicial task, the interpretation of a treaty provision. It is not concerned with the motives which may have inspired this request, nor with the considerations which, in the concrete cases submitted for examination to the Security Council, formed the subject of the exchange of views which took place in that body. It is the duty of the Court to envisage the question submitted to it only in the abstract form which has been given to it; nothing which is said in the present opinion refers, either directly or indirectly, to concrete cases or to particular circumstances.

It has also been contended that the Court should not deal with a question couched in abstract terms. That is a mere affirmation devoid of any justification. According to Article 96 of the Charter and Article 65 of the Statute, the Court may give an advisory opinion on any legal question, abstract or otherwise.

Lastly, it has also been maintained that the Court cannot reply to the question put because it involves an interpretation of the Charter. Nowhere is any provision to be found forbidding the Court, "the principal judicial organ of the United Nations", to exercise in regard to Article 4 of the Charter, a multilateral treaty, an interpretative function which falls within the normal exercise of its judicial powers.

Accordingly, the Court holds that it is competent, on the basis of Article 96 of the Charter and Article 65 of the Statute, and [p. 62] considers that there are no reasons why it should decline to answer the question put to it.

In framing this answer, it is necessary first to recall the "conditions" required, under paragraph 1 of Article 4, of an applicant for admission. This provision reads as follows:

> "Membership in the United Nations is open to all other peace-loving States which accept the obligations contained in the present Charter and, in the judgment of the Organization, are able and willing to carry out these obligations."

The requisite conditions are five in number: to be admitted to membership in the United Nations, an applicant must (1) be a State; (2) be peace-loving; (3) accept the obligations of the Charter; (4) be able to carry out these obligations; and (5) be willing to do so.

All these conditions are subject to the judgment of the Organization. The judgment of the Organization means the judgment of the two organs mentioned in paragraph 2 of Article 4, and, in the last analysis, that of its Members. The question put is concerned with the individual attitude of each Member called upon to pronounce itself on the question of admission.

Having been asked to determine the character, exhaustive or otherwise, of the conditions stated in Article 4, the Court must in the first place consider the text of that Article. The English and French texts of paragraph 1 of Article 4 have the same meaning, and it is impossible to find any conflict between them. The text of this paragraph, by the enumeration which it contains and the choice of its terms, clearly demonstrates the intention of its authors to establish a legal rule which, while it fixes the conditions of admission, determines also the reasons for which admission may be refused; for the text does not differentiate between these two cases and any attempt to restrict it to one of them would be purely arbitrary.

The terms "Membership in the United Nations is open to all other peace-loving States which ..." and "Peuvent devenir Membres des Nations unies tous autres Etats pacifiques", indicate that States which fulfil the conditions stated have the qualifications requisite for admission. The natural meaning of the words used leads to the conclusion that these conditions constitute an exhaustive enumeration and are not merely stated by way of guidance or example. The provision would lose its significance and weight, if other conditions, unconnected with those laid down, could be demanded. The conditions stated in paragraph 1 of Article 4 must therefore be regarded not merely as the necessary conditions, but also as the conditions which suffice.

Nor can it be argued that the conditions enumerated represent only an indispensable minimum, in the sense that political considerations could be superimposed upon them, and prevent the admission of an applicant which fulfils them. Such an interpretation [p. 63] would be inconsistent with the terms of paragraph 2 of Article 4, which provide for the admission of "tout Etat remplissant ces conditions" – "any such State". It would lead to conferring upon Members an indefinite and practically unlimited power of discretion in the imposition of new conditions. Such a power would be inconsistent with the very character of paragraph 1 of Article 4 which, by reason of the close connexion which it establishes between membership and the observance of the principles and obligations of the Charter, clearly constitutes a legal regulation of the question of the admission of new States. To warrant an interpretation other than that which ensues from the natural meaning of the words, a decisive reason would be required which has not been established.

Moreover, the spirit as well as the terms of the paragraph preclude the idea that considerations extraneous to these principles and obligations can prevent the admission of a State which complies with them. If the authors of the Charter had meant to leave Members free to import into the application of this provision considerations extraneous to the conditions laid down therein, they would undoubtedly have adopted a different wording.

The Court considers that the text is sufficiently clear; consequently, it does not feel that it should deviate from the consistent practice of the Permanent Court of International Justice, according to which there is no occasion to resort to preparatory work if the text of a convention is sufficiently clear in itself.

The Court furthermore observes that Rule 60 of the Provisional Rules of Procedure of the Security Council is based on this interpretation. The first paragraph of this Rule reads as follows:

> "The Security Council shall decide whether in its judgment the applicant

is a peace-loving State and is able and willing to carry out the obligations contained in the Charter, and accordingly whether to recommend the applicant State for membership."

It does not, however, follow from the exhaustive character of paragraph 1 of Article 4 that an appreciation is precluded of such circumstances of fact as would enable the existence of the requisite conditions to be verified.

Article 4 does not forbid the taking into account of any factor which it is possible reasonably and in good faith to connect with the conditions laid down in that Article. The taking into account of such factors is implied in the very wide and very elastic nature of the prescribed conditions; no relevant political factor – that is to say, none connected with the conditions of admission – is excluded.

[p. 64]

It has been sought to deduce either from the second paragraph of Article 4, or from the political character of the organ recommending or deciding upon admission, arguments in favour of an interpretation of paragraph 1 of Article 4, to the effect that the fulfilment of the conditions provided for in that Article is necessary before the admission of a State can be recommended or decided upon, but that it does not preclude the Members of the Organization from advancing considerations of political expediency, extraneous to the conditions of Article 4.

But paragraph 2 is concerned only with the procedure for admission, while the preceding paragraph lays down the substantive law. This procedural character is clearly indicated by the words "will be effected", which, by linking admission to the decision, point clearly to the fact that the paragraph is solely concerned with the manner in which admission is effected, and not with the subject of the judgment of the Organization, nor with the nature of the appreciation involved in that judgment, these two questions being dealt with in the preceding paragraph. Moreover, this paragraph, in referring to the "recommendation" of the Security Council and the "decision" of the General Assembly, is designed only to determine the respective functions of these two organs which consist in pronouncing upon the question whether or not the applicant State shall be admitted to membership after having established whether or not the prescribed conditions are fulfilled.

The political character of an organ cannot release it from the observance of the treaty provisions established by the Charter when they constitute limitations on its powers or criteria for its judgment. To ascertain whether an organ has freedom of choice for its decisions, reference must be made to the terms of its constitution. In this case, the limits of this freedom are fixed by Article 4 and allow for a wide liberty of appreciation. There is therefore no conflict between the functions of the political organs, on the one hand, and the exhaustive character of the prescribed conditions, on the other.

It has been sought to base on the political responsibilities assumed by the Security Council, in virtue of Article 24 of the Charter, an argument justifying the necessity for according to the Security Council as well as to the General Assembly complete freedom of appreciation in connexion with the admission of new Members. But Article 24, owing to the very general nature of its terms, cannot, in the absence of any provision, affect the special rules for admission which emerge from Article 4. The foregoing considerations establish the exhaustive character of the conditions prescribed in Article 4.

* * *

The second part of the question concerns a demand on the part of a Member making its consent to the admission of an applicant dependent on the admission of other applicants.

[p. 65]

Judged on the basis of the rule which the Court adopts in its interpretation of Article 4, such a demand clearly constitutes a new condition, since it is entirely unconnected with those prescribed in Article 4. It is also in an entirely different category from those conditions, since it makes admission dependent, not on the conditions required of applicants, qualifications which are supposed to be fulfilled, but on an extraneous consideration concerning States other than the applicant State.

The provisions of Article 4 necessarily imply that every application for admission should be examined and voted on separately and on its own merits; otherwise it would be impossible to determine whether a particular applicant fulfils the necessary conditions. To subject an affirmative vote for the admission of an applicant State to the condition that other States be admitted with that State would prevent Members from exercising their judgment in each case with complete liberty, within the scope of the prescribed conditions. Such a demand is incompatible with the letter and spirit of Article 4 of the Charter.

Notes

- What question is the court being asked? How can the court review a question of this nature that is inherently political? How do politics and law interact in this opinion?
- What does the court mean by the "judgment" of the organization? The question in the case sounds more like the judgment of the member states, not the judgment of the organization. Whose judgment is being exercised here? And what is the mechanism for exercising that judgment?
- Is this case more focused on legal questions or factual questions? Does the court identify legal issues that are in controversy and need to be resolved? Or does the court need to determine whether there are certain facts on the qualifications of potential members that must be settled?
- Does the court leave any room to argue for membership requirements outside of those listed in the UN Charter?

4.2.4 Procedural law of the decision on qualification

The cases above discussed the substantive qualifications, and the assessment of substantive qualifications, in order for an entity to become a member of an international organization. Aside from the substantive matters, the other question for matters of admission involves procedural issues. Whether an entity is a state or is able to discharge its obligations are quite different matters from whether the entity has correctly filed an application and received a decision from the correct organ. In matters of admission, the UN Charter lays down the following procedural rule:

Charter of the United Nations
24 October 1945
1 UNTS 16[11]

Chapter II Membership
Article 4.

2. The admission of any such state to membership in the United Nations will be effected by a decision of the General Assembly upon the recommendation of the Security Council.

This provision appears to grant the Security Council considerable power over questions of admission, depending on how we interpret the meaning of a "recommendation" by that organ. Is the recommendation merely advisory, or a threshold for a decision? Which organ acts first and has the power of initiative? In the early years of the UN, there was an attempt to argue that the General Assembly held the right of decision and that the Security Council was merely advisory. Inevitably, this led to a request for an advisory opinion from the International Court of Justice:

Competence of the General Assembly for the
Admission of a State to the United Nations
["Second Admissions Case"]
Advisory Opinion
1950 ICJ Reps. 4
International Court of Justice, 3 March 1950

[p. 6]

...

The Request for an Opinion calls upon the Court to interpret Article 4, paragraph 2, of the Charter. Before examining the merits of the question submitted to it, the Court must first consider the objections that have been made to its doing so, either on the ground that it is not competent to interpret the provisions of the Charter, or on the ground of the alleged political character of the question.

So far as concerns its competence, the Court will simply recall that, in a previous Opinion which dealt with the interpretation of Article 4, paragraph 1, it declared that, according to Article 96 of

---

11 From United Nations Treaty Series, by the United Nations © 1945 United Nations. Reprinted with the permission of the United Nations.

the Charter and Article 65 of the Statute, it may give an Opinion on any legal question and that there is no provision which prohibits it from exercising, in regard to Article 4 of the Charter, a multilateral treaty, an interpretative function falling within the normal exercise of its judicial powers (I.C.J. Reports 1947–1948, p. 61).

With regard to the second objection, the Court notes that the General Assembly has requested it to give the legal interpretation of paragraph 2 of Article 4. As the Court stated in the same Opinion, it "cannot attribute a political character to a request [p. 7] which, framed in abstract terms, invites it to undertake an essentially judicial task, the interpretation of a treaty provision".

Consequently, the Court, in accordance with its previous declarations, considers that it is competent on the basis of Articles 96 of the Charter and 65 of its Statute and that there is no reason why it should not answer the question submitted to it.

This question has been framed by the General Assembly in the following terms:

> "Can the admission of a State to membership in the United Nations, pursuant to Article 4, paragraph 2, of the Charter, be effected by a decision of the General Assembly when the Security Council has made no recommendation for admission by reason of the candidate failing to obtain the requisite majority or of the negative vote of a permanent Member upon a resolution so to recommend?"

The Request for an Opinion envisages solely the case in which the Security Council, having voted upon a recommendation, has concluded from its vote that the recommendation was not adopted because it failed to obtain the requisite majority or because of the negative vote of a permanent Member. Thus the Request refers to the case in which the General Assembly is confronted with the absence of a recommendation from the Security Council.

It is not the object of the Request to determine how the Security Council should apply the rules governing its voting procedure in regard to admissions or, in particular, that the Court should examine whether the negative vote of a permanent Member is effective to defeat a recommendation which has obtained seven or more votes. The question, as it is formulated, assumes in such a case the non-existence of a recommendation.

The Court is, therefore, called upon to determine solely whether the General Assembly can make a decision to admit a State when the Security Council has transmitted no recommendation to it.

Article 4, paragraph 2, is as follows:

> "The admission of any such State to membership in the United Nations will be effected by a decision of the General Assembly upon the recommendation of the Security Council."

The Court has no doubt as to the meaning of this text. It requires two things to effect admission: a "recommendation" of the Security Council and a "decision" of the General Assembly. It is in the nature of things that the recommendation should come before the decision. The word "recommendation", and the word "upon" preceding it, imply the idea that the recommendation is the foundation of the decision to admit, and that the latter rests upon the recommendation. Both these acts are indispensable to form the judgment of the Organization to which the previous [p. 8] paragraph of Article 4 refers. The text under consideration means that the General Assembly can only decide to admit upon the recommendation of the Security Council; it determines the respective roles of the two organs whose combined action is required before admission can be effected: in other words, the recommendation of the Security Council is the condition precedent to the decision of the Assembly by which the admission is effected.

In one of the written statements placed before the Court, an attempt was made to attribute to paragraph 2 of Article 4 a different meaning. The Court considers it necessary to say that the first duty of a tribunal which is called upon to interpret and apply the provisions of a treaty, is to endeavour to give effect to them in their natural and ordinary meaning in the context in which they occur ....

...

The General Assembly and the Security Council are both principal organs of the United Nations. The Charter does not place the Security Council in a subordinate position. Article 24 confers upon it "primary responsibility for the maintenance of international [p. 9] peace and security", and the Charter grants it for this purpose certain powers of decision. Under Articles 4, 5, and 6, the Security Council co-operates with the General Assembly in matters of admission to membership, of suspension from the exercise of the rights and privileges of membership, and of expulsion from the Organization. It has power, without the concurrence of the General Assembly, to reinstate the Member which was the object of the suspension, in its rights and privileges.

The organs to which Article 4 entrusts the judgment of the Organization in matters of admission have consistently interpreted the text in the sense that the General Assembly can decide to admit only on the basis of a recommendation of the Security Council. In particular, the Rules of Procedure of the General Assembly provide for consideration of the merits of an application and of the decision to be made upon it only "if the Security Council recommends the applicant State for membership" (Article 125). The Rules merely state that if the Security Council has not recommended the admission, the General Assembly may send back the application to the Security Council for further consideration (Article 126). This last step has been taken several times: it was taken in Resolution 296 (IV), the very one that embodies this Request for an Opinion.

To hold that the General Assembly has power to admit a State to membership in the absence of a recommendation of the Security Council would be to deprive the Security Council of an important power which has been entrusted to it by the Charter. It would almost nullify the role of the Security Council in the exercise of one of the essential functions of the Organization. It would mean that the Security Council would have merely to study the case, present a report, give advice, and express an opinion. This is not what Article 4, paragraph 2, says.

The Court cannot accept the suggestion made in one of the written statements submitted to the Court, that the General Assembly, in order to try to meet the requirement of Article 4, paragraph 2, could treat the absence of a recommendation as equivalent to what is described in that statement as an "unfavourable recommendation", upon which the General Assembly could base a decision to admit a State to membership.

Reference has also been made to a document of the San Francisco Conference, in order to put the possible case of an unfavourable recommendation being voted by the Security Council: such a recommendation has never been made in practice. In the opinion of the Court, Article 4, paragraph 2, envisages a favourable recommendation of the Security Council and that only. An unfavourable recommendation would not correspond to the provisions of Article 4, paragraph 2.

While keeping within the limits of a Request which deals with the scope of the powers of the General Assembly, it is enough for [p. 10] the Court to say that nowhere has the General Assembly received the power to change, to the point of reversing, the meaning of a vote of the Security Council.

In consequence, it is impossible to admit that the General Assembly has the power to attribute to a vote of the Security Council the character of a recommendation when the Council itself considers that no such recommendation has been made.

Notes

- Is it clear from this case what the General Assembly was attempting to do? Why would the General Assembly attempt to take that approach? Consider the dates when this matter arose, the membership of the Security Council at the time, and the political dynamics within the Council then. Why would the Security Council not give a recommendation? Surely it is very interested in potential new members.
- The court finds that the language in the UN Charter is clear. There must be both a "recommendation" and a "decision." Is this really an obvious conclusion from the text of the Charter? Can we develop any argument that the text does not require both? This excerpt from the case omits the court's discussion on how it interprets the ordinary meaning and structure of the text in the Charter. That material was included in Chapter 2 on the law of treaties, including treaty interpretation.
- How does the court determine that a recommendation naturally precedes a decision? What sources of law does the court draw on for this conclusion? What principles of treaty interpretation does the court apply? Recall the discussion on the application of the law of treaties to international organizations in Chapter 2. Does the court at all rely on the "family" structure of the UN? Is the court correct?
- What is the substance of a "recommendation" by the Security Council? Is it advisory, meaning that the Council can render positive or negative advice on the

qualifications of the applicant? Or is the recommendation more in the nature of the decision, producing either an acceptance or rejection?
- What relationship does this opinion envision between the General Assembly and the Security Council? Can the Security Council effectively block an entity from membership, regardless of the views of the General Assembly? Could the General Assembly also block an entity for membership that has the support of the Security Council? Recall that the General Assembly operates on the principle of one state, one vote, whereas the Security Council votes by majority, and gives the permanent five members a veto. How does the membership application procedure produced by this opinion affect the legitimacy of membership decisions, and the organization itself?

The case above characterized membership decisions as decisions of the organ(s) involved. Even though a permanent member of the Security Council might have a veto over membership applications, those acts appear to be considered acts of the organ, and thus acts of the organization. But a permanent member of the Security Council might veto a membership application in its own self-interest, rather than being primarily motivated by its role in the organ and organization. In the case of the former Yugoslav Republic of Macedonia (FYROM), Greece objected to that country's name as provided under its Constitution, the "Republic of Macedonia," for being provocative and aggressive against the Greek region of Makedonia. Accordingly, Greece objected to any membership applications, for example to NATO, where FYROM applied using its constitutional name rather than FYROM. The question of the Greek objections was eventually taken to the International Court of Justice:

Application of the Interim Accord of 13 September 1995
The Former Yugoslav Republic of Macedonia v Greece
Judgment
2011 ICJ Reps. 644
International Court of Justice, 5 December 2011

1. On 17 November 2008, the former Yugoslav Republic of Macedonia (hereinafter the "Applicant") filed in the Registry of the Court an Application instituting proceedings against the Hellenic Republic (hereinafter the "Respondent") in respect of a dispute concerning the interpretation and implementation of the Interim Accord signed by the Parties on 13 September 1995, which entered into force on 13 October 1995 (hereinafter the "Interim Accord"). In particular, the Applicant sought "to establish the violation by the Respondent of its legal obligations under Article 11, paragraph 1, of the Interim Accord and to ensure that the Respondent abides by its obligations under Article 11 of the Interim Accord in relation to invitations or applications that might be made to or by the Applicant for membership of NATO or any other international, multilateral or regional organization or institution of which the Respondent is a member."

2. In its Application, the Applicant, referring to Article 36, paragraph 1, of the Statute, relied on Article 21, paragraph 2, of the Interim Accord to found the jurisdiction of the Court. ...

* * *

I. Introduction

15. Before 1991, the Socialist Federal Republic of Yugoslavia comprised six constituent republics, including the "Socialist Republic of Macedonia". In the course of the break-up of Yugoslavia, the Assembly of the Socialist Republic of Macedonia adopted (on 25 January 1991) the "Declaration on the Sovereignty of the Socialist Republic of Macedonia", which asserted sovereignty and the right of self-determination. On 7 June 1991, the Assembly of the Socialist Republic of Macedonia enacted a constitutional amendment, changing the name "Socialist Republic of Macedonia" to the "Republic of Macedonia". The Assembly then adopted a declaration asserting the sovereignty and independence of the new State and sought international recognition.

16. On 30 July 1992, the Applicant submitted an application for membership in the United Nations. The Respondent stated on 25 January 1993 that it objected to the Applicant's admission on the basis of the Applicant's adoption of the name "Republic of Macedonia", among other factors. The Respondent explained that its opposition was based *inter alia* on its view that the term "Macedonia" referred to a geographical region in south-east Europe that included an important part of the territory and population of the Respondent and of certain third States. The Respondent further indicated that once a settlement had been reached on these issues, it would no longer oppose the Applicant's admission to the United Nations. The Respondent had also expressed opposition on similar grounds to the Applicant's recognition by the member States of the European Community.

17. On 7 April 1993, in accordance with Article 4, paragraph 2, of the Charter, the Security Council adopted resolution 817 (1993), concerning the "application for admission to the United Nations" of the Applicant. In that resolution, noting that "a difference has arisen over the name of the [Applicant], which needs to be resolved in the interest of the maintenance of peaceful and good-neighbourly relations in the region", the Security Council: ...

2. *Recommend[ed]* to the General Assembly that the State whose application is contained in document S/25147 be admitted to membership in the United Nations, this State being provisionally referred to for all purposes within the United Nations as "the former Yugoslav Republic of Macedonia" pending settlement of the difference that has arisen over the name of the State; ...

18. On 8 April 1993, the Applicant was admitted to the United Nations, following the adoption by the General Assembly, on the recommendation of the Security Council, of resolution A/RES/47/225.

...

20. Against this backdrop, on 13 September 1995, the Parties signed the Interim Accord, providing for the establishment of diplomatic relations between them and addressing other related issues.

...

21. In the Interim Accord, the Parties also addressed the admission of, and membership by, the Applicant in international organizations and institutions of which the Respondent was a member. In this regard, Article 11, paragraph 1, of the Interim Accord provides:

> "Upon entry into force of this Interim Accord, the Party of the First Part agrees not to object to the application by or the membership of the Party of the Second Part in international, multilateral and regional organizations and institutions of which the Party of the First Part is a member; however, the Party of the First Part reserves the right to object to any membership referred to above if and to the extent 2 the Party of the Second Part is to be referred to in such organization or institution differently than in paragraph 2 of United Nations Security Council resolution 817 (1993)." (*United Nations Treaty Series (UNTS)*, Vol. 1891, p. 7; original English)

22. In the period following the adoption of the Interim Accord, the Applicant was granted membership in a number of international organizations of which the Respondent was already a member. On the invitation of the North Atlantic Treaty Organization, the Applicant in 1995 joined the Organization's Partnership for Peace (a programme that promotes co-operation between NATO and partner countries) and, in 1999, the Organization's Membership Action Plan (which assists prospective NATO members). The Applicant's NATO candidacy was considered in a meeting of NATO member States in Bucharest (hereinafter the "Bucharest Summit") on 2 and 3 April 2008 but the Applicant was not invited to begin talks on accession to the Organization. The communique issued at the end of the Summit stated that an invitation would be extended to the Applicant "as soon as a mutually acceptable solution to the name issue has been reached". ...

*

41. In order to examine the Respondent's objection, the Court has to consider the specific object of the Application. The Applicant claims that "the Respondent, through its State organs and agents, has violated its obligations under Article 11, paragraph 1, of the Interim Accord" and requests the Court to make a declaration to this effect and to order the Respondent to "take all necessary steps to comply with its obligations under Article 11, paragraph 1, of the Interim Accord".

...

43. Similarly, the Court does not need to determine the responsibility of NATO or of its member States in order to assess the conduct of the Respondent. In this respect, the Respondent's argument that the rights and interests of a third party (which it identifies as NATO and/or the member States of NATO) would form the subject-matter of any decision which the Court might take, with the result that the Court should decline to hear the case under the principle developed in the case of the *Monetary Gold Removed from Rome in 1943*, is misplaced. The present case can be distinguished from the *Monetary Gold* case since the Respondent's conduct can be assessed independently of NATO's decision, and the rights and obligations of NATO and its member States other than Greece do not form the subject-matter of

the decision of the Court on the merits of the case (*Monetary Gold Removed from Rome in 1943 (Italy v. France; United Kingdom and United States of America), Preliminary Question, Judgment, I.C.J. Reports 1954*, p. 19; *East Timor (Portugal v. Australia), Judgment, I.C.J. Reports 1995*, p. 105, para. 34); nor would the assessment of their responsibility be a "prerequisite for the determination of the responsibility" of the Respondent (*Certain Phosphate Lands in Nauru (Nauru v. Australia), Preliminary Objections, Judgment, I.C.J. Reports 1992*, p. 261, para. 55). Therefore, the Court considers that the conduct forming the object of the Application is the Respondent's alleged objection to the Applicant's admission to NATO, and that, on the merits, the Court will only have to determine whether or not that conduct demonstrates that the Respondent failed to comply with its obligations under the Interim Accord, irrespective of NATO's final decision on the Applicant's membership application.

44. The Court accordingly finds that the Respondent's objection based on the argument that the dispute relates to conduct attributable to NATO and its member States or that NATO and its member States are indispensable third parties not before the Court cannot be upheld.

1. *The Respondent's Obligation under Article 11, Paragraph 1, of the Interim Accord not to Object to the Applicant's Admission to NATO*

A. *The meaning of the first clause of Article 11, paragraph 1, of the Interim Accord*

67. The first clause of Article 11, paragraph 1, of the Interim Accord obliges the Respondent not to object to "the application by or membership of" the Applicant in NATO. The Court notes that the Parties agree that the obligation "not to object" does not require the Respondent actively to support the Applicant's admission to international organizations.

In addition, the Parties agree that the obligation "not to object" is not an obligation of result, but rather one of conduct. ...

*

70. The Court does not accept the general proposition advanced by the Respondent that special rules of interpretation should apply when the Court is examining a treaty that limits a right that a party would otherwise have. Turning to the Respondent's specific arguments in regard to the first clause of Article 11, paragraph 1, the Court observes that nothing in the text of that clause limits the Respondent's obligation not to object to organizations that use a voting procedure to decide on the admission of new members. There is no indication that the Parties intended to exclude from Article 11, paragraph 1, organizations like NATO that follow procedures that do not require a vote. Moreover, the question before the Court is not whether the decision taken by NATO at the Bucharest Summit with respect to the Applicant's candidacy was due exclusively, principally, or marginally to the Respondent's objection. As the Parties agree, the obligation under the first clause of Article 11, paragraph 1, is one of conduct, not of result. Thus, the question before the Court is whether the Respondent, by its own conduct, did not comply with the obligation not to object contained in Article 11, paragraph 1, of the Interim Accord. ...

*

81. In the view of the Court, the evidence submitted to it demonstrates that through formal diplomatic correspondence and through statements of its senior officials, the Respondent made clear before, during and after the Bucharest Summit that the resolution of the difference over the name was the "decisive criterion" for the Respondent to accept the Applicant's admission to NATO. The Respondent manifested its objection to the Applicant's admission to NATO at the Bucharest Summit, citing the fact that the difference regarding the Applicant's name remained unresolved.

82. Moreover, the Court cannot accept that the Respondent's statements regarding the admission of the Applicant were not objections, but were merely observations aimed at calling the attention of other NATO member States to concerns about the Applicant's eligibility to join NATO. The record makes abundantly clear that the Respondent went beyond such observations to oppose the Applicant's admission to NATO on the ground that the difference over the name had not been resolved.

83. The Court therefore concludes that the Respondent objected to the Applicant's admission to NATO, within the meaning of the first clause of Article 11, paragraph 1, of the Interim Accord.

Notes

- What is the "Interim Accord"? What does it oblige Greece and FYROM/Macedonia to do?
- How does the court view a decision on membership? Is it an act of an organ, or an act of the organization? Or is it an identifiable act of the state, for which a state could be responsible?
- Why is the voting of other member states of NATO not at issue? Surely those other states either supported or acquiesced in the acts of Greece. If those other states did act in this way, then would they also be responsible?
- Does the Interim Accord have any effect on the usual rights of states participating in international organizations to object? Is this case unique to the Greek–FYROM/Macedonian context or does it have larger relevance for procedural questions of admission?

4.2.5 Succession to membership

The members of international organizations are not static entities. Although it is unusual, from time to time a state will dissolve or secede from another state. One of the most important periods in the development of the United Nations was the decolonization movement that led to the admission to the UN of a large number of newly independent states.

Generally, when a new state emerges in the international community, its request to participate in an international organization is treated as a new admission request. Recall the discussion in Chapter 2 on the law of treaties as it applies to international organizations. When a newly independent state secures independence from its former state, the new state may choose whether to continue to apply treaties that had bound that territory when it was part of the former state. States usually notify the depositary that they will succeed to the treaty, if they want the treaty to continue to apply. However, in the case of adherence to a treaty creating an international organization and membership in that organization, the process is handled differently. Membership is not simply a matter of treaty participation to which a new state can merely succeed, but also a matter of membership and governance of the international organization. Newly independent states do not have a right of option to continue membership in an international organization. For example, when Ghana achieved its independence from the UK, it applied for new admission to the UN, even though the UK was a member of the UN. In this way, most authorities have concluded that if Scotland were to ever secede from the UK, then it would not automatically succeed to the UK's membership in the UN and EU, and would need to make a fresh application to join both organizations.

However, in cases where a state dissolves, the situation is different. In the previous example, the original state remained, albeit in a reduced territorial scope, but in this case, the original state ceases to exist. One of its successor states may seek to succeed to the original state's membership rather than apply for new admission. The distinction between succession and new admission can have important legal consequences.

For example, consider the case of the former Yugoslavia. The former Socialist Federal Republic of Yugoslavia (SFR Yugoslavia) had been a party to the Genocide Convention since 1948. By the early 1990s, the SFR Yugoslavia was in the process of dissolution. The UN Security Council determined that the state was collapsing in 1991.[12] The newly proclaimed Federal Republic of Yugoslavia (FR Yugoslavia) had previously claimed on 27 April 1992 that it was succeeding to the SFR Yugoslavia, and thus necessarily to all of its treaty commitments, including the Genocide Convention.

On 22 May 1992, Bosnia and Herzegovina, as one of the states seceding from the former SFR Yugoslavia, was admitted as a member of the United Nations. On 30 May 1992, the UN Security Council determined that the SFR Yugoslavia no longer existed as a state.[13] The General Assembly came to the same conclusion.[14] Several months later, on 29 December 1992, Bosnia and Herzegovina notified the Secretary-General of the United Nations that it wished to succeed to adherence to the Genocide Convention, which was duly accepted.

However, the precise position of "Yugoslavia" was unclear. On the one hand, the FR Yugoslavia claimed to be the successor to the SFR Yugoslavia. On the other hand, just having a similar name to the original state and also basing its capital city in Belgrade was not substantive succession to the entirety of the prior state's personality. The SFR Yugoslavia had dissolved entirely, which implies that there was no

---

12 See UN Security Council Resolution 713 (25 September 1991).
13 See UN Security Council Resolution 757 (30 May 1992); UNSC Resolution 777 (19 September 1992).
14 See UN General Assembly Resolution 47/1 (22 September 1992).

successor that could continue its personality. And, even though the SFR Yugoslavia appeared to be extinct, it was still a party to the Genocide Convention and a member of the United Nations, although those facts might not have any relevance for an extinct state.

In March 1993, Bosnia and Herzegovina brought a case against the FR Yugoslavia at the ICJ, arguing that it had committed genocide against Bosnia and Herzegovina during the armed conflict. In July 1996, the ICJ found that both states were party to the Genocide Convention and that the court therefore had jurisdiction over the case.[15] In particular, the FR Yugoslavia was found to be the correct respondent in the case.

Several years later, while the *Genocide* case above was still pending, the FR Yugoslavia brought a complaint to the ICJ against Belgium and a number of other states that were conducting bombing missions over the territory of the FR Yugoslavia, under a NATO cooperation action. The FR Yugoslavia contended that the bombing constituted the unlawful use of force against it, as the action was neither in self-defense nor pursuant to a UN Security Council Chapter VII Resolution. The ICJ should have jurisdiction over the claim involving the FR Yugoslavia as the successor to the SFR Yugoslavia, just like it did in the *Genocide* case.[16] The court made the distinction between whether there was a violation of the prohibition of the use of force, on the one hand, from whether the court had jurisdiction over the complaint, on the other. The court held that "it is not disputed that both Yugoslavia and Belgium are parties to the Genocide Convention without reservation," but that the issue of the use of force was not *prima facie* an issue of "the interpretation, application or fulfilment" of the Convention. It refused the request for provisional measures, but permitted the case to proceed to the merits.

In October 2000, following large protests, Slobodan Milošević resigned as president of the FR Yugoslavia in favor of Vojislav Koštunica, and a long process of negotiations over the future of the state began. In 2002, the various groups reached a decision to reorganize the state as a confederacy or commonwealth, with the two constituent states of Serbia and Montenegro operating with far more autonomy. On 4 February 2003, the Federal Assembly of the FR Yugoslavia voted to adopt this new constitutional arrangement, and the state changed its name to the State Union of Serbia and Montenegro (Serbia and Montenegro), finally retiring the name Yugoslavia definitively.

During this time, on 27 October 2000, President Koštunica sent a letter to the UN Secretary-General applying for admission of the FR Yugoslavia as a member of the UN. He specifically noted the recent change in government:

---

15 *See* Case Concerning Application of the Convention on the Prevention and Punishment of the Crime of Genocide, Bosnia and Herzegovina v Yugoslavia [Serbia and Montenegro], Preliminary Objections, Judgment, 1996 ICJ Reps. 595 (International Court of Justice, 11 July 1996).

16 *See* Case Concerning Legality of Use of Force, Yugoslavia [Serbia and Montenegro] v Belgium, Request for the Indication of Provisional Measures, Order, 1999 ICJ Reps. 124 (International Court of Justice, 2 June 1999). Also see parallel cases filed against Canada, France, Germany, Italy, The Netherlands, Portugal, Spain, the UK, and the US.

In the wake of fundamental democratic changes that took place in the Federal Republic of Yugoslavia, in the capacity of President, I have the honour to request the admission of the Federal Republic of Yugoslavia to membership in the United Nations in light of the implementation of Security Council resolution 777 (1992).[17]

On 31 October 2000, the UN Security Council recommended the FR Yugoslavia's admission,[18] and on 1 November 2000, the General Assembly admitted the state to membership.[19] In reaching this decision, the General Assembly noted that "The admission of the FRY to membership of the United Nations on 1 November 2000 put an end to Yugoslavia's *sui generis* position within the United Nations."[20]

Having now been admitted to the UN, the FR Yugoslavia applied to the ICJ for a revision of the preliminary objections in the *Genocide* case where the court had held that it was the proper respondent. In that application, the court applied the standard that it uses for applications for revision: whether there are new facts which existed at the time of the previous decision, but were unknown and would have bearing on the outcome. The FR Yugoslavia argued that the new fact was the nature of its legal personality and membership in the United Nations as of 1996. This new fact was only discovered when the UN Security Council and General Assembly took the decision in 2000 to admit the FR Yugoslavia to membership. It would have consequences for the court's decision because it means that the court could not have had jurisdiction over the state, since it was not a UN member or party to the statute of the court. The court disagreed that this was the discovery of a new fact, with the following argument:

Application for Revision of the Judgment of 11 July 1996 in the Case Concerning Application of the Convention on the Prevention and Punishment of the Crime of Genocide
Bosnia & Herzegovina v. Yugoslavia
Preliminary Objections, Judgment
2003 ICJ Reps. 7
International Court of Justice, 3 February 2003

70. Furthermore the Court notes that the admission of the FRY [FR Yugoslavia] to membership of the United Nations took place more than four years after the Judgment which it is seeking to have revised. At the time when that Judgment was given, the situation obtaining was that created by General Assembly resolution 47/1. In this regard the Court observes that the difficulties which arose regarding the FRY's status between the adoption of that resolution

---

17 Vojislav Koštunica, President of the FR Yugoslavia, Letter to the UN Secretary-General, United Nations Doc. A/55/528-S/2000/1043 (27 October 2000).
18 *See* United Nations Security Council Resolution 1326 (31 October 2000).
19 *See* United Nations General Assembly Resolution 55/12 (1 November 2000).
20 *Ibid.*

and its admission to the United Nations on 1 November 2000 resulted from the fact that, although the FRY's claim to continue the international legal personality of the Former Yugoslavia was not "generally accepted" (see paragraph 28 above), the precise consequences of this situation were determined on a case-by-case basis (for example, non-participation in the work of the General Assembly and ECOSOC and in the meetings of States parties to the International Covenant on Civil and Political Rights, etc.).

Resolution 47/1 did not *inter alia* affect the FRY's right to appear before the Court or to be a party to a dispute before the Court under the conditions laid down by the Statute. Nor did it affect the position of the FRY in relation to the Genocide Convention. To "terminate the situation created by resolution 47/1", the FRY had to submit a request for admission to the United Nations as had been done by the other Republics composing the SFRY. All these elements were known to the Court and to the FRY at the time when the Judgment was given. Nevertheless, what remained unknown in July 1996 was if and when the FRY would apply for membership in the United Nations and if and when that application would be accepted, thus terminating the situation created by General Assembly resolution 47/1.

71. The Court wishes to emphasize that General Assembly resolution 55/12 of 1 November 2000 cannot have changed retroactively the *sui generis* position which the FRY found itself in vis-à-vis the United Nations over the period 1992 to 2000, or its position in relation to the Statute of the Court and the Genocide Convention. Furthermore, the letter of the Legal Counsel of the United Nations dated 8 December 2000, cannot have affected the FRY's position in relation to treaties.

The Court also observes that, in any event, the said letter did not contain an invitation to the FRY to accede to the relevant conventions, but rather to "undertake treaty actions, as appropriate, ... as a successor State".

72. It follows from the foregoing that it has not been established that the request of the FRY is based upon the discovery of "some fact" which was "when the judgment was given, unknown to the Court and also to the party claiming revision". The Court therefore concludes that one of the conditions for the admissibility of an application for revision prescribed by paragraph 1 of Article 61 of the Statute has not been satisfied.

Notes

- This is a rather complex case, both procedurally and substantively. You may want to first ensure that you fully follow where this case is procedurally, as well as the *Use of Force* case. What kind of an application is this? How does that kind of application relate to previous decisions in this same case? And how do those decisions relate to the overall case?
- Keep in mind the legal standard for convincing the court to reconsider a decision that it has rendered. The court observes the length of time between the previous

decision and this application. Why does that amount of time make a difference? Does it?
- Is the FR Yugoslavia's membership a fact? Or is it a legal interpretation of events? Is its statehood a fact? Or a legal interpretation?
- Why is the admission to membership not a new fact? Surely whether the FR Yugoslavia was a member of the UN or not is a fact. Does the decision in 2000 establish the fact, prove the fact, or clarify the fact?
- What legal effect does the court view the membership admission as having? Does it mean that the FR Yugoslavia was not a member before the application? Or was it somehow a member up until the new application?
- The court does not mention the constitutional changes underway in the state at the same time as the case was pending. Is it relevant that the very next day after this judgment was rendered, the Federal Assembly voted to reorganize the state as "Serbia and Montenegro," and abolish "Yugoslavia."

Running in parallel to the continuing *Genocide* case, the FR Yugoslavia, now of course using the name Serbia and Montenegro, continued to litigate the *Use of Force* case. Since the court had decided that FR Yugoslavia/Serbia and Montenegro was not *not* a UN member for purposes of the *Genocide* case, Serbia and Montenegro argued that it must have been a party to the statute of the court when it filed its application in the *Use of Force* case.

Case Concerning Legality of Use of Force
Serbia & Montenegro v. Belgium
Preliminary Objections, Judgment
2004 ICJ Reps. 279
International Court of Justice, 15 December 2004

45. The Court accordingly turns to the questions of jurisdiction arising in the present case. ...

46. The Court notes that in several cases it referred to "its freedom to select the ground upon which it will base its judgment" (*Application of the Convention of 1902 Governing the Guardianship of Infants, Judgment, I.C.J. Reports 1958*, p. 62; *Application for Revision and Interpretation of the Judgment of 24 February 1982 in the Case concerning the* Continental Shelf (Tunisia/Libyan Arab Jamahiriya) *(Tunisia v. Libyan Arab Jamahiriya), Judgment, I.C.J. Reports 1985*, p. 207, para. 29; *Oil Platforms (Islamic Republic of Iran v. United States of America), Judgment, I.C.J. Reports 2003*, p. 180, para. 37). By the same token, the Court in the past pointed out that when its jurisdiction is challenged on diverse grounds, it is free to base its decision on one or more grounds of its own choosing, in particular "the ground which in its judgment is more direct and conclusive" (*Certain Norwegian Loans (France v. Norway), Judgment, I.C.J. Reports 1957*, p. 25; see also *Aerial Incident of 27 July 1955 (Israel v. Bulgaria), Judgment, I.C.J. Reports 1959*, p. 127;

Aegean Sea Continental Shelf (Greece v. Turkey), Judgment, I.C.J. Reports 1978, pp. 16–17, paras. 39–40, and *Aerial Incident of 10 August 1999 (Pakistan v. India), Jurisdiction, Judgment, I.C.J. Reports 2000*, p. 24, para. 26). But in those instances, the parties to the cases before the Court were, *without doubt*, parties to the Statute of the Court and the Court was thus open to them under Article 35, paragraph 1, of the Statute. That is not the case in the present proceedings in which an objection has been made regarding the right of the Applicant to have access to the Court. And it is this issue of access to the Court which distinguishes the present case from all those referred to above.

As the Court observed earlier (see paragraph 30 above), the question whether Serbia and Montenegro was or was not a party to the Statute of the Court at the time of the institution of the present proceedings is fundamental; for if it were not such a party, the Court would not be open to it under Article 35, paragraph 1, of the Statute. In that situation, subject to any application of paragraph 2 of that Article, Serbia and Montenegro could not have properly seised the Court, whatever title of jurisdiction it might have invoked, for the simple reason that Serbia and Montenegro did not have the right to appear before the Court.

The Court can exercise its judicial function only in respect of those States which have access to it under Article 35 of the Statute. And only those States which have access to the Court can confer jurisdiction upon it.

It is the view of the Court that it is incumbent upon it to examine first of all the question whether the Applicant meets the conditions laid down in Articles 34 and 35 of the Statute and whether the Court is thus open to it. Only if the answer to that question is in the affirmative will the Court have to deal with the issues relating to the conditions laid down in Articles 36 and 37 of the Statute of the Court (see *Application of the Convention on the Prevention and Punishment of the Crime of Genocide (Bosnia and Herzegovina v. Yugoslavia (Serbia and Montenegro)), Provisional Measures, Order of 8 April 1993, I.C.J. Reports 1993*, p. 11 *et seq.*, paras. 14 *et seq.*). There is no doubt that Serbia and Montenegro is a State for the purpose of Article 34, paragraph 1, of the Statute. However, the objection was raised by certain Respondents (see paragraphs 49, 51, 93, 96 and 97 below) that Serbia and Montenegro did not meet, at the time of the filing of its Application on 29 April 1999, the conditions set down in Article 35 of the Statute.

47. No specific assertion was made in the Application that the Court was open to Serbia and Montenegro under Article 35, paragraph 1, of the Statute of the Court, but it was later made clear that the Applicant claimed to be a Member of the United Nations and thus a party to the Statute of the Court, by virtue of Article 93, paragraph 1, of the Charter, at the time of filing of the Application. As indicated earlier (paragraph 28 above) this position was expressly stated in the Memorial filed by Serbia and Montenegro on 4 January 2000 (Memorial, Part III, paras. 3.1.17 and 3.1.18).

48. A request for the indication of provisional measures of protection was submitted by Serbia and Montenegro on the day of the filing of its Application in the present case, i.e. 29 April 1999

(see paragraph 2 above). The Court, by its Order of 2 June 1999, rejected this request (see paragraph 8 above), on the ground that, on the basis of the original Application, it had no prima facie jurisdiction to entertain it and that it could not take account of the additional basis of jurisdiction contained in the "Supplement to the Application" in view of the late stage at which it was invoked. ...

49. In the course of the proceedings on this request, however, the Respondent raised the issue of whether the Applicant was a party to the Statute of the Court, and contended that

> "the Court's jurisdiction in this case cannot in any event be based, even prima facie, on Article 36, paragraph 2, of the Statute, for under this provision only 'States ... parties to the ... Statute' may subscribe to the optional clause for compulsory jurisdiction contained therein." (*ibid.*, p. 135, para. 31)

Belgium referred, *inter alia*, to United Nations General Assembly resolution 47/1 of 22 September 1992, and contended that "'the Federal Republic of Yugoslavia is not the continuator State of the former Socialist Federal Republic of Yugoslavia' as regards membership of the United Nations", and that "not having duly acceded to the Organization, Yugoslavia is in consequence not a party to the Statute of the Court" (*ibid.*).

50. Notwithstanding this contention by the Respondent, the Court did not, in its Order on provisional measures, carry out any examination of it, confining itself to observing that in view of its finding relating to the lack of prima facie jurisdiction *ratione temporis* under Article 36, paragraph 2, "the Court need not consider this question for the purpose of deciding whether or not it can indicate provisional measures in the present case" (*I.C.J. Reports 1999 (I)*, p. 136, para. 33).

51. Belgium subsequently argued as its first preliminary objection to the jurisdiction of the Court, *inter alia*, that:

> "The FRY is not now and has never been a member of the United Nations. This being the case, there is no basis for the FRY's claim to be a party to the *Statute* of the Court pursuant to Article 93 (1) of the *Charter*. The Court is not therefore, on this basis open to the FRY in accordance with Article 35 (1) of the *Statute*." (Preliminary Objections of Belgium, p. 69, para. 206; original emphasis)

52. The Court notes that it is, and has always been, common ground between the Parties that Serbia and Montenegro has not claimed to have become a party to the Statute on any other basis than by membership in the United Nations. Therefore the question raised in this first preliminary objection is simply whether or not the Applicant was a Member of the United Nations at the time when it instituted proceedings in the present case.

53. In addressing the question whether Serbia and Montenegro had access to the Court under Article 35, paragraph 1, of the Statute, the Court will consider the arguments put forward in this case and any other legal issue which it deems relevant to consider with a view to arriving at its conclusion on this point, including the issues raised in the other cases referred to in paragraph 3 above.

54. The Court will first recapitulate the sequence of events relating to the legal

position of Serbia and Montenegro vis-à-vis the United Nations – events already examined, so far as was necessary to the Court, in the context of another case (see Judgment in the case concerning *Application for Revision, I.C.J. Reports 2003*, pp. 14–26, paras. 24–53).

...

64. As is clear from the sequence of events summarized in the above paragraphs (paragraphs 55–63), the legal position of the Federal Republic of Yugoslavia within the United Nations and vis-à-vis that Organization remained highly complex during the period 1992–2000. In fact, it is the view of the Court that the legal situation that obtained within the United Nations during that eight-year period concerning the status of the Federal Republic of Yugoslavia, after the break-up of the Socialist Federal Republic of Yugoslavia, remained ambiguous and open to different assessments. This was due, *inter alia*, to the absence of an authoritative determination by the competent organs of the United Nations defining clearly the legal status of the Federal Republic of Yugoslavia vis-à-vis the United Nations.

...

73. To sum up, all these events testify to the rather confused and complex state of affairs that obtained within the United Nations surrounding the issue of the legal status of the Federal Republic of Yugoslavia in the Organization during this period. It is against this background that the Court, in its Judgment of 3 February 2003, referred to the "*sui generis* position which the FRY found itself in" during the period between 1992 and 2000.

74. It must be stated that this qualification of the position of the Federal Republic of Yugoslavia as "*sui generis*", which the Court employed to describe the situation during this period of 1992 to 2000, is not a prescriptive term from which certain defined legal consequences accrue; it is merely descriptive of the amorphous state of affairs in which the Federal Republic of Yugoslavia found itself during this period. No final and definitive conclusion was drawn by the Court from this descriptive term on the amorphous status of the Federal Republic of Yugoslavia vis-à-vis or within the United Nations during this period. The Court did not commit itself to a definitive position on the issue of the legal status of the Federal Republic of Yugoslavia in relation to the Charter and the Statute in its pronouncements in incidental proceedings, in the cases involving this issue which came before the Court during this anomalous period. For example, the Court stated in its Order of 2 June 1999 on the request for the indication of provisional measures in the present case as follows:

> "Whereas Belgium contends that the Court's jurisdiction in this case cannot in any event be based, even prima facie, on Article 36, paragraph 2, of the Statute, for, under this provision, only 'States ... parties to the ... Statute' may subscribe to the optional clause for compulsory jurisdiction contained therein
>
> ...
>
> Whereas, in view of its finding in paragraph 30 above, the Court need not consider this question for the purpose of deciding whether or not it can indicate provisional measures in the

present case." (*I.C.J. Reports 1999 (I)*, pp. 135–136, paras. 31–33)

75. This situation, however, came to an end with a new development in 2000 ....

78. This new development effectively put an end to the *sui generis* position of the Federal Republic of Yugoslavia within the United Nations, which, as the Court has observed in earlier pronouncements, had been fraught with "legal difficulties" throughout the period between 1992 and 2000 (cf. *Application of the Convention on the Prevention and Punishment of the Crime of Genocide (Bosnia and Herzegovina v. Yugoslavia (Serbia and Montenegro))*, *Provisional Measures, Order of 8 April 1993, I.C.J. Reports 1993*, p. 14, para. 18). The Applicant thus has the status of membership in the United Nations as from 1 November 2000. However, its admission to the United Nations did not have, and could not have had, the effect of dating back to the time when the Socialist Federal Republic of Yugoslavia broke up and disappeared; there was in 2000 no question of restoring the membership rights of the Socialist Federal Republic of Yugoslavia for the benefit of the Federal Republic of Yugoslavia. At the same time, it became clear that the *sui generis* position of the Applicant could not have amounted to its membership in the Organization.

79. In the view of the Court, the significance of this new development in 2000 is that it has clarified the thus far amorphous legal situation concerning the status of the Federal Republic of Yugoslavia vis-à-vis the United Nations. It is in that sense that the situation that the Court now faces in relation to Serbia and Montenegro is manifestly different from that which it faced in 1999. If, at that time, the Court had had to determine definitively the status of the Applicant vis-à-vis the United Nations, its task of giving such a determination would have been complicated by the legal situation, which was shrouded in uncertainties relating to that status. However, from the vantage point from which the Court now looks at the legal situation, and in light of the legal consequences of the new development since 1 November 2000, the Court is led to the conclusion that Serbia and Montenegro was not a Member of the United Nations, and in that capacity a State party to the Statute of the International Court of Justice, at the time of filing its Application to institute the present proceedings before the Court on 29 April 1999.

80. A further point to consider is the relevance to the present case of the Judgment in the *Application for Revision* case, of 3 February 2003. There is no question of that Judgment possessing any force of *res judicata* in relation to the present case. Nevertheless, the relevance of that judgment to the present case has to be examined, inasmuch as Serbia and Montenegro raised, in connection with its Application for revision, the same issue of its access to the Court under Article 35, paragraph 1, of the Statute, and the judgment of the Court was given in 2003 at a time when the new development described above had come to be known to the Court.

...

86. In the Judgment in the *Application for Revision* case, the Court found the Application for revision inadmissible ...

...

89. ... The Court thus made its position clear that there could have been no retroactive modification of the situation in 2000, which would amount to a new fact, and that therefore the conditions of Article 61 were not satisfied. This, however, did not entail any finding by the Court, in the revision proceedings, as to what that situation actually was.

90. Given the specific characteristics of the procedure under Article 61 of the Statute, in which the conditions for granting an application for revision of a judgment are strictly circumscribed, there is no reason to treat the Judgment in the *Application for Revision* case as having pronounced upon the issue of the legal status of Serbia and Montenegro vis-à-vis the United Nations. Nor does the Judgment pronounce upon the status of Serbia and Montenegro in relation to the Statute of the Court.

91. For all these reasons, the Court concludes that, at the time of filing of its Application to institute the present proceedings before the Court on 29 April 1999, the Applicant in the present case, Serbia and Montenegro, was not a Member of the United Nations, and, consequently, was not, on that basis, a State party to the Statute of the International Court of Justice. It follows that the Court was not open to Serbia and Montenegro under Article 35, paragraph 1, of the Statute.

Notes

- What does the court acknowledge is the significance of FR Yugoslavia (or Serbia and Montenegro) being a member state of the UN (or party to the Statute of the ICJ)?
- Did the states in this litigation ever raise the issue of the membership of the FR Yugoslavia/Serbia and Montenegro? Can this matter be raised at this point? And what is the legal effect of raising a matter at this point in the litigation?
- The court says that the FR Yugoslavia's status was "highly complex" and "*sui generis*." What does it mean for an entity's status to be *sui generis*? How can we argue in favor of and against this proposition?
- We already discussed under the *Genocide* case preliminary objections judgment of 2003 whether the clarification of the FR Yugoslavia's status was a new fact. How does the court review the clarification of its status in this case?
- Can the court reopen findings of law or fact at a later stage of proceedings? What does the court mean when it says "*res judicata*"? What would be the argument against it having this power? In considering this question, you may want to take note that this book will discuss in later chapters how we analyze the powers of international organizations, especially those of judicial organs. But without necessarily having read those sections yet, how should we analyze whether the ICJ has the power to reopen its decisions? What premises and assumptions do you draw on when you consider this question?
- This case also highlights a distinction between succession to a regular treaty from succession to a treaty creating an international organization. Why is succession to a regular treaty relatively easier? Is this difference in treatment justified, either politically or under the law of treaties?

In May 2006, Montenegro voted in favor of independence from its union with Serbia, and in June 2006, the State Union came to an end, with Serbia and Montenegro becoming independent states.

We will now switch back to the *Genocide* case once more, where the court issued its final judgment in the case a little more than two years later:

Case Concerning Application of the Convention on the Prevention and Punishment of the Crime of Genocide
Bosnia & Herzegovina v. Serbia & Montenegro
Judgment
2007 ICJ Reps 43
International Court of Justice, 26 February 2007

130. That does not however signify that in 1996 the Court was unaware of the fact that the solution adopted in the United Nations to the question of continuation of the membership of the SFRY "[was] not free from legal difficulties", as the Court had noted in its Order of 8 April 1993 indicating provisional measures in the case (*I.C.J. Reports 1993*, p. 14, para. 18; above, paragraph 105). The FRY was, at the time of the proceedings on its preliminary objections culminating in the 1996 Judgment, maintaining that it was the continuator State of the SFRY. As the Court indicated in its Judgments in the cases concerning the *Legality of Use of Force*,

...

131. The "legal difficulties" referred to were finally dissipated when in 2000 the FRY abandoned its former insistence that it was the continuator of the SFRY, and applied for membership in the United Nations (paragraph 98 above).

...

133. In the view of the Court, the express finding in the 1996 Judgment that the Court had jurisdiction in the case *ratione materiae*, on the basis of Article IX of the Genocide Convention, seen in its context, is a finding which is only consistent, in law and logic, with the proposition that, in relation to both Parties, it had jurisdiction *ratione personae* in its comprehensive sense, that is to say, that the status of each of them was such as to comply with the provisions of the Statute concerning the capacity of States to be parties before the Court. As regards Bosnia and Herzegovina, there was no question but that it was a party to the Statute at the date of filing its Application instituting proceedings; and in relation to the Convention, the Court found that it "could ... become a party to the Convention" from the time of its admission to the United Nations (*I.C.J. Reports 1996 (II)*, p. 611, para. 19), and had in fact done so. As regards the FRY, the Court found that it "was bound by the provisions of the Convention", i.e. was a party thereto, "on the date of the filing of the Application" (*ibid.*, p. 610, para. 17); in this respect the Court took note of the declaration made by the FRY on 27 April 1992, set out in paragraph 89 above, whereby the FRY "continuing the State, international legal and political personality" of the SFRY, declared that it would "strictly abide by" the

international commitments of the SFRY. The determination by the Court that it had jurisdiction under the Genocide Convention is thus to be interpreted as incorporating a determination that all the conditions relating to the capacity of the Parties to appear before it had been met.

...

136. The Court thus considers that the 1996 Judgment contained a finding, whether it be regarded as one of jurisdiction *ratione personae*, or as one anterior to questions of jurisdiction, which was necessary as a matter of logical construction, and related to the question of the FRY's capacity to appear before the Court under the Statute. The force of *res judicata* attaching to that judgment thus extends to that particular finding.

137. However it has been argued by the Respondent that even were that so,

"the fundamental nature of access as a precondition for the exercise of the Court's judicial function means that positive findings on access cannot be taken as definitive and final until the final judgment is rendered in proceedings"

...

138. It appears to the Court that these contentions are inconsistent with the nature of the principle of *res judicata*. That principle signifies that once the Court has made a determination, whether on a matter of the merits of a dispute brought before it, or on a question of its own jurisdiction, that determination is definitive both for the parties to the case, in respect of the case (Article 59 of the Statute), and for the Court itself in the context of that case. However fundamental the question of the capacity of States to be parties in cases before the Court may be, it remains a question to be determined by the Court, in accordance with Article 36, paragraph 6, of the Statute, and once a finding in favour of jurisdiction has been pronounced with the force of *res judicata*, it is not open to question or re-examination, except by way of revision under Article 61 of the Statute. There is thus, *as a matter of law*, no possibility that the Court might render "its final decision with respect to a party over which it cannot exercise its judicial function", because the question whether a State is or is not a party subject to the jurisdiction of the Court is one which is reserved for the sole and authoritative decision of the Court.

139. Counsel for the Respondent contended further that, in the circumstances of the present case, reliance on the *res judicata* principle "would justify the Court's *ultra vires* exercise of its judicial functions contrary to the mandatory requirements of the Statute". However, the operation of the "mandatory requirements of the Statute" falls to be determined by the Court in each case before it; and once the Court has determined, with the force of *res judicata*, that it has jurisdiction, then for the purposes of that case no question of *ultra vires* action can arise, the Court having sole competence to determine such matters under the Statute. For the Court *res judicata pro veritate habetur*, and the judicial truth within the context of a case is as the Court has determined it, subject only to the provision in the Statute for revision of judgments. This result is required by the nature of the judicial function, and the universally recognized need for stability of legal relations.

Notes

- In the *Use of Force* case preliminary objections judgment of 2004, we already discussed the question of *res judicata*. How does the court deal with that principle in this case? Is that consistent with the approach that it took in the *Use of Force* case?
- How should the court deal with contemporaneous cases that might have bearing on each other? Surely litigants should not have to prove the same fact in both proceedings with the same burden? Or should they?
- Both of the questions above are matters of judicial practice, but are they law, or judicial policy? How would we distinguish those two? What guidance can be drawn to make a determination of how this practice should be applied?
- The decisions above are referred to as "judgments," but the court also issues "orders." Is there any meaning behind these different terms?
- The court also refers to an expression "*ultra vires*." What does this expression mean? You want to keep this term in mind when you study Chapter 5 on powers of international organizations.
- Now that you have reviewed this entire case study of the FR Yugoslavia, its purported succession to the SFR Yugoslavia's UN membership, and the *Genocide* and *Use of Force* cases, are you satisfied with the outcome in these cases? How would these cases have been decided differently if the disintegration of Yugoslavia had a different characterization? For example, would it have any bearing on the outcome if the FR Yugoslavia had been the successor to the SFR Yugoslavia in terms of its UN membership? What kind of facts would have to exist in order for the FR Yugoslavia to have been a successor?

The above discussion focused on membership and the rights and duties that flowed from that membership. Recall the discussion at the beginning of this chapter that sometimes there are different categories of members, and that these different categories may have slightly different rights and obligations. This distinction would make succession even more significant for states that could successfully lay claim to it. For example, the permanent five members of the UN Security Council alone have the right of veto over substantive matters. On 24 December 1991, Boris Yeltsin wrote the following letter to the UN Secretary-General:

Boris N. Yeltsin, President of the Russian Federation, Letter to the UN Secretary-General
24 December 1991
IAEA Doc. INFCIRC/397 (9 January 1992) Attachment 2[21]

The membership of the Union of Soviet Socialist Republics in the United Nations, including the Security Council and all other organs and organizations of the United Nations system, is being continued by the

---

21 Information Circular No. 397 (9 January 1992) © IAEA, 1992, *available at* www.iaea.org/sites/default/files/infcirc397.pdf.

Russian Federation (RSFSR) with the support of the countries of the Commonwealth of Independent States. In this connection, I request that the name "Russian Federation" should be used in the United Nations in place of the name "the Union of Soviet Socialist Republics". The Russian Federation maintains full responsibility for all the rights and obligations of the USSR under the Charter of the United Nations, including the financial obligations. I request that you consider this letter as confirmation of the credentials to represent the Russian Federation in United Nations organs for all the persons currently holding the credentials of representatives of the USSR to the United Nations.

One month later, the UN Security Council resumed session, and in an unusual exercise, the various heads of state of each member of the Security Council attended in person to represent their state. John Major, the Prime Minister of the UK, chaired the meeting:

**United Nations Security Council,
Provisional verbatim record of the 2046th meeting
held at Headquarters, New York, on Friday, 31 January 1992, at 10:30 a.m.
UN Doc. S/PV.3046 (31 January 1992)[22]**

[p. 42]

The PRESIDENT: [Mr. MAJOR (United Kingdom of Great Britain and Northern Ireland)] ... I now invite the President and Chairman of the Government of the Russian Federation to address the Security Council.

President YELTSIN ... : This summit meeting of the Security Council, the first of its kind on the political Olympus of the contemporary world, is a historic and unprecedented event. The end of the twentieth century is a time of great promise and new anxieties.

...

I am grateful to the world community for its support of our efforts and for understanding that the future not only of the people of Russia but of the [p. 43] entire planet largely depends on whether or not these reforms are successful.

I am also grateful to the people of Russia for their courage and steadfastness. They should take a great deal of credit for the fact that the world community is moving ever farther away from the totalitarian past, ...

[p. 48]

... It is a historical irony that the Russian Federation, a State with centuries-long experience in foreign policy and diplomacy, has only just appeared on the political map of the world. I am confident that the world community will find in Russia, as an equal participant in

---

22 From UN Document S/PV.3046, by the United Nations © 1992 United Nations. Reprinted with the permission of the United Nations.

international relations and as a permanent member' of the Security Council, a firm and steadfast champion of freedom, democracy and humanism.

...

In conclusion, permit me to wish Mr. Boutros-Ghali every success in his important post of Secretary-General of the United Nations.

The PRESIDENT: Mr. President, thank you, I know the Council would wish me to welcome Russia as a permanent member of our Council. You are very welcome indeed.

...

[p. 102]

... I now invite the Prime Minister of Japan to address the Council.

Mr. MIYAZAWA (Japan): The year 1992 marks a point of departure towards a promising future for the United Nations.

...

I should also like to extend a heartfelt welcome to President Boris Yeltsin, who is here at the United Nations for the first time as the leader of the Russian Federation. The political and economic stability of the Federation is of great importance to the peace and stability of the entire world. I am confident that Russia will successfully discharge its awesome responsibilities, not only as a Member of the United Nations but also as a permanent member of the Security Council.

...

[p. 136]

[The PRESIDENT:] ... We celebrate too a new world Power: the Russian Federation, the Power which has now emerged from an aberration that lasted for 70 years.

Notes

- How does Russia, and then other UN member states, characterize its succession? Did Russia secede from the USSR? Did the USSR abandon Russia? Some states seem to refer to Russia as a "new world Power," but does Russia view itself as "new"? If it is not new, where was it before? Reflecting once more on Yeltsin's letter, is this better understood as simply a matter of changing the name plates from "USSR" to "Russia"? Consider, for example, that Bolivia was initially declared the "Republic of Bolívar"(from Simón Bolívar, of course) before being quickly revised as the "Republic of Bolivia." In 2009, the state adopted a new constitution which changed its name to the "Plurinational State of Bolivia," in recognition of its indigenous peoples and multiethnic nature. Naturally, Bolivia did not have to reapply for admission to the UN following a name change and new constitution. How is this different for Russia?
- Why did Russia have a relatively easier time succeeding to the USSR's membership? One would think that succeeding to the membership of one of the

permanent five members of the UN Security Council would be such a serious matter that the issue of succession would be far more controversial. And certainly the USSR dissolved; Russia did not secede from the USSR. Can you think of any reason why succession to one of the permanent five seats would be far less controversial than other membership succession? Is it just because they have nuclear weapons?

- A cynic might point to Yeltsin's assumption of the full financial obligations of the former USSR to the UN as a key factor in its succession. Would you agree that this is relevant, both politically and legally? Perhaps you might want to review once more Legal Opinion No. 15 of the UN Office of Legal Counsel on questions regarding the financial contributions of Belarus and Ukraine, reproduced above. Does this opinion inform your view on the role of finances in state succession to membership?

4.2.6 Representation and credentials

While states and other qualifying entities are members of international organizations, they clearly need some representative to speak on their behalf. This question is distinct from that of membership. Consider, for example, the case of a state in the midst of a civil war, such as Libya. The state remains a member of the organization throughout the conflict, although it may be unclear which of two delegations may actually speak for the state. Because this issue arises in the context of the exercise of membership rights, it will be addressed in this section on membership.

The first question about representation is how to determine which delegation represents the state. Recall from the UN Charter that one of the original members, and one of the permanent members of the Security Council, was the "Republic of China." The representatives from Beijing at the time the UN was founded were credentialed and correctly represented their state. However, during the civil war in China, the "Republic of China" government retreated from Beijing to the island of Taiwan, where it remains to this day in continuous operation. The new government that took over in Beijing renamed the state the "People's Republic of China." These two governments, one in Beijing and the other in Taipei, both officially maintain the position that they are the government of one Chinese state. Throughout this chain of events, the delegates from the "Republic of China" continued to be credentialed at the UN as the representatives of all of China, in line with previous practice. By the early 1970s, this practice was viewed as untenable. The drafters of the UN Charter had most likely intended for the vast state of continental China to be represented both in the General Assembly and Security Council, and the small, residual government on the island of Taiwan was no longer in effective control of virtually all of the territory of China. Accordingly, the UN General Assembly issued the following resolution:

United Nations General Assembly Resolution 2758 (XXVI) (25 October 1971) Restoration of the lawful rights of the People's Republic of China in the United Nations[23]

The General Assembly,

Recalling the principles of the Charter of the United Nations,

Considering that the restoration of the lawful rights of the People's Republic of China is essential both for the protection of the Charter of the United Nations and for the cause that the United Nations must serve under the Charter,

Recognizing that the representatives of the Government of the People's Republic of China are the only lawful representatives of China to the United Nations and that the People's Republic of China is one of the five permanent members of the Security Council

Decides to restore all its rights to the People's Republic of China and to recognize the representatives of its Government as the only legitimate representatives of China to the United Nations, and to expel forthwith the representatives of Chiang Kai-shek from the place which they unlawfully occupy at the United Nations and in all the organizations related to it.

In addition to the question of which delegation correctly represents the state, there are also sometimes questions of whether the particular delegates selected by the state are acceptable under the rules of the organization. While there might not be any controversy that they were selected by the government in effective control of the state, the question is whether the state is empowering and sending individuals in compliance with the constitutive instrument of the organization.

In one particular notorious case, the delegates to the International Labour Conference from Germany in 1933 were challenged. The International Labour Conference, as the governing body of the International Labour Organization, has a particularly unusual policy on representation. Not only do state governments send official delegates, but also representatives from employers and employees, in keeping with the unique competences of the organization. Just to be clear, the representatives from employers and employees are not observers, but are full voting delegates, independent from instructions by their national governments. Of course, the controversy in 1933 for the delegates from Germany would have been their independence from

---

23 From UN General Assembly Resolution 2758 (XXVI), by the United Nations © 1971 United Nations. Reprinted with the permission of the United Nations.

the Nazi Government, and thus their *bona fide* qualification as independent delegates from employers and employees. In most organizations, these types of matters are dealt with by a credentials committee that is empowered to reach binding decisions on which delegates are correctly accepted to participate by their nominating state. In the case of the German delegates, the Credentials Committee rejected the proposed delegates. There was precedent at the ILO for such an action challenging the delegates, although in that case, the Committee and the Conference accepted the delegates nominated by the state.[24]

The rejection of proposed delegates stands in contrast with the freedom that states have in appointing the representatives before international organizations. In the WTO case *EC-Bananas III*, some of the litigants challenged the right of St. Lucia to hire outside legal counsel to represent it before the Dispute Settlement Body's Appellate Body. Before the WTO had been reconstituted as a full-fledged international organization, it operated as a minimal secretariat office overseeing the General Agreement on Tariffs and Trade of 1947 (GATT 1947). That entity had not been understood as an international organization, although it did have some independent exercise of competences. Practice at the GATT 1947 secretariat excluded private independent legal counsel from disputes, on the grounds that they were not delegates of the state party. The Appellate Body (now of the WTO rather than the GATT 1947 secretariat) notified the complaining states that St. Lucia's counsel would be permitted to participate, stating that:

> [10]… we can find nothing in the *Marrakesh Agreement Establishing the World Trade Organization* …, the *DSU* or the *Working Procedures*, nor in customary international law or the prevailing practice of international tribunals, which prevents a WTO Member from determining the composition of its delegation in Appellate Body proceedings … we rule that it is for a WTO Member to decide who should represent it as members of its delegation in an oral hearing of the Appellate Body.[25]

Practice since then has consistently permitted states to retain outside, independent legal counsel to represent it in proceedings.

---

24 *See* Designation of the Workers' Delegate for The Netherlands at the Third Session of the International Labour Conference, Advisory Opinion, 1922 PCIJ (Ser. B) No. 1, para. 24 (Permanent Court of International Justice, 31 July 1922) (finding that "The Article throws upon the Government of the State the duty of deciding, on the data at its disposal, what organisations are, in point of fact, the most representative. Its decision on this question may however, be reviewed under the seventh paragraph of this Article, and the Conference has the power, by a two-thirds majority, to refuse to admit any delegate whom it deems not to have been nominated in accordance with the Article").
25 European Communities – Regime for the Importation, Sale and Distribution of Bananas ["EC-Bananas III"], WTO Case. AB-1997-3, Report of the Appellate Body, WTO Doc. WT/DS27/AB/R (World Trade Organization, 9 September 1997).

Although this practice above is widely applicable, it might have particular importance in the case of the European Union. The EU, of course, is an unusual case in that it is an international organization, yet it also participates as a member of other international organizations, alongside states. While unitary and federal states have their own internal rules on representatives that might take account of their constitutional organization (consider, for example, the enhanced participation of Flanders and Wallonia in Belgian diplomatic practice), the EU is neither a unitary nor a federal state. Its members are sovereign states, and the organization acts on a variety of competences, carefully balanced with the sovereign discretion of those Member States. The EU must often argue for its inclusion in organizations where decisions will be taken in the areas of the EU's competence. There may even be disagreements among the Member States about the participation of the EU within an organization. Other non-EU Member States may perceive an effort for Europe generally to dominate the organization if both the EU and Member States are represented.

4.3 SUSPENSION OR TERMINATION OF MEMBERSHIP

In this final section of this chapter, we will briefly consider whether and when a state may be denied participation or outright removed from membership.

4.3.1 Extinction of the state

The first, most obvious, case of a state being removed from membership is when the state becomes extinct. In this regard, you may wish to review the succession issues in the case of the former Yugoslavia and USSR above. In particular, there is the notion that a state might be extinct and yet still remain a party to a treaty or a member of an organization pending a definitive decision on the matter. Other cases that come to mind are the former Czechoslovakia, and the brief existence of the United Arab Republic, being a union of Syria and Egypt. Visitors to the Peace Palace in The Hague will find the old chair reserved for the Austro-Hungarian Empire on display in the museum as a former member of the Permanent Court of Arbitration.

4.3.2 Suspension of membership

A less grave action than removal can be suspension of membership and/or voting rights. Most organizations have some provision for suspending a misbehaving member, or one seriously deficient in paying dues. The EU, for example, may suspend a Member State that has made a "clear risk of a serious breach by a Member State of the [values of respect for human dignity, freedom, democracy, equality, the rule of law and respect for human rights]."[26] Another possibility is for the constitutive instrument to permit suspension when the state suffers a non-democratic or unconstitutional change of government. For example, the Organization of American States may suspend a member when its "democratically constituted government has been overthrown by force,"[27] or in the case of the African Union, when the government of a member state has "come to power through unconstitutional means."[28] In the latter case, the AU did suspend Madagascar when that state suffered a *coup d'état* in 2009. In the case of the UN, the provision reads as follows:

Charter of the United Nations
24 October 1945
1 UNTS 16[29]

Chapter II Membership
Article 5.

A Member of the United Nations against which preventive or enforcement action has been taken by the Security Council may be suspended from the exercise of the rights and privileges of membership by the General Assembly upon the recommendation of the Security Council. The exercise of these rights and privileges may be restored by the Security Council.

4.3.3 Termination of membership

However, the graver outcome can be the termination of the state's membership in an international organization. This termination can come about in one of several ways. A state might wish to end its membership by withdrawing. A state might also refuse to ratify an amendment to the constitutive instrument, and such refusal could potentially function as the equivalent to a withdrawal of membership. Surprisingly, many organizations do not stipulate any terms on how a state might withdraw its membership.

Some withdrawals are relatively straightforward and not controversial, but others are complex and divisive. As of this writing, the United Kingdom is attempting to negotiate a withdrawal from the European Union, the so-called "Brexit," which is proving to be incredibly difficult, partly due to the high level of the UK's integration into the EU.

---

26 Treaty on European Union, article 7.
27 Charter of the Organization of American States, 30 April 1948, 119 UNTS 3, article 9.
28 African Union Constitutive Act, 11 July 2000, 2158 UNTS 37733, article 30.
29 From the United Nations Treaty Series, by the United Nations © 1945 United Nations. Reprinted with the permission of the United Nations.

Indonesia is the only state to ever attempt to withdraw from the UN. On 1 January 1965, the Deputy Prime Minister and Minister for Foreign Affairs of Indonesia, under the direction of President Sukarno, notified UN Secretary-General Thant that the state was stopping its participation in the UN. At the heart of the matter was Indonesia's tense relationship with Malaysia, and Malaysia's election as a nonpermanent member of the UN Security Council. The Secretary-General acknowledged receipt of the notice and cooperated with Indonesia's request, noting that he hoped Indonesia would "resume full cooperation" in the future. President Sukarno then attempted to create a new international organization as an alternative to the UN, named CONEFO (Conference of the New Emerging Forces). Subsequently, in 1966, President Sukarno was removed as president by General Suharto, who then notified the UN Secretary-General that Indonesia would "resume full cooperation with the UN and … resume participation in its activities." Rather than insist that Indonesia had to reapply to become a member, the UN General Assembly President interpreted this chain of events as a "cessation of cooperation," not a true withdrawal, and the representatives of Indonesia were seated when they appeared at that organ in September 1966. Thus, one method for managing membership withdrawal is to treat it as a kind of self-imposed suspension or non-cooperation.

In addition to complete withdrawal, there are a few partial withdrawal options. For example, when Denmark joined the European Union, it included Greenland as a part of its territories to which EU rights and obligations would apply, although it excluded the Faroe Islands. In time, Greenland acquired additional autonomy rights and chose to remove itself from the EU and seek a new status. Denmark duly negotiated with the EU and the other Member States for this outcome, and in 2006, Greenland effectively left the European Union and was reorganized as an excluded overseas territory.[30]

A final way in which a state's membership may be terminated is when the state violates the constitutive instrument so significantly that the other members of the organization expel the state. For example, the UN charter states the following:

---

30 Council Decision 2006/526/EC of 17 July 2006 on relations between the European Community and Greenland.

Charter of the United Nations
24 October 1945
1 UNTS 16[31]

Chapter II Membership
Article 6.

A Member of the United Nations which has persistently violated the Principles contained in the present Charter may be expelled from the Organization by the General Assembly upon the recommendation of the Security Council.

No state has ever been expelled from the UN for persistent violation, despite some particularly bold violations that we can think of from the history of the UN. This practice suggests that a persistent violation would have to be shockingly severe to trigger such a remedy.

---

[31] From the United Nations Treaty Series, by the United Nations © 1945 United Nations. Reprinted with the permission of the United Nations.

Powers

5.1 SOURCES OF POWERS

International organizations are based on the goal of more efficient international cooperation, and for this purpose they exercise a variety of powers. These powers range from the more mundane, such as negotiating headquarters agreements with the host state, that are fairly common among all international organizations, to the more specialized and specific, such as authorizing the use of force or international financial loans, that are more unique to particular organizations. The founders of any international organization operate under several constraints when they provide for the powers of an international organization. First, they cannot possibly predict how the organization will grow and develop in the international community, and the role that it will fill, so they may not be able to imagine all the powers the organization may need. Second, the founders tend to focus on the more significant powers the organization will have, and cannot make an express provision for all of the minute tasks an organization must accomplish. Sometimes the founders must just assume that the organization will have certain powers.

When an organization acts in some way, it is always exercising one of its powers. However, because an organization has limited competences, we must always ensure that the organization has legal authority to act as it proposes to do. This means that any time an organization acts, we must find the legal basis for the powers of an organization that authorizes the action, or else the organization will have taken an action that is beyond its powers, *ultra vires*, rendering the act invalid.

This chapter will study the legal basis for the powers of an organization, the methodology for determining whether an organization has a proposed power, and the approach for determining whether an act is *ultra vires*. First, the chapter will examine the sources of the powers of international organizations.

Initially, international organizations approached the question of their powers as merely a treaty interpretation problem. The organization was created by a treaty, and drew its personality and powers from that instrument. For example, when it was asked whether the International Labour Organization had certain competences, the

Permanent Court of International Justice (PCIJ) looked for the grant of those competences to the organization in its constitutive instrument:

Competence of the International Labour Organization in Regard to International Regulation of the Conditions of Labour of Persons Employed in Agriculture
Advisory Opinion
1922 PCIJ (Ser. B) No. 2
Permanent Court of International Justice, 12 August 1922

[20] The question before the Court relates simply to the competency of the International Labour Organisation as to agricultural labour. No point arises on this question as to the expediency or the opportuneness of the application to agriculture of any particular proposal.

[21] The Treaty of Peace between the Allied and Associated Powers, on the one hand, and Germany on the other, signed at Versailles on June 28th, 1919, is divided into fifteen Parts, of which Part XIII relates to Labour. Part XIII is composed of two sections, the first of which, opening with a Preamble, embraces Articles 387–426, while the second, consisting of Article 427, enunciates certain "General Principles". Section I, which is entitled "Organisation of Labour", provides for a "permanent organisation", international in character, commonly called the International Labour Organisation. This organisation consists (1) of a General Conference, to be held at least once a year, of Representatives of the Members of the International Labour Organisation, and (2) of an International Labour Office, controlled by a Governing Body.

...

[24] In considering the question before the Court upon the language of the Treaty, it is obvious that the Treaty must be read as a whole, and that its meaning is not to be determined merely upon particular phrases which, if detached from the context, may be interpreted in more than one sense.

[25] It was much urged in argument that the establishment of the International Labour Organisation involved an abandonment of rights derived from national sovereignty, and that the competence of the Organisation therefore should not be extended by interpretation. There may be some force in this argument, but the question in every case must resolve itself into what the terms of the Treaty actually mean, and it is from this point of view that the Court proposes to examine the question.

[26] As Part XIII expressly declares, the design of the Contracting Parties was to establish a permanent labour organisation. This in itself strongly militates against the argument that agriculture, which is, beyond all question, the most ancient and the greatest industry in the world, employing more than half of the world's wage-earners, is to be considered as left outside the scope of the International Labour Organisation because it is not expressly mentioned by name.

[27] The comprehensive character of Part XIII is clearly shown in the Preamble, which declares that "conditions of

labour", (conditions de travail), exist "involving such injustice, hardship and privation to large numbers of persons as to produce unrest so great that the peace and harmony of the world are imperilled". An improvement of these conditions the Preamble declares to be urgently required in various particulars, the examples given being (1) "the regulation of the hours of work, including the establishment of a maximum working day and week"; (2) "the regulation of the labour supply"; (3) the "prevention of unemployment"; (4) the "provision of an adequate living wage"; (5) the "protection of the worker against sickness, disease and injury arising out of his employment"; (6) the "protection of children, young persons and women"; (7) "provision for old-age and injury"; (8) "protection of the interests of workers when employed in countries other than their own"; (9) "recognition of the principle of the freedom of association"; and (10) the "organisation of vocational and technical education".

[28] The Preamble then goes on to state that the reason for dealing with the enumerated measures internationally is that "the failure of any nation to adopt humane conditions of labour is an obstacle in the way of other nations which desire to improve the conditions in their own countries". This in itself is as applicable to navigation as to any industry, and it is also applicable to some extent to fishing and to agriculture. The adoption of humane conditions of labour in any of these three industries might to some extent be retarded by the danger that such conditions would form a handicap against the nations which had adopted them and in favour of those which had not, in the competition of the markets of the world.

[29] "Moved", then, so the Preamble declares, "by sentiments of justice and humanity as well as by the desire to secure the permanent peace of the world", the High Contracting Parties proceeded, in the very next clauses of the Treaty (Articles 387, 388) to establish the "permanent organisation", "for the promotion of the objects set forth in the Preamble".

[30] These are the terms in which the Treaty expressly defines the competence of the International Labour Organisation, and language could hardly be more comprehensive.

Notes

- Why does the International Labour Organization have the powers it does? What grants and/or limits those powers? Why does that instrument have the ability to legally authorize exercise of certain powers?
- How does the Permanent Court of International Justice determine whether the organization has the proposed powers? What does it consider, and by using what interpretive methodology?

This case is fairly typical of the period of international law when states were regarded as the primary, if not only, relevant actors. States, of course, have a much wider range of competences under international law than organizations.

Organizations were understood to be incredibly efficient treaty mechanisms, not actors in international law in their own right.

This traditional view of the role of international organizations continues to this day. We can find the distinction in, for example, the Vienna Convention pertaining to treaties between states, which provides in article 6 that "Every State possesses capacity to conclude treaties," and the Vienna Convention for International Organizations, which provides in its article 6 that "The capacity of an international organization to conclude treaties is governed by the rules of that organization." This difference suggests that international organizations participate in international law insofar as states wish them to. They do not have an inherent right to participate. Therefore, in the case above, the Permanent Court of International Justice found that the ILO's range of competences was expressed in its founding treaty, and there was no room to understand powers beyond the clear terms of the treaty. This kind of thinking was still predominant around the time of the founding of the United Nations and continues until today, though other views have since emerged to dispute it as the only way of interpreting the powers of an organization.

Consider, for example, the following case:

Conditions of Admission of a State to Membership in the United Nations (Article 4 of the Charter)
["First Admissions Case"]
Advisory Opinion
1948 ICJ Reps. 57
International Court of Justice, 28 May 1948

[p. 61]... The question put is in effect confined to the following point only: are the conditions stated in paragraph 1 of Article 4 exhaustive in character in the sense that an affirmative reply would lead to the conclusion that a Member is not legally entitled to make admission dependent on conditions not expressly provided for in that Article, while a negative reply would, on the contrary, authorize a Member to make admission dependent also on other conditions ....

[p. 63]... Moreover, the spirit as well as the terms of the paragraph preclude the idea that considerations extraneous to these principles and obligations can prevent the admission of a State which complies with them. If the authors of the Charter had meant to leave Members free to import into the application of this provision considerations extraneous to the conditions laid down therein, they would undoubtedly have adopted a different wording.

In this opinion, we see that states clearly determine the competences of the organization, and that determination can be found in the text of the constitutive instrument.

Why should the powers of an international organization be limited at all? Surely the member states can control the organization and dictate its mandate, objectives, and strategy through their participatory governance. In the following case, an arbitral tribunal explained why an organization's powers are limited:

United Nations Educational, Scientific and Cultural Organization [UNESCO] (Constitution) Case
16 International Law Reports 331
Special Arbitral Tribunal, 19 September 1949[1]

The Facts – The first paragraph of Article V of the Constitution of the United Nations Educational, Scientific and Cultural Organization (UNESCO) provides that the Executive Board shall consist of eighteen members elected by the General Conference from among the delegates appointed by the Member States. Paragraph 4 lays down that a substitute for a member who dies or resigns shall be appointed "from among the delegates of the Member State concerned". Paragraph 3 establishes the eligibility of elected members of the Executive Board for re-election for a second term, but without the express condition that such persons shall be members of their country's delegation to the Session of the Conference at which such election takes place. Differences having arisen on the subject, the Executive Board of UNESCO set up a Special Arbitral Tribunal to decide on the following question: "May an outgoing member of the Executive Board be re-elected even though he is not a member of his country's delegation to the Session of the Conference at which such election takes place?"

...

VI. *Consideration of Sovereignty of States* – Assuming that the above considerations had not been convincing and that a doubt subsisted, again, in the Tribunal's opinion, that doubt must be resolved in conformity with the interpretation set out above, since paragraph 1 of Article V affords States a guarantee that none of their nationals will be elected a member of the Executive Board of Unesco without having been proposed by his government, indirectly at least, by his nomination as a delegate to the General Conference. To deprive Member States of Unesco of that right where the original mandate of a member of the Executive Board was renewed would amount to a restriction of their sovereignty. It is an established rule of law that such a restriction cannot be presumed (*North Atlantic Coast Fisheries* – Permanent Court of Arbitration, 1910, No. 7, pages 114 and 122 – Cf. Permanent Court of International Justice – *Mosul Case*, Advisory Opinion of 21 November 1925 – *Lotus case*, Judgment of 7 September 1927. Reports of the Court, Series A/B, No. 17, page 25, No. 22, page 18).

---

[1] © Sir E. Lauterpacht, published by Cambridge University Press. Reproduced with permission of The Licensor through PLSclear.

Notes

- What does this special arbitral tribunal understand to be the limitation on the powers of the organization? Are the powers limited by the constitutive treaty, or some other concern?
- What is the role of the relationship between member states and the organization in determining the powers of the organization?

5.1.1 Express attribution of powers

In determining what powers an international organization has, the primary approach is to begin with the text of the constitutive instrument, as we saw above. This approach would apply the normal textual interpretive techniques provided for in the Vienna Convention, considering not only the text of the agreement, but also the context and the object and purpose of the agreement. It might also be relevant to consult the preparatory works, subsequent agreements or practice, and perhaps even other rules of international law, to determine the meaning of the various provisions of the treaty. Through this approach, one would be able to determine whether the drafters of the constitutive instrument expressly provided for the attribution of certain powers to the organization.

In the following case, the Court of Justice of the EU had to determine whether certain acts regarding tobacco advertising regulation by organs of the European Union fell within their powers:

Case C-376/98, Federal Republic of Germany v European Parliament and Council of the European Union
[*In re* "Tobacco Directive"]
Judgment
Court of Justice of the European Communities [Union], 5 October 2000[2]

Grounds

1 By application lodged at the Registry of the Court on 19 October 1998, the Federal Republic of Germany brought an action under Article 173 of the EC Treaty (now, after amendment, Article 230 EC) for the annulment of Directive 98/43/EC of the European Parliament and of the Council of 6 July 1998 on the approximation of the laws, regulations and administrative provisions of the Member States relating to the advertising and sponsorship of tobacco products (OJ 1992 L 213, p. 9, hereinafter the Directive)

....

3 The Directive was adopted on the basis of Article 57(2) of the EC Treaty (now, after amendment, Article 47(2) EC), Article 66 of the EC Treaty (now Article 55 EC) and Article 100a of the

---

2 https://eur-lex.europa.eu, © European Union 1998–2020.

EC Treaty (now, after amendment, Article 95 EC).

...

5 According to Article 3 of the Directive:

1. Without prejudice to Directive 89/552/EEC, all forms of advertising and sponsorship [of tobacco products] shall be banned in the Community.

...

9 In support of its application, the Federal Republic of Germany puts forward seven pleas in law alleging, respectively, that Article 100a of the Treaty is not an appropriate legal basis for the Directive, infringement of Article 57(2) and Article 66 of the Treaty, breach of the principles of proportionality and subsidiarity, breach of fundamental rights, infringement of Articles 30 and 36 of the EC Treaty (now, after amendment, Articles 28 EC and 30 EC) and infringement of Article 190 of the EC Treaty (now Article 253 EC).

...

The Court's analysis

The choice of Articles 100a, 57(2) and 66 of the Treaty as a legal basis and judicial review thereof

76 The Directive is concerned with the approximation of laws, regulations and administrative provisions of the Member States relating to the advertising and sponsorship of tobacco products. The national measures affected are to a large extent inspired by public health policy objectives.

77 The first indent of Article 129(4) of the Treaty excludes any harmonisation of laws and regulations of the Member States designed to protect and improve human health.

78 But that provision does not mean that harmonising measures adopted on the basis of other provisions of the Treaty cannot have any impact on the protection of human health. Indeed, the third paragraph of Article 129(1) provides that health requirements are to form a constituent part of the Community's other policies.

79 Other articles of the Treaty may not, however, be used as a legal basis in order to circumvent the express exclusion of harmonisation laid down in Article 129(4) of the Treaty.

80 In this case, the approximation of national laws on the advertising and sponsorship of tobacco products provided for by the Directive was based on Articles 100a, 57(2) and 66 of the Treaty.

81 Article 100a(1) of the Treaty empowers the Council, acting in accordance with the procedure referred to in Article 189b (now, after amendment, Article 251 EC) and after consulting the Economic and Social Committee, to adopt measures for the approximation of the provisions laid down by law, regulation or administrative action in Member States which have as their object the establishment and functioning of the internal market.

82 Under Article 3(c) of the EC Treaty (now, after amendment, Article 3(1)(c) EC), the internal market is characterised by the abolition, as between Member States, of all obstacles to the free movement of goods, persons, services and capital. Article 7a of the EC Treaty (now, after amendment, Article 14 EC), which provides for the measures to be taken

with a view to establishing the internal market, states in paragraph 2 that that market is to comprise an area without internal frontiers in which the free movement of goods, persons, services and capital is ensured in accordance with the provisions of the Treaty.

83 Those provisions, read together, make it clear that the measures referred to in Article 100a(1) of the Treaty are intended to improve the conditions for the establishment and functioning of the internal market. To construe that article as meaning that it vests in the Community legislature a general power to regulate the internal market would not only be contrary to the express wording of the provisions cited above but would also be incompatible with the principle embodied in Article 3b of the EC Treaty (now Article 5 EC) that the powers of the Community are limited to those specifically conferred on it.

...

85 So, in considering whether Article 100a was the proper legal basis, the Court must verify whether the measure whose validity is at issue in fact pursues the objectives stated by the Community legislature (see, in particular, Spain v Council, cited above, paragraphs 25 to 41, and Case C-233/94 Germany v Parliament and Council [1997] ECR I-2405, paragraphs 10 to 21).

86 It is true, as the Court observed in paragraph 35 of its judgment in Spain v Council, cited above, that recourse to Article 100a as a legal basis is possible if the aim is to prevent the emergence of future obstacles to trade resulting from multifarious development of national laws. However, the emergence of such obstacles must be likely and the measure in question must be designed to prevent them.

...

89 It is therefore necessary to verify whether, in the light of the foregoing, it was permissible for the Directive to be adopted on the basis of Articles 100a, 57(2) and 66 of the Treaty.

The Directive

90 In the first recital in the preamble to the Directive, the Community legislature notes that differences exist between national laws on the advertising and sponsorship of tobacco products and observes that, as a result of such advertising and sponsorship transcending the borders of the Member States, the differences in question are likely to give rise to barriers to the movement of the products which serve as the media for such activities and the exercise of freedom to provide services in that area, as well as to distortions of competition, thereby impeding the functioning of the internal market.

91 According to the second recital, it is necessary to eliminate such barriers, and, to that end, approximate the rules relating to the advertising and sponsorship of tobacco products, whilst leaving Member States the possibility of introducing, under certain conditions, such requirements as they consider necessary in order to guarantee protection of the health of individuals.

92 Article 3(1) of the Directive prohibits all forms of advertising and sponsorship of tobacco products and Article 3(4) prohibits any free distribution having the purpose or the effect of promoting such products. However, its scope does not extend to communications between

professionals in the tobacco trade, advertising in sales outlets or in publications published and printed in third countries which are not principally intended for the Community market (Article 3 (5)).

...

94   Pursuant to Article 5, the Directive is not to preclude Member States from laying down, in accordance with the Treaty, such stricter requirements concerning the advertising or sponsorship of tobacco products as they deem necessary to guarantee the health protection of individuals.

95   It therefore necessary to verify whether the Directive actually contributes to eliminating obstacles to the free movement of goods and to the freedom to provide services, and to removing distortions of competition.

Elimination of obstacles to the free movement of goods and the freedom to provide services

96   It is clear that, as a result of disparities between national laws on the advertising of tobacco products, obstacles to the free movement of goods or the freedom to provide services exist or may well arise.

...

99   However, for numerous types of advertising of tobacco products, the prohibition under Article 3 (1) of the Directive cannot be justified by the need to eliminate obstacles to the free movement of advertising media or the freedom to provide services in the field of advertising. That applies, in particular, to the prohibition of advertising on posters, parasols, ashtrays and other articles used in hotels, restaurants and cafés, and the prohibition of advertising spots in cinemas, prohibitions which in no way help to facilitate trade in the products concerned.

100   Admittedly, a measure adopted on the basis of Articles 100a, 57(2) and 66 of the Treaty may incorporate provisions which do not contribute to the elimination of obstacles to exercise of the fundamental freedoms provided that they are necessary to ensure that certain prohibitions imposed in pursuit of that purpose are not circumvented. It is, however, quite clear that the prohibitions mentioned in the previous paragraph do not fall into that category.

101   Moreover, the Directive does not ensure free movement of products which are in conformity with its provisions.

102   Contrary to the contentions of the Parliament and Council, Article 3(2) of the Directive, relating to diversification products, cannot be construed as meaning that, where the conditions laid down in the Directive are fulfilled, products of that kind in which trade is allowed in one Member State may move freely in the other Member States, including those where such products are prohibited.

103   Under Article 5 of the Directive, Member States retain the right to lay down, in accordance with the Treaty, such stricter requirements concerning the advertising or sponsorship of tobacco products as they deem necessary to guarantee the health protection of individuals.

104   Furthermore, the Directive contains no provision ensuring the free movement of products which conform to its provisions, in contrast to other directives allowing Member States to adopt

stricter measures for the protection of a general interest (see, in particular, Article 7(1) of Council Directive 90/239/EEC of 17 May 1990 on the approximation of the laws, regulations and administrative provisions of the Member States concerning the maximum tar yield of cigarettes (OJ 1990 L 137, p. 36) and Article 8(1) of Council Directive 89/622/EEC of 13 November 1989 on the approximation of the laws, regulations and administrative provisions of the Member States concerning the labelling of tobacco products (OJ 1989 L 359, p. 1)).

105 In those circumstances, it must be held that the Community legislature cannot rely on the need to eliminate obstacles to the free movement of advertising media and the freedom to provide services in order to adopt the Directive on the basis of Articles 100a, 57(2) and 66 of Treaty.

Elimination of distortion of competition

106 In examining the lawfulness of a directive adopted on the basis of Article 100a of the Treaty, the Court is required to verify whether the distortion of competition which the measure purports to eliminate is appreciable (Titanium Dioxide, cited above, paragraph 23).

107 In the absence of such a requirement, the powers of the Community legislature would be practically unlimited. National laws often differ regarding the conditions under which the activities they regulate may be carried on, and this impacts directly or indirectly on the conditions of competition for the undertakings concerned. It follows that to interpret Articles 100a, 57(2) and 66 of the Treaty as meaning that the Community legislature may rely on those articles with a view to eliminating the smallest distortions of competition would be incompatible with the principle, already referred to in paragraph 83 of this judgment, that the powers of the Community are those specifically conferred on it.

108 It is therefore necessary to verify whether the Directive actually contributes to eliminating appreciable distortions of competition.

109 First, as regards advertising agencies and producers of advertising media, undertakings established in Member States which impose fewer restrictions on tobacco advertising are unquestionably at an advantage in terms of economies of scale and increase in profits. The effects of such advantages on competition are, however, remote and indirect and do not constitute distortions which could be described as appreciable. They are not comparable to the distortions of competition caused by differences in production costs, such as those which, in particular, prompted the Community legislature to adopt Council Directive 89/428/EEC of 21 June 1989 on procedures for harmonising the programmes for the reduction and eventual elimination of pollution caused by waste from the titanium dioxide industry (OJ 1989 L 201, p. 56).

110 It is true that the differences between certain regulations on tobacco advertising may give rise to appreciable distortions of competition. As the Commission and the Finnish and United Kingdom Governments have submitted, the fact that sponsorship is prohibited in some Member States and authorised in others gives rise, in particular, to certain sports events being relocated, with considerable repercussions on the conditions

of competition for undertakings associated with such events.

111 However, such distortions, which could be a basis for recourse to Article 100a of the Treaty in order to prohibit certain forms of sponsorship, are not such as to justify the use of that legal basis for an outright prohibition of advertising of the kind imposed by the Directive.

...

114 In those circumstances, it must be held that the Community legislature cannot rely on the need to eliminate distortions of competition, either in the advertising sector or in the tobacco products sector, in order to adopt the Directive on the basis of Articles 100a, 57(2) and 66 of the Treaty.

115 In view of all the foregoing considerations, a measure such as the directive cannot be adopted on the basis of Articles 100a, 57(2) and 66 of the Treaty.

Notes

- This case concerns the European Union. Does that make a difference when it comes to an analysis of powers? The European Union, while it is clearly an organization founded by a treaty, also contains elements of a supranational, perhaps even federal, state. Given its unique nature, could it be more appropriate to apply an interpretive approach more in line with a "living constitution" approach?
- One important reason why international organizations are created is to make international cooperation more efficient. Does this objective necessarily imply a certain degree of independence of the organization? Surely we need international organizations to have the flexibility to craft suitable solutions for complex international problems, and it would be potentially less efficient if member states of an organization were required to vote on each and every action taken by the organization. The founders of an international organization could not have anticipated all of the needs of the organization in advance. But if we take a very strict approach of only looking for expressly provided powers, then doesn't such an approach restrict the independence of the organization? If organizations only have narrow, expressly provided powers, then why do states bother to create organizations?

5.1.2 Implied powers

Until this point, the powers of international organizations were always understood to arise from the express grant in the constitutive treaty, in keeping with the limited coordinating role that organizations played. In Chapter 3 on creation of international organizations and legal personality, we discussed the *Reparations* case. However, that case is also relevant here. In order for the UN to make a claim under international law against a non-state member, not only must it have international legal personality, it also needs the capacity to make claims against states under international law. This question is a question of powers. The following text shows the court's reasoning:

Reparation for Injuries Suffered in the Service of the United Nations
Advisory Opinion
1949 ICJ Reps. 174
International Court of Justice, 11 April 1949

The questions asked of the Court relate to the "capacity to bring an international claim"; accordingly, we must begin by defining what is meant by that capacity, and consider the characteristics of the Organization, so as to determine whether, in general, these characteristics do, or do not, include for the Organization a right to present an international claim.

Competence to bring an international claim is, for those possessing it, the capacity to resort to the customary methods recognized by international law for the establishment, the presentation and the settlement of claims. Among these methods may be mentioned protest, request for an enquiry, negotiation, and request for submission to an arbitral tribunal or to the Court in so far as this may be authorized by the Statute.

This capacity certainly belongs to the State; a State can bring an international claim against another State. Such a claim takes the form of a claim between two political entities, equal in law, similar [p. 178] in form, and both the direct subjects of international law. It is dealt with by means of negotiation, and cannot, in the present state of the law as to international jurisdiction, be submitted to a tribunal, except with the consent of the States concerned.

When the Organization brings a claim against one of its Members, this claim will be presented in the same manner, and regulated by the same procedure. It may, when necessary, be supported by the political means at the disposal of the Organization. In these ways the Organization would find a method for securing the observance of its rights by the Member against which it has a claim.

But, in the international sphere, has the Organization such a nature as involves the capacity to bring an international claim? In order to answer this question, the Court must first enquire whether the Charter has given the Organization such a position that it possesses, in regard to its Members, rights which it is entitled to ask them to respect. In other words, does the Organization possess international personality? This is no doubt a doctrinal expression, which has sometimes given rise to controversy. But it will be used here to mean that if the Organization is recognized as having that personality, it is an entity capable of availing itself of obligations incumbent upon its Members.

To answer this question, which is not settled by the actual terms of the Charter, we must consider what characteristics it was intended thereby to give to the Organization.

The next question is whether the sum of the international rights of the Organization comprises the right to bring the kind of international claim described in the Request for this Opinion. That is a claim against a State to obtain reparation in respect of the [p. 180] damage caused by the injury of an agent of the Organization in the course of the performance of his duties. Whereas a State possesses the totality of international rights and duties recognized by international law, the rights and duties of an entity such as the Organization must depend upon its purposes and functions as specified or implied in its constituent documents and developed in practice. The functions of the Organization are of such a character that they could not be effectively discharged if they involved the concurrent action, on the international plane, of fifty-eight or more Foreign Offices, and the Court concludes that the Members have endowed the Organization with capacity to bring international claims when necessitated by the discharge of its functions.

What is the position as regards the claims mentioned in the request for an opinion? Question I is divided into two points, which must be considered in turn.

* * *

Question I (a) is as follows:

> "In the event of an agent of the United Nations in the performance of his duties suffering injury in circumstances involving the responsibility of a State, has the United Nations, as an Organization, the capacity to bring an international claim against the responsible de jure or de facto government with a view to obtaining the reparation due in respect of the damage caused (a) to the United Nations …?"

The question is concerned solely with the reparation of damage caused to the Organization when one of its agents suffers injury at the same time. It cannot be doubted that the Organization has the capacity to bring an international claim against one of its Members which has caused injury to it by a breach of its international obligations towards it. The damage specified in Question I (a) means exclusively damage caused to the interests of the Organization itself, to its administrative machine, to its property and assets, and to the interests of which it is the guardian. It is clear that the Organization has the capacity to bring a claim for this damage. As the claim is based on the breach of an international obligation on the part of the Member held responsible by the Organization, the Member cannot contend that this obligation is governed by municipal law, and the Organization is justified in giving its claim the character of an international claim.

When the Organization has sustained damage resulting from a breach by a Member of its international obligations, it is impossible to see how it can obtain reparation unless it possesses capacity to bring an international claim. It cannot be supposed that in such an event all the Members of the Organization, save the defendant State, must combine to bring a claim against the defendant for the damage suffered by the Organization.

The Court is not called upon to determine the precise extent of the reparation which the Organization would be entitled to recover. It may, however, be said that the measure of the reparation should depend upon the amount of the damage which the Organization has suffered as the result of the wrongful act or omission of the defendant State and should be calculated in accordance with the rules of international law. Amongst other things, this damage would include the reimbursement of any reasonable compensation which the Organization had to pay to its agent or to persons entitled through him. Again, the death or disablement of one of its agents engaged upon a distant mission might involve very considerable expenditure in replacing him. These are mere illustrations, and the Court cannot pretend to forecast all the kinds of damage which the Organization itself might sustain.

* * *

Question I (b) is as follows:

> "... has the United Nations, as an Organization, the capacity to bring an international claim ... in respect of the damage caused ... (b) to the victim or to persons entitled through him?"

In dealing with the question of law which arises out of Question I (b), it is unnecessary to repeat the considerations which led to an affirmative answer being given to Question I (a). It can now be assumed that the Organization has the capacity to bring a claim on the international plane, to negotiate, to conclude a special agreement and to prosecute a claim before an international tribunal. The only legal question which remains to be considered is whether, in the course of bringing an international claim of this kind, the Organization can recover "the reparation due in respect of the damage caused ... to the victim ...".

The traditional rule that diplomatic protection is exercised by the national State does not involve the giving of a negative answer to Question I (b).

In the first place, this rule applies to claims brought by a State. But here we have the different and new case of a claim that would be brought by the Organization.

In the second place, even in inter-State relations, there are important exceptions to the rule, for there are cases in which protection may be exercised by a State on behalf of persons not having its nationality.

In the third place, the rule rests on two bases. The first is that the defendant State has broken an obligation towards the national State in respect of its nationals. The second is that only the party [p. 182] to whom an international obligation is due can bring a claim in respect of its breach. This is precisely what happens when the Organization, in bringing a claim for damage suffered by its agent, does so by invoking the breach of an obligation towards itself. Thus, the rule of the nationality of claims affords no reason against recognizing that the Organization has the right to bring a claim for the damage referred to in Question I (b). On the contrary, the principle underlying this rule leads to the recognition of this capacity as belonging to the Organization, when the Organization invokes, as the ground of its claim, a breach of an obligation towards itself.

Nor does the analogy of the traditional rule of diplomatic protection of nationals abroad justify in itself an affirmative reply. It is not possible, by a strained use of the concept of allegiance, to assimilate the legal bond which exists, under Article 100 of the Charter, between the Organization on the one hand, and the Secretary-General and the staff on the other, to the bond of nationality existing between a State and its nationals.

The Court is here faced with a new situation. The questions to which it gives rise can only be solved by realizing that the situation is dominated by the provisions of the Charter considered in the light of the principles of international law.

The question lies within the limits already established; that is to say it presupposes that the injury for which the reparation is demanded arises from a breach of an obligation designed to help an agent of the Organization in the performance of his duties. It is not a case in which the wrongful act or omission would merely constitute a breach of the general obligations of a State concerning the position of aliens; claims made under this head would be within the competence of the national State and not, as a general rule, within that of the Organization.

The Charter does not expressly confer upon the Organization the capacity to include, in its claim for reparation, damage caused to the victim or to persons entitled through him. The Court must therefore begin by enquiring whether the provisions of the Charter concerning the functions of the Organization, and the part played by its agents in the performance of those functions, imply for the Organization power to afford its agents the limited protection that would consist in the bringing of a claim on their behalf for reparation for damage suffered in such circumstances. Under international law, the Organization must be deemed to have those powers which, though not expressly provided in the Charter, are conferred upon it by necessary implication as being essential to the performance of its duties. This principle of law was applied by the Permanent Court of International Justice to the International Labour Organization in its Advisory Opinion No. 13 of July 23rd, [p. 183] 1926 (Series B., No. 13, p. 18), and must be applied to the United Nations.

Having regard to its purposes and functions already referred to, the Organization may find it necessary, and has in fact found it necessary, to entrust its agents with important missions to be performed in disturbed parts of the world. Many missions, from their very nature, involve the agents in unusual dangers to which ordinary persons are not exposed. For the same reason, the injuries suffered by its agents in these circumstances will sometimes have occurred in such a manner that their national State would not be justified in bringing a claim for reparation on the ground of diplomatic protection, or, at any rate, would not feel disposed to do so. Both to ensure the efficient and independent performance of these missions and to afford effective support to its agents, the Organization must provide them with adequate protection.

This need of protection for the agents of the Organization, as a condition of the performance of its functions, has already been realized, and the Preamble to the Resolution of December 3rd, 1948 (supra, p. 175), shows that this was the unanimous view of the General Assembly.

For this purpose, the Members of the Organization have entered into certain undertakings, some of which are in the Charter and others in complementary agreements. The content of these undertakings need not be described here; but the Court must stress the importance of the duty to render to the Organization "every assistance" which is accepted by the Members in Article 2, paragraph 5, of the Charter. It must be noted that the effective working of the Organization – the accomplishment of its task, and the independence and effectiveness of the work of its agents – require that these undertakings should be strictly observed. For that purpose, it is necessary that, when an infringement occurs, the Organization should be able to call upon the responsible State to remedy its default, and, in particular, to obtain from the State reparation for the damage that the default may have caused to its agent.

In order that the agent may perform his duties satisfactorily, he must feel that this protection is assured to him by the Organization, and that he may count on it. To ensure the independence of the agent, and, consequently, the independent action of the Organization itself, it is essential that in performing his duties he need not have to rely on any other protection than that of the Organization (save of course for the more direct and immediate protection due from the State in whose territory he may be). In particular, he should not have to rely on the protection of his own State. If he had to rely on that State, his independence might well be compromised, contrary to the principle applied by Article 100 of the Charter. And lastly, it is essential that – [p. 184] whether the agent belongs to a powerful or to a weak State; to one more affected or less affected by the complications of international life; to one in sympathy or not in sympathy with the mission of the agent – he should know that in the performance of his duties he is under the protection of the Organization. This assurance is even more necessary when the agent is stateless.

Upon examination of the character of the functions entrusted to the Organization and of the nature of the missions of its agents, it becomes clear that the capacity of the Organization to exercise a measure of functional protection of its agents arises by necessary intendment out of the Charter.

The obligations entered into by States to enable the agents of the Organization to perform their duties are undertaken not in the interest of the agents, but in that of the Organization. When it claims redress for a breach of these obligations, the Organization is invoking its own right, the right that the obligations due to it should be respected. On this ground, it asks for reparation of the injury suffered, for "it is a principle of international law that the breach of an engagement involves an obligation to make reparation in an adequate form"; as was stated by the Permanent Court in its Judgment No. 8 of July 26th, 1927 (Series A., No. 9, p. 21). In claiming reparation based on the injury suffered by its agent, the Organization does not represent the agent, but is asserting its own right, the right to secure respect for undertakings entered into towards the Organization.

Having regard to the foregoing considerations, and to the undeniable right of the Organization to demand that its Members shall fulfil the obligations entered into by them in the interest of the good working of the Organization, the Court is of the opinion that, in the case of a breach of these obligations, the Organization has the capacity to claim adequate reparation, and that in assessing this reparation it is authorized to include the damage suffered by the victim or by persons entitled through him.

Notes

- The court observes that making a claim is normally a state prerogative. How can an international organization have a power normally reserved to states?
- What interpretive technique is the court using to determine whether the power exists in the constitutive treaty?
- Does the power exist for the organization because the states granted it, but failed to mention it? Why would they fail to mention it? Did they forget? Or assume that it was included? On what basis could they assume that? Why not simply include it expressly? How could such a significant power be forgotten?
- Or does the power exist because the organization needs it, regardless of whether the states granted it specifically or not? Or does the power exist because the powers the organization received require it, but do not contain it?
- Is this power really necessary? How would the organization operate without it? Could it operate without it? What would be the repercussions of not having it? Does the court demand this level of necessity, or does it demand a lower bar for necessity? Does that not contravene the intention of the drafters? What if the power did not exist in the UN to demand reparations: who or what could demand reparations on the international plane? Is that not just as effective?
- Does the fact that the court is an organ of the UN make a difference? Does the court inherently have a view on the value and role of the UN in the international system? Is the UN more than just a coordinating body for the activities of the state of the world? Is the UN unique in that regard? Is that view correct? If we take a different view, does that affect whether this power is correctly understood to exist?
- Is the fact that the UN is an international legal person relevant for the analysis of whether it has a power or not? Why does the court need to answer this question before considering its powers? Does personality impact whether an entity has powers?

In the *Reparations* case above, the court relied on the implied powers theory. Under this theory, when the power is not expressly provided in the constitutive instrument, it might nonetheless be employed because it is necessary to achieve the objectives of the organization. We can consider, for example, whether the UN has the power to enter into a contract to lease an automobile or subscribe to an internet service provider. Neither of these powers are provided in the UN Charter, but surely the organization must have them in order to fulfill all the other tasks listed in the Charter. While simple contracts are more obvious, what is less obvious is whether the organization can take up the claim of one of its employees against another state for injuries.

All states have the power to exercise "diplomatic protection" over their nationals. Despite the use of the term "diplomatic," diplomatic protection is not limited to the protection of diplomats. In fact, it means rather the reverse: protection of nationals by their states through the actions of their diplomats. In exercising this power, states adopt an injury to one of their nationals as if it was an injury to the state itself, although in some sense, injuring a national is an injury suffered by the state. In the *Reparations* case above, the injured UN representative was a national of Sweden, and that state could have taken up his claim. However, for the reasons the court discussed, the UN preferred to adopt his claim, rather than rely on Sweden to do so. The question was whether or not this power, which was normally reserved to the states, could be understood to have been granted to the organization by implication.

The *Reparations* case was not completely without precedent. In several cases before the Permanent Court of International Justice,[3] the court held that provisions in a treaty could have been understood and implied without the need to expressly state them. We can imagine that if we excluded implied provisions, many treaties might cease to function effectively. The drafters could have hardly thought of everything, and the need to articulate everything would be quite burdensome. While it might be somewhat surprising that an organization would enjoy a power by implication, this interpretive technique could be seen as a normal approach to treaty interpretation, searching for the intention of the drafters. After all, if the founders of the organization truly did intend for an organization to have a certain power, then it should be able to effectively exercise it.

The UN employs thousands of international civil servants in hundreds of roles all over the world. From time to time, as with any civil service, employees have genuine legal grievances about their employment. These claims could range from failure to pay salary or pension to serious employment discrimination or mistreatment by superiors. One difficulty, as explored later in Chapter 8, is that the UN is immune from lawsuit, so employees of the UN do not have a clear legal remedy despite having an employment contract. For this reason, the United Nations created an Administrative Tribunal in order to assess these claims. Although it was created by the United Nations General Assembly (UNGA), it operates independently of the UNGA, rendering impartial decisions based on the law of employment contracts that bind the organization:

Effect of Awards of Compensation Made by the United Nations Administrative Tribunal
Advisory Opinion
1954 ICJ Reps. 47
International Court of Justice, 13 July 1954

[p. 56]

...

The Court must now examine the principal contentions which have been put forward, in the written and in the oral statements, by the Governments that take the position that there are grounds which would justify the General Assembly in refusing to give effect to awards of the Administrative Tribunal.

---

3 *See e.g.* Competence of the International Labour Organization to Regulate, Incidentally, the Personal Work of the Employer, Advisory Opinion, 1926 PCIJ (Ser. B) No. 13 (Permanent Court of International Justice, 23 June 1926); Jurisdiction of the European Commission of the Danube Between Galatz and Braila, Advisory Opinion, 1927 PCIJ (Ser. B) No. 14 (Permanent Court of International Justice, 8 December 1927); Interpretation of the Greco-Turkish Agreement of December 1st, 1926 (Final Protocol, Article IV), Advisory Opinion, 1928 PCIJ (Ser. B) No. 16 (Permanent Court of International Justice, 28 August 1928).

The legal power of the General Assembly to establish a tribunal competent to render judgments binding on the United Nations has been challenged. Accordingly, it is necessary to consider whether the General Assembly has been given this power by the Charter.

There is no express provision for the establishment of judicial bodies or organs and no indication to the contrary. However, in its Opinion – Reparation for Injuries suffered in the Service of the United Nations, Advisory Opinion: I.C.J. Reports 1949, p. 182 – the Court said:

> "Under international law, the Organization must be deemed to have those powers which, though not expressly provided in the Charter, are conferred upon it by necessary implication as being essential to the performance of its duties."

The Court must therefore begin by enquiring whether the provisions of the Charter concerning the relations between the staff members and the Organization imply for the Organization the power to establish a judicial tribunal to adjudicate upon disputes arising out of the contracts of service.

[p. 57]
Under the provisions of Chapter XV of the Charter, the Secretariat, which is one of the principal organs of the United Nations, comprises the Secretary-General and the staff. The Secretary-General is appointed by the General Assembly, upon the recommendation of the Security Council, and he is "the chief administrative officer of the Organization". The staff members are "appointed by the Secretary-General under regulations established by the General Assembly". In the words of Article 101 (3) of the Charter, "The paramount consideration in the employment of the staff and in the determination of the conditions of service shall be the necessity of securing the highest standards of efficiency, competence and integrity".

The contracts of service between the Organization and the staff members are contained in letters of appointment. Each appointment is made subject to terms and conditions provided in the Staff Regulations and Staff Rules, together with such amendments as may be made from time to time.

When the Secretariat was organized, a situation arose in which the relations between the staff members and the Organization were governed by a complex code of law. This code consisted of the Staff Regulations established by the General Assembly, defining the fundamental rights and obligations of the staff, and the Staff Rules, made by the Secretary-General in order to implement the Staff Regulations. It was inevitable that there would be disputes between the Organization and staff members as to their rights and duties. The Charter contains no provision which authorizes any of the principal organs of the United Nations to adjudicate upon these disputes, and Article 105 secures for the United Nations jurisdictional immunities in national courts. It would, in the opinion of the Court, hardly be consistent with the expressed aim of the Charter to promote freedom and justice for individuals and with the constant preoccupation of the United Nations Organization to promote this aim that it should afford no judicial or arbitral remedy to its own staff for the settlement of any disputes which may arise between it and them.

In these circumstances, the Court finds that the power to establish a tribunal, to do justice as between the Organization and the staff members, was essential to ensure the efficient working of the Secretariat, and to give effect to the paramount consideration of securing the highest standards of efficiency, competence and integrity. Capacity to do this arises by necessary intendment out of the Charter.

The existence of this capacity leads to the further enquiry as to the agency by which it may be exercised. Here, there can be no room for doubt.

[p. 58]
In Article 7 of the Charter, after naming the six principal organs, it is provided in paragraph (2):

> "Such subsidiary organs as may be found necessary may be established in accordance with the present Charter."

Article 22 provides:

> "The General Assembly may establish such subsidiary organs as it deems necessary for the performance of its functions."

Further, in Article 101, paragraph 1, the General Assembly is given power to regulate staff relations:

> "The Staff shall be appointed by the Secretary-General under regulations established by the General Assembly."

Accordingly, the Court finds that the power to establish a tribunal to do justice between the Organization and the staff members may be exercised by the General Assembly.

...

[p. 76]
Dissenting Opinion by Judge Hackworth

...
[p. 90]
...

The Court is asked to consider only the abstract question of right to decline to make an appropriation to satisfy an award. To this I have answered that there is no justification for concluding that the General Assembly is bound to effectuate a decision which is not juridically sound, and which, because of the absence of juridical plausibility, does not command the respect of the Assembly. A proper administration of justice within the Secretariat must be the guiding criterion. A denial of justice in the sense of the prevailing jurisprudence on the subject should find no place in the United Nations Organization.

If I am correct in my conclusion stated above, that the Assembly has a right to review a decision of the Tribunal, as a corollary to [p. 91] its duty to "consider and approve the budget of the Organization" and to maintain a high standard of efficiency and integrity, it must follow that it may "lawfully" exercise that right with respect to any decision which does not commend itself to respectful and favorable consideration.

The principal grounds upon which the Assembly may lawfully exercise a right to decline to give effect to an award may be simply stated as follows:

(1) That the award is ultra vires;

(2) That the award reveals manifest defects or deficiency in the administration of justice;

(3) That the award does not reflect a faithful application of the Charter, the Statute of the Tribunal, or the Staff Rules and Regulations, to the facts of the case; and

(4) That the amount of the award is obviously either excessive or inadequate.

Notes

- Once more, what interpretative technique and legal analysis does the court employ to reach this decision?
- Is it truly necessary to have this power? Does this application of necessity show a relaxation in the demands of necessity compared to the *Reparations* case?
- Why does Judge Hackworth disagree with the court? Why would the General Assembly not have the power to create a subsidiary organ? Or this particular subsidiary organ?

In the 1960s the UN took on a role that has now become widespread and in many ways one of its most significant: peacekeeping. However peacekeeping does not appear in the UN Charter.

Certain Expenses of the United Nations
(Article 17, Paragraph 2, of the Charter)
Advisory Opinion
1962 ICJ Reps. 151
International Court of Justice, 20 July 1962

... The question on which the Court is asked to give its opinion is whether certain expenditures which were authorized by the General Assembly to cover the costs of the United Nations operations in the Congo (hereinafter referred to as ONUC) and of the operations of the United Nations Emergency Force in the Middle East (hereinafter referred to as UNEF), "constitute 'expenses of the Organization' within the meaning of Article 17, paragraph 2, of the Charter of the United Nations". ...

[p. 157]

*   *   *

Turning to the question which has been posed, the Court observes that it involves an interpretation of Article 17, paragraph 2, of the Charter. On the previous occasions when the Court has had to interpret the Charter of the United Nations, it has followed the principles and rules applicable in general to the interpretation of treaties, since it has recognized that the Charter is a multilateral treaty, albeit a treaty having certain special characteristics. In interpreting Article 4 of the Charter, the Court was led to consider "the structure of the Charter" and "the relations established by it between the General Assembly and the Security Council"; a comparable problem confronts the Court in the instant matter. The Court sustained its interpretation of Article 4 by considering the manner in which the organs concerned "have consistently interpreted the text" in their practice (Competence of the General Assembly for the Admission of a State to the United Nations, I.C.J. Reports 1950, pp. 8–9).

The text of Article 17 is in part as follows:

"1. The General Assembly shall consider and approve the budget of the Organization.

2. The expenses of the Organization shall be borne by the Members as apportioned by the General Assembly."

Although the Court will examine Article 17 in itself and in its relation to the rest of the Charter, it should be noted that at least three separate questions might arise in the interpretation of paragraph 2 of this Article. One question is that of identifying what are "the expenses of the Organization"; a second question might [p. 158] concern apportionment by the General Assembly; while a third question might involve the interpretation of the phrase "shall be borne by the Members". It is the second and third questions which directly involve "the financial obligations of the Members", but it is only the first question which is posed by the request for the advisory opinion. The question put to the Court has to do with a moment logically anterior to apportionment, just as a question of apportionment would be anterior to a question of Members' obligation to pay.

...

[p. 162]

* * *

Passing from the text of Article 17 to its place in the general structure and scheme of the Charter, the Court will consider whether in that broad context one finds any basis for implying a limitation upon the budgetary authority of the General Assembly which in turn might limit the meaning of "expenses" in paragraph 2 of that Article.

The general purposes of Article 17 are the vesting of control over the finances of the Organization, and the levying of apportioned amounts of the expenses of the Organization in order to enable it to carry out the functions of the Organization as a whole acting through its principal organs and such subsidiary organs as may be established under the authority of Article 22 or Article 29.

Article 17 is the only article in the Charter which refers to budgetary authority or to the power to apportion expenses, or otherwise to raise revenue, except for Articles 33 and 35, paragraph 3, of the Statute of the Court which have no bearing on the point here under discussion. Nevertheless, it has been argued before the Court that one type of expenses, namely those resulting from operations for the maintenance of international peace and security, are not "expenses of the Organization" within the meaning of Article 17, paragraph 2, of the Charter, inasmuch as they fall to be dealt with exclusively by the Security Council, and more especially through agreements negotiated in accordance with Article 43 of the Charter.

The argument rests in part upon the view that when the maintenance of international peace and security is involved, it is only the Security Council which is authorized to decide on any action relative thereto. It is argued further that since the General Assembly's power is limited to discussing, considering, studying and recommending, it cannot impose an obligation to pay the expenses which result from the implementation of its recommendations. This [p. 163] argument leads to an examination of the respective functions of the General Assembly and of the Security Council under the Charter, particularly with respect to the maintenance of international peace and security.

Article 24 of the Charter provides:

"In order to ensure prompt and effective action by the United Nations, its Members confer on the Security Council primary responsibility for the maintenance of international peace and security ..."

The responsibility conferred is "primary", not exclusive. This primary responsibility is conferred upon the Security Council, as stated in Article 24, "in order to ensure prompt and effective action". To this end, it is the Security Council which is given a power to impose an explicit obligation of compliance if for example it issues an order or command to an aggressor under Chapter VII. It is only the Security Council which can require enforcement by coercive action against an aggressor.

The Charter makes it abundantly clear, however, that the General Assembly is also to be concerned with international peace and security. Article 14 authorizes the General Assembly to "recommend measures for the peaceful adjustment of any situation, regardless of origin, which it deems likely to impair the general welfare or friendly relations among nations, including situations resulting from a violation of the provisions of the present Charter setting forth the purposes and principles of the United Nations". The word "measures" implies some kind of action, and the only limitation which Article 14 imposes on the General Assembly is the restriction found in Article 12, namely, that the Assembly should not recommend measures while the Security Council is dealing with the same matter unless the Council requests it to do so. Thus while it is the Security Council which, exclusively, may order coercive action, the functions and powers conferred by the Charter on the General Assembly are not confined to discussion, consideration, the initiation of studies and the making of recommendations; they are not merely hortatory. Article 18 deals with "decisions" of the General Assembly "on important questions". These "decisions" do indeed include certain recommendations, but others have dispositive force and effect. Among these latter decisions, Article 18 includes suspension of rights and privileges of membership, expulsion of Members, "and budgetary questions". In connection with the suspension of rights and privileges of membership and expulsion from membership under Articles 5 and 6, it is the Security Council which has only the power to recommend and it is the General Assembly which decides and whose decision determines status; but there is a close collaboration between the two organs. Moreover, these powers of decision of the General Assembly under Articles [p. 164] 5 and 6 are specifically related to preventive or enforcement measures.

By Article 17, paragraph 1, the General Assembly is given the power not only to "consider" the budget of the Organization, but also to "approve" it. The decision to "approve" the budget has a close connection with paragraph 2 of Article 17, since thereunder the General Assembly is also given the power to apportion the expenses among the Members and the exercise of the power of apportionment creates the obligation, specifically stated in Article 17, paragraph 2, of each Member to bear that part of the expenses which is apportioned to it by the General Assembly. When those expenses include expenditures for the maintenance of peace and security, which are not otherwise provided for, it is the General Assembly which has the authority to apportion the latter amounts among the Members. The provisions of the Charter which distribute functions and powers to the Security Council and to the General Assembly give no support to the view that such distribution excludes from the powers of the General Assembly the power to provide for the financing of measures designed to maintain peace and security.

The argument supporting a limitation on the budgetary authority of the General Assembly with respect to the maintenance of international peace and security relies especially on the reference to "action" in the last sentence of Article 11, paragraph 2. This paragraph reads as follows:

> "The General Assembly may discuss any questions relating to the maintenance of international peace and security brought before it by any Member of the United Nations, or by the Security Council, or by a State which is not a Member of the United Nations in accordance with Article 35, paragraph 2, and, except as provided in Article 12, may make recommendations with regard to any such question to the State or States concerned or to the Security Council, or to both. Any such question on which action is necessary shall be referred to the Security Council by the General Assembly either before or after discussion."

The Court considers that the kind of action referred to in Article 11, paragraph 2, is coercive or enforcement action. This paragraph, which applies not merely to general questions relating to peace and security, but also to specific cases brought before the General Assembly by a State under Article 35, in its first sentence empowers the General Assembly, by means of recommendations to States or to the Security Council, or to both, to organize peacekeeping operations, at the request, or with the consent, of the States concerned. This power of the General Assembly is a special power which in no way derogates from its general powers under Article 10 [p. 165] or Article 14, except as limited by the last sentence of Article 11, paragraph 2. This last sentence says that when "action" is necessary the General Assembly shall refer the question to the Security Council. The word "action" must mean such action as is solely within the province of the Security Council. It cannot refer to recommendations which the Security Council might make, as for instance under Article 38, because the General Assembly under Article 11 has a comparable power. The "action" which is solely within the province of the Security Council is that which is indicated by the title of Chapter VII of the Charter, namely "Action with respect to threats to the peace, breaches of the peace, and acts of aggression". If the word "action" in Article 11, paragraph 2, were interpreted to mean that the General Assembly could make recommendations only of a general character affecting peace and security in the abstract, and not in relation to specific cases, the paragraph would not have provided that the General Assembly may make recommendations on questions brought before it by States or by the Security Council. Accordingly, the last sentence of Article 11, paragraph 2, has no application where the necessary action is not enforcement action.

The practice of the Organization throughout its history bears out the foregoing elucidation of the term "action" in the last sentence of Article 11, paragraph 2. Whether the General Assembly proceeds under Article 11 or under Article 14, the implementation of its recommendations for setting up commissions or other bodies involves organizational activity – action – in connection with the maintenance of international peace and security. Such implementation is a normal feature of the functioning of the United Nations. Such committees, commissions or other bodies or individuals, constitute, in some cases, subsidiary organs established under the authority of Article 22 of the Charter. The functions of the General Assembly for which it may establish such subsidiary organs include, for example, investigation, observation and supervision, but the way in which such subsidiary organs are utilized depends on the consent of the State or States concerned.

The Court accordingly finds that the argument which seeks, by reference to Article 11, paragraph 2, to limit the budgetary authority of the General Assembly in respect of the maintenance of international peace and security, is unfounded.

...

[p. 167]

* * *

The Court has considered the general problem of the interpretation of Article 17, paragraph 2, in the light of the general structure of the Charter and of the respective functions assigned by the Charter to the General Assembly and to the Security Council, with a view to determining the meaning of the phrase "the expenses of the Organization". The Court does not find it necessary to go further in giving a more detailed definition of such expenses. The Court will, therefore, proceed to examine the expenditures enumerated in the request for the advisory opinion. In determining whether the actual expenditures authorized constitute "expenses of the Organization within the meaning of Article 17, paragraph 2, of the Charter", the Court agrees that such expenditures must be tested by their relationship to the purposes of the United Nations in the sense that if an expenditure were made for a purpose which is not one of the purposes of the United Nations, it could not be considered an "expense of the Organization".

The purposes of the United Nations are set forth in Article 1 of the Charter. The first two purposes as stated in paragraphs 1 [p. 168] and 2, may be summarily described as pointing to the goal of international peace and security and friendly relations. The third purpose is the achievement of economic, social, cultural and humanitarian goals and respect for human rights. The fourth and last purpose is: "To be a center for harmonizing the actions of nations in the attainment of these common ends."

The primary place ascribed to international peace and security is natural, since the fulfilment of the other purposes will be dependent upon the attainment of that basic condition. These purposes are broad indeed, but neither they nor the powers conferred to effectuate them are unlimited. Save as they have entrusted the Organization with the attainment of these common ends, the Member States retain their freedom of action. But when the Organization takes action which warrants the assertion that it was appropriate for the fulfilment of one of the stated purposes of the United Nations, the presumption is that such action is not ultra vires the Organization.

If it is agreed that the action in question is within the scope of the functions of the Organization but it is alleged that it has been initiated or carried out in a manner not in conformity with the division of functions among the several organs which the Charter prescribes, one moves to the internal plane, to the internal structure of the Organization. If the action was taken by the wrong organ, it was irregular as a matter of that internal structure, but this would not necessarily mean that the expense incurred was not an expense of the Organization. Both national and international law contemplate cases in which the body corporate or politic may be bound, as to third parties, by an ultra vires act of an agent.

In the legal systems of States, there is often some procedure for determining the validity of even a legislative or governmental act, but no analogous procedure is to be found in the structure of the United Nations. Proposals made during the drafting of the Charter to place the ultimate authority to interpret the Charter in the International Court of Justice were not accepted; the opinion which the Court is in course of rendering is an advisory opinion. As anticipated in 1945, therefore, each organ must, in the first place at least, determine its own jurisdiction. If the Security Council, for example, adopts a resolution purportedly for the maintenance of international peace and security and if, in accordance with a mandate or authorization in such resolution, the Secretary-General incurs financial obligations, these amounts must be presumed to constitute "expenses of the Organization".

The Financial Regulations and Rules of the United Nations, adopted by the General Assembly, provide:

"Regulation 4.1: The appropriations voted by the General Assembly shall constitute an authorization to the Secretary-[p. 169]General to incur obligations and make payments for the purposes for which the appropriations were voted and up to the amounts so voted."

Thus, for example, when the General Assembly in resolution 1619 (XV) included a paragraph reading:

"3. Decides to appropriate an amount of $100 million for the operations of the United Nations in the Congo from 1 January to 31 October 1961",

this constituted an authorization to the Secretary-General to incur certain obligations of the United Nations just as clearly as when in resolution 1590 (XV) the General Assembly used this language:

"3. Authorizes the Secretary-General ... to incur commitments in 1961 for the United Nations operations in the Congo up to the total of $24 million ..."

On the previous occasion when the Court was called upon to consider Article 17 of the Charter, the Court found that an award of the Administrative Tribunal of the United Nations created an obligation of the Organization and with relation thereto the Court said that:

"the function of approving the budget does not mean that the General Assembly has an absolute power to approve or disapprove the expenditure proposed to it; for some part of that expenditure arises out of obligations already incurred by the Organization, and to this extent the General Assembly has no alternative but to honour these engagements. (Effects of awards of compensation made by the United Nations Administrative Tribunal, I.C.J. Reports 1954, p. 59.)

Similarly, obligations of the Organization may be incurred by the Secretary-General, acting on the authority of the Security Council or of the General Assembly, and the General Assembly "has no alternative but to honour these engagements".

The obligation is one thing: the way in which the obligation is met – that is from what source the funds are secured – is another. The General Assembly may follow any one of several alternatives: it may apportion the cost of the item according to the ordinary scale of assessment; it may apportion the cost according to some special scale of assessment; it may utilize funds which are voluntarily contributed to the Organization; or it may find some other method or combination of methods for providing the necessary funds. In this context, it is of no legal significance whether, as a matter of book-keeping or accounting, the General Assembly chooses to have the item in question included under one of the standard' established sections of the "regular" budget or whether it is separately listed in some special account or fund. The significant fact is that the item is an expense of the Organization and under [p. 170] Article 17, paragraph 2, the General Assembly therefore has authority to apportion it.

...
[p. 182]

Separate Opinion of Judge Sir Percy Spender

...
[p. 195]
...

Apart from a practice which is of a peaceful, uniform and undisputed character accepted in fact by all current Members, a consideration of which is not germane to the present examination, I accordingly entertain considerable doubt whether practice of an organ of the United Nations has any probative value either as providing evidence of the intentions of the original Member States or otherwise a criterion of interpretation. As presently advised I think it has none.

If however it has probative value, what is the measure of its value before this Court?

An organ of the United Nations, whether it be the General Assembly, the Security Council, the Economic and Social Council, the Secretariat or its subsidiary organs, has in practice to interpret its authority in order that it may effectively function. So, throughout the world, have countless governmental and administrative [p. 196] organs and officials to interpret theirs. The General Assembly may thus in practice, by majority vote, interpret Charter provisions as giving it authority to pursue a certain course of action. It may continue to give the same interpretation to these Charter provisions in similar or different situations as they arise. In so doing action taken by it may be extended to cover circumstances and situations which had never been contemplated by those who framed the Charter. But this would not, for reasons which have already been given, necessarily involve any departure from the terms of the Charter.

On the other hand, the General Assembly may in practice construe its authority beyond that conferred upon it, either expressly or impliedly, by the Charter. It may, for example, interpret its powers to permit it to enter a field prohibited to it under the Charter or in disregard of the procedure prescribed in the Charter. Action taken by the General Assembly (or other organs) may accordingly on occasions be beyond power.

The Charter establishes an Organization. The Organization must function through its constituted organs. The functions and authorities of those organs are set out in the Charter. However the Charter is otherwise described the essential fact is that it is a multilateral treaty. It cannot be altered at the will of the majority of the Member States, no matter how often that will is expressed or asserted against a protesting minority and no matter how large be the majority of Member States which assert its will in this manner or how small the minority.

It is no answer to say that the protesting minority has the choice of remaining in or withdrawing from the Organization and that if it chooses to remain or because it pays its contributions according to apportionment under Article 17 (2) the Members in the minority "acquiesce" in the practice or must be deemed to have done so. They are bound to pay these contributions and the minority has a right to remain in the Organization and at the same time to assert what it claims to be any infringement of its rights under the Charter or any illegal use of power by any organ of the United Nations.

In practice, if the General Assembly (or any organ) exceeds its authority there is little that the protesting minority may do except to protest and reserve its rights whatever they may be. If, however, the authority purported to be exercised against the objection of any Member State is beyond power it remains so.

So, if the General Assembly were to "intervene in matters which are essentially within the domestic jurisdiction of any State" within the meaning of Article 2 (7) of the Charter, whatever be the meaning to be given to these words, that intervention would be the [p. 197] entering into a field prohibited to it under the Charter and be beyond the authority of the General Assembly. This would continue to be so, no matter how frequently and consistently the General Assembly had construed its authority to permit it to make intervention in matters essentially within the domestic jurisdiction of any States. The majority has no power to extend, alter or disregard the Charter.

Each organ of the United Nations, of course, has an inherent right to interpret the Charter in relation to its authority and functions. But the rule that they may do so is not in any case applicable without qualification. Their interpretation of their respective authorities under the Charter may conceivably conflict one with the other. They may agree. They may, after following a certain interpretation for many years, change it. In any case, their right to interpret the Charter gives them no power to alter it.

The question of constitutionality of action taken by the General Assembly or the Security Council will rarely call for consideration except within the United Nations itself, where a majority rule prevails. In practice this may enable action to be taken which is beyond power.

When, however, the Court is called upon to pronounce upon a question whether certain authority exercised by an organ of the Organization is within the power of that organ, only legal considerations may be invoked and de facto extension of the Charter must be disregarded.

* * *

Once a request for an Advisory Opinion is made to this Court and it decides to respond to that request, the question on which the Opinion has been sought passes, as is claimed by the Republic of France in its written statement in this case, on to the legal plane and takes on a new character, in the determination of which legal considerations and legal considerations only may be invoked.

In the present case, it is sufficient to say that I am unable to regard any usage or practice followed by any organ of the United Nations which has been determined by a majority therein against the will of a minority as having any legal relevance or probative value.

...

Notes

- How does the court regard peacekeeping missions? Are peacekeeping operations among the expressly provided powers of the UN in the UN Charter? If not, how can the UN have those powers by implication? Where does the court find the purposes of the UN and its organs? Are these correct? Are purposes a sufficient basis for finding implied powers? Compare purposes to the needs that formed the basis for the implied powers in the *Reparations* case. Are those needs more or less significant? And more or less needed? For argument's sake, could the UN fulfill its objectives without peacekeepers?
- This discussion is partly about the powers of the UN, but also the powers of the UN organs specifically. Is the consideration of organ powers different from the implied powers approach in *Reparations* above? If so, is there an additional concern about using implied powers theory to determine the various powers of organs when exercising implied powers of the organization? If an organ exercised powers beyond its capacity, could those powers still be powers of the organization, and thus not *ultra vires* the organization?
- Greatly simplified, the complaint was that some states did not want to pay for peacekeeping operations. In the end, do they have to pay? Why? Surely states are the masters of their organization, so how can a state be forced by an international organization to pay for operations against its will?
- The court also cites the practice of the organization. Is this the practice of the organization as such, or of the states within the organization? How is practice relevant for understanding the UN Charter and the powers granted to the organization and its organs?

Having read the *Certain Expenses* case above that was heard by the International Court of Justice, now consider *Case 22/70, Commission v Council [ERTA]* before the EU Court of Justice. Keep in mind that the EU is an international organization just like the UN, but then it is also quite different, and even unique among organizations. Sometimes it is even called a "supranational" organization. How is this special status reflected in the way the court applies the implied powers theory?

Case C-22/70, Commission of the European Communities v Council of the European Communities
[*In re* European Road Transport Agreement (ERTA or AETR)]
Judgment
Court of Justice of the European Communities [Union], 31 March 1971[4]

1 – The initial question

6 The Commission takes the view that Article 75 of the Treaty, which conferred on the Community powers defined in wide terms with a view to implementing the common transport policy, must apply to external relations just as much as to domestic measures in the sphere envisaged.

7 It believes that the full effect of this provision would be jeopardized if the powers which it confers, particularly that of laying down "any appropriate provisions", within the meaning of subparagraph (1) (c) of the article cited, did not extend to the conclusion of agreements with third countries.

8 Even if, it is argued, this power did not originally embrace the whole sphere of transport, it would tend to become general and exclusive as and where the common policy in this field came to be implemented.

9 The Council, on the other hand, contends that since the Community only has such powers as have been conferred on it, authority to enter into agreements with third countries cannot be assumed in the absence of an express provision in the Treaty.

10 More particularly, Article 75 relates only to measures internal to the Community, and cannot be interpreted as authorizing the conclusion of international agreements.

11 Even if it were otherwise, such authority could not be general and exclusive, but at the most concurrent with that of the Member States.

12 In the absence of specific provisions of the Treaty relating to the negotiation and conclusion of international agreements in the sphere of transport policy – a category into which, essentially, the AETR [European Agreement Concerning the Work of Crews of Vehicles Engaged in International Road Transport] falls – one must turn to the general system of Community law in the sphere of relations with third countries.

13 Article 210 provides that "The Community shall have legal personality".

14 This provision, placed at the head of Part Six of the Treaty, devoted to "General and Final Provisions", means that in its external relations the Community enjoys the capacity to establish contractual links with third countries over the whole field of objectives defined in

---

4 https://eur-lex.europa.eu, © European Union 1998–2020.

Part One of the Treaty, which Part Six supplements.

15 To determine in a particular case the Community's authority to enter into international agreements, regard must be had to the whole scheme of the Treaty no less than to its substantive provisions.

16 Such authority arises not only from an express conferment by the Treaty – as is the case with Articles 113 and 114 for tariff and trade agreements and with Article 238 for association agreements – but may equally flow from other provisions of the Treaty and from measures adopted, within the framework of those provisions, by the Community institutions.

17 In particular, each time the Community, with a view to implementing a common policy envisaged by the Treaty, adopts provisions laying down common rules, whatever form these may take, the Member States no longer have the right, acting individually or even collectively, to undertake obligations with third countries which affect those rules.

18 As and when such common rules come into being, the Community alone is in a position to assume and carry out contractual obligations towards third countries affecting the whole sphere of application of the Community legal system.

19 With regard to the implementation of the provisions of the Treaty the system of internal Community measures may not therefore be separated from that of external relations.

20 Under Article 3 (e), the adoption of a common policy in the sphere of transport is specially mentioned amongst the objectives of the Community.

21 Under Article 5, the Member States are required on the one hand to take all appropriate measures to ensure fulfilment of the obligations arising out of the Treaty or resulting from action taken by the institutions and, on the other, hand, to abstain from any measure which might jeopardize the attainment of the objectives of the Treaty.

22 If these two provisions are read in conjunction, it follows that to the extent to which Community rules are promulgated for the attainment of the objectives of the Treaty, the Member States cannot, outside the framework of the Community institutions, assume obligations which might affect those rules or alter their scope.

23 According to Article 74, the objectives of the Treaty in matters of transport are to be pursued within the framework of a common policy.

24 With this in view, Article 75 (1) directs the Council to lay down common rules and, in addition, "any other appropriate provisions".

25 By the terms of subparagraph (a) of the same provision, those common rules are applicable "to international transport to or from the territory of a Member State or passing across the territory of one or more Member States".

26 This provision is equally concerned with transport from or to third countries, as regards that part of the journey which takes place on Community territory.

27 It thus assumes that the powers of the Community extend to relationships arising from international law, and hence involve the need in the sphere in question for agreements with the third countries concerned.

28   Although it is true that Articles 74 and 75 do not expressly confer on the Community authority to enter into international agreements, nevertheless the bringing into force, on 25 March 1969, of Regulation No 543/69 of the Council on the harmonization of certain social legislation relating to road transport (OJ L 77, p. 49) necessarily vested in the Community power to enter into any agreements with third countries relating to the subject-matter governed by that regulation.

29   This grant of power is moreover expressly recognized by Article 3 of the said regulation which prescribes that: "The Community shall enter into any negotiations with third countries which may prove necessary for the purpose of implementing this regulation".

30   Since the subject-matter of the AETR falls within the scope of Regulation No 543/69, the Community has been empowered to negotiate and conclude the agreement in question since the entry into force of the said regulation.

31   These Community powers exclude the possibility of concurrent powers on the part of Member States, since any steps taken outside the framework of the Community institutions would be incompatible with the unity of the Common Market and the uniform application of Community law.

Notes

- What power is the court questioning? Is it the power to adopt internal policies, or a common policy among the Member States, or an external treaty?
- Why is the fact that the European Community (now European Union) has legal personality relevant to whether it enjoys a certain power? Compare this question in the case of the EU to the similar question in the case of the UN in the *Reparations* case. What power was the UN attempting to exercise? How does that power compare to the power in this case?
- How does the court propose to proceed when the treaty is silent on whether a particular power has been granted to the organization or not? What is the "general system of Community law"? What is its source? Can it create a power that was not delegated in the constitutive instrument?
- In prior cases, the court looked to the necessity of the power given the duties or functions of the organization. Here the court looks at the "whole scheme of the Treaty." Which "Treaty" is the court referring to? Is this correct? The court also observes that transport is an "objective" of the EU. Does this satisfy the necessity for implied powers? What is the difference among a power being necessary for a duty, being helpful for a function, and being useful for an objective?
- It also considers the other measures adopted by the Community (Union), and holds that powers "may equally flow ... from measures adopted, within the framework of those provisions, by the Community institutions." Is this correct? Does this mean that the EU can give itself powers? Is the role of adopting a "common policy" making a difference?

The common thread from all of these cases on implied powers is the degree of necessity for the power. However, one area of inconsistency appears to be the way that this necessity is understood from case to case. In the *Reparations* case, the ICJ found any power could be implied if it was central to the performance of the organization's duties. In the *Effect of Awards* case, the court seemed to apply a somewhat less demanding test, asking only if the Secretary-General, not the UN as a whole, would find the power useful for the organ's purposes. In *Case 22/70 Commission v Council [ERTA]*, the court may have been even less demanding, looking to the European Union objectives of community solidarity.

Just as implied powers theory seems to empower organizations, it is still based on the notion that the organization only enjoys those powers that were granted to it by the states. Implied powers theory is only trying to discover powers that the states granted the organization but did not include expressly in the constitutive instrument because it was thought so obvious, so trivial, or so clearly necessary for the discharge of the other tasks. While there is a degree of flexibility in assessing necessity, there are limitations to the implied powers theory.

In the last case above, *Case 22/70 Commission v Council [ERTA]*, the court was determining whether the EU had the power to conclude an international agreement. It was not an agreement with or among the EU Member States only, but one among a collection of EU and non-EU states in Europe. Just because the court found a power to exist for a specific purpose does not mean that the EU is now competent generally to enter into treaties on any subject:

Opinion 2/94 [*In re* competence of the Community to accede to the European Convention for the Protection of Human Rights and Fundamental Freedoms (ECHR)] Court of Justice of the European Communities [Union], 28 March 1996[5]

23 It follows from Article 3 b of the Treaty, which states that the Community is to act within the limits of the powers conferred upon it by the Treaty and of the objectives assigned to it therein, that it has only those powers which have been conferred upon it.

24 That principle of conferred powers must be respected in both the internal action and the international action of the Community.

25 The Community acts ordinarily on the basis of specific powers which, as the Court has held, are not necessarily the express consequence of specific provisions of the Treaty but may also be implied from them.

26 Thus, in the field of international relations, at issue in this request for an Opinion, it is settled case-law that the competence of the Community to enter into international commitments may not only flow from express provisions of the Treaty but also be implied from those provisions. The Court has held, in particular, that, whenever Community

---

5 https://eur-lex.europa.eu, © European Union 1998–2020.

law has created for the institutions of the Community powers within its internal system for the purpose of attaining a specific objective, the Community is empowered to enter into the international commitments necessary for attainment of that objective even in the absence of an express provision to that effect (see Opinion 2/91 of 19 March 1993 [1993] ECR I-1061, paragraph 7).

27 No Treaty provision confers on the Community institutions any general power to enact rules on human rights or to conclude international conventions in this field.

28 In the absence of express or implied powers for this purpose, it is necessary to consider whether Article 235 of the Treaty may constitute a legal basis for accession.

29 Article 235 is designed to fill the gap where no specific provisions of the Treaty confer on the Community institutions express or implied powers to act, if such powers appear none the less to be necessary to enable the Community to carry out its functions with a view to attaining one of the objectives laid down by the Treaty.

30 That provision, being an integral part of an institutional system based on the principle of conferred powers, cannot serve as a basis for widening the scope of Community powers beyond the general framework created by the provisions of the Treaty as a whole and, in particular, by those that define the tasks and the activities of the Community. On any view, Article 235 cannot be used as a basis for the adoption of provisions whose effect would, in substance, be to amend the Treaty without following the procedure which it provides for that purpose.

31 It is in the light of those considerations that the question whether accession by the Community to the Convention may be based on Article 235 must be examined.

32 It should first be noted that the importance of respect for human rights has been emphasized in various declarations of the Member States and of the Community institutions (cited in point III.5 of the first part of this Opinion). Reference is also made to respect for human rights in the preamble to the Single European Act and in the preamble to, and in Article F(2), the fifth indent of Article J. 1(2) and Article K.2(1) of, the Treaty on European Union. Article F provides that the Union is to respect fundamental rights, as guaranteed, in particular, by the Convention. Article 130u(2) of the EU Treaty provides that Community policy in the area of development cooperation is to contribute to the objective of respecting human rights and fundamental freedoms.

33 Furthermore, it is well settled that fundamental rights form an integral part of the general principles of law whose observance the Court ensures. For that purpose, the Court draws inspiration from the constitutional traditions common to the Member States and from the guidelines supplied by international treaties for the protection of human rights on which the Member States have collaborated or of which they are signatories. In that regard, the Court has stated that the Convention has special significance (see, in particular, the judgment in

Case C-260/89 *ERT* [1991] ECR I-2925, paragraph 41).

34 Respect for human rights is therefore a condition of the lawfulness of Community acts. Accession to the Convention would, however, entail a substantial change in the present Community system for the protection of human rights in that it would entail the entry of the Community into a distinct international institutional system as well as integration of all the provisions of the Convention into the Community legal order.

35 Such a modification of the system for the protection of human rights in the Community, with equally fundamental institutional implications for the Community and for the Member States, would be of constitutional significance and would therefore be such as to go beyond the scope of Article 235. It could be brought about only by way of Treaty amendment.

36 It must therefore be held that, as Community law now stands, the Community has no competence to accede to the Convention.

Notes

- Why does the EU not have this competence? It may be helpful to note that the EU is charged with protecting fundamental rights as a part of its mission. Why is this mission not broad enough for the EU to have the competence to enter into a treaty protecting those rights?
- Does this opinion perhaps represent a trend to move away from a liberal interpretation of necessity underpinning implied powers?

After this opinion, the Treaty on European Union was amended by the Lisbon Treaty to permit the EU to adhere to the European Convention on Human Rights. In fact, the now-amended article 6(2) states that the EU "shall accede to the European Convention for the Protection of Human Rights and Fundamental Freedoms."[6] However, the same provision continues to state that "Such accession shall not affect the Union's competences as defined in the Treaties." How is this possible?

Notes

- As noted above, the EU is meant to protect human rights. The current version of the treaty on European Union, article 6(1) also states that the EU "recognises the rights, freedoms and principles set out in the Charter of Fundamental Rights of the European Union of 7 December 2000, as adapted at Strasbourg, on 12 December 2007, which shall have the same legal value as the Treaties."[7] The

---

6 *See* Consolidated Version of the Treaty on European Union, Official Journal of the European Union C 115/13 (9 May 2008).
7 *Ibid.*

- Charter is yet another treaty on human rights, but this time the EU is held to the protections. How is this possible? And why the Charter, but not the ECHR? Once again, the same provision in the Treaty on European Union states: "The provisions of the Charter shall not extend in any way the competences of the Union as defined in the Treaties." Is this argument tenable?
- Furthermore, the same article 6, but paragraph 3, even includes "Fundamental rights, as guaranteed by the European Convention for the Protection of Human Rights and Fundamental Freedoms and as they result from the constitutional traditions common to the Member States, shall constitute general principles of the Union's law."
- All of the Member States of the EU are parties to the ECHR. It is a condition to their being members of the other European organization, the Council of Europe. If all of the Member States of the EU are already parties to the ECHR, why is it that the EU cannot adhere itself? What would change?
- Lastly, the Treaty on European Union, article 5(1) states that "The limits of Union competences are governed by the principle of conferral. The use of Union competences is governed by the principles of subsidiarity and proportionality," and adds in paragraph 2 that:

> Under the principle of conferral, the Union shall act only within the limits of the competences conferred upon it by the Member States in the Treaties to attain the objectives set out therein. Competences not conferred upon the Union in the Treaties remain with the Member States.[8]

This statement is not too surprising given the discussion on implied powers so far, however, note that the EU has an additional requirement in its powers analysis: subsidiarity. In paragraph 3, the Treaty on European Union states:

> Under the principle of subsidiarity, in areas which do not fall within its exclusive competence, the Union shall act only if and in so far as the objectives of the proposed action cannot be sufficiently achieved by the Member States, either at central level or at regional and local level, but can rather, by reason of the scale or effects of the proposed action, be better achieved at Union level.[9]

What does this add? Is the fact that the limitations of conferred powers is itself expressly observed in the constitutive instrument, a very rare addition, make any difference? Otherwise why include it?

---

8 *Ibid.*
9 *Ibid.*

Returning to the *Reparations* case, Judge Hackworth made some observations in his dissenting opinion on the implied powers theory, and some inherent limitations on it.

Reparation for Injuries Suffered in the Service of the United Nations
Advisory Opinion
1949 ICJ Reps. 174
International Court of Justice, 11 April 1949

[p. 196]

Dissenting Opinion by Judge Hackworth

I concur, but for different reasons, in the conclusion of the Court that the United Nations Organization has capacity to bring an international claim against the responsible government, with a view to obtaining reparation due in respect of damage caused by that government to the Organization. But I regret that I am unable to concur in that part of the Opinion having to do with the capacity of the Organization to sponsor an international claim in behalf of one of its agents.

The authority of the Organization to make a claim for damage caused to it by the wrongful act of a State can be very simply stated, as follows:

(1) Article 104 of the Charter gives the Organization "such legal capacity as may be necessary for the exercise of its functions and the fulfilment of its purposes".

(2) Paragraphs 1 and 2 of Article 105 specify that the Organization "shall enjoy in the territory of each of its Members such privileges and immunities as are necessary for the fulfilment of its purposes", and that officials of the Organization shall "similarly enjoy such privileges and immunities as are necessary for the independent exercise of their functions in connexion with the Organization".

(3) The Convention on Privileges and Immunities, adopted by the General Assembly on February 13th, 1946, recognizes that the United Nations shall possess juridical personality, with capacity (a) to contract; (b) to acquire and dispose of immovable and movable property; and (c) to institute legal proceedings; also that the Organization and its officials shall enjoy certain specified privileges and immunities.

The Convention has not been approved by all the Members of the Organization, but we may assume, for present purposes, that it is fairly representative of the views of most of them.

(4) It stands to reason that, if the Organization is to make contracts, to acquire and dispose of property, to institute legal proceedings, and to claim the benefits of the privileges and immunities to which it is entitled, it must be able to carry on negotiations with governments as well as with private parties. It must therefore be able to assert claims in its own behalf. No other conclusion consistent with the specified powers and with the inherent right of self-preservation could possibly be drawn. The Organization must have and does have ample authority to [p. 197] take needful steps for its protection against wrongful acts for which Member States are responsible. Any

damage suffered by the Organization by reason of wrongful acts committed against an agent, while in the performance of his duties, would likewise be within its competence.

This is a proper application of the doctrine of implied powers.

(5) I, therefore, find no difficulty in giving an affirmative answer to Question I (a) of the Assembly's request.

Such a claim by the United Nations would include any element of damage susceptible of proof under customary rules relating to damages in international claims. It would include any reasonable payments made by the Organization to the victim of the wrongful act or to those entitled through him, provided that such payments were made pursuant to contractual undertakings of the Organization, or on the basis of an established policy in such cases.

(6) Thus it would appear that under I (a) the Organization has ample and unquestionable authority to safeguard itself against derelictions by States, and to vindicate the dignity, honour and authority of the Organization. To this extent I am in agreement with the conclusions of the majority of the Court.

* * *

As to Question I (b), having to do with a claim for reparation due in respect of damage caused to the victim of a wrongful act or to persons entitled through him, as distinguished from a claim on behalf of the Organization itself, a different situation is presented.

The Court is asked to state its opinion as to whether the Organization has capacity to espouse such a claim. In giving our answer, we must look to the traditional international practice of nations with respect to private claims, and to the express treaty stipulations as regards the Organization.

As to international practice, we find at once that heretofore only States have been regarded as competent to advance such international claims.

As to the Organization, we find nothing to suggest that it too has capacity in this field. Certainly there is no specific provision in the Charter, nor is there provision in any other agreement of which I am aware, conferring upon the Organization authority to [p. 198] assume the role of a State, and to represent its agents in the espousal of diplomatic claims on their behalf. I am equally convinced that there is no implied power to be drawn upon for this purpose.

It is stated in the majority opinion that the Charter does not expressly provide that the Organization should have capacity to include, in "its claim for reparation", damage caused to the victim or to persons entitled through him, but the conclusion is reached that such power is conferred by necessary implication. This appears to be based on the assumption that, to ensure the efficient and independent performance of missions entrusted to agents of the Organization, and to afford them moral support, the exercise of this power is necessary.

The conclusion that power in the Organization to sponsor private claims is conferred by "necessary implication" is not believed to be warranted under rules laid down by tribunals for filling lacunae in specific grants of power.

There can be no gainsaying the fact that the Organization is one of delegated and enumerated powers. It is to be presumed that such powers as the Member States desired to confer upon it are stated either in the Charter or in complementary agreements concluded by them. Powers not expressed cannot freely be implied. Implied powers flow from a grant of expressed powers, and are limited to those that are "necessary" to the exercise of powers expressly granted. No necessity for the exercise of the power here in question has been shown to exist. There is no impelling reason, if any at all, why the Organization should become the sponsor of claims on behalf of its employees, even though limited to those arising while the employee is in line of duty. These employees are still nationals of their respective countries, and the customary methods of handling such claims are still available in full vigour. The prestige and efficiency of the Organization will be safeguarded by an exercise of its undoubted right under point I (a) supra. Even here it is necessary to imply power, but, as stated above, the necessity is self-evident. The exercise of an additional extraordinary power in the field of private claims has not been shown to be necessary to the efficient performance of duty by either the Organization or its agents.

But we are presented with an analogy between the relationship of a State to its nationals and the relationship of the Organization [p. 199] to its employees; also an analogy between functions of a State in the protection of its nationals and functions of the Organization in the protection of its employees.

The results of this liberality of judicial construction transcend, by far, anything to be found in the Charter of the United Nations, as well as any known purpose entertained by the drafters of the Charter.

These supposed analogies, even assuming that they may have some semblance of reality, which I do not admit, cannot avail to give jurisdiction, where jurisdiction is otherwise lacking. Capacity of the Organization to act in the field here in question must rest upon a more solid foundation.

...

Article 100 of the Charter, which, it should be remarked, relates only to the Secretary-General and the staff, cannot be drawn upon to claim for the Organization by indirection an authority which obviously cannot be claimed under any direct authorization. [p. 201] The most charitable, and indeed the most realistic construction to be given the article is that it is designed to place service with the United Nations on a high plane of loyalty and fidelity and to require Member States to respect this status and not to seek to influence the Secretary-General or members of the staff in the discharge of their duties.

This bond between the Organization and its employees, which is an entirely proper and natural one, does not have and cannot have the effect of expatriating the employee or of substituting allegiance to the Organization for allegiance to his State. Neither the State nor the employee can be said to have contemplated such a situation. There is nothing inconsistent between continued allegiance to the national State and complete fidelity to the Organization. The State may still protect its national under international law. One can even visualize a situation where that protection might be directed against acts by the Organization itself.

...

[p. 203]

It is generally admitted that the State of the employee's nationality has a right to sponsor a claim, such as is here in question, and the General Assembly obviously envisaged the possibility of complications in this respect, as is shown by its second question, wherein it inquires how, in the event of an affirmative reply on point I (b), action by the United Nations is "to be reconciled with [p. 204] such rights as may be possessed by the State of which the victim is a national".

The answer which I have suggested for point I (a) would probably give the Organization all that it needs from a practical point of view.

If it desires to go further and to espouse claims on behalf of employees, the conventional method is open. If the States should agree to allow the Organization to espouse claims on behalf of their nationals who are in the service of the Organization, no one could question its authority to do so. The respondent State would be relieved of the possibility of demands from two sources, the employee or his dependants would know to whom to look for assistance, and the whole procedure would be free from uncertainty and irregularity.

Notes

- What is Hackworth's critique? Does he accept implied powers doctrine? How would he limit it further?
- How does Hackworth propose for the UN to make a claim for reparations for the injury of one of its agents? Is it not necessary, and thus an implied power, for the UN to have an independent means of making such a claim?

The more unusual cases that reach the ICJ are UN staff employment disputes. These are usually resolved at a lower level, but can be appealed to the highest UN court. In the *Judgment No. 273* case (*Mortished* case), a UN staff member did not receive the repatriation grant he expected. The UN General Assembly had in the meantime adopted Resolution 34/165, and Staff Regulations and Rules had been adopted pursuant to the resolution that deprived him of his expected compensation. The UN Administrative Tribunal had rendered its decision, and the court was asked to review the refusal of his claim. The difficulty for the ICJ was that the request fell outside its competence. The application would, in effect, ask it:[10]

> to retry the case with a view to deciding whether to substitute the Court's view of the merits of the case for that of the Tribunal. This, for the reasons explained above, is not the business of this Court. It is not the business of

---

10 Application for Review of Judgment No. 273, Advisory Opinion, 1982 ICJ Reps. 325 (International Court of Justice, 20 July 1982).

this Court to decide whether the Tribunal's Judgement involves an error in its interpretation of the relevant instruments, unless it involves an error on a question of law relating to the provisions of the United Nations Charter.

The ICJ concluded that:[11]

> Certainly the Tribunal must accept and apply the decisions of the General Assembly ... Certainly there can be no question of the Tribunal possessing any "powers of judicial review or appeal in respect of the decisions" taken by the General Assembly, powers which the Court itself does not possess (I.C.J. Reports 1971, p. 45, para. 89). Nor did the Tribunal suppose that it had any such competence. ... The question is not whether the Tribunal was right or wrong in the way it performed this task in the case before it; the question – indeed, the only matter on which the Court can pass – is whether the Tribunal erred on a question of law relating to the provisions of the Charter of the United Nations. This it clearly did not do when it attempted only to apply to Mr. Mortished's case what it found to be the relevant Staff Regulations and Rules made under the authority of the General Assembly.

Did it apply its analysis of powers in the usual way? Why did the ICJ not adopt an implied powers analysis in this matter?

5.1.3 Inherent powers

The final category of methodology for determining powers is far more controversial. Perhaps there are powers that an organization holds inherently? These would not be powers the organization received by express grant or implication, but those it holds as a result of its nature and being. This theory overturns the assumption we have held from the outset of this chapter, that organizations can only enjoy powers they are given. Even if we accept this view, we are then faced with the problem of enumerating which powers could be inherent. Some powers seem to be good candidates for this approach, such as the treaty-making power. But other powers, more unique to each

---

11 *Ibid.*, para. 76.

organization, would be more difficult to identify. Consider the following case from the International Criminal Tribunal for the former Yugoslavia (ICTY):

Prosecutor v Tadić, Case No. IT-94-1-A-R77,
Judgment on Allegations of Contempt against prior counsel, Milan Vujin
International Criminal Tribunal for the Former Yugoslavia,
Appeals Chamber, 31 January 2000[12]

12. Contempt of the Tribunal is dealt with in Rule 77 of the Tribunal's Rules of Procedure and Evidence. That Rule identifies a number of specific situations which are stated to constitute contempt of the Tribunal, but Rule 77(E) provides:

> Nothing in this Rule affects the inherent power of the Tribunal to hold in contempt those who knowingly and wilfully interfere with its administration of justice.

It has not been submitted in this case that, if established, the allegations against the Respondent in the present case would not constitute contempt of the Tribunal in that general sense. There was, however, argument as to whether the various changes made to Rule 77 over the relevant period qualified such an inherent power and increased the extent of the conduct which amounts to contempt, to the prejudice of the Respondent's rights. [footnote 10 – Rule 6(D) of the Rules of Procedure and Evidence provides that an amendment made to the Rules shall not operate to prejudice the rights of the accused in any pending case.] Reference will be made to that argument later, as it is necessary, first, to consider generally the Tribunal's jurisdiction to deal with contempt.

13. There is no mention in the Tribunal's Statute of its power to deal with contempt. The Tribunal does, however, possess an inherent jurisdiction, deriving from its judicial function, to ensure that its exercise of the jurisdiction which is expressly given to it by that Statute is not frustrated and that its basic judicial functions are safeguarded. [footnote 11 – *Nuclear Tests Case*, ICJ Reports 1974, pp 259–260, par 23, followed by the Appeals Chamber in *Prosecutor v Blaškić*, Case IT-95-14-AR108*bis*, Judgment on the Request of the Republic of Croatia for Review of the Decision of Trial Chamber 11 of 18 July 1997, 29Oct 1997 ("*Blaškić Subpoena Decision*"), footnote 27 at par 25. See also *Northern Cameroons Case*, ICJ Reports 1963, p 29.] As an international criminal court, the Tribunal must therefore possess the inherent power to deal with conduct which interferes with its administration of justice. The content of that inherent power may be discerned by reference to the usual sources of international law.

14. There is no specific customary international law directly applicable to this issue. There is an international analogue available, by way of conventional international law, in the Charter of the International Military Tribunal (an annexure to the 1945 London Agreement) [footnote 12 – Agreement by the Government of the United States of

---

[12] From the United Nations International Residual Mechanism for Criminal Tribunals, archives of the International Criminal Tribunal for the former Yugoslavia.

America, the Provisional Government of the French Republic, the Government of the United Kingdom of Great Britain and Northern Ireland and the Government of the Union of Soviet Socialist Republics for the Prosecution and Punishment of the Major War Criminals of the European Axis, 8 August 1945.] which gave to that tribunal the power to deal summarily with "any contumacy" by "imposing appropriate punishment, including exclusion of any Defendant or his Counsel from some or all further proceedings, but without prejudice to the determination of the charges". [footnote 13 – Article 18(c).] Although no contempt matter arose before the International Military Tribunal itself, three contempt matters were dealt with by United States Military Tribunals sitting in Nürnberg in accordance with the Allied Control Council Law No 10 (20 December 1945), whereby war crimes trials were heard by the four Allied Powers in their respective zones of occupation in Germany. That Law incorporated the Charter of the International Military Tribunal. The US Military Tribunals interpreted their powers as including the power to punish contempt of court. [footnote 14 – All references are taken from "Trials of War Criminals Before the Nuernberg Military Tribunals under Control Council Law No 10": *US v Karl Brandt*, 27 June 1947, at 968–970 (where a prosecution witness assaulted one of the accused in court); *US v Joseph Altstoetter*, 17 July 1947, at 974–975, 978, 992 (where defence counsel and a private individual attempted improperly to influence an expert medical witness by making false representations, and mutilated an expert report in an attempt to influence the signatories of the report to join in altering it); and *US v Alfried Krupp von Bohlen und Halbach*, 21 January 1948, at 1003, 1005–1006, 1088, 1011 (where defence counsel staged a walk out, and then failed to appear, in protest of a ruling against their clients, but which conduct was ultimately dealt with on a disciplinary basis).]

15. It is otherwise of assistance to look to the general principles of law common to the major legal systems of the world, as developed and refined (where applicable) in international jurisprudence. [footnote 15 – cf *Prosecutor v Blaškić*, Case IT-95-14-PT, Decision on the Objection of the Republic of Croatia to the Issuance of Subpoenae Duces Tecum, TC II, 18 July 1997, par 152; *Prosecutor v Furundžija*, Case IT-95-17I1, 10 December 1998, Judgment, pars 177–178.] Historically, the law of contempt originated as, and has remained, a creature of the common law. The general concept of contempt is said to be unknown to the civil law, but many civil law systems have legislated to provide offences which produce a similar result.

16. In a passage widely accepted as a correct assessment of the purpose and scope of the law of contempt at common law as developed over the centuries, the Report of the (UK) Committee on Contempt of Court, published in 1974, described it as:

> ... a means whereby the courts may act to prevent or punish conduct which tends to obstruct, prejudice or abuse the administration of justice either in relation to a particular case or generally.

[footnote 16 – Report of the Committee on Contempt of Court, UK Cmnd 5794 (1974) ("Phillimore Committee Report"), par 1. That passage has been accepted as a correct assessment of the purpose and scope of the law of contempt by the European Court of Human Rights, in *Sunday Times v United Kingdom*, Series A Vol 30 at pars 18 and 55, (1979) 2 EHRR 245 at 256, 274, by the English House of Lords, in *Attorney-General v Times Newspaper Ltd* [1992] 1 AC 191 at 207–209 (per Lord Ackner), and by the Ontario Court of Appeal, in *Regina v Glasner* (1994) 119 DLR (4th) 113 at 128–129. See also *AMIEU v Mudginberri Station Pty Ltd* (1986) 161 CLR 98 at 106 (High Court of Australia); *Witham v Holloway* (1995) 183 CLR 525 at 533 (per joint judgment), 538–539 (per McHugh J) (High Court of Australia); *US v Dixon & Foster* 509 US 688 (1993) at 694 (Supreme Court of the United States).]

The rule of law, which lies at the heart of society, is necessary to ensure peace and good order, and that rule is directly dependent upon the ability of courts to enforce their process and to maintain their dignity and respect. To maintain their process and respect, the common law courts have, since the twelfth century, exercised a power to punish for contempt. [footnote 17 – *United Nurses of Alberta v Attorney-General for Alberta* (1992) 89 DLR (4th) 609 at 636 (per McLachlin J, for the majority of the Supreme Court of Canada).] In order to avoid any misconception, it is perhaps necessary to emphasise that the law of contempt as developed at common law is not designed to buttress the dignity of the judges or to punish mere affronts or insults to a court or tribunal; rather, it is justice itself which is flouted by a contempt of court, not the individual court or judge who is attempting to administer justice. [footnote 18 – *Attorney-General v Leveller Magazine Ltd* [1979] AC 440 at 449 (per Lord Diplock). This statement has frequently been quoted with approval.]

17. Although the law of contempt has now been partially codified in the United Kingdom, [footnote omitted] the power to deal with contempt at common law has essentially remained one which is part of the inherent jurisdiction of the superior courts of record, rather than based upon statute. On the other hand, the analogous control exercised in the civil law systems over conduct which interferes with the administration of justice is based solely upon statute, and the statutory provisions, in general, enact narrow offences dealing with precisely defined conduct where the jurisdiction of the courts has been or would be frustrated by that conduct. [footnote 20 – For example, the German Penal Code punishes as a principal offender anyone who incites a witness to make a false statement (§§ 26, 153). The Criminal Law of the People's Republic of China punishes anyone who entices a witness to give false testimony (Article 306). The French *Nouveau Code Pénal* punishes those who pressure a witness to give false evidence or to abstain from giving truthful evidence (Article 434–15). More general statutory provisions exist which deal with such things as the control of the hearing (*police de l'audience*), "affronts" (*outrages*), offences committed during the hearings (for example, *delits d'audience*) and the publication of comments tending to exert pressure (*pression*) on the testimony of witnesses or on the decision of any court. The Russian Criminal Code punishes interference in any form whatsoever with the activities of the court where the purpose is to

obstruct the effectuation of justice (Article 294), and also provides more specific offences such as the falsification of evidence (Article 303).]

18. A power in the Tribunal to punish conduct which tends to obstruct, prejudice or abuse its administration of justice is a necessity in order to ensure that its exercise of the jurisdiction which is expressly given to it by its Statute is not frustrated and that its basic judicial functions are safeguarded. Thus the power to deal with contempt is clearly within its inherent jurisdiction. [footnote 21 – The Appeals Chamber has already held this to be so, but as an *obiter dictum* only, in the *Blaškić Subpoena Decision*, par 59.] That is not to say that the Tribunal's powers to deal with contempt or conduct interfering with the administration of justice are in every situation the same as those possessed by domestic courts, because its jurisdiction as an international court must take into account its different setting within the basic structure of the international community. [footnote 22 – *Blaškić Subpoena Decision*, par 40.]

19. This Tribunal has, since its creation, assumed the right to punish for contempt. The original Rules of Procedure and Evidence, adopted on 11 February 1994, provided by Rule 77 ("Contempt of Court") for a fine or a term of imprisonment where – subject to the provisions of what is now Rule 90(F), which permits a witness to object to making any statement which may tend to incriminate him or her – a witness "refuses or fails contumaciously to answer a question relevant to the issue before a Chamber". In January 1995, such punishment was also made applicable to a person who attempts to interfere with or intimidate a witness, and any judgment of a Chamber under Rule 77 was made subject to appeal. [footnote 23 – The heading of the rule was corrected to read "Contempt of the Tribunal".] In July 1997, such punishment was also made applicable to any party, witness or other person participating in proceedings before a Chamber who discloses information relating to the proceedings in violation of an order of the Chamber. Both of these additions expressly identified the relevant conduct as "contempt".

Notes

- What theory of powers does the ICTY apply in this case? Is the tribunal finding these powers because the drafters of the statute of the tribunal intended for the power to be vested in the tribunal? And if so, is that an application of implied powers? Or does the tribunal find the powers granted in some other way?
- Or perhaps were they ever granted? And if this is the case, then how does the tribunal come to have those powers? So far, our discussion of powers has always understood organizations to operate on the principle of speciality, i.e. that they are constituted for a particular purpose and have limited powers granted to them for that purpose.
- Like many international courts and tribunals, the judges of the tribunal are specifically empowered by the Statute to draft the rules of procedure and evidence of the tribunal. Is this decision simply the exercise of this power? Is this merely a

procedural issue, or one of substantial power? Consider that if the judges chose to revise the rules and grant the ability to hold a person in contempt, how could they apply that new penal sanction retroactively, *ex post facto*, to the individual?

5.1.4 Balance of powers with member states

Before concluding the consideration of powers, we should observe that organizations are granted powers when they are constituted, and while we try to find the precise division of powers between states and organizations, in reality those powers often overlap. This problem will be discussed again in Chapter 9 on responsibility for violations of international law, especially when states and organizations exercise overlapping powers. In this chapter on powers, however, we can consider that one way that powers are allocated when they are overlapping is to find some kind of balance between the powers held by the state and those held by the organization:

Case C-159/90, Society for the Protection of Unborn Children [SPUC] Ireland Ltd v Grogan et al.
Judgment
Court of Justice of the European Communities [Union], 4 October 1991[13]

Grounds

1 By order dated 5 March 1990, which was received at the Court on 23 May 1990, the High Court of Ireland referred to the Court for a preliminary ruling under Article 177 of the EEC Treaty three questions on the interpretation of Community law, in particular Article 60 of the EEC Treaty.

2 The questions arose in proceedings brought by the Society for the Protection of Unborn Children Ireland Ltd ("SPUC") against Stephen Grogan and fourteen other officers of students associations in connection with the distribution in Ireland of specific information relating to the identity and location of clinics in another Member State where medical termination of pregnancy is carried out.

3 Abortion has always been prohibited in Ireland, first of all at common law, then by statute. The relevant provisions at present in force are Sections 58 and 59 of the Offences Against the Person Act 1861, as reaffirmed in the Health (Family Planning) Act 1979.

4 In 1983 a constitutional amendment approved by referendum inserted in Article 40, Section 3, of the Irish Constitution a third subsection worded as follows: "The State acknowledges the right to life of the unborn and, with due regard to the equal right to life of the mother, guarantees in its laws to respect, and, as far as practicable, by its laws to defend and vindicate that right."

5 According to the Irish courts (High Court, judgment of 19 December 1986, and Supreme Court, judgment of 16

---

[13] https://eur-lex.europa.eu, © European Union 1998–2020.

March 1988, The Attorney General (at the relation of the Society for the Protection of Unborn Children Ireland Ltd) v Open Door Counselling Ltd and Dublin Wellwoman Centre Ltd [1988] Irish Reports 593), to assist pregnant women in Ireland to travel abroad to obtain abortions, inter alia by informing them of the identity and location of a specific clinic or clinics where abortions are performed and how to contact such clinics, is prohibited under Article 40.3.3 of the Irish Constitution.

6   SPUC, the plaintiff in the main proceedings, is a company incorporated under Irish law whose purpose is to prevent the decriminalization of abortion and to affirm, defend and promote human life from the moment of conception. In 1989/90 Stephen Grogan and the other defendants in the main proceedings were officers of students associations which issued certain publications for students. Those publications contained information about the availability of legal abortion in the United Kingdom, the identity and location of a number of abortion clinics in that country and how to contact them. It is undisputed that the students associations had no links with clinics in another Member State.

7   In September 1989 SPUC requested the defendants, in their capacity as officers of their respective associations, to undertake not to publish information of the kind described above during the academic year 1989/90. The defendants did not reply, and SPUC then brought proceedings in the High Court for a declaration that the distribution of such information was unlawful and for an injunction restraining its distribution.

8   By a judgment of 11 October 1989 the High Court decided to refer certain questions to the Court of Justice for a preliminary ruling under Article 177 of the EEC Treaty before ruling on the injunction applied for by the plaintiff. An appeal was brought against that judgment and, on 19 December 1989, the Supreme Court granted the injunction applied for but did not overturn the High Court's decision to refer questions to the Court of Justice for a preliminary ruling. Moreover, each of the parties was given leave to apply to the High Court in order to vary the decision of the Supreme Court in the light of the preliminary ruling to be given by the Court of Justice.

...

First question

16   In its first question, the national court essentially seeks to establish whether medical termination of pregnancy, performed in accordance with the law of the State where it is carried out, constitutes a service within the meaning of Article 60 of the EEC Treaty.

17   According to the first paragraph of that provision, services are to be considered to be "services" within the meaning of the Treaty where they are normally provided for remuneration, in so far as they are not governed by the provisions relating to freedom of movement for goods, capital or persons. Indent (d) of the second paragraph of Article 60 expressly states that activities of the professions fall within the definition of services.

18   It must be held that termination of pregnancy, as lawfully practised in several Member States, is a medical activity

which is normally provided for remuneration and may be carried out as part of a professional activity. In any event, the Court has already held in the judgment in Luisi and Carbone (Joined Cases 286/82 and 26/83 Luisi and Carbone v Ministero del Tesoro [1984] ECR 377, paragraph 16) that medical activities fall within the scope of Article 60 of the Treaty.

19 SPUC, however, maintains that the provision of abortion cannot be regarded as being a service, on the grounds that it is grossly immoral and involves the destruction of the life of a human being, namely the unborn child.

20 Whatever the merits of those arguments on the moral plane, they cannot influence the answer to the national court's first question. It is not for the Court to substitute its assessment for that of the legislature in those Member States where the activities in question are practised legally.

21 Consequently, the answer to the national court's first question must be that medical termination of pregnancy, performed in accordance with the law of the State in which it is carried out, constitutes a service within the meaning of Article 60 of the Treaty.

Second and third questions

22 Having regard to the facts of the case, it must be considered that, in its second and third questions, the national court seeks essentially to establish whether it is contrary to Community law for a Member State in which medical termination of pregnancy is forbidden to prohibit students associations from distributing information about the identity and location of clinics in another Member State where medical termination of pregnancy is lawfully carried out and the means of communicating with those clinics, where the clinics in question have no involvement in the distribution of the said information.

23 Although the national court's questions refer to Community law in general, the Court takes the view that its attention should be focused on the provisions of Article 59 et seq. of the EEC Treaty, which deal with the freedom to provide services, and the argument concerning human rights, which has been treated extensively in the observations submitted to the Court.

24 As regards, first, the provisions of Article 59 of the Treaty, which prohibit any restriction on the freedom to supply services, it is apparent from the facts of the case that the link between the activity of the students associations of which Mr Grogan and the other defendants are officers and medical terminations of pregnancies carried out in clinics in another Member State is too tenuous for the prohibition on the distribution of information to be capable of being regarded as a restriction within the meaning of Article 59 of the Treaty.

25 The situation in which students associations distributing the information at issue in the main proceedings are not in cooperation with the clinics whose addresses they publish can be distinguished from the situation which gave rise to the judgment in GB-INNO-BM (Case C-362/88 GB-INNO-BM v Confédération du Commerce Luxembourgeois [1990] I-667), in which the Court held that a prohibition on the distribution of advertising was capable of constituting a barrier to the free movement of goods

and therefore had to be examined in the light of Articles 30, 31 and 36 of the EEC Treaty.

26 The information to which the national court's questions refer is not distributed on behalf of an economic operator established in another Member State. On the contrary, the information constitutes a manifestation of freedom of expression and of the freedom to impart and receive information which is independent of the economic activity carried on by clinics established in another Member State.

27 It follows that, in any event, a prohibition on the distribution of information in circumstances such as those which are the subject of the main proceedings cannot be regarded as a restriction within the meaning of Article 59 of the Treaty.

28 Secondly, it is necessary to consider the argument of the defendants in the main proceedings to the effect that the prohibition in question, inasmuch as it is based on a constitutional amendment approved in 1983, is contrary to Article 62 of the EEC Treaty, which provides that Member States are not to introduce any new restrictions on the freedom to provide services in fact attained at the date when the Treaty entered into force.

29 It is sufficient to observe, as far as that argument is concerned, that Article 62, which is complementary to Article 59, cannot prohibit restrictions which do not fall within the scope of Article 59.

30 Thirdly and lastly, the defendants in the main proceedings maintain that a prohibition such as the one at issue is in breach of fundamental rights, especially of freedom of expression and the freedom to receive and impart information, enshrined in particular in Article 10(1) of the European Convention on Human Rights.

31 According to, inter alia, the judgment of 18 June 1991 in Elliniki Radiophonia Tileorasi (Case C-260/89 Elliniki Radiophonia Tileorasi v Dimotiki Etairia Pliroforissis [1991] ECR I-2951, paragraph 42), where national legislation falls within the field of application of Community law the Court, when requested to give a preliminary ruling, must provide the national court with all the elements of interpretation which are necessary in order to enable it to assess the compatibility of that legislation with the fundamental rights – as laid down in particular in the European Convention on Human Rights – the observance of which the Court ensures. However, the Court has no such jurisdiction with regard to national legislation lying outside the scope of Community law. In view of the facts of the case and of the conclusions which the Court has reached above with regard to the scope of Articles 59 and 62 of the Treaty, that would appear to be true of the prohibition at issue before the national court.

32 The reply to the national court's second and third questions must therefore be that it is not contrary to Community law for a Member State in which medical termination of pregnancy is forbidden to prohibit students associations from distributing information about the identity and location of clinics in another Member State where voluntary termination of pregnancy is lawfully carried out and the means of communicating with those clinics, where the clinics in question have no involvement in the distribution of the said information.

Notes

- Is the medical procedure at issue a "service"? What if a state provides such procedure through a state-funded medical service that is free to the patient? If the procedure was any other act that was unlawful under a Member State's laws, such as a contract for murder, would it still constitute a service? Does it matter that this procedure is lawful in the state where it would be done, whereas a contract to murder is not lawful in any Member State? Consider a service that is less controversial, but also only lawful in some Member States, such as gambling.
- The end result of this case is that Ireland must tolerate advertising for unlawful services (even immoral services, contrary to public order, in its view). Does this solution strike the right balance between the powers of the Union and those of the Member States? Is there any other way to balance these powers? Does this outcome mean that the EU protects whatever laws are the most liberal in the Union? Is there any way that the EU might find any service provided in a Member State to be too extreme for protection under Union law? Consider that some Member States might restrict the right of lawyers to advertise their services. How should this practice be resolved in cases of cross-border advertising within the Union?
- If there was no overlap of powers, would that change the outcome? Would the EU have greater powers without the conflict with Ireland's laws?

In *SPUC v Grogan*, the question was the balance between powers of a state to prohibit a service and the power of the Union to also regulate the cross-border offering of the same service. Keeping that case in mind, consider the following case:

Case C-205/06, Commission of the European Communities v Austria
[*In re* bilateral agreements with third countries]
Judgment
Court of Justice of the European Union (Grand Chamber), 3 March 2009[14]

Legal framework

2 Prior to its accession to the European Union, the Republic of Austria entered into bilateral investment agreements with the People's Republic of China (this agreement entered into force on 11 October 1986 (BGBl. 537/1986)), Malaysia (this agreement entered into force on 1 January 1987 (BGBl. 601/1986)), the Russian Federation (this agreement entered into force on 1 September 1991 (BGBl. 387/1991), initially concluded with the former Union of Soviet Socialist Republics and made applicable between the Republic of Austria and the Russian Federation pursuant to an exchange of letters (BGBl. 257/1994)), the Republic of Korea (this agreement entered into force on 1 November 1991 (BGBl. 523/1991)), the Republic of Turkey (this agreement entered into force on 1 January 1992 (BGBl. 612/1991)) and the Republic of Cape Verde (this agreement entered into force on 1 April 1993 (BGBl. 83/1993)).

---

14 https://eur-lex.europa.eu, © European Union 1998–2020.

3   Each of those agreements contains a clause under which each party guarantees to the investors of the other party, without undue delay, the free transfer, in freely convertible currency, of payments connected with an investment.

...

Findings of the Court

24   The various investment agreements at issue concluded by the Republic of Austria contain equivalent provisions which guarantee the free transfer, without undue delay and in freely convertible currency, of payments connected with an investment.

25   In particular, the following matters are thus guaranteed: the free transfer of funds in order to create, manage or extend an investment; the freedom to repatriate the income from that investment; and the freedom to transfer the funds necessary to repay loans and the funds arising from the liquidation or assignment of that investment.

26   Those agreements are to that extent consistent with the wording of Article 56(1) EC, according to which "... all restrictions on the movement of capital between Member States and between Member States and third countries shall be prohibited", and of Article 56(2) EC, under which "all restrictions on payments between Member States and between Member States and third countries shall be prohibited", and are in line with the objective pursued by that article.

27   It is true that the Treaty provisions to which the present action by the Commission refers grant the Council the power to restrict, in certain circumstances, the movement of capital and payments between Member States and third countries, including the movements covered by the transfer clauses here at issue.

28   The provisions in question, contained in Articles 57(2) EC, 59 EC and 60(1) EC, introduce, with a view to protecting the general Community interest and enabling the Community to comply, as appropriate, with its international obligations and with those of the Member States, exceptions to the principle of free movement of capital and payments between Member States and between Member States and third countries.

29   Article 57(2) EC allows the Council, acting by qualified majority on a proposal from the Commission, to adopt certain measures restricting the movement of capital to or from third countries involving, inter alia, direct investment. Where those measures constitute a "step back" in Community law as regards the liberalisation of the movement of capital to or from third countries, unanimity is required.

30   Article 59 EC authorises the Council, on a proposal from the Commission and after consulting the European Central Bank, to take safeguard measures where movements of capital to or from third countries "cause, or threaten to cause, serious difficulties for the operation of economic and monetary union", provided that they are strictly necessary and that they relate to a period "not exceeding six months".

31   Article 60(1) EC allows the Council, on a proposal from the Commission, in order to implement a common position or a joint action in the area of the common foreign and security policy, to take "necessary urgent measures" on the movement of capital and on payments.

Such action could, for example, be required in order to give effect to a resolution of the Security Council of the United Nations Organisation.

32 It is common ground that the agreements at issue do not contain any provision reserving such possibilities for the Community to restrict movements of funds connected with investments. It is therefore necessary to examine whether the Republic of Austria was, for that reason, under an obligation to take the appropriate steps to which the second paragraph of Article 307 EC refers.

33 Under the first paragraph of Article 307 EC, the rights and obligations arising from an agreement concluded before the date of accession of a Member State between it and a third country are not affected by the provisions of the Treaty. The purpose of that provision is to make it clear, in accordance with the principles of international law, that application of the Treaty is not to affect the duty of the Member State concerned to respect the rights of third countries under a prior agreement and to perform its obligations thereunder (see Case 812/79 *Burgoa* [1980] ECR 2787, paragraph 8; Case C-84/98 *Commission v Portugal* [2000] ECR I-5215, paragraph 53; and Case C-216/01 *Budějovický Budvar* [2003] ECR I-13617, paragraphs 144 and 145).

34 The second paragraph of Article 307 EC obliges the Member States to take all appropriate steps to eliminate incompatibilities with Community law which have been established in agreements concluded prior to their accession. Under that provision, the Member States are required, where necessary, to assist each other to that end and, where appropriate, to adopt a common attitude.

35 The provisions of Articles 57(2) EC, 59 EC and 60(1) EC confer on the Council the power to restrict, in certain specific circumstances, movements of capital and payments between Member States and third countries.

36 In order to ensure the effectiveness of those provisions, measures restricting the free movement of capital must be capable, where adopted by the Council, of being applied immediately with regard to the States to which they relate, which may include some of the States which have signed one of the agreements at issue with the Republic of Austria.

37 Accordingly, those powers of the Council, which consist in the unilateral adoption of restrictive measures with regard to third countries on a matter which is identical to or connected with that covered by an earlier agreement concluded between a Member State and a third country, reveal an incompatibility with that agreement where, first, the agreement does not contain a provision allowing the Member State concerned to exercise its rights and to fulfil its obligations as a member of the Community and, second, there is also no international-law mechanism which makes that possible.

38 Contrary to what is contended by the Republic of Austria, the measures put forward by it and which, in its view, are such as to enable it to fulfil its Community obligations do not appear to guarantee that this will be the case.

39   In the first place, the periods of time necessarily involved in any international negotiations which would be required in order to reopen discussion of the agreements at issue are inherently incompatible with the practical effectiveness of those measures.

40   In the second place, the possibility of relying on other mechanisms offered by international law, such as suspension of the agreement, or even denunciation of the agreements at issue or of some of their provisions, is too uncertain in its effects to guarantee that the measures adopted by the Council could be applied effectively.

41   Moreover, as it pointed out again at the hearing, the Republic of Austria intends to introduce, in the investment agreements under negotiation or when the existing agreements are renewed, a clause which would reserve certain powers to regional organisations and would, therefore, make it possible to apply any measures restricting movements of capital and payments which might be adopted by the Council.

42   While acknowledging that such a clause should, in principle, as the Commission admitted at the hearing, be considered capable of removing the established incompatibility, it is common ground that, in the cases referred to by the Commission, the Republic of Austria has not taken any steps, within the period prescribed by the Commission in its reasoned opinion, with regard to the third countries concerned, designed to eliminate the risk of conflict with measures liable to be adopted by the Council under Articles 57(2) EC, 59 EC and 60(1) EC which may arise from the application of the investment agreements concluded with those third countries.

43   It must be added that, as follows from the judgment delivered today in Case C-249/06 *Commission* v *Sweden* [2009] ECR I-0000, the incompatibilities with the Treaty to which the investment agreements with third countries give rise and which militate against the application of the restrictions on movement of capital and on payments which the Council may adopt under Articles 57(2) EC, 59 EC and 60(1) EC are not limited to the Member State which is the defendant in the present case.

44   It must therefore be stated that, in accordance with the second paragraph of Article 307 EC, where necessary, the Member States must assist each other with a view to eliminating the incompatibilities established and must adopt, where appropriate, a common attitude. In the context of its duty, under Article 211 EC, to ensure that the provisions of the Treaty are applied, it is for the Commission to take any steps which may facilitate mutual assistance between the Member States concerned and their adoption of a common attitude.

45   It follows from the foregoing that, by not having taken appropriate steps to eliminate incompatibilities concerning the provisions on transfer of capital contained in the investment agreements entered into with the Republic of Korea, the Republic of Cape Verde, the People's Republic of China, Malaysia, the Russian Federation and the Republic of Turkey, the Republic of Austria has failed to fulfil its obligations under the second paragraph of Article 307 EC.

Notes

- What is the basis for this decision? Is it a power that was expressly specified in the Treaties on European Union? Or a power that was decided later by the Commission and/or Council? If this is a Council/Commission decision, is it within the powers of the EU? Are those organs granting themselves powers?
- What theory of powers does the ECJ apply here? How does the Union come to hold these particular powers?
- Compare this case to *SPUC v Grogan*. How is this case different? Is there no way to apply the same kind of balancing of powers in *SPUC* to the case above on bilateral agreements?
- Are the bilateral agreements still in force after this decision? Does the EU have the power to void them? If they are still in effect, then how do the EU Member States eliminate the conflict?
- Is there really any overlap of powers here between the EU and the Member State? What is the precise overlap if there is one, and how can we resolve it?

5.1.5 Other limitations on powers

In addition to the inherent powers above, there may also be inherent limitations on powers. An example could be those rules of international law that are *jus cogens* norms. Consider the separate opinion of Judge *ad hoc* Lauterpacht in the *Bosnia Genocide* case:

Case Concerning Application of the Convention on the Prevention and Punishment of the Crime of Genocide
Bosnia & Herzegovina v. Yugoslavia (Serbia & Montenegro)
Further Requests for the Indication of Provisional Measures, Order
1993 ICJ Reps. 325
International Court of Justice, 13 September 1993

Separate Opinion of Judge Lauterpacht

...

97. The Applicant's request gives rise to two questions: one is whether any challenge to the Security Council resolution is possible in the present context; the other is how, as a matter of form, the Court could give operative effect to its views on this matter within the procedural framework of bilateral litigation between the present two Parties. Although the Court has taken the position that it can make a suitable order without entering into these questions, I believe that some consideration should be given to them.

A. *The effect of the Security Council resolution*

98. On the face of it, Security Council resolution 713 (1991) is a valid prohibition of the supply of arms and military equipment to those involved in the Yugoslav conflict and is binding on all Members of the United Nations. Although the resolution is open to the comments expressed above in paragraphs 91–96, it cannot be said with certainty that in

themselves these comments affect the continuing validity of the resolution. The fact that some of the members of the Security Council indicated that they would not have supported the resolution in the absence of the consent of Yugoslavia, in relation to whose territory the embargo was adopted, could only be relevant in the absence of a determination by the Security Council that the situation fell within Chapter VII of the Charter. Once the Security Council indicated that it was acting "under Chapter VII", it was no longer constrained by the necessity of obtaining the consent of any State to the measures that it considered the circumstances to require.

99. This is not to say that the Security Council can act free of all legal controls but only that the Court's power of judicial review is limited. That the Court has some power of this kind can hardly be doubted, though there can be no less doubt that it does not embrace any right of the Court to substitute its discretion for that of the Security Council in determining the existence of a threat to the peace, a breach of the peace or an act of aggression, or the political steps to be taken following such a determination. But the Court, as the principal judicial organ of the United Nations, is entitled, indeed bound, to ensure the rule of law within the United Nations system and, in cases properly brought before it, to insist on adherence by all United Nations organs to the rules governing their operation. The Court has already, in the Lockerbie case, given an extensive interpretation of the powers of the Security Council when acting under Chapter VII, in holding that a decision of the Council is, by virtue of Articles 25 and 103 of the Charter, able to prevail over the obligations of the parties under any other international agreement (see *Questions of Interpretation and Application of the 1971 Montreal Convention arising from the Aerial Incident at Lockerbie (Libyan Arab Jamahiriya v. United Kingdom), Provisional Measures, Order of 14 April 1992, I.C.J. Reports 1992*, p. 15, para. 39).

100. The present case, however, cannot fall within the scope of the doctrine just enunciated. This is because the prohibition of genocide, unlike the matters covered by the Montreal Convention in the Lockerbie case to which the terms of Article 103 could be directly applied, has generally been accepted as having the status not of an ordinary rule of international law but of *jus cogens*. Indeed, the prohibition of genocide has long been regarded as one of the few undoubted examples of *jus cogens*. Even in 1951, in its Advisory Opinion on *Reservations to the Convention on the Prevention and Punishment of the Crime of Genocide*, the Court affirmed that genocide was "contrary to moral law and to the spirit and aims of the United Nations" (a view repeated by the Court in paragraph 51 of today's Order) and that "the principles underlying the Convention are provisions which are recognized by civilized nations as binding on States even without any conventional obligation" (*I.C.J. Reports 1951*, p. 22). An express reference to the special quality of the prohibition of genocide may also be seen in the work of the International Law Commission in the preparation of Article 50 of the draft articles on the Law of Treaties (*Yearbook of the International Law Commission*, 1966, Vol. II, pp. 248–249) which eventually materialized in Article 53 of the Vienna Convention on the Law

of Treaties and in the same Commission's commentary on Article 19 (international crimes and delicts) of the draft articles on State Responsibility (*Yearbook of the International Law Commission*, 1976, Vol. II, Pt. 2, p. 103). The concept of *jus cogens* operates as a concept superior to both customary international law and treaty. The relief which Article 103 of the Charter may give the Security Council in case of conflict between one of its decisions and an operative treaty obligation cannot – as a matter of simple hierarchy of norms – extend to a conflict between a Security Council resolution and *jus cogens*. Indeed, one only has to state the opposite proposition thus – that a Security Council resolution may even require participation in genocide – for its unacceptability to be apparent.

101. Nor should one overlook the significance of the provision in Article 24 (2) of the Charter that, in discharging its duties to maintain international peace and security, the Security Council shall act in accordance with the Purposes and Principles of the United Nations. Amongst the Purposes set out in Article 1 (3) of the Charter is that of achieving international co-operation "in promoting and encouraging respect for human rights and for fundamental freedoms for all without distinction as to race, sex, language or religion".

102. Now, it is not to be contemplated that the Security Council would ever deliberately adopt a resolution clearly and deliberately flouting a rule of *jus cogens* or requiring a violation of human rights. But the possibility that a Security Council resolution might inadvertently or in an unforeseen manner lead to such a situation cannot be excluded. And that, it appears, is what has happened here.

On this basis, the inability of Bosnia-Herzegovina sufficiently strongly to fight back against the Serbs and effectively to prevent the implementation of the Serbian policy of ethnic cleansing is at least in part directly attributable to the fact that Bosnia-Herzegovina's access to weapons and equipment has been severely limited by the embargo. Viewed in this light, the Security Council resolution can be seen as having in effect called on Members of the United Nations, albeit unknowingly and assuredly unwillingly, to become in some degree supporters of the genocidal activity of the Serbs and in this manner and to that extent to act contrary to a rule of *jus cogens*.

103. What legal consequences may flow from this analysis? One possibility is that, in strict logic, when the operation of paragraph 6 of Security Council resolution 713 (1991) began to make Members of the United Nations accessories to genocide, it ceased to be valid and binding in its operation against Bosnia-Herzegovina; and that Members of the United Nations then became free to disregard it. Even so, it would be difficult to say that they then became positively obliged to provide the Applicant with weapons and military equipment.

104. There is, however, another possibility that is, perhaps, more in accord with the realities of the situation. It must be recognized that the chain of hypotheses in the analysis just made involves some debatable links – elements of fact, such as that the arms embargo has led to the imbalance in the possession of arms by the two sides and that that imbalance has contributed in greater or lesser degree to genocidal activity such as ethnic cleansing; and elements of law, such as that genocide is *jus cogens* and that

a resolution which becomes violative of jus cogens must then become void and legally ineffective. It is not necessary for the Court to take a position in this regard at this time. Instead, it would seem sufficient that the relevance here of *jus cogens* should be drawn to the attention of the Security Council, as it will be by the required communication to it of the Court's Order, so that the Security Council may give due weight to it in future reconsideration of the embargo.

Notes

- This view is, in itself, a bold statement. It may very well be correct, though the precise legal foundation for many *jus cogens* norms and their application is a bit elusive. How does Lauterpacht know that genocide is *jus cogens*?
- If indeed it is correct, then what is the legal framework for analyzing the question? Is it a question of the Security Council not having the power because it is not possible to legally enjoy such a power? Or is it a question of the law of treaties, in that a treaty provision permitting a *jus cogens* violation is invalid? Or is it only a question of responsibility, meaning that every subject of international law has the power (not authority) to commit such violations, and if they do, then they are held responsible?
- Also note Lauterpacht's view on the relationship between the UN Security Council and the ICJ. How would you describe his interpretation of this relationship? If the Security Council was to violate a *jus cogens* norm, would the court have a role? If so, how, according to his view? If not, then how is the UN ensuring compliance with *jus cogens* norms, the most important legal rules in the international community?

5.2 ISSUES OF *ULTRA VIRES* ACTS

Having examined the basis for the legal powers of international organizations, we will now turn to the *ultra vires* analysis. Early on in the history of international organizations, it was not entirely clear that an organization was even capable of acting *ultra vires*. After all, the organization was limited by its powers and could not act beyond them. However, it quickly became apparent that organizations might attempt to act beyond their powers, or might act where their powers were unclear.

At this initial stage, it is helpful to distinguish *ultra vires* issues from issues of lawfulness. *Ultra vires* is a question of the validity of the act within the internal legal order of the organization. Lawfulness is a question of whether the act (valid or not) violates rules of international law governing the organization's engagement in the international legal system. The question of lawfulness is a question of responsibility, and will be addressed in more detail in Chapter 9 on responsibility. In this section, we only deal with the question of *ultra vires*, or the validity of an act.

One of the first considerations in making an *ultra vires* assessment is to determine which actor may raise an objection on *ultra vires* grounds. Member states of the organization may protest an act of the organization within the internal governance mechanisms as being *ultra vires*. Non-member states do not have access to these internal governance mechanisms and are not able to raise an *ultra vires* argument. It is the member states that decide what powers have been granted to the organization, so they are empowered to assess *ultra vires* questions. Non-member states are limited to complaining of responsibility for violations of international law, but not *ultra vires* issues. Recall the *Tobacco Directive* case above. Within the European Union legal order, the Court of Justice has the competence to determine whether or not the Union has acted within its powers, and only Member States of the Union may seize the court. Thus, this was a case brought by Germany challenging the exercise of powers by the European Parliament and Council. However, non-member states of the International Criminal Court may object to the court exercising jurisdiction over their nationals. In this case, is the non-member state making an *ultra vires* argument, or is it arguing that the court is violating international law? Sometimes the distinction between *ultra vires* and international responsibility is difficult to see. Consider whether the non-member state is really arguing that the court chambers have exceeded powers granted to them under the constitutive instrument, or is it really arguing that the court is risking violating international law on jurisdiction for international crimes?

A second question is which organization or organ has the competence to make a decision whether an act is *ultra vires* or not. When an organ has acted, its decisions about its own competence are presumptively correct.[15] In some situations, the constitutive instrument identifies the organ or organization with competence to assess *ultra vires*.[16] Did the Court of Justice respect this presumption in the following case?

Opinion 2/00, [*In re* accession to the Cartagena Protocol on Biosafety] Court of Justice of the European Communities [Union], 6 December 2001[17]

[i] The Court of Justice has received a request for an Opinion, lodged at the Court Registry on 27 October 2000 by the Commission of the European Communities pursuant to Article 300(6) EC, which provides:

"The Council, the Commission or a Member State may obtain the opinion of the Court of Justice as to whether an agreement envisaged is compatible with the provisions of this Treaty. Where the opinion of the Court of Justice is adverse, the agreement may enter into force only in accordance with Article 48 of the Treaty on European Union."

---

15 *See* Certain Expenses of the United Nations (Article 17, Paragraph 2, of the Charter), Advisory Opinion, 1962 ICJ Reps. 151 (International Court of Justice, 20 July 1962).
16 *See* Appeal Relating to the Jurisdiction of the ICAO [International Civil Aviation Organization] Council (India v. Pakistan) Judgment, 1972 ICJ Reps. 46 (International Court of Justice, 18 August 1972).
17 https://eur-lex.europa.eu, © European Union 1998–2020.

...

[ii] The Convention on Biological Diversity (hereinafter "the Convention") was signed on 5 June 1992 by the European Economic Community and its Member States at the United Nations Conference on Environment and Development (UNCED), the "Earth Summit", which took place in Rio de Janeiro (Brazil), and was approved on behalf of the Community by Council Decision 93/626/EEC of 25 October 1993 (OJ 1993 L 309, p. 1). That decision was adopted on the basis of Article 130s of the EC Treaty (now, after amendment, Article 175 EC).

...

B – Cartagena Protocol

[vii] On 17 November 1997, the Conference of the Parties to the Convention adopted decision II/5 mandating the parties to negotiate "a protocol on biosafety, specifically focusing on transboundary movement, of any living modified organism resulting from modern biotechnology that may have adverse effect on the conservation and sustainable use of biological diversity, setting out for consideration, in particular, appropriate procedure for advance informed agreement".

[viii] The negotiations led to the adoption, on 29 January 2000 in Montreal (Canada), of the Cartagena Protocol on Biosafety (hereinafter "the Protocol"), which was opened for signature in Nairobi (Kenya) on 15 May 2000 and signed on behalf of the European Community and the Member States on 24 May 2000.

...

II – The Commission's questions and the procedure before the Court

A – The Commission's questions

[xx] Before submitting to the Council a proposal for a decision concluding the Protocol, the Commission, represented by A. Rosas, G. Zur Hausen and M. Afonso, acting as Agents, brought before the Court, under Article 300(6) EC, a request for an Opinion relating to the choice of the most appropriate legal basis for that purpose, given the divergence in the views of the Commission and the Council which had become apparent when the decision authorising signature of the Protocol on behalf of the Community was discussed and adopted by the Council. While the Commission's proposal was based on Articles 133 EC and 174(4) EC, in conjunction with the first subparagraph of Article 300(2) EC, on 15 May 2000 the Council unanimously adopted that decision on the basis of Article 175(1) EC alone, in conjunction with the abovementioned provision of Article 300 EC.

[xxi] Since the Commission considered that removal of Article 133 EC from the legal basis for the decision concluding the Protocol would undermine the external competence conferred on the Community by the EC Treaty with regard to common commercial policy, it decided to ask the Court the following questions:

"(1) Do Articles 133 and 174(4), in conjunction with the relevant provisions of Article 300 of the EC Treaty, constitute the appropriate legal basis for the act concluding, on behalf of the European Community, the Cartagena Biosafety Protocol?"

...

Opinion of the Court

...

II – Substance

20 According to the Commission, the Protocol essentially falls within the scope of Article 133(3) EC, but it does not rule out that certain matters more specifically related to environmental protection fall outside that provision. It therefore maintains that Articles 133 and 174(4) EC constitute the appropriate legal basis for concluding the Protocol.

21 That interpretation is contested by the Council and by the Member States which have submitted observations. They argue that, principally on account of its purpose and content, the Protocol can be concluded only on the basis of Article 175(1) EC. The Parliament also contends that this provision constitutes the appropriate legal basis for the measure concluding the Protocol, but it does not rule out referring in addition to Article 133 EC in so far as it is established that the Protocol's effects on trade in LMOs [living modified organisms] are a significant additional factor over and above environmental protection, which is its primary objective.

22 It is settled case-law that the choice of the legal basis for a measure, including one adopted in order to conclude an international agreement, does not follow from its author's conviction alone, but must rest on objective factors which are amenable to judicial review. Those factors include in particular the aim and the content of the measure (see Portugal v Council, cited above, paragraph 22, Case C-269/97 Commission v Council [2000] ECR I-2257, paragraph 43, and Spain v Council, cited above, paragraph 58).

...

24 Since interpretation of an international agreement is at issue, it should also be recalled that, under Article 31 of the Vienna Convention on the Law of Treaties, "a treaty shall be interpreted in good faith in accordance with the ordinary meaning to be given to the terms of the treaty in their context and in the light of its object and purpose".

25 In the present case, application of those criteria amounts to asking whether the Protocol, in the light of its context, its aim and its content, constitutes an agreement principally concerning environmental protection which is liable to have incidental effects on trade in LMOs, whether, conversely, it is principally an agreement concerning international trade policy which incidentally takes account of certain environmental requirements, or whether it is inextricably concerned both with environmental protection and with international trade.

...

43 As the Court has already held (see Peralta, cited above, paragraph 57, and Safety Hi-Tech, cited above, paragraph 43), Article 174 EC defines the objectives to be pursued in the context of environmental policy, while Article 175 EC constitutes the legal basis on which Community measures are adopted. It is true that Article 174(4) EC specifically provides that the "arrangements for Community cooperation" with non-member countries and international organisations "may be the subject of agreements ... negotiated and concluded

in accordance with Article 300". However, in the present case, the Protocol does not merely establish "arrangements for cooperation" regarding environmental protection, but lays down, in particular, precise rules on control procedures relating to transboundary movements, risk assessment and management, handling, transport, packaging and identification of LMOs.

44 Consequently, Article 175(1) EC is the appropriate legal basis for conclusion of the Protocol on behalf of the Community.

Notes

- In this case, which organ, organization or state made the complaint about the exercise of powers? Was that actor alleging an *ultra vires* issue?
- Did the court presume that the actor's assessment of powers was correct? Why, or why not? Did it apply the presumption, but find that it was overcome? Or did it disregard the presumption?
- Is the fact that this was the European Union significant? Or that this was a judicial organ of the organization?

Lastly, what is the result if an act is considered *ultra vires*? If the organ itself determines that the exercise of powers would be *ultra vires*, then the action is not taken, but in cases where a different organ (or organization) has been granted the competence to determine the validity of the act, what is the legal effect on such a decision?

In *Case 45/86, Commission v. Council,* the court held:

> that the contested regulations do not satisfy the requirements laid down in Article 190 of the Treaty with regard to the statement of reasons and that, moreover, they were not adopted on the correct legal basis. Consequently, they must be declared void.[18]

This means that the EU regulations were "annulled." This case appears rather straightforward. If an organization exceeds its powers, then the act must be invalid.

---

18 Case 45/86, Commission of the European Communities v Council of the European Communities [*In re* Generalised Tariff Preferences] (Court of Justice of the European Communities [Union], 26 March 1987).

In this light, consider the following case before the ICJ. The ICJ was specifically empowered to review the constitution of the Inter-Governmental Maritime Consultative Organization (IMCO) Maritime Safety Committee because it was requested by the IMCO to issue an advisory opinion on the matter:

Constitution of the Maritime Safety Committee of the Inter-Governmental Maritime Consultative Organization
Advisory Opinion
1960 ICJ Reps 150
International Court of Justice, 8 June 1960

[p. 152]

...

The question submitted to the Court in the Request for an Advisory Opinion, cast though it is in a general form, is directed [p. 153] to a particular case, and may be formulated in the following manner: has the Assembly, in not electing Liberia and Panama to the Maritime Safety Committee, exercised its electoral power in a manner in accordance with the provisions of Article 28 (*a*) of the Convention of 6 March 1948, for the Establishment of the Inter-Governmental Maritime Consultative Organization?

...

The Maritime Safety Committee's principal duties are set out in Article 29. They include the consideration of any matter within the scope of the Organization and concerned with aids to navigation, construction and equipment of vessels, manning from a safety standpoint, rules for prevention of collisions, handling of dangerous cargoes, maritime safety procedures and requirements and any other matters directly affecting maritime safety. It is called upon to maintain close relationship with such other inter-governmental bodies concerned with transport and communications as may further the object of the Organization in promoting maritime safety.

[p. 154]

The composition of the Committee and the mode of designating its Members are governed by Article 28 (*a*) which reads as follows:

> "The Maritime Safety Committee shall consist of fourteen Members elected by the Assembly from the Members, governments of those nations having an important interest in maritime safety, of which not less than eight shall be the largest ship-owning nations, and the remainder shall be elected so as to ensure adequate representation of Members, governments of other nations with an important interest in maritime safety, such as nations interested in the supply of large numbers of crews or in the carriage of large numbers of berthed and unberthed passengers, and of major geographical areas."

The Court is called upon to appreciate whether, in not electing Liberia and Panama to the Maritime Safety Committee, the Assembly complied with that provision. For this purpose, the Court must, in the first place, recall the circumstances in which the Assembly proceeded to the election of the Committee and asked for an advisory opinion.

...

The words of Article 28 (*a*) must be read in their natural and ordinary meaning, in the sense which they would normally have in their context. It is only if, when this is done, the words of the [p. 160] Article are ambiguous in any way that resort need be had to other methods of construction. (*Competence of the General Assembly for the Admission of a State to the United Nations, I.C.J. Reports* 1950, p. 8)

From the terms of Article 28 (*a*) it is clear that the draftsmen deliberately contemplated that the preponderant control of the Committee was in all circumstances to be vested in "the largest ship-owning nations". This control was to be secured by the provision that not less than eight of the fourteen seats had to be filled by them. The language employed – "of which not less than eight shall be the largest ship-owning nations" – in its natural and ordinary meaning conveys this intent of the draftsmen.

...

In order to determine which nations are the largest ship-owning nations, it is apparent that some basis of measurement must be applied. The rationale of the situation is that when Article 28 (*a*) speaks of "the largest ship-owning nations", it can only have in mind a comparative size vis-à-vis other nations owners of tonnage. There is no other practical means by which the size of ship-owning nations may be measured. The largest ship-owning nations are to be elected on the strength of their tonnage, the tonnage which is owned by or belongs to them. The only question is in what sense Article 28 (*a*) contemplates it should be owned by or belong to them.

...

The practice followed by the Assembly in relation to other Articles reveals the reliance placed upon registered tonnage.

...

The conclusion the Court reaches is that where in Article 28 (*a*) "ship-owning nations" are referred to, the reference is solely to registered tonnage. The largest ship-owning nations are the nations having the largest registered ship tonnage.

...

The Assembly elected to the Committee neither Liberia nor Panama, in spite of the fact that, on the basis of registered tonnage, these two States were included among the eight largest ship-owning nations. By so doing the Assembly failed to comply with Article 28 (*a*) of the Convention which, as the Court has established, must be interpreted as requiring the determination of the largest ship-owning nations to be made solely on the basis of registered tonnage.

Notes

- How does the ICJ have the power to adjudicate on the election of another international organization? Where does this power come from?
- Did the IMCO Assembly act within or outside its powers in the view of the ICJ? Why did the court find that to be the case?

- The ICJ concluded that the committee was incorrectly elected and, in principle, voided the election. Afterwards, a new election was held and Liberia and Panama were elected. What should happen to the decisions the committee took during its tenure until its election was annulled? When the committee was correctly elected, the new members adopted and confirmed all of the decisions taken by the previous committee. Was this necessary?
- After this case, the IMCO was reorganized and re-constituted under a revised treaty, and re-named the International Maritime Organization. Its governing council was also revised to include a better "geographical representation" and include developing nations. Would election now need to include states from these categories to be valid? How would you assess this question in light of the opinion above?

CHAPTER 6

Legal effects of acts

6.1 BASIS FOR LEGAL EFFECT

This chapter will examine the legal effect of acts of international organizations. At first glance, it might not be obvious that this is a question. Surely if states created an organization for better international cooperation, then the states would comply with the decision of the organization. However, as this study of international organizations reveals, states are both obliged to cooperate with the organization and yet also serve as the masters of the organization. This tension is also apparent in the legal effect of the organization's acts. Sometimes, organizations are empowered to make decisions that oblige the states to comply under international law, and at other times, the organization is not empowered to do so. The question in this chapter is: when is a state obliged under international law to follow the decision of an international organization?

The issue of obligation is not purely a yes or no question. Certainly, whether there is a legal obligation is one or the other, but the nature of the obligation might vary from organization to organization and from type of decision to type of decision. For example, an organization might be empowered to require states to comply with decisions on matters of peace and security and on matters of the budget, yet only be able to request cooperation on matters of international coordination. However, the states could have an obligation to cooperate in good faith with the organization, meaning that complete disregard without consideration of the request would violate an obligation to the organization. This chapter will not only identify when decisions are binding or not, but also the various nuances in the nature of the states' obligations to cooperate with the organization.

The first issue is the legal basis for any decision of an organization to have legal force at all:

Railway Traffic between Lithuania and Poland
(Railway Sector Landwarów-Kaisiadorys)
Advisory Opinion
1931 PCIJ (Ser. A/B) No. 42
Permanent Court of International Justice, 15 October 1931

[1] THE COURT, composed as above, gives the following opinion: ...

* * *

[11] The question put to the Court is, substantially, as follows: "Do the international engagements in force oblige Lithuania, in the present circumstances,

to open for traffic the Landwarów-Kaisiadorys railway sector?"

...

[14] After the war, the whole of this part of Europe was thrown into confusion by political events: the disappearance as a Russian naval port of Libau, which became a Latvian commercial port; the establishment of frontiers between new and old States, Latvia, Lithuania, Poland and Germany, where formerly German and Russian territory had been contiguous; events in Russia with their political and economic consequences. Trade exchanges were, accordingly, profoundly modified, both as regards their importance and the routes which they formerly followed.

[15] Such was the situation when, on 15 October 1927, Lithuania, under Article 11 of the Covenant, brought before the Council of the League of Nations, which had already often had to consider relations between Lithuania and Poland, a new dispute between the two Governments regarding events which had occurred in the Vilna territory. As a result, a Resolution was adopted by the Council on 10 December 1927, with the concurrence of the two Parties concerned. ...

* * *

[20] The representatives of the Lithuanian Government have declared in Court that Lithuania, on the ground of her present relations with Poland, does not intend to restore to use the Landwarów-Kaisiadorys railway sector, so far as it lies in her territory; she adopts this attitude as a form of pacific reprisals and believes herself to be entitled to persist in it "until the question of the allocation of Vilna and the adjoining territory has been settled by arbitration or by a decision given by the Court at the request of the two Governments concerned". It is however to be observed that the question whether Lithuania is or is not entitled to exercise reprisals, inter alia, by keeping the Landwarów-Kaisiadorys railway sector out of use, only arises if it is shown that the international engagements in force oblige Lithuania to open this sector for traffic. Should the Court arrive at the conclusion that no international engagements of this nature exist for Lithuania, the argument based on the alleged right of that country to engage in pacific reprisals ceases to be of any importance.

* * *

[21] Having regard to the conditions set out above, it is for the Court to consider whether there are any international engagements obliging Lithuania "to take the necessary measures to open for traffic the Landwarów-Kaisiadorys railway sector".

[22] The question put to the Court makes no mention of any particular international engagement; it refers not to the application of rules resulting from general international law, but to any contractual engagements in force which may create for Lithuania the obligation in question.

[23] According to the Advisory and Technical Committee, this obligation ensues from Article 23 (e) of the Covenant of the League of Nations and from the Convention of Paris of 8 May 1924, concerning Memel.

[24] To these instruments, the Polish Government adds the Resolution of the Council of the League of Nations of 10 December 1927.

[25] The Court will first of all consider this Resolution and then take Article 23 (e) of the Covenant, and the Convention concerning Memel, in that order.

1. – Council's Resolution of 10 December 1927.

[26] The Council's Resolution of 10 December 1927, is as follows

"The Council of the League of Nations

Declares that a state of war between two Members of the League is incompatible with the spirit and the letter of the Covenant, by which Lithuania and Poland are bound;

Takes note of the solemn declarations made by the Lithuanian representative that Lithuania does not consider herself in a state of war with Poland and that in consequence peace exists between their respective countries;

Takes note of the solemn declarations of the Polish representative that the Polish Republic fully recognizes and respects the political independence and territorial integrity of the Lithuanian Republic;

Recommends the two Governments to enter into direct negotiations as soon as possible in order to establish such relations between the two neighbouring States as will ensure "the good understanding between nations upon which peace depends";

Places at the disposal of the two Parties the good offices of the League and of its technical organs should their assistance be desired in the negotiations which it recommends;

Decides that the Lithuanian Government's complaints regarding the treatment of persons of Lithuanian race or speech, referred to in its appeal, shall be examined by a Committee, consisting of the Acting President of the Council and two other members of the Council appointed by him. This Committee will report to the Council in due course.

Decides that, in the event of a frontier incident or threat of an incident, the Secretary-General of the League of Nations may, at the request of one of the Parties, consult the Acting President of the Council and the Rapporteur, who shall then advise any steps they consider necessary to bring about a better state of feeling. The Council notes that both Parties have agreed to facilitate any enquiry by the League of Nations.

Notes with satisfaction the Polish representative's declarations to the effect that the Polish nationals referred to in the Lithuanian Government's appeal will be authorized to return to Poland without hindrance. In case of unforeseen difficulties, the Rapporteur would place his good offices at the disposal of the Parties with a view to removing those difficulties.

The Council declares that the present Resolution in no way affects questions on which the two Governments have differences of opinion."

[27] The representatives of Lithuania and of Poland participated in the adoption of this Resolution of the Council.

[28] The two Governments concerned being bound by their acceptance of the Council's Resolution, the Court must examine the scope of this engagement.

[29] The Council's Resolution recommends the two Governments "to enter

into direct negotiations as soon as possible in order to establish such relations between the two neighbouring States as will ensure 'the good understanding between nations upon which peace depends'."

[30] According to the view maintained before the Court on behalf of the Polish Government, Poland and Lithuania, in accepting this recommendation, undertook not only to negotiate but also to come to an agreement, with the result – it is alleged – that Lithuania has incurred an obligation to open the Landwarów-Kaisiadorys railway sector to traffic – a conclusion which would decide the question on which the Court is asked for an opinion.

[31] The Court is indeed justified in considering that the engagement incumbent on the two Governments in conformity with the Council's Resolution is not only to enter into negotiations, but also to pursue them as far as possible, with a view to concluding agreements. This point of view appears, moreover, to have been that adopted by the Council at its subsequent meetings. But an obligation to negotiate does not imply an obligation to reach an agreement, nor in particular does it imply that Lithuania, by undertaking to negotiate, has assumed an engagement, and is in consequence obliged to conclude the administrative and technical agreements indispensable for the re-establishment of traffic on the Landwarów-Kaisiadorys railway sector.

[32] There is therefore no justification for maintaining that the acceptance by the two Governments concerned of the Council's Resolution of 10 December 1927, implies that Lithuania has incurred an obligation to restore to use and to open to traffic the railway sector in question.

[33] The Court, having arrived at this conclusion, is not called upon to express an opinion with regard to the interpretation of the last paragraph of the Resolution to the effect that the Resolution "in no way affects questions on which the two Governments have differences of opinion". Indeed, only if the Court considered that the Resolution created, otherwise, for Lithuania fan obligation to restore the line in question to use would the arguments based on the clause in question be relevant.

* * *

2. – Article 23 (e) of the Covenant of the League of Nations.

[34] During the year 1928, the Council of the League noted the meagre results produced by the negotiations which had been entered into and carried on at Königsberg between Lithuania and Poland, in pursuance of the Council Resolution of 10 December 1927. The Council accordingly accepted the conclusions of its Rapporteur, M. Beelaerts van Blokland, and basing itself on the provisions of Article 23 (e) of the Covenant and on the Resolution of the Assembly of the League of Nations of 9 December 1920 – by which the Advisory and Technical Committee was instructed "to consider and propose measures calculated to ensure freedom of communications and transit at all times" – decided to request that Committee to present a report on the practical steps which might be adopted, account being taken of the international agreements in force.

[35] It was in pursuance of that invitation of the Council that the Advisory

Committee drew up its report dated 4 September 1930, in which it expressed the opinion, inter alia, that the railway sector Landwarów-Kaisiadorys should be restored, in order to serve for the international transit of goods coming from or going to the districts of Grodno and Vilna, or going to and coming from Königsberg, Memel, Libau and Riga.

[36] The Committee, whilst therefore holding that the interruption of goods transit has the effect of completely stopping certain forms of transport which cannot use these latter ports owing to the heavy cost of sending the goods by a roundabout route, considers that goods traffic between Poland and Lithuania other than transit traffic can continue to be carried on indirectly without any serious difficulty, and that it is not advisable at the present moment to resume passenger traffic.

[37] Accordingly, the Committee's report sets forth the following conclusions:

"1. They should remove these obstacles to freedom of transit ... in order to put an end to a situation which seems contrary to the objects of Article 23 (e) of the Covenant of the League of Nations and incompatible with the international engagements to which they have subscribed.

2. They should with this object proceed more especially:

(a) to draw up regulations on timber-floating on the Niemen, in conformity with the provisions of Articles 332 to 337 of the Treaty of Versailles;

(b) to conclude administrative and technical agreements essential for re-establishing, on the railway through Landwarów-Kaisiadorys, a continuous service which shall meet the requirements of international transit."

[38] As M. Silvain Dreyfus, President of the Advisory and Technical Committee, reaffirmed in his statement in Court at the hearing on 16 September 1931, the Committee considers that Lithuania is bound to open this railway sector to inter-national traffic under Article 23 (e) of the Covenant. It considers that if it were once admitted that certain countries would be at liberty, on the ground of political disagreements, to suppress international railway connections during long periods, the interests of third States, Members of the League, might suffer, since they would no longer enjoy the benefits of freedom of transit and communications to which they are, in principle, entitled under Article 23 (e) of the Covenant.

[39] Nevertheless, no third State has considered it necessary or expedient to intervene and to claim that Article 23 (e) has been violated by Lithuania.

[40] The Polish Government, however, basing itself on the opinion of the Advisory and Technical Committee, contends that Article 23 (e) of the Covenant constitutes an international engagement, obliging the Lithuanian State to open this line.

[41] But it should be observed that Article 23 (e) of the Covenant – whatever may be the obligations which do arise from it for States Members of the League of Nations – does not imply any specific obligations for these States to open any particular lines of communication.

[42] The actual wording of this article of the Covenant is as follows:

> "Article 23. – Subject to and in accordance with the provisions of international conventions existing or hereafter to be agreed upon, the Members of the League: ...
>
> (e) will make provision to secure and maintain freedom of communications and of transit and equitable treatment for the commerce of all Members of the League ...."

[43] Specific obligations can therefore only arise, as this text clearly states, from "international conventions existing or hereafter to be agreed upon", for instance from "general conventions to which other Powers may accede at a later date", as is stated in the Preamble to the Barcelona Convention on freedom of transit. If this interpretation is correct, it is impossible to deduce from the general rule contained in Article 23 (e) of the Covenant an obligation for Lithuania to open the Landwarów-Kaisiadorys railway sector for inter-national traffic, or for part of such traffic; such obligation could only result from a special agreement.

[44] In these circumstances, it is unnecessary for the Court to consider whether a State refusing to establish any communication with one or more other States, also Members of the League, would not be contravening Article 23 (e) of the Covenant, even if it had not signed any convention prescribing freedom of communications and transit. In this connection, the Court desires to emphasize that the present Opinion is not to be construed as giving any view in regard to the opinion expressed on behalf of the Advisory and Technical Committee, to the effect that, by the terms of Article 23 (e), "the Members of the League have certainly the right to request any Members at least to refrain from acting in opposition to the objects of this article".

3. – Application of the Convention of Paris of 8 May 1924, concerning Memel.

[45] Thirdly and lastly, certain provisions of the so-called Memel Convention, signed at Paris on 8 May 1924, between the British Empire, France, Italy and Japan of the one part, and Lithuania of the other part, for the establishment of the régime of the territory and port of Memel, have been relied on to prove the existence of an obligation incumbent upon Lithuania.

[46] Article 3 of Annex III of the Memel Convention lays down that "the Lithuanian Government shall ensure the freedom of transit by sea, by water or by rail, of traffic coming from or destined for the Memel territory or in transit through the said territory, and shall conform in this respect with the rules laid down by the Statute and Convention on the Freedom of Transit adopted by the Barcelona Conference ...".

[47] The Statute of Barcelona to which reference is thus made in the Memel Convention, and which is to this extent applicable to Lithuania, lays down, in Article 2, that contracting States "shall facilitate free transit, by rail or waterway, on routes in use convenient for international transit".

[48] The question therefore arises whether the Landwarów-Kaisiadorys railway sector is in use. On this point the very terms of the question submitted to the Court clearly establish that the line is not in use, for if it were in use, there

would be no reason for discussing the possibility of reopening it for traffic. But can it be said that the railway of which it forms part is in use as a whole, though the sector in question is not? That is a distinction which appears too subtle and which it is therefore impossible to draw, especially seeing that the question referred to the Court solely concerns the Landwarów-Kaisiadorys railway sector taken by itself.

[49]   Again, it is clear that this railway or railway sector is scarcely convenient for international transit to or from Memel, which alone is in question, since it only affords communication with Memel by means of a detour or by means of reloading on to barges at Kovno.

[50]   It follows therefore from the above that neither the Memel Convention nor the Statute of Barcelona to which the former refers can be adduced to prove that the Lithuanian Government is under an obligation to restore the Landwarów-Kaisiadorys railway sector to use and to open it for international traffic.

[51]   Furthermore, it must be remembered that, under the last paragraph of Article 3 of Annex III to the Memel Convention, to which reference has been made above, the Lithuanian Government undertakes "to permit and to grant all facilities for the traffic on the river to or from or in the port of Memel, and not to apply, in respect of such traffic, on the ground of the present political relations between Lithuania and Poland, the stipulations of Articles 7 and 8 of the Barcelona Statute on the Freedom of Transit and Article 13 of the Barcelona Recommendations relative to Ports placed under an International Régime".

[52]   These are obviously circumstances calculated to promote freedom of transit via the port of Memel, for the provisions which Lithuania abandons her right to apply are designed to place certain restrictions on this freedom. But it is to be observed that this clause in the Memel Convention applies solely to waterways and not to railways.

[53]   As regards railways, on the contrary, which might be in use and of importance to the port of Memel, regard is had to the present political relations between Lithuania and Poland, and it is clearly for this reason that Lithuania did not wish to abandon – as she had done with regard to waterways – her right to apply to them certain measures restricting freedom of traffic.

[54]   Seeing that the Memel Convention expressly forbids Lithuania to invoke Article 7 of the Barcelona Statute, with reference to freedom of transit by waterway, it is clear, on the other hand, that she might avail herself of it with regard to rail-ways of importance to the Memel territory. And, accordingly, even if the Landwarów-Kaisiadorys railway sector were in use and could serve Memel traffic, Lithuania would be entitled to invoke Article 7, as a ground for refusing to open this sector for traffic or for certain categories of traffic, in case of an emergency affecting her safety or vital interests.

[55]   From this point of view also, Lithuania is therefore not at present under the Memel Convention under any obligation to restore to use and open for traffic the railway sector in question.

*   *   *

[56] As appears from the foregoing considerations, the Court, after examining the engagements which have been invoked with regard to the re-opening for traffic, or for certain categories of traffic, of the Landwarów-Kaisiadorys railway sector, has reached the conclusion that, in the present circumstances, the obligation, which is alleged to be incumbent on Lithuania, does not exist.

[57] FOR THESE REASONS,

The Court,

unanimously,

is of opinion that the international engagements in force do not oblige Lithuania in the present circumstances to take the necessary steps to open for traffic or for certain categories of traffic the Landwarów-Kaisiadorys railway sector.

Notes

- In the view of the court, what is the relationship between the organization and its member states? Is it one of delegation of powers, or more effective treaty-making, or administration of legislative competence, and the necessary legal effect of that kind of power relationship?
- What kind of legal effect does the relevant act have? Is it binding, non-binding, or is it unclear? And why does it have that effect? What is the legal basis?

Now we will consider the perspective from within a national system. In the *Avena* case, the ICJ ordered the US, specifically Texas, to not execute an individual who was convicted without having had his consular officer notified, as required by the Vienna Convention on Consular Relations.[1] Following the *Avena* decision by the ICJ, the US President requested Texas to comply with the ICJ judgment, but Texas resisted, arguing that the US President did not have the power under the US Constitution to order compliance. The case went before the US Supreme Court:

Medellín v Texas
Case No. 06-984, Judgment
552 US 491 (2008)
US Supreme Court, 25 March 2008

CHIEF JUSTICE ROBERTS delivered the opinion of the Court.

The International Court of Justice (ICJ), located in the Hague, is a tribunal established pursuant to the United Nations Charter to adjudicate disputes between member states. In the *Case Concerning Avena and Other Mexican Nationals* (*Mex. v. U. S.*), 2004 I. C. J. 12 (Judgment of Mar. 31) (*Avena*), that tribunal considered a claim brought by Mexico against the United States. The ICJ held that, based on violations of the Vienna Convention, 51 named Mexican nationals were entitled to review and reconsideration of their state-court convictions and

---

1 Case Concerning Avena and Other Mexican Nationals (Mexico v US), Judgment, 2004 ICJ Reps 12 (International Court of Justice, 31 March 2004); Vienna Convention on Consular Relations, 24 April 1963, 596 UNTS 261.

sentences in the United States. This was so regardless of any forfeiture of the right to raise Vienna Convention claims because of a failure to comply with generally applicable state rules governing challenges to criminal convictions.

In *Sanchez-Llamas* v. *Oregon*, 548 U. S. 331 (2006) – issued after *Avena* but involving individuals who were not named in the *Avena* judgment – we held that, contrary to the ICJ's determination, the Vienna Convention did not preclude the application of state default rules. After the *Avena* decision, President George W. Bush determined, [p. 2] through a Memorandum to the Attorney General [citation omitted], that the United States would "discharge its international obligations" under *Avena* "by having State courts give effect to the decision."

Petitioner José Ernesto Medellín, who had been convicted and sentenced in Texas state court for murder, is one of the 51 Mexican nationals named in the Avena decision. Relying on the ICJ's decision and the President's Memorandum, Medellín filed an application for a writ of habeas corpus in state court. The Texas Court of Criminal Appeals dismissed Medellín's application as an abuse of the writ under state law, given Medellín's failure to raise his Vienna Convention claim in a timely manner under state law. We granted certiorari to decide two questions. *First*, is the ICJ's judgment in *Avena* directly enforceable as domestic law in a state court in the United States? ... We conclude that neither *Avena* nor the President's Memorandum constitutes directly enforceable federal law that preempts state limitations on the filing of successive habeas petitions. We therefore affirm the decision below.

...

I

A

...

The ICJ is "the principal judicial organ of the United Nations." United Nations Charter, Art. 92, 59 Stat. 1051, T. S. No. 993 (1945). It was established in 1945 pursuant to the United Nations Charter. The ICJ Statute – annexed to the U. N. Charter – provides the organizational framework and governing procedures for cases brought before the ICJ. Statute of the International Court of Justice (ICJ Statute), 59 Stat. 1055, T. S. No. 993 (1945).

Under Article 94(1) of the U. N. Charter, "[e]ach Member of the United Nations undertakes to comply with the decision of the [ICJ] in any case to which it is a party." 59 Stat. 1051. The ICJ's jurisdiction in any particular case, however, is dependent upon the consent of the parties. See Art. 36, 59 Stat. 1060. The ICJ Statute delineates two ways in which a nation may consent to ICJ jurisdiction: It may consent generally to jurisdiction on any question arising under a treaty or general international law, Art. [p. 4] 36(2), *ibid.*, or it may consent specifically to jurisdiction over a particular category of cases or disputes pursuant to a separate treaty, Art. 36(1), *ibid*. The United States originally consented to the general jurisdiction of the ICJ when it filed a declaration recognizing compulsory jurisdiction under Art. 36(2) in 1946. The United States withdrew from general ICJ jurisdiction in 1985. See U. S. Dept. of State Letter and Statement Concerning Termination of Acceptance of ICJ Compulsory Jurisdiction (7 October 1985), reprinted in 24 I. L. M. 1742 (1985). By ratifying the Optional Protocol to the Vienna Convention, the United States consented to the specific jurisdiction of the ICJ with respect to claims arising out of the Vienna Convention. On 7 March 2005, subsequent to the ICJ's judgment in *Avena*, the United States gave notice of withdrawal from the Optional Protocol to the Vienna Convention. Letter from Condoleezza Rice, Secretary of State, to Kofi A. Annan, Secretary-General of the United Nations.

...

II

...

No one disputes that the *Avena* decision – a decision that flows from the treaties through which the United States submitted to ICJ jurisdiction with respect to Vienna Convention disputes – constitutes an *international* law obligation on the part of the United States. But not all international law obligations automatically constitute binding federal law enforceable in United States courts. The question we confront here is whether the *Avena* judgment has automatic *domestic* legal effect such that the judgment of its own force applies in state and federal courts.

This Court has long recognized the distinction between treaties that automatically have effect as domestic law, and those that – while they constitute international law commitments – do not by themselves function as binding federal law. The distinction was well explained by Chief Justice Marshall's opinion in *Foster* v. *Neilson*, 2 Pet. 253, 315 (1829), overruled on other grounds, *United States* v. *Percheman*, 7 Pet. 51 (1833), which held that a treaty is "equivalent to an act of the legislature," and hence self-executing, when it "operates of itself without the aid of any legislative provision." *Foster, supra*, at 314. When, in contrast, "[treaty] stipulations are not self-executing they can only be enforced pursuant to legislation to carry them into effect." *Whitney* v. *Robertson*, 124 U. S. 190, 194 (1888). In sum, while treaties "may comprise international commitments ... they are not domestic law unless Congress has either enacted implementing statutes or the [p. 9] treaty itself conveys an intention that it be 'self-executing' and is ratified on these terms." *Igartúa-De La Rosa* v. *United States*, 417 F. 3d 145, 150 (CA1 2005) (en banc) (Boudin, C. J.). [footnote 2 – The label "self-executing" has on occasion been used to convey different meanings. What we mean by "self-executing" is that the treaty has automatic domestic effect as federal law upon ratification. Conversely, a "non-self-executing" treaty does not by itself give rise to domestically enforceable federal law. Whether such a treaty has domestic effect depends upon implementing legislation passed by Congress. [footnote omitted] Even when treaties are self-executing in the sense that they create federal law, the background presumption is that "[i]nternational agreements, even those directly benefiting private persons, generally do not create private rights or provide for a private cause of action in domestic courts." 2 Restatement (Third) of Foreign Relations Law of the United States §907, Comment *a*, p. 395 (1986) (hereinafter Restatement). Accordingly, a number of the Courts of Appeals have presumed that treaties do not create privately enforceable rights in the absence of express language to the contrary. See, *e.g., United States* v. *Emuegbunam*, 268 F. 3d 377, 389 (CA6 2001); *United States* v. *Jimenez Nava*, 243 F. 3d 192, 195 (CA5

2001); *United States* v. *Li*, 206 F. 3d 56, 60–61 (CA1 2000) (en banc); *Goldstar (Panama) S. A.* v. *United States*, 967 F. 2d 965, 968 (CA4 1992); *Canadian Transp. Co.* v. *United States*, 663 F. 2d 1081, 1092 (CADC 1980); *Mannington Mills, Inc.* v. *Congoleum Corp.*, 595 F. 2d 1287, 1298 (CA3 1979). [footnote omitted] The question is whether the *Avena* judgment has binding effect in domestic courts under the Optional Protocol, ICJ Statute, and U.N. Charter. Consequently, it is unnecessary to resolve whether the Vienna Convention is itself "self-executing" or whether it grants Medellín individually enforceable rights. [citation omitted] As in *Sanchez-Llamas*, 548 U. S., at 342–343, we thus assume, without deciding, that Article 36 grants foreign nationals "an individually enforceable right to request that their consular officers be notified of their detention, and an accompanying right to be informed by authorities of the availability of consular notification."]

A treaty is, of course, "primarily a compact between independent nations." *Head Money Cases*, 112 U. S. 580, 598 (1884). It ordinarily "depends for the enforcement of its provisions on the interest and the honor of the governments which are parties to it." *Ibid.*; see also The Federalist No. 33, p. 207 (J. Cooke ed. 1961) (A. Hamilton) (comparing laws that individuals are "bound to observe" as "the supreme law of the land" with "a mere treaty, dependent on the good faith of the parties"). "If these [interests] fail, its infraction becomes the subject of international negotiations and reclamations. ... It is obvious that with all this the judicial courts have nothing to do and can give no redress." *Head Money Cases, supra*, at 598. Only "[i]f the treaty contains stipulations which are self-executing, that is, require no legislation to make them operative, [will] they have the force and effect of a legislative enactment." *Whitney, supra*, at 194. [footnote omitted] [p. 10] ...

[p. 11] ... The obligation on the part of signatory nations to comply with ICJ judgments derives not from the Optional Protocol, but rather from Article 94 of the United Nations Charter – the provision that specifically addresses the effect of ICJ decisions. Article 94(1) provides that "[e]ach Member [p. 12] of the United Nations *undertakes to comply* with the decision of the [ICJ] in any case to which it is a party." 59 Stat. 1051 (emphasis added). The Executive Branch contends that the phrase "undertakes to comply" is not "an acknowledgement that an ICJ decision will have immediate legal effect in the courts of U.N. members," but rather "a *commitment* on the part of U. N. Members to take *future* action through their political branches to comply with an ICJ decision." Brief for United States as *Amicus Curiae* in *Medellín I*, O. T. 2004, No. 04–5928, p. 34.

We agree with this construction of Article 94. The Article is not a directive to domestic courts. It does not provide that the United States "shall" or "must" comply with an ICJ decision, nor indicate that the Senate that ratified the U. N. Charter intended to vest ICJ decisions with immediate legal effect in domestic courts. Instead, "[t]he words of Article 94 ... call upon governments to take certain action." *Committee of United States Citizens Living in Nicaragua* v. *Reagan*, 859 F. 2d 929, 938 (CADC 1988) (quoting *Diggs* v. *Richardson*, 555 F. 2d 848, 851 (CADC 1976); internal quotation marks omitted). See also *Foster*, 2 Pet., at 314, 315 (holding a treaty non-self executing because its text – "'all ... grants of land ... shall be ratified and confirmed'" – did not "act directly on the grants" but rather "pledge[d] the faith of the United States to pass acts which shall ratify and confirm them"). In other words, the U. N. Charter reads like "a compact between independent nations" that "depends for the enforcement of its provisions on the interest and the honor of the governments which are parties to it." *Head Money Cases*, 112 U. S., at 598. [footnote 5 – We do not read "undertakes" to mean that "'"[t]he United States ... shall be at liberty to make respecting th[e] matter, such laws as they think proper."'" *Post*, at 17–18 (BREYER, J., dissenting) (quoting *Todok v. Union State Bank of Harvard*, 281 U. S. 449, 453, 454 (1930) (holding that a treaty with Norway did *not* "operat[e] to override the law of [Nebraska] as to the disposition of homestead property")). Whether or not the United States "undertakes" to comply with a treaty says nothing about what laws it may enact. The United States is *always* "at liberty to make ... such laws as [it] think[s] proper." *Id.*, at 453. Indeed, a later-in-time federal statute supersedes inconsistent treaty provisions. See, *e.g., Cook v. United States*, 288 U. S. 102, 119–120 (1933). Rather, the "undertakes to comply" language confirms that further action to give effect to an ICJ judgment was contemplated, contrary to the dissent's position that such judgments constitute directly enforceable federal law, without more. See also *post*, at 1–3 (STEVENS, J., concurring in judgment).]

The remainder of Article 94 confirms that the U. N. Charter does not contemplate the automatic enforceability of ICJ decisions in domestic courts. [footnote omitted] Article 94(2) – the enforcement provision – provides the sole remedy for noncompliance: referral to the United Nations Security Council by an aggrieved state. 59 Stat. 1051.

The U. N. Charter's provision of an express diplomatic – that is, nonjudicial remedy is itself evidence that ICJ judgments were not meant to be enforceable in domestic courts. See *Sanchez-Llamas*, 548 U. S., at 347. And even this "quintessentially *international* remed[y]," *id.*, at 355, is not absolute. First, the Security Council must "dee[m] necessary" the issuance of a recommendation or measure to effectuate the judgment. Art. 94(2), 59 Stat. 1051. Second, as the President and Senate were undoubtedly aware in subscribing to the U. N. Charter and Optional Protocol, the United States retained the unqualified right to exercise its veto of any Security Council resolution.

...

If ICJ judgments were instead regarded as automatically enforceable domestic law, they would be immediately and directly binding on state and federal courts pursuant to the Supremacy Clause. Mexico or the ICJ would have no need to proceed to the Security Council to enforce the judgment in this case. Noncompliance with an ICJ judgment through exercise of the Security Council veto – always regarded as an option by the Executive and ratifying Senate during and after consideration of the U. N. Charter, Optional Protocol, and ICJ Statute – would no longer be a viable alternative. There would be nothing to veto. In light of the U. N. Charter's remedial scheme, there is no reason to believe that the President and Senate signed up for such a result.

In sum, Medellín's view that ICJ decisions are automatically enforceable as domestic law is fatally under[p. 15]mined by the enforcement structure established by Article 94. His construction would eliminate the option of noncompliance contemplated by Article 94(2), undermining the ability of the political branches to determine whether and how to comply with an ICJ judgment. Those sensitive foreign policy decisions would instead be transferred to state and federal courts charged with applying an ICJ judgment directly as domestic law. And those courts would not be empowered to decide whether to comply with the judgment – again, always regarded as an option by the political branches – any more than courts may consider whether to comply with any other species of domestic law. This result would be particularly anomalous in light of the principle that "[t]he conduct of the foreign relations of our Government is committed by the Constitution to the Executive and Legislative – 'the political' – Departments." *Oetjen* v. *Central Leather Co.*, 246 U. S. 297, 302 (1918).

...

[p. 19]

...

Our Framers established a careful set of procedures that must be followed before federal law can be created under the Constitution – vesting that decision in the political branches, subject to checks and balances. U. S. Const., Art. I, §7. They also recognized that treaties could create federal law, but again through the political branches, with the President making the treaty and the Senate approving it. Art. II, §2. The dissent's understanding of the treaty route, depending on an ad hoc judgment of the judiciary without looking to the treaty language – the very language negotiated by the President and approved by the Senate – cannot readily be ascribed to those same Framers.

...

[p. 22]

...

In sum, while the ICJ's judgment in *Avena* creates an international law obligation on the part of the United States, it does not of its own force constitute binding federal law that pre-empts state restrictions on the filing of successive habeas petitions. As we noted in *Sanchez-Llamas*, a contrary conclusion would be extraordinary, given that basic rights guaranteed by our own Constitution do not have the effect of displacing state procedural rules. See 548 U. S., at 360. Nothing in the text, background, negotiating and drafting history, or practice among signatory nations suggests that the President or Senate intended the improbable result of giving the judgments of an international tribunal a higher status than that enjoyed by "many of our most fundamental constitutional protections." *Ibid.*

Notes

- What is the Supreme Court's view on international law and international organizations specifically? Consider whether the Supreme Court looks at the relationship between the US and the UN as one of subject and legislature, or

delegation of international legislative powers, or just a more effective form of international cooperation.
- Where in the UN Charter does it say that the decisions of the ICJ should have this effect?

Thus, acts taken in the international legal system by an entity empowered to do so are binding within international law, but do not necessarily extend binding force, or give individuals a right of action, in domestic legal systems.

The key distinction in the legal effect of acts is therefore the distinction between binding and non-binding effect within the international legal system.

6.2 LEGAL VALUE OF THE ACT

Having concluded that organizations can hold legal authority from states to, in turn, impose obligations on states, we next turn to interpreting whether an organization has legal authority to bind the states and, if so, on which matters.

In some constitutive instruments, whether an organization has binding authority on a given matter is quite clearly articulated, but for others, the precise legal authority is vague. Usually, the legal effect of being binding or non-binding is expressly stated in the constitutive instrument creating the organization. For example, the Treaty Establishing the European Coal and Steel Community, states quite clearly that:

> In order to carry out the tasks assigned to it the High Authority shall, in accordance with the provisions of this Treaty, take decisions, make recommendations or deliver opinions. Decisions shall be binding in their entirety. Recommendations shall be binding as to the aims to be pursued but shall leave the choice of the appropriate methods for achieving these aims to those to whom the recommendations are addressed. Opinions shall have no binding force. In cases where the High Authority is empowered to take a decision, it may confine itself to making a recommendation.[2]

On the basis of this provision, a "decision" is binding, but a "recommendation" is only binding insofar as outcome is concerned, not conduct, and "opinions" are not binding at all.

Similarly, the European Union can clearly adopt binding and non-binding acts. The Treaty of the Functioning of the European Union states that:

> To exercise the Union's competences, the institutions shall adopt regulations, directives, decisions, recommendations and opinions.
> A regulation shall have general application. It shall be binding in its entirety and directly applicable in all Member States.

---

2 Treaty Establishing the European Coal and Steel Community, 18 April 1951, article 14. https://eur-lex.europa.eu, © European Union 1998–2020.

> A directive shall be binding, as to the result to be achieved, upon each Member State to which it is addressed, but shall leave to the national authorities the choice of form and methods.
>
> A decision shall be binding in its entirety upon those to whom it is addressed.
>
> Recommendations and opinions shall have no binding force.[3]

Therefore, under the EU legal order, a "regulation" is binding in terms of conduct and directly applies within Member State legal orders, a "decision" is also binding in terms of conduct but does not direct apply within Member State legal orders, a "directive" is binding in terms of outcome, and a "recommendation" or "opinion" is not binding.

Yet the Convention on International Civil Aviation takes a different view on "recommendations," and instead provides that:

> If the Council is of the opinion that the airports or other air navigation facilities, including radio and meteorological services, of a contracting State are not reasonably adequate for the safe, regular, efficient, and economical operation of international air services, present or contemplated, the Council shall consult with the State directly concerned, and other States affected, with a view to finding means by which the situation may be remedied, and may make recommendations for that purpose. No contracting State shall be guilty of an infraction of this Convention if it fails to carry out these recommendations.[4]

In this instrument, a "recommendation" is not binding in terms of outcome or conduct.

This approach is almost identical to that taken at the UN. If we look at the UN Charter, to be discussed in more detail below, we find that "recommendations" under articles 10–14, 58 and 105, are only authorizations to trigger other acts. This means that they are binding in a sense, in that subsequent action cannot occur without their adoption, but clearly they alone do not impose an obligation.

Also consider the Convention of the World Meteorological Organization, which states that:

> *(a)* All Members shall do their utmost to implement the decisions of [the WMO] Congress;
>
> *(b)* If, however, any Member finds it impracticable to give effect to some requirement in a technical resolution adopted by Congress, such Member

---

3 The Treaty of the Functioning of the European Union (consolidated version), Official Journal of the European Union C 326/47 (26 October 2012), article 288 https://eur-lex.europa.eu, © European Union 1998–2020.
4 Convention on International Civil Aviation, 7 December 1944 ("Chicago Convention"), 15 UNTS 102, ICAO Doc. 7300/9, article 69. Reproduced with permission of the International Civil Aviation Organization.

shall inform the Secretary-General of the Organization whether its inability to give effect to it is provisional or final, and state its reasons therefor.[5]

So, for the WMO, a "decision" imposes an obligation of conduct, but not outcome.

Some organizations can adopt binding decisions against individuals, such as the International Criminal Court. Consider the Rome Statute of the International Criminal Court, where it lays out its binding power using the terminology of jurisdiction, responsibility and international cooperation:

Article 25 Individual criminal responsibility

1. The Court shall have jurisdiction over natural persons pursuant to this Statute.
2. A person who commits a crime within the jurisdiction of the Court shall be individually responsible and liable for punishment in accordance with this Statute.
3. In accordance with this Statute, a person shall be criminally responsible and liable for punishment for a crime within the jurisdiction of the Court if that person: (a) Commits such a crime ... (b) Orders, solicits or induces the commission of such a crime ... (c) ... aids, abets or otherwise assists in its commission ... (d) In any other way contributes to the commission ... (e) In respect of the crime of genocide, directly and publicly incites others to commit genocide; (f) Attempts to commit such a crime ...
4. No provision in this Statute relating to individual criminal responsibility shall affect the responsibility of States under international law.

Article 86 General obligation to cooperate

States Parties shall, in accordance with the provisions of this Statute, cooperate fully with the Court in its investigation and prosecution of crimes within the jurisdiction of the Court.[6]

In this case, the Rome Statute does not specify that its acts in regards to individuals are binding because it is not addressing states, but in the case of acts in regards to states, it invokes cooperation.

---

5 Convention of the World Meteorological Organization, 11 October 1946, 77 UNTS 143, *as amended*, article 9, Execution of Congress decisions. Reproduced with permission of the World Meteorological Organization.
6 Rome Statute of the International Criminal Court, 17 July 1998, 2187 UNTS 90. International Criminal Court, *available at* www.icc-cpi.int/resource-library/Documents/RS-Eng.pdf.

In contrast to the acts above, the Organization for the Prohibition of Chemical Weapons does not itself adopt binding decisions as it is not an enforcement organization. Instead, the OPCW is a reporting, investigation, and referral body that monitors state party obligations under the Chemical Weapons Convention. Specifically, article XII (Measures to Redress a Situation and to Ensure Compliance, including Sanctions) states that:

1. The Conference [of States Parties to the Convention on the Prohibition of the Development, Production, Stockpiling and Use of Chemical Weapons and on their Destruction (CWC)] shall take the necessary measures, as set forth in paragraphs 2, 3 and 4, to ensure compliance with this Convention and to redress and remedy any situation which contravenes the provisions of this Convention. In considering action pursuant to this paragraph, the Conference shall take into account all information and recommendations on the issues submitted by the Executive Council [of the OPCW].
2. In cases where a State Party has been requested by the Executive Council to take measures to redress a situation raising problems with regard to its compliance, and where the State Party fails to fulfil the request within the specified time, the Conference may, inter alia, upon the recommendation of the Executive Council, restrict or suspend the State Party's rights and privileges under this Convention until it undertakes the necessary action to conform with its obligations under this Convention.
3. In cases where serious damage to the object and purpose of this Convention may result from activities prohibited under this Convention, in particular by Article I, the Conference may recommend collective measures to States Parties in conformity with international law.
4. The Conference shall, in cases of particular gravity, bring the issue, including relevant information and conclusions, to the attention of the United Nations General Assembly and the United Nations Security Council.[7]

Based on this brief survey of various organizations, we see that each may be empowered to adopt binding or non-binding acts, with varying normativity, and with a variety of names. Each constitutive instrument, and each applicable legal regime, thus determines the legal value of the various relevant legal acts. Whether the act is called "decision," "recommendation," or "opinion" is not solely determinative.

In addition to the existence of legal authority, we must also consider whether the organization actually exercised its full authority in any given act. It may be that

---

[7] Convention on the Prohibition of the Development, Production, Stockpiling and Use of Chemical Weapons and on their Destruction (Chemical Weapons Convention), 27 September 2005, 1974 UNTS 45. From the United Nations Treaty Series, by the United Nations © 2005 United Nations. Reprinted with the permission of the United Nations.

the organization was empowered to make binding decisions on a particular matter, but chooses not to vest its decision with obligatory force. For example, in the ICJ *East Timor* case,[8] the court declined to decide whether the relevant Security Council resolutions could potentially be binding, because the Security Council had clearly not intended for the resolutions to be binding. Nowadays, the Security Council is usually careful to explain the basis for its exercise of power and makes it explicit whether the act is intended to be binding or not. But in the first use of its Chapter VII powers, the decision on North Korea, the Security Council was fairly vague about which powers it was exercising and what legal effect it meant for the resolution to have:

United Nations Security Council Resolution 82 (25 June 1950)

The Security Council,

Recalling the finding of the General Assembly ... that the Government of the Republic of Korea is a lawfully established government having effective control and jurisdiction ...

Noting with grave concern the armed attack on the Republic of Korea by forces from North Korea,

Determines that this action constitutes a breach of the peace; and ...

Calls for the immediate cessation of hostilities;

Calls upon the authorities in North Korea to withdraw forthwith their armed forces to the 38th parallel; ...

Requests the United Nations Commission on Korea:

(a) To communicate its fully considered recommendations on the situation with the least possible delay;
(b) To observe the withdrawal of North Korean forces to the 38th parallel;
(c) To keep the Security Council informed on the execution of this resolution:

Calls upon all Member States to render every assistance to the United Nations in the execution of this resolution and. to refrain from giving assistance to the North Korean authorities

The Security Council Resolution mentioned above is not particularly controversial, but it presents the need to interpret the effect of an act. In determining the legal effect of an act of an international organization, we must be careful to identify the precise legal effect the organization can impose within a possible range of options, and ask whether the organization has in fact exercised its authority to its fullest extent.

---

8 *See* Case Concerning East Timor (Portugal v Australia), Judgment, 1995 ICJ Reps. 90, at 104, para. 32 (International Court of Justice, 30 June 1995).

6.2.1 Binding legal effect

An international organization might have the authority to issue a legally binding decision or non-legally binding recommendation. In the case of the United Nations, and following the discussion above, the UN Charter makes a distinction between acts taken under Chapter VI and Chapter VII of the Charter and between "decisions" and "recommendations," and makes distinctions between the authority held by the UN Security Council and the General Assembly. In general, the UN General Assembly can issue non-binding recommendations under Chapter VI, and the UN Security Council can issue either non-binding recommendations under Chapter VI or binding decisions under Chapter VII. This statement is, however, an oversimplification, and the precise boundaries between these powers are still subject to some discussion. This chapter will focus on the United Nations as a case study. Other international organizations, such as those mentioned above, will have a similar analysis by analogy.

6.2.1.1 United Nations Security Council

First we will begin with the Security Council, and consider the opinion of the ICJ in the *Namibia* case. Note that this advisory opinion is different from the *International Status of South West Africa* advisory opinion issued in 1950. That earlier case dealt with the succession of the UN to the mandate system of the League of Nations. This present opinion, coming more than 20 years later, was requested after the UN General Assembly terminated the mandate and the Security Council found that the continued presence of South Africa in Namibia (South West Africa) was unlawful. The question was the legal effect of the act of the Security Council:

**Legal Consequences for States of the Continued Presence
of South Africa in Namibia (South West Africa)
Notwithstanding Security Council Resolution 276 (1970)
Advisory Opinion
1971 ICJ Reps. 16
International Court of Justice, 21 June 1971**

1. The question upon which the advisory opinion of the Court has been asked was laid before the Court by a letter dated 29 July 1970, filed in the Registry on 10 August, and addressed by the Secretary-General of the United Nations to the President of the Court. In his letter the Secretary-General informed the Court that, by resolution 284 (1970) adopted on 29 July 1970, certified true copies of the English and French texts of which were transmitted with his letter, the Security Council of the United Nations had decided to submit to the Court, with the request for an advisory opinion to be transmitted to the Security Council at an early date, the question set out in the resolution …

* * *

…

42. Having established that it is properly seised of a request for an advisory opinion, the Court will now proceed to an analysis of the question placed before it: "What are the legal consequences for

States of the continued presence of South Africa in Namibia, notwithstanding Security Council resolution 276 (1970)?"

43. The Government of South Africa in both its written and oral statements has covered a wide field of history, going back to the origin and functioning of the Mandate. The same and similar problems were dealt with by other governments, the Secretary-General of the United Nations and the Organization of African Unity in their written and oral statements.

44. A series of important issues is involved: the nature of the Mandate, its working under the League of Nations, the consequences of the demise of the League and of the establishment of the United Nations and the impact of further developments within the new organization. While the Court is aware that this is the sixth time it has had to deal with the issues involved in the Mandate for South West Africa, it has nonetheless reached the conclusion that it is necessary for it to consider and summarize some of the issues underlying the question addressed to it. In particular, the Court will examine the substance and scope of Article 22 of the League Covenant and the nature of "C" mandates.

45. ... As the Court recalled in its 1950 Advisory Opinion on the International Status of South-West Africa, in the setting-up of the mandates system "two principles were considered to be of paramount importance: the principle of non-annexation and the principle that the well-being and development of such peoples form 'a sacred trust of civilization'" (I.C.J. Reports 1950, p. 131).

46. It is self-evident that the "trust" had to be exercised for the benefit of the peoples concerned, who were admitted to have interests of their own and to possess a potentiality for independent existence on the attainment of a certain stage of development: the mandates system was designed to provide peoples "not yet" able to manage their own affairs with the help and guidance necessary to enable them to arrive at the stage where they would be "able to stand by themselves". ... This made it clear that those Powers which were to undertake the task envisaged would be acting exclusively as mandatories on behalf of the League. As to the position of the League, the Court found in its 1950 Advisory Opinion that: "The League was not, as alleged by [the South African] Government, a 'mandator' in the sense in which this term is used in the national law of certain States." The Court pointed out that: "The Mandate was created, in the interest of the inhabitants of the territory, and of humanity in general, as an international institution with an international object – a sacred trust of civilisation." Therefore, the Court found, the League "had only assumed an international function of supervision and control" (I.C.J. Reports 1950, p. 132). ...

* * *

55. The Court will now turn to the situation which arose on the demise of the League and with the birth of the United Nations. As already recalled, the League of Nations was the international organization entrusted with the exercise of the supervisory functions of the Mandate. Those functions were an indispensable element of the Mandate. But that does not mean that the mandates institution was to collapse with the disappearance of the original supervisory machinery. To the question whether the continuance of a mandate was inseparably linked with the existence of the League, the answer must

be that an institution established for the fulfilment of a sacred trust cannot be presumed to lapse before the achievement of its purpose. The responsibilities of both mandatory and supervisor resulting from the mandates institution were complementary, and the disappearance of one or the other could not affect the survival of the institution. ... In the particular case, specific provisions were made and decisions taken for the transfer of functions from the organization which was to be wound up to that which came into being.

56. Within the framework of the United Nations an international trusteeship system was established and it was clearly contemplated that mandated territories considered as not yet ready for independence would be converted into trust territories under the United Nations international trusteeship system. This system established a wider and more effective international supervision than had been the case under the mandates of the League of Nations.

57. It would have been contrary to the overriding purpose of the mandates system to assume that difficulties in the way of the replacement of one regime by another designed to improve international supervision should have been permitted to bring about, on the dissolution of the League, a complete disappearance of international supervision. To accept the contention of the Government of South Africa on this point would have entailed the reversion of mandated territories to colonial status, and the virtual replacement of the mandates regime by annexation, so determinedly excluded in 1920.

...

60. Article 80, paragraph 1, of the Charter was thus interpreted by the Court as providing that the system of replacement of mandates by trusteeship agreements, resulting from Chapter XII of the Charter, shall not "be construed in or of itself to alter in any manner the rights whatsoever of any States or any peoples" ...

* * *

73. ... As stated in the Court's 1962 Judgment:

"... the League of Nations in ending its own existence did not terminate the Mandates but ... definitely intended to continue them by its resolution of 18 April 1946." (I.C.J. Reports 1962, p. 334)

...

78. In the light of the foregoing review, there can be no doubt that, as consistently recognized by this Court, the Mandate survived the demise of the League, and that South Africa admitted as much for a number of years. Thus the supervisory element, an integral part of the Mandate, was bound to survive, and the Mandatory continued to be accountable for the performance of the sacred trust. To restrict the responsibility of the Mandatory to the sphere of conscience or of moral obligation would amount to conferring upon that Power rights to which it was not entitled, and at the same time to depriving the peoples of the Territory of rights which they had been guaranteed. It would mean that the Mandatory would be unilaterally entitled to decide the destiny of the people of South West Africa at its discretion. ...

* * *

84. Where the United Nations is concerned, the records show that, throughout a period of twenty years, the General Assembly, by virtue of the powers vested

in it by the Charter, called upon the South African Government to perform its obligations arising out of the Mandate. ... These proposals were rejected by South Africa, which refused to accept the principle of the supervision of its administration of the Territory by the United Nations.

...

86. To complete this brief summary of the events preceding the present request for advisory opinion, it must be recalled that in 1955 and 1956 the Court gave at the request of the General Assembly two further advisory opinions on matters concerning the Territory. Eventually the General Assembly adopted resolution 2145 (XXI) on the termination of the Mandate for South West Africa. Subsequently the Security Council adopted resolution 276 (1970), which declared the continued presence of South Africa in Namibia to be illegal and called upon States to act accordingly. ...

* * *

105. General Assembly resolution 2145 (XXI), after declaring the termination of the Mandate, added in operative paragraph 4 "that South Africa has no other right to administer the Territory". This part of the resolution has been objected to as deciding a transfer of territory. That in fact is not so. The pronouncement made by the General Assembly is based on a conclusion, referred to earlier, reached by the Court in 1950:

> "The authority which the Union Government exercises over the Territory is based on the Mandate. If the Mandate lapsed, as the Union Government contends, the latter's authority would equally have lapsed." (I.C.J. Reports 1950, p. 133)

This was confirmed by the Court in its Judgment of 21 December 1962 in the South West Africa cases (Ethiopia v. South Africa; Liberia v. South Africa) (I.C.J. Reports 1962, p. 333). Relying on these decisions of the Court, the General Assembly declared that the Mandate having been terminated "South Africa has no other right to administer the Territory". This is not a finding on facts, but the formulation of a legal situation. For it would not be correct to assume that, because the General Assembly is in principle vested with recommendatory powers, it is debarred from adopting, in specific cases within the framework of its competence, resolutions which make determinations or have operative design.

* * *

106. By resolution 2145 (XXI) the General Assembly terminated the Mandate. However, lacking the necessary powers to ensure the withdrawal of South Africa from the Territory, it enlisted the co-operation of the Security Council by calling the latter's attention to the resolution, thus acting in accordance with Article 11, paragraph 2, of the Charter.

107. The Security Council responded to the call of the General Assembly. It "took note" of General Assembly resolution 2145 (XXI) in the preamble of its resolution 245 (1968); it took it "into account" in resolution 246 (1968); in resolutions 264 (1969) and 269 (1969) it adopted certain measures directed towards the implementation of General Assembly resolution 2145 (XXI) and, finally, in resolution 276 (1970), it reaffirmed resolution 264 (1969) and recalled resolution 269 (1969).

108 Resolution 276 (1970) of the Security Council, specifically mentioned

in the text of the request, is the one essential for the purposes of the present advisory opinion. Before analysing it, however, it is necessary to refer briefly to resolutions 264 (1969) and 269 (1969), since these two resolutions have, together with resolution 276 (1970), a combined and a cumulative effect. Resolution 264 (1969), in paragraph 3 of its operative part, calls upon South Africa to withdraw its administration from Namibia immediately. Resolution 269 (1969), in view of South Africa's lack of compliance, after recalling the obligations of Members under Article 25 of the Charter, calls upon the Government of South Africa, in paragraph 5 of its operative part, "to withdraw its administration from the territory immediately and in any case before 4 October 1969". The preamble of resolution 276 (1970) reaffirms General Assembly resolution 2145 (XXI) and espouses it, by referring to the decision, not merely of the General Assembly, but of the United Nations "that the Mandate of South-West Africa was terminated". In the operative part, after condemning the non-compliance by South Africa with General Assembly and Security Council resolutions pertaining to Namibia, the Security Council declares, in paragraph 2, that "the continued presence of the South African authorities in Namibia is illegal" and that consequently all acts taken by the Government of South Africa "on behalf of or concerning Namibia after the termination of the Mandate are illegal and invalid". In paragraph 5 the Security Council "Calls upon all States, particularly those which have economic and other interests in Namibia, to refrain from any dealings with the Government of South Africa which are inconsistent with operative paragraph 2 of this resolution".

109. It emerges from the communications bringing the matter to the Security Council's attention, from the discussions held and particularly from the text of the resolutions themselves, that the Security Council, when it adopted these resolutions, was acting in the exercise of what it deemed to be its primary responsibility, the maintenance of peace and security, which, under the Charter, embraces situations which might lead to a breach of the peace. (Art. 1, para. 1.) In the preamble of resolution 264 (1969) the Security Council was "Mindful of the grave consequences of South Africa's continued occupation of Namibia" and in paragraph 4 of that resolution it declared "that the actions of the Government of South Africa designed to destroy the national unity and territorial integrity of Namibia through the establishment of Bantustans are contrary to the provisions of the United Nations Charter". In operative paragraph 3 of resolution 269 (1969) the Security Council decided "that the continued occupation of the territory of Namibia by the South African authorities constitutes an aggressive encroachment on the authority of the United Nations, ...". In operative paragraph 3 of resolution 276 (1970) the Security Council declared further "that the defiant attitude of the Government of South Africa towards the Council's decisions undermines the authority of the United Nations".

110. As to the legal basis of the resolution, Article 24 of the Charter vests in the Security Council the necessary authority to take action such as that taken in the present case. The reference in paragraph 2 of this Article to specific powers of the Security Council under certain chapters of the Charter does not exclude the

existence of general powers to discharge the responsibilities conferred in paragraph 1. Reference may be made in this respect to the Secretary-General's Statement, presented to the Security Council on 10 January 1947, to the effect that "the powers of the Council under Article 24 are not restricted to the specific grants of authority contained in Chapters VI, VII, VIII and XII ... the Members of the United Nations have conferred upon the Security Council powers commensurate with its responsibility for the maintenance of peace and security. The only limitations are the fundamental principles and purposes found in Chapter I of the Charter."

111. As to the effect to be attributed to the declaration contained in paragraph 2 of resolution 276 (1970), the Court considers that the qualification of a situation as illegal does not by itself put an end to it. It can only be the first, necessary step in an endeavour to bring the illegal situation to an end.

112. It would be an untenable interpretation to maintain that, once such a declaration had been made by the Security Council under Article 24 of the Charter, on behalf of all member States, those Members would be free to act in disregard of such illegality or even to recognize violations of law resulting from it. When confronted with such an internationally unlawful situation, Members of the United Nations would be expected to act in consequence of the declaration made on their behalf. The question therefore arises as to the effect of this decision of the Security Council for States Members of the United Nations in accordance with Article 25 of the Charter.

113. It has been contended that Article 25 of the Charter applies only [p. 53] to enforcement measures adopted under Chapter VII of the Charter. It is not possible to find in the Charter any support for this view. Article 25 is not confined to decisions in regard to enforcement action but applies to "the decisions of the Security Council" adopted in accordance with the Charter. Moreover, that Article is placed, not in Chapter VII, but immediately after Article 24 in that part of the Charter which deals with the functions and powers of the Security Council. If Article 25 had reference solely to decisions of the Security Council concerning enforcement action under Articles 41 and 42 of the Charter, that is to say, if it were only such decisions which had binding effect, then Article 25 would be superfluous, since this effect is secured by Articles 48 and 49 of the Charter.

114. It has also been contended that the relevant Security Council resolutions are couched in exhortatory rather than mandatory language and that, therefore, they do not purport to impose any legal duty on any State nor to affect legally any right of any State. The language of a resolution of the Security Council should be carefully analysed before a conclusion can be made as to its binding effect. In view of the nature of the powers under Article 25, the question whether they have been in fact exercised is to be determined in each case, having regard to the terms of the resolution to be interpreted, the discussions leading to it, the Charter provisions invoked and, in general, all circumstances that might assist in determining the legal consequences of the resolution of the Security Council.

115. Applying these tests, the Court recalls that in the preamble of resolution 269 (1969), the Security Council was "Mindful of its responsibility to take

necessary action to secure strict compliance with the obligations entered into by States Members of the United Nations under the provisions of Article 25 of the Charter of the United Nations". The Court has therefore reached the conclusion that the decisions made by the Security Council in paragraphs 2 and 5 of resolutions 276 (1970), as related to paragraph 3 of resolution 264 (1969) and paragraph 5 of resolution 269 (1969), were adopted in conformity with the purposes and principles of the Charter and in accordance with its Articles 24 and 25. The decisions are consequently binding on all States Members of the United Nations, which are thus under obligation to accept and carry them out.

116. In pronouncing upon the binding nature of the Security Council decisions in question, the Court would recall the following passage in its Advisory Opinion of 11 April 1949 on Reparation for Injuries Suffered in the Service of the United Nations:

> "The Charter has not been content to make the Organization created by it merely a centre 'for harmonizing the actions of nations in the attainment of these common ends' (Article 1, para. 4). It has equipped that centre with organs, and has given it special tasks. It has defined the position of the Members in relation to the Organization [p. 54] by requiring them to give it every assistance in any action undertaken by it (Article 2, para. 5), and to accept and carry out the decisions of the Security Council." (I.C.J. Reports 1949, p. 178)

Thus when the Security Council adopts a decision under Article 25 in accordance with the Charter, it is for member States to comply with that decision, including those members of the Security Council which voted against it and those Members of the United Nations who are not members of the Council. To hold otherwise would be to deprive this principal organ of its essential functions and powers under the Charter.

* * *

117. Having reached these conclusions, the Court will now address itself to the legal consequences arising for States from the continued presence of South Africa in Namibia, notwithstanding Security Council resolution 276 (1970). A binding determination made by a competent organ of the United Nations to the effect that a situation is illegal cannot remain without consequence. Once the Court is faced with such a situation, it would be failing in the discharge of its judicial functions if it did not declare that there is an obligation, especially upon Members of the United Nations, to bring that situation to an end. As this Court has held, referring to one of its decisions declaring a situation as contrary to a rule of international law: "This decision entails a legal consequence, namely that of putting an end to an illegal situation" (I.C.J. Reports 1951, p. 82).

118. South Africa, being responsible for having created and maintained a situation which the Court has found to have been validly declared illegal, has the obligation to put an end to it. It is therefore under obligation to withdraw its administration from the Territory of Namibia. ...

119. The member States of the United Nations are, for the reasons given in paragraph 115 above, under obligation to recognize the illegality and invalidity

of South Africa's continued presence in Namibia. They are also under obligation to refrain from lending any support or any form of assistance to South Africa with reference to its occupation of Namibia, subject to paragraph 125 below.

...

126. As to non-member States, although not bound by Articles 24 and 25 of the Charter, they have been called upon in paragraphs 2 and 5 of resolution 276 (1970) to give assistance in the action which has been taken by the United Nations with regard to Namibia. In the view of the Court, the termination of the Mandate and the declaration of the illegality of South Africa's presence in Namibia are opposable to all States in the sense of barring erga omnes the legality of a situation which is maintained in violation of international law: in particular, no State which enters into relations with South Africa concerning Namibia may expect the United Nations or its Members to recognize the validity or effects of such relationship, or of the consequences thereof. The Mandate having been terminated by decision of the international organization in which the supervisory authority over its administration was vested, and South Africa's continued presence in Namibia having been declared illegal, it is for non-member States to act in accordance with those decisions.

Notes

- What kind of act was at issue: "decision," "recommendation," "opinion," or another? Does that act permit binding obligations? And did the Security Council exercise its binding authority?
- Why is the act having the value it does? Is it based on the UN Charter, or another source?
- Does the Security Council have the competence over the subject matter (*ratione materiae*) in this case to issue a binding order? And does the Security Council have authority over the subject of the order (*ratione personae*) in this case?
- Why does the court find that a "binding determination ... cannot remain without consequence"? How is it binding? Did the UN Security Council have that power and exercise that power? Perhaps it is interesting to note that the French version of the Court's judgment, which is equally authoritative, used the expression "*décision*" as the translation of "determination." Does that change our view?
- Is it legally binding or politically binding? Or is it binding in the sense of not being subject to further discussion? The court continues to say that "there is an obligation ... to bring the situation to an end."
- Is it more helpful to distinguish between whether the act is binding from what the content of the obligation is? Whether or not you believe the ICJ was correct about the binding authority of the Security Council's act, what did the act request the state to do? How is that different from whether the act was binding or not?

- How does the ICJ view the relationship between the UN and the state? Is it a legislative or delegation question, or is it a view on how to more efficiently conduct international cooperation?

The UN Security Council has authority over matters concerning peace and security. Thus, in order for an act of the UN Security Council to have legal effect, it must fall within its competences. Consider the following excerpt from the *Wall* advisory opinion:

Legal Consequences of the Construction of a Wall in the Occupied Palestinian Territory
Advisory Opinion
2004 ICJ Reps. 136
International Court of Justice, 9 July 2004

26. Under Article 24 of the Charter the Security Council has "primary responsibility for the maintenance of international peace and security". In that regard it can impose on States "an explicit obligation of compliance if for example it issues an order or command ... under Chapter VII" and can, to that end, "require enforcement by coercive action" (*Certain Expenses of the United Nations (Article 17, paragraph 2, of the Charter), Advisory Opinion, I. C. J. Reports 1962*, p. 163). However, the Court would emphasize that Article 24 refers to a primary, but not necessarily exclusive, competence. The General Assembly does have the power, *inter alia*, under Article 14 of the Charter, to "recommend measures for the peaceful adjustment" of various situations *(ibid)*. "[T]he only limitation which Article 14 imposes on the General Assembly is the restriction found in Article 12, namely, that the Assembly should not recommend measures while the Security Council is dealing with the same matter unless the Council requests it to do so." (*I. C. J. Reports 1962*, p. 163.)

27. As regards the practice of the United Nations, both the General Assembly and the Security Council initially interpreted and applied Article 12 to the effect that the Assembly could not make a recommendation on a question concerning the maintenance of international peace and security while the matter remained on the Council's agenda. Thus the Assembly during its fourth session refused to recommend certain measures on the question of Indonesia, on the ground, *inter alia*, that the Council remained seised of the matter (*Official Records of the General Assembly, Fourth Session*, Ad Hoc Political Committee, Summary Records of Meetings, 27 September–7 December 1949, 56th Meeting, 3 December 1949, p. 339, para. 118). As for the Council, on a number of occasions it deleted items from its agenda in order to enable the Assembly to deliberate on them (for example, in respect of the Spanish question *(Official Records of the Security Council, First Year: Second Series, No. 21*, 79th Meeting, 4 November 1946, p. 498), in connection with incidents on the Greek border *(Official Records of the Security Council, Second Year, No. 89*, 202nd Meeting, 15 September 1947, pp. 2404–2405) and in regard to the Island of Taiwan (Formosa) *(Official Records of*

the Security Council, Fifth Year, No. 48, 506th Meeting, 29 September 1950, p. 5)). In the case of the Republic of Korea, the Council decided on 31 January 1951 to remove the relevant item from the list of matters of which it was seised in order to enable the Assembly to deliberate on the matter (*Official Records of the Security Council, Sixth Year*, S/PV.531, 53 1st Meeting, 3 1 January 0195 1, p. 11–12, para. 57).

However, this interpretation of Article 12 has evolved subsequently. Thus the General Assembly deemed itself entitled in 1961 to adopt recommendations in the matter of the Congo (resolutions 1955 (XV) and 1600 (XVI)) and in 1963 in respect of the Portuguese colonies (resolution 1913 (XVIII)) while those cases still appeared on the Council's agenda, without the Council having adopted any recent resolution concerning them. In response to a question posed by Peru during the twenty-third session of the General Assembly, the Legal Counsel of the United Nations confirmed that the Assembly interpreted the words "is exercising the functions" in Article 12 of the Charter as meaning "is exercising the functions at this moment" (General Assembly, Twenty-third Session, Third Committee, 1637th meeting, A/C.3/SR.1637, para. 9). Indeed, the Court notes that there has been an increasing tendency over time for the General Assembly and the Security Council to deal in parallel with the same matter concerning the maintenance of international peace and security (see, for example, the matters involving Cyprus, South Africa, Angola, Southern Rhodesia and more recently Bosnia and Herzegovina and Somalia). It is often the case that, while the Security Council has tended to focus on the aspects of such matters related to international peace and security, the General Assembly has taken a broader view, considering also their humanitarian, social and economic aspects.

28. The Court considers that the accepted practice of the General Assembly, as it has evolved, is consistent with Article 12, paragraph 1, of the Charter.

The Court is accordingly of the view that the General Assembly, in adopting resolution ES-10114, seeking an advisory opinion from the Court did not contravene the provisions of Article 12, paragraph 1, of the Charter. The Court concludes that by submitting that request the General Assembly did not exceed its competence.

...

120. As regards these settlements, the Court notes that Article 49, paragraph 6, of the Fourth Geneva Convention provides: "The Occupying Power shall not deport or transfer parts of its own civilian population into the territory it occupies.

...

The Security Council has thus taken the view that such policy and practices "have no legal validity". It has also called upon "Israel, as the occupying Power, to abide scrupulously" by the Fourth Geneva Convention.

...

The Council reaffirmed its position in resolutions 452 (1979) of 20 July 1979 and 465 (1980) of 1 March 1980. Indeed, in the latter case it described "Israel's policy and practices of settling parts of its population and new immigrantis in [the occupied] territories" as a "flagrant violation" of the Fourth Geneva Convention.

The Court concludes that the Israeli settlements in the Occupied Palestinian Territory (including East Jerusalem) have been established in breach of international law.

...

132. From the information submitted to the Court, particularly the report of the Secretary-General, it appears that the construction of the wall has led to the destruction or requisition of properties under conditions which contravene the requirements of Articles 46 and 52 of the Hague Regulations of 1907 and of Article 53 of the Fourth Geneva Convention.

133. That construction, the establishment of a closed area between the Green Line and the wall itself and the creation of enclaves have moreover imposed substantial restrictions on the freedom of movement of the inhabitants of the Occupied Palestinian Territory (with the exception of [p. 58] Israeli citizens and those assimilated thereto). Such restrictions are most marked in urban areas, such as the Qalqiliya enclave or the City of Jerusalem and its suburbs. They are aggravated by the fact that the access gates are few in number in certain sectors and opening hours appear to be restricted and unpredictably applied. For example, according to the Special Rapporteur of the Commission on Human Rights on the situation of human rights in the Palestinian territories occupied by Israel since 1967, "Qalqiliya, a city with a population of 40,000, is completely surrounded by the Wall and residents can only enter and leave through a single military checkpoint open from 7 a.m. to 7 p.m." (Report of the Special Rapporteur of the Commission on Human Rights, John Dugard, on the situation of human rights in the Palestinian territories occupied by Israel since 1967, submitted in accordance with Commission resolution 1993/2 A and entitled "Question of the Violation of Human Rights in the Occupied Arab Territories, including Palestine", E/CN.4/2004/6, 8 September 2003, para. 9.)

There have also been serious repercussions for agricultural production, as is attested by a number of sources. According to the Special Committee to Investigate Israeli Practices Affecting the Human Rights of the Palestinian People and Other Arabs of the Occupied Territories

"an estimated 100,000 dunums [approximately 10,000 hectares] of the West Bank's most fertile agricultural land, confiscated by the Israeli Occupation Forces, have been destroyed during the first phase of the wall construction, which involves the disappearance of vast amounts of property, notably private agricultural land and olive trees, wells, citrus grows and hothouses upon which tens of thousands of Palestinians rely for their survival." (Report of the Special Committee to Investigate Israeli Practices Affecting the Human Rights of the Palestinian People and Other Arabs of the Occupied Territories, A/58/311, 22 August 2003, para. 26)

Further, the Special Rapporteur on the situation of human rights in the Palestinian territories occupied by Israel since 1967 states that "Much of the Palestinian land on the Israeli side of the Wall consists of fertile agricultural land and some of the most important water wells in the region" and adds that "Many fruit and olive trees had been destroyed in the course of building the barrier." (E/CN.4/2004/6, 8 September 2003, para. 9.) The Special Rapporteur on the Right to Food of the United Nations Commission on Human Rights states that construction of the wall "cuts off Palestinians from their agricultural lands, wells and means of subsistence" (Report by the Special Rapporteur of the United Nations Commission on Human Rights, Jean Ziegler, "The Right to Food", Addendum, Mission to the Occupied Palestinian Territories, E/CN.4/2004/10/Add.2, 31 October 2003, para. 49). In a recent survey conducted by the World Food Programme, it is stated that the situation has aggra-[p. 59]vated food insecurity in the region, which reportedly numbers 25,000 new beneficiaries of food aid (report of the Secretary-General, para. 25).

It has further led to increasing difficulties for the population concerned regarding access to health services, educational establishments and primary sources of water. This is also attested by a number of different information sources. Thus the report of the Secretary-General states generally that "According to the Palestinian Central Bureau of Statistics, so far the Barrier has separated 30 localities from health services, 22 from schools, 8 from primary water sources and 3 from electricity networks." (Report of the Secretary-General, para. 23.) The Special Rapporteur of the United Nations Commission on Human Rights on the situation of human rights in the Palestinian territories occupied by Israel since 1967 states that "Palestinians between the Wall and Green Line will effectively be cut off from their land and workplaces, schools, health clinics and other social services." (E/CN.4/2004/6, 8 September 2003, para. 9.) In relation specifically to water resources, the Special Rapporteur on the Right to Food of the United Nations Commission on Human Rights observes that "By constructing the fence Israel will also effectively annex most of the western aquifer system (which provides 51 per cent of the West Bank's water resources)."   (E/CN.4/2004/10/Add.2, 31 October 2003, para. 51.) Similarly, in regard to access to health services, it has been stated that, as a result of the enclosure of Qalqiliya, a United Nations hospital in that town has recorded a 40 per cent decrease in its caseload (report of the Secretary-General, para. 24).

At Qalqiliya, according to reports furnished to the United Nations, some 600 shops or businesses have shut down, and 6,000 to 8,000 people have already left the region (E/CN.4/2004/6, 8 September 2003, para. 10; E/CN.4/2004/10/Add.2, 31 October 2003, para. 51). The Special Rapporteur on the Right to Food of the United Nations Commission on Human Rights has also observed that "With the fence/wall cutting communities off from their land and water without other [p. 54] means of subsistence, many of the Palestinians living in these areas will be forced to leave." (E/CN.4/2004/10/Add.2, 31 October 2003, para. 51.) In this respect also the construction of the wall would effectively deprive a significant number of Palestinians of the "freedom to choose [their] residence". In addition, however, in the view of the Court, since a significant number of Palestinians have already been compelled by the construction of the wall and its associated régime to depart from certain areas, a process that will continue as more of the wall is built, that construction, coupled with the establishment of the Israeli settlements mentioned in paragraph 120 above, is tending to alter the demographic composition of the Occupied Palestinian Territory.

134. To sum up, the Court is of the opinion that the construction of the wall and its associated régime impede the liberty of movement of the inhabitants of the Occupied Palestinian Territory (with the exception [p. 60] of Israeli citizens

and those assimilated thereto) as guaranteed under Article 12, paragraph 1, of the International Covenant on Civil and Political Rights. They also impede the exercise by the persons concerned of the right to work, to health, to education and to an adequate standard of living as proclaimed in the International Covenant on Economic, Social and Cultural Rights and in the United Nations Convention on the Rights of the Child. Lastly, the construction of the wall and its associated régime, by contributing to the demographic changes referred to in paragraphs 122 and 133 above, contravene Article 49, paragraph 6, of the Fourth Geneva Convention and the Security Council resolutions cited in paragraph 120 above.

Notes

- What is the kind of act that is at issue? What kind of legal value does such an act potentially have? Does the court respect that value? The court held that Israel had "contravened" Security Council Resolutions, even though those resolutions were not Chapter VII resolutions. Without being taken under Chapter VII, the resolutions could not have been binding, and thus could not have been contravened, could they?
- Does the text of the judgment suggest a better explanation of the intention of the act, and prescribe its normativity?
- If not, then does the court reach a decision on legal effect? What is it? And what is the basis for this legal value?

One question is whether the Security Council could issue a binding order to a non-member of the UN. Does the Security Council have the authority to issue a binding order against a UN Member State that is not a member of the Security Council or, as member of the Security Council, voted against the resolution? What about against a non-member of the UN? In this regard, recall the *Reparations* case discussion on personality in Chapter 3 on the creation of an international organization. Is objective personality relevant? Or is it a question of powers? Or membership?

Turning from decisions to recommendations, in the *Lockerbie* case, the ICJ held that a recommendation of the Security Council had a different value:

Case Concerning Questions of Interpretation and Application of the 1971 Montreal Convention Arising from the Aerial Incident at Lockerbie
Libya v United Kingdom
Preliminary Objections, Judgment
1988 ICJ Reps. 9
International Court of Justice, 27 February 1998

40. The Court will now proceed to consider the objection of the United Kingdom that the Libyan Application is not admissible.

...

43. Libya furthermore draws the Court's attention to the principle that "The critical

date for determining the admissibility of an application is the date on which it is filed" (Border and Transborder Armed Actions, (Nicaragua v. Honduras), Jurisdiction and Admissibility, I.C.J. Reports 1988, p. 95, para. 66). It points out in this connection that its Application was filed on 3 March 1992; that Security Council resolutions 748 (1992) and 883 (1993) were adopted on 31 March 1992 and 11 November 1993, respectively; and that resolution 731 (1992) of 21 January 1992 was not adopted under Chapter VII of the United Nations Charter and was only a mere recommendation. Consequently, Libya argues, its Application is admissible in any event.

44. In the view of the Court, this last submission of Libya must be upheld. The date, 3 March 1992, on which Libya filed its Application, is in fact the only relevant date for determining the admissibility of the Application. Security Council resolutions 748 (1992) and 883 (1993) cannot be taken into consideration in this regard since they were adopted at a later date. As to Security Council resolution 731 (1992), adopted before the filing of the Application, it could not form a legal impediment to the admissibility of the latter because it was a mere recommendation without binding effect, as was recognized moreover by the United Kingdom itself. Consequently, Libya's Application cannot be held inadmissible on these grounds.

45. In the light of the foregoing, the Court concludes that the objection to admissibility derived by the United Kingdom from Security Council resolutions 748 (1992) and 883 (1993) must be rejected, and that Libya's Application is admissible.

Notes

- What is the "critical date," and why is it relevant? Can the court consider events following the submission of the case? Why, or why not?
- What was the legal effect of the various Security Council resolutions? Is this correct? Why is this legal effect relevant for determining the admissibility of the case? Surely a case is decided on its merits, not depending on the legal effect of an act of the UN Security Council?
- Does this case evidence a particular view on the legal effect of acts of organizations? Are the Security Council resolutions viewed more as equivalents to treaties or delegated decision-makers for states? Or is this more like a legislative body's acts?

In light of the discussion above, consider the legal effect of certain acts by the International Civil Aviation Organization (ICAO). Article 12 of the Chicago Convention that grants ICAO its legal authority provides that "over the high seas, the rules in force shall be those established under this Convention."[9] In turn, this grants the ICAO

---

9   Convention on International Civil Aviation, 7 December 1944 ("Chicago Convention"), 15 UNTS 102, ICAO Doc. 7300/9, article 12 © International Civil Aviation Organization. Reproduced with permission of ICAO.

Council the power to legislate international rules on flights above the high seas. Such expansive authority makes sense, because otherwise international air travel would follow various, potentially conflicting, rules when flying overseas. However, the Chicago Convention was only adopted by 52 states. How can this organization with limited membership create international law? Do states only follow the ICAO rules out of practical safety concerns, or are they legally bound to?

6.2.1.2 United Nations General Assembly

Having considered the Security Council, we now move to the General Assembly. We initially observed that the legal effects of its acts were generally non-binding. While the General Assembly has largely non-binding powers, it does have the authority to make binding acts concerned the budget of the UN, voting procedure, and admission or expulsion of members.[10] The question of legal value of General Assembly acts becomes a bit more difficult when faced with questions of a different nature.

Let us examine the *South West Africa* cases. These are distinct from the *International Status of South West Africa* and *Namibia* advisory opinions issued in 1950 and 1971 respectively. These cases were contentious, and were brought in the early 1960s, after the *International Status of South West Africa* advisory opinion, but before the *Namibia* advisory opinion. They were brought by the two remaining, non-colonialized states in Africa, Liberia and Ethiopia, against South Africa for its continuing colonial governance system, including its policy of *apartheid*, in Namibia (South West Africa). After filing, the two cases were litigated in parallel, hence the plural designation "*South West Africa* cases." The court issued two judgments in the cases: the first, in 1962, was addressed only to the preliminary objections, and the second, in 1966, was addressed to the merits of the cases. The 1962 preliminary objections judgment will be discussed later in this chapter, in Section 6.2.2 on non-binding legal effect. Here we discuss the 1966 merits judgment on the legal effect of UN General Assembly Resolutions:

South West Africa Cases
Ethiopia v. South Africa; Liberia v. South Africa
Second Phase [Merits], Judgment
1966 ICJ Reps. 6
International Court of Justice, 18 July 1966

1. In the present proceedings the two applicant States, the Empire of Ethiopia and the Republic of Liberia (whose cases are identical and will for present purposes be treated as one case), acting in the capacity of States which were members of the former League of Nations, put forward various allegations of contraventions of the League of Nations Mandate for South West Africa, said to

---

10 *See* Competence of the General Assembly for the Admission of a State to the United Nations ["Second Admissions Case"], Advisory Opinion, 1950 ICJ Reps. 4, 8 (International Court of Justice, 3 March 1950).

have been committed by the respondent State, the Republic of South Africa, as the administering authority.

2. In an earlier phase of the case, which took place before the Court in 1962, four preliminary objections were advanced, based on Article 37 of the Court's Statute and the jurisdictional clause (Article 7, paragraph 2) of the Mandate for South West Africa, which were all of them argued by the Respondent and treated by the Court as objections to its jurisdiction. The Court, by its Judgment of 21 December 1962, rejected each of these objections, and thereupon found that it had "jurisdiction to adjudicate upon the merits of the dispute".

3. In the course of the proceedings on the merits, comprising the exchange of written pleadings, the oral arguments of the Parties and the hearing of a considerable number of witnesses, the Parties put forward various contentions on such matters as whether the Mandate for South West Africa was still in force, – and if so, whether the Mandatory's obligation under Article 6 of the Mandate to furnish annual reports to the Council of the former League of Nations concerning its administration of the mandated territory had become transformed by one means or another into an obligation to furnish such reports to the General Assembly of the United Nations, or had, on the other hand, lapsed entirely; – whether there had been any contravention by the Respondent of the second paragraph of Article 2 of the Mandate which required the Mandatory to "promote to the utmost the material and moral well-being and the social progress of the inhabitants of the territory", – whether there had been any contravention of Article 4 of the Mandate, prohibiting (except for police and local defence purposes) the "military training of the natives", and forbidding the establishment of military or naval bases, or the erection of fortifications in the territory. The Applicants also alleged that the Respondent had contravened paragraph 1 of Article 7 of the Mandate (which provides that the Mandate can only be modified with the consent of the Council of the League of Nations) by attempting to modify the Mandate without the consent of the General Assembly of the United Nations which, so it was contended, had replaced the Council of the League for this and other purposes. There were other allegations also, which it is not necessary to set out here.

...

98. It has also been sought to explain why certain trusteeship agreements do not contain the jurisdictional clause by a further appeal to the "necessity" argument. This clause was no longer necessary, so it was contended, because the United Nations voting rule was different. In the League Council, decisions could not be arrived at without the concurrence of the mandatory, whereas in the United Nations the majority voting rule ensured that a resolution could not be blocked by any single vote. This contention would not in any event explain why the clause was accepted for some trusteeships and not for others. But the whole argument is misconceived. If decisions of the League Council could not be arrived at without the concurrence, express or tacit, of the mandatory, they were, when arrived at, binding: and if resolutions of the United Nations General Assembly (which on this hypothesis would be the relevant organ) can be arrived at without the concurrence of the administering authority, yet when so arrived at – and

subject to certain exceptions not here material – they are not binding, but only recommendatory in character. The persuasive force of Assembly resolutions can indeed be very considerable, – but this is a different thing. It operates on the political not the legal level: it does not make these resolutions binding in law. If the "necessity" argument were valid therefore, it would be applicable as much to trusteeships as it is said to be to mandates, because in neither case could the administering authority be coerced by means of the ordinary procedures of the organization. The conclusion to be drawn is obvious.

Notes

- What kind of act was at issue in these cases – "decision," "recommendation," "opinion," or another? Does that act permit binding obligations? And did the Security Council exercise its binding authority? Why is this legal effect relevant for these cases?
- Why does the act have the value it does? Is it based on the UN Charter, or another source? Does the court have an explicit or implied view on the reason for why acts of organizations have legal effect? Recall the discussion above for the *Lockerbie* case. Does the court here apply a treaty equivalency, delegated decision-making, or legislative model?

Both the UN Security Council and General Assembly can therefore issue orders in some form, although in differing areas of competence, but their authority may go further. Certainly, in the cases mentioned above, the member states must comply with the content of what was ordered. There are other acts of the organization that might result in *de facto* binding decisions, though not necessarily specifically designated as such.

One such act is making a finding of fact. Such an act can carry significant authority because it means, in essence, that the actor views some fact as existing. One particularly important example of reaching a decision on a finding of fact is the need for the Security Council to make a finding that a threat to the peace, breach of the peace, or act of aggression has occurred in order to be authorized to use Chapter VII powers.

United Nations Security Council Resolution 1973 (17 March 2011)

The Security Council,

Recalling its resolution 1970 (2011) of 26 February 2011,
Deploring the failure of the Libyan authorities to comply with resolution 1970 (2011),
Expressing grave concern at the deteriorating situation, the escalation of violence, and the heavy civilian casualties,
Reiterating the responsibility of the Libyan authorities to protect the Libyan population and *reaffirming* that parties to armed conflicts bear the

primary responsibility to take all feasible steps to ensure the protection of civilians,

Condemning the gross and systematic violation of human rights, including arbitrary detentions, enforced disappearances, torture and summary executions,

...

Considering that the widespread and systematic attacks currently taking place in the Libyan Arab Jamahiriya against the civilian population may amount to crimes against humanity,

Recalling paragraph 26 of resolution 1970 (2011) in which the Council expressed its readiness to consider taking additional appropriate measures, as necessary, to facilitate and support the return of humanitarian agencies and make available humanitarian and related assistance in the Libyan Arab Jamahiriya,

...

Recalling its decision to refer the situation in the Libyan Arab Jamahiriya since 15 February 2011 to the Prosecutor of the International Criminal Court, and *stressing* that those responsible for or complicit in attacks targeting the civilian population, including aerial and naval attacks, must be held to account,

...

Determining that the situation in the Libyan Arab Jamahiriya continues to constitute a threat to international peace and security,

Acting under Chapter VII of the Charter of the United Nations,

1. *Demands* the immediate establishment of a cease-fire and a complete end to violence and all attacks against, and abuses of, civilians;

...

4. *Authorizes* Member States that have notified the Secretary-General, acting nationally or through regional organizations or arrangements, and acting in cooperation with the Secretary-General, to take all necessary measures, notwithstanding paragraph 9 of resolution 1970 (2011), to protect civilians and civilian populated areas under threat of attack in the Libyan Arab Jamahiriya, including Benghazi, while excluding a foreign occupation force of any form on any part of Libyan territory, and *requests* the Member States concerned to inform the Secretary-General immediately of the measures they take pursuant to the authorization conferred by this paragraph which shall be immediately reported to the Security Council;

...

6. *Decides* to establish a ban on all flights in the airspace of the Libyan Arab Jamahiriya in order to help protect civilians; ...

Notes

- What was the purpose of the resolution? What triggered it? We see that the Security Council invoked a threat to peace as a basis for using its Chapter VII powers. What was the threat to peace? Does this threat justify the measures in the resolution? And does this conclusion then explain not only whether the resolution is binding, but what the addressees must do?

- Was the referral to the ICC binding? Was the factual finding of crimes against humanity binding? How could the ICC reach an independent judicial determination on this issue?

In many ways the Libya resolution above is a straightforward exercise of Security Council powers with a largely predictable effect, but reconsider the determinations of the ICJ in the *Namibia* advisory opinion above at paragraphs 105–117.

The discussions above looked at whether the commands of the organs had binding effect. This next section looks at findings and factual determinations of the organs, and considers whether those findings might have binding effect.

In general, factual findings contained in recommendations are non-binding. For example, when it comes to admissions to membership, the Security Council makes a recommendation to the General Assembly. Within that recommendation, the Security Council must make certain findings whether the candidate state is eligible for UN membership under article 4(1) of the UN Charter. Following the Security Council's recommendation, the General Assembly makes a "decision." However, the General Assembly is not bound by the recommendation of the Security Council, and – important for the question of binding effect – the General Assembly is not bound to reach the same factual conclusion that the candidate state is eligible for UN membership under the UN Chapter criteria.[11] That being said, certain factual findings in a recommendation or decision would have probative value.[12]

In light of the effect of factual findings, reconsider the legal effect of the factual finding in Security Council Resolution 1973 that "the widespread and systematic attacks currently taking place in the Libyan Arab Jamahiriya against the civilian population may amount to crimes against humanity," mentioned above. While the statement is conditioned by "may," it is contained in a binding resolution and was sufficient to trigger the jurisdiction of the ICC.

In addition to the effect of findings in decisions, recommendations, and referrals, organizations might also have the authority to authorize or "de-authorize" certain permissive actions. Here again, the organization might not have been expressly vested with the authority to bind the member states to the content of its act, but its permissive authorization may be necessary in order for the states to act.

---

11 *See* Conditions of Admission of a State to Membership in the United Nations (Article 4 of the Charter) ["First Admissions Case"], Advisory Opinion, 1948 ICJ Reps. 57, 64 (International Court of Justice, 28 May 1948).

12 *See* Case Concerning Military and Paramilitary Activities in and against Nicaragua (Nicaragua v United States), Merits, Judgment, 1986 ICJ Reps. 14, para. 72 (International Court of Justice, 27 June 1986): "The declarations to which the Court considers it may refer are not limited to those made in the pleadings and the oral argument addressed to it in the successive stages of the case, nor are they limited to statements made by the Parties. ... But the Court considers that, in its quest for the truth, it may also take note of statements of representatives of the Parties (or of other States) in international organizations, as well as the resolutions adopted or discussed by such organizations, in so far as factually relevant, whether or not such material has been drawn to its attention by a Party."

The International Court of Justice cannot act on a case on its own initiative *sua sponte*. Its jurisdiction must be triggered by bringing a case or advisory request to it. If a UN organ or affiliated entity requests an advisory opinion, then the organ has authorized the ICJ to act. The court is not, however, bound to issue an opinion. It can refuse. And the opinion the court issues is not itself binding in the sense of constituting an order. Instead, it is a very authoritative statement of the law.[13]

In addition, organs might also have the ability to issue acts removing authorization, if they choose to retain that power:

**Effect of Awards of Compensation
Made by the United Nations Administrative Tribunal
Advisory Opinion
1954 ICJ Reps. 47
International Court of Justice, 13 July**

[p. 57]

In these circumstances, the Court finds that the power to establish a tribunal, to do justice as between the Organization and the staff members, was essential to ensure the efficient working of the Secretariat, and to give effect to the paramount consideration of securing the highest standards of efficiency, competence and integrity. Capacity to do this arises by necessary intendment out of the Charter.

The existence of this capacity leads to the further enquiry as to the agency by which it may be exercised. Here, there can be no room for doubt.

[p. 58]

*

But that does not dispose of the problem before the Court. Some of the Governments that take the position that there are grounds which would justify the General Assembly in refusing to give effect to awards, agree that the powers of the General Assembly, and particularly its power to establish regulations under Article 101, imply the power to set up an administrative tribunal. They agree that the General Assembly would be able to establish a tribunal competent to hear and decide staff grievances, to prescribe its jurisdiction, and to authorize it to give a final decision, in the sense that no appeal could be taken as of right. They nevertheless contend that the implied power does not enable the General Assembly to establish a tribunal with authority to make decisions binding on the General Assembly itself.

...

But the function of approving the budget does not mean that the General Assembly has an absolute power to approve or disapprove the expenditure proposed to it; for some part of that expenditure arises out of obligations already incurred by the Organization, and to this extent

---

13 *See* Legal Consequences of the Construction of a Wall in the Occupied Palestinian Territory, Advisory Opinion, 2004 ICJ Reps. 136 paras. 43–65 (9 July). *Also see* Security Council Resolution 1973 (regarding triggering the ICC's jurisdiction, discussed above).

the General Assembly has no alternative but to honour these engagements. The question, therefore, to be decided by the Court is whether these obligations comprise the awards of compensation made by the Administrative Tribunal in favour of staff members. The reply to this question must be in the affirmative. The obligatory character of these awards has been established by the considerations set out above relating to the authority of res judicata and the binding effect of the judgments of this Tribunal upon the United Nations Organization.

The Court therefore considers that the assignment of the budgetary function to the General Assembly cannot be regarded as conferring upon it the right to refuse to give effect to the obligation arising out of an award of the Administrative Tribunal.

...

[p. 60]

It has been argued that an authority exercising a power to make regulations is inherently incapable of creating a subordinate body competent to make decisions binding its creator. There can be no doubt that the Administrative Tribunal is subordinate in the sense that the General Assembly can abolish the Tribunal by repealing the Statute, that it can amend the Statute and provide for review of the-future decisions of the Tribunal and that it can amend the Staff Regulations and make new ones. There is no lack of power to deal effectively with any problem that may arise. But the contention that the General Assembly is inherently incapable of creating a tribunal competent to make decisions binding on itself cannot be accepted. It cannot be justified by analogy to national laws, for it is common practice in national legislatures to create courts with the capacity to render decisions legally binding on the legislatures which brought them into being. The question cannot be determined on the basis of the description of the relationship between the General Assembly and the Tribunal, that is, by considering whether the Tribunal is to be regarded as a subsidiary, a subordinate, or a secondary organ, or on the basis of the fact that it was established by the General Assembly. It depends on the intention of the General Assembly in establishing the Tribunal, and on the nature of the functions conferred upon it by its Statute. An examination of the language of the Statute of the Administrative Tribunal has shown that the General Assembly intended to establish a judicial body; moreover, it had the legal capacity under the Charter to do so.

Notes

- What kind of acts are we discussing here – recommendations, decisions, etc.? Are these acts binding? Where does that power or authority come from? And why do the acts have the legal effect they do?
- If the UN Administrative Tribunal (UNAT) is subsidiary to the General Assembly, then it can only exercise those powers of the General Assembly that were delegated to it, so how do the UNAT acts come to have the legal effect they do? The General Assembly does not have this power.

- In addition, as a subsidiary, the UNAT is subject to reversal by the General Assembly. In essence, the UN General Assembly can disempower the UNAT. It can abolish it at any time and amend its operating statute. How does the ICJ view this power and the legal effects?

6.2.1.3 International Court of Justice

Similar to the ICC, mentioned above, the International Court of Justice can issue binding judgments. The Statute of the ICJ provides explicitly that its judgments are binding and final, but only in the dispute between the parties, i.e., not laying down legal precedent for other litigants. Other international organizations that are empowered to issue binding orders and judgments have similarly delegated powers in their constitutive instruments, and the same is true for *ad hoc* arbitral tribunals. What was initially controversial is whether the court could issue binding orders for interim measures, or whether those orders were only politically binding:

LaGrand Case
Germany v United States of America
Jurisdiction and Admissibility, Judgment
2001 ICJ Reps. 466
International Court of Justice, 27 June 2001

[p. 475]

14. On 7 January 1982, Karl LaGrand and Walter LaGrand were arrested in the United States by law enforcement officers on suspicion of having been involved earlier the same day in an attempted armed bank robbery in Marana, Arizona, in the course of which the bank manager was murdered and another bank employee seriously injured. They were subsequently tried before the Superior Court of Pitna County, Arizona, which, on 17 February 1984, convicted them both of murder in the first degree, attempted murder in the first degree, attempted armed robbery and two counts of kidnaping. On 14 December 1984, each was sentenced to death for first degree murder and to concurrent sentences of imprisonment for the other charges.

15. At all material times, Germany as well as the United States were parties to both the Vienna Convention on Consular Relations and the Optional Protocol to that Convention. Article 36, paragraph 1*(b)*, of the Vienna Convention provides that:

> "if he so requests, the competent authorities of the receiving State shall, without delay. inform the consular post of the sending State if, within its consular district, a national of that State is arrested or committed to prison or to custody pending trial or is detained in any other manner. Any communication addressed to the consular post by the person arrested, in prison, custody or detention shall be forwarded by the said authorities without delay. The said authorities shall inform the person concerned without delay of his rights under this subparagraph."

It is not disputed that at the time the LaGrands were convicted and sentenced, the competent United States authorities had failed to provide the LaGrands with the information required by this provision of the Vienna Convention, and had not informed the relevant German consular post of the LaGrands' arrest. The United States concedes that the competent authorities failed to do so, even after becoming aware that the LaGrands were German nationals and not United States nationals, and admits that [p. 476] the United States has therefore violated its obligations under this provision of the Vienna Convention.

...

18. The convictions and sentences pronounced by the Superior Court of Pima County, Arizona, were subsequently challenged by the LaGrands in three principal sets of legal proceedings.

...

[p. 478]

25. On 15 January 1999, the Supreme Court of Arizona decided that Karl LaGrand was to be executed on 24 February 1999, and that Walter LaGrand was to be executed on 3 March 1999. Germany claims that the German Consulate learned of these dates on 19 January 1999.

...

30. On 2 March 1999, the day before the scheduled date of execution of Walter LaGrand, at 7.30 p.m. (The Hague time), Germany filed in the Registry of this Court the Application instituting the present proceedings against the United States (see paragraph 1 above), accompanied by a request for the following provisional measures:

...

[p. 479]

"The United States should take all measures at its disposal to ensure that Walter LaGrand is not executed pending the final decision in these proceedings, and should inform the Court of all the measures which it has taken in implementation of that Order."

...

34. On that same day, proceedings were also instituted in the United [p. 480] States Supreme Court by Walter LaGrand. These proceedings were decided against him. Later that day, Walter LaGrand was executed.

...

[p. 498]

92. The Court will now consider Germany's third submission, in which it asks the Court to adjudge and declare:

"that the United States, by failing to take all measures at its disposal to ensure that Walter LaGrand was not executed pending the final decision of the International Court of Justice on the matter, violated its international legal obligation to comply with the Order on provisional measures issued by the Court on 3 March 1999, and to refrain from any action which might interfere with the subject matter of a dispute while judicial proceedings are pending."

...

[p. 501]

98. Neither the Permanent Court of International Justice, nor the present Court to date, has been called upon to determine the legal effects of orders

made under Article 41 of the Statute. As Germany's third submission refers expressly to an international legal obligation "to comply with the Order on Provisional Measures issued by the Court on 3 March 1999", and as the United States disputes the existence of such an obligation, the Court is now called upon to rule expressly on this question.

99. The dispute which exists between the Parties with regard to this point essentially concerns the interpretation of Article 41, which is worded in identical terms in the Statute of each Court (apart from the respective references to the Council of the League of Nations and the Security Council). This interpretation has been the subject of extensive controversy in the literature. The Court will therefore now proceed to the interpretation of Article 41 of the Statute. It will do so in accordance with customary international law, reflected in Article 31 of the 1969 Vienna Convention on the Law of Treaties. According to paragraph 1 of Article 31, a treaty must be interpreted in good faith in accordance with the ordinary meaning to be given to its terms in their context and in the light of the treaty's object and purpose.

100. The French text of Article 41 reads as follows:

"1. La Cour a le pouvoir *d'indiquer*, si elle estime que les circons-[p. 502] tances l'exigent, quelles mesures conservatoires du droit de chacun *doivent être prises* à titre provisoire.

2. En attendant l'arrêt définitif, l'indication de ces mesures est immédiatement notifiée aux parties et au Conseil de sécurité." (Emphasis added.)

In this text, the terms "indiquer" and "l'indication" may be deemed to be neutral as to the mandatory character of the measure concerned; by contrast the words "doivent être prises" have an imperative character. For its part, the English version of Article 41 reads as follows:

"1. The Court shall have the power to *indicate*, if it considers that circumstances so require, any provisional measures which *ought to be taken* to preserve the respective rights of either party.

2. Pending the final decision, notice of the measures suggested shall forthwith be given to the parties and to the Security Council." (Emphasis added.)

...

101. Finding itself faced with two texts which are not in total harmony, the Court will first of all note that according to Article 92 of the Charter, the Statute "forms an integral part of the present Charter". Under Article 111 of the Charter, the French and English texts of the latter are "equally authentic". The same is equally true of the Statute. In cases of divergence between the equally authentic versions of the Statute, neither it nor the Charter indicates how to proceed. In the absence of agreement between the parties in this respect, it is appropriate to refer to paragraph 4 of Article 33 of the Vienna Convention on the Law of Treaties, which in the view of the Court again reflects customary international law. This provision reads "when a comparison of the authentic texts discloses a difference of meaning which the application of Articles 31 and 32 does not remove the meaning which best reconciles the texts, having regard to

the object and purpose of the treaty, shall be adopted".

The Court will therefore now consider the object and purpose of the Statute together with the context of Article 41.

102. The object and purpose of the Statute is to enable the Court to fulfil the functions provided for therein, and, in particular, the basic function of judicial settlement of international disputes by binding decisions in accordance with Article 59 of the Statute. The context in which Article 41 has to be seen within the Statute is to prevent the Court from [p. 503] being hampered in the exercise of its functions because the respective rights of the parties to a dispute before the Court are not preserved. It follows from the object and purpose of the Statute, as well as from the terms of Article 41 when read in their context, that the power to indicate provisional measures entails that such measures should be binding, inasmuch as the power in question is based on the necessity, when the circumstances call for it, to safeguard, and to avoid prejudice to, the rights of the parties as determined by the final judgment of the Court. The contention that provisional measures indicated under Article 41 might not be binding would be contrary to the object and purpose of that Article.

103. A related reason which points to the binding character of orders made under Article 41 and to which the Court attaches importance is the existence of a principle which has already been recognized by the Permanent Court of International Justice when it spoke of

> "the principle universally accepted by international tribunals and likewise laid down in many conventions ... to the effect that the parties to a case must abstain from any measure capable of exercising a prejudicial effect in regard to the execution of the decision to be given, and, in general, not allow any step of any kind to be taken which might aggravate or extend the dispute." (*Electricity Company of Sofia and Bulgaria, Order of 5 December 1939, P.C.I.J., Series A/B, No. 79, p. 199*)

...

104. Given the conclusions reached by the Court above in interpreting the text of Article 41 of the Statute in the light of its object and purpose, it does not consider it necessary to resort to the preparatory work in order to determine the meaning of that Article. The Court would nevertheless point out that the preparatory work of the Statute [p. 504] does not preclude the conclusion that orders under Article 41 have binding force.

105. The initial preliminary draft of the Statute of the Permanent Court of International Justice, as prepared by the Committee of Jurists established by the Council of the League of Nations, made no mention of provisional measures. A provision to this effect was inserted only at a later stage in the draft prepared by the Committee, following a proposal from the Brazilian jurist Raul Fernandes. ... The Drafting Committee prepared a new version of this text, to which two main amendments were made: on the one hand, the words "la Cour pourra ordonner" ("the Court may ... order") were replaced by "la Cour a le pouvoir d'indiquer" ("the Court shall have the power to suggest"), while, on the other, a second paragraph was added providing for notice to be given to the parties and to

the Council of the "measures suggested" by the Court. ... [p. 505] The Committee of Jurists eventually adopted a draft Article 39, which amended the former Article 2bis only in its French version: in the second paragraph, the words "cette suggestion" were replaced in French by the words "l'indication".

106. When the draft Article 39 was examined by the Sub-Committee of the Third Committee of the first Assembly of the League of Nations, a number of amendments were considered. Raul Fernandes suggested again to use the word "ordonner" in the French version. The Sub-Committee decided to stay with the word "indiquer", the Chairman of the Sub-Committee observing that the Court lacked the means to execute its decisions. The language of the first paragraph of the English version was then made to conform to the French text: thus the word "suggest" was replaced by "indicate", and "should" by "ought to". However, in the second paragraph of the English version, the phrase "measures suggested" remained unchanged.

The provision thus amended in French and in English by the Sub-Committee was adopted as Article 41 of the Statute of the Permanent Court of International Justice. It passed as such into the Statute of the present Court without any discussion in 1945.

107. The preparatory work of Article 41 shows that the preference given in the French text to "indiquer" over "ordonner" was motivated by the consideration that the Court did not have the means to assure the execution of its decisions. However, the lack of means of execution and the lack of binding force are two different matters. Hence, the fact that the Court does not itself have the means to ensure the execution of orders made pursuant to Article 41 is not an argument against the binding nature of such orders.

108. The Court finally needs to consider whether Article 94 of the United Nations Charter precludes attributing binding effect to orders indicating provisional measures. That Article reads as follows:

"1. Each Member of the United Nations undertakes to comply with the decision of the International Court of Justice in any case to which it is a party.

2. If any party to a case fails to perform the obligations incumbent upon it under a judgment rendered by the Court, the other party may have recourse to the Security Council, which may, if it [p. 506] deems necessary, make recommendations or decide upon measures to be taken to give effect to the judgment."

The question arises as to the meaning to be attributed to the words "the decision of the International Court of Justice" in paragraph 1 of this Article. This wording could be understood as referring not merely to the Court's judgments but to any decision rendered by it, thus including orders indicating provisional measures. It could also be interpreted to mean only judgments rendered by the Court as provided in paragraph 2 of Article 94. In this regard, the fact that in Articles 56 to 60 of the Court's Statute both the word "decision" and the word "judgment" are used does little to clarify the matter.

Under the first interpretation of paragraph 1 of Article 94, the text of the paragraph would confirm the binding nature of provisional measures; whereas the second interpretation would in no way preclude their being accorded binding force under Article 41 of the Statute. The Court accordingly concludes that Article 94 of the Charter does not prevent orders made under Article 41 from having a binding character.

109. In short, it is clear that none of the sources of interpretation referred to in the relevant Articles of the Vienna Convention on the Law of Treaties, including the preparatory work, contradict the conclusions drawn from the terms of Article 41 read in their context and in the light of the object and purpose of the Statute. Thus, the Court has reached the conclusion that orders on provisional measures under Article 41 have binding effect.

Notes

- On what basis does the court find that its orders for provisional measures are binding? Is this analysis different from that of other legal effects of acts of international organizations? Why is that? Is it really just a matter of treaty interpretation?
- For students of the French language, does the French text really have the same meaning that the court attributes?
- Does the negotiating history provided above (admittedly in abbreviated form), support the conclusion of the court?
- Is the nature of the ICJ as a judicial organ of an international organization relevant to this analysis? Is this part of the object and purpose of the Statute? Or is the source of law general principles of law relevant to judicial institutions?
- Under the law of international organizations, the key question is whether the states party to the constitutive instrument of the international organization have granted the power to the organization and accepted the legal effect of the act. Has this happened?
- The court cites the ability of the parties to an ICJ case to submit the ICJ judgment to the Security Council for enforcement. This has never happened in the history of the UN, because states almost always comply, but it is possible. However, what kind of act can the Security Council adopt in reaction to a failure to comply with an ICJ judgment? Is that act binding? How does this impact our understanding of the ICJ's analysis in this case?

6.2.2 Non-binding legal effect

As discussed above, only certain types of acts, such as "decisions" in the case of Security Council acts, carry binding legal effect in general. Other acts may have incidental effects. But what about purely non-binding acts? Are member states permitted to completely ignore non-binding acts? Clearly, they are not under an obligation to comply, but can they safely ignore them? Or obstruct them?

Consider the separate opinions by Judges Klaestad and Lauterpacht in the *Voting Procedure* case. This advisory opinion is yet another case in the long-running series of cases regarding the South African mandate and governance of South West Africa (Namibia). This opinion was issued after the *International Status of South West Africa* opinion in 1950, and before the *South West Africa* cases in 1962–1966 and the *Namibia* advisory opinion in 1971. We will only study the separate opinions here, and not the controlling opinion, for the views of the judges on non-binding legal effects.

Voting Procedure on Questions Relating to Reports and Petitions Concerning the Territory of South-West Africa
Advisory Opinion
1955 ICJ Reps. 67
International Court of Justice, 7 July 1955

[p. 84]

Separate Opinion of Judge Klaestad

I have arrived at the same final conclusion as the Court; but as my approach to the matter is entirely different, I consider it my duty to state as briefly as possible the reasons upon which I base my opinion.

1. In the Resolution by which the present Request for an Advisory Opinion was adopted, the General Assembly of the United Nations referred to a statement made by the Court in giving the reasons on which its Advisory Opinion of July 11th, 1950, was based – a statement which, for the purpose of answering the Question now put to the Court, calls for a brief comment. After having expressed the view that South-West Africa was still to be considered as a territory under the Mandate of December 17th, 1920, and that the Union of South Africa was under an obligation to submit to the supervision and control of the General Assembly, the Court stated:

"The degree of supervision to be exercised by the General Assembly should not therefore exceed that which applied under the Mandates System, and should conform as far as possible to the procedure followed in this respect by the Council of the League of Nations. These observations are particularly applicable to annual reports and petitions."

...

[p. 87]

...

In its Advisory Opinion of 1950 the Court stated that the competence of the General Assembly to exercise supervisory functions with regard to a mandated territory and to receive and examine reports is derived from the provisions of Article 10 of the Charter, which authorizes the General Assembly to discuss any questions within the scope of the Charter and to make recommendations on these questions to the Members of the United Nations. Such recommendations relating to reports and petitions concerning the Territory of South-West Africa shall, as already mentioned, in accordance with the General Assembly's Resolution 844 (IX) of October 11th, 1954, be regarded as important questions within the meaning of Article 18, §2, of the Charter and therefore be made by a two thirds majority of the Members present and voting.

Article 18 does not make any distinction between "decisions" and "recommendations". It refers to "decisions" as including "recommendations". These decisions of the General Assembly on [p. 88] "important questions" are of different categories. Some are decisions with a final and binding effect, such as, for instance, the election of members of the various organs of the United Nations or decisions approving the budget of the Organization by virtue of Article 17. Some other decisions are recommendations in the ordinary sense of that term, having no binding force. Recommendations adopted by virtue of Article 10 concerning reports and petitions relating to the Territory of South-West Africa belong in my opinion to the last-mentioned category. They are not legally binding on the Union of South Africa in its capacity as Mandatory Power. Only if the Union Government by a concurrent vote has given its consent to the recommendation can that Government become legally bound to comply with it. In that respect the legal situation is the same as it was under the supervision of the League. Only a concurrent vote can create a binding legal obligation for the Union of South Africa.

It is true that against a negative vote of the Union Government no decision could be reached in the League, while a decision in the United Nations can be made by a two-thirds majority of the General Assembly without the concurrent vote of that Government. But such a decision (recommendation) adopted by the General Assembly without the concurrent vote of the Union Government does not create a binding legal obligation for that Government. Its effects are, in my view, not of a legal nature in the usual sense, but rather of a moral or political character. This does not, however, mean that such a recommendation is without real significance and importance, and that the Union Government can simply disregard it. As a Member of the United Nations, the Union of South Africa is in duty bound to consider in good faith a recommendation adopted by the General Assembly under Article 10 of the Charter and to inform the General Assembly with regard to the attitude which it has decided to take in respect of the matter referred to in the recommendation. But a duty of such a nature, however real and serious it may be, can hardly be considered as involving a true legal obligation, and it does not in any case involve a binding legal obligation to comply with the recommendation.

...

[p. 90]

Separate Opinion of Judge Lauterpacht

...

I have considered it incumbent upon me to append the present Separate Opinion. for, while I concur in the unanimous Opinion of the Court inasmuch as it gives an affirmative answer to the question put to it, I do so on grounds and by a method substantially different – and differing – from those on which that Opinion is based. On the subject of method I find it necessary to devote some preliminary observations to the question as to the legal issues which ought to find an answer in the Opinion of the Court. This matter raises the more general question of the character of the function of the Court and the nature of its judicial pronouncements.

...

[p. 118]

In the first instance, not all the resolutions of the General Assembly in the matter are in the form of recommendations addressed to the Administering Authority. They are often, in form and in substance, directives addressed to the organs of the United Nations such as the Trusteeship Council or the Secretary-General. As such, they are endowed with legal validity and effect. They are measures of supervision of a force comparable with the legal effects of such acts of the General Assembly as the election of members of the Trusteeship Council or the confirmation of the Trusteeship Agreements. A survey of the resolutions passed by the General Assembly in the sphere of trusteeship shows the frequency of this aspect of the supervisory function of the General Assembly.

However, even in relation to the Administering Authority the question of the effect of the decision of the General Assembly cannot accurately be answered by the simple statement that they are not legally binding. In general it is clear that as the General Assembly has no power of decision – as distinguished from recommendation – imposing itself with binding force upon the substantive action of the Member States, its Resolutions have *per se* no binding force in relation to the Administering State. Thus that State is not bound to comply with any specific Resolution recommending it to undertake or to abstain from any particular legislative or administrative action. As stated, no considerations of practical persuasiveness permit any different interpretation of the existing law on the subject. I have referred to cases in which the Administering Authority has expressly declined to act upon the recommendation addressed to it. Its right to do so has never been challenged. What has been challenged – and, I believe, properly challenged – is its right simply to ignore the recommendations and to abstain from adducing reasons for not putting them into effect or for not submitting them for examination with the view to giving effect to them. What has been questioned is the opinion that a recommendation is of no legal effect whatsoever. A Resolution recommending to an Administering State a specific course of action creates *some* legal obligation which, however rudimentary, elastic [p. 119] and imperfect, is nevertheless a legal obligation and constitutes a measure of supervision. The State in question, while not bound to accept the recommendation, is bound to give it due consideration in good faith. If, having regard to its own ultimate responsibility for the good government of the territory, it decides to disregard it, it is bound to explain the reasons for its decision. These obligations appear intangible and almost nominal when compared with the ultimate discretion of the Administering Authority. They nevertheless constitute an obligation; they have been acknowledged as such by the Administering Authorities. This appears with some clarity from the searching discussion at the Sixth General Assembly in 1952 which followed upon the presentation by the Secretary-General, in pursuance of a previous recommendation of the General Assembly, of a series of documents entitled *Information on the Implementation of Trusteeship Council and General Assembly Resolutions relating to Trust Territories* (Documents A/1903; A/1903/Add.1; A/1903/Add.2;

October 1952. In Resolution 436(V) of 2 December 1950, the General Assembly requested the Secretary-General to report to it on the measures taken by the Administering Authorities to implement the Resolutions of the General Assembly and the Trusteeship Council and if there had been no action on the part of an Administering Authority in respect of any particular Resolution to set forth the reasons given concerning that matter). While pointing to the difficulties in the way of giving effect to some of the recommendations, and while affirming their own final responsibility and their own right of ultimate decision, various delegations of the Administering States made no attempt to assert that these recommendations were *bruta fulmina* devoid of any element of legal obligation. Thus at the Sixth General Assembly, in the course of the debate of the Trusteeship Committee, the representative of the United Kingdom stated as follows: "The United Kingdom considered that, in cases where the Trusteeship Council and the General Assembly had adopted Resolutions concerning the Trust Territories, they were perfectly entitled to be informed of the decisions taken by the Administering Authorities in regard to them." (245th Meeting of 12 January 1952; *Sixth General Assembly*, IVth Committee, p. 295.)

Although, as stated, the Trusteeship Agreements do not provide for a legal obligation of the Administering Authority to comply with the decisions of an organ of the United Nations, they are not in this respect devoid of an element of legal obligation. In practically all of them the Administering Authority undertakes to collaborate fully with the General Assembly and the Trusteeship Council in the discharge of their functions, to facilitate periodic missions, and the like. Such collaboration, which is a matter of legal duty, is initiated by decisions of the organs of the United Nations.

[p. 120]

Both principle and practice would thus appear to suggest that the discretion which, in the sphere of the administration of Trust Territories or territories assimilated thereto is vested in the Members of the United Nations in respect of the Resolutions of the General Assembly, is not a discretion tantamount to unrestricted freedom of action. It is a discretion to be exercised in good faith. Undoubtedly, the degree of application of good faith in the exercise of full discretion does not lend itself to rigid legal appreciation. This fact does not destroy altogether the legal relevance of the discretion thus to be exercised. This is particularly so in relation to a succession of recommendations, on the same subject and with regard to the same State, solemnly reaffirmed by the General Assembly. Whatever may be the content of the recommendation and whatever may be the nature and the circumstances of the majority by which it has been reached, it is nevertheless a legal act of the principal organ of the United Nations which Members of the United Nations are under a duty to treat with a degree of respect appropriate to a Resolution of the General Assembly. The same considerations apply to Resolutions in the sphere of territories administered by virtue of the principles of the System of Trusteeship. Although there is no automatic obligation to accept fully a particular recommendation or series of recommendations, there is a legal obligation to act in good faith in accordance with the principles of the Charter and of the System of Trusteeship. An administering State may not be acting illegally by declining to act upon a recommendation or series of recommendations on the same subject. But in doing so it acts at its peril when a point is reached when the cumulative effect of the persistent disregard of the articulate opinion of the Organization is such as to foster the conviction that the State in question has become guilty of disloyalty to the Principles and Purposes of the Charter. Thus an Administering State which consistently sets itself above the solemnly and repeatedly expressed judgment of the Organisation, in particular in proportion as that judgment approximates to unanimity, may find that it has overstepped the imperceptible line between impropriety and illegality, between discretion and arbitrariness, between the exercise of the legal right to disregard the recommendation and the abuse of that right, and that it has exposed itself to consequences legitimately following as a legal sanction.

Notes

- What are differences in the views of the two judges? Both come to the same conclusion, do they not? But how are they distinct?
- Is there more than one obligation, in the view of the judges? What discrete steps are states obliged to take in reaction to a formally non-binding act? Must they participate in the adoption of the act, read and disseminate the act to relevant governmental departments, consider the act, etc.? It might be useful to consult the UN Charter articles 1(3), 1(4), 13, 55, 56 and 60 in this regard.
- Lauterpacht even goes so far as to seemingly blur the distinction between a non-binding effect and a binding effect. When does a non-binding effect become binding, in his view? Why? Or is it that the non-binding act does not take on binding quality, but takes on some other quality? Or that its implementation – or lack thereof – creates other, different, and binding obligations distinct from the requests in the non-binding act?

Both of these opinions were not in the majority, although they agreed with the majority outcome. In the next case, the majority on the court held the following:

Interpretation of the Agreement of 25 March 1951
Between the WHO and Egypt
Advisory Opinion
1980 ICJ Reps. 73
International Court of Justice, 20 December 1980

43. By the mutual understandings reached between Egypt and the [World Health] Organization from 1949 to 1951 with respect to the Regional

Office of the Organization in Egypt, whether they are regarded as distinct agreements or as separate parts of one transaction, a contractual legal régime was created between Egypt and the Organization which remains the basis of their legal relations today. Moreover, Egypt was a member – a founder member – of the newly created World Health Organization when, in 1949, it transferred the operation of the Alexandria Sanitary Bureau to the Organization; and it has continued to be a member of the Organization ever since. The very fact of Egypt's membership of the Organization entails certain mutual obligations of co-operation and good faith incumbent upon Egypt and upon the Organization. Egypt offered to become host to the Regional Office in Alexandria and the Organization accepted that offer: Egypt agreed to provide the privileges, immunities and facilities necessary for the independence and effectiveness of the Office. As a result the legal relationship between Egypt and the Organization became, and now is, that of a host State and an international organization, the very essence of which is a body of mutual obligations of co-operation and good faith. In the present instance Egypt became host to the Organization's Regional Office, with its attendant advantages, and the Organization acquired a valuable seat for its office by the handing over to the Organization of an existing Egyptian Sanitary Bureau established in Alexandria, and the element of mutuality in the legal régime thus created between Egypt and the WHO is underlined by the fact that this was effected through common action based on mutual consent. This special legal régime of mutual rights and obligations has been in force between Egypt and WHO for over thirty years. The result is that there now exists in Alexandria a substantial WHO institution employing a large staff and discharging health functions important both to the Organization and to Egypt itself. In consequence, any transfer of the WHO Regional Office from the territory of Egypt necessarily raises practical problems of some importance. These problems are, of course, the concern of the Organization and of Egypt rather than of the Court. But they also concern the Court to the extent that they may have a bearing on the legal conditions under which a transfer of the Regional Office from Egypt may be effected.

...

46. In considering these provisions, the Court feels bound to observe that in future closer attention might with advantage be given to their drafting. Nevertheless, despite their variety and imperfections, the provisions of host agreements regarding their revision, termination or denunciation are not without significance in the present connection. In the first place, they confirm the recognition by international organizations and host States of the existence of mutual obligations incumbent upon them to resolve the problems attendant upon a revision, termination or denunciation of a host agreement. But they do more, since they must be presumed to reflect the views of organizations and host States as to the implications of those obligations in the contexts in which the provisions are intended to apply. In the view of the Court, therefore, they provide certain general indications of what the mutual obligations of organizations and host States to co-operate in good faith may

involve in situations such as the one with which the Court is here concerned.

47. A further general indication as to what those obligations may entail is to be found in the second paragraph of Article 56 of the Vienna Convention on the Law of Treaties and the corresponding provision in the International Law Commission's draft articles on treaties between States and international organizations or between international organizations. Those provisions, as has been mentioned earlier, specifically provide that, when a right of denunciation is implied in a treaty by reason of its nature, the exercise of that right is conditional upon notice, and that of not less than twelve months. Clearly, these provisions also are based on an obligation to act in good faith and have reasonable regard to the interests of the other party to the treaty.

48. In the present case, as the Court has pointed out, the true legal question submitted to it in the request is: What are the legal principles and rules applicable to the question under what conditions and in accordance with what modalities a transfer of the Regional Office from Egypt may be effected? Moreover, as it has also pointed out, differing views have been expressed concerning both the relevance in this connection of the 1951 Agreement and the interpretation of Section 37 of that Agreement. Accordingly, in formulating its reply to the request, the Court takes as its starting point the mutual obligations incumbent upon Egypt and the Organization to co-operate in good faith with respect to the implications and effects of the transfer of the Regional Office from Egypt. The Court does so the more readily as it considers those obligations to be the very basis of the legal relations between the Organization and Egypt under general international law, under the Constitution of the Organization and under the agreements in force between Egypt and the Organization. The essential task of the Court in replying to the request is, therefore, to determine the specific legal implications of the mutual obligations incumbent upon Egypt and the Organization in the event of either of them wishing to have the Regional Office transferred from Egypt.

49. The Court considers that in the context of the present case the mutual obligations of the Organization and the host State to co-operate under the applicable legal principles and rules are as follows:

– In the first place, those obligations place a duty both upon the Organization and upon Egypt to consult together in good faith as to the question under what conditions and in accordance with what modalities a transfer of the Regional Office from Egypt may be effected.

– Secondly, in the event of its being finally decided that the Regional Office shall be transferred from Egypt, their mutual obligations of co-operation place a duty upon the organization and Egypt to consult together and to negotiate regarding the various arrangements needed to effect the transfer from the existing to the new site in an orderly manner and with a minimum of prejudice to the work of the Organization and the interests of Egypt.

– Thirdly, those mutual obligations place a duty upon the party which wishes to effect the transfer to give a reasonable period of notice to the other party for the termination of the existing situation regarding the Regional Office at Alexandria, taking due account of all the practical arrangements needed to effect an orderly and equitable transfer of the Office to its new site.

Those, in the view of the Court, are the implications of the general legal principles and rules applicable in the event of the transfer of the seat of a Regional Office from the territory of a host State. Precisely what periods of time may be involved in the observance of the duties to consult and negotiate, and what period of notice of termination should be given, are matters which necessarily vary according to the requirements of the particular case. In principle, therefore, it is for the parties in each case to determine the length of those periods by consultation and negotiation in good faith. Some indications as to the possible periods involved, as the Court has said, can be seen in provisions of host agreements, including Section 37 of the Agreement of 25 March 0195 1, as well as in Article 56 of the Vienna Convention on the Law of Treaties and in the corresponding article of the International Law Commission's draft articles on treaties between States and international organizations or between international organizations. But what is reasonable and equitable in any given case must depend on its particular circumstances. Moreover, the paramount consideration both for the Organization and the host State in every case must be their clear obligation to co-operate in good faith to promote the objectives and purposes of the Organization as expressed in its Constitution; and this too means that they must in consultation determine a reasonable period of time to enable them to achieve an orderly transfer of the Office from the territory of the host State.

Notes

- What act of an organization is at issue in this case? Does the court find that the obligations of the WHO and Egypt are binding? If they are binding, why? If they are not binding, then what are Egypt and the WHO obliged to do, and why do they have those obligations from a non-binding obligation?
- Where do these obligations come from? Is this a principle of the law of international organizations? Or of the law of treaties? Or a general principle of law? Or some other source? How can this rule be applied to situations of other international organizations? Suppose an organization issued a non-binding recommendation and a state chose not to comply. Is this a problem? In what situation would it be a violation of the state's obligations to the organization?
- And consider what is the precise obligation on the state(s) in reaction to a formally non-binding act. Is the obligation in the *WHO/Egypt* advisory opinion articulated as the same as the obligation(s) in the *Voting Procedure* case?
- What if a state, upon reflection and consideration, decides that it is honestly not in its interest to comply with the formally non-binding act, and acts contrary to it? Has the state violated any obligation to the organization or to the other member states of the organization?

The *WHO/Egypt* advisory opinion was not unique. In the *Certain Expenses* case, the court found that member states of an organization still had a duty to cover the expenses of the organization, even for acts they voted against. This is not precisely a duty to comply with a non-binding act, but an on-going duty to assist the organization. Would US withdrawal of funding from the UN, UNESCO, the World Health Organization, or one of the various other UN bodies violate this obligation?

Surely where an organization adopts an act that calls for a state to comply with its existing obligations under international law, the state must comply. For example, the UN General Assembly might adopt a resolution demanding a state comply with UN Charter article 2(4), prohibiting the state from unlawfully using force. The state must comply not because of the organization's act, but because of another binding source of law. In this light, consider also General Assembly Resolution 95(I) (1946), which confirmed the law and principles applied by the Nuremberg Tribunal that tried the Nazi leadership for war crimes. Surely the law applied at Nuremberg in 1945 must have been binding even without the General Assembly's resolution.

And this discussion must include cases where the state accepts the decision of the organization as binding. While the organization might not inherently have the power to issue a binding decision, the member state might make the act binding by consenting to its legal force.[14]

Lastly, consider the separate views of Judge Jessup in the *South West Africa* cases. This separate opinion comes from the 1962 preliminary phase of the *South West Africa* cases discussed above:

South West Africa Cases
Ethiopia v. South Africa; Liberia v. South Africa
Preliminary Objections, Judgment
1962 ICJ Reps. 319
International Court of Justice, 21 December

[p. 387]

Separate Opinion of Judge Jessup

I agree with the decision of the Court that it has jurisdiction to hear the present cases on the merits and that the four preliminary objections are not well founded and should be dismissed. Since, however, the Opinion of the Court does not embrace all the questions of fact and of law which I find essential to reaching the decision, I find it my duty to deliver this separate Opinion.

...

[p. 418]

...

---

14 *See* Railway Traffic between Lithuania and Poland (Railway Sector Landwarów-Kaisiadorys), Advisory Opinion, 1931 PCIJ (Ser. A/B) No. 42 at 116, para. 28 (Permanent Court of International Justice, 15 October 1931) ("The two Governments concerned being bound by their acceptance of the Council's Resolution, the Court must examine the scope of this engagement").

This was an undertaking of an international character by which the Union of South Africa assumed an international obligation. The Permanent Court held in the *Free Zones* case that binding force attached to a declaration made in the Court by the Agent of a State (A/B No. 46, at p. 170). The Permanent Court held in *Eastern Greenland* that a declaration by a Foreign Minister to the Ambassador of another State created a binding international obligation (A/B No. 53 (1953), at p. 71).

Surely a formal pledge of the kind just quoted made by the representative of a State to the Assembly of the League also constituted a binding international obligation. As quoted above from McNair, *Law of Treaties*, "a declaration contained in the minutes of a conference" may embody a binding international engagement.

There was reliance on this and other similar declarations as revealed by the fourth paragraph of the League Assembly's resolution of 18 April, in which the Assembly:

"4. Takes note of the expressed intentions of the members of the League now administering territories under mandate to continue to administer them for the well-being and development of the peoples concerned *in accordance with the obligations contained in the respective mandates* until other arrangements have been agreed between the United Nations and the respective mandatory powers." (Preliminary Objections, p. 43. Italics supplied.)

Now one of the "obligations" under the Mandate which the Union of South Africa thus newly agreed to respect after the dissolution of the League, was the obligation under Article 7 to submit to the jurisdiction of the Court; by accepting the Charter, it had already agreed to substitute the International Court of Justice for the Permanent Court. In its pledge to the Assembly, the Union of South Africa pointed out that the disappearance of certain organs of the League would prevent full compliance with the letter of the Mandate. Since the Permanent Court had by agreement (Article 37 of the Statute) been replaced by the International Court, the disappearance of the Permanent Court in no way prevented full compliance with the letter of Article 7, so far as concern the basic consent to the jurisdiction of the Court.

Notes

- What is the basis for the act to be binding in this case, in the view of Jessup? Is it consent to delegate a binding decision to the organization? Or is it the creation of a new obligation by promise? Or is it estoppel? If so, what would serve as detrimental reliance?
- Note that Jessup was not writing for the majority in this instance. What would be the argument against his view?

In all of the cases above, the member states were not obliged to comply with the content of the act. It was, after all, non-binding, and yet the member states had obligations, linked to the general obligation to participate in the organization in good faith, to take certain actions. The ICJ upheld this distinction between complying with the substantive obligations and participating in good faith in the *Border and Transborder Activities* case.

Perhaps it goes without saying that a final way a non-binding act can have some legal consequences can be serving as evidence of law. Indeed, the obligations stated in the act are non-binding, but they are binding insofar as they also exist as one of the formal sources of international law, such as customary international law. See the discussion on this issue in the *Nicaragua* case:

Case Concerning Military and Paramilitary Activities in and against Nicaragua
Nicaragua v United States of America
Merits, Judgment
1986 ICJ Reps. 14
International Court of Justice, 27 June 1986

187. The Court must therefore determine, first, the substance of the customary rules relating to the use of force in international relations, applicable to the dispute submitted to it. The United States has argued that, on this crucial question of the lawfulness of the use of force in inter-State relations, the rules of general and customary international law, and those of the United Nations Charter, are in fact identical. In its view this identity is so complete that, as explained above (paragraph 173), it constitutes an argument to prevent the Court from applying this customary law, because it is indistinguishable from the multilateral treaty law which it may not apply. In its Counter-Memorial on jurisdiction and admissibility the United States asserts that "Article 2 (4) of the Charter *is* customary and general international law". ...

...

188. The Court thus finds that both Parties take the view that the principles as to the use of force incorporated in the United Nations Charter correspond, in essentials, to those found in customary international law. The Parties thus both take the view that the fundamental principle in this area is expressed in the terms employed in Article 2, paragraph 4, of the United Nations Charter. They therefore accept a treaty-law obligation to refrain in their international relations from the threat or use of force against the territorial integrity or political independence of any State, or in any other manner inconsistent with the purposes of the United Nations. The Court has however to be satisfied that there exists in customary international law an *opinio juris* as to the binding character of such abstention. This *opinio juris* may, though with all due caution, be deduced from, inter alia, the attitude of the Parties and the attitude of States towards certain General Assembly resolutions, and particularly resolution 2625 (XXV) entitled "Declaration on Principles of International Law concerning Friendly Relations and Co-operation among States in accordance with the Charter

of the United Nations". The effect of consent to the text of such resolutions cannot be understood as merely that of a "reiteration or elucidation" of the treaty commitment undertaken in the Charter. On the contrary, it may be understood as an acceptance of the validity of the rule or set of rules declared by the resolution by themselves. The principle of non-use of force, for example, may thus be regarded as a principle of customary international law, not as such conditioned by provisions relating to collective security, or to the facilities or armed contingents to be provided under Article 43 of the Charter. It would therefore seem apparent that the attitude referred to expresses an *opinio juris* respecting such rule (or set of rules), to be thenceforth treated separately from the provisions, especially those of an institutional kind, to which it is subject on the treaty-law plane of the Charter.

189. As regards the United States in particular, the weight of an expression of *opinio juris* can similarly be attached to its support of the resolution of the Sixth International Conference of American States condemning aggression (18 February 1928) and ratification of the Montevideo Convention on Rights and Duties of States (26 December 1933). Article 11 of which imposes the obligation not to recognize territorial acquisitions or special advantages which have been obtained by force. Also significant is United States acceptance of the principle of the prohibition of the use of force which is contained in the declaration on principles governing the mutual relations of States participating in the Conference on Security and Co-operation in Europe (Helsinki, 1 August 1975), whereby the participating States undertake to "refrain in their mutual relations, *as well as in their international relations in general*," (emphasis added) from the threat or use of force. Acceptance of a text in these terms confirms the existence of an *opinio juris* of the participating States prohibiting the use of force in international relations. ...

191. As regards certain particular aspects of the principle in question, it will be necessary to distinguish the most grave forms of the use of force (those constituting an armed attack) from other less grave forms. In determining the legal rule which applies to these latter forms, the Court can again draw on the formulations contained in the Declaration on Principles of International Law concerning Friendly Relations and Co-operation among States in accordance with the Charter of the United Nations (General Assembly resolution 2625 (XXV), referred to above). As already observed, the adoption by States of this text affords an indication of their *opinio juris* as to customary international law on the question. Alongside certain descriptions which may refer to aggression, this text includes others which refer only to less grave forms of the use of force. ...

192. Moreover, in the part of this same resolution devoted to the principle of non-intervention in matters within the national jurisdiction of States, a very similar rule is found:

> "Also, no State shall organize, assist, foment, finance, incite or tolerate subversive, terrorist or armed activities directed towards the violent overthrow of the régime of another State, or interfere in civil strife in another State."

In the context of the inter-American system, this approach can be traced back at least to 1928 (Convention on the Rights and Duties of States in the Event of Civil Strife, Art. 1 (1)); it was confirmed by resolution 78 adopted by the General Assembly of the Organization of American States on 21 April 1972. ...

193. The general rule prohibiting force allows for certain exceptions. In view of the arguments advanced by the United States to justify the acts of which it is accused by Nicaragua, the Court must express a view on the content of the right of self-defence, and more particularly the right of collective self-defence. First, with regard to the existence of this right, it notes that in the language of Article 51 of the United Nations Charter, the inherent right (or "droit naturel") which any State possesses in the event of an armed attack, covers both collective and individual self-defence. Thus, the Charter itself testifies to the existence of the right of collective self-defence in customary international law. Moreover, just as the wording of certain General Assembly declarations adopted by States demonstrates their recognition of the principle of the prohibition of force as definitely a matter of customary international law, some of the wording in those declarations operates similarly in respect of the right of self-defence (both collective and individual). Thus, in the declaration quoted above on the Principles of International Law concerning Friendly Relations and Cooperation among States in accordance with the Charter of the United Nations, the reference to the prohibition of force is followed by a paragraph stating that:

"nothing in the foregoing paragraphs shall be construed as enlarging or diminishing in any way the scope of the provisions of the Charter concerning cases in which the use of force is lawful."

This resolution demonstrates that the States represented in the General Assembly regard the exception to the prohibition of force constituted by the right of individual or collective self-defence as already a matter of customary international law ....

195. In the case of individual self-defence, the exercise of this right is subject to the State concerned having been the victim of an armed attack. Reliance on collective self-defence of course does not remove the need for this. There appears now to be general agreement on the nature of the acts which can be treated as constituting armed attacks. In particular, it may be considered to be agreed that an armed attack must be understood as including not merely action by regular armed forces across an international border, but also "the sending by or on behalf of a State of armed bands, groups, irregulars or mercenaries, which carry out acts of armed force against another State of such gravity as to amount to" (*inter alia*) an actual armed attack conducted by regular forces, "or its substantial involvement therein". This description, contained in Article 3, paragraph (g), of the Definition of Aggression annexed to General Assembly resolution 3314 (XXIX), may be taken to reflect customary international law. The Court sees no reason to deny that, in customary law, the prohibition of armed attacks may apply to the sending by a State of armed bands to the territory of another State, if such an operation, because of its scale and effects, would have been classified as an armed attack rather than

as a mere frontier incident had it been carried out by regular armed forces. But the Court does not believe that the concept of "armed attack" includes not only acts by armed bands where such acts occur on a significant scale but also assistance to rebels in the form of the provision of weapons or logistical or other support. Such assistance may be regarded as a threat or use of force, or amount to intervention in the internal or external affairs of other States. It is also clear that it is the State which is the victim of an armed attack which must form and declare the view that it has been so attacked. There is no rule in customary international law permitting another State to exercise the right of collective self-defence on the basis of its own assessment of the situation. Where collective self-defence is invoked, it is to be expected that the State for whose benefit this right is used will have declared itself to be the victim of an armed attack.

Notes

- How is customary international law formed? What is *opinio juris*? What kinds of evidence would be proof of the existence of customary international law? Can customary international law be deduced, or do we use an inductive inference?
- What is the basis for the General Assembly resolutions and Organization of American States resolution to be binding law? Are they binding, or not? Distinguish between formally binding and politically binding if that is helpful.
- Is the law being created by the organizations, clarified by the organizations, amended by the organizations, restated by the organizations, or interpreted by the organizations? Are there really any differences among these kinds of acts?
- Or is the organization, as an independent actor itself, doing anything in relation to the law on the use of force? It was the states that voted and took this decision.
- Is the fact that Nicaragua and the US, or both or neither, voted positively in favor of the resolutions relevant? Does positive voting on such a resolution constitute consent to the creation of law, or *opinio juris*? If so, then does this conclusion change our view on whether the organization is creating law, or merely restating law?

CHAPTER 7
Organs

7.1 DEFINITION OF ORGANS

International organizations generally have at least one, and often more than one, organ. These are the bodies within the organization that exercise the different functions and competences of the organization as a whole. Some organs are charged with setting policy, whereas others administer the day-to-day operations or settle disputes within the organization.

In the Draft Articles on the Responsibility of International Organizations, the International Law Commission defined an organ as follows:

International Law Commission,
Draft Articles on the Responsibility of International Organizations
II(2) Yearbook of the International Law Commission (2011)
UN Doc. A/CN.4/SER.A/2011/Add.1 (Part 2)[1]

Article 2 Use of terms

For the purposes of the present draft articles, ...
(c) "organ of an international organization" means any person or entity which has that status in accordance with the rules of the organization;

This is not a particularly helpful definition other than to simply point us to the organization's constitutive instrument as controlling. Thus, an organ is an organ if the organization's constitutive instrument says it is an organ.

Some organizations, such as the UN, list their principal organs in their constitutive instrument. For example, we can consult article 53 of the constitutive instrument of the Organization of American States, which specifies the organs: General Assembly, the Meeting of Consultation of Ministers of Foreign Affairs, the Councils, the Inter-American Juridical Committee, the Inter-American Commission on Human Rights, the General Secretariat, the Specialized Conferences, and the Specialized Organizations. Others, however, might not use the term "organ," leaving

---

1   © (2011) United Nations. Reprinted with the permission of the United Nations.

the interpreter to determine whether the entity was created as an organ within the meaning of the Draft Articles. Subsidiary organs may be created in the constitutive instrument or in subsequent acts of the organization creating them. They also may or may not be described as organs. The North Atlantic Treaty creating NATO, however, only specifies the Council in article 9 as an organ, and empowers the Council to create other "bodies" as necessary.

While some bodies within an international organization may obviously be organs, some other bodies might not. In fact, sometimes international organizations seem to treat their member states as if they were quasi-organs, for example when the Member States of the EU implement policies adopted by the EU within its exclusive competences.

There are a variety of considerations for organs, which in turn can have an impact on the precise role of the organ within the organization, the precise powers of the organization it exercises, and its function and limitations. For each of these considerations, we must have regard to the nature of the organ. For example, when we consider the powers of the organization, we are looking at the powers the organization as a whole can exercise. But just because an organization has certain powers does not mean that all the organs of the organization can exercise those powers, so we have to consider the nature of the particular organ and its relation to other organs in order to determine whether it can exercise those powers of the organization.

A variety of considerations are relevant for determining the organ's role and competences, such as the composition and governance of the organ. This chapter will only look at the role of the organ within the organization's "family" structure and the function of the organ.

7.2 "FAMILY" STRUCTURE

Organizations having more than one organ necessarily have relationships among and between their organs. The constitutive instrument may specify different competences and fields of expertise, but it does not always specify how the various organs should interact, especially when they disagree either on issues of competences or on substantive outcomes.

Around the same time, the UN General Assembly and the World Health Organization (a UN agency empowered to request advisory opinions), both requested advisory opinions from the International Court of Justice on a highly similar question, being whether the use of nuclear weapons was lawful. One preliminary issue the ICJ felt it needed to address was whether the advisory opinions were correctly requested, and whether the content of the request fell within the competences of each organ or agency:

Legality of the Use by a State of Nuclear Weapons in Armed Conflict
[on request of the World Health Organization]
Advisory Opinion
1996 ICJ Reps. 66
International Court of Justice, 8 July 1996

21. Interpreted in accordance with their ordinary meaning, in their context and in the light of the object and purpose of the WHO Constitution, as well as of the practice followed by the Organization, the provisions of its Article 2 may be read as authorizing the Organization to deal with the effects on health of the use of nuclear weapons, or of any other hazardous activity, and to take preventive measures aimed at protecting the health of populations in the event of such weapons being used or such activities engaged in.

The question put to the Court in the present case relates, however, *not to the effects* of the use of nuclear weapons on health, but to the *legality* of the use of such weapons *in view of their health and environmental effects*. Whatever those effects might be, the competence of the WHO to deal with them is not dependent on the legality of the acts that caused them. Accordingly, it does not seem to the Court that the provisions of Article 2 of the WHO Constitution, interpreted in accordance with the criteria referred to above, can be understood as conferring upon the Organization a competence to address the legality of the use of nuclear weapons, and thus in turn a competence to ask the Court about that.22. World Health Assembly resolution WHA46.40, by which the Court has been seised of this request for an opinion, expressly refers, in its Preamble, to the functions indicated under subparagraphs (a), (k), (p) and (v) of Article 2 under consideration. These functions are defined as:

"(a) to act as the directing and co-ordinating authority on international health work;

...

(k) to propose conventions, agreements and regulations, and make recommendations with respect to international health matters and to perform such duties as may be assigned thereby to the Organization and are consistent with its objective;

...

(p) to study and report on, in co-operation with other specialized agencies where necessary, administrative and social techniques affecting public health and medical care from preventive and curative points of view, including hospital services and social security;

...

[and]

(v) generally to take all necessary action to attain the objective of the Organization."

In the view of the Court, none of these functions has a sufficient connection with the question before it for that question to be capable of being considered as arising "within the scope of [the] activities" of the WHO. The causes of the deterioration of human health are numerous and varied; and the legal or illegal character of these causes is essentially immaterial to the measures which the WHO must in any case take in an attempt to remedy their effects. In particular, the legality or illegality of the use of nuclear weapons in no way determines the specific measures, regarding health or otherwise (studies, plans, procedures, etc.), which could be necessary in order to seek to prevent or cure some of their effects. Whether nuclear weapons are used legally or illegally, their effects on health would be the same. Similarly, while it is probable that the use of nuclear weapons might seriously prejudice the WHO's material capability to deliver all the necessary services in such an eventuality, for example, by making the affected areas inaccessible, this does not raise an issue falling within the scope of the Organization's activities within the meaning of Article 96, paragraph 2, of the Charter. The reference in the question put to the Court to the health and environmental effects, which according to the WHO the use of a nuclear weapon will always occasion, does not make the question one that falls within the WHO's functions.

23. However, in its Preamble, resolution WHA46.40 refers to "primary prevention" in the following terms:

> "Recalling that primary prevention is the only appropriate means to deal with the health and environmental effects of the use of nuclear weapons." [footnote 2 – See *Effects of Nuclear War on Health and Health Services* (2nd ed.), Geneva, WHO, 1987]

Realizing that primary prevention of the health hazards of nuclear weapons requires clarity about the status in international law of their use, and that over the last 48 years marked differences of opinion have been expressed by Member States about the lawfulness of the use of nuclear weapons;

The document entitled *Effects of Nuclear War on Health and Health Services*, to which the Preamble refers, is a report prepared in 1987 by the Management Group created by the Director-General of the WHO in Pursuance of World Health Assembly resolution WHA36.28: this report updates another report on the same topic, which had been prepared in 1983 by an international committee of experts in medical sciences and public health, and whose conclusions had been approved by the Assembly in its above-mentioned resolution. As several States have observed during the present proceedings, the Management Group does indeed emphasize in its 1987 report that "the only approach to the treatment of health effects of nuclear warfare is primary prevention, that is, the prevention of nuclear war" (Summary, p. 5, para. 7). However, the Group states that "it is not for [it] to outline the political steps by which this threat can be removed or the preventive measures to be implemented" (*ibid.*, para. 8); and the Group concludes:

> "However, WHO can make important contributions to this process by systematically distributing information on the health consequences of nuclear warfare and by expanding and intensifying international cooperation in the field of health." (*Ibid.*, para. 9)

24. The WHO could only be competent to take those actions of "primary prevention" which fall within the functions of the Organization as defined in Article 2 of its Constitution. In consequence, the references to this type of prevention

which are made in the Preamble to resolution WHA46.40 and the link there suggested with the question of the legality of the use of nuclear weapons do not affect the conclusions reached by the Court in paragraph 22 above.

25. The Court need hardly point out that international organizations are subjects of international law which do not, unlike States, possess a general competence. International organizations are governed by the "principle of speciality", that is to say, they are invested by the States which create them with powers, the limits of which are a function of the common interests whose promotion those States entrust to them. The Permanent Court of International Justice referred to this basic principle in the following terms:

> "As the European Commission is not a State, but an international institution with a special purpose, it only has the functions bestowed upon it by the Definitive Statute with a view to the fulfilment of that purpose, but it has power to exercise these functions to their full extent, in so far as the Statute does not impose restrictions upon it." (*Jurisdiction of the European Commission of the Danube, Advisory Opinion, P.C.I.J., Series B, No. 14*, p. 64)

The powers conferred on international organizations are normally the subject of an express statement in their constituent instruments. Nevertheless, the necessities of international life may point to the need for organizations, in order to achieve their objectives, to possess subsidiary powers which are not expressly provided for in the basic instruments which govern their activities. It is generally accepted that international organizations can exercise such powers, known as "implied" powers. As far as the United Nations is concerned, the Court has expressed itself in the following terms in this respect:

> "Under international law, the Organization must be deemed to have those powers which, though not expressly provided in the Charter, are conferred upon it by necessary implication as being essential to the performance of its duties. This principle of law was applied by the Permanent Court of International Justice to the International Labour Organization in its Advisory Opinion No. 13 of July 23rd, 1926 (Series B, No. 13, p. 18), and must be applied to the United Nations." (*Reparation for Injuries Suffered in the Service of the United Nations, Advisory Opinion, I. C. J. Reports 1949*, pp. 182–183; cf. *Effect of Awards of Compensation Made by the United Nations Administrative Tribunal, Advisory Opinion, I. C. J. Reports 1954*, p. 57)

In the opinion of the Court, to ascribe to the WHO the competence to address the legality of the use of nuclear weapons – even in view of their health and environmental effects – would be tantamount to disregarding the principle of speciality; for such competence could not be deemed a necessary implication of the Constitution of the Organization in the light of the purposes assigned to it by its member States.

Before considering the discussion notes on this case, also review the court's opinion on the parallel General Assembly request below:

Legality of the Threat or Use of Nuclear Weapons
[on request of the United Nations General Assembly]
Advisory Opinion
1996 ICJ Reps. 226
International Court of Justice, 8 July 1996

14. Article 65, paragraph 1, of the Statute provides: "The Court *may* give an advisory opinion ..." (Emphasis added.) This is more than an enabling provision. As the Court has repeatedly emphasized, the Statute leaves a discretion as to whether or not it will give an advisory opinion that has been requested of it, once it has established its competence to do so. In this context, the Court has previously noted as follows:

"The Court's Opinion is given not to the States, but to the organ which is entitled to request it; the reply of the Court, itself an "organ of the United Nations", represents its participation in the activities of the Organization, and, in principle, should not be refused." (*Interpretation of Peace Treaties with Bulgaria, Hungary and Romania, First Phase, Advisory Opinion, I.C.J. Reports 1950*, p. 71; see also *Reservations to the Convention on the Prevention and Punishment of the Crime of Genocide, Advisory Opinion, I.C.J. Reports 1951*, p. 19; *Judgments of the Administrative Tribunal of the ILO upon Complaints Made against Unesco, Advisory Opinion, I.C.J. Reports 1956*, p. 86; *Certain Expenses of the United Nations (Article 17, paragraph 2, of the Charter), Advisory Opinion, I.C.J. Reports 1962*, p. 155; and *Applicability of Article VI, Section 22, of the Convention on the Privileges and Immunities of the United Nations, Advisory Opinion, I.C.J. Reports 1989*, p. 189)

The Court has constantly been mindful of its responsibilities as "the principal judicial organ of the United Nations" (Charter, Art. 92). When considering each request, it is mindful that it should not, in principle, refuse to give an advisory opinion. In accordance with the consistent jurisprudence of the Court, only "compelling reasons" could lead it to such a refusal (*Judgments of the Administrative Tribunal of the ILO upon Complaints Made against Unesco, Advisory Opinion, I.C.J. Reports 1956*, p. 86; *Certain Expenses of the United Nations (Article 17, paragraph 2, of the Charter), Advisory Opinion, I.C.J. Reports 1962*, p. 155; *Legal Consequences for States of the Continued Presence of South Africa in Namibia (South West Africa) notwithstanding Security Council Resolution 276 (1970), Advisory Opinion, I.C.J. Reports 1971*, p. 27; *Application for Review of Judgement No. 158 of the United Nations Administrative Tribunal, Advisory Opinion, I.C.J. Reports 1973*, p. 183; *Western Sahara, Advisory Opinion, I.C.J. Reports 1975*, p. 21; and *Applicability of Article VI, Section 22, of the Convention on the Privileges and Immunities of the United Nations, Advisory Opinion, I.C.J. Reports 1989*, p. 191). There has been no refusal, based on the discretionary power of the Court, to act upon a request for advisory opinion in the history of the present Court; in the case concerning the *Legality of the Use by a State of Nuclear Weapons in Armed Conflict*, the refusal to give the

World Health Organization the advisory opinion requested by it was justified by the Court's lack of jurisdiction in that case. The Permanent Court of International Justice took the view on only one occasion that it could not reply to a question put to it, having regard to the very particular circumstances of the case, among which were that the question directly concerned an already existing dispute, one of the States parties to which was neither a party to the Statute of the Permanent Court nor a Member of the League of Nations, objected to the proceedings, and refused to take part in any way (*Status of Eastern Carelia, P.C.I.J., Series B, No. 5*).

15. Most of the reasons adduced in these proceedings in order to persuade the Court that in the exercise of its discretionary power it should decline to render the opinion requested by General Assembly resolution 49/75K were summarized in the following statement made by one State in the written proceedings:

> "The question presented is vague and abstract, addressing complex issues which are the subject of consideration among interested States and within other bodies of the United Nations which have an express mandate to address these matters. An opinion by the Court in regard to the question presented would provide no practical assistance to the General Assembly in carrying out its functions under the Charter. Such an opinion has the potential of undermining progress already made or being made on this sensitive subject and, therefore, is contrary to the interests of the United Nations Organization." (United States of America, Written Statement, pp. 1–2; cf. pp. 3–7, II. See also United Kingdom, Written Statement, pp. 9–20, paras. 2.23–2.45; France, Written Statement, pp. 13–20, paras. 5–9; Finland, Written Statement, pp. 1–2; Netherlands, Written Statement, pp. 3–4, paras. 6–13; Germany, Written Statement, pp. 3–6, para. 2 *(b)*))

In contending that the question put to the Court is vague and abstract, some States appeared to mean by this that there exists no specific dispute on the subject-matter of the question. In order to respond to this argument, it is necessary to distinguish between requirements governing contentious procedure and those applicable to advisory opinions. The purpose of the advisory function is not to settle – at least directly – disputes between States, but to offer legal advice to the organs and institutions requesting the opinion (cf. *Interpretation of Peace Treaties with Bulgaria, Hungary and Romania, First Phase, Advisory Opinion, I.C.J. Reports 1950*, p. 71). The fact that the question put to the Court does not relate to a specific dispute should consequently not lead the Court to decline to give the opinion requested.

Moreover, it is the clear position of the Court that to contend that it should not deal with a question couched in abstract terms is "a mere affirmation devoid of any justification", and that "the Court may give an advisory opinion on any legal question, abstract or otherwise" (*Conditions of Admission of a State to Membership in the United Nations (Article 4 of Charter), Advisory Opinion, 1948, I.C.J. Reports 1947–1948*, p. 61; see also *Effect of Awards of Compensation Made by the United Nations Administrative Tribunal, Advisory Opinion, I.C.J. Reports 1954*, p. 51; and *Legal Consequences for States of the Continued Presence of South*

Africa in Namibia (South West Africa) notwithstanding Security Council Resolution 276 (1970), Advisory Opinion, I.C.J. Reports 1971, p. 27, para. 40).

Certain States have however expressed the fear that the abstract nature of the question might lead the Court to make hypothetical or speculative declarations outside the scope of its judicial function. The Court does not consider that, in giving an advisory opinion in the present case, it would necessarily have to write "scenarios", to study various types of nuclear weapons and to evaluate highly complex and controversial technological, strategic and scientific information. The Court will simply address the issues arising in all their aspects by applying the legal rules relevant to the situation.

16. Certain States have observed that the General Assembly has not explained to the Court for what precise purposes it seeks the advisory opinion. Nevertheless, it is not for the Court itself to purport to decide whether or not an advisory opinion is needed by the Assembly for the performance of its functions. The General Assembly has the right to decide for itself on the usefulness of an opinion in the light of its own needs.

Equally, once the Assembly has asked, by adopting a resolution, for an advisory opinion on a legal question, the Court, in determining whether there are any compelling reasons for it to refuse to give such an opinion, will not have regard to the origins or to the political history of the request, or to the distribution of votes in respect of the adopted resolution.

17. It has also been submitted that a reply from the Court in this case might adversely affect disarmament negotiations and would, therefore, be contrary to the interest of the United Nations. The Court is aware that, no matter what might be its conclusions in any opinion it might give, they would have relevance for the continuing debate on the matter in the General Assembly and would present an additional element in the negotiations on the matter. Beyond that, the effect of the opinion is a matter of appreciation. The Court has heard contrary positions advanced and there are no evident criteria by which it can prefer one assessment to another. That being so, the Court cannot regard this factor as a compelling reason to decline to exercise its jurisdiction.

18. Finally, it has been contended by some States that in answering the question posed, the Court would be going beyond its judicial role and would be taking upon itself a law-making capacity. It is clear that the Court cannot legislate, and, in the circumstances of the present case, it is not called upon to do so. Rather its task is to engage in its normal judicial function of ascertaining the existence or otherwise of legal principles and rules applicable to the threat or use of nuclear weapons. The contention that the giving of an answer to the question posed would require the Court to legislate is based on a supposition that the present *corpus juris* is devoid of relevant rules in this matter. The Court could not accede to this argument; it states the existing law and does not legislate. This is so even if, in stating and applying the law, the Court necessarily has to specify its scope and sometimes note its general trend.

19. In view of what is stated above, the Court concludes that it has the authority to deliver an opinion on the question posed by the General Assembly, and that there exist no "compelling reasons"

which would lead the Court to exercise its discretion not to do so.

An entirely different question is whether the Court, under the constraints placed upon it as a judicial organ, will be able to give a complete answer to the question asked of it. However, that is a different matter from a refusal to answer at all.

...

64. The Court will now turn to an examination of customary international law to determine whether a prohibition of the threat or use of nuclear weapons as such flows from that source of law. As the Court has stated, the substance of that law must be "looked for primarily in the actual practice and *opinio juris* of States" (*Continental Shelf (Libyan Arab Jamahiriya/Malta), Judgment, I.C.J. Reports 1985*, p. 29, para. 27).

65. States which hold the view that the use of nuclear weapons is illegal have endeavoured to demonstrate the existence of a customary rule prohibiting this use. They refer to a consistent practice of non-utilization of nuclear weapons by States since 1945 and they would see in that practice the expression of an *opinio juris* on the part of those who possess such weapons.

66. Some other States, which assert the legality of the threat and use of nuclear weapons in certain circumstances, invoked the doctrine and practice of deterrence in support of their argument. They recall that they have always, in concert with certain other States, reserved the right to use those weapons in the exercise of the right to self-defence against an armed attack threatening their vital security interests. In their view, if nuclear weapons have not been used since 1945, it is not on account of an existing or nascent custom but merely because circumstances that might justify their use have fortunately not arisen.

67. The Court does not intent to pronounce here upon the practice known as the "policy of deterrence". It notes that it is a fact that a number of States adhered to that practice during the greater part of the Cold War and continue to adhere to it. Furthermore, the members of the international community are profoundly divided on the matter of whether non-recourse to nuclear weapons over the past 50 years constitutes the expression of an *opinio juris*. Under these circumstances the Court does not consider itself able to find that there is such an *opinio juris*.

68. According to certain States, the important series of General Assembly resolutions, beginning with resolution 1653 (XVI) of 24 November 1961, that deal with nuclear weapons and that affirm, with consistent regularity, the illegality of nuclear weapons, signify the existence of a rule of international customary law which prohibits recourse to those weapons. According to other States, however, the resolutions in question have no binding character on their own account and are not declaratory of any customary rule of prohibition of nuclear weapons; some of these States have also pointed out that this series of resolutions not only did not meet with the approval of all of the nuclear-weapon States but of many other States as well.

69. States which consider that the use of nuclear weapons is illegal indicated that those resolutions did not claim to create any new rules, but were confined to a confirmation of customary law

relating to the prohibition of means or methods of warfare which, by their use, overstepped the bounds of what is permissible in the conduct of hostilities. In their view, the resolutions in question did no more than apply to nuclear weapons the existing rules of international law applicable in armed conflict; they were no more than the "envelope" or *instrumentum* containing certain pre-existing customary rules of international law. For those States it is accordingly of little importance that the *instrumentum* should have occasioned negative votes, which cannot have the effect of obliterating those customary rules which have been confirmed by treaty law.

70. The Court notes that General Assembly resolutions, even if they are not binding, may sometimes have normative value. They can, in certain circumstances, provide evidence important for establishing the existence of a rule or the emergence of an *opinio juris*. To establish whether this is true of a given General Assembly resolution, it is necessary to look at its content and the conditions of its adoption; it is also necessary to see whether an *opinio juris* exists as to its normative character. Or a series of resolutions may show the gradual evolution of the *opinio juris* required for the establishment of a new rule.

71. Examined in their totality, the General Assembly resolutions put before the Court declare that the use of nuclear weapons would be "a direct violation of the Charter of the United Nations"; and in certain formulations that such use "should be prohibited". The focus of these resolutions has sometimes shifted to diverse related matters; however, several of the resolutions under consideration in the present case have been adopted with substantial numbers of negative votes and abstentions; thus, although those resolutions are a clear sign of deep concern regarding the problem of nuclear weapons, they still fall short of establishing the existence of an *opinio juris* on the illegality of the use of such weapons.

72. The Court further notes that the first of the resolutions of the General Assembly expressly proclaiming the illegality of the use of nuclear weapons, resolution 1653 (XVI) of 24 November 1961 (mentioned in subsequent resolutions), after referring to certain international declarations and binding agreements, from the Declaration of St. Petersburg of 1868 to the Geneva Protocol of 1925, proceeded to qualify the legal nature of nuclear weapons, determine their effects, and apply general rules of customary international law to nuclear weapons in particular. That application by the General Assembly of general rules of customary law to the particular case of nuclear weapons indicates that, in its view, there was no specific rule of customary law which prohibited the use of nuclear weapons; if such a rule had existed, the General Assembly could simply have referred to it and would not have needed to undertake such an exercise of legal qualification.

73. Having said this, the Court points out that the adoption each year by the General Assembly, by a large majority, of resolutions recalling the content of resolution 1653 (XVI), and requesting the member States to conclude a convention prohibiting the use of nuclear weapons in any circumstance, reveals the desire of a very large section of the

international community to take, by a specific and express prohibition of the use of nuclear weapons, a significant step forward along the road to complete nuclear disarmament. The emergence, as *lex lata*, of a customary rule specifically prohibiting the use of nuclear weapons as such is hampered by the continuing tensions between the nascent *opinio juris* on the one hand, and the still strong adherence to the practice of deterrence on the other.

Notes

- Why does the WHO not have the competence to request this advisory opinion? Are there different rules for advisory opinion requests? Does the ICJ apply its usual powers analysis here?
- The ICJ does not mention it expressly, but the UNGA requested an advisory opinion on the same question at the same time as the WHO request. Did that fact make it easier to reject the request? Politically easier or legally easier?
- Did the ICJ take the correct approach? Did it really have to decide whether the organ or agency had the capacity to request the opinion? Surely whether or not a legal question was interesting and important to an organ/agency was within that body's ability to assess. Why does the ICJ feel a need to second-guess that decision?
- Is this really a question of competences? The WHO certainly has the competence to request an advisory opinion. Why would that competence be limited by the subject matter of the agency's mission?
- The ICJ appears to rely on a "family" structure consideration. What is the "family" relationship between the UNGA and the WHO? How does this add to our understanding of the powers that might be granted expressly or by implication to the WHO? The WHO was established on 7 April 1948 based on its own constitution, an international treaty. Previously, there had been a Health Organization agency of the League of Nations, and the WHO inherited the mandate and resources of its predecessor, but the two are legally distinct. The WHO thus has its own constitutive instrument adopted in 1946, although it is a specialized agency of the UN. It is not an organ of the UN. Does the fact that the UN was created first make a difference? Does it make a difference that the WHO was created as a specialized agency of the UN at its founding, and was not created independently and absorbed at a later date?

7.2.1 Principal organs

One distinction can be made between organs: some are superior. An organization's constitutive instrument will generally bring some organs into existence and may place certain organs above others in a kind of constitutional hierarchy. These organs are the principal organs. They do not depend on any other organ for their role, powers, or existence.

7.2.1.1 Limited competences

That being said, the principal organs each exercise certain functions and powers of the organization as a whole. In this way, we can say that each organ exercises limited competence within the organization.

Case C-327/91, French Republic v. Commission of the European Communities
Judgment
Court of Justice of the European Communities [Union], 9 August 1994[2]

Grounds

1 By application lodged at the Court Registry on 16 December 1991, the French Republic brought an action under the first paragraph of Article 173 of the EEC Treaty and Article 33 of the ECSC Treaty for a declaration that the Agreement signed on 23 September 1991 by the Commission of the European Communities and the Government of the United States of America regarding the application of their competition laws (hereinafter "the Agreement" is void.

…

5 The purpose of the Agreement is to promote cooperation and coordination and lessen the possibility or impact of differences between the parties in the application of their competition laws (Article I(1)).

…

Substance

18 The French Government puts forward three pleas in support of its application. The first plea alleges that the Commission was not competent to conclude such an agreement, …

The first plea

19 Article 228(1) of the EEC Treaty, in the version in force at the time of the events material to this case, provided as follows:

"Where this Treaty provides for the conclusion of agreements between the Community and one or more States or an international organization, such agreements shall be negotiated by the Commission. Subject to the powers vested in the Commission in this field, such agreements shall be concluded by the Council, after consulting the European Parliament where required by this Treaty."

20 The French Republic argues that that provision expressly reserves to the Council the power to conclude international agreements. Consequently, by concluding the Agreement, the Commission, which is empowered merely to conduct negotiations in that field, exceeded its powers.

21 The Commission contends that the Agreement in fact constitutes an administrative agreement which it is competent to conclude …

…

---

2 https://eur-lex.europa.eu, © European Union, 1998–2020.

24 Next, it is the Community alone, having legal personality pursuant to Article 210 of the Treaty, which has the capacity to bind itself by concluding agreements with a non-member country or an international organization.

...

26 That being so, the question is whether the Commission was competent under Community law to conclude such an agreement.

27 As the Court explained in Opinion 1/75 of 11 November 1975 ([1975] ECR 1355), Article 228 uses the expression "agreement" in a general sense to indicate any undertaking entered into by entities subject to international law which has binding force, whatever its formal designation.

28 Furthermore, as the Advocate General has pointed out in paragraph 37 of his Opinion, Article 228 constitutes, as regards the conclusion of treaties, an autonomous general provision, in that it confers specific powers on the Community institutions. With a view to establishing a balance between those institutions, it provides that agreements between the Community and one or more States are to be negotiated by the Commission and then concluded by the Council, after consulting the European Parliament where required by the Treaty. However, the power to conclude agreements is conferred on the Council "subject to the powers vested in the Commission in this field".

29 According to the French Government, those powers vested in the Commission are limited to agreements to be concluded by the Commission for the recognition of Community laissez-passer (Article 7 of the Protocol on the Privileges and Immunities of the European Communities). The French Government acknowledges that those powers may also extend to the conclusion of agreements which it describes as administrative or working agreements and which include, by way of example, the establishment of relations with the organs of the United Nations and the other international organizations referred to in Article 229 of the EEC Treaty.

30 The Commission, relying on what it describes as international administrative agreements, maintains, first, that the exception provided for in Article 228 should not be interpreted in the restrictive manner suggested by the French Government. It points out that, if those who drafted the Treaty had really sought to limit its power to conclude treaties, the French version of Article 228 would have conferred power on the Council "sous réserve des compétences attribuées à la Commission" and not "reconnues à la Commission".

31 Instead, the use of the term "reconnues" in the French version shows, according to the Commission, that it may derive its powers from sources other than the Treaty, such as the practices followed by the institutions. Moreover, reasoning by analogy from the third paragraph of Article 101 of the Euratom Treaty, the Commission considers that it can itself negotiate and conclude agreements or contracts whose implementation does not require action by the Council and can be effected within the limits of the relevant budget without giving rise to any new financial obligations on the part of the Community, provided that it keeps the Council informed.

32 That argument cannot be accepted.

33 First, the expression "sous réserve des compétences reconnues à la Commission" derogates from the rule

empowering the Council to conclude international agreements.

34 Second, according to the second subparagraph of Article 4(1) of the EEC Treaty, "each institution shall act within the limits of the powers conferred upon it by this Treaty". Consequently, the term "reconnues" in the French version of Article 228 of the Treaty cannot have any meaning other than "attribuées".

35 Third, other language versions of Article 228 use terms suggesting that the powers in question are "attribuées" rather than "reconnues". That is the case in particular as regards the versions in Danish ("som paa dette omraade er tillagt Kommissionen"), German ("der Zustaendigkeit, welche die Kommission auf diesem Gebiet besitzt"), Dutch ("van de aan de Commissie te dezer zake toegekende bevoegheden") and English ("the powers vested in the Commission in this field").

36 Fourth, and in any event, a mere practice cannot override the provisions of the Treaty.

37 It follows from the foregoing that the Commission cannot claim to derive from Article 228 of the Treaty powers analogous to those which it enjoys by virtue of the third paragraph of Article 101 of the Euratom Treaty.

38 First, as the Advocate General has pointed out in paragraph 26 of his Opinion, Article 101 provides for a procedure which is quite different from that referred to in Article 228 of the EEC Treaty.

39 Second, the EEC and the Euratom Treaties were negotiated simultaneously and signed on the same day; accordingly, if those negotiating the two treaties had intended to grant the Commission the same powers, they would have done so expressly.

40 The Commission's final argument against the French Government's plea is that its power to conclude international agreements is all the more clear-cut in the present case, since the EEC Treaty has conferred on it specific powers in the field of competition. Under Article 89 of the Treaty and Regulation No 17 of the Council of 6 February 1962, the first regulation implementing Articles 85 and 86 of the EEC Treaty (OJ, English Special Edition 1959–1962, p. 87), the Commission is entrusted with the task of ensuring the application of the principles laid down in Articles 85 and 86 of the EEC Treaty and the application of Council Regulation (EEC) No 4064/89 of 21 December 1989 on the control of concentrations between undertakings (OJ 1990 L 257, p. 14).

41 That argument cannot be accepted either. Even though the Commission has the power, internally, to take individual decisions applying the rules of competition, a field covered by the Agreement, that internal power is not such as to alter the allocation of powers between the Community institutions with regard to the conclusion of international agreements, which is determined by Article 228 of the Treaty.

42 The plea alleging lack of competence on the part of the Commission to conclude the Agreement at issue must therefore be upheld.

43 It follows, without there being any need to examine the other pleas relied on by the French Republic, that the act whereby the Commission sought to conclude the Agreement with the United States regarding the application of the competition laws of the European Communities and the United States must be declared void.

Notes

- Why is this case being decided by the EU Court of Justice? How did this case get to the court, and why does the court have competence to decide the question on the powers of European Union organs? This question may not be clearly apparent in the excerpt above, so what can you infer from the initial paragraphs?
- Which organs of which organization are at issue in this case? And which powers are we discussing?
- How does the Court of Justice determine which powers belong to which organ? Does it only apply the normal rules on treaty interpretation? Or does it apply other considerations? How does the Court of Justice deal with the question of the express delegation of competence over competition?
- Do the organs of the organization have their own legal personality? How can they act in their own name?
- Following from the court's decision on the competence to enter into international agreements, what now is the result for the agreement at issue? Is that agreement annulled? Where would such a result leave the other party to the agreement, the United States? Would voiding the treaty be the correct result under international law? How can we distinguish the questions of the power of an organ within the organization's constitutional framework from the power of the organization under international law?

Another question that may not be readily apparent from the excerpt above would be to wonder why the drafters of the Treaty on European Union created different organs, rather than one organ. What possible purpose could multiple organs serve? Contrast the governance of the EU with the notion of separation of powers within states. But doesn't the EU differ significantly from states in terms of its internal governance and democratic accountability? Consider that the EU has a Council where European governments are represented, a Commission which constitutes a form of executive bureaucracy, and the Parliament elected by the people of Europe, in addition to the Court of Justice. In *Case 9/56, Meroni v. High Authority*,[3] the Court of Justice had to address these very concerns, and determined that the objective of organs is institutional balance of powers.

7.2.1.2 Institutional balance

Following from this notion of separate organs with limited competence, the various organs must necessarily interact with each other in discharging the organization's powers. It might be that one principal organ has exclusive competence to exercise one of the powers of the organization, or that one principal organ might have the final say, but more commonly, the various organs exercise those powers through some form of institutional balance. In many cases, the precise competences are provided

---

3 *See* Case 9/56, Meroni & Co., Industrie Metallurgiche, S.p.A v. High Authority of the European Coal and Steel Community, Judgment (Court of Justice of the European Communities [Union], 13 June 1958).

in the constitutive instrument, but inevitably there will be gray areas where certain competences overlap.

Re-read the excerpt from the ICJ *Second Admissions* case in Chapter 4 on membership. In that chapter, we reviewed the case for its contribution to understanding the differences between "recommendations" and "decisions." Here we want to consider the same case from the perspective of the balance between organs within an organization.

Notes

- Why is this case being decided by the ICJ? How did this case get to the court, and why does the court have competence to decide the question?
- Which organs of which organization are at issue in this case? And which powers are we discussing?
- How does the ICJ determine which powers belong to which organ? Does it only apply the normal rules on treaty interpretation? Or does it apply other considerations? Compare the approach of the ICJ to that of the Court of Justice of the EU. Is it the same, or different?
- What is the purpose of the distinct roles for different organs? Does the court suggest a view? Consider its heavy reliance on the text of the UN Charter and the use of the terms "principal" and "subordinate," and the concern that to hold otherwise would "deprive" the Security Council of its powers or "nullify" its "role." What are the respective roles of the General Assembly and Security Council in membership applications?
- What is the result of this case? Does the ICJ here definitively determine the status of intra-organization competences and potentially void the action? Or is this merely advisory?
- Compare this outcome as well with that in the EU case above. What would be the difference in outcome, if any, and why would there be a difference?

Keeping in mind the views of the ICJ above in the *Second Admissions* case, consider the *Certain Expenses* case below and the views of the court on the relationship between the General Assembly and the Security Council:

Certain Expenses of the United Nations
(Article 17, Paragraph 2, of the Charter)
Advisory Opinion
1962 ICJ Reps. 151
International Court of Justice, 20 July 1962

[p. 162]

...

Passing from the text of Article 17 to its place in the general structure and scheme of the Charter, the Court will consider whether in that broad context one finds any basis for implying a limitation upon the budgetary authority of the General Assembly which in turn might limit the meaning of "expenses" in paragraph 2 of that Article.

The general purposes of Article 17 are the vesting of control over the finances of the Organization, and the levying of apportioned amounts of the expenses of the Organization in order to enable it to carry out the functions of the Organization as a whole acting through its principal organs and such subsidiary organs as may be established under the authority of Article 22 or Article 29.

Article 17 is the only article in the Charter which refers to budgetary authority or to the power to apportion expenses, or otherwise to raise revenue, except for Articles 33 and 35, paragraph 3, of the Statute of the Court which have no bearing on the point here under discussion. Nevertheless, it has been argued before the Court that one type of expenses, namely those resulting from operations for the maintenance of international peace and security, are not "expenses of the Organization" within the meaning of Article 17, paragraph 2, of the Charter, inasmuch as they fall to be dealt with exclusively by the Security Council, and more especially through agreements negotiated in accordance with Article 43 of the Charter.

The argument rests in part upon the view that when the maintenance of international peace and security is involved, it is only the Security Council which is authorized to decide on any action relative thereto. It is argued further that since the General Assembly's power is limited to discussing, considering, studying and recommending, it cannot impose an obligation to pay the expenses which result from the implementation of its recommendations. This [p. 163] argument leads to an examination of the respective functions of the General Assembly and of the Security Council under the Charter, particularly with respect to the maintenance of international peace and security.

Article 24 of the Charter provides:

> "In order to ensure prompt and effective action by the United Nations, its Members confer on the Security Council primary responsibility for the maintenance of international peace and security ..."

The responsibility conferred is "primary", not exclusive. This primary responsibility is conferred upon the Security Council, as stated in Article 24, "in order to ensure prompt and effective action". To this end, it is the Security Council which is given a power to impose an explicit obligation of compliance if for example it issues an order or command to an aggressor under Chapter VII. It is only the Security Council which can require enforcement by coercive action against an aggressor.

The Charter makes it abundantly clear, however, that the General Assembly is also to be concerned with international peace and security. Article 14 authorizes the General Assembly to "recommend measures for the peaceful adjustment of any situation, regardless of origin, which it deems likely to impair the general welfare or friendly relations among nations, including situations resulting from a violation of the provisions of the present Charter setting forth the purposes and principles of the United Nations." The word "measures" implies some kind of action, and the only limitation which Article 14 imposes on the General Assembly is the restriction found in Article 12, namely, that the Assembly should not recommend measures while the Security Council is dealing with the same matter unless the Council requests it to do so. Thus while it is the Security Council which, exclusively, may order coercive action, the functions and powers conferred by the Charter on the General Assembly are not confined to discussion, consideration, the initiation of studies and the making of recommendations; they are not merely hortatory. Article 18 deals with "decisions" of the General Assembly "on important questions". These "decisions" do indeed include certain recommendations, but others have dispositive force and effect. Among these latter decisions, Article 18 includes suspension of rights and privileges of membership, expulsion of Members, "and budgetary questions". In connection with the suspension of rights and privileges of membership and expulsion from membership under Articles 5 and 6, it is the Security Council which has only the power to recommend and it is the General Assembly which decides and whose decision determines status; but there is a close collaboration between the two organs. Moreover, these powers of decision of the General Assembly under Articles [p. 164] 5 and 6 are specifically related to preventive or enforcement measures.

By Article 17, paragraph 1, the General Assembly is given the power not only to "consider" the budget of the Organization, but also to "approve" it. The decision to "approve" the budget has a close connection with paragraph 2 of Article 17, since thereunder the General Assembly is also given the power to apportion the expenses among the Members and the exercise of the power of apportionment creates the obligation, specifically stated in Article 17, paragraph 2, of each Member to bear that part of the expenses which is apportioned to it by the General Assembly. When those expenses include expenditures for the maintenance of peace and security, which are not otherwise provided for, it is the General Assembly which has the authority to apportion the latter amounts among the Members. The provisions of the Charter which distribute functions and powers to the Security Council and to the General Assembly give no support to the view that such distribution excludes from the powers of the General Assembly the power to provide for the financing of measures designed to maintain peace and security.

The argument supporting a limitation on the budgetary authority of the General Assembly with respect to the maintenance of international peace and security relies especially on the reference to "action" in the last sentence of Article 11, paragraph 2. This paragraph reads as follows:

"The General Assembly may discuss any questions relating to the maintenance of international peace and security brought before it by any Member of the United Nations, or by the Security Council, or by a State which is not a Member of the United Nations in accordance with Article 35, paragraph 2, and, except as provided in Article 12, may make recommendations with regard to any such question to the State or States concerned or to the Security Council, or to both. Any such question on which action is necessary shall be referred to the Security Council by the General Assembly either before or after discussion."

The Court considers that the kind of action referred to in Article 11, paragraph 2, is coercive or enforcement action. This paragraph, which applies not merely to general questions relating to peace and security, but also to specific cases brought before the General Assembly by a State under Article 35, in its first sentence empowers the General Assembly, by means of recommendations to States or to the Security Council, or to both, to organize peacekeeping operations, at the request, or with the consent, of the States concerned. This power of the General Assembly is a special power which in no way derogates from its general powers under Article 10 [p. 165] or Article 14, except as limited by the last sentence of Article 11, paragraph 2. This last sentence says that when "action" is necessary the General Assembly shall refer the question to the Security Council. The word "action" must mean such action as is solely within the province of the Security Council. It cannot refer to recommendations which the Security Council might make, as for instance under Article 38, because the General Assembly under Article 11 has a comparable power. The "action" which is solely within the province of the Security Council is that which is indicated by the title of Chapter VII of the Charter, namely "Action with respect to threats to the peace, breaches of the peace, and acts of aggression". If the word "action" in Article 11, paragraph 2, were interpreted to mean that the General Assembly could make recommendations only of a general character affecting peace and security in the abstract, and not in relation to specific cases, the paragraph would not have provided that the General Assembly may make recommendations on questions brought before it by States or by the Security Council. Accordingly, the last sentence of Article 11, paragraph 2, has no application where the necessary action is not enforcement action.

The practice of the Organization throughout its history bears out the foregoing elucidation of the term "action" in the last sentence of Article 11, paragraph 2. Whether the General Assembly proceeds under Article 11 or under Article 14, the implementation of its recommendations for setting up commissions or other bodies involves organizational activity – action – in connection with the maintenance of international peace and security. Such implementation is a normal feature of the functioning of the United Nations. Such committees, commissions or other bodies or individuals, constitute, in some cases, subsidiary organs established under the authority of Article 22 of the Charter. The functions of the General Assembly for which it may establish such subsidiary organs include, for example, investigation, observation and supervision, but the way in which such subsidiary organs are utilized depends on the consent of the State or States concerned.

The Court accordingly finds that the argument which seeks, by reference to Article 11, paragraph 2, to limit the budgetary authority of the General Assembly in respect of the maintenance of international peace and security, is unfounded.

...

[p. 167]

The Court has considered the general problem of the interpretation of Article 17, paragraph 2, in the light of the general structure of the Charter and of the respective functions assigned by the Charter to the General Assembly and to the Security Council, with a view to determining the meaning of the phrase "the expenses of the Organization". The Court does not find it necessary to go further in giving a more detailed definition of such expenses. The Court will, therefore, proceed to examine the expenditures enumerated in the request for the advisory opinion. In determining whether the actual expenditures authorized constitute "expenses of the Organization within the meaning of Article 17, paragraph 2, of the Charter", the Court agrees that such expenditures must be tested by their relationship to the purposes of the United Nations in the sense that if an expenditure were made for a purpose which is not one of the purposes of the United Nations, it could not be considered an "expense of the Organization".

The purposes of the United Nations are set forth in Article 1 of the Charter. The first two purposes as stated in paragraphs 1 [p. 168] and 2, may be summarily described as pointing to the goal of international peace and security and friendly relations. The third purpose is the achievement of economic, social, cultural and humanitarian goals and respect for human rights. The fourth and last purpose is: "To be a center for harmonizing the actions of nations in the attainment of these common ends."

The primary place ascribed to international peace and security is natural, since the fulfilment of the other purposes will be dependent upon the attainment of that basic condition. These purposes are broad indeed, but neither they nor the powers conferred to effectuate them are unlimited. Save as they have entrusted the Organization with the attainment of these common ends, the Member States retain their freedom of action. But when the Organization takes action which warrants the assertion that it was appropriate for the fulfilment of one of the stated purposes of the United Nations, the presumption is that such action is not ultra vires the Organization.

If it is agreed that the action in question is within the scope of the functions of the Organization but it is alleged that it has been initiated or carried out in a manner not in conformity with the division of functions among the several organs which the Charter prescribes, one moves to the internal plane, to the internal structure of the Organization. If the action was taken by the wrong organ, it was irregular as a matter of that internal structure, but this would not necessarily mean that the expense incurred was not an expense of the Organization. Both national and international law contemplate cases in which the body corporate or politic may be bound, as to third parties, by an ultra vires act of an agent.

In the legal systems of States, there is often some procedure for determining the validity of even a legislative or governmental act, but no analogous procedure is to be found in the structure of the United Nations. Proposals made during the drafting of the Charter to place the ultimate authority to interpret the Charter in the International Court of Justice were not accepted; the opinion which the Court is in course of rendering is an advisory opinion. As anticipated in 1945, therefore, each organ must, in the first place at least, determine its own jurisdiction. If the Security Council, for example, adopts a resolution purportedly for the maintenance of international peace and security and if, in accordance with a mandate or authorization in such resolution, the Secretary-General incurs financial obligations, these amounts must be presumed to constitute "expenses of the Organization".

The Financial Regulations and Rules of the United Nations, adopted by the General Assembly, provide:

> "Regulation 4.1: The appropriations voted by the General Assembly shall constitute an authorization to the Secretary-[p. 169]General to incur obligations and make payments for the purposes for which the appropriations were voted and up to the amounts so voted."

Thus, for example, when the General Assembly in resolution 1619 (XV) included a paragraph reading:

> "3. Decides to appropriate an amount of $100 million for the operations of the United Nations in the Congo from 1 January to 31 October 1961",

this constituted an authorization to the Secretary-General to incur certain obligations of the United Nations just as clearly as when in resolution 1590 (XV) the General Assembly used this language:

> "3. Authorizes the Secretary-General ... to incur commitments in 1961 for the United Nations operations in the Congo up to the total of $24 million ..."

On the previous occasion when the Court was called upon to consider Article 17 of the Charter, the Court found that an award of the Administrative Tribunal of the United Nations created an obligation of the Organization and with relation thereto the Court said that:

> "the function of approving the budget does not mean that the General Assembly has an absolute power to approve or disapprove the expenditure proposed to it; for some part of that expenditure arises out of obligations already incurred by the Organization, and to this extent the General Assembly has no alternative but to honour these engagements." (Effects of awards of compensation made by the United Nations Administrative Tribunal, I.C.J. Reports 1954, p. 59.)

Similarly, obligations of the Organization may be incurred by the Secretary-General, acting on the authority of the Security Council or of the General Assembly, and the General Assembly "has no alternative but to honour these engagements."

The obligation is one thing: the way in which the obligation is met – that is from what source the funds are secured – is another. The General Assembly may follow any one of several alternatives: it may apportion the cost of the item according to the ordinary scale of assessment; it may apportion the cost according to some special scale of assessment; it may utilize funds which are voluntarily contributed to the Organization; or it may find some other method or combination of methods for providing the necessary funds. In this context, it is of no legal significance whether, as a matter of book-keeping or accounting, the General Assembly chooses to have the item in question included under one of the standard' established sections of the "regular" budget or whether it is separately listed in some special account or fund. The significant fact is that the item is an expense of the Organization and under [p. 170] Article 17, paragraph 2, the General Assembly therefore has authority to apportion it.

The reasoning which has just been developed, applied to the resolutions mentioned in the request for the advisory opinion, might suffice as a basis for the opinion of the Court. The Court finds it appropriate, however, to take into consideration other arguments which have been advanced.

Notes

- Once again, reflect on the methodology the court is using to determine the relative competences of the organs, and the kind of institutional balance that has been constructed. Is this normal treaty interpretation, or something different? Why should it be different, if it is? What additional considerations can you identify that the court draws on?
- What power is really at issue in this case? Is it a budgetary power, or does it concern powers over the underlying acts that incur a budgetary consequence?
- And is "power" really the right concept to discuss the court's appreciation of institutional balance here? What concept might be better? Responsibility? Competence? We have already studied some legal principles around examining the powers of international organizations, so we use a concept different than powers; what legal principles do we apply? Does this case strike you in any way as similar to any cases you may have studied in a constitutional law course?
- Does the General Assembly really have any authority over international peace and security? Why is it that the Security Council does not have exclusive competence?
- Are the expressions "primary" or "secondary" very helpful in describing or understanding the balance of powers between organs?
- How is the structure of the UN Charter relevant for assessing powers of the General Assembly? How can the General Assembly and Security Council balance "primary" and secondary authority? How could the General Assembly have any role in peace and security?
- These notes have been discussing international peace and security as a general competence, yet that vague statement of competence rests on a basket of discrete tasks and responsibilities. When it comes to the particular responsibilities, does the Security Council exercise any exclusive competence? And the General Assembly?
- It might be helpful to observe that at the time of the decision, the UN Security Council was largely unable to operate due to the Cold War. In essence, the NATO states on the one hand and the USSR on the other hand vetoed each other's initiatives. It is into this void of activity that the UN General Assembly stepped. Does this reality change our understanding of the reasoning of the court in the *Certain Expenses* case? Should it? How is a political stalemate relevant to interpreting powers in the UN Charter? Also recall that the UN General Assembly does not have a veto mechanism. But does this consideration mean that the UN General Assembly can now act in lieu of the Security Council? Or does it still operate within certain limitations?

Shifting back to the European Union, it also has some of the same institutional balance issues when it comes to certain areas of decision-making. For example, the European Parliament must be consulted by the European Commission before the Commission submits proposals or measures to the European Council. However, the Commission is not required to follow the views of the Parliament. In order to act contrary to Parliament's views, the Commission must rule unanimously.

7.2.1.3 Judicial review

In addition to tensions between organs due to institutional balance, in some organizations the various organs may have powers of review over the other organs. For example, in the European Union, the Court of Justice is understood to be the check that the EU is exercising its powers in compliance with the Treaty on European Union. Consider, for example, *Case C-327/91, France v. Commission*,[4] where the Court of Justice held that the commission had acted *ultra vires*, and annulled its action.

In light of that case, re-read *Case C-376/98, Germany v Parliament*, otherwise known as the *Tobacco Directive* case, which is excerpted in Chapter 5 on powers. In that chapter, *Germany v Parliament* was introduced to discuss whether the EU had acted within its powers by regulating tobacco advertising. In this section, that case is also relevant for the judicial review of EU acts by the Court of Justice.

Notes

- What is the Directive at issue, and what is the basis for the challenge?
- What role for judicial review does the court exercise? Does the court simply substitute its view for that of the European Parliament and Council? What standard of review is applied? What is the constraint on the exercise of this power?
- Does the court express any methodology to determine the relative competences of the organs, including review competences, and the kind of institutional balance under the Treaty on European Union. Does it apply the law of treaties to reach this conclusion?
- Does the Directive concern a topic that falls within the competence of the EU? Is this not a concern of the internal market? Surely advertising differences between Member States impedes the free flow of goods? The court seems to agree that differences in advertising would not necessary impede the movement of goods.
- And why does the distortion of competition not pose a problem?

However, just because this particular kind of institutional balance is available does not mean that the organization was crafted along those lines. In fact, the Court of Justice of the European Union is not fully empowered to review all acts of the other organs.

---

4 Case C-327/91, French Republic v. Commission of the European Communities, Judgment (Court of Justice of the European Communities [Union], 9 August 1994).

In Chapter 6, we already examined the *Lockerbie* judgment, but in the excerpt below, we will read a different selection from the same case discussing the view of the International Court of Justice on whether it can review its sister organ, the Security Council.

Case Concerning Questions of Interpretation and Application of the 1971 Montreal Convention Arising from the Aerial Incident at Lockerbie
Libya v. United Kingdom
Preliminary Objections, Judgment
1998 ICJ Reps. 9
International Court of Justice, 27 February 1998

46. In dealing with admissibility, the Agent of the United Kingdom also stated that his Government "ask[ed] the Court to rule that the intervening resolutions of the Security Council have rendered the Libyan claims without object".

The Court has already acknowledged, on several occasions in the past, that events subsequent to the filing of an application may "render an application without object" (Border and Transborder Armed Actions (Nicaragua v. Honduras), Jurisdiction and Admissibility, Judgment, I.C.J. Reports 1988, p. 95, para. 66) and "therefore the Court is not called upon to give a decision thereon" (Nuclear Tests (Australia v. France), Judgment, I.C.J. Reports 1974, p. 272, para. 62) (cf. Northern Cameroons, Judgment, I.C.J. Reports 1963, p. 38).

In the present case, the United Kingdom puts forward an objection aimed at obtaining from the Court a decision not to proceed to judgment on the merits, which objection must be examined within the framework of this jurisprudence.

...

50. The Court must therefore ascertain whether, in the present case, the United Kingdom's objection based on the Security Council decisions contains "both preliminary aspects and other aspects relating to the merits" or not.

That objection relates to many aspects of the dispute. By maintaining that Security Council resolutions 748 (1992) and 883 (1993) have rendered the Libyan claims without object, the United Kingdom seeks to obtain from the Court a decision not to proceed to judgment on the [p. 29] merits, which would immediately terminate the proceedings. However, by requesting such a decision, the United Kingdom is requesting, in reality, at least two others which the decision not to proceed to judgment on the merits would necessarily postulate: on the one hand a decision establishing that the rights claimed by Libya under the Montreal Convention are incompatible with its obligations under the Security Council resolutions; and, on the other hand, a decision that those obligations prevail over those rights by virtue of Articles 25 and 103 of the Charter.

The Court therefore has no doubt that Libya's rights on the merits would not only be affected by a decision, at this stage of the proceedings, not to proceed to judgment on the merits, but would constitute, in many respects, the very subject-matter of that decision. The objection raised by the United Kingdom on that point has the character of a defence on the merits. In the view of the Court, this objection does much more than "touch[ing] upon subjects belonging to the merits of the case" (Certain German Interests in Polish Upper Silesia, Jurisdiction, Judgment No. 6, 1925, P.C.I.J., Series A, No. 6, p. 15); it is "inextricably interwoven" with the merits (Barcelona Traction, Light and Power Company, Limited Preliminary Objections, Judgment, I.C.J. Reports 1964, p. 46).

The Court notes furthermore that the United Kingdom itself broached many substantive problems in its written and oral pleadings in this phase, and pointed out that those problems had been the subject of exhaustive exchanges before the Court; the United Kingdom Government thus implicitly acknowledged that the objection raised and the merits of the case were "closely interconnected" (Barcelona Traction, Light and Power Company, Limited, Preliminary Objections, Judgment, I.C.J. Reports 1964, p. 46, and the reference to Pajzs, Csaky, Esterhazy, Order of 23 May 1936, P.C.I.J., Series A/B, No. 66, p. 9).

If the Court were to rule on that objection, it would therefore inevitably be ruling on the merits; in relying on the provisions of Article 79 of the Rules of Court, the Respondent has set in motion a procedure the precise aim of which is to prevent the Court from so doing.

The Court concludes from the foregoing that the objection of the United Kingdom according to which the Libyan claims have been rendered without object does not have "an exclusively preliminary character" within the meaning of that Article.

51. Having established its jurisdiction and concluded that the Application is admissible, the Court will be able to consider this objection when it reaches the merits of the case.

...

[p. 64]

Dissenting Opinion of President Schwebel

JUDICIAL REVIEW

That last spectre raises the question of whether the Court is empowered to exercise judicial review of the decisions of the Security Council, a question as to which I think it right to express my current views. The Court is not generally so empowered, and it is particularly without power to overrule or undercut decisions of the Security Council made by it in pursuance of its authority under Articles 39, 41 and 42 of the Charter to determine the existence of any threat to the peace, breach of the peace, or [p. 74] act of aggression and to decide upon responsive measures to be taken to maintain or restore international peace and security. The Court more than once has disclaimed possessing a power of judicial review. In its Advisory Opinion in the case concerning *Certain Expenses of the United Nations (Article 17, paragraph 2, of the Charter)*, the Court declared:

> "In the legal systems of States, there is often some procedure for determining the validity of even a legislative or governmental act, but no analogous procedure is to be found in the structure of the United Nations. Proposals made during the drafting of the Charter to place the ultimate authority to interpret the Charter in the International Court of Justice were

not accepted; the opinion which the Court is in course of rendering is an *advisory* opinion. As anticipated in 1945, therefore, each organ must, in the first place at least, determine its own jurisdiction. If the Security Council, for example, adopts a resolution purportedly for the maintenance of international peace and security and if, in accordance with a mandate or authorization in such resolution, the Secretary-General incurs financial obligations, these amounts must be presumed to constitute 'expenses of the Organization'." (*I.C.J. Reports 1962*, p. 168)

In its Advisory Opinion on *Legal Consequences for States of the Continued Presence of South Africa in Namibia (South West Africa) notwithstanding Security Council Resolution 276 (1970)*, the Court reiterated that: "Undoubtedly, the Court does not possess powers of judicial review or appeal in respect of the decisions taken by the United Nations organs concerned." (*I.C.J. Reports 1971*, p. 45.)

...

[p. 80]

The conclusions to which the *travaux préparatoires* and text of the Charter lead are that the Court was not and was not meant to be invested with a power of judicial review of the legality or effects of decisions of the Security Council. Only the Security Council can determine what is a threat to or breach of the peace or act of aggression under Article 39, and under Article 39 only it can "decide what measures shall be taken ... to maintain or restore international peace and security". Two States at variance in the interpretation of the Charter may submit a dispute to the Court, but that facility does not empower the Court to set aside or second-guess the determinations of the Security Council under Article 39. Contentious cases may come before the Court that call for its passing upon questions of law raised by Council decisions and for interpreting pertinent Council resolutions. But that power cannot be equated with an authority to review and confute the decisions of the Security Council.

It may of course be maintained that the Charter is a living instrument; that the present-day interpreters of the Charter are not bound by the intentions of its drafters of 50 years ago; that the Court has interpreted the powers of the United Nations constructively in other respects, and could take a constructive view of its own powers in respect of judicial review or some variation of it. The difficulty with this approach is that for the Court to engraft upon the Charter régime a power to review, and revise the reach of, resolutions of the Security Council would not be evolutionary but revolutionary. It would be not a development but a departure, and a great and grave departure. It would not be a development even arguably derived from the terms or structure of the Charter and Statute. It would not be a development arising out of customary international law, which has no principle of or provision for judicial review. It would not be a development drawn from the general principles of law. Judicial review, in varying forms, is found in a number of democratic polities, most famously that of the United States, where it was developed by the Supreme Court itself. But it is by no means a universal or even general principle of government or law. It is hardly found outside the democratic world and is not uniformly found in it. Where it exists internationally, as in the European Union, it is expressly provided for by treaty in specific terms. The United Nations is far from being a government, or an international organization comparable in its integration to the European Union, and it is not democratic ....

Notes

- How did this case get to the ICJ? What is the issue being litigated? Construct the timeline, and distinguish the various actors.
- Can the ICJ review the acts of the UN Security Council? Would the ICJ need to review the UN Security Council to reach a decision in this case? Or is it avoidable? If it cannot be avoided, what is a better outcome?
- What other kind of limits can there be to the exercise of powers by the Security Council? Surely it is limited politically, and the legal limitations in the Charter on its powers could be enforced by the member states themselves by simply refusing to adopt acts that were not in compliance with the Charter.
- Is this question limited by the nature of the proceedings? Is this a decision for the merits, or for a different question? How would that change the question? And how would that change the powers the ICJ can exercise?

7.2.2 Subsidiary organs

Contrasted with principal organs are subsidiary organs. As their name suggests, they play a role under the principal organs, deriving their powers and duties from the principal organs. They may be created in the constitutive instrument itself (for example, the Military Staff Committee in the UN Charter) or by subsequent decision of the principal organ (for example, the decision of the Security Council to create the ICTY or the decision of the UN General Assembly to create the UNEP). In the latter case, their continued existence depends on the decision of the principal organ, which may dissolve the subsidiary.

Despite this power of constitution and dissolution, one question that arises is whether the principal organs can review or revise decisions by subsidiary organs. While this power of review might be less objectionable over subsidiary political organs, though not without controversy, any power of review over a subsidiary organ of a judicial nature becomes quite problematic. The International Court of Justice had to deal with just this question in the *Effect of Awards* advisory opinion. In this matter, the ICJ addressed whether the UN General Assembly had to give effect to awards of compensation made by the UN Administrative Tribunal. Recall that this tribunal was established by the General Assembly so that the UN remained accountable as an employer to its employees for respecting their labor rights.

Re-read the excerpt from the *Effect of Awards* case from Chapter 5 on powers. In that section, we considered the interpretative techniques used by the court and the powers of the UN General Assembly to create the Administrative Tribunal. In this section, the question to focus on is the power of the General Assembly to create a subsidiary organ.

Notes

- The Administrative Tribunal is a judicial organ. Does the UN have any power to create such subsidiary organ? Does the General Assembly have any such power? Recall the discussion in Chapter 6 on the powers of an organization, and compare that with the discussion in this chapter on the powers of an organ of an organization.
- Are the powers of an organ to create subsidiary organs unlimited? What would limit those powers? How can we analyze whether powers are correctly exercised or not?

7.2.2.1 Independence

Despite subsidiary organs falling under the review and control of another organ, there can be times when it would be better for the subsidiary to have a degree of independence. Some subsidiary organs have been empowered to enter into agreements in their own name, and, seemingly, within their own capacity. See, for example, the practice of the UN Interim Administration Mission in Kosovo (UNMIK), which operated as an effectively independent government of Kosovo. This practice can even be extended to interactions between subsidiary organs, for example the relationship between UNMIK and the ICTY in providing for provisional release of the accused Haradinaj.[5] This practice may be due to other considerations, though. The ICTY and Administrative Tribunal are judicial institutions, and other judicial organs have operated with a high degree of independence. For example, the ICJ has entered into its own agreement with The Netherlands as host state and another agreement with the Carnegie Foundation, the private foundation that owns the Peace Palace. Also, organs such as UNMIK are, more or less, essentially the governments of territories and also necessarily need a high degree of independence.

Continuing with the *Effect of Awards* advisory opinion, the International Court of Justice next had to examine the relationship of a subsidiary organ to a principal organ in the unusual case where the subsidiary was intended to operate with a degree of independence from the principal. Even more surprising, it appeared that the subsidiary was empowered to bind the principal organ:

---

5 *See* Prosecutor v Haradinaj et al., Case No. IT-04-84-AR65.1, Decision on Ramush Haradinaj's Modified Provisional Release, paras. 14, 77, 103–4 (International Criminal Tribunal for the former Yugoslavia, Appeals Chamber, 10 March 2006).

Effect of Awards of Compensation Made by the United Nations Administrative Tribunal
Advisory Opinion
1954 ICJ Reps. 47
International Court of Justice, 13 July 1954

[p. 58]

...

But that does not dispose of the problem before the Court. Some of the Governments that take the position that there are grounds which would justify the General Assembly in refusing to give effect to awards, agree that the powers of the General Assembly, and particularly its power to establish regulations under Article 101, imply the power to set up an administrative tribunal. They agree that the General Assembly would be able to establish a tribunal competent to hear and decide staff grievances, to prescribe its jurisdiction, and to authorize it to give a final decision, in the sense that no appeal could be taken as of right. They nevertheless contend that the implied power does not enable the General Assembly to establish a tribunal with authority to make decisions binding on the General Assembly itself.

In the first place, it is contended that there was no need to go so far, and that an implied power can only be exercised to the extent that the particular measure under consideration can be regarded as absolutely essential. There can be no doubt that the General Assembly in the exercise of its power could have set up a tribunal without giving finality to its judgments. In fact, however, it decided, after long deliberation, to invest the Tribunal with power to render judgments which would be "final and without appeal", and which would be binding on the United Nations. The precise nature and scope of the measures by which the power of creating a tribunal was to be exercised, was a matter for determination by the General Assembly alone.

*

[p. 59]

In the second place, it has been argued that, while an implied power of the General Assembly to establish an administrative tribunal may be both necessary and essential, nevertheless, an implied power to impose legal limitations upon the General Assembly's express Charter powers is not legally admissible.

It has been contended that the General Assembly cannot, by establishing the Administrative Tribunal, divest itself of the power conferred by paragraph (1) of Article 17 of the Charter, which reads:

> "The General Assembly shall consider and approve the budget of the Organization."

This provision confers a power on the General Assembly, for the exercise of which Article 18 requires the vote of a two-thirds majority. Accordingly, the establishment of a tribunal competent to make an award of compensation to which the General Assembly was bound to give effect would, it has been argued, contravene the provisions relating to the budgetary power. The Court is unable to accept this contention.

The Court notes that Article 17 of the Charter appears in a section of Chapter IV relating to the General Assembly, which is entitled "Functions and Powers". This Article deals with a function of the General Assembly and provides for the consideration and approval by it of the budget of the Organization. Consideration of the budget is thus an act which must be performed and the same is true of its approval, for without such approval there can be no budget.

But the function of approving the budget does not mean that the General Assembly has an absolute power to approve or disapprove the expenditure proposed to it; for some part of that expenditure arises out of obligations already incurred by the Organization, and to this extent the General Assembly has no alternative but to honour these engagements. The question, therefore, to be decided by the Court is whether these obligations comprise the awards of compensation made by the Administrative Tribunal in favour of staff members. The reply to this question must be in the affirmative. The obligatory character of these awards has been established by the considerations set out above relating to the authority of res judicata and the binding effect of the judgments of this Tribunal upon the United Nations Organization.

The Court therefore considers that the assignment of the budgetary function to the General Assembly cannot be regarded as conferring upon it the right to refuse to give effect to the obligation arising out of an award of the Administrative Tribunal.

*

[p. 60]

It has also been contended that the implied power of the General Assembly to establish a tribunal cannot be carried so far as to enable the tribunal to intervene in matters falling within the province of the Secretary-General. The Court cannot accept this contention.

The General Assembly could at all times limit or control the powers of the Secretary-General in staff matters, by virtue of the provisions of Article 101. Acting under powers conferred by the Charter, the General Assembly authorized the intervention of the Tribunal to the extent that such intervention might result from the exercise of jurisdiction conferred upon the Tribunal by its Statute. Accordingly, when the Tribunal decides that particular action by the Secretary-General involves a breach of the contract of service, it is in no sense intervening in a Charter power of the Secretary-General, because the Secretary-General's legal powers in staff matters have already been limited in this respect by the General Assembly.

*

A similar problem is involved in the contention that the General Assembly cannot authorize and the Secretary-General cannot enter into contracts of service which are not in conformity with the Charter. The Staff Regulations are made a part of the contracts of service and No. 11.2 reads as follows:

> "The United Nations Administrative Tribunal shall, under conditions prescribed in its Statute, hear and pass judgment upon applications from staff members alleging non-observance of their terms of appointment, including all pertinent regulations and rules."

It is contended that the incorporation, in the contracts of service, of the right to rely on the Statute of the Administrative Tribunal would conflict with the powers conferred on the General Assembly and on the Secretary-General by the Charter. In view of the foregoing considerations, the Court cannot accept this contention. There can be no doubt that, by virtue of the terms thus incorporated in the contracts of service, and so long as the Statute of the Administrative Tribunal in its present form is in force, the staff members are entitled to resort to the Tribunal and rely on its judgments.

*

In the third place, the view has been put forward that the Administrative Tribunal is a subsidiary, subordinate, or secondary organ; and that, accordingly, the Tribunal's judgments cannot bind the General Assembly which established it.

[p. 61]

This view assumes that, in adopting the Statute of the Administrative Tribunal, the General Assembly was establishing an organ which it deemed necessary for the performance of its own functions. But the Court cannot accept this basic assumption. The Charter does not confer judicial functions on the General Assembly and the relations between staff and Organization come within the scope of Chapter XV of the Charter. In the absence of the establishment of an Administrative Tribunal, the function of resolving disputes between staff and Organization could be discharged by the Secretary-General by virtue of the provisions of Articles 97 and 101. Accordingly, in the three years or more preceding the establishment of the Administrative Tribunal, the Secretary-General coped with this problem by means of joint administrative machinery, leading to ultimate decision by himself. By establishing the Administrative Tribunal, the General Assembly was not delegating the performance of its own functions: it was exercising a power which it had under the Charter to regulate staff relations. In regard to the Secretariat, the General Assembly is given by the Charter a power to make regulations, but not a power to adjudicate upon, or otherwise deal with, particular instances.

It has been argued that an authority exercising a power to make regulations is inherently incapable of creating a subordinate body competent to make decisions binding its creator. There can be no doubt that the Administrative Tribunal is subordinate in the sense that the General Assembly can abolish the Tribunal by repealing the Statute, that it can amend the Statute and provide for review of the future decisions of the Tribunal and that it can amend the Staff Regulations and make new ones. There is no lack of power to deal effectively with any problem that may arise. But the contention that the General Assembly is inherently incapable of creating a tribunal competent to make decisions binding on itself cannot be accepted. It cannot be justified by analogy to national laws, for it is common practice in national legislatures to create courts with the capacity to render decisions legally binding on the legislatures which brought them into being.

...

The question cannot be determined on the basis of the description of the relationship between the General Assembly and the Tribunal, that is, by considering whether the Tribunal is to be regarded as a subsidiary, a subordinate, or a secondary organ, or on the basis of the fact that it was established by the General Assembly. It depends on the intention of the General Assembly in establishing the Tribunal, and on the nature of the functions conferred upon it by its Statute. An examination of the language of the Statute of the Administrative Tribunal has shown that the General Assembly intended to establish a judicial body; moreover, it had the legal capacity under the Charter to do so.

...

[p. 76]

Dissenting Opinion by Judge Hackworth

...

The Court is asked to consider only the abstract question of right to decline to make an appropriation to satisfy an award. To this I have answered that there is no justification for concluding that the General Assembly is bound to effectuate a decision which is not juridically sound, and which, because of the absence of juridical plausibility, does not command the respect of the Assembly. A proper administration of justice within the Secretariat must be the guiding criterion. A denial of justice in the sense of the prevailing jurisprudence on the subject should find no place in the United Nations Organization.

If I am correct in my conclusion stated above, that the Assembly has a right to review a decision of the Tribunal, as a corollary to [p. 91] its duty to "consider and approve the budget of the Organization" and to maintain a high standard of efficiency and integrity, it must follow that it may "lawfully" exercise that right with respect to any decision which does not commend itself to respectful and favorable consideration.

The principal grounds upon which the Assembly may lawfully exercise a right to decline to give effect to an award may be simply stated as follows:

(1) That the award is ultra vires;

(2) That the award reveals manifest defects or deficiency in the administration of justice;

(3) That the award does not reflect a faithful application of the Charter, the Statute of the Tribunal, or the Staff Rules and Regulations, to the facts of the case; and

(4) That the amount of the award is obviously either excessive or inadequate.

Notes

- The court says that the purpose of the tribunal is to "do justice." What does this mean in the context of an international organization and its employees? Is the Administrative Tribunal a judicial organ? Or something else?
- If it is a judicial organ, then what significance does that have? Assuming that the General Assembly can create a judicial body, what would we normally expect from a judiciary? Are those expectations compatible with the organ being subsidiary to a political body?
- On what grounds could the General Assembly refuse to give effect to an award of the Administrative Tribunal? What type of grounds are possible: procedural or substantive?
- If the General Assembly can no longer refuse to give effect to decisions of the Administrative Tribunal, then what oversight powers does it retain? Can it still abolish the subsidiary organ? If it can, then is that power limited to abolishing the organ on non-substantive grounds? But then how would we distinguish abolishing the tribunal due to legitimate management concerns versus abolishing the tribunal due to disagreement with its views?

- Can the Administrative Tribunal issue decisions that would bind the General Assembly? Is this power only limited to certain decisions within the Tribunal's competence? How can we determine if something was within the Tribunal's competence?
- Looking specifically at Judge Hackworth's dissenting opinion, why does Hackworth disagree with the majority? Try to answer that question from the perspective of the creation of subsidiary organs rather than the perspective of powers. Does he disagree with the power to create the organ? Or the power to review the organ? And what does he think would be the constraints on such a power from a powers theory or organs theory perspective?
- Recalling the discussion on *ultra vires* exercise of powers from Chapter 5 on powers, what is the view of the ICJ on *ultra vires* acts? How does the ICJ believe *ultra vires* issues are resolved within the UN family? Do *ultra vires* acts nonetheless attract the responsibility of the organization?

7.2.2.2 Judicial review of a principal organ

Having examined the relationship between a principal and subsidiary organ, and the ability of the principal to review decisions of the subsidiary, we now consider the reverse – whether the subsidiary may review the acts of the principal organ:

Prosecutor v. Tadić a/k/a "Dule", Case No. IT-94-1
Decision on the Defence Motion for Interlocutory Appeal on Jurisdiction
International Criminal Tribunal for the former Yugoslavia,
Appeals Chamber, 2 October 1995

II. UNLAWFUL ESTABLISHMENT OF THE INTERNATIONAL TRIBUNAL

9. The first ground of appeal attacks the validity of the establishment of the International Tribunal.

A. Meaning Of Jurisdiction

10. In discussing the Defence plea to the jurisdiction of the International Tribunal on grounds of invalidity of its establishment by the Security Council, the Trial Chamber declared:

"There are clearly enough matters of jurisdiction which are open to determination by the International Tribunal, questions of time, place and nature of an offence charged. These are properly described as jurisdictional, whereas the validity of the creation of the International Tribunal is not truly a matter of jurisdiction but rather the lawfulness of its creation [...]." (Decision at Trial, at para. 4)

There is a *petitio principii* underlying this affirmation and it fails to explain the criteria by which it the Trial Chamber disqualifies the plea of invalidity of the establishment of the International Tribunal as a plea to jurisdiction. What is more important, that proposition implies a narrow concept of jurisdiction reduced to pleas based on the limits of its scope in time and space and as to persons and subject-matter (*ratione temporis, loci, personae and materiae*). But jurisdiction is not merely an ambit or sphere (better described in this case as "competence"); it is basically – as is visible from the Latin origin of the word itself, *jurisdictio* – a legal power, hence necessarily a legitimate power, "to state the law" (*dire le droit*) within this ambit, in an authoritative and final manner. This is the meaning which it carries in all legal systems. Thus, historically, in common law, the Termes de la ley provide the following definition: "jurisdiction' is a dignity which a man hath by a power to do justice in causes of complaint made before him." (Stroud's Judicial Dictionary, 1379 (5th ed. 1986).) The same concept is found even in current dictionary definitions:

> "[Jurisdiction] is the power of a court to decide a matter in controversy and presupposes the existence of a duly constituted court with control over the subject matter and the parties." Black's Law Dictionary, 712 (6th ed. 1990) (citing Pinner v. Pinner, 33 N.C. App. 204, 234 S.E.2d 633).)

11. A narrow concept of jurisdiction may, perhaps, be warranted in a national context but not in international law. International law, because it lacks a centralized structure, does not provide for an integrated judicial system operating an orderly division of labour among a number of tribunals, where certain aspects or components of jurisdiction as a power could be centralized or vested in one of them but not the others. In international law, every tribunal is a self-contained system (unless otherwise provided). This is incompatible with a narrow concept of jurisdiction, which presupposes a certain division of labour. Of course, the constitutive instrument of an international tribunal can limit some of its jurisdictional powers, but only to the extent to which such limitation does not jeopardize its "judicial character", as shall be discussed later on. Such limitations cannot, however, be presumed and, in any case, they cannot be deduced from the concept of jurisdiction itself.

12. In sum, if the International Tribunal were not validly constituted, it would lack the legitimate power to decide in time or space or over any person or subject-matter. The plea based on the invalidity of constitution of the International Tribunal goes to the very essence of jurisdiction as a power to exercise the judicial function within any ambit. It is more radical than, in the sense that it goes beyond and subsumes, all the other pleas concerning the scope of jurisdiction. This issue is a preliminary to and conditions all other aspects of jurisdiction.

B. Admissibility Of Plea Based On The Invalidity Of The Establishment Of The International Tribunal

13. Before the Trial Chamber, the Prosecutor maintained that:

(1) the International Tribunal lacks authority to review its establishment by the Security Council (Prosecutor Trial Brief, at 10–12); and that in any case (2) the question whether the Security Council in establishing the International Tribunal complied with the United Nations Charter raises "political questions" which are "nonjusticiable" (id. at 12–14).

The Trial Chamber approved this line of argument.

This position comprises two arguments: one relating to the power of the International Tribunal to consider such a plea; and another relating to the classification of the subject-matter of the plea as a "political question" and, as such, "nonjusticiable", i.e., regardless of whether or not it falls within its jurisdiction.

1. Does The International Tribunal Have Jurisdiction?

14. In its decision, the Trial Chamber declares:

> "[I]t is one thing for the Security Council to have taken every care to ensure that a structure appropriate to the conduct of fair trials has been created; it is an entirely different thing in any way to infer from that careful structuring that it was intended that the International Tribunal be empowered to question the legality of the law which established it. The competence of the International Tribunal is precise and narrowly defined; as described in Article 1 of its Statute, it is to prosecute persons responsible for serious violations of international humanitarian law, subject to spatial and temporal limits, and to do so in accordance with the Statute. That is the full extent of the competence of the International Tribunal." (Decision at Trial, at para. 8)

Both the first and the last sentences of this quotation need qualification. The first sentence assumes a subjective stance, considering that jurisdiction can be determined exclusively by reference to or inference from the intention of the Security Council, thus totally ignoring any residual powers which may derive from the requirements of the "judicial function" itself. That is also the qualification that needs to be added to the last sentence. Indeed, the jurisdiction of the International Tribunal, which is defined in the middle sentence and described in the last sentence as "the full extent of the competence of the International Tribunal", is not, in fact, so. It is what is termed in international law "original" or "primary" and sometimes "substantive" jurisdiction. But it does not include the "incidental" or "inherent" jurisdiction which derives automatically from the exercise of the judicial function.

15. To assume that the jurisdiction of the International Tribunal is absolutely limited to what the Security Council "intended" to entrust it with, is to envisage the International Tribunal exclusively as a "subsidiary organ" of the Security Council (see United Nations Charter, Arts. 7(2) & 29), a "creation" totally fashioned to the smallest detail by its "creator" and remaining totally in its power and at its mercy. But the Security Council not only decided to establish a subsidiary organ (the only legal means available to it for setting up such a body), it also clearly intended to establish a special kind of "subsidiary organ": a tribunal.

16. In treating a similar case in its advisory opinion on the *Effect of Awards of the United Nations Administrative Tribunal*, the International Court of Justice declared:

> "[T]he view has been put forward that the Administrative Tribunal is a subsidiary, subordinate, or secondary organ; and that, accordingly, the Tribunal's judgements cannot bind the General Assembly which established it.
>
> [...]
>
> The question cannot be determined on the basis of the description of the relationship between the General Assembly and the Tribunal, that is, by considering whether the Tribunal is to be regarded as a subsidiary, a subordinate, or a secondary organ, or on the

basis of the fact that it was established by the General Assembly. It depends on the intention of the General Assembly in establishing the Tribunal and on the nature of the functions conferred upon it by its Statute. An examination of the language of the Statute of the Administrative Tribunal has shown that the General Assembly intended to establish a judicial body." (Effect of Awards of Compensation Made by the United Nations Administrative Tribunal, 1954 I.C.J. Reports 47, at 60–1 (Advisory Opinion of 13 July) (hereinafter *Effect of Awards*))

17. Earlier, the Court had derived the judicial nature of the United Nations Administrative Tribunal ("UNAT") from the use of certain terms and language in the Statute and its possession of certain attributes. Prominent among these attributes of the judicial function figures the power provided for in Article 2, paragraph 3, of the Statute of UNAT: "In the event of a dispute as to whether the Tribunal has competence, the matter shall be settled by the decision of the Tribunal." (Id. at 51–2, *quoting* Statute of the United Nations Administrative Tribunal, art. 2, para. 3.)

18. This power, known as the principle of "*Kompetenz-Kompetenz*" in German or "*la compétence de la competence*" in French, is part, and indeed a major part, of the incidental or inherent jurisdiction of any judicial or arbitral tribunal, consisting of its "jurisdiction to determine its own jurisdiction." It is a necessary component in the exercise of the judicial function and does not need to be expressly provided for in the constitutive documents of those tribunals, although this is often done (see, e.g., Statute of the International Court of Justice, Art. 36, para. 6). But in the words of the International Court of Justice:

> "[T]his principle, which is accepted by the general international law in the matter of arbitration, assumes particular force when the international tribunal is no longer an arbitral tribunal [...] but is an institution which has been pre-established by an international instrument defining its jurisdiction and regulating its operation." (Nottebohm Case (Liech. v. Guat.), 1953 I.C.J. Reports 7, 119 (21 March))

This is not merely a power in the hands of the tribunal. In international law, where there is no integrated judicial system and where every judicial or arbitral organ needs a specific constitutive instrument defining its jurisdiction, "the first obligation of the Court – as of any other judicial body – is to ascertain its own competence." (Judge Cordova, dissenting opinion, advisory opinion on Judgements of the Administrative Tribunal of the I.L.O. upon complaints made against the U.N.E.S.C.O., 1956 I.C.J. Reports, 77, 163 (Advisory Opinion of 23 October)(Cordova, J., dissenting).)

19. It is true that this power can be limited by an express provision in the arbitration agreement or in the constitutive instruments of standing tribunals, though the latter possibility is controversial, particularly where the limitation risks undermining the judicial character or the independence of the Tribunal. But it is absolutely clear that such a limitation, to the extent to which it is admissible, cannot be inferred without an express provision allowing the waiver or the shrinking of such a well entrenched principle of general international law.

As no such limitative text appears in the Statute of the International Tribunal, the International Tribunal can and indeed has to exercise its "*compétence de la competence*" and examine the jurisdictional plea of the Defence, in order to ascertain its jurisdiction to hear the case on the merits.

20. It has been argued by the Prosecutor, and held by the Trial Chamber that:

> "[T]his International Tribunal is not a constitutional court set up to scrutinise the actions of organs of the United Nations. It is, on the contrary, a criminal tribunal with clearly defined powers, involving a quite specific and limited criminal jurisdiction. If it is to confine its adjudications to those specific limits, it will have no authority to investigate the legality of its creation by the Security Council." (Decision at Trial, at para. 5; *see also* paras. 7, 8, 9, 17, 24, *passim*)

There is no question, of course, of the International Tribunal acting as a constitutional tribunal, reviewing the acts of the other organs of the United Nations, particularly those of the Security Council, its own "creator." It was not established for that purpose, as is clear from the definition of the ambit of its "primary" or "substantive" jurisdiction in Articles 1 to 5 of its Statute. But this is beside the point. The question before the Appeals Chamber is whether the International Tribunal, in exercising this "incidental" jurisdiction, can examine the legality of its establishment by the Security Council, solely for the purpose of ascertaining its own "primary" jurisdiction over the case before it.

21. The Trial Chamber has sought support for its position in some dicta of the International Court of Justice or its individual Judges, (see Decision at Trial, at paras. 10–13), to the effect that: "Undoubtedly, the Court does not possess powers of judicial review or appeal in respect of decisions taken by the United Nations organs concerned." (Legal Consequences for States of the Continued Presence of South Africa in Namibia (South-West Africa) Notwithstanding Security Council Resolution 276 (1970), 1971 I.C.J. Reports 16, at para. 89 (Advisory Opinion of 21 June) (hereafter the *Namibia Advisory Opinion*).) All these dicta, however, address the hypothesis of the Court exercising such judicial review as a matter of "primary" jurisdiction. They do not address at all the hypothesis of examination of the legality of the decisions of other organs as a matter of "incidental" jurisdiction, in order to ascertain and be able to exercise its "primary" jurisdiction over the matter before it. Indeed, in the *Namibia Advisory Opinion*, immediately after the dictum reproduced above and quoted by the Trial Chamber (concerning its "primary" jurisdiction), the International Court of Justice proceeded to exercise the very same "incidental" jurisdiction discussed here:

> "[T]he question of the validity or conformity with the Charter of General Assembly resolution 2145 (XXI) or of related Security Council resolutions does not form the subject of the request for advisory opinion. However, in the exercise of its judicial function and since objections have been advanced the Court, in the course of its reasoning, will consider these objections before determining any legal consequences arising from those resolutions." (Id. at para. 89)

The same sort of examination was undertaken by the International Court of Justice, *inter alia,* in its advisory opinion on the *Effect of Awards Case*:

> "[T]he legal power of the General Assembly to establish a tribunal competent to render judgements binding on the United Nations has been challenged. Accordingly, it is necessary to consider whether the General Assembly has been given this power by the Charter." (Effect of Awards, at 56)

Obviously, the wider the discretion of the Security Council under the Charter of the United Nations, the narrower the scope for the International Tribunal to review its actions, even as a matter of incidental jurisdiction. Nevertheless, this does not mean that the power disappears altogether, particularly in cases where there might be a manifest contradiction with the Principles and Purposes of the Charter.

22. In conclusion, the Appeals Chamber finds that the International Tribunal has jurisdiction to examine the plea against its jurisdiction based on the invalidity of its establishment by the Security Council.

2. Is The Question At Issue Political And As Such Non-Justiciable?

23. The Trial Chamber accepted this argument and classification. (See Decision at Trial, at para. 24.)

24. The doctrines of "political questions" and "non-justiciable disputes" are remnants of the reservations of "sovereignty", "national honour", etc. in very old arbitration treaties. They have receded from the horizon of contemporary international law, except for the occasional invocation of the "political question" argument before the International Court of Justice in advisory proceedings and, very rarely, in contentious proceedings as well. The Court has consistently rejected this argument as a bar to examining a case. It considered it unfounded in law. As long as the case before it or the request for an advisory opinion turns on a legal question capable of a legal answer, the Court considers that it is duty-bound to take jurisdiction over it, regardless of the political background or the other political facets of the issue. On this question, the International Court of Justice declared in its advisory opinion on *Certain Expenses of the United Nations*:

> "[I]t has been argued that the question put to the Court is intertwined with political questions, and that for this reason the Court should refuse to give an opinion. It is true that most interpretations of the Charter of the United Nations will have political significance, great or small. In the nature of things it could not be otherwise. The Court, however, cannot attribute a political character to a request which invites it to undertake an essentially judicial task, namely, the interpretation of a treaty provision." (Certain Expenses of the United Nations, 1962 I.C.J. Reports 151, at 155 (Advisory Opinion of 20 July))

This dictum applies almost literally to the present case.

25. The Appeals Chamber does not consider that the International Tribunal is barred from examination of the Defence jurisdictional plea by the so-called "political" or "non-justiciable" nature of the issue it raises.

C. The Issue Of Constitutionality

26. Many arguments have been put forward by Appellant in support of the contention that the establishment of the International Tribunal is invalid under the Charter of the United Nations or that it was not duly established by law. Many of these arguments were presented orally and in written submissions before the Trial Chamber. Appellant has asked this Chamber to incorporate into the argument before the Appeals Chamber all the points made at trial. (See Appeal Transcript, 7 September 1995, at 7.) Apart from the issues specifically dealt with below, the Appeals Chamber is content to allow the treatment of these issues by the Trial Chamber to stand.

27. The Trial Chamber summarized the claims of the Appellant as follows:

> "It is said that, to be duly established by law, the International Tribunal should have been created either by treaty, the consensual act of nations, or by amendment of the Charter of the United Nations, not by resolution of the Security Council. Called in aid of this general proposition are a number of considerations: that before the creation of the International Tribunal in 1993 it was never envisaged that such an ad hoc criminal tribunal might be set up; that the General Assembly, whose participation would at least have guaranteed full representation of the international community, was not involved in its creation; that it was never intended by the Charter that the Security Council should, under Chapter VII, establish a judicial body, let alone a criminal tribunal; that the Security Council had been inconsistent in creating this Tribunal while not taking a similar step in the case of other areas of conflict in which violations of international humanitarian law may have occurred; that the establishment of the International Tribunal had neither promoted, nor was capable of promoting, international peace, as the current situation in the former Yugoslavia demonstrates; that the Security Council could not, in any event, create criminal liability on the part of individuals and that this is what its creation of the International Tribunal did; that there existed and exists no such international emergency as would justify the action of the Security Council; that no political organ such as the Security Council is capable of establishing an independent and impartial tribunal; that there is an inherent defect in the creation, after the event, of ad hoc tribunals to try particular types of offences and, finally, that to give the International Tribunal primacy over national courts is, in any event and in itself, inherently wrong." (Decision at Trial, at para. 2)

These arguments raise a series of constitutional issues which all turn on the limits of the power of the Security Council under Chapter VII of the Charter of the United Nations and determining what action or measures can be taken under this Chapter, particularly the establishment of an international criminal tribunal. Put in the interrogative, they can be formulated as follows:

1. was there really a threat to the peace justifying the invocation of Chapter VII as a legal basis for the establishment of the International Tribunal?

2. assuming such a threat existed, was the Security Council authorized, with a view to restoring or maintaining peace, to take any measures at its own discretion,

or was it bound to choose among those expressly provided for in Articles 41 and 42 (and possibly Article 40 as well)?

3. in the latter case, how can the establishment of an international criminal tribunal be justified, as it does not figure among the ones mentioned in those Articles, and is of a different nature?

1. The Power Of The Security Council To Invoke Chapter VII

28. Article 39 opens Chapter VII of the Charter of the United Nations and determines the conditions of application of this Chapter. It provides:

> "The Security Council shall determine the existence of any threat to the peace, breach of the peace, or act of aggression and shall make recommendations, or decide what measures shall be taken in accordance with Articles 41 and 42, to maintain or restore international peace and security." (United Nations Charter, 26 June 1945, Art. 39)

It is clear from this text that the Security Council plays a pivotal role and exercises a very wide discretion under this Article. But this does not mean that its powers are unlimited. The Security Council is an organ of an international organization, established by a treaty which serves as a constitutional framework for that organization. The Security Council is thus subjected to certain constitutional limitations, however broad its powers under the constitution may be. Those powers cannot, in any case, go beyond the limits of the jurisdiction of the Organization at large, not to mention other specific limitations or those which may derive from the internal division of power within the Organization. In any case, neither the text nor the spirit of the Charter conceives of the Security Council as *legibus solutus* (unbound by law). In particular, Article 24, after declaring, in paragraph 1, that the Members of the United Nations "confer on the Security Council primary responsibility for the maintenance of international peace and security", imposes on it, in paragraph 3, the obligation to report annually (or more frequently) to the General Assembly, and provides, more importantly, in paragraph 2, that:

> "In discharging these duties the Security Council shall act in accordance with the Purposes and Principles of the United Nations. The specific powers granted to the Security Council for the discharge of these duties are laid down in Chapters VI, VII, VIII, and XII." (Id., Art. 24(2))

The Charter thus speaks the language of specific powers, not of absolute fiat.

29. What is the extent of the powers of the Security Council under Article 39 and the limits thereon, if any? The Security Council plays the central role in the application of both parts of the Article. It is the Security Council that makes the determination that there exists one of the situations justifying the use of the "exceptional powers" of Chapter VII. And it is also the Security Council that chooses the reaction to such a situation: it either makes recommendations (i.e., opts not to use the exceptional powers but to continue to operate under Chapter VI) or decides to use the exceptional powers by ordering measures to be taken in accordance with Articles 41 and 42 with a view to maintaining or restoring international peace and security. The situations justifying resort to the powers

provided for in Chapter VII are a "threat to the peace", a "breach of the peace" or an "act of aggression." While the "act of aggression" is more amenable to a legal determination, the "threat to the peace" is more of a political concept. But the determination that there exists such a threat is not a totally unfettered discretion, as it has to remain, at the very least, within the limits of the Purposes and Principles of the Charter.

30. It is not necessary for the purposes of the present decision to examine any further the question of the limits of the discretion of the Security Council in determining the existence of a "threat to the peace", for two reasons. The first is that an armed conflict (or a series of armed conflicts) has been taking place in the territory of the former Yugoslavia since long before the decision of the Security Council to establish this International Tribunal. If it is considered an international armed conflict, there is no doubt that it falls within the literal sense of the words "breach of the peace" (between the parties or, at the very least, would be a as a "threat to the peace" of others). But even if it were considered merely as an "internal armed conflict", it would still constitute a "threat to the peace" according to the settled practice of the Security Council and the common understanding of the United Nations membership in general. Indeed, the practice of the Security Council is rich with cases of civil war or internal strife which it classified as a "threat to the peace" and dealt with under Chapter VII, with the encouragement or even at the behest of the General Assembly, such as the Congo crisis at the beginning of the 1960s and, more recently, Liberia and Somalia. It can thus be said that there is a common understanding, manifested by the "subsequent practice" of the membership of the United Nations at large, that the "threat to the peace" of Article 39 may include, as one of its species, internal armed conflicts.

The second reason, which is more particular to the case at hand, is that Appellant has amended his position from that contained in the Brief submitted to the Trial Chamber. Appellant no longer contests the Security Council's power to determine whether the situation in the former Yugoslavia constituted a threat to the peace, nor the determination itself. He further acknowledges that the Security Council "has the power to address to such threats [...] by appropriate measures." [Defence] Brief to Support the Notice of (Interlocutory) Appeal, 25 August 1995 (Case No. IT-94-1-AR72), at para. 5.4 (hereinafter *Defence Appeal Brief*).) But he continues to contest the legality and appropriateness of the measures chosen by the Security Council to that end.

2. The Range of Measures Envisaged Under Chapter VII

31. Once the Security Council determines that a particular situation poses a threat to the peace or that there exists a breach of the peace or an act of aggression, it enjoys a wide margin of discretion in choosing the course of action: as noted above (see para. 29) it can either continue, in spite of its determination, to act via recommendations, i.e., as if it were still within Chapter VI ("*Pacific Settlement of Disputes*") or it can exercise its exceptional powers under Chapter VII. In the words of Article 39, it would then "decide what measures shall be taken in accordance with Articles 41

and 42, to maintain or restore international peace and security." (United Nations Charter, art. 39.) A question arises in this respect as to whether the choice of the Security Council is limited to the measures provided for in Articles 41 and 42 of the Charter (as the language of Article 39 suggests), or whether it has even larger discretion in the form of general powers to maintain and restore international peace and security under Chapter VII at large. In the latter case, one of course does not have to locate every measure decided by the Security Council under Chapter VII within the confines of Articles 41 and 42, or possibly Article 40. In any case, under both interpretations, the Security Council has a broad discretion in deciding on the course of action and evaluating the appropriateness of the measures to be taken. The language of Article 39 is quite clear as to the channelling of the very broad and exceptional powers of the Security Council under Chapter VII through Articles 41 and 42. These two Articles leave to the Security Council such a wide choice as not to warrant searching, on functional or other grounds, for even wider and more general powers than those already expressly provided for in the Charter. These powers are coercive *vis-à-vis* the culprit State or entity. But they are also mandatory *vis-à-vis* the other Member States, who are under an obligation to cooperate with the Organization (Article 2, paragraph 5, Articles 25, 48) and with one another (Articles 49), in the implementation of the action or measures decided by the Security Council.

3. The Establishment Of The International Tribunal As A Measure Under Chapter VII

32. As with the determination of the existence of a threat to the peace, a breach of the peace or an act of aggression, the Security Council has a very wide margin of discretion under Article 39 to choose the appropriate course of action and to evaluate the suitability of the measures chosen, as well as their potential contribution to the restoration or maintenance of peace. But here again, this discretion is not unfettered; moreover, it is limited to the measures provided for in Articles 41 and 42. Indeed, in the case at hand, this last point serves as a basis for the Appellant's contention of invalidity of the establishment of the International Tribunal. In its resolution 827, the Security Council considers that "in the particular circumstances of the former Yugoslavia", the establishment of the International Tribunal "would contribute to the restoration and maintenance of peace" and indicates that, in establishing it, the Security Council was acting under Chapter VII (S.C. Res. 827, U.N. Doc. S/RES/827 (1993)). However, it did not specify a particular Article as a basis for this action. Appellant has attacked the legality of this decision at different stages before the Trial Chamber as well as before this Chamber on at least three grounds:

a) that the establishment of such a tribunal was never contemplated by the framers of the Charter as one of the measures to be taken under Chapter VII; as witnessed by the fact that it figures nowhere in the provisions of that Chapter, and more particularly in Articles 41 and 42 which detail these measures;

b) that the Security Council is constitutionally or inherently incapable of creating a judicial organ, as it is conceived in the Charter as an executive organ, hence not possessed of judicial powers which can be exercised through a subsidiary organ;

c) that the establishment of the International Tribunal has neither promoted, nor was capable of promoting, international peace, as demonstrated by the current situation in the former Yugoslavia.

(a) What Article of Chapter VII Serves As A Basis For The Establishment Of A Tribunal?

33. The establishment of an international criminal tribunal is not expressly mentioned among the enforcement measures provided for in Chapter VII, and more particularly in Articles 41 and 42. Obviously, the establishment of the International Tribunal is not a measure under Article 42, as these are measures of a military nature, implying the use of armed force. Nor can it be considered a "provisional measure" under Article 40. These measures, as their denomination indicates, are intended to act as a "holding operation", producing a "stand-still" or a "cooling-off" effect, "without prejudice to the rights, claims or position of the parties concerned." (United Nations Charter, art. 40.) They are akin to emergency police action rather than to the activity of a judicial organ dispensing justice according to law. Moreover, not being enforcement action, according to the language of Article 40 itself ("before making the recommendations or deciding upon the measures provided for in Article 39"), such provisional measures are subject to the Charter limitation of Article 2, paragraph 7, and the question of their mandatory or recommendatory character is subject to great controversy; all of which renders inappropriate the classification of the International Tribunal under these measures.

34. *Prima facie*, the International Tribunal matches perfectly the description in Article 41 of "measures not involving the use of force." Appellant, however, has argued before both the Trial Chamber and this Appeals Chamber, that:

> "... [I]t is clear that the establishment of a war crimes tribunal was not intended. The examples mentioned in this article focus upon economic and political measures and do not in any way suggest judicial measures." (Brief to Support the Motion [of the Defence] on the Jurisdiction of the Tribunal before the Trial Chamber of the International Tribunal, 23 June 1995 (Case No. IT-94-1-T), at para. 3.2.1 (hereinafter *Defence Trial Brief*))

It has also been argued that the measures contemplated under Article 41 are all measures to be undertaken by Member States, which is not the case with the establishment of the International Tribunal.35. The first argument does not stand by its own language. Article 41 reads as follows:

> "The Security Council may decide what measures not involving the use of armed force are to be employed to give effect to its decisions, and it may call upon the Members of the United Nations to apply such measures. These may include complete or partial interruption of economic relations and of rail, sea, air, postal, telegraphic, radio, and other means of communication, and the severance of diplomatic relations." (United Nations Charter, art. 41)

It is evident that the measures set out in Article 41 are merely illustrative examples which obviously do not exclude other measures. All the Article requires is that they do not involve "the use of force." It is a negative definition. That the examples do not suggest judicial measures goes some way towards the other argument that the Article does not contemplate institutional measures implemented directly by the United Nations through one of its organs but, as the given examples suggest, only action by Member States, such as economic sanctions (though possibly coordinated through an organ of the Organization). However, as mentioned above, nothing in the Article suggests the limitation of the measures to those implemented by States. The Article only prescribes what these measures cannot be. Beyond that it does not say or suggest what they have to be. Moreover, even a simple literal analysis of the Article shows that the first phrase of the first sentence carries a very general prescription which can accommodate both institutional and Member State action. The second phrase can be read as referring particularly to one species of this very large category of measures referred to in the first phrase, but not necessarily the only one, namely, measures undertaken directly by States. It is also clear that the second sentence, starting with "These [measures]" not "Those [measures]", refers to the species mentioned in the second phrase rather than to the "genus" referred to in the first phrase of this sentence.

36. Logically, if the Organization can undertake measures which have to be implemented through the intermediary of its Members, it can a fortiori undertake measures which it can implement directly via its organs, if it happens to have the resources to do so. It is only for want of such resources that the United Nations has to act through its Members. But it is of the essence of "collective measures" that they are collectively undertaken. Action by Member States on behalf of the Organization is but a poor substitute *faute de mieux*, or a "second best" for want of the first. This is also the pattern of Article 42 on measures involving the use of armed force. In sum, the establishment of the International Tribunal falls squarely within the powers of the Security Council under Article 41.

(b) Can The Security Council Establish A Subsidiary Organ With Judicial Powers?

37. The argument that the Security Council, not being endowed with judicial powers, cannot establish a subsidiary organ possessed of such powers is untenable: it results from a fundamental misunderstanding of the constitutional set-up of the Charter. Plainly, the Security Council is not a judicial organ and is not provided with judicial powers (though it may incidentally perform certain quasi-judicial activities such as effecting determinations or findings). The principal function of the Security Council is the maintenance of international peace and security, in the discharge of which the Security Council exercises both decision-making and executive powers.

38. The establishment of the International Tribunal by the Security Council does not signify, however, that the Security Council has delegated to it some of its own functions or the exercise of some of its own powers. Nor does it mean, in reverse, that the Security Council was usurping for itself part of a judicial function which does not belong to it but

to other organs of the United Nations according to the Charter. The Security Council has resorted to the establishment of a judicial organ in the form of an international criminal tribunal as an instrument for the exercise of its own principal function of maintenance of peace and security, i.e., as a measure contributing to the restoration and maintenance of peace in the former Yugoslavia. The General Assembly did not need to have military and police functions and powers in order to be able to establish the United Nations Emergency Force in the Middle East ("UNEF") in 1956. Nor did the General Assembly have to be a judicial organ possessed of judicial functions and powers in order to be able to establish UNAT. In its advisory opinion in the *Effect of Awards,* the International Court of Justice, in addressing practically the same objection, declared:

> "[T]he Charter does not confer judicial functions on the General Assembly [...] By establishing the Administrative Tribunal, the General Assembly was not delegating the performance of its own functions: it was exercising a power which it had under the Charter to regulate staff relations." (Effect of Awards, at 61)

(c) Was The Establishment Of The International Tribunal An Appropriate Measure?

39. The third argument is directed against the discretionary power of the Security Council in evaluating the appropriateness of the chosen measure and its effectiveness in achieving its objective, the restoration of peace. Article 39 leaves the choice of means and their evaluation to the Security Council, which enjoys wide discretionary powers in this regard; and it could not have been otherwise, as such a choice involves political evaluation of highly complex and dynamic situations. It would be a total misconception of what are the criteria of legality and validity in law to test the legality of such measures *ex post facto* by their success or failure to achieve their ends (in the present case, the restoration of peace in the former Yugoslavia, in quest of which the establishment of the International Tribunal is but one of many measures adopted by the Security Council).

40. For the aforementioned reasons, the Appeals Chamber considers that the International Tribunal has been lawfully established as a measure under Chapter VII of the Charter.

4. Was The Establishment Of The International Tribunal Contrary To The General Principle Whereby Courts Must Be "Established By Law"?

41. Appellant challenges the establishment of the International Tribunal by contending that it has not been established by law. The entitlement of an individual to have a criminal charge against him determined by a tribunal which has been established by law is provided in Article 14, paragraph 1, of the International Covenant on Civil and Political Rights. It provides:

> "In the determination of any criminal charge against him, or of his rights and obligations in a suit at law, everyone shall be entitled to a fair and public hearing by a competent, independent and impartial tribunal established by law." (ICCPR, art. 14, para. 1)

Similar provisions can be found in Article 6(1) of the European Convention on Human Rights, which states:

"In the determination of his civil rights and obligations or of any criminal charge against him, everyone is entitled to a fair and public hearing within a reasonable time by an independent and impartial tribunal established by law [...]" (European Convention for the Protection of Human Rights and Fundamental Freedoms, 4 November 1950, art. 6, para. 1, 213 U.N.T.S. 222 (hereinafter ECHR))

and in Article 8(1) of the American Convention on Human Rights, which provides:

"Every person has the right to a hearing, with due guarantees and within a reasonable time, by a competent, independent and impartial tribunal, previously established by law." (American Convention on Human Rights, 22 November 1969, art. 8, para. 1, O.A.S. Treaty Series No. 36, at 1, O.A.S. Off. Rec. OEA/Ser. L/V/II.23 doc. rev. 2 (hereinafter ACHR))

Appellant argues that the right to have a criminal charge determined by a tribunal established by law is one which forms part of international law as a "general principle of law recognized by civilized nations", one of the sources of international law in Article 38 of the Statute of the International Court of Justice. In support of this assertion, Appellant emphasises the fundamental nature of the "fair trial" or "due process" guarantees afforded in the International Covenant on Civil and Political Rights, the European Convention on Human Rights and the American Convention on Human Rights. Appellant asserts that they are minimum requirements in international law for the administration of criminal justice.

42. For the reasons outlined below, Appellant has not satisfied this Chamber that the requirements laid down in these three conventions must apply not only in the context of national legal systems but also with respect to proceedings conducted before an international court. This Chamber is, however, satisfied that the principle that a tribunal must be established by law, as explained below, is a general principle of law imposing an international obligation which only applies to the administration of criminal justice in a municipal setting. It follows from this principle that it is incumbent on all States to organize their system of criminal justice in such a way as to ensure that all individuals are guaranteed the right to have a criminal charge determined by a tribunal established by law. This does not mean, however, that, by contrast, an international criminal court could be set up at the mere whim of a group of governments. Such a court ought to be rooted in the rule of law and offer all guarantees embodied in the relevant international instruments. Then the court may be said to be "established by law."

43. Indeed, there are three possible interpretations of the term "established by law." First, as Appellant argues, "established by law" could mean established by a legislature. Appellant claims that the International Tribunal is the product of a "mere executive order" and not of a "decision making process under democratic control, necessary to create a judicial organisation in a democratic society." Therefore Appellant maintains that the International Tribunal not been "established by law." (Defence Appeal Brief, at para. 5.4.) The case law applying the words "established by law" in

the European Convention on Human Rights has favoured this interpretation of the expression. This case law bears out the view that the relevant provision is intended to ensure that tribunals in a democratic society must not depend on the discretion of the executive; rather they should be regulated by law emanating from Parliament. (See Zand v. Austria, App. No. 7360/76, 15 Eur. Comm'n H.R. Dec. & Rep. 70, at 80 (1979); Piersack v. Belgium, App. No. 8692/79, 47 Eur. Ct. H.R. (ser. B) at 12 (1981); Crociani, Palmiotti, Tanassi and D'Ovidio v. Italy, App. Nos. 8603/79, 8722/79, 8723/79 & 8729/79 (joined) 22 Eur. Comm'n H.R. Dec. & Rep. 147, at 219 (1981).) Or, put another way, the guarantee is intended to ensure that the administration of justice is not a matter of executive discretion, but is regulated by laws made by the legislature. It is clear that the legislative, executive and judicial division of powers which is largely followed in most municipal systems does not apply to the international setting nor, more specifically, to the setting of an international organization such as the United Nations. Among the principal organs of the United Nations the divisions between judicial, executive and legislative functions are not clear cut. Regarding the judicial function, the International Court of Justice is clearly the "principal judicial organ" (*see* United Nations Charter, art. 92). There is, however, no legislature, in the technical sense of the term, in the United Nations system and, more generally, no Parliament in the world community. That is to say, there exists no corporate organ formally empowered to enact laws directly binding on international legal subjects. It is clearly impossible to classify the organs of the United Nations into the above-discussed divisions which exist in the national law of States. Indeed, Appellant has agreed that the constitutional structure of the United Nations does not follow the division of powers often found in national constitutions. Consequently the separation of powers element of the requirement that a tribunal be "established by law" finds no application in an international law setting. The aforementioned principle can only impose an obligation on States concerning the functioning of their own national systems.

44. A second possible interpretation is that the words "established by law" refer to establishment of international courts by a body which, though not a Parliament, has a limited power to take binding decisions. In our view, one such body is the Security Council when, acting under Chapter VII of the United Nations Charter, it makes decisions binding by virtue of Article 25 of the Charter.

According to Appellant, however, there must be something more for a tribunal to be "established by law." Appellant takes the position that, given the differences between the United Nations system and national division of powers, discussed above, the conclusion must be that the United Nations system is not capable of creating the International Tribunal unless there is an amendment to the United Nations Charter. We disagree. It does not follow from the fact that the United Nations has no legislature that the Security Council is not empowered to set up this International Tribunal if it is acting pursuant to an authority found within its constitution, the United Nations Charter. As set out above (paras. 28–40) we are of the view that the Security Council was endowed with the power to create this International Tribunal as a measure under Chapter VII in the light of its determination that there exists a threat to the peace. In addition, the establishment of the International Tribunal has been repeatedly approved and endorsed by the "representative" organ of the United Nations, the General Assembly: this body not only participated in its setting up, by electing the Judges and approving the budget, but also expressed its satisfaction with, and encouragement of the activities of the International Tribunal in various resolutions. (See G.A. Res. 48/88 (20 December 1993) and G.A. Res. 48/143 (20 December 1993), G.A. Res. 49/10 (8 November 1994) and G.A. Res. 49/205 (23 December 1994).)

45. The third possible interpretation of the requirement that the International Tribunal be "established by law" is that its establishment must be in accordance with the rule of law. This appears to be the most sensible and most likely meaning of the term in the context of international law. For a tribunal such as this one to be established according to the rule of law, it must be established in accordance with the proper international standards; it must provide all the guarantees of fairness, justice and even-handedness, in full conformity with internationally recognized human rights instruments. This interpretation of the guarantee that a tribunal be "established by law" is borne out by an analysis of the International Covenant on Civil and Political Rights. As noted by the Trial Chamber, at the time Article 14 of the International Covenant on Civil and Political Rights was being drafted, it was sought, unsuccessfully, to amend it to require that tribunals should be "pre-established" by law and not merely "established by law" (Decision at Trial, at para. 34). Two similar proposals to this effect were made (one by the representative of Lebanon and one by the representative of Chile); if adopted, their effect would have been to prevent all *ad hoc* tribunals. In response, the delegate from the Philippines noted the disadvantages of using the language of "pre-established by law":

"If [the Chilean or Lebanese proposal was approved], a country would never be able to reorganize its tribunals. Similarly it could be claimed that the Nürnberg tribunal was not in existence at the time the war criminals had committed their crimes." (*See* E/CN.4/SR 109. United Nations Economic and Social Council, Commission on Human Rights, 5th Sess., Sum. Rec. 8 June 1949, U.N. Doc. 6)

As noted by the Trial Chamber in its Decision, there is wide agreement that, in most respects, the International Military Tribunals at Nuremberg and Tokyo gave the accused a fair trial in a procedural sense (Decision at Trial, at para. 34). The important consideration in determining whether a tribunal has been "established by law" is not whether it was pre-established or established for a specific purpose or situation; what is important is that it be set up by a competent organ in keeping with the relevant legal procedures, and should that it observes the requirements of procedural fairness. This concern about *ad hoc* tribunals that function in such a way as not to afford the individual before them basic fair trial guarantees also underlies United Nations Human Rights Committee's interpretation of the phrase "established by law" contained in Article 14, paragraph 1, of the International Covenant on Civil and Political Rights. While the Human Rights Committee has not determined that "extraordinary" tribunals or "special" courts are incompatible with the requirement that tribunals be established by law, it has taken the position that the provision is intended to ensure that any court, be it "extraordinary" or not, should genuinely afford the accused the full guarantees of fair trial set out in Article 14 of the International Covenant on Civil and Political Rights. (See General Comment on Article 14, H.R. Comm. 43rd Sess., Supp. No. 40, at para. 4, U.N. Doc. A/43/40 (1988), Cariboni v. Uruguay H.R.Comm. 159/83. 39th Sess. Supp. No. 40 U.N. Doc. A/39/40.) A similar approach has been taken by the Inter-American Commission. (*See*, e.g., Inter-Am C.H.R., Annual Report 1972, OEA/Ser. P, AG/doc. 305/73 rev. 1, 14 March 1973, at 1; Inter-Am C.H.R., Annual Report 1973, OEA/Ser. P, AG/doc. 409/174, 5 March 1974, at 2–4.) The practice of the Human Rights Committee with respect to State reporting obligations indicates its tendency to scrutinise closely "special" or "extraordinary" criminal courts in order to ascertain whether they ensure compliance with the fair trial requirements of Article 14.

46. An examination of the Statute of the International Tribunal, and of the Rules of Procedure and Evidence adopted pursuant to that Statute leads to the conclusion that it has been established in accordance with the rule of law. The fair trial guarantees in Article 14 of the International Covenant on Civil and Political Rights have been adopted almost verbatim in Article 21 of the Statute. Other fair trial guarantees appear in the Statute and the Rules of Procedure and Evidence. For example, Article 13, paragraph 1, of the Statute ensures the high moral character, impartiality, integrity and competence of the Judges of the International Tribunal, while various other provisions in the Rules ensure equality of arms and fair trial.

47. In conclusion, the Appeals Chamber finds that the International Tribunal has been established in accordance with the appropriate procedures under the United Nations Charter and provides all the necessary safeguards of a fair trial. It is thus "established by law."

48. The first ground of Appeal: unlawful establishment of the International Tribunal, is accordingly dismissed.

Notes

- What is the tribunal specifically being asked in this case? Was it asked to review a decision of the Security Council? How does this question come before the tribunal? The objective of the ICTY was to prosecute certain individuals who bore the highest responsibility for international crimes committed in the former

Yugoslavia. How can a question of review of the Security Council arise under such a mandate?
- This is a decision of the ICTY Appeals Chamber. The matter was previously also addressed before the Trial Chamber. Diligent students of international law may want to investigate that decision as well, because the chamber took a very different approach. What would the argument be to refuse to even consider reviewing the Security Council decision?
- As a judicial body, the ICTY judgment can only rest on foundations of international law. What is the legal basis for the Tribunal's judgment in this case? Why does it have power to examine this question?
- In principle, the crimes at issue are international crimes with universal jurisdiction, meaning that any state in the world would have jurisdiction to prosecute this accused for this offense. If a domestic legal system had set up a special court to prosecute this case, would the special court apply similar reasoning? Could the tribunal review the political decision to create the special court? If not, then why should the ICTY in this case be able to do the same regarding a Security Council decision?
- If the tribunal had decided that the Security Council decision was wrongful, what would the outcome of such a decision be? Would the case against the accused be dismissed? What would become of the ICTY as a subsidiary body? Would the UN or Security Council be responsible for violating international law?
- Recall once more the ICJ *Effect of Awards* advisory opinion and consider this question about the *Tadić* judgment above. Does the fact that this organ is a judicial organ have any significance? If this organ had been created as a political organ, would it have the same powers?

7.3 FUNCTION OF THE ORGAN

In the previous sections in this chapter, it was suggested that different organs have different types of functions, and that this difference can have an impact on how we appreciate the powers and legal effects of the organ's acts. In the *Effect of Awards* advisory opinion and *Tadić* case, the ICJ and ICTY had to appreciate the role of the subsidiary organs differently due to their judicial function. The discussion above focused on the role of the "family" structure in informing us of the powers of the organ. This structure was in tension with the function. You may wish to review those cases again, and argue both sides. In this regard, it would also be interesting to review the *Bustani* case from Chapter 3 on the creation of international organizations and wonder what kind of function the ILO Administrative Tribunal believes it has, and what the consequences of that function are.

Following *Bustani*, consider the *First Admissions* case:

Conditions of Admission of a State to Membership in the United Nations (Article 4 of the Charter)
["First Admissions Case"]
Advisory Opinion
1948 ICJ Reps. 57
International Court of Justice, 28 May 1948

[p. 61]

The clause of the General Assembly's Resolution, referring to "the exchange of views which has taken place ...", is not understood as an invitation to the Court to say whether the views thus referred to are well founded or otherwise. The abstract form in which the question is stated precludes such an interpretation.

The question put is in effect confined to the following point only: are the conditions stated in paragraph 1 of Article 4 exhaustive in character in the sense that an affirmative reply would lead to the conclusion that a Member is not legally entitled to make admission dependent on conditions not expressly provided for in that Article, while a negative reply would, on the contrary, authorize a Member to make admission dependent also on other conditions.

...

Lastly, it has also been maintained that the Court cannot reply to the question put because it involves an interpretation of the Charter. Nowhere is any provision to be found forbidding the Court, "the principal judicial organ of the United Nations", to exercise in regard to Article 4 of the Charter, a multilateral treaty, an interpretative function which falls within the normal exercise of its judicial powers.

Accordingly, the Court holds that it is competent, on the basis of Article 96 of the Charter and Article 65 of the Statute, and [p. 62] considers that there are no reasons why it should decline to answer the question put to it.

...

But paragraph 2 is concerned only with the procedure for admission, while the preceding paragraph lays down the substantive law. This procedural character is clearly indicated by the words "will be effected", which, by linking admission to the decision, point clearly to the fact that the paragraph is solely concerned with the manner in which admission is effected, and not with the subject of the judgment of the Organization, nor with the nature of the appreciation involved in that judgment, these two questions being dealt with in the preceding paragraph. Moreover, this paragraph, in referring to the "recommendation" of the Security Council and the "decision" of the General Assembly, is designed only to determine the respective functions of these two organs which consist in pronouncing upon the question whether or not the applicant State shall be admitted to membership after having established whether or not the prescribed conditions are fulfilled.

The political character of an organ cannot release it from the observance of the treaty provisions established by the Charter when they constitute limitations on its powers or criteria for its judgment. To ascertain whether an organ has freedom of choice for its decisions, reference must be made to the terms of its constitution. In this case, the limits of this freedom are fixed by Article 4 and allow for a wide liberty of appreciation. There is therefore no conflict between the functions of the political organs, on the one hand, and the exhaustive character of the prescribed conditions, on the other.

It has been sought to base on the political responsibilities assumed by the Security Council, in virtue of Article 24 of the Charter, an argument justifying the necessity for according to the Security Council as well as to the General Assembly complete freedom of appreciation in connexion with the admission of new Members. But Article 24, owing to the very general nature of its terms, cannot, in the absence of any provision, affect the special rules for admission which emerge from Article 4.

The foregoing considerations establish the exhaustive character of the conditions prescribed in Article 4.

...

[p. 82]

Dissenting Opinion of Judges Basdevant, Winiarski, Sir Arnold McNair and Read

...

7. The first conclusion that emerges from a reading of Article 4 in its entirety is that the Charter does not follow the model of the multilateral treaties which create international unions and frequently contain an accession clause by virtue of which a declaration of accession made by a third State involves automatically the acquisition of membership of the union by that State. On the contrary, the Charter, following the example of the Covenant of the League of Nations and having due regard to the fact that it is designed to create a political international organization, has adopted a different and more complex system, namely, the system of admission. Assuming that a request is made by a State desiring to be admitted, the system involves a decision by the General Assembly whereby admission "will be effected"; this decision is taken upon a recommendation made by the Security Council; that recommendation cannot be made, and that decision cannot be taken, unless certain qualifications specified in paragraph 1 of Article 4 are possessed by the applicant State.

8. The essential feature of this system is the decision of the General Assembly whereby the admission "will be effected". The provisions of paragraph 2 of Article 4, which fix the respective powers of the General Assembly and the Security Council in this matter, do not treat the admission of new Members as a mere matter of the routine application of rules of admission. It would only be possible to attribute such a meaning to this Article if it had adopted a system of accession and not of admission; and if accession had been the system adopted it would have been better to have placed the Secretary-General in control of the procedure. This [p. 85] Article does not create a system of accession, but the entirely different system of admission. In the working of this system the Charter requires the intervention of the two principal political organs of the United Nations, one for the purpose of making

a recommendation and then the other for the purpose of effecting the admission. It is impossible by means of interpretation to regard these organs as mere pieces of procedural machinery like the Committee for Admissions established by the Security Council. In the system adopted by the Charter, admission is effected by the decision of the General Assembly, which can only act upon a recommendation of the Security Council, and after both these organs are satisfied that the applicant State possesses the qualifications required by paragraph 1 of Article 4.

9. The resolutions which embody either a recommendation or a decision in regard to admission are decisions of a political character; they emanate from political organs; by general consent they involve the examination of political factors, with a view to deciding whether the applicant State possesses the qualifications prescribed by paragraph 1 of Article 4; they produce a political effect by changing the condition of the applicant State in making it a Member of the United Nations. Upon the Security Council, whose duty it is to make the recommendation, there rests by the provisions of Article 24 of the Charter "primary responsibility for the maintenance of international peace and security" – –a purpose inscribed in Article 1 of the Charter as the first of the Purposes of the United Nations. The admission of a new Member is pre-eminently a political act, and a political act of the greatest importance.

The main function of a political organ is to examine questions in their political aspect, which means examining them from every point of view. It follows that the Members of such an organ who are responsible for forming its decisions must consider questions from every aspect, and, in consequence, are legally entitled to base their arguments and their vote upon political considerations. That is the position of a member of the Security Council or of the General Assembly who raises an objection based upon reasons other than the lack of one of the qualifications expressly required by paragraph 1 of Article 4.

That does not mean that no legal restriction is placed upon this liberty. We do not claim that a political organ and those who contribute to the formation of its decisions are emancipated from all duty to respect the law. The Security Council, the General Assembly and the Members who contribute by their votes to the decisions of these bodies are clearly bound to respect paragraph 1 of Article 4, and, in consequence, bound not to admit a State which fails to possess the conditions required in this paragraph.

Notes

- What question is the court being asked in this case? How does that relate to the organ's function?
- What is the function of the organ in this case? Is it political, administrative, judicial, or something else? How does the court determine the function? And does it reach the correct conclusion?

- In the previous section, we saw that an organ, characterized as a judicial body, might enjoy a certain role and powers due to its function. In this case, what role and powers does the organ enjoy due to its function? Do those come about necessarily because of the function? Or is the function used to interpret the organ's role and powers?
- Review the *Tadić* and *Effect of Awards* cases above again. Do the tribunal and the court have any view on their function(s)? Is there any tension between their function(s) and their place in the "family" structure?

Privileges and immunities

8.1 LEGAL BASIS FOR PRIVILEGES AND IMMUNITIES

Before we can examine the precise privileges and immunities of international organizations and their staff, and the process for assessing protections, we need to review the legal basis for privileges and immunities in general.

8.1.1 Jurisdiction

Privileges and immunities, whether of international organizations, states, or their agents, are based in the law on jurisdiction. Specifically, they are exceptions to jurisdiction. What is jurisdiction, and how is it manifested? Jurisdiction is the lawful authority to demand consequences for actions. That definition is, of course, hopelessly vague, so jurisdiction is best examined by breaking down the concept.

There are three main types of jurisdiction. Common law lawyers and civil law lawyers will likely disagree on this number of classifications, since both traditions view jurisdiction in slightly different ways. However, this analysis will continue using these three types to better discuss the questions on an international level. The first type of jurisdiction is prescription. This type is the lawful authority to regulate an act by law. The second type is adjudicative. This type is the authority to judge an act, meaning to determine in a binding fashion whether acts qualify for the legal regulation. The third type is enforcement jurisdiction. This type is the authority to ensure that the consequences of the regulation are realized, such as through imprisonment or seizure of assets. Each of these various types of jurisdiction can be exercised in one of two forms, either civil or criminal.

In addition to the broad types and forms of jurisdiction, jurisdiction can also be limited in its scope. Jurisdiction can be *ratione personae*, regarding certain person(s); *ratione materiae*, regarding a certain subject matter or issue; or *ratione temporis*, regarding a certain timeframe. In addition, there are more variations to the exercise of jurisdiction, including such topics as territory, that can limit the scope.

For every kind of exercise of jurisdiction, be it an attempt to prescribe civil consequences for acts of minors or to enforce a judgment regarding a certain subject matter, the lawful authority vested with jurisdiction must determine if it has sufficient links in order to exercise that jurisdiction. Those links could be territorial, nationality, protective interests, or universal jurisdiction. Territorial jurisdiction could be based on the presence of the individual in the territory of the state or the fact that extraterritorial acts have effects in the territory of the state. Nationality jurisdiction could be based on the nationality of the actor or the nationality of the victim. In all of these cases, different types and forms of attempted exercises of jurisdiction within certain scopes will be lawful based on certain links. For example, acts may usually be prescribed as long as there is some arguable link, although enforcement of those prescriptions may be limited only to cases where the individual or the individual's assets are present in the territory of the state.

8.1.2 Privileges and immunities

Keeping in mind the various ways in which jurisdiction is manifested, we can now turn to privileges and immunities. We so often hear of "privileges and immunities" as a single expression that it is important to distinguish between the two concepts. The distinction rests in the form of jurisdiction from which the entity and its agents are being exempted. A privilege is an exemption from prescriptive jurisdiction, meaning that the laws do not apply. It could be that the laws do not apply to that particular person, or that laws on a particular subject matter do not apply. An immunity is an exemption from enforcement jurisdiction, meaning that the laws do apply, but the person may not be subjected to legal process for violating them. Here as well, it could be that the individual is entirely exempt from legal process, or that an individual will be exempted for certain subject matter.

In addition to "privileges and immunities," we often hear the expression "inviolable." Literally, this word means that something may not be violated. This term is generally used to describe protections of the person from being arrested or impeded, or for an organization or mission from having the police enter its building without its consent, or having its archives or communications examined, etc.

8.2 JUSTIFICATION FOR PRIVILEGES AND IMMUNITIES OF INTERNATIONAL ORGANIZATIONS

An initial, and perhaps strange, question is why do international organizations and their staff enjoy immunities at all? States are sovereign equals, and respect immunity in a reciprocal relationship among themselves. International organizations are neither sovereign equals nor have the capacity to respect immunities reciprocally. Or is that not the case? Are the employees of an international organization really comparable to diplomats?

8.2.1 Functional necessity for independence

The usual explanation for privileges and immunities is that the organization needs them in order to operate independently without the undue influence of any government, especially the government of the host state. The following case, *Porru*, concerns the UN Food and Agriculture Organization (FAO):

Porru v. Food and Agriculture Organization
Case No. 4961, Judgment
1969 UN Juridical Yearbook 238
Rome Court of First Instance (Labour Section), Italy, 25 June 1969[1]

The plaintiff was an Italian national who, for a period of years had been employed by FAO as a messenger or lift operator under short term appointments which, with one exception, never exceeded three months. Under FAO's rules, short-term staff members are normally paid on a daily or monthly basis and are not covered by certain social security benefits provided for by the Organization. The latter fact is, however, taken into account when calculating the daily rates. The plaintiff complained that he had been refused permanent employment which would have entitled him to benefits such as medical coverage and participation in the United Nations Joint Staff Pension Fund and claimed an amount equivalent to certain Italian social security benefits.

The plaintiff followed the internal appeals procedure provided for by FAO's rules and his appeal was rejected by the Director-General acting upon the recommendation of the Organization's Appeals Committee. He did not bring his case before the Administrative Tribunal of the International Labour Organisation which has competence to hear disputes between staff members and FAO relating to their terms and conditions of employment. Instead he brought an action against the Organization before the Italian courts. The Organization maintained that it was in all respects immune from the jurisdiction of the Italian courts under the Headquarters Agreement it had concluded with Italy on 31 July 1950. [footnote omitted]

The Court dismissed the case for lack of jurisdiction but observed that there was "no rule of customary international law under which foreign States and subjects of international law in general are to be considered as immune from the jurisdiction of another State". Such immunity could only be recognized with regard to public law activities i.e., in the case of an international organization, with regard to the activities by which it pursues its specific purposes (*jure imperii*) but not with regard to private law activities where the Organization acts on an equal footing with private individuals (*uti privatus*). In this respect the situation of subjects of international law was analogous to that of the Italian State.

Interpreting article VIII, section 16, of the Headquarters Agreement which provides that "FAO ... shall enjoy immunity from every form of legal process except in so far as in any particular case FAO shall have expressly waived its immunity", the Court considered that this provision merely confirmed the general rules of customary international law but could not be understood as granting immunity from jurisdiction for all activities regardless of the distinction made above.

With regard to the issue in the present case, i.e. the legal relations between FAO and the plaintiff, the Court held that the acts by which an international

---

1   © (1969) United Nations. Reprinted with the permission of the United Nations.

organization arranges its internal structure fall undoubtedly in the category of acts performed in the exercise of its established functions and that in this respect therefore the Organization enjoyed immunity from jurisdiction.

Notes

- Why would this employee bring his action before the courts of Italy?
- What is the source of law that the Italian courts relied on?
- Is the distinction between public and private acts correct for an international organization? Are not all acts of an international organization public acts, since the organization is constituted for a limited public purpose?
- Why does the court find that the organization enjoyed immunity in this case?

However, although the justification discussed above is helpful in explaining privileges and immunities, is it really the case that this need alone is the source of the law? That is to say, do organizations have immunities because they need them, or does the need for independence inspire states to grant concessions of immunity?

Branno v Ministry of War
1954-I Giurisprudenza Italiana 1, 904; 22 International Law Reports 756
Court of Cassation (United Chambers), Italy, 14 June 1954[2]

This Court finds that the dispute under consideration is subject to the jurisdiction of the Italian courts and, in particular, of the Tribunal of Naples.

The North Atlantic Treaty Organization – which is a union of various States adhering to the North Atlantic Treaty, one organ of which is the General Headquarters for Southern Europe – was established by a Treaty signed in Washington on 4 April 1949, which was ratified and brought into operation in Italy by Law No. 465 of 1 August 1949. It is an international organization, its main purpose being the mutual defence of its members. The North Atlantic Treaty Organization is, therefore, a subject of international law, and it is autonomous with respect to each and all of the member countries. Therefore none of the members – one of which is Italy – may interfere with the activities of the North Atlantic Treaty Organization; the member States cannot exercise judicial functions with regard to any public law activity of the North Atlantic Treaty Organization connected with its organization or with regard to acts performed on the basis of its sovereignty.

The Italian courts will not exercise jurisdiction with respect to cases arising out of public law activities of a subject of international law possessing both *jus imperii* and a legal system of its own. But

---

[2] © Sir E. Lauterpacht, published by Cambridge University Press. Reproduced with permission of The Licensor through PLSclear.

the North Atlantic Treaty Organization, like any foreign State, may expressly or implicitly renounce such an immunity whenever it makes clear that it does not wish to take advantage of the special status which it has as a subject of international law, and, instead, act *more privatorum*; it may thus enter into contracts with Italian nationals on a basis which excludes any idea of sovereignty. In such an event, the North Atlantic Treaty Organization would come under consideration as a subject of our internal legal system.

Subjects of international law and public bodies alike, in order to achieve the purposes for which they were established, may not only perform acts of a public law nature, but when they do not take advantage of their special status they may perform acts of a private law nature, including entering into contracts which are regulated by rules of private law. In such a case, there is a waiver by the subject of international law of its jurisdictional immunity: when it enters into contracts with private individuals it thereby agrees to be subject to the laws of Italian civil law which regulate such contracts, and therefore, it agrees also to submit to the jurisdiction of the courts.

In the present case, it appears from the documents produced that the contract out of which the dispute arises is not one in respect to which foreign States and other subjects of international law are exempted from Italian jurisdiction by the operation of particular rules of internal or international law (*e.g.*, the Rome Convention of 29 May 1933, limiting liability for surface damage done by aircraft, brought into operation in Italy by Law No. 993 of 28 May 1936). Moreover, the General Headquarters of the Armed Forces for Southern Europe, in providing canteen facilities for its staff in the building in Naples which it occupies, was not performing an act of sovereignty connected with its public law activity. In particular it was not, while granting the concession to the plaintiff, intending to reserve all rights in respect of its sovereignty; it intended rather to divest itself of that attribute. Therefore, it intended to contract as an individual, under a private law, and to create a true contract regulated by civil law and by the contractual will of the parties.

Notes

- Compare this case to *Porru*. Why does the court in this case find the organization is immune? What is the significance of the organization having "a legal system of its own"?
- Does the organization need immunity in this case? Did the organization receive a grant of immunity from the states that created it? Or is need for immunity merely a description of why the organization received immunity from states?

Other cases take a different approach than functionalism:

Cristiani v Italian Latin-American Institute, Case No 5819/1985
1986 Rivista di diritto internazionale 146, 149; 87 International Law Reports 20
Court of Cassation (plenary session), Italy, 25 November 1985[3]

1. It is well known that neither the doctrine nor the jurisprudence reflect any discernible *communis opinio* as to the requisite correlation between international legal personality and immunity.

[1.1.] The traditional theory, which our jurisprudence has consistently followed, maintains that immunity depends on international personality and applies to international organizations the principle, commonly recognized in relation to States, of *par in parem non habet jurisdictionem* (Court of Cassation, plenary session, Cases No 5399, 18 October 1982; No 1266, 8 April 1975; No 4502, 21 October 1977).

[1.2.] Others do not recognize international personality for international organizations and oppose the concept that the principle of immunity is fundamentally inherent in the status of sovereign entities, in accordance with the so-called theory of absolute immunity which considers that States, as sovereign entities, are basically exempt from the exercise of civil jurisdiction by other States. Instead jurisdictional immunity is justified as being necessarily conferred on international organizations in order to protect the independent and autonomous exercise of their functions from control by the individual Member States' judicial authorities.

[1.3.] Others argue that the jurisdictional immunity of international organizations is dependent upon explicit treaty provisions or is implicit, at least in relation to the essential functions of the organization. They observe that the States concerned, in creating the organization, must have intended that those functions entrusted to it should be exercised under conditions of independence from the jurisdictional organs of the Member States.

[1.4.] But whatever the basis of jurisdictional immunity may be, generally it is recognized by the doctrine and jurisprudence that it may be relied upon by unions of States, either when they enjoy legal personality or when they form a collectivity of States. In the latter case, a general rule concerning the recognition of immunity to all Member States would also be applicable to States *pur sempre* acting as a third party [agent]. On the question of the limits of immunity, the rule is that immunity will govern and cover all acts and relationships entered into in the exercise of the essential functions of the organization.

2. In the present case, the appellant denies that the IILA [Italian Latin-American Institute] is a subject of international law and entitled to jurisdictional immunity, on the ground of its lack of territory and the lack of any visible sign indicating sovereign status.

[2.1.] But this view is positively contradicted by the text of the Convention of 1 June 1966 concluded between the Italian Republic and twenty Latin

---

3 © Sir E. Lauterpacht, published by Cambridge University Press. Reproduced with permission of The Licensor through PLSclear.

American Republics (Argentina, Bolivia, Brazil, Chile, Colombia, Costa Rica, Cuba, Ecuador, El Salvador, Guatemala, Haiti, Honduras, Mexico, Nicaragua, Panama, Paraguay, Peru, the Dominican Republic, Uruguay and Venezuela), ratified by Italy by Law No 794 of 4 October 1966.

[2.2.] This Convention, which is now part of the Italian legal order, unequivocally states that the Institute is "an international organization", established with a view to developing research and documentation on the problems and achievements of the Member States in the cultural, scientific, technical and social fields, in order to identify possibilities for exchanges and common action amongst Member States in these areas, and for the purpose of formulating proposals, requests and recommendations to be addressed to the respective governments (Article I). The Convention also states explicitly that the IILA is endowed with legal personality (Article II).

[2.3.] The so-called "institutionalist" theory, which the appellant refers to in his pleadings, affirms that legal personality in international law is acquired through a process of self-qualification, on the basis of the effective position enjoyed by the entity within the international community. Therefore the behaviour of the Member States is the fundamental pointer in order to establish such personality.

[2.4.] In the case at issue there is no doubt that, even if the appellant's theory were accepted as regards the acquisition of legal personality by international organizations, in no way could the IILA's legal personality in relation to Member States be denied on the ground of doubt, given the presence of an international agreement which has generated various institutions, shaping them as a collective unit distinct from the Member States (see Court of Cassation, Case No 804, 20 February 1978).

[2.5.] Such a unit is derived from a system of rules of special international law, governing so-called social organs which are conceived as distinct from those of each Member State rather than merely common institutions of all the Member States. These bodies are therefore the independent organs of a union of States (see Articles III *et seq.* of the Convention).

3. Once it has been ascertained that the IILA does indeed have legal personality, there is no doubt that it is also entitled to jurisdictional immunity (irrespective of the presence or absence of treaty provisions explicitly granting that right) pursuant to the rule of customary international law *par in parem non habet jurisdictionem* which, by virtue of Article 10 of the Italian Constitution, is automatically incorporated into the Italian legal order (Court of Cassation, plenary session, Cases No 1266 of 1975, No 4212 of 1977 and No 5399 of 1982).

[3.3.] In conformity with the most recent tendencies of doctrine and jurisprudence, this Court has gradually moved away from a concept of absolute immunity to the more recent concept of restrictive immunity, granting immunity only for acts performed in the exercise of sovereign functions. But at the same time this Court has taken the view that this criterion cannot be applicable to international organizations with regard to their employment relationships,

> ... by reason of their inherent connection with the functions of such

organizations, since it is a characteristic of international organizations that their organizational functions are of an eminently "Unitarian" nature. (Court of Cassation, Case No 4212 of 1977)

[3.4.] Consequently more complete immunity is generally granted in favour of international organizations as regards employment relationships when the employees have a stable contract and are fully integrated into the structure of the entity. Exceptions to this tendency are constituted by either occasional or temporary forms of collaboration, or by purely menial types of work (Court of Cassation, Case No 1266, 8 April 1975).

Notes

- What theories of personality and immunity does the court identify? What is the importance of the relationship between states and international organizations for purposes of immunity? How are international organizations different from states, and how does this difference impact immunity?
- What is the legal basis for immunity in this case? Is this domestic or international law? And what are the limitations?
- How do we reconcile this case with *Porru* and *Branno*? Can all three be said to fall within a single legal framework?

Food and Agriculture Organization v. INPDAI [Istituto Nazionale di Previdenza per I Dirigenti di Aziende Industrialia (Italy)], Case No. 5399 1983 Rivista di diritto internazionale 187; 87 International Law Reports 1 Court of Cassation (plenary session), Italy, 18 October 1982[4]

Firstly the FAO, in its request for a preliminary ruling on the jurisdictional issue, declares that it is an international organization entitled to its own distinct legal personality and endowed with a legal framework which is separate from both municipal law and international law.

Secondly the FAO contends that, pursuant to Article XV of its Constitution signed at Quebec on 16 October 1945 (ratified in Italy by Law No 546 of 16 May 1947):

1. The Organization shall have the capacity of a legal person to perform any legal act appropriate to its purpose which is not beyond the powers granted to it by this Constitution.

2. Each Member nation undertakes, in so far as it may be possible under its constitutional procedure, to accord to the Organization all the immunities and facilities which it accords to diplomatic missions, including inviolability of premises and archives,

---

4 © Sir E. Lauterpacht, published by Cambridge University Press. Reproduced with permission of The Licensor through PLSclear.

immunity from suit and exemption from taxation.

By virtue of Article VIII (Section 16) of the Headquarters Agreement signed in Washington on 31 October 1950 (ratified in Italy by Law No 11 of 9 January 1951):

> FAO and its property, wherever located and by whomsoever held, shall enjoy immunity from every form of legal process except in so far as in any particular case FAO shall have expressly waived its immunity. It is, however, understood that no waiver of immunity shall extend to any measure of execution.

...

Accordingly the FAO invokes the settled principle of international law, according to which jurisdictional immunity is granted only to activities carried out by an international body in fulfilment of its institutional purposes and to tasks performed in order to create an administrative structure aimed at pursuing those functions. It follows that the initiatives undertaken by the FAO, with a view to finding appropriate premises for its offices designated to provide specific public services, form part of the public tasks pursued by the organization and, as such, are immune from the jurisdiction of the Italian judge. The proceedings instituted by INPDAI against the FAO before the Examining Magistrate of Rome concern a contract entered into by the FAO for the furtherance of its own institutional purposes, which is covered by immunity for the reasons mentioned above.

This Court dismisses the preliminary objection to the exercise of jurisdiction, which is unfounded. If it is necessary to establish whether or not the pending action at first instance before the Examining Magistrate of Rome, brought by INPDAI against the FAO, is subject to Italian jurisdiction, then Article XV of the Quebec Convention (which contains the Constitution of the FAO) is irrelevant, as it fails to offer any decisive criterion. This Article defines the FAO as a body endowed with its own distinct legal personality and capacity to perform any legal act, appropriate to its purpose, which is not beyond the powers granted to it by its Constitution. In relation to this legal status, Article XV binds the Member States to accord to the Organization (in so far as their constitutional procedures allow) the same immunities which are ordinarily granted to diplomatic missions, including inviolability of premises and archives, jurisdictional immunity and exemption from taxation. It is to be observed that this Article delineates a status but does not confer immediate and general immunity to the FAO with respect to each Member State.

Firstly Article XV simply grants the same immunity recognized to diplomatic missions, that is to say a type of immunity which is invested in diplomatic premises and individuals, but not in the State itself. In this context it is to be noted that Decision No 48 of 18 June 1979, handed down by the Constitutional Court and invoked by the claimant in support of its contentions, declared groundless the argument of lack of conformity to the Constitution raised against Article 2 of Law No 804 of 9 August 1967 in so far as it enacted the provisions of Article 31(1) and (3) of the Vienna Convention on Diplomatic Immunity, concerning immunity from the civil jurisdiction of the receiving State. Indeed this judgment merely refers to the immunity enjoyed by diplomatic envoys.

Secondly Article XV explicitly limits the commitment of the Member nations to the extent allowed by their constitutions. In the case of Italy, the State accepts the generally recognized rules of customary international law which are incorporated under Article 10(1) of the Italian Constitution, but requires that the immunity accorded to States or international organizations must not infringe the basic tenor of the guarantee of effective judicial protection to which nationals are entitled with regard to their rights and legitimate interests (Article 24 of the Italian Constitution).

Neither can absolute immunity from jurisdiction be given effect, on the basis of Article VIII of the Headquarters Agreement between the Government of the Italian Republic and the FAO, signed in Washington on 31 October 1950 and ratified by Law No 11 of 9 January 1951, if the Court takes into account the subject-matter of the case at issue, that is to say the seat of the FAO. Even considering this Agreement, there is no doubt that the scope of the immunity which it grants from Italian jurisdiction cannot be wider than the scope of diplomatic immunity. The concept of diplomatic immunity is applicable to the seat and to individuals carrying out their diplomatic and consular functions, as Article VIII clearly points out in mentioning the FAO and its assets, wherever their location and by whomsoever held.

Article VII (Section 14) of the same Agreement confirms this line of reasoning by stating that:

The Government recognizes the juridical personality of FAO and, in particular, its capacity:

(a) to contract;

(b) to acquire and dispose of movable and immovable property;

(c) to institute legal proceedings.

This last rule clearly assumes that the FAO is subject to Italian jurisdiction and implicitly denies its supposed entitlement to absolute and general immunity.

...

The problematic issue of the extent to which the FAO is entitled to jurisdictional immunity needs to be tackled and solved on the basis of the same principles of international law (which were not derogated from by the Conventions mentioned above, and which Italian law is bound to respect, pursuant to Article 10 of the Constitution). Such rules on immunity have been developed in favour of both States and international organizations. In addition the Court observes that the FAO, in its capacity as a specialized body endowed with its own separate legal personality in international law, enjoys autonomous sovereign powers and, whilst acting in the exercise of those powers, is not subject to the sovereignty of Member States, including Italy as the receiving State.

A settled orientation in earlier case-law has established that this Court upholds the competence of the Italian judge over claims where one of the parties is either a public or private foreign entity, wherever that organization enters a contract acting as a private individual and implicitly waiving its sovereign powers (Court of Cassation, Cases Nos 1996/54, 1178/63 and 2830/66). On other occasions immunity claimed by a foreign State (and its public bodies) is granted in relation to activities intended to achieve their public functions. On the other hand, the same immunity is denied with respect to merely private activities (Court of Cassation, Case No 1653/74). In these judgments the purpose for which the activity was performed was emphasized, and not the private or public nature of the activity itself.

What mattered was whether or not that purpose was directly connected with the institutional aims normally pursued by the entity at issue, although the established principle *par in parem non habet jurisdictionem* was also referred to.

As far as employment relationships are concerned ..., it has been pointed out that, in relations of employment established with an international organization, those relationships which form part of the basic internal structure of the entity and are performed in furtherance of institutional or sovereign functions must be distinguished from relationships whereby only manual tasks are carried out by auxiliary personnel in order to permit the normal daily functioning of offices overseas.

The latter relationships are not exempt from jurisdiction, whilst the former relationships are exempt. In particular, the nature of the tenancy agreement must be ascertained, that is to say the purpose pursued by the organization in entering into such agreements (Court of Cassation, Case No 4502/77).

Accordingly, as far as non-liability to taxation is concerned, it has been stated that the exercise of activities *jure gestionis* is irrelevant. On the contrary, what matters is the fact that the acts at issue were either closely connected with the exercise of sovereign functions or carried out with a view to accomplishing the institutional purposes of the entity, rather than merely to achieve private aims (Case No 2051/78). A subsequent decision (Case No 979/79) referred to the exercise of "sovereign functions" and held that so-called "functional activities", whose performance arose from normal contracts, were exempt when they were performed to achieve the institutional aims of a foreign organization endowed with legal personality.

From the findings summarized above different conclusions may be drawn. Doctrine and jurisprudence are mostly oriented towards a concept of restrictive immunity, connected with the dichotomy between "acts *jure imperii* and *jure gestionis*", and do not grant immunity where the foreign body enters into a contract of private law with an Italian national. Another view expressed is that sovereignty is not related to the nature of the legal instruments which are executed, but to the purpose they are designated for, on the basis of a concept of so-called functional immunity. Regardless of the conclusion which may be reached on the views outlined above there is no doubt in the present case that the Italian judge has jurisdiction over the dispute between the parties. Whichever of the two concepts of international law should prevail, either restrictive or functional immunity, is irrelevant since both views lead to identical solutions.

It is sufficient to contemplate the circumstance that the FAO, whose main seat is established in via Terme di Caracalla [in Rome], rented the premises situated in via Cristoforo Colombo [in Rome] for the relocation of some of its auxiliary offices and entered into a tenancy agreement with INPDAI, negotiating with the lessor the inclusion of various clauses which are typical of leases concluded between private parties. The lessor INPDAI brought an action against the lessee, the FAO, before the Examining Magistrate of Rome in his function as judge responsible for regulated tenancies and rent limits, with a view to obtaining a specific increase in rent, provided for by one of the aforementioned clauses. This is a claim which lies entirely within the domain of private law.

It is not disputed that, according to the traditional approach which distinguishes between acts *jure imperii* and acts *jure gestionis*, the Italian courts have jurisdiction, and an identical conclusion is reached taking into account the purpose, i.e. the relocation of offices, which the FAO intended to pursue by concluding the tenancy agreement.

The *ratio* of immunity lies in the assumption that the Italian State shall not interfere in the fulfilment of institutional purposes carried out by the FAO, whenever this international organization acts in the exercise of its sovereign powers. On the other hand, in order to grant immunity to activities performed by the FAO in furtherance of its institutional aims, the existence of a close, direct and necessary connection between those activities and its purposes must first be ascertained and proved. The claimant's contention, however, is based on the *a priori* affirmation of the absolute existence, under all circumstances, of an instrumental relationship between activities and purposes, irrespective of the type of activity which is performed and of the objective which is pursued, on the ground that any activity is *lato sensu* carried out by an international organization to achieve its sovereign functions. If ever such a contention were to be accepted, a concept of absolute immunity would thereby implicitly be acknowledged, whereas such an approach seemingly conflicts with the very provisions enshrined in the international conventions which govern the FAO. The rule of international law which was previously mentioned in the claimant's application would inevitably assume a character which was not originally intended nor provided for, and the natural evolution of doctrine and jurisprudence would be utterly disregarded.

The only activity whose performance qualifies for immunity from jurisdiction is an activity closely affecting the institutional purposes of the organization. In other words, immunity is granted only to those activities which, were they to be carried out differently or employing other methods, would compromise the accomplishment of the organization's aims or would achieve them in a less appropriate manner.

In accordance with the above considerations there is no doubt that activities relating to the internal organization of offices and the definition of responsibilities with regard to tasks and services are closely and necessarily connected with the institutional purposes and sovereign powers of the entity at issue, and therefore fall within its organizational autonomy. The same reasoning cannot apply, however, to an activity such as the one performed by entering into a contract of tenancy, whose aim is solely logistic and pertains to the external arrangement and management of offices, not to their inner functioning and structure. It is evident that the choice of location of an office is a factor which is extraneous to the primary functions pursued by the international organization and which does not affect the autonomy and the structural planning of the entity under consideration. It follows logically that the Italian State is entitled, in this case, to exercise its sovereignty and jurisdiction.

...

In conclusion, the Italian courts must be held to have jurisdiction in this case whereby an action, brought by INPDAI against the FAO and regarding a claim for a rent increase under a contract of lease, is presently pending before the Tribunal of Rome (first instance) awaiting a decision by the judge responsible for regulated tenancies and rent limits.

Notes

- What is the claim in this lawsuit? Does that issue sound like *jure imperii*, or something else? Is *jure imperii* the correct theoretical framework to understand the acts of an international organization?
- Before we can analyze the issue of immunity as a procedural bar against the exercise of jurisdiction, the court must have jurisdiction. Does it have jurisdiction in this case?
- Is this immunity assimilated to that of diplomatic immunity? Why is that a good idea, or a problematic one?
- Is this issue functionally necessary for the FAO to perform? Could it operate without it? Would it be unreasonably burdensome to operate without it?

A different view on the legal basis for privileges and immunities might be that states have delegated certain sovereign functions to the organization. If those functions would have enjoyed immunity when exercised by states, should not they also enjoy immunity when exercised by a delegatee?

Bank Bumiputra Malaysia Bhd. v. International Tin Council and Another
[1987] 2 Malaya Law Journal 732; 80 International Law Reports 24
High Court, Malaysia, 13 January 1987[5]

The plaintiff bank had caused to issue in this Court a writ against the International Tin Council as the 1st named defendant with Datuk Keramat Smelting Sdn. Bhd. as the 2nd defendant.

It is alleged in the statement of claim that since 1976 the plaintiff bank had provided banking facilities to the International Tin Council (ITC) which is an organization established as a result of agreement arrived at between various countries, one of which is Malaysia. The ITC has its headquarters in London and apparently functions from there.

The plaintiff bank has a branch in London and the said banking facilities

---

5 © Sir E. Lauterpacht, published by Cambridge University Press. Reproduced with permission of The Licensor through PLSclear.

were said to have been arranged through that branch and executed in London.

It is alleged by the plaintiff that as at 10 March 1986, there was due and owing from the ITC to the Bank in respect of the said facilities the sum of £76,127,721.29 with interest accruing. ...

The plaintiffs contend that ITC had deposited with them a number of what is referred to as tin warrants which they appear to contend to be documents of title to the tin referred to in each of the warrants. ... It is the contention of the plaintiff that by virtue of the pledge of those warrants and/or of the tin, to the plaintiffs by ITC, the plaintiffs were entitled on the failure to meet the demand of the amount owing, to possession of the tin in respect of which the warrants were issued.

...

It is a general rule that the jurisdiction of the courts over persons is territorial. It is restricted to those upon whom its process may be served within the territorial jurisdiction of the courts. See *Siskina (Cargo Owners) v. Distos S.A.* [1979] AC 210, 254; also see *Re Busfield* (1886) 32 ChD 123. To this general rule there are exceptions, to be found in Order 11 of the Rules of High Court. Order 11 gives the Court the discretionary jurisdiction to allow the process of the Court to be served outside its territorial jurisdiction. For the discretion to be exercised the action must fall within one of the sub-paragraphs of Order 11 rule 1.

I think it amounts to an abuse of the process to have allowed the service of the writ outside the jurisdiction so long as the money claim is tagged on to that part of the plaintiffs' claim properly made against both defendants. ...

Now, that ITC enjoys immunity from being sued in England and that accordingly if the Malaysian courts refuse to allow the writ to be served on ITC in London the Bank may be left without a remedy is a fact that is not relevant in deciding whether that part of the action brought against ITC for the money claim falls within the ambit of any of the sub-paragraphs of Order 11 rule 1.

It would have been otherwise if it was necessary for the Bank to obtain a judgment before they are entitled to enforce the securities. But that is not the case for the plaintiffs. The case against the 2nd defendant is that upon demand made on ITC they are entitled to enforce the securities.

Encik Yeoh attempted to use *inter alia* the immunity that ITC enjoys in England to persuade me to allow his application. Shortly stated his contention was that because there was the statutory immunity accorded to ITC from being sued in the English courts to allow it to be sued here would run foul of international comity or courtesy. I reject that argument. The relevant international agreements as a result of which ITC was established specifically provided for ITC to enjoy certain immunities in the United Kingdom. Provisions were made in respect of the position of ITC in the other member countries and immunity from suit was not one of them. The parties to the agreements appear to have treated the host country (*i.e.* the United Kingdom) in a different way from the other member countries. Immunity from suits in the other member countries does not appear to have been sought or given. In the circumstances I am inclined to what Lord Denning has called the modern rule in *Trendtex Corpn. v. Central Bank* [1977] 2 WLR 356, 368.

He referred to his own judgments in *Rahimtoola v. Nizam of Hyderabad* [1958] AC 379, 422, and *Thai-Europe Tapioca Service Ltd. v. Government of Pakistan* [1975] 1 WLR 1485, 1491, and said:

> ... a foreign sovereign has no immunity when it enters into a commercial transaction with a trader here and a dispute arises which is properly within the territorial jurisdiction of our courts ... international comity requires that it (*i.e.* the foreign sovereign) should abide by the rules of the market.

Encik Yeoh had contended that sub-paragraph (k) has no relevance. He pointed out that in the letters of pledge the word "charge" is not used. That may be so but it seems to me that there can be no doubt that in fact the Bank had provided what in effect was a charge over what they held out to be their tin held by the 2nd defendant in favour of the banks. In my view in respect of the claim in respect of the tin the plaintiff is entitled to seek to serve the writ on ITC outside the Court's territorial jurisdiction invoking either (j) or (k).

Notes

- What is the claim against the organization in this case? Whose rights are infringed?
- What source of immunity law is being applied here? And why is that important? Is the issue of service of process relevant?
- What is the implied, underlying theory of immunity? Is this functional necessity?

Lastly, as discussed in Section 3.1.1 on international legal personality in Chapter 3 on the creation of international organizations, organizations are legal persons in the international legal order. While states have a general personality and organizations have a particular, functional personality, and notwithstanding the differences in their creation, both are comparable persons. Do states derive their immunity from a grant by other states? Perhaps international organizations should enjoy a similar inherent immunity as states?

8.2.2 Limitations of the functional theory

Even if we accept that functionalism is the correct theory for assessing immunities, the model has limitations, i.e. some actions might not be protected where they are not functionally necessary.

While we largely accept the notion that international organizations are expressions of state cooperation, and are thus a positive contribution to the international community, that conclusion does not mean that organizations are without fault. In Section 8.2.1, we looked at the application of functional necessity. Perhaps, however, there are situations where functional necessity is not the correct analytical framework. Can you really argue that violations of law are functionally "necessary"? Consider, for example, where the employees of an international organization working in a regulated industry (physicians, engineers, lawyers, etc.) are monitored for professional standards compliance by a licensing and disciplinary authority. Surely it can never be necessary for a bar regulation authority to be prohibited from enforcing professional standards on lawyers within its jurisdiction. Or consider that some international organizations (for example, Europol or Interpol) exercise police powers, powers inherent to statehood, and are universally understood to necessarily be subject to judicial control. How can the exercise of police authority ever be immune? Similar considerations apply in cases of internationally recognized labor rights or, as will be discussed in more detail below, human rights. What about the tension between a person's fundamental human rights and the acts of an international organization? States are party to human rights treaties and can be held to account for human rights violations, having often waived their immunity from suit. International organizations are largely not party to human rights treaties:

Waite & Kennedy v. Germany, Application No. 26083/94
Judgment
European Court of Human Rights (Grand Chamber), 18 February 1999[6]

AS TO THE FACTS

10. Mr Richard Waite is a British national, born in 1946 and resident in Griesheim. Mr Terry Kennedy is also a British national, born in 1950 and resident in Darmstadt.

I. *The Circumstances of the Case*

11. In 1977 the applicants, systems programmers by profession and employed by the British company SPM, were placed at the disposal of the European Space Agency ("the ESA") to perform services at the European Space Operations Centre in Darmstadt.

12. The ESA with headquarters in Paris, formed out of the European Space Research Organization ("the ESRO") and the European Organization for the Development and Construction of Space Vehicle Launchers ("the ELDO"), was established under the Convention for the Establishment of a European Space Agency, 1975 ("the ESA Convention") (Paris, 30 May 1975; UNTS 1983 vol. 1297, I-no 21524). The ESA runs the European Space Operations Centre ("the ESOC") as an independent operation in Darmstadt (under the Agreement concerning the European Space Operations Centre of 1967 ("the ESOC Agreement") (*Bundesgesetzblatt* II no 3, 18.1.1969)).

13. In 1979 the applicants' contracts were taken over from SPM by CDP, a limited company established in Dublin. In 1982 the applicants founded Storepace, a limited company with its registered office in Manchester, which contracted with CDP on the services to be performed by the applicants for the ESA and on the payment due. As from 1984 the ESA participated in the above contractual relations through Science System, a firm associated with it. Subsequently, the applicants liquidated Storepace, replacing it by Network Consultants, a company with its registered office on the island of Jersey. These

---

6 © Council of Europe.

changes in contractual relations had no bearing on the applicants' services at the ESOC.

14. By letter of 12 October 1990, CDP informed the applicants that the cooperation with their company Network Consultants would terminate on 31 December 1990, when the term of their contracts expired.

15. The applicants thereupon instituted proceedings before the Darmstadt Labour Court (*Arbeitsgericht*) against the ESA, arguing that, pursuant to the German Provision of Labour (Temporary Staff) Act (*Arbeitnehmer-Überlassungsgesetz*), they had acquired the status of employees of the ESA. In their submission, the termination of their contracts by the company CDP had no bearing on their labour relationship with the ESA.

16. In the Labour Court proceedings, the ESA relied on its immunity from jurisdiction under Article XV(2) of the ESA Convention and its Annex I.

17. On 10 April 1991 the Darmstadt Labour Court, following a hearing, declared the applicants' actions inadmissible, considering that the ESA had validly relied on its immunity from jurisdiction. In its reasoning, the Labour Court considered in particular that the ESA had been established in 1975 as a new and independent international organization. It therefore rejected the applicants' argument that the ESA was bound by Article 6(2) of the ESOC agreement, which had subjected the former ESRO to German jurisdiction in cases of disputes with its employees which were outside the competence of its appeals board.

18. On 20 May 1992 the Frankfurt am Main Labour Appeals Court (*Landes-Ärbeitsgericht*) dismissed the applicants'

appeal. It gave leave to an appeal on points of law (Revision) to the Federal Labour Court (*Bundesarbeitsgericht*).

...

22. The Federal Labour Court considered that immunity from jurisdiction was an impediment to court proceedings, and that an action against a defendant who enjoyed immunity from jurisdiction, and had not waived this immunity, was inadmissible. According to Section 20(2) of the Courts Act, German jurisdiction did not extend to international organizations which were exempted in accordance with international agreements. In this respect, the Federal Labour Court noted that, pursuant to Article XV(2) of the ESA Convention, the ESA had the immunities provided for in Annex I of the said Convention, and that it had not waived immunity under Article IV(1)(a) of that Annex.

...

26. Sitting as a panel of three members, on 11 May 1994 the Federal Constitutional Court (*Bundesverfassungsgericht*) declined to accept the applicants' appeal (*Verfassungsbeschwerde*) for adjudication.

...

II. *Relevant Law*

1. *Provision of Labour (Temporary Staff) Act*

29. Section 1 (1)(1) of the Provision of Labour (Temporary Staff) Act (*Arbeitnekmerüberlassungsgesetz*) provides that an employer who, on a commercial basis (*gewerbsmäßlig*), intends to hire out his employees to third persons – hiring employers (*Entleiher*) – must obtain official permission. Section 1(9)(1) provides that contracts between the hirer-out

(*Verleiher*) and the hiring employer and between the hirer-out and the employee hired out (*Leiharbeitnehmer*) are void if no official permission has been obtained as required by Section 1(1)(1). If the contract between a hirer-out and an employee hired out is void under Section 1(9)(1), a contract between the hiring employer and the employee hired out is deemed to have been concluded (*gilt als zustande gekommen*) as from the envisaged start of employment (Section 1(10)(1)(1)). Section 1(10)(2) further provides for a claim in damages against the hirer-out in respect of any loss suffered as a consequence of having relied on the validity of the contract, except where the employee hired out was aware of the factor rendering the contract void.

2. *Immunity from jurisdiction*

30. Sections 18 to 20 of the German Courts Act (*Gerichtsverfassungsgesetz*) regulate immunity from jurisdiction (*Exterritorialität*) in German court proceedings. Sections 18 and 19 concern the members of diplomatic and consular missions, and Section 20(1) other representatives of States staying in Germany upon the invitation of the German Government. Section 20(2) provides that other persons shall have immunity from jurisdiction according to the rules of general international law, or pursuant to international agreements or other legal rules.

3. *The ESA Convention*

31. The ESA Convention came into force on 30 October 1980, when ten States, members of the ESRO or the ELDO, had signed it and had deposited their instruments of ratification or acceptance.

32. The purpose of the ESA is to provide for and to promote, for exclusively peaceful purposes, co-operation among European States in space research and technology and their space applications, with a view to their being used for scientific purposes and for operational space applications systems (Article II of the ESA Convention). For the execution of the programmes entrusted to it, the agency shall maintain the internal capability required for the preparation and supervision of its tasks and, to this end, shall establish and operate such establishments and facilities as are required for its activities (Article VI(1)(a)).

33. Article XV regulates the legal status, privileges and immunities of the agency. According to paragraph 1, the agency shall have legal personality. Paragraph 2 provides that the agency, its staff members and experts, and the representatives of its Member States, shall enjoy the legal capacity, privileges and immunities provided for in Annex I. Agreements concerning the headquarters of the agency and the establishments set up in accordance with Article VI shall be concluded between the agency and the Member States on whose territory the headquarters and the establishments are situated (Article VI(3)).

34. Article XVII concerns the arbitration procedure in case of disputes between two or more Member States, or between any of them and the ESA, concerning the interpretation or application of the ESA Convention or its annexes, and disputes arising out of damage caused by the ESA, or involving any other responsibility of the ESA, which are not settled by or through the Council (see Article XXVI of Annex I).

35. Article XIX provides that on the date of entry into force of the ESA Convention, the agency shall take over all the rights and obligations of the ESRO.

36. Annex I relates to the privileges and immunities of the agency.

37. According to Article I of Annex I, the agency shall have legal personality, in particular the capacity to contract, to acquire and to dispose of movable and immovable property, and to be a party to legal proceedings.

38. Pursuant to Article IV(1)(a) of Annex I, the agency shall have immunity from jurisdiction and execution, except to the extent that it shall, by decision of the Council, have expressly waived such immunity in a particular case; the Council has the duty to waive this immunity in all cases where reliance upon it would impede the course of justice and it can be waived without prejudicing the interests of the agency.

39. Article XXV of Annex I provides for arbitration with regard to written contracts other than those concluded in accordance with the staff regulations. Moreover, any Member State may submit to the International Arbitration Tribunal referred to in Article XVII of the ESA Convention any dispute, *inter alia*, arising out of damage caused by the agency, or involving any other non-contractual responsibility of the agency. According to Article XXVII of Annex I, the agency shall make suitable provision for the satisfactory settlement of disputes arising between the agency and the Director General, staff members or experts in respect of their conditions of service.

40. Chapter VIII of the ESA staff regulations concerns disputes within the ESA (regs. 33–41). As regards the competence of its appeals board, reg. 33 provides as follows:

(1) There shall be set up an Appeals Board, independent of the Agency, to hear disputes relating to any explicit or implicit decision taken by the Agency and arising between it and a staff member, a former staff member or persons entitled under him.

(2) The Appeals Board shall rescind any decision against which there has been an appeal if the decision is contrary to the Staff Regulations; Rules or Instructions or to the claimant's terms of appointment or vested rights; and if the claimant's personal interests are affected.

(3) The Appeals Board may also order the Agency to repair any damage suffered by the claimant as a result of the decision referred to in paragraph 2 above.

(4) Should the Agency – or the claimant – maintain that execution of a rescinding decision would raise major difficulties the Appeals Board may, if it considers the argument valid, award compensation to the claimant for the damage he has suffered.

(5) The Appeals Board shall also be competent in the case where a staff member wishes to sue another staff member and such action has been prevented by the Director General's refusal to waive the immunity of the latter.

(6) The Appeals Board shall also be competent to settle disputes concerning its jurisdiction, as defined in these Regulations, or any question of procedure.

4. *The ESOC Agreement*

41. The ESOC Agreement was concluded between the Government of the Federal Republic of Germany and the ESRO for the purpose of establishing a European Space Operations Centre, including the European Space Data Centre.

Articles 1 to 4 of the Agreement concern the site for construction of the ESOC buildings and related matters.

42. Part III of the ESOC Agreement contains general provisions. Article 6 provides as follows:

(1) Subject to the provisions of the Protocol on Privileges and Immunities of the Organisation and of any complementary Agreement between the Federal Republic of Germany and the Organisation according to Article 30 of that Protocol, the activities of the Organisation in the Federal Republic of Germany shall be governed by German law. If the terms of employment of a staff member of the Organisation are not governed by the Organisation's staff regulations, then they shall be subject to German laws and regulations.

(2) Disputes between the Organisation and such staff members of the organisation in the Federal Republic of Germany who are not within the competence of the Organisation's Appeals Board, shall be subject to German jurisdiction.

...

AS TO THE LAW

I. *Alleged Violation of Article 6(1) of the Convention*

...

B. *Compliance with Article 6(1)*

50. Article 6(1) secures to everyone the right to have any claim relating to his civil rights and obligations brought before a court or tribunal. In this way the article embodies the "right to a court", of which the right of access, that is, the right to institute proceedings before courts in civil matters, constitutes one aspect only (see *Golder v. UK* (1975) 1 EHRR 524 at 536 and *Osman v. UK* (1998) 5 BHRC 293 at 326).

51. The applicants had access to the Darmstadt Labour Court and then the Frankfurt am Main Labour Appeals Court and the Federal Labour Court, only to be told that their action was barred by operation of law (sec paras. 17–25, above). The Federal Constitutional Court declined to accept their case for adjudication on the grounds that it did not raise a matter of general importance and that the alleged violation of their constitutional rights was not of special importance (see paras. 26–8, above).

The proceedings before the German labour courts had thus concentrated on the question of whether or not the ESA could validly rely on its immunity from jurisdiction.

...

57. The Court observes that the ESA was formed out of the ESRO and the ELDO as a new and single organization (see para. 12, above). According to its constituent instrument, the ESA enjoys immunity from jurisdiction and execution except, *inter alia*, to the extent that the ESA Council expressly waives immunity in a particular case (see paras. 33 and 36–8, above). Considering the exhaustive rules in Annex I to the ESA Convention and also the wording of Article 6(2) of the ESOC Agreement, the reasons advanced by the German labour courts to give effect to the immunity from jurisdiction of the ESA under Article XV of

the ESA Convention and its Annex I cannot be regarded as arbitrary (see para. 42, above).

58. Admittedly, the applicants were able to argue the question of immunity at three levels of German jurisdiction. However, the Court must next examine whether this degree of access limited to a preliminary issue was sufficient to secure the applicants' "right to a court", having regard to the rule of law in a democratic society (see *Golder v. UK* (1975) 1 EHRR 524 at 534–6).

59. The Court recalls that the right of access to the courts secured by Article 6(1) of the Convention is not absolute, but may be subject to limitations, these are permitted by implication since the right of access by its very nature calls for regulation by the State. In this respect, the Contracting States enjoy a certain margin of appreciation, although the final decision as to the observance of the Convention's requirements rests with the Court. It must be satisfied that the limitations applied do not restrict or reduce the access left to the individual in such a way or to such an extent that the very essence of the right is impaired. Furthermore, a limitation will not be compatible with Article 6(1) if it does not pursue a legitimate aim and if there is not a reasonable relationship of proportionality between the means employed and the aim sought to be achieved (see *Osman v. UK* (1998) 5 BHRC 293 at 329 and the recapitulation of the relevant principles in *Fayed v. U.K.* (1994) 18 EHRR 393 at 429–30).

...

63. Like the Commission, the Court points out that the attribution of privileges and immunities to international organizations is an essential means of ensuring the proper functioning of such organizations free from unilateral interference by individual governments.

The immunity from jurisdiction commonly accorded by States to international organizations under the organizations' constituent instruments or supplementary agreements is a long-standing practice established in the interest of the good working of these organizations. The importance of this practice is enhanced by a trend towards extending and strengthening international co-operation in all domains of modern society.

Against this background, the Court finds that the rule of immunity from jurisdiction, which the German courts applied to the ESA in the present case, has a legitimate objective.

64. As to the issue of proportionality, the Court must assess the contested limitation placed on Article 6 in the light of the particular circumstances of the case.

...

66. The Commission in substance agreed with the Government that in private law disputes involving the ESA, judicial or equivalent review could be obtained, albeit in procedures adapted to the special features of an international organization and therefore different from the remedies available under domestic law.

67. The Court is of the opinion that where States establish international organizations in order to pursue or strengthen their co-operation in certain fields of activities, and where they attribute to these organizations certain competences and accord them immunities, there may be implications as to

the protection of fundamental rights. It would be incompatible with the purpose and object of the Convention, however, if the Contracting States were thereby absolved from their responsibility under the Convention in relation to the field of activity covered by such attribution. It should be recalled that the Convention is intended to guarantee not theoretical or illusory rights, but rights that are practical and effective. This is particularly true for the right of access to the courts in view of the prominent place held in a democratic society by the right to a fair trial (see, as recent authority, *Aït-Mouhoub v. France (Case No 103/1997/887/1099)* (28 October 1998, unreported) (para. 52) referring to *Airey v. Ireland* (1979) 2 EHRR 305 t 314–15).

68. For the Court, a material factor in determining whether granting the ESA immunity from German jurisdiction is permissible is whether the applicants had available to them reasonable alternative means to protect effectively their rights under the Convention.

69. The ESA Convention, together with its Annex I, expressly provides for various modes of settlement of private-law disputes, in staff matters as well as in other litigation (see paras. 31–40, above).

Since the applicants argued an employment relationship with the ESA, they could and should have had recourse to the ESA appeals board. In accordance with reg. 33(1) of the ESA staff regulations, the ESA appeals board, which is "independent of the Agency", has jurisdiction "to hear disputes relating to any explicit or implicit decision taken by the agency and arising between it and a staff member" (see para. 40, above).

As to the notion of "staff member", it would have been for the ESA appeals board, under reg. 33(6) of the ESA staff regulations, to settle the question of its jurisdiction and, in this connection, to rule whether in substance the applicants fell within the notion of "staff members".

70. Moreover, it is in principle open to temporary workers to seek redress from the firms that have employed them and hired them out. Relying on general labour regulations or, more particularly, on the German Provision of Labour (Temporary Staff) Act, temporary workers can file claims in damages against such firms. In such court proceedings, a judicial clarification of the nature of the labour relationship can be obtained. The fact that any such claims under the Provision of Labour (Temporary Staff) Act are subject to a condition of good faith does not generally deprive this kind of litigation of reasonable prospects of success (see para. 29, above).

71. The significant feature of the instant case is that the applicants, after having performed services at the premises of ESOC in Darmstadt for a considerable time on the basis of contracts with foreign firms, attempted to obtain recognition of permanent employment by the ESA on the basis of the above-mentioned special German legislation for the regulation of the German labour market.

72. The Court shares the Commission's conclusion that, bearing in mind the legitimate aim of immunities of international organizations, the test of proportionality cannot be applied in such a way as to compel an international organization to submit itself to national litigation in relation to employment

conditions prescribed under national labour law (see para. 63, above). To read Article 6(1) of the Convention and its guarantee of access to court as necessarily requiring the application of national legislation in such matters would, in the Court's view, thwart the proper functioning of international organizations and run counter to the current trend towards extending and strengthening international co-operation.

73. In view of all these circumstances, the Court finds that, in giving effect to the immunity from jurisdiction of the ESA on the basis of Section 20(2) of the Courts Act, the German courts did not exceed their margin of appreciation. Taking into account in particular the alternative means of legal process available to the applicants, it cannot be said that the limitation on their access to the German courts with regard to the ESA impaired the essence of their "right to a court" or was disproportionate for the purposes of Article 6(1).

74. Accordingly, there has been no violation of that provision.

Notes

- How did the European Court of Human Rights resolve the need for immunity on the one hand with the need for human rights accountability on the other? Note that in recent years, many international organizations have established internally administered tribunals to address issues of labor law, for example the UN and World Bank. The International Labour Organization has also created its own administrative tribunal that is open for the use of other organizations should they choose not to create their own internal system. While it was initially unclear whether organizations had implied power to create internal judicial mechanisms, this question was largely settled in the ICJ *Effect of Awards* case.
- These tribunals are largely closed to non-employees, with the ILO being an exception. However, some tribunals are beginning to open their international organizations up to complaints from non-employees.[7]
- However, does an internal administrative tribunal fulfill the human right of a fair trial in the sense of an impartial and independent tribunal?
- In addition to protecting individual rights, perhaps the rights of states are not being adequately protected when the entities they create and supposedly control are immune from suit?
- Are our international organizations in general well served by enjoying immunity? Because the analogy with diplomatic and state immunity is not completely applicable, some enforcement mechanisms might not be available. In addition, international organizations are designed to serve the international community, and in particular humans and their human rights. Following the notion that power corrupts, does immunity create incentives for international

---

[7] *See e.g.* Teixera v. Secretary-General of the United Nations, Judgment No. 230 (UN Administrative Tribunal, 14 October 1977).

organizations not to serve their mandates? After all, most organizations must engage with private companies for the provision of various services, and effective accountability might increase the willingness to work with the organization.

In addition to human rights concerns, employees of international organizations often attempt to have alleged violations of their employment contracts adjudicated in domestic courts, especially where international organizations have not set up their own internal employment administrative tribunals. However, when these cases get to a domestic court, that body must consider choice of forum issues,[8] its competence to adjudicate on matters of international law,[9] in addition to its jurisdiction over an international organization.[10] In some cases, the court must also consider whether it is capable of reviewing the decision of an international organization.[11] In light of many of these concerns, the United Nations and most major international organizations have set up administrative tribunals. Those that have not done so often subscribe to the Administrative Tribunal of the International Labour Organization instead, for efficiency reasons.

8.3 PRIVILEGES AND IMMUNITIES ENJOYED BY DIFFERENT ACTORS

Having addressed the basis for and sources of privileges and immunities, as well as some potential limitations on those rights, we will now examine how the immunities regime differs depending on the type of actor. International organizations, as distinct persons themselves enjoy the fullest scope of immunity available. Employees and others serving an international organization may derive some immunity from the immunity of the organization. That is to say, these individuals may have a form of immunity based on their link to the organization.

---

8 *See e.g.* International Civil Aviation Organization [ICAO] v. Tripal Systems Pty Ltd et al., CLOUT Case No. 182 (Superior Court of Quebec, Canada, 9 September 1994).
9 *See e.g.* Case 25/60, De Bruyn v. European Parliamentary Assembly [Parliament], Judgment (Court of Justice of the European Communities [Union] (First Chamber), 1 March 1962); United States v. Gereschi, 1978 Rivista di diritto internazionale 573, (1978–9) 4 Italian Yearbook of International Law 173, 77 International Law Reports 598 (Court of Cassation (Joint Session), Italy, 14 October 1977).
10 *See e.g.* Chemidlin v. International Bureau of Weights and Measures, Gazette du Palais (16 October 1945), 12 International Law Reports 281 (Tribunal Civil of Versailles, France, 27 July 1945); Klarsfeld v. Office Franco-Allemand pour la Jeunesse, 1969 (II) Juris-Classeur Périodique 15725, 72 International Law Reports 191 (Court of Appeal of Paris (21st Chamber), France, 18 June 1968).
11 *See e.g.* Dalfino v. Governing Council of European Schools and European School of Brussels I, 1982 RACE 1544, 108 International Law Reports 638 (Conseil d'Etat, Belgium, 17 November 1982).

8.3.1 International organizations

In this section, we will first look at the organization as an actor, before we look at employees and experts of the organization:

Broadbent, et al v. Organization of American States, et al
628 F. 2d 27 (1980); 63 International Law Reports 337
Court of Appeals, District of Columbia, United States, 8 January 1980[12]

This is an appeal from a District Court judgment dismissing an action by the appellants claiming they had been improperly discharged by the Organization of American States (OAS). The district court held that OAS was absolutely immune from suit. We affirm on the ground that, even assuming for discussion the applicability of the lesser, "restrictive" immunity doctrine, which permits a lawsuit based on "commercial" activity to be maintained against a sovereign without its consent, this case does not present such "commercial" activity.

I. BACKGROUND

The plaintiffs-appellants are seven former staff members of the General Secretariat of OAS. Before their termination, they had been employed at the permanent headquarters of the organization in Washington, D. C., for periods ranging from six to twenty four years. They are all United States citizens or foreign nationals admitted to permanent residency in the United States.

The appellants were dismissed from the Secretariat on 31 August 1976, due to a reduction in force mandated by the OAS General Assembly. At various times between October 31 and 8 November 1976, they filed complaints with the Administrative Tribunal of the OAS, the internal court created to resolve personnel disputes. On 1 June 1977, the Tribunal held that the discharges had been improper and that the appellants should be reinstated at the grades they held when they were separated from service. In accordance with its governing statute, the Tribunal also fixed an indemnity to be paid to each appellant should the Secretary General choose to exercise the option of refusing to reinstate them. Subsequently, the Secretary General denied reinstatement, and each appellant received the indicated indemnity ....

II. ANALYSIS

...

B. *The Immunity of International Organizations*

The International Organizations Immunities Act of 1945, 22 U.S.C. § 288a(b) (1979) [IOIA], grants to international organizations which are designated by the President [footnote 10 – By Executive Order 10533 (3 June 1954), 19 Fed Reg. 3289 (1954), President Eisenhower designated the OAS an international organization entitled to the privileges and immunities conferred by the IOIA] "the same immunity from suit and every form of judicial process as is enjoyed by

---

12 © Sir E. Lauterpacht, published by Cambridge University Press. Reproduced with permission of The Licensor through PLSclear.

foreign governments, except to the extent that such organizations may expressly waive their immunity for the purpose of any proceedings or by the terms of any contract." [footnote 11 – The legislative history of the Act makes clear the Act was passed to fill a then existing void in our domestic law with respect to the legal status of international organizations. H.Rep. No. 1203. 79th Cong., 1st Sess. 2 (1945), U.S.Code Cong. Serv. 1945. p. 946. 1976, [footnote 12 – *See, e. g.*, The "Tate Letter," 26 Dept. State Bull. 984–85 (1952), quoted in *Alfred Dunhill of London, Inc. v. Cuba*, 425 U.S. 682, 711, 96 S.Ct. 1854, 48 L.Ed.2d 301 (1975).] had come to be the immunity enjoyed by sovereign states – *restrictive* immunity. The central feature of restrictive immunity is the distinction between the governmental or sovereign activities of a state (acts *jure imperii*) and its commercial activities (acts *jure gestionis*). Foreign states may not be found liable for their governmental activities by American courts; but they enjoy no immunity from liability for their commercial activities.] As of 1945, the statute granted absolute immunity to international organizations, for that was the immunity then enjoyed by foreign governments.

The Foreign Sovereign Immunities Act of 1976, 28 U.S.C. § 1602 *et seq.* (1979) [FSIA], codified what, in the period between 1946 and the privileges, exemptions, and immunities to which international organizations shall be entitled shall be those accorded under similar circumstances to foreign governments.

...

First, the FSIA is generally silent about international organizations. No reference to such organizations is made in the elaborate definition of "state" in § 1603, and only § 1611 even alludes to their existence. True, § 1611, dealing as it does with the attachment of property belonging to international organizations, presupposes a successful action against an international organization. However, that could follow a waiver of immunity. Alternatively, § 1611 would have application in case of an attempt to execute a judgment against a foreign state by attaching funds of that foreign state held by an international organization.

Second, by its own terms the IOIA provides for the modification, where appropriate, of the immunity enjoyed by one or move international organizations.

Under the statute, the President can withdraw or restrict the immunity and privileges thereby conferred. Specifically, it provides:

> The president (is) authorized, in the light of the functions performed by any such international organization, by appropriate executive order to withhold or withdraw from any such organization or its officers or employees any of the privileges, exemptions, and immunities provided for in this title ... or to condition or limit the enjoyment by any such organization or its officers or employees of any such privilege, exemption, or immunity.

The Senate Report on the IOIA stated: "This provision will permit the adjustment or limitation of the privileges in the event that any international organization should engage for example, in activities of a commercial nature." [footnote 18 – 18. S.R.Rep. No. 861, 79th Cong., 1st Sess. 2 (1945).] And, in floor debate on the legislation, its supporters pointed again to this provision as a limitation on commercial abuses by an international organization. [footnote 19 – *See* 91 Cong.Rec. 12,432 (daily ed. 20 December 1945) and 12,530 (daily ed. 21 December 1945).] Hence this provision may reveal that Congress intended to grant absolute immunity to international organizations giving to the President the authority to relax that immunity, including removal or restriction of immunity in cases involving the commercial activities of international organizations.

Finally, Congress may have concluded that the policies and considerations that led to the development of the restrictive immunity concept for foreign nations do not apply to international organizations like the OAS. [footnote 20 – Prior to its modification, the absolute immunity of states was justified by "the desirability of avoiding adjudication which might affront a foreign nation and thus embarrass the executive branch in its conduct of foreign relations." *See* Hearings on H.R. 11315 before the Subcommittee on Administrative Law and Governmental Relations, House Committee on the Judiciary, 94th Cong., 2d Sess. 29 (1976). As sovereign nations become more and more involved in the market place, as merchants rather than sovereigns, claims arising out of commercial transactions do not affront the sovereignty of the nations involved. *Id.* Recognition of this growing involvement in commercial activity was the basis of the movement to a restrictive concept. Moreover, most other commercial nations embrace restrictive immunity with regard to sovereigns. Thus, when our government and its instrumentalities are sued abroad in commercial litigation, the sovereign immunity defense is rarely available. H.R. Rep. No. 94–2487, 94th Cong., 2d Sess. 9 (1976). Congressional proponents of the restrictive immunity could thus indicate that use of the restrictive immunity concept would bring the United States into step with foreign nations. *Id.* at 54. But neither rationale for adopting the restrictive notion of immunity would seem to apply to international organizations. Such organizations do not regularly engage in commercial activities, nor do other nations apply the concept of restrictive immunity to them. *Cf Alfred Dunhill of London. Inc. v. Cuba* 425 U S. 682. 699 702. 96 S.Ct. 1854, 48 L.Ed.2d 301 (1975)]

We need not decide this difficult question of statutory construction. On *either* theory of immunity – absolute or restrictive – an immunity exists sufficient to shield the organization from lawsuit on the basis of acts involved here.

C. The "Commercial" Activity Concept in the Restrictive Immunity Doctrine

Even under the restrictive immunity doctrine, there is immunity from lawsuits based on governmental or sovereign activities – the *jure imperii* – as distinct from commercial activities. We discuss the narrower standard of restrictive immunity not because it is necessarily the governing principle, but because we discern that an organization conducting the activities at issue in this case is shielded even under the restrictive immunity formula, and *a fortiori* on the absolute immunity theory.

Section 1605 of the FSIA provides that foreign states shall not be immune from the jurisdiction of American courts in any case based upon their commercial activity in the United States, with the commercial character of an activity determined by reference to its "nature" rather than to its "purpose." The conceptual difficulties involved in differentiating *jure questionis* from *jure imperii* have led some commentators to declare the distinction unworkable. The restrictive immunity doctrine is designed to accommodate the legal interests of citizens doing business with foreign governments on the one hand, with the interests of foreign states in avoiding the embarrassment of defending the propriety of political acts before a foreign court.

In our view, the employment by a foreign state or international organization of internal administrative personnel –civil servants – is not properly characterized as "doing business." That view is supported by the legislative history of the FSIA, and the definition of "commercial activity" in § 1603. The House Report commented:

> (d) *Commercial activity.* – Paragraph (c) of section 1603 defines the term "commercial activity" as including a broad spectrum of endeavor, from an individual commercial transaction or act to a regular course of commercial conduct. A "regular course of commercial conduct" includes the carrying on of a commercial enterprise such as a mineral extraction company, an airline or a state trading corporation. Certainly, if an activity is customarily carried on for profit, its commercial nature could readily be assumed. At the other end of the spectrum, a single contract, if of the same character as a contract which might be made by a private person, could constitute a "particular transaction or act."
>
> As the definition indicates, the fact that goods or services to be procured through a contract are to be used for a public purpose is irrelevant; it is the essentially commercial nature of an activity or transaction that is critical. Thus, a contract by a foreign governmental to buy provisions or equipment for its armed forces or to construct a government building constitutes a commercial activity. The same would be true of a contract to make repairs on an embassy building. Such contracts should be considered to be commercial contracts, even if their ultimate object is to further a public function.
>
> [34] By contrast, a foreign state's mere participation in a foreign assistance program administered by the Agency for International Development (AID) is an activity whose essential nature is public or governmental, and it would not itself constitute a commercial activity. By the same token, a foreign state's activities in and "contacts" with the United States resulting from or necessitated by participation in such a program would not in themselves constitute a sufficient commercial nexus with the United States so as to give rise to jurisdiction (see sec. 1330) or to assets which could be subjected to attachment or execution with respect to unrelated commercial transactions (see sec. 1610(b)). However, a transaction to obtain goods or services from private parties would not lose its otherwise commercial character because it was entered into in connection with an AID program. *Also public or governmental and not commercial in nature, would be the employment of diplomatic, civil service*, or military personnel, but not the employment of American citizens or third country nationals by the foreign state in the United States.[footnote

23 – H.Rep. No. 94–1487, 94th Cong., 2d Sess. 16 (1976) (emphasis added), U.S.Code Cong. & Admin. News 1976, p. 6614.]

This report clearly marks employment of civil servants as noncommercial for purposes of restrictive immunity. The Committee Reports establish an exception from the general rule in the case of employment of American citizens or third country nationals by foreign states. The exception leaves foreign states free to conduct "governmental" matters through their own citizens. A comparable exception is not applicable to international organizations, because their civil servants are inevitably drawn from either American citizens or "third" country nations. In the case of international organizations, such an exception would swallow up the rule of immunity for civil service employment disputes.

The United States has accepted without qualification the principles that international organizations must be free to perform their functions and that no member state may take action to hinder the organization. [footnote 24 – *See e. g.* XIII Documents of the United Nations Conference on International Organizations 704–05 (1945), *reprinted in* 13 Whitman, Digest of International Law 36 (1968).] The unique nature of the *international* civil service is relevant. International officials should be as free as possible, within the mandate granted by the member states, to perform their duties free from the peculiarities of national politics. The OAS charter, for example, imposes constraints on the organization's employment practices. [footnote 25 – *See e. g.* OAS Charter, Article 143 (forbidding discrimination on the basis of "race, creed or sex"). Article 126 (requiring staff recruitment on as wide a geographic basis as possible).]

Such constraints may not coincide with the employment policies pursued by its various member states.[footnote 26 – For example, the Age Discrimination in Employment Act of 1978, (ADEA) 29 U.S.C. § 621 *et seq.*, forbids in most circumstances a requirement that a person retire at a particular age. Yet other countries consider early retirement an important social goal, the achievement of which facilities advancement by younger people. Since there is no inconsistent provision in the OAS Charter (and since, even if there were the ADEA was enacted after the latest amendment to the OAS Charter), the ADEA presumably would govern, and unless its provisions were construed not to cover international employment, see 29 U.S.C. §§ 630 and 633a, the OAS and other international organizations who are thought not immune from suit would be required to abide by the terms of the Act in their employment here. Or for another example, the rigid quotas employed as an integral part of recruiting a "balanced" international civil service, *see, e. g.*, General Assembly resolution 33/143, 18 December 1978, might run afoul of the emerging law of "affirmative action" in the United States.] It would seem singularly inappropriate for the international organization to bind itself to the employment law of any particular member, and we have no reason to think that either the President or Congress intended this result. An attempt by the courts of one nation to adjudicate the personnel claims of international civil servants would entangle those courts in the internal administration of those organizations. Denial of immunity opens the door to divided decisions of the courts of different member states passing judgment on the rules, regulations, and decisions of the international bodies. Undercutting uniformity in the application of staff rules or regulations would undermine the ability of the organization to function effectively. [footnote 27 – Treatise writers on the law of international organizations have recognized the force of the argument made in text. *See, e. g.*, M. B. Akehurst, The Law Governing Employment in International Organizations 12 (1967), which discusses suits such as the instant case in the following terms:

> At first sight, disputes of this sort could be referred to municipal tribunals. The organization normally possesses immunity, but immunity can be waived. However, the special nature of the law governing employment in international organizations, closely linked as it is with delicate questions of administrative policy, makes municipal tribunals totally unsuited to deal with it. It would be like an English court trying to judge a dispute between the French Government and one of its officials. Courts in all countries usually refuse to handle questions of foreign *public* law, and, in the same way, a number of municipal courts have held themselves incompetent to judge claims brought by international civil servants against the organizations which employ them, not on the grounds of immunity, but on the grounds of the special law applicable.
>
> There is therefore a vacuum which needs to be filled by the organizations themselves. The creation of an independent body, empowered to make binding decisions in legal disputes between an organization and its staff, is by no means an altruistic gesture from the organization's point of view; without it, officials might suffer from a sense of injustice which would impair the smooth running of the Secretariat.

The court notes that the OAS, like most international organizations, has established elaborate internal grievance machinery.]

We hold that the relationship of an international organization with its internal administrative staff is noncommercial, and, absent waiver, activities defining or arising out of that relationship may not be the basis of an action against the organization – regardless of whether international organizations enjoy absolute or restrictive immunity.

D. *The Activities at Issue Here*

The appellants were staff members of the General Secretariat of the OAS. Their appointments, terms of employment, salaries and allowances, and the termination of employment were governed by detailed "Staff Rules of the General Secretariat" promulgated by the OAS. The Staff Rules further establish an elaborate grievance procedure within the OAS, with ultimate appeal to the Administrative Tribunal of the OAS.

The Tribunal is competent to determine the lawfulness of an employee's termination of employment. If an employee has been wrongfully discharged, the Tribunal may order reinstatement. If reinstatement is ordered, the Tribunal may also establish an indemnity to be paid to the employee in the event the Secretary

General exercises his authority to indemnify the employee rather than effect the reinstatement.

The employment disputes between the appellants and OAS were disputes concerning the internal administrative staff of the Organization. The internal administration of the OAS is a non-commercial activity shielded by the doctrine of immunity. There was no waiver, and accordingly the appellant's action had to be dismissed.

Notes

- Which entity is claiming immunity? Does that entity qualify?
- Who is Broadbent, and what was/is his role? Would he have had any expectation regarding the terms of his employment when he was hired?
- Is it correct that the President may withdraw or restrict immunity of an international organization? This is a question of what legal system?
- What was the action that served as the basis for the complaint? Is it really true that it is necessary for the organization to engage in that action? What threshold of necessity is required here?

Firstly, it is crucial to observe that the organization as such is immune. This entity can be distinguished from its organs, employees, or representatives. Immunity for an organization includes immunity from adjudication[13] and enforcement.[14] Privileges often cover currency movement, fiscal and taxation measures,[15] and communications.[16] Inviolability generally covers the premises of the organization, and also specifically its archives.[17]

8.3.2 State representatives

But privileges and immunities are not only for the organization and its organs, they are also enjoyed by the (individual) representatives of states accredited to the organization.

---

13 *See e.g.* Austria E GmbH v. European Patent Organization, Judgment, 7 Ob 627/91, (1992) 47 Österreichische Juristenzeitung 661 (Supreme Court [OGH], Austria, 11 June 1992).

14 *See e.g.* Mininni v Bari Institute of the International Centre for Advanced Mediterranean Agronomic Studies, 1981 Rivista di diritto internazionale 685, 78 International Law Reports 112 (Tribunal of Bari (Labor Chamber), Italy, 20 June 1981); International Institute of Refrigeration v. Elkaim, 77 International Law Reports 498 (Court of Appeal of Paris, France, 7 February 1984) (Cour de Cassation, France, 8 November 1988).

15 *See e.g.* International Bank for Reconstruction and Development Articles of Agreement, article VII(4)).

16 *See e.g.* Juan Ysmael & Co. Inc. v. Government of the Republic of Indonesia, [1955] AC 72, [1954] 3 WLR 531, 21 International Law Reports 95 (Judicial Committee of the Privy Council, 7 October 1954)

17 *See e.g.* Shearson Lehman Brothers Inc. and Another v Maclaine Watson & Co. Ltd and Another (No. 2), [1988] 1 WLR 16, 77 International Law Reports 107 (High Court, Queen's Bench Division, England, 29 June 1987).

Re Pisani Balestra Di Mottola
1971 Rivista di diritto internazionale 691; 71 International Law Reports 571
Court of Cassation (Criminal), Italy, 10 July 1969[18]

As regards the position of the resident representative of a Member Nation accredited to the FAO with the rank of Ambassador (...), the [Headquarters] Agreement provides that such persons shall be entitled to the same privileges and immunities as are accorded to members of diplomatic missions of comparable rank accredited to the Italian Government. In other words what is applicable is the international norm on diplomatic immunity comprising the exemption from Italian criminal jurisdiction of diplomatic agents and their families living with them.

Cases of the exclusion or limitation of diplomatic immunity are in general dependent upon international norms. However, in the case of the FAO, the Contracting Parties to the Washington Agreement (the FAO and the Italian Government) agreed to establish special cases where immunity was to be limited and such provisions, as special norms, take precedence over the general norms. It is therefore irrelevant to ascertain what limitations might be provided for according to the rules of customary international law and under the supervening norms of the Vienna Convention, which basically reproduces customary international law, whilst being innovative on certain points (for instance, with regard to the limitations resulting from "permanent residence"). The examination is to be conducted exclusively on the basis of the provisions of the Washington Agreement.

The statement contained in the Washington Agreement (which is in any case not made in relation to the particular immunity under discussion here) to the effect that the immunities are accorded in the interests of the FAO and not for the personal benefit of the individuals themselves, is not a criteria for limiting those immunities but rather an affirmation of the scope of the purpose for which they are granted, which is to guarantee the independence of an international organization which has its seat within the territory of a sovereign State. It involves the application to a particular situation of the principle *ne impediatur legatio*. The true causes of limitation of immunity are contained in Article XI, Section 24 (c) of the Agreement:

> Whenever the resident representatives of Member Nations or members of their missions are Italian citizens, or are engaged in any trade or industry within the Italian Republic, the privileges and immunities recognized by international law shall apply to the extent authorized by international law as accepted by the Government.

According to this provision it is for the Italian Government to determine in fact to what extent immunity should be limited in each case. In the case in point the Government has not decided to limit the

---

18 © Sir E. Lauterpacht, published by Cambridge University Press. Reproduced with permission of The Licensor through PLSclear.

immunity of Ambassador Di Mottola ... On the contrary, the possible existence of a reason to limit immunity based on the exercise of a trade or industry can be excluded. In the judgment under appeal it was implicitly held that such a reason did not exist.

With regard to the question of citizenship the judgment under appeal substantially recognized that Carlo Di Mottola acquired Costa Rican citizenship on 25 September 1958 and simultaneously lost Italian citizenship (Article 8 (1) of Law No. 555 of 13 June 1912). It confirmed, however, that the minor Leopoldo, naturalized as a Costa Rican on 4 November 1958 at the request of his father, had acquired foreign citizenship "without his own consent" within the meaning of Article 8 (2) of Law No. 555 so that, by reason of the lack of proper renunciation, he had not lost his original Italian citizenship.

Notes

- Who is claiming immunity specifically? On what basis does that individual have immunity? What is the legal source?
- What is the legal principle of "*ne impediatur legatio*"? How is it relevant, and what is its source? How does this relate to the question above?
- The court observes that the organization "has its seat within the territory of a sovereign State." Why is this relevant for the analysis of immunity?
- The court also observes whether the representative is an Italian citizen or not. Why is this relevant for the analysis of immunity? Surely all representatives are from sovereign equal states, so why even discuss this question?

Sometimes, the individuals appointed are objectionable, and sometimes the state (or entity) that the person represents are objectionable, either to the host state or the organization, or both. Where a nominee to be a diplomat is objectionable, the nominating state usually withdraws the appointment, but for international organizations, the solution is not so clear. The person might be accredited to the organization only, or in some cases, to both the organization and the host state. Furthermore, the state sending the representative surely has some right to govern the organization it created in its discretion. Yet the nominee will reside in a foreign country. In these cases, the host state and the organization must work together.

8.3.3 Employees of international organizations

In addition to the representatives of states to the international organization, the organization also employs its own staff directly. These individuals are intended to be independent of their state governments, although their nationality may be taken into consideration for purposes of maintaining a balanced, diverse, and globally representative staff.

Staff of an international organization are sometimes divided into two categories. The first category are the highest officers of the organization, for example the United

Nations Secretary-General. These individuals might receive immunity comparable to that of a diplomat, i.e. immunity *ratione personae*, under relevant agreements and practice. However, it cannot be assumed that simply because an individual is the administrative head of an organization (or within a small circle of organizational leadership) he/she will enjoy that level of immunity.[19]

World Health Organization and Verstuyft v. Aquino and Others
69 Official Gazette 1914; 48 Supreme Court Reps. Annotated 242;
52 International Law Reports 389
Supreme Court, Philippines, 29 November 1972[20]

[i] An original action for certiorari and prohibition to set aside respondent judge's refusal to quash a search warrant issued by him at the instance of respondents COSAC (Constabulary Offshore Action Center) officers for the search and seizure of the personal effects of petitioner official of the WHO (World Health Organization) notwithstanding his being entitled to diplomatic immunity, as duly recognized by the executive branch of the Philippine Government, and to prohibit respondent judge from further proceedings in the matter.

...

[iii] Respondents COSAC officers filed their answer joining issue against petitioners and seeking to justify their act of applying for and securing from respondent judge the warrant for the search and seizure of ten crates consigned to petitioner Verstuyft and stored at the Eternit Corporation warehouse on the ground that they "contain large quantities of highly dutiable goods" beyond the official needs of said petitioner "and the only lawful way to reach these articles and effects for purpose of taxation is through a search warrant." [footnote omitted]...

[v] It is undisputed in the record that petitioner Dr. Leonce Verstuyft, who was assigned on 6 December 1971 by the WHO from his last station in Taipei to the Regional Office in Manila as Acting Assistant Director of Health Services, is entitled to diplomatic immunity, pursuant to the Host Agreement executed on 22 July 1951 between the Philippine Government and the World Health Organization.

[vi] Such diplomatic immunity carries with it, among other diplomatic privileges and immunities, personal inviolability, inviolability of the official's properties, exemption from local jurisdiction, and exemption from taxation and customs duties.

[vii] When petitioner Verstuyft's personal effects contained in twelve crates entered the Philippines as unaccompanied

---

19 *See e.g.* The People of New York v Dominique Strauss-Kahn, Indictment No. 02526/2011, Recommendation for Dismissal (Supreme Court, New York, 22 August 2011) (individual being Managing Director of the International Monetary Fund at the time of arrest in New York; immunities were not raised and case was dismissed due to unreliable evidence).

20 © Sir E. Lauterpacht, published by Cambridge University Press. Reproduced with permission of The Licensor through PLSclear.

baggage on 10 January 1972, they were accordingly allowed free entry from duties and taxes. The crates were directly stored at the Eternit Corporation's warehouse at Mandaluyong, Rizal, "pending his relocation into permanent quarters upon the offer of Mr. Berg, Vice President of Eternit, who was once a patient of Dr. Verstuyft in the Congo." [footnote omitted]

[viii] Nevertheless, as above stated, respondent judge issued on 3 March 1972 upon application on the same date of respondents COSAC officers search warrant No. 72–138 for alleged violation of Republic Act 4712 amending section 3601 of the Tariff and Customs Code [footnote omitted] directing the search and seizure of the dutiable items in said crates.

[ix] Upon protest of 6 March 1972 of Dr. Francisco Dr, WHO Regional Director for the Western Pacific with station in Manila, Secretary of Foreign Affairs Carlos P. Romulo personally wired on the same date respondent judge advising that "Dr. Verstuyft is entitled to immunity from search in respect of his personal baggage as accorded to members of diplomatic missions" pursuant to the Host Agreement and requesting suspension of the search warrant order "pending clarification of the matter from the ASAC."

[x] Respondent judge set the Foreign Secretary's request for hearing and heard the same on 16 March 1972, but notwithstanding the official plea of diplomatic immunity interposed by a duly authorized representative of the Department of Foreign Affairs who furnished the respondent judge with a list of the articles brought in by petitioner Verstuyft, respondent judge issued his order of the same date maintaining the effectivity of the search warrant issued by him, unless restrained by a higher court. [footnote 1 – Respondent judge's justification in his said order reads in part as follows:

"From the reply submitted by Captain Pedro S. Navarro and Antonio G. Relieve of the COSAC, it appears that the articles contained in the two baggages allegedly belonging to Dr. Verstuyft so far opened by them, are 120 bottles of assorted foreign wine and 15 tins of PX goods which are said to be dutiable under the Customs and Tariff Code of the Philippines. The two COSAC officers further manifested that they positively believe that there are more contraband items in the nine other huge crates which are still unopened. ... The Court is certain that the World Health Organization would not tolerate violations of local laws by its officials and/or representatives under a claim of immunity granted to them by the host agreement. Since the right of immunity invoked by the Department of Foreign Affairs is admittedly relative and not absolute, and there are strong and positive indications of violation of local laws, the Court declines to suspend the effectivity of the search warrant issued in the case at bar."]

...

[xi] At the hearing thereof held on 8 May 1972, the Office of the Solicitor General appeared and filed an extended comment stating the official position of the executive branch of the Philippine Government that petitioner Verstuyft

is entitled to diplomatic immunity, he did not abuse his diplomatic immunity, [footnote 2 – Aside from the Foreign Affairs Department's certification that the importation of 120 bottles of wine is "ordinary in diplomatic practice," the Solicitor General took pains to inform the lower court that the packing of Dr. Verstuyft's baggages and personal effects was done "by a packing company in Taipei ... (and) Dr. Verstuyft had no hand in the preparation of the packing list of his personal effects which has been assailed by ASAC agents. ...."] and that court proceedings in the receiving or host State are not the proper remedy in the case of abuse of diplomatic immunity [footnote omitted][.] ...

1. The executive branch of the Philippine Government has *expressly* recognized that petitioner Verstuyft is entitled to diplomatic immunity pursuant to the provisions of the Host Agreement. The Department of Foreign Affairs formally advised respondent judge of the Philippine Government's official position that accordingly "Dr. Verstuyft cannot be the subject of a Philippine court summons without violating an obligation in international law of the Philippine Government" and asked for the quashal of the search warrant, since his personal effects and baggages, after having been allowed free entry from all customs duties and taxes, may not be baselessly claimed to have been "unlawfully imported" in violation of the tariff and customs code as claimed by respondents COSAC officers. The Solicitor-General, as principal law officer of the Government, [footnote omitted] likewise expressly affirmed said petitioner's right to diplomatic immunity and asked for the quashal of the search warrant.

[1.1.] It is a recognized principle of international law and under our system of separation of powers that diplomatic immunity is essentially a political question and courts should refuse to look beyond a determination by the executive branch of the government, [footnote omitted] ... Hence, ... it is accepted doctrine that "in such cases the judical department of (this) government follows the action of the political branch and will not embarrass the latter by assuming an antagonistic jurisdiction." [footnote omitted]

[2.1.] As already stated above, and brought to respondent court's attention, the Philippine Government is bound by the procedure laid down in Article VII of the Convention on the Privileges and Immunities of the Specialized Agencies of the United Nations [footnote omitted] for consultations between the Host State and the United Nations agency concerned to determine in the first instance the fact of occurrence of the abuse alleged, and if so, to ensure that no repetition occurs and for other recourses. This is a treaty commitment voluntarily assumed by the Philippine Government and, as such, has the force and effect of law.

[2.2.] Hence, even assuming *arguendo* as against the categorical assurance of the executive branch of government that respondent judge had some ground to prefer respondents COSAC officers' suspicion that there had been an abuse of diplomatic immunity, the continuation of the search warrant proceedings before him was not the proper remedy. He should, nevertheless, in deference to the exclusive competence and jurisdiction of the executive branch of government to act on the matter, have acceded to the quashal of the search warrant, and forwarded his findings or grounds to believe that there had been such abuse of diplomatic immunity to the Department of Foreign Affairs for it to deal with, in accordance with the aforementioned Convention, if so warranted.

...

[2.5.] The Court, therefore, holds that respondent judge acted without jurisdiction and with grave abuse of discretion in not ordering the quashal of the search warrant issued by him in disregard of the diplomatic immunity of petitioner Verstuyft.

Notes

- What specifically did the individual do that he wishes to seek immunity from? Why did the government intervene in this matter? Did it have good reason to suspect criminal activity?
- Is this a question of immunity, inviolability, or privilege? Which person, organization, or organ is responsible for serving and defending immunity in such a case?
- Is this really a matter of international law, or domestic law, and what is the role of the executive determination? Is it legally determinative, or evidentiary?
- The court holds that the lower court acted "without jurisdiction." Is this correct?
- Did the individual benefit from *ratione personae* or *materiae* protection? What was his office or function? Is the form of protection correct?

The second category of international organization staff is the more frequently encountered: the regular staff. These individuals do not receive diplomatic level immunity, but instead receive functional community, i.e. immunity *ratione materiae*.

Curran v City of New York, et al.
191 Misc. 229; 77 NYS 2d 206; 14 International Law Reports 154
Supreme Court (Special Term) of Queen's County,
New York, United States, 29 December 1947[21]

The Department of State, the political branch of our Government, having, without any reservation or qualification whatsoever, recognized and certified the immunity of the United Nations and the defendant Lie to judicial process, there is no longer any question for independent determination by this Court. *United States of Mexico v. Schmuck*, 294 N.Y. 265, 62 N.E. 2d. 64, reaffirming 293 N.Y. 264, 56 N.E. 2d. 577.

The judicial branch of our Government follows the political branch in dealing with sovereign immunity and will not embarrass the latter by assuming an antagonistic jurisdiction. *United States v. Lee*, 106 U.S. 196, 209. Neither will

---

21 © Sir E. Lauterpacht, published by Cambridge University Press. Reproduced with permission of The Licensor through PLSclear.

the judicial branch embarrass the executive arm of the Government. *Ex parte Republic of Peru*, 318 U.S. 578–588.

The case at bar demonstrates the wisdom of the rule that such determination by the State Department is final and controlling. The complaint herein raises delicate questions pertaining to the foreign policy of the United States and to its internal processes incident thereto. To be allowed to raise such issues in a court of this country can serve but to embarrass the United States in the conduct of its relations with the other nations of the world. *In re Baiz*, 135 U.S. 403; *United States v. Pink*, 315 U.S. 203, at page 223; *United States v. Belmont*, 301 U.S. 324; *Wulfsohn v. Russian Socialist Federated Soviet Republic*, 234 N.Y. 372, at page 376, 138 N.E. 24, at page 26.

It follows that the Court is bound to accord recognition to, and uphold, the suggestion of immunity presented by the Department of State, through the United States Attorney for the Eastern District of New York.

This brings us to a consideration of the motion made by the City of New York.

...

The allegations of the complaint must be viewed in respect of their sufficiency in the light of existing law. In 1945, in the exercise of the President's power "by and with the Advice and Consent of the Senate, to make Treaties", United States Constitution, Article 2, Section 2, Clause 2, the United States signed and ratified the multilateral treaty known as the Charter of the United Nations. The treaty came into force on 24 October 1945, upon the deposit of the number of ratifications required by Article no of the Charter.

"... By the terms of this treaty, the United States became a party, *inter alia*, to Articles 104 and 105 of the Charter, These provide:

> 'Article 104. The Organisation shall enjoy in the territory of each of its Members such legal capacity as may be necessary for the exercise of its functions and the fulfillment of its purposes.
>
> Article 105. 1. The Organization shall enjoy in the territory of each of its Members such privileges and immunities as are necessary for the fulfillment of its purposes.'

That these provisions, in a treaty made under the authority of the United States, are the law of the land, needs no argument. Article 6, Clause 2, of the Constitution of the United States provides:

> 'This Constitution, and the Laws of the United States which shall be made in pursuance thereof; and all Treaties made, or which shall be made, under the Authority of the United States, shall be the supreme Law of the Land; and the Judges in every State shall be bound thereby, anything in the Constitution or Laws of any State to the Contrary notwithstanding.'

Even without further action by Congress or by the State, the effect of Article 104 would be to give to the United Nations the legal status and capacity to own land in the United States. Also, that without further action by Congress or the State, the immunities 'necessary for the fulfillment of its purposes', conferred upon the United Nations by Article 105, include immunity from taxation.

Furthermore, in implementation of the Charter, Congress passed the 'International

Organizations Immunities Act', Public Law 291, 79th Congress, which, pursuant to its terms, was made applicable to the United Nations by Executive Order 9698 of 19 February 1946. This, too, then, as a law of the United States, is the supreme law of the land.

By H. Con. Res. 75, 10 December 2011, 1945, the Congress invited the United Nations 'to locate the seat of the United Nations within the United States'. To effectuate this resolution the Congress, by Public Law 357, 80th Congress, 61 Stat. 756, authorized the President of the United States to bring into effect a 'Headquarters Agreement', negotiated by the Secretary of State and Secretary General of the United Nations. These acts of national legislation were in furtherance of our national policy, and they were further clarified by the Legislature of the State of New York in enacting Chapters 23, 24 and 25 of the Laws of 1947" [which provide that the interests of the State and the City of New York would be promoted by the granting to the United Nations of the land to be used as a headquarters site, that the real property of the United Nations should be exempt from taxation, and that the State should cede its jurisdiction with respect to such land when used for the headquarters of the United Nations].

Notes

- How does this court explain the relationship between the judiciary and the executive when it comes to matters of immunity? What does it mean for the executive to "suggest" immunity?
- Is it a matter of international law, or domestic law (statutory, or constitutional)? If it is domestic law, then why does the court hold that Congress does not need to take any action for there to be a legal effect?

In addition to immunity, regular staff of an organization may also receive certain privileges:

Case 85/86, Commission of the European Communities v Board of Governors of the European Investment Bank (EIB)
Court of Justice of the European Communities [Union], 3 March 1988[22]

1   By an application lodged at the Court Registry on 21 March 1986, the Commission of the European Communities brought an action under Article 180 (b) and Article 173 of the EEC Treaty for a declaration that the decision of the Board of Governors of the European Investment Bank (hereinafter referred to as "the Board of Governors") of 30 December 1985 on the disposal of the proceeds of the income tax withheld by the Bank from salaries and pensions paid to its staff is void.

---

22 https://eur-lex.europa.eu, © European Union, 1998–2020.

2 The proceedings arise from a disagreement between the parties concerning the application of the provisions of the Protocol on the Privileges and Immunities of the European Communities of 8 April 1965 (Journal Officiel 1967, 152, p. 13) ("the Protocol") as regards the tax on the remuneration of staff of the Communities and the application of that tax to staff of the European Investment Bank ("the Bank").

3 The first paragraph of Article 13 of the Protocol provides as follows:

> "Officials and other servants of the Communities shall be liable to a tax for the benefit of the Communities on salaries, wages and emoluments paid to them by the Communities, in accordance with the conditions and procedure laid down by the Council, acting on a proposal from the Commission".

Article 22 provides that:

> "This Protocol shall also apply to the European Investment Bank, to the members of its organs, to its staff and to the representatives of the Member States taking part in its activities, without prejudice to the provisions of the Protocol on the Statute of the Bank".

4 Pursuant to Article 13 of the Protocol, the Council of the European Communities adopted Regulation No 260/68 of 29 February 1968 laying down the conditions and procedure for applying the tax for the benefit of the European Communities (Official Journal, English Special Edition 1968 (I), p. 37). Article 9 of that regulation provides that the proceeds of the tax are to be entered as revenue in the budgets of the Communities. According to Article 12, the regulation is to apply to members of the organs of the Bank, and to members of its staff and recipients of the pensions it pays, with regard to salaries, wages, emoluments and pensions.

5 The aforementioned provisions replace the corresponding articles of the Protocol of 17 April 1957 on the Privileges and Immunities of the European Economic Community and of Council Regulation No 32/61/EEC and 12/61/EAEC of 18 December 1961 (Journal Officiel 1962, p. 1461), the content of which was identical.

6 Since 1962 the Bank has withheld the aforesaid tax from the salaries, wages, pensions and emoluments which it pays to its staff and each year has entered the sums deducted on the liabilities side of its balance sheet under the heading "Miscellaneous".

7 Since the 1960s the Commission had repeatedly made it clear in contacts with representatives of the Bank that it intended to assert the Communities' rights. Between 1981 and 1985 it made various approaches to the Board of Governors with a view to securing payment of the sums withheld into the general budget of the Communities. Its approaches were unsuccessful.

8 On 30 December 1985 the Board of Governors adopted the contested decision providing that the proceeds of the tax withheld by the Bank up until the end of 1985 and entered on the liabilities side of its balance sheet were to be transferred to the reserves. The decision further provided that as from the 1986 financial year amounts withheld by the Bank from salaries, wages, pensions and emoluments paid by the Bank were to

be accounted for as Bank income and entered as such on the profit and loss account.

9   Reference is made to the Report for the Hearing for a fuller account of the facts of the case, the procedure and the submissions and arguments of the parties, which are mentioned or discussed hereinafter only in so far as is necessary for the reasoning of the Court.

...

Substance

17   In support of its application the Commission argues in the first place that by providing for the transfer to the Bank's reserves of the proceeds of the tax levied on the remuneration of its staff for the benefit of the Communities, the contested decision infringes Article 13 of the Protocol and Articles 9 and 12 of Regulation No 260/68. In its view, Article 22 of the Protocol extends the class of persons covered by the Protocol so as to include the Bank and its staff but without changing the intended purpose of the tax.

18   The Board of Governors contends that under the first paragraph of Article 22 of the Protocol the privileges and immunities set out in the Protocol are granted to the Bank and its staff and to the Communities alike. Without adopting a definitive position on the question whether the Board of Governors was itself empowered to determine the conditions for collecting the tax in question, the Board of Governors considers that the tax should be collected for the benefit of the Bank in any event. In its view, Regulation No 260/68 must be interpreted to that effect.

19   In order to assess the merits of the application it must be observed in the first place that the conditions and procedure for applying the tax for the benefit of the European Communities are laid down in Council Regulation No 260/68, which is based on the Protocol and in particular on Article 13 thereof. According to its preamble, the regulation is intended to subject to the Community tax not only officials and other servants of the Communities but also persons to whom Article 13 of the Protocol is also applicable, those persons including, *inter alios*, the staff of the Bank.

20   As far as wages and salaries paid by the Communities to their officials and other servants are concerned, Article 9 of the regulation provides that the tax proceeds are to be entered as revenue in the budget of the Communities, which, under Article 20 of the Treaty establishing a Single Council and a Single Commission of the European Communities, took the place of the budgets of the individual Communities. Article 12 of the regulation provides that the regulation is to apply to members of the organs of the Bank and to members of its staff and recipients of the pensions it pays "with regard to salaries, wages and emoluments and to disability, retirement and survivors' pensions paid by the Bank". Consequently, the regulation unequivocally appropriates to the Communities' budget the proceeds of the tax withheld by the Bank from the wages and salaries paid to its staff.

21   The defence submitted by the Board of Governors raises the question whether the Council was empowered under the Protocol to determine the conditions and procedure for taxing the wages and salaries paid by the Bank and to allot to the Communities' budget the sums so withheld.

22 In order to answer that question it is necessary to consider the scope of Article 13 of the Protocol and the effect of its application to the Bank having regard to Article 22 of the Protocol.

23 The second paragraph of Article 13 of the Protocol provides that salaries, wages and emoluments (hereinafter abbreviated to "salaries") paid by the Communities are to be exempt from national taxes. However, the first paragraph of Article 13 subjects those salaries to a tax for the benefit of the Communities, in accordance with the conditions and procedure which are to be laid down by the Council, acting on a proposal from the Commission. It follows from the relationship between those two paragraphs that in the interests of the Communities' independence and equal treatment of their staff Article 13 is to replace national taxes by a Community tax which is applicable to the Communities' staff on the basis of uniform conditions.

24 Those considerations are equally valid as regards the application of Article 13 of the Protocol to the staff of the Bank pursuant to Article 22 of the Protocol. In its judgment of 15 June 1976 in Case 110/75 *(Mills* v *European Investment Bank* [1976] ECR 955) the Court held that the Bank was a Community body established and endowed with legal personality by the Treaty. Consequently, the Bank's staff had to be exempted from national taxes just like the Community's staff and be subjected to a Community tax. Since the Protocol contains no provisions to the contrary, the result of the application of Article 13 to the staff of the Bank must be that the Council has the power to extend the scope of the conditions and the procedure adopted pursuant to that article so as to cover the staff of the Bank.

25 As regards the intended purpose of the tax to which staff of the Communities are subject, Article 13 of the Protocol provides that the tax is to be collected "for the benefit of the Communities". Article 22 of the Protocol is silent as to the purpose to which the tax withheld from staff of the Bank is to be put but merely provides that Article 13 is to apply, in particular, to the Bank.

26 It should be observed in this context that it does not follow from the aim of Article 13 of the Protocol, which is that the national taxes which would normally be applicable to the salaries of staff of the Communities should be replaced by a uniform tax, that the proceeds of that tax should be allotted to the bodies in which the staff concerned are employed. Since the rights and privileges arising out of the Protocol were conferred on the Bank only in its capacity as a body which, according to Article 130 of the Treaty, acts in the interest of the Communities, Articles 13 and 22 of the Protocol must be interpreted as meaning that the tax on salaries paid by the Bank is also levied for the benefit of the Communities.

27 The Bank opposes that interpretation, arguing that it is neither an institution nor a department of the Communities; rather, it enjoys autonomy *vis-à-vis* the Communities by virtue of its legal status, its composition and its institutional structure, as well as by virtue of the nature and origin of its resources, which are absolutely independent of the Communities' budget.

28 It is true that under Article 129 of the Treaty the Bank has legal personality distinct from that of the Community

and that it is administered and managed by organs of its own in accordance with its statute. In order to perform the tasks assigned to it by Article 130 of the Treaty the Bank must be able to act in complete independence on the financial markets, like any other bank. Indeed, the Bank is not financed out of the budget but from its own resources, which consist in particular of the capital subscribed by the Member States and funds borrowed on the financial markets. Lastly, the Bank draws up annual accounts and a profit and loss account which are audited annually by a committee appointed by the Board of Governors.

29   Nevertheless, the fact that the Bank has that degree of operational and institutional autonomy does not mean that it is totally separated from the Communities and exempt from every rule of Community law. It is clear in particular from Article 130 of the Treaty that the Bank is intended to contribute towards the attainment of the Community's objectives and thus by virtue of the Treaty forms part of the framework of the Community.

30   The position of the Bank is therefore ambivalent inasmuch as it is characterized on the one hand by independence in the management of its affairs, in particular in the sphere of financial operations, and on the other by a close link with the Community as regards its objectives. It is entirely compatible with the ambivalent nature of the Bank that the provisions generally applicable to the taxation of staff at the Community level should also apply to the staff of the Bank. This is true in particular of the rule that the tax in question is collected for the benefit of the Communities' budget. Contrary to the contentions of the Board of Governors, the fact that the tax is allotted to that purpose is not liable to undermine the operational autonomy and reputation of the Bank as an independent institution on the financial markets since it does not affect the capital or the actual management of the Bank.

31   The Board of Governors resists that conclusion by adducing a number of arguments based on the fact that the payment of the proceeds of the tax in question to the Communities' budget would diminish the Bank's assets, which are intended to cover its operating costs and in particular the salaries of its staff and which the Member States would be entitled to claim in the event of the winding-up of the Bank.

32   Those arguments cannot be accepted. The transfer of the proceeds of the tax to the Communities' budget affects only the sums withheld from salaries paid by the Bank to its staff and not the Bank's own resources or the capital amounts which would be payable to the Member States if the Bank's activities were suspended or it went into liquidation. Consequently, the collection by the Bank of tax on the gross salaries of its staff for the benefit of the Communities has a neutral effect on the Bank's financial position.

33   It follows from the foregoing that the Council had the power, under the combined provisions of Articles 13 and 22 of the Protocol, to determine in Regulation No 260/68 the conditions and procedure for levying the tax on the salaries of the staff of the Bank and to allot the proceeds of that tax to the Communities' budget. In those circumstances,

it is unnecessary to consider the significance of the agreement which the President of the Bank is said to have given to the entry of the tax proceeds as revenue in the Communities' budget on which the Commission relies in support of its argument.

34 The decision of the Board of Governors of the European Investment Bank of 30 December 1985 on the disposal of the proceeds of the income tax withheld by the Bank from salaries and pensions paid to its staff must therefore be declared void.

Notes

- Is this case about immunity, or privileges? Or inviolability?
- Why does the Bank withhold tax assessments on employees' salaries? What entity is taxing the staff? Does that entity have taxing powers? Is it a tax?
- What are the sources of law in this case? What is their legal value? How do they relate to each other? That is to say, what source of law provides for exemption from taxation?

Taxation is one of the biggest issues in the law on privileges and immunities. Sometimes, questions arise whether a particular assessment is a tax or a fee for services, or perhaps something else.[23] Further, even if salary is exempt from taxation, the local tax authority may wish to consider the income when it determines the applicable tax rate within a system of progressive tax rates.[24]

8.3.4 Experts on mission

However, an organization does not only employ staff directly. Most international organizations make use of extensive teams of interns. These individuals are not paid, nor do they exist within a formal employment relationship, but for most other purposes they are assimilated to regular staff. In addition, an international organization may request the services of an independent expert, often on an unpaid basis, to consult or discharge certain functions on behalf of the organization, yet without becoming an employee of the organization. These individuals are usually termed "Experts on Mission".

---

23 *See. e.g.* Evangelical Church (Augburg and Helvitic Confessions) in Austria v. Grezda, 6 Ob 302/63, 38 International Law Reports 453 (Supreme Court, Austria, 27 February 1964)

24 *See e.g.* Karl M. v. Provincial Revenue Office for Vienna, Case No. Zl. 1509/69, 71 International Law Reports 573 (Administrative Court, Austria, 20 November 1970); Case 6/60, Jean-E. Humblet v. Belgian State, Judgment (Court of Justice of the European Communities [Union], 16 December 1960).

Difference Relating to Immunity from Legal Process of a Special Rapporteur of the Commission on Human Rights ["Cumaraswamy case"]
Advisory Opinion
1999 ICJ Reps. 62
International Court of Justice, 29 April 1999

10. In its decision 1998/297, the Council asked the Court to take into account, for purposes of the advisory opinion requested, the "circumstances set out in paragraphs 1 to 15 of the note by the Secretary-General" (E/1998/94). Those paragraphs read as follows:

"1. In its resolution 22A(I) of 13 February 1946, the General Assembly adopted, pursuant to Article 105(3) of the Charter of the United Nations, the Convention on the Privileges and Immunities of the United Nations (the Convention). Since then, 137 Member States have become parties to the Convention, and its provisions have been incorporated by reference into many hundreds of agreements relating to the headquarters or seats of the United Nations and its organs, and to activities carried out by the Organization in nearly every country of the world.

2. That Convention is, *inter alia*, designed to protect various categories of persons, including 'Experts on Mission for the United Nations', from all types of interference by national authorities. In particular, Section 22*(b)* of Article VI of the Convention provides:

'*Section 22*: Experts (other than officials coming within the scope of Article V) performing missions for the United Nations shall be accorded such privileges and immunities as are necessary for the independent exercise of their functions during the period of their missions, including time spent on journeys in connection with their missions. In particular they shall be accorded:

...

(b) in respect of words spoken or written and acts done by them in the course of the performance of their mission, immunity from legal process of every kind. This immunity from legal process shall continue to be accorded notwithstanding that the persons concerned are no longer employed on missions for the United Nations.'

3. In its Advisory Opinion of 14 December 1989, on the *Applicability of Article VI, Section 22, of the Convention on the Privileges and Immunities of the United Nations* (the so-called '*Mazilu* case'), the International Court of Justice held that a Special Rapporteur of the Subcommission on the Prevention of Discrimination and Protection of Minorities of the Commission on Human Rights was an 'expert on mission' within the meaning of Article VI of the Convention.

4. The Commission on Human Rights, by its resolution 1994/41 of 4 March 1994, endorsed by the Economic and Social Council in its decision 1994/251 of 22 July 1994, appointed Dato' Param Cumaraswamy, a Malaysian jurist, as the Commission's Special Rapporteur on the Independence of Judges and Lawyers. His mandate consists of tasks including, *inter alia*, to inquire into

substantial allegations concerning, and to identify and record attacks on, the independence of the judiciary, lawyers and court officials. Mr. Cumaraswamy has submitted four reports to the Commission on the execution of his mandate: E/CN.4/1995/39, E/CN.4/1996/37, E/CN.4/1997/32 and E/CN.4/1998/39. After the third report containing a section on the litigation pending against him in the Malaysian civil courts, the Commission at its fifty-fourth session, in April 1997, renewed his mandate for an additional three years.

5. In November 1995 the Special Rapporteur gave an interview to *International Commercial Litigation*, a magazine published in the United Kingdom of Great Britain and Northern Ireland but circulated also in Malaysia, in which he commented on certain litigations that had been carried out in Malaysian courts. As a result of an article published on the basis of that interview, two commercial companies in Malaysia asserted that the said article contained defamatory words that had "brought them into public scandal, odium and contempt". Each company filed a suit against him for damages amounting to M$30 million (approximately US$12 million each), "including exemplary damages for slander".

6. Acting on behalf of the Secretary-General, the Legal Counsel considered the circumstances of the interview and of the controverted passages of the article and determined that Dato' Param Cumaraswamy was interviewed in his official capacity as Special Rapporteur on the Independence of Judges and Lawyers, that the article clearly referred to his United Nations capacity and to the Special Rapporteur's United Nations global mandate to investigate allegations concerning the independence of the judiciary and that the quoted passages related to such allegations. On 15 January 1997, the Legal Counsel, in a note verbale addressed to the Permanent Representative of Malaysia to the United Nations, therefore "requested the competent Malaysian authorities to promptly advise the Malaysian courts of the Special Rapporteur's immunity from legal process" with respect to that particular complaint. On 20 January 1997, the Special Rapporteur filed an application in the High Court of Kuala Lumpur (the trial court in which the said suit had been filed) to set aside and/or strike out the plaintiffs' writ, on the ground that the words that were the subject of the suits had been spoken by him in the course of performing his mission for the United Nations as Special Rapporteur on the Independence of Judges and Lawyers. The Secretary-General issued a note on 7 March 1997 confirming that "the words which constitute the basis of plaintiffs' complaint in this case were spoken by the Special Rapporteur in the course of his mission" and that the Secretary-General "therefore maintains that Dato' Param Cumaraswamy is immune from legal process with respect thereto". The Special Rapporteur filed this note in support of his above-mentioned application.

7. After a draft of a certificate that the Minister for Foreign Affairs proposed to file with the trial court had been discussed with representatives of the Office of Legal Affairs, who had indicated that the draft set out the immunities of the Special Rapporteur incompletely and inadequately, the Minister nevertheless on 12 March 1997 filed the certificate in the form originally proposed: in particular the final sentence of that certificate in

effect invited the trial court to determine at its own discretion whether the immunity applied, by stating that this was the case "*only* in respect of words spoken or written and acts done by him in the course of the performance of his mission" (emphasis added). In spite of the representations that had been made by the Office of Legal Affairs, the certificate failed to refer in any way to the note that the Secretary-General had issued a few days earlier and that had in the meantime been filed with the court, nor did it indicate that in this respect, i.e. in deciding whether particular words or acts of an expert fell within the scope of his mission, the determination could exclusively be made by the Secretary-General, and that such determination had conclusive effect and therefore had to be accepted as such by the court. In spite of repeated requests by the Legal Counsel, the Minister for Foreign Affairs refused to amend his certificate or to supplement it in the manner urged by the United Nations.

8. On 28 June 1997, the competent judge of the Malaysian High Court for Kuala Lumpur concluded that she was "unable to hold that the Defendant is absolutely protected by the immunity he claims", in part because she considered that the Secretary-General's note was merely "an opinion" with scant probative value and no binding force upon the court and that the Minister for Foreign Affairs' certificate "would appear to be no more than a bland statement as to a state of fact pertaining to the Defendant's status and mandate as a Special Rapporteur and appears to have room for interpretation". The Court ordered that the Special Rapporteur's motion be dismissed with costs, that costs be taxed and paid forthwith by him and that he file and serve his defence within 14 days.

On 8 July, the Court of Appeal dismissed Mr. Cumaraswamy's motion for a stay of execution.

9. On 30 June and 7 July 1997, the Legal Counsel thereupon sent notes verbales to the Permanent Representative of Malaysia, and also held meetings with him and his Deputy. In the latter note, the Legal Counsel, *inter alia*, called on the Malaysian Government to intervene in the current proceedings so that the burden of any further defence, including any expenses and taxed costs resulting therefrom, be assumed by the Government; to hold Mr. Cumaraswamy harmless in respect of the expenses he had already incurred or that were being taxed to him in respect of the proceedings so far; and, so as to prevent the accumulation of additional expenses and costs and the further need to submit a defence until the matter of his immunity was definitively resolved between the United Nations and the Government, to support a motion to have the High Court proceedings stayed until such resolution. The Legal Counsel referred to the provisions for the settlement of differences arising out of the interpretation and application of the 1946 Convention that might arise between the Organization and a Member State, which are set out in Section 30 of the Convention, and indicated that if the Government decided that it cannot or does not wish to protect and to hold harmless the Special Rapporteur in the indicated manner, a difference within the meaning of those provisions might be considered to have arisen between the Organization and the Government of Malaysia.

10. Section 30 of the Convention provides as follows:

> "*Section 30:* All differences arising out of the interpretation or application of the present convention shall be

referred to the International Court of Justice, unless in any case it is agreed by the parties to have recourse to another mode of settlement. If a difference arises between the United Nations on the one hand and a Member on the other hand, a request shall be made for an advisory opinion on any legal question involved in accordance with Article 96 of the Charter and Article 65 of the Statute of the Court. The opinion given by the Court shall be accepted as decisive by the parties."

11. On 10 July yet another lawsuit was filed against the Special Rapporteur by one of the lawyers mentioned in the magazine article referred to in paragraph 5 above, based on precisely the same passages of the interview and claiming damages in an amount of M$60 million (US$24 million). On 11 July, the Secretary-General issued a note corresponding to the one of 7 March 1997 (see para. 6 above) and also communicated a note verbale with essentially the same text to the Permanent Representative of Malaysia with the request that it be presented formally to the competent Malaysian court by the Government.

12. On 23 October and 21 November 1997, new plaintiffs filed a third and fourth lawsuit against the Special Rapporteur for M$100 million (US$40 million) and M$60 million (US$24 million) respectively. On 27 October and 22 November 1997, the Secretary-General issued identical certificates of the Special Rapporteur's immunity.

13. On 7 November 1997, the Secretary-General advised the Prime Minister of Malaysia that a difference might have arisen between the United Nations and the Government of Malaysia and about the possibility of resorting to the International Court of Justice pursuant to Section 30 of the Convention. Nonetheless on 19 February 1998, the Federal Court of Malaysia denied Mr. Cumaraswamy's application for leave to appeal stating that he is neither a sovereign nor a full-fledged diplomat but merely "an unpaid, part-time provider of information".

40. Pursuant to Article 105 of the Charter of the United Nations:

"1. The Organization shall enjoy in the territory of each of its Members such privileges and immunities as are necessary for the fulfilment of its purposes.

2. Representatives of the Members of the United Nations and officials of the Organization shall similarly enjoy such privileges and immunities as are necessary for the independent exercise of their functions in connexion with the Organization.

3. The General Assembly may make recommendations with a view to determining the details of the application of paragraphs 1 and 2 of this Article or may propose conventions to the Members of the United Nations for this purpose."

Acting in accordance with Article 105 of the Charter, the General Assembly approved the General Convention on 13 February 1946 and proposed it for accession by each Member of the United Nations. Malaysia became a party to the General Convention, without reservation, on 28 October 1957.

41. The General Convention contains an Article VI entitled "Experts on

Missions for the United Nations". It is comprised of two Sections (22 and 23). Section 22 provides:

> "Experts (other than officials coming within the scope of Article V) performing missions for the United Nations shall be accorded such privileges and immunities as are necessary for the independent exercise of their functions during the period of their missions, including time spent on journeys in connection with their missions. In particular they shall be accorded:
>
> ...
>
> (b) in respect of words spoken or written and acts done by them in the course of the performance of their mission, immunity from legal process of every kind. This immunity from legal process shall continue to be accorded notwithstanding that the persons concerned are no longer employed on missions for the United Nations. ..."

42. In its Advisory Opinion of 14 December 1989 on the *Applicability of Article VI, Section 22, of the Convention on the Privileges and Immunities of the United Nations*, the Court examined the applicability of Section 22 *ratione personae, ratione temporis* and *ratione loci*.

In this context the Court stated:

> "The purpose of Section 22 is ... evident, namely, to enable the United Nations to entrust missions to persons who do not have the status of an official of the Organization, and to guarantee them 'such privileges and immunities as are necessary for the independent exercise of their functions ...'. The essence of the matter lies not in their administrative position but in the nature of their mission." (*I.C.J. Reports 1989*, p. 194, para. 47)

In that same Advisory Opinion, the Court concluded that a Special Rapporteur who is appointed by the Sub-Commission on Prevention of Discrimination and Protection of Minorities and is entrusted with a research mission must be regarded as an expert on mission within the meaning of Article VI, Section 22, of the General Convention (*ibid.*, p. 197, para. 55).

43. The same conclusion must be drawn with regard to Special Rapporteurs appointed by the Human Rights Commission, of which the Sub-Commission is a subsidiary organ. It may be observed that Special Rapporteurs of the Commission usually are entrusted not only with a research mission but also with the task of monitoring human rights violations and reporting on them. But what is decisive is that they have been entrusted with a mission by the United Nations and are therefore entitled to the privileges and immunities provided for in Article VI, Section 22, that safeguard the independent exercise of their functions.

44. By a letter of 21 April 1994, the Chairman of the Commission informed the Assistant Secretary-General for Human Rights of Mr. Cumaraswamy's appointment as Special Rapporteur. The mandate of the Special Rapporteur is contained in resolution 1994/41 of the Commission entitled "Independence and Impartiality of the Judiciary, Jurors and Assessors and the Independence of Lawyers". This resolution was endorsed by the Council in its decision 1994/251 of 22 July 1994. The Special Rapporteur's mandate consists of the following tasks:

"(a) to inquire into any substantial allegations transmitted to him or her and report his or her conclusions thereon;

(b) to identify and record not only attacks on the independence of the judiciary, lawyers and court officials but also progress achieved in protecting and enhancing their independence, and make concrete recommendations, including accommodations for the provision of advisory services or technical assistance when they are requested by the State concerned;

(c) to study, for the purpose of making proposals, important and topical questions of principle with a view to protecting and enhancing the independence of the judiciary and lawyers".

45. The Commission extended by resolution 1997/23 of 11 April 1997 the Special Rapporteur's mandate for a further period of three years.

In the light of these circumstances, the Court finds that Mr. Cumaraswamy must be regarded as an expert on mission within the meaning of Article VI, Section 22, as from 21 April 1994, that by virtue of this capacity the provisions of this Section were applicable to him at the time of his statements at issue, and that they continue to be applicable.

46. The Court observes that Malaysia has acknowledged that Mr. Cumaraswamy, as Special Rapporteur of the Commission, is an expert on mission and that such experts enjoy the privileges and immunities provided for under the General Convention in their relations with States parties, including those of which they are nationals or on the territory of which they reside. Malaysia and the United Nations are in full agreement on these points, as are the other States participating in the proceedings.

*

47. The Court will now consider whether the immunity provided for in Section 22(b) applies to Mr. Cumaraswamy in the specific circumstances of the case; namely, whether the words used by him in the interview, as published in the article in *International Commercial Litigation* (November issue 1995), were spoken in the course of the performance of his mission, and whether he was therefore immune from legal process with respect to these words.

48. During the oral proceedings, the Solicitor General of Malaysia contended that the issue put by the Council before the Court does not include this question. She stated that the correct interpretation of the words used by the Council in its request

"does not extend to inviting the Court to decide whether, assuming the Secretary-General to have had the authority to determine the character of the Special Rapporteur's action, he had properly exercised that authority"

and added:

"Malaysia observes that the word used was '*applicability*' not '*application*'. 'Applicability' means 'whether the provision is applicable to someone' not 'how it is to be applied'."

49. The Court does not share this interpretation. It follows from the terms of the request that the Council wishes to be informed of the Court's opinion as to whether Section 22(b) is applicable to the

Special Rapporteur, in the circumstances set out in paragraphs 1 to 15 of the note of the Secretary-General and whether, therefore, the Secretary-General's finding that the Special Rapporteur acted in the course of the performance of his mission is correct.

50. In the process of determining whether a particular expert on mission is entitled, in the prevailing circumstances, to the immunity provided for in Section 22(b), the Secretary-General of the United Nations has a pivotal role to play. The Secretary-General, as the chief administrative officer of the Organization, has the authority and the responsibility to exercise the necessary protection where required. This authority has been recognized by the Court when it stated:

> "Upon examination of the character of the functions entrusted to the Organization and of the nature of the missions of its agents, it becomes clear that the capacity of the Organization to exercise a measure of functional protection of its agents arises by necessary intendment out of the Charter." (*Reparation for Injuries Suffered in the Service of the United Nations, Advisory Opinion, I.C.J. Reports 1949*, p. 184)

51. Article VI, Section 23, of the General Convention provides that "[p]rivileges and immunities are granted to experts in the interests of the United Nations and not for the personal benefit of the individuals themselves". In exercising protection of United Nations experts, the Secretary-General is therefore protecting the mission with which the expert is entrusted. In that respect, the Secretary-General has the primary responsibility and authority to protect the interests of the Organization and its agents, including experts on mission. As the Court held:

> "In order that the agent may perform his duties satisfactorily, he must feel that this protection is assured to him by the Organization, and that he may count on it. To ensure the independence of the agent, and, consequently, the independent action of the Organization itself, it is essential that in performing his duties he need not have to rely on any other protection than that of the Organization ...." (*Ibid.*, p. 183)

52. The determination whether an agent of the Organization has acted in the course of the performance of his mission depends upon the facts of a particular case. In the present case, the Secretary-General, or the Legal Counsel of the United Nations on his behalf, has on numerous occasions informed the Government of Malaysia of his finding that Mr. Cumaraswamy had spoken the words quoted in the article in *International Commercial Litigation* in his capacity as Special Rapporteur of the Commission and that he consequently was entitled to immunity from "every kind" of legal process.

53. As is clear from the written and oral pleadings of the United Nations, the Secretary-General was reinforced in this view by the fact that it has become standard practice of Special Rapporteurs of the Commission to have contact with the media. This practice was confirmed by the High Commissioner for Human Rights who, in a letter dated 2 October 1998, included in the dossier, wrote that: "it is more common than not for Special Rapporteurs to speak to the press about matters pertaining to their investigations, thereby keeping the general public informed of their work".

54. As noted above (see paragraph 13), Mr. Cumaraswamy was explicitly referred to several times in the article "Malaysian Justice on Trial" in *International Commercial Litigation* in his capacity as United Nations Special Rapporteur on the Independence of Judges and Lawyers. In his reports to the Commission (see paragraph 18 above), Mr. Cumaraswamy had set out his methods of work, expressed concern about the independence of the Malaysian judiciary, and referred to the civil lawsuits initiated against him. His third report noted that the Legal Counsel of the United Nations had informed the Government of Malaysia that he had spoken in the performance of his mission and was therefore entitled to immunity from legal process.

55. As noted in paragraph 18 above, in its various resolutions the Commission took note of the Special Rapporteur's reports and of his methods of work. In 1997, it extended his mandate for another three years (see paragraphs 18 and 45 above). The Commission presumably would not have so acted if it had been of the opinion that Mr. Cumaraswamy had gone beyond his mandate and had given the interview to *International Commercial Litigation* outside the course of his functions. Thus the Secretary-General was able to find support for his findings in the Commission's position.

56. The Court is not called upon in the present case to pass upon the aptness of the terms used by the Special Rapporteur or his assessment of the situation. In any event, in view of all the circumstances of this case, elements of which are set out in paragraphs 1 to 15 of the note by the Secretary-General, the Court is of the opinion that the Secretary-General correctly found that Mr. Cumaraswamy, in speaking the words quoted in the article in *International Commercial Litigation*, was acting in the course of the performance of his mission as Special Rapporteur of the Commission. Consequently, Article VI, Section 22*(b)*, of the General Convention is applicable to him in the present case and affords Mr. Cumaraswamy immunity from legal process of every kind.

* *

57. The Court will now deal with the second part of the Council's question, namely, "the legal obligations of Malaysia in this case".

58. Malaysia maintains that it is premature to deal with the question of its obligations. It is of the view that the obligation to ensure that the requirements of Section 22 of the Convention are met is an obligation of result and not of means to be employed in achieving that result. It further states that Malaysia has complied with its obligation under Section 34 of the General Convention, which provides that a party to the Convention must be "in a position under its own law to give effect to [its] terms", by enacting the necessary legislation; finally it contends that the Malaysian courts have not yet reached a final decision as to Mr. Cumaraswamy's entitlement to immunity from legal process.

59. The Court wishes to point out that the request for an advisory opinion refers to "the legal obligations of Malaysia in this case". The difference which has arisen between the United Nations and Malaysia originated in the Government of Malaysia not having informed the competent Malaysian judicial authorities of the Secretary-General's finding that Mr. Cumaraswamy had spoken the words at issue in the course of the performance of his mission and was, therefore, entitled to immunity from legal process

(see paragraph 17 above). It is as from the time of this omission that the question before the Court must be answered.

60. As the Court has observed, the Secretary-General, as the chief administrative officer of the Organization, has the primary responsibility to safeguard the interests of the Organization; to that end, it is up to him to assess whether its agents acted within the scope of their functions and, where he so concludes, to protect these agents, including experts on mission, by asserting their immunity. This means that the Secretary-General has the authority and responsibility to inform the Government of a member State of his finding and, where appropriate, to request it to act accordingly and, in particular, to request it to bring his finding to the knowledge of the local courts if acts of an agent have given or may give rise to court proceedings.

61. When national courts are seised of a case in which the immunity of a United Nations agent is in issue, they should immediately be notified of any finding by the Secretary-General concerning that immunity. That finding, and its documentary expression, creates a presumption which can only be set aside for the most compelling reasons and is thus to be given the greatest weight by national courts.

The governmental authorities of a party to the General Convention are therefore under an obligation to convey such information to the national courts concerned, since a proper application of the Convention by them is dependent on such information.

Failure to comply with this obligation, among others, could give rise to the institution of proceedings under Article VIII, Section 30, of the General Convention.

62. The Court concludes that the Government of Malaysia had an obligation, under Article 105 of the Charter and under the General Convention, to inform its courts of the position taken by the Secretary-General. According to a well-established rule of international law, the conduct of any organ of a State must be regarded as an act of that State. This rule, which is of a customary character, is reflected in Article 6 of the Draft Articles on State Responsibility adopted provisionally by the International Law Commission on first reading, which provides:

"The conduct of an organ of the State shall be considered as an act of that State under international law, whether that organ belongs to the constituent, legislative, executive, judicial or other power, whether its functions are of an international or an internal character, and whether it holds a superior or a subordinated position in the organization of the State." (*Yearbook of the International Law Commission*, 1973, Vol. II, p. 193)

Because the Government did not transmit the Secretary-General's finding to the competent courts, and the Minister for Foreign Affairs did not refer to it in his own certificate, Malaysia did not comply with the above-mentioned obligation.

63. Section 22(b) of the General Convention explicitly states that experts on mission shall be accorded immunity from legal process of every kind in respect of words spoken or written and acts done by them in the course of the performance of their mission. By necessary implication, questions of immunity are therefore preliminary issues which must be expeditiously decided *in limine litis*. This is a generally recognized principle of

procedural law, and Malaysia was under an obligation to respect it. The Malaysian courts did not rule *in limine litis* on the immunity of the Special Rapporteur (see paragraph 17 above), thereby nullifying the essence of the immunity rule contained in Section 22*(b)*. Moreover, costs were taxed to Mr. Cumaraswamy while the question of immunity was still unresolved. As indicated above, the conduct of an organ of a State – even an organ independent of the executive power – must be regarded as an act of that State. Consequently, Malaysia did not act in accordance with its obligations under international law.

*

64. In addition, the immunity from legal process to which the Court finds Mr. Cumaraswamy entitled entails holding Mr. Cumaraswamy financially harmless for any costs imposed upon him by the Malaysian courts, in particular taxed costs.

*

65. According to Article VIII, Section 30, of the General Convention, the opinion given by the Court shall be accepted as decisive by the parties to the dispute. Malaysia has acknowledged its obligations under Section 30.

Since the Court holds that Mr. Cumaraswamy is an expert on mission who under Section 22*(b)* is entitled to immunity from legal process, the Government of Malaysia is obligated to communicate this advisory opinion to the competent Malaysian courts, in order that Malaysia's international obligations be given effect and Mr. Cumaraswamy's immunity be respected.

*

66. Finally, the Court wishes to point out that the question of immunity from legal process is distinct from the issue of compensation for any damages incurred as a result of acts performed by the United Nations or by its agents acting in their official capacity.

The United Nations may be required to bear responsibility for the damage arising from such acts. However, as is clear from Article VIII, Section 29, of the General Convention, any such claims against the United Nations shall not be dealt with by national courts but shall be settled in accordance with the appropriate modes of settlement that "[t]he United Nations shall make provisions for" pursuant to Section 29.

Furthermore, it need hardly be said that all agents of the United Nations, in whatever official capacity they act, must take care not to exceed the scope of their functions, and should so comport themselves as to avoid claims against the United Nations.

Notes

- What is this person's job and/or function? Why does the court reach the conclusion that he is qualified as an expert on mission? Is that decision based on the court's assessment, or does the court simply accept his status as asserted by the Secretary-General?
- Why is the Secretary-General the responsible officer in this matter? Surely the Council and Commission have a role to play?

- Previously, the court held that an expert on mission may have immunity from his or her state of nationality.[25] Why would that be a question? If individuals must have immunity in order to discharge their function, then why is the nationality of the expert a matter of concern?
- Consider again the reasoning for having immunity in the first place. Is the immunity granted as a necessary prerequisite for independence? Or is it necessary in order that the expert may "feel" independent? And in the latter case, would that lead to a subjective regime of immunity?
- Does this litigation really interfere with the Special Rapporteur's work?
- Were the acts of the individual truly within the scope of his employment? And what entity (or what organ of an entity) has the capacity to make a definitive decision on this matter? Could that decision ever be ignored?
- Why does the court invoke the Draft Articles on State Responsibility?

The case of lawyers serving as defense counsel for persons accused of international crimes before international tribunals presents a small challenge for classifying this role. On the one hand, these individuals are certainly experts who are not employed by the organization, yet provide an indispensable expertise and potentially need to be protected from interference. On the other hand, these individuals are employed directly by their clients, and must be independent of the organization and operate to challenge the actions of the organization. The following case was heard at the Appeals Chamber of the International Criminal Tribunal for Rwanda (ICTR):

Bagosora, Ntabakuze & Nsengiyumva v. Prosecutor, Case No. ICTR-98-41-A, Decision on Aloys Ntabakuze's Motion for Injunctions, Against the Government of Rwanda Regarding the Arrest and Investigation of Lead Counsel Peter Erlinder
International Criminal Tribunal for Rwanda, Appeals Chamber, 6 October 2010[26]

A. Background

2. On 28 May 2010, Erlinder was arrested in Kigali by Rwandan authorities on allegations of "genocide denial". [footnote omitted] At the time of his arrest, Erlinder was in Rwanda for reasons unrelated to his work at the tribunal. [footnote omitted]

3. On 31 May 2010, the Registrar of the Tribunal ("Registrar") addressed a *note verbale* to the Rwandan Ministry of Foreign Affairs and Cooperation requesting clarification of the motives of Erlinder's arrest and, in particular, inquiring whether the arrest was related to Erlinder's mandate as Defence Counsel

---

25 *See* Applicability of Article VI, Section 22, of the Convention on the Privileges and Immunities of the United Nations ["Mazilu case"], Advisory Opinion, 1989 ICJ Reps. 177 (International Court of Justice, 15 December 1989).

26 From the United Nations International Residual Mechanism for Criminal Tribunals, archives of the International Criminal Tribunal for Rwanda.

at the tribunal. [footnote omitted] On 2 June 2010, the Prosecutor General of Rwanda responded to the *note verbale* indicating that the arrest of Erlinder was "not at all related to his assignments at the ICTR".[footnote omitted]

4. On 3 June 2010, Ntabakuze filed the present Motion.

5. On 7 June 2010, the High Court of Gasabo (Rwanda), sitting in Kabuga and at first instance, found that "the Prosecution's grounds establishing that there is prima facie evidence of guilt against Carl Peter Erlinder, charged with the crime of denying and minimizing the genocide and that of spreading rumours likely to disrupt the security of Rwandans, have merit" and ordered that Erlinder be provisionally detained for 30 days. [footnote omitted] In the course of the provisional release hearing, the Rwandan Prosecutor's allegations against Erlinder focused on his writings but also made specific references to Erlinder's statements as Defence Counsel before the Tribunal. [footnote omitted] Upon review of the Decision of the High Court of Gasabo, the Registrar sent a second note verbale to the Rwandan Ministry of Foreign Affairs and Cooperation requesting a formal copy of the charges against Erlinder. [footnote omitted]

6. On 9 June 2010, the Appeals Chamber instructed the Registrar to request the assistance of the Rwandan authorities in obtaining information regarding the nature and basis of the charges against Erlinder. [footnote omitted] The Registrar immediately transmitted the Appeals Chamber's Order of 9 June 2010 to the Rwandan Ministry of Foreign Affairs and Cooperation via a third *note verbale*. [footnote omitted] On 11 June 2010, the Registrar filed submissions pursuant to Rule 33(B) of the Rules of Procedure and Evidence of the Tribunal ("Rules") setting out the steps taken thus far. [footnote omitted]

7. On 11 June 2010, the Prosecution responded to the Motion, arguing that it should be dismissed in its entirety. [footnote omitted] Ntabakuze filed his Reply on 15 June 2010. [footnote omitted]

8. On 15 June 2010, the Registrar filed further submissions indicating that the Registry had consulted with the Office of Legal Affairs of the United Nations regarding the possible immunity of Erlinder on the basis of the Decision of the High Court of Gasabo and that the Office of Legal Affairs had advised the Tribunal to assert Erlinder's immunity without delay. [footnote omitted] The Registrar accordingly sent a fourth note verbale to the Rwandan Ministry of Foreign Affairs and Cooperation asserting that Erlinder benefited from immunity and requesting his immediate release. [footnote omitted]

…

C. Discussion

18. The Appeals Chamber emphasizes that it will not lightly intervene in the domestic jurisdiction of a state. As the Chamber seized of Ntabakuze's appeal, however, it has the duty to ensure the fairness of the proceedings in this case. To this end, it has competence under Article 28 of the Statute of the Tribunal ("Statute") and Rules 54 and 107 of the Rules to issue any related order. Accordingly, the Appeals Chamber will only consider whether Rwanda's exercise of its domestic jurisdiction in Erlinder's case threatens the fairness of the proceedings

in this case. The Appeals Chamber will therefore not address Ntabakuze's arguments that are not relevant to this enquiry. The Appeals chamber thus turns to consider Ntabakuze's arguments that Erlinder benefits from functional immunity and that the legal process against Erlinder in Rwanda will impede his ability to adequately represent Ntabakuze in this case, thereby resulting in the infringement of Ntabakuze's right to a fair trial.

19. Article 29 of the Statute, addressing the status, privileges, and immunities of the Tribunal, provides that:

> Other persons, including the accused, required at the seat or meeting place of the International Tribunal for Rwanda shall be accorded such treatment as is necessary for the proper functioning of the International Tribunal for Rwanda. [footnote 44 – Statute, Article 29(4)]

The Appeals Chamber considers that Defence Counsel fall within the category of persons required at the seat or meeting place of the Tribunal and as such must be accorded such treatment as is necessary for the proper functioning of the Tribunal. The proper functioning of the Tribunal requires that Defence Counsel be able to investigate and present arguments in support of their client's case without fear of repercussions against them for these actions. Without such assurance, Defence Counsel cannot be reasonably expected to adequately represent their clients.

20. Additionally, the Memorandum of Understanding Between the United Nations and the Republic of Rwanda to Regulate Matters of Mutual Concern Relating to the Office in Rwanda of the International Tribunal for Rwanda of 3 June 1999 ("Memorandum of Understanding"), [footnote omitted] which governs the privileges and immunities of the Tribunal's operations in Rwanda, should also be taken into account. Of particular relevance to the present situation, the Memorandum of Understanding provides that the government of Rwanda shall extend:

> To other persons assigned to the Office whose names shall be communicated to the Government of Rwanda for that purpose, the privileges and immunities accorded to experts on mission for the United Nations, in accordance with Article VI of the Convention. [footnote omitted]

With respect to whether Defence Counsel fall within the meaning of "other persons assigned to the Office", the Appeals Chamber notes that while Defence Counsel are not employees of the Tribunal they are assigned or appointed by the Tribunal to their positions as Defence Counsel. Furthermore, the procedures associated with Defence Counsel going on mission to Rwanda indicate that the Tribunal considers Defence Counsel to be acting in official capacity and on assignment in association with the Tribunal. For instance, Defence Counsel may request logistical support from the Tribunal while performing their missions in Rwanda. [footnote omitted]

21. The Appeals Chamber further notes that the Memorandum of Understanding sets out the rights and facilities granted to the Tribunal by the Government of Rwanda on its territory. These rights and facilities include various access rights such as the "right to question victims and witnesses, to gather evidence and all useful information and

to conduct investigations in the field". [footnote omitted] The Appeals Chamber considers that, as the rights of access to undertake investigations are fundamental to the preparation of the Defence case, in concluding the Memorandum of Understanding it was contemplated that it applied to Defence Counsel as well as officials of the Tribunal. Indeed, if the Memorandum of Understanding did not extend to Defence Counsel, the right of equality of arms would be meaningless as the Defence would have no guarantee of access to potential witnesses and evidence to allow them to prepare their case.

22. In light of the procedural practice of the Tribunal as well as the purpose of the Memorandum of Understanding, the Appeals Chamber finds that Defence Counsel fall within the meaning of "other persons assigned to the Office" and therefore are to be accorded the privileges and immunities due to experts performing missions for the United Nations pursuant to Article VI of the Convention. [footnote 49 – Convention on the Privileges and Immunities of the United Nations, adopted by General Assembly Resolution A/RES/22(I)A, 13 February 1946]

23. This is further supported by the interpretation of the International Court of Justice as to who can be considered an expert according to Section 22 of the Convention:

> The purpose of Section 22 is nevertheless evident, namely, to enable the United Nations to entrust missions to persons who do not have the status of an official of the Organization, and to guarantee them "such privileges and immunities as are necessary for the independent exercise of their functions". The experts thus appointed or elected may or may not be remunerated, may or may not have a contract, may be given a task requiring work over a lengthy period or a short time. The essence of the matter lies not in their administrative position but in the nature of their mission. [footnote 50 – Applicability of Article VI, Section 22, of the Convention on the Privileges and Immunities of the United Nations, Advisory Opinion, I.C.J. Reports 1989, para. 47.]

Applying this reasoning to Defence Counsel on mission, the Appeals Chamber concludes that they are to be considered experts on mission within the meaning of the Convention. While Defence Counsel are not officials of the Tribunal, some guarantee is necessary for the independent exercise of their Tribunal assigned functions which are integral to its functioning. Accordingly, the nature of their mission, which is to engage in preparations for proceedings before the Tribunal, is the defining factor in granting them such privileges and immunities as granted to experts on mission – not their administrative status with the Tribunal.

24. The Appeals Chamber also notes that the response of the Prosecutor General of Rwanda to the Registrar's invocation of the Memorandum of Understanding as affording to persons carrying out functions on behalf of the Tribunal, such as Defence Counsel, the immunities provided for in Article VI of the conventions [footnote omitted] reflects support for the application of the relevant provisions of the Memorandum

of Understanding to Defence Counsel of the Tribunal operating in Rwanda:

> [...] I wish to state on record, that [Erlinder's] arrest is not at all related to his assignments at the ICTR and that we remain in full compliance with the provisions of the memorandum of understanding [g]overn[]ing our cooperation. [footnote omitted]

25. Article VI of the Convention provides that experts performing missions for the United Nations shall be accorded such privileges and immunities as are necessary for the independent exercise of their functions during the period of their missions. In particular, Section 22 of Article VI of the Convention, invoked in the Registrar's *note verbale* of 15 June 2010, [footnote omitted] provides that:

> Experts (other than officials coming within the scope of Article V) performing missions for the United Nations shall be accorded such privileges and immunities as are necessary for the independent exercise of their functions during the period of their missions, including the time spent on journeys in connection with their missions. In particular they shall be accorded:
>
> (a) immunity from personal arrest or detention and from seizure of their personal baggage;
>
> (b) in respect of words spoken or written and acts done by them in the course of the performance of their mission, immunity from legal process of every kind. This immunity from legal process shall continue to be accorded notwithstanding that the persons concerned are no longer employed on missions for the United Nations; [...]

26. Accordingly, Defence Counsel benefit from immunity from personal arrest or detention while performing their duties assigned by the Tribunal and also with respect to words spoken or written and acts done by them in the course of the performance of their duties as Defence counsel before the Tribunal, in order to allow for the proper functioning of the Tribunal in accordance with Article 29 of the Statute. In light of this, the Appeals Chamber turns to consider whether Erlinder benefited from immunity in relation to his arrest and investigation in Rwanda.

27. The Appeals Chamber recalls that, at the time of his arrest, Erlinder was not in Rwanda in his capacity as Ntabakuze's Defence Counsel. He was therefore not immune from personal arrest or detention as provided for under Section 22(a) of Article VI of the Convention. Nonetheless, Erlinder benefits from immunity from legal process in respect of words spoken or written and acts done by him in the course of his representation of Ntabakuze before the Tribunal.

28. The vast majority of the material submitted by Rwanda as forming the basis for the investigation of Erlinder consists of articles written in Erlinder's private or academic capacity on issues ranging from the Rwandan presidential candidate, Victoire Ingabire, [footnote omitted] the alleged role played by Rwanda in the Democratic Republic of the Congo, [footnote omitted] the alleged role of the Rwandan Patriotic Front ("RPF") and President Paul Kagame in the shooting down of President Juvénal Habyarimana's plane and the ensuing genocide, [footnote omitted] and the alleged related cover-up by the United States and the United Kingdom. [footnote omitted] Some of the documents

are also media reports by other authors on similar issues referring to Erlinder, [footnote omitted] and conference programmes and notes on conference proceedings in which Erlinder participated. There is also a copy of a case filed in the United States against President Paul Kagame and others by the widows of Presidents Habyarimana and Ntaryarnira whom Erlinder is representing. [footnote omitted] While some of these documents comment upon the *Bagosora et al.* case and in some cases refer to evidence tendered in that case, [footnote omitted] they constitute private commentary on the case rather than words spoken or written in the course of Erlinder's representation of Ntabakuze in the *Bagosora et al.* case. Accordingly, Erlinder does not benefit from immunity from legal process in respect of those materials.

29. However, there is one document entitled "Military I – Convicting Major Ntabakuze Would be an 'Offence to Common Sense'" which is an Hirondelle News article dated 31 May 2007 reporting on the closing arguments Erlinder made on behalf of Ntabakuze in the *Bagosora et al.* case. [footnote omitted] The article summarises Erlinder's arguments before the Tribunal and quotes some of his submissions in the case. The Appeals Chamber finds that proceeding against Erlinder on the basis of submissions he made in the course of Ntabakuze's closing arguments before the Tribunal violates his functional immunity from legal process for words spoken or written in the course of his functions before the Tribunal. The Appeals Chamber considers that this interferes with the proper functioning of the Tribunal, which requires that Defence Counsel be free to advance arguments in their client's case without fear of prosecution.

30. The Appeals Chamber recalls Rwanda's intention to respect Erlinder's functional immunity, [footnote omitted] and stresses the need to respect it. Ntabakuze's right to a fair trial cannot be protected where Erlinder faces investigation or prosecution in Rwanda on the basis of words spoken or written in the course of his representation of Ntabakuze before the Tribunal.

Notes

- What is this person's job and/or function? Was he hired by the tribunal? Was he advising or assisting the tribunal? How is this case similar to other experts and different from other experts?
- Who decided on his immunity, and through what process? How does that compare to the *Cumaraswamy* case? Was immunity in the *Erlinder* case above handled correctly?
- Is the conclusion correct? Perhaps it is interesting to observe that initially the ICTR held that he was immune, and only later issued the decision above with a more nuanced view.
- What was the effect of this decision? Any immunity that Erlinder would enjoy is immunity that he would derive from the international organization because it was functionally necessary for him to have immunity in order to perform his expert duties. Does the decision by the ICTR permit the government to interfere with his expert duties? What is the correct scope of the immunity?

8.3.5 Waiver

Even if an organization enjoys immunity, or an individual derives immunity from the organization, this situation only grants a right to the organization to claim its immunity. It does not require the organization to exercise its immunity. This is particularly significant for individuals. The right to immunity does not belong to them, but rather to the organization. (Although representatives to organizations will also derive immunity from their state.) Thus, an organization could waive the immunity that one of its employees would otherwise enjoy. Waiver of immunity is clearly a major decision because of the gravity of exercising jurisdiction over an international person or its employee, so such a waiver must be made expressly.

CHAPTER 9

Responsibility

9.1 RESPONSIBILITY IN INTERNATIONAL LAW

This chapter concerns the "responsibility" of international organizations. The notion of responsibility is not always immediately obvious to most students. They might wonder why this additional step is necessary in seeking a remedy. Just because a norm of international law has been violated, does not mean that we can point to any particular state that should bear the burden, the "guilt" for lack of a better term, for the violation. Much like guilt in criminal law, responsibility in international law is the need to identify whether a state has violated its international obligations. This is equally true for international organizations, but, due to their nature, it might be somewhat more difficult to establish responsibility for an international organization. Consider when an international organization adopts an act that falls within its powers and has obligatory legal effect, and the state complies, but such compliance violates a different, distinct norm of international law. Is the state or the organization to blame? Surely the state was obliged to comply, yet the organization might not have been bound by the same obligation the state was. Even worse, what if the state had used the fact that the organization was not bound as a means to adopt a decision the state would otherwise be prohibited from adopting? And in so doing, pass the blame to the organization?

One preliminary question is whether organizations can even claim that other actors have violated international law. It could be that they are charged with certain duties and fulfill those duties, but not that they engage with states as equals. In this regard, consider the *Reparations* case again. From the case, it seems clear that an international organization, or at least the UN, can invoke the responsibility of a state for violations of international law.

9.1.1 Possibility for responsibility

The next question is whether organizations can be held responsible if they violate international law. In 2002, the ILC placed the topic of international organization responsibility on its agenda and the Draft Articles on the Responsibility of International Organizations were completed in 2011.[1] This book has already referred to the

---

1 *See* International Law Commission, Draft articles on the responsibility of international organizations, II(2) Yearbook of the International Law Commission (2011), UN Doc. A/CN.4/SER.A/2011/Add.1 (Part 2).

Draft Articles several times for different issues, but their underlying purpose was to codify the rules on the responsibility of international organizations.

During the work on the Draft Articles, the ILC identified the need to distinguish states from organizations in terms of responsibility, and perhaps also to formulate special rules on the responsibility of international organizations. At first, it was unclear whether international organizations could attract responsibility, given their restrictive competence to undertake certain delineated tasks. Surely it was not possible for them to violate international law at all? As of 1963, the ILC Special Rapporteur, Roberto Ago, argued that was the case.[2] However, by 1996, the UN Secretary-General accepted that the organization could bear responsibility.[3]

> 6. The international responsibility of the United Nations for the activities of United Nations forces is an attribute of its international legal personality and its capacity to bear international rights and obligations. It is also a reflection of the principle of State responsibility – widely accepted to be applicable to international organizations – that damage caused in breach of an international obligation and which is attributable to the State (or to the Organization), entails the international responsibility of the State (or of the Organization) and its liability in compensation.

In turn, the ILC eventually also concluded that:

International Law Commission,
Draft articles on the responsibility of international organizations
II(2) Yearbook of the International Law Commission (2011)
UN Doc. A/CN.4/SER.A/2011/Add.1 (Part 2)[4]

Article 43. Invocation of responsibility by an injured
State or international organization

A State or an international organization is entitled as an injured State or an injured international organization to invoke the responsibility of another international organization if the obligation breached is owed to:
(a) that State or the former international organization individually;

---

2 *See* International Law Commission, Sub-Committee on State Responsibility, Summary record of the second meeting (Monday, 7 January 1963, at 3 p.m.), II Yearbook of the International Law Commission 229 (1963), UN Doc. A/CN.4/SER.A/1963/ADD.1, Annex I, Report by Mr. Roberto Ago (16 January 1963), UN Doc. A/CN.4/152, Appendix I.
3 *See* UN General Assembly, Report of the Secretary-General, Financing of the United Nations Protection Force, the United Nations Confidence Restoration Operation in Croatia, the United Nations Preventive Deployment Force and the United Nations Peace Forces Headquarters, UN Doc. A/51/389 p. 4 (20 September 1996).
4 From the Yearbook of the International Law Commission, by the International Law Commission © 2011 United Nations. Reprinted with the permission of the United Nations.

(b) a group of States or international organizations including that State or the former international organization, or the international community as a whole, and the breach of the obligation:
  (i) specially affects that State or that international organization; or
  (ii) is of such a character as radically to change the position of all the other States and international organizations to which the obligation is owed with respect to the further performance of the obligation.

In studying the responsibility of international organizations, this chapter will generally follow the Draft Articles, although some articles will be reordered or regrouped for clarity and brevity.

9.1.2 General and special rules of responsibility

The Draft Articles on International Organization Responsibility are, by default, general rules. There may be cases where an organization alters the rule and imposes a different rule on responsibility, tailored for that organization. Alternatively, there does not seem to a prohibition on a particular rule of responsibility for an organization being formed by customary international law. While examples may be difficult to imagine, perhaps the EU would fall into such a category:

**International Law Commission,
Draft articles on the responsibility of international organizations
II(2) Yearbook of the International Law Commission (2011)
UN Doc. A/CN.4/SER.A/2011/Add.1 (Part 2)**[5]

Article 64 Lex specialis

These draft articles do not apply where and to the extent that the conditions for the existence of an internationally wrongful act or the content or implementation of the international responsibility of an international organization, or of a State in connection with the conduct of an international organization, are governed by special rules of international law. Such special rules of international law may be contained in the rules of the organization applicable to the relations between an international organization and its members.

Article 65 Questions of international responsibility not regulated by these draft articles

The applicable rules of international law continue to govern questions concerning the responsibility of an international organization or a State for an internationally wrongful act to the extent that they are not regulated by these draft articles.

---

5 Ibid.

Notes

- Does this article mean that states could draft a *lex specialis* rule on responsibility for an organization that permits it to violate international law?
- Does it mean that states could create such a *lex specialis* rule in order to delegate their responsibility to the organization, and thus escape responsibility for unlawful behavior?
- Does this article exempt the organization from the *lex generalis* rule in relation to violations of international law against its members or states not members of the organization? Or to other organizations or subjects of international law?

9.2 GENERAL RULES ON RESPONSIBILITY OF INTERNATIONAL ORGANIZATIONS

Keeping in mind that there may be *lex specialis* rules for any of the following general rules in the Draft Articles, we will now go through some of the key substantive provisions.

The general rule for establishing responsibility of an organization comprises two elements:

**International Law Commission,
Draft articles on the responsibility of international organizations
II(2) Yearbook of the International Law Commission (2011)
UN Doc. A/CN.4/SER.A/2011/Add.1 (Part 2)[6]**

Article 4 Elements of an internationally wrongful act of an international organization

There is an internationally wrongful act of an international organization when conduct consisting of an action or omission:
(a) is attributable to that organization under international law; and
(b) constitutes a breach of an international obligation of that organization.

The rule does not contain an element of damage in order to establish responsibility. Certainly, damage is important criterion, but it pertains to the substance of the violation, i.e. the primary obligation being violated, not to the establishment of responsibility.[7]

---

6 *Ibid.*
7 International Law Commission, II(2) Yearbook of the International Law Commission, para. 77 (2001), article 2, commentary para. (9).

9.2.1 Existence of a binding international obligation

The first element in the Draft Articles is the requirement that there is an obligation binding the organization under international law and that this obligation is violated. Within this element, one question is whether there is an obligation that binds the organization:

**International Law Commission,
Draft articles on the responsibility of international organizations
II(2) Yearbook of the International Law Commission (2011)
UN Doc. A/CN.4/SER.A/2011/Add.1 (Part 2)**[8]

Article 11 International obligation in force for an international organization

> An act of an international organization does not constitute a breach of an international obligation unless the organization is bound by the obligation in question at the time the act occurs.

What rules of international law bind international organizations? Recalling Chapter 2 on the law of treaties, we know that an international organization can be bound by a treaty obligation to which it freely consents. However, can it also be bound to the general rules of customary international law and general principles of law just as states are?

**International Law Commission,
Draft articles on the responsibility of international organizations
II(2) Yearbook of the International Law Commission (2011)
UN Doc. A/CN.4/SER.A/2011/Add.1 (Part 2)**[9]

Article 10 Existence of a breach of an international obligation

1. There is a breach of an international obligation by an international organization when an act of that international organization is not in conformity with what is required of it by that obligation, regardless of the origin or character of the obligation concerned.
2. Paragraph 1 includes the breach of any international obligation that may arise for an international organization towards its members under the rules of the organization.

---

8 From the Yearbook of the International Law Commission, by the International Law Commission © 2011 United Nations. Reprinted with the permission of the United Nations.
9 *Ibid.*

Notes

- This article in the Draft Articles suggests that rules are binding "regardless of the[ir] origin or character." Does this include general rules of customary international law and general principles of law? What other meaning could this phrase have? And why would the article take an effort to make this clear?
- Recall the *WHO/Egypt Agreement* case discussed in Chapter 6, where the court opined that "International organizations are subjects of international law and, as such, are bound by any obligations incumbent upon them under general rules of international law, under their constitutions or under international agreements to which they are parties."[10] Did the court need to express such a wide view in order to reach an opinion in the matter? You may wish to review the case and ask on what basis did the court reason.
- Can an international organization be bound by customary international law? Does an international organization contribute to the formation of customary international law? Isn't customary international law relevant to inter-state relations, not the internal governance of an international organization? You could consider that in the *Reservations to the Genocide Convention* advisory opinion, the ICJ looked to the practice of the UN Secretary-General as depositary of treaties for evidence of customary international law on the law of treaties.[11] This question of contribution to customary international law seems to imply the need for reciprocity of the subjects of the law with the creators of the law. Is that a requirement for the formation of customary international law?

In *Case C-327/91, France v Commission*, the European Commission argued an agreement concluded between the Commission and third parties, was merely an "administrative agreement" and would not result "in an international claim capable of giving rise to liability on the part of the Community, but merely in termination of the Agreement."[12] The Court rejected this argument, holding that:[13]

> There is no doubt, therefore, that the Agreement is binding on the European Communities. It falls squarely within the definition of an international agreement concluded between an international organization and a State, within the meaning of Article 2(1)(a)(i) of the Vienna Convention of 21 March 1986 on the Law of Treaties between States and International

---

10 Interpretation of the Agreement of 25 March 1951 Between the WHO and Egypt, Advisory Opinion, 1980 ICJ Reps. 73, 89–90, para. 37 (International Court of Justice, 20 December 1980).
11 *See* Reservations to the Convention on Genocide, Advisory Opinion, 1951 ICJ Reps 15, 25 (International Court of Justice, 1951).
12 Case C-327/91, French Republic v Commission (Court of Justice of the European Communities [Union], 9 August 1994)
13 *Ibid.*

Organizations or between International Organizations. In the event of non-performance of the Agreement by the Commission, therefore, the Community could incur liability at international level.

Could there be any international obligation on an international organization, especially one adopted by agreement, that would not result in responsibility? Surely violation of an international agreement would justify the other party terminating the agreement in case of a significant breach, but does termination of the agreement mean that events preceding the termination were not violations attracting responsibility?

As already discussed in this textbook, a number of rules of international law are raised to the level of being *jus cogens* norms. Even if international organizations are bound to normal rules of international law, would they also be bound by *jus cogens* norms as *lex superior*? Recall Judge Lauterpacht's separate opinion in the *Bosnian Genocide* case in Chapter 5 on powers, where he expressed the view that the UN Security Council could not violate a *jus cogens* norm.[14] The ILC adopted his view:

International Law Commission, Draft articles on the responsibility of international organizations II(2) Yearbook of the International Law Commission (2011) UN Doc. A/CN.4/SER.A/2011/Add.1 (Part 2)[15]

Chapter III Serious breaches of obligations under peremptory norms of general international law

Article 41 Application of this Chapter

1. This Chapter applies to the international responsibility which is entailed by a serious breach by an international organization of an obligation arising under a peremptory norm of general international law.
2. A breach of such an obligation is serious if it involves a gross or systematic failure by the responsible international organization to fulfil the obligation.

Article 42 Particular consequences of a serious breach of an obligation under this Chapter

1. States and international organizations shall cooperate to bring to an end through lawful means any serious breach within the meaning of article 41.

---

14 *See* Case Concerning Application of the Convention on the Prevention and Punishment of the Crime of Genocide (Bosnia & Herzegovina v. Yugoslavia (Serbia & Montenegro)), Further Requests for the Indication of Provisional Measures, Order, 1993 ICJ Reps. 325 (International Court of Justice, 13 September 1993) (Lauterpacht, J. *ad hoc*, separate opinion)
15 From the Yearbook of the International Law Commission, by the International Law Commission © 2011 United Nations. Reprinted with the permission of the United Nations.

2. No State or international organization shall recognize as lawful a situation created by a serious breach within the meaning of article 41, nor render aid or assistance in maintaining that situation.
3. This article is without prejudice to the other consequences referred to in this Part and to such further consequences that a breach to which this Chapter applies may entail under international law.

Notes

- What do you recall about the nature of *jus cogens* norms under international law? How do they form, and what is their source? How do we assess whether they are regular norms or norms *jus cogens*?
- It is clear what *jus cogens* norm is at issue here? Would the UN Security Council ever adopt a resolution violating this norm? What would such a resolution look like?
- Recall the *Kadi* case.[16] The Grand Chamber of the EU Court of Justice held that, while the Court of Justice could not review the legality of a UN Security Council resolution directly, it can review an EU regulation, and it can annul a regulation that is unlawful. If the Court of Justice found the regulation was violating *jus cogens*, then does it not follow that the UN is responsible for violating *jus cogens*? How is the ILC approaching this question?
- Recall also Judge Lauterpacht's view in the *Bosnian Genocide* case. Is the ILC really adopting his view fully? Why did he think the Security Council was limited by *jus cogens*, and what was the consequence? Is that the same as or different from the ILC provision?
- Also consider the decision by the ICC to refer an asylum claim by a witness to the host state, The Netherlands, and then, once The Netherlands had refused the claim on grounds of lack of jurisdiction, to return the witness to the state he sought protection from.[17] If *non-refoulement*, or expulsion of a person to a situation of torture or mistreatment, is *jus cogens*, then has the ICC violated a rule of *jus cogens*? Is the ICC even capable (not competent or authorized, but capable) of refusing to expel a person to a risky state and instead hosting the vulnerable person on its territory indefinitely?

---

16 *See* Joined cases C-402/05 and C-415/05 P, Kadi and Al Barakaat International Foundation v Council and Commission of the European Union, Judgment (Court of Justice of the European Communities [Union] (Grand Chamber), 3 September 2008).
17 *See* Prosecutor v Lubanga Dyilo, Situation in the Democratic Republic of the Congo, Case No.: ICC-01/04-01/06, Redacted Decision on the request by DRC-DOl-WWWW-0019 for special protective measures relating to his asylum application (International Criminal Court, Trial Chamber, 5 August 2011); [Mbodina Iribi] v. staatssecretaris van Veiligheid en Justitie [Secretary of State of Security and Justice], Ruling 201310217/1/V1 (ECLI:NL:RVS:2014:2427) (Supreme Court [*Raad van Staat*], Netherlands, 27 June 2014).

Finally, what about the rules of international law that are part of the rules in the treaty that constituted the organization? If an organization violates the rules in its constitutive instrument, for example by acting *ultra vires*, surely this act is also a violation of international law, and thus an issue of responsibility as well. However, for this question, we could distinguish between rules of international law that look to the default rules on responsibility, and "internal" rules of the international organization that can be resolved through the internal mechanisms of the organization, including member state oversight and governance. The distinction between normal international law and "internal" law is drawn in the Advisory Opinion on the *Kosovo* case.[18] In this case, the court found that Security Council Resolution 1244, while on the one hand an act of an international organization with its own legal effects, was also, on the other hand, the internal, domestic law of Kosovo. The ILC Draft Articles largely avoid the issue of the rules of the organization and suggest that violations of the rules of the organizations might not be violations of international law to which the Draft Articles are applicable.

9.2.2 Attribution of an internationally wrongful act

This following section is one of the most controversial in the law on responsibility. As we recall from the sections above, there are two elements to establishing responsibility of an international organization: there must be an obligation under international binding the organization, and the organization must violate that obligation either by act or omission. Within this second element, there are two sub-elements: that there must be an act or omission contrary to the international legal obligation, and that the act or omission be attributable to the organization.[19] We will now examine these two sub-elements.

9.2.2.1 Internationally wrongful act

The first sub-element of an internationally wrongful act or omission is the easier of the two sub-elements to establish. What can sometimes be difficult to determine is what the obligation requires, and whether the organization really did or failed to do the prescribed act. More specifically, did the obligation require the organization to act or refrain from acting?

Second, does the international legal obligation impose a requirement that the organization achieve some result, or does it only require the organization to act in a certain manner, regardless of outcome?

Consider the *Mothers of Srebrenica v Netherlands* case, where an action was brought against The Netherlands and the UN for the failure of the Dutch military

---

18 *See* Accordance with International Law of the Unilateral Declaration of Independence by the Provisional Institutions of Self-Government of Kosovo, Advisory Opinion, 2010 ICJ Reps. 403 (International Court of Justice, 22 July 2010).
19 *See* International Law Commission, Draft articles on the responsibility of international organizations, art. 4, II(2) Yearbook of the International Law Commission (2011), UN Doc. A/CN.4/SER.A/2011/Add.1 (Part 2).

unit (DUTCHBAT), acting under a UN peacekeeping mandate, to protect the inhabitants of Srebrenica during the 1990s armed conflict in the former Yugoslavia. The court excused the UN as a party because of its immunity and maintained the suit only against The Netherlands; however, the court then proceeded to consider the scope of the obligation. Although the UN was not party, its immunity only served as a procedural bar against the action, not an exemption from the law (recall Chapter 8 on immunities), and the question is whether the responsibility in the case was also incurred by the UN.

[A] et al. and the Association of Citizens Mothers of Srebrenica v. State of The Netherlands (Ministry of General Affairs) and the United Nations
Case No. 295247 / HA ZA 07–2973; LJN: BD6796
Judgment
Rechtbank 's-Gravenhage (District Court in the Hague), Civil Law Section, Netherlands, 10 July 2008

2. The claim in the principal proceedings

...

2.2. The Association et al. motivate this – in summary – as follows. In July 1995 the worst act of genocide in Europe since the Second World War was committed in the East Bosnian enclave of Srebrenica. The State (with the Netherlands UN battalion Dutchbat) and the UN are responsible for the fall of the enclave in which Dutchbat had its base, as well as for the consequences, namely the murder by Bosnian Serbs of 8,000–10,000 citizens of Bosnia-Herzegovina who had taken refuge within the enclave. The State and the UN's acts (and omissions) in the context of the implementation of various UN resolutions according to which the enclave Srebrenica was declared a "Safe area" are in violation of promises made and, even besides that, are wrongful towards Fejzi? et al. – all of whom are surviving relatives of men murdered by Bosnian Serbs – and towards the Association representing the interests of the victims' relatives.

...

5. The assessment

...

5.18. The Genocide Convention comprises as principal rule the penalization of genocide. From article 1 of this Convention it is clear that the parties to the treaty, including the Netherlands, undertake to prevent genocide – and therefore not to commit the crime themselves – as well as to punish it.

5.19. Neither the text of the Genocide Convention or any other treaty, nor international customary law or the practice of states offer scope in this respect for the obligation of a Netherlands court to enforce the standards of the Genocide Convention by means of a civil action. The Contracting parties are obliged to punish all acts defined by this Convention as genocide within the boundaries set in article VI of the Convention. Also, as stated before, the states are bound to prevent genocide and therefore to refrain from committing it themselves. The states are also bound to clearly set out obligations on the extradition of suspects of genocide, but the Convention does not provide for (any obligation pertaining to) the enforcement of the standards of enforcing the prohibition on genocide via a civil law action. It should be noted here that the International Court of Justice expressed an opinion in 2007 about the substance of obligations of parties to the Genocide Convention and in that context omitted to discuss any obligation by states to enforce the Convention in civil law actions (ruling of 26 February 2007 on the application of the Convention on the Prevention and Punishment of the Crime of Genocide in the case of Bosnia and Herzegovina v. Serbia and Montenegro, paragraphs 155–179).

Notes

- What was the obligation binding The Netherlands and the UN? Did that obligation truly bind both The Netherlands and the UN?
- Was that obligation one of conduct or result? Did the obligation impose a duty to act, or a duty to refrain from acting? So would an act or omission constitute a violation of the obligation?
- Did The Netherlands and the UN intend for the horrible outcome in Srebrenica? Is that relevant?

9.2.2.2 Attribution of the act

The second sub-element of an internationally wrongful act or omission is attribution. Here, the question is whether some behavior by some person or entity is, in actuality, the act of the international organization. Clearly, an international organization is a fictional legal person. It can only act as a collective and only through natural persons. When do the acts of those natural persons implicate the organization, and when are they done in a personal capacity? Or, alternatively, in a capacity that implicates a state? For example, during the NATO bombing campaign in the former Yugoslavia, were the individual states that released bombs responsible for any violations of the laws of war, or was NATO responsible for coordinating the campaign?

One question that can arise is whether the rules on attribution are attributing the responsibility or the conduct of the actor to the organization. Take a look at how the Draft Articles discuss attribution. Are they written with attribution of conduct or responsibility in mind?

In addition, the rules on responsibility seem largely written to identify a single actor that is responsible for wrongful conduct. In reality, states and international organizations often act in coordinated ways, and responsibility might be diffused among the actors. Provided that the rules on responsibly are satisfied, there is no prohibition on multiple actors bearing responsibility.

Now we will turn to the various actors and their relationship to the organization that may give rise to attribution. First, the actions of agents and organs of an international organization are clearly those of the organization.

International Law Commission,
Draft articles on the responsibility of international organizations
II(2) Yearbook of the International Law Commission (2011)
UN Doc. A/CN.4/SER.A/2011/Add.1 (Part 2)[20]

Article 6 Conduct of organs or agents of an international organization

1. The conduct of an organ or agent of an international organization in the performance of functions of that organ or agent shall be considered an act of that organization under international law, whatever position the organ or agent holds in respect of the organization.
2. The rules of the organization apply in the determination of the functions of its organs and agents.

The Draft Articles establish that organs and agents of the organization can impute the responsibility of the organization. Recall from Chapter 7 on organs that the Draft Articles define an organ as "any person or entity which has that status in accordance with the rules of the organization." For more discussion on which entities qualify as organs, consult Chapter 7.

In addition to organs, the Draft Articles also attribute conduct of the agents of the organization to the organization. In article 2, the Draft Articles define an agent thus:

International Law Commission,
Draft articles on the responsibility of international organizations
II(2) Yearbook of the International Law Commission (2011)
UN Doc. A/CN.4/SER.A/2011/Add.1 (Part 2)[21]

Article 2 Use of terms

For the purposes of the present draft articles, ...
(d) "agent of an international organization" means an official or other person or entity, other than an organ, who is charged by the organization with carrying out, or helping to carry out, one of its functions, and thus through whom the organization acts.

One important distinction in this definition is between agents who perform duties that fulfill the organization's functions and those that do not. This distinction is in keeping with the functional analysis of international organizations, referring back to the *Reparations* case, identifying the core tasks of the organization that discharge its

---

20 From the Yearbook of the International Law Commission, by the International Law Commission © 2011 United Nations. Reprinted with the permission of the United Nations.
21 *Ibid.*

mandate, and those that are performed, but not necessarily critical. In fact, in *Reparations*, the ICJ said that it:

> understands the word "agent" in the most liberal sense, that is to say, any person who, whether a paid official or not, and whether permanently employed or not, has been charged by an organ of the organization with carrying out, or helping to carry out, one of its functions – in short, any person through whom it acts.[22]

Later, the ICJ considered two advisory opinions on the privileges and immunities of experts on mission. These opinions were discussed in Chapter 8 on privileges and immunities. Suffice it to say that the court focused not on the formal title or even administrative position of the actor, but on the "nature of their mission," i.e. their duties, to determine whether the individual was an agent.[23] Thus, the definition of agent is not limited to officials or those with certain employment contracts, but to those individuals acting in a certain capacity to fulfill the organization's functions.

Two final observations are in order. Firstly, that attribution of the conduct or responsibility of the agent to the organization does not mean that the individual is entirely excused. Most acts by individuals do not amount to violations of international law, as they are not usually addressees of international law. However, in the case of international criminal law, individuals can be responsible under international law, and cannot escape that responsibility by attributing their conduct to a state or organization.

Secondly, the acts of the organ or agent can be attributed to the organization, even if the organ or agent exceeded their mandate by acting *ultra vires*. The ILC accepted this view.

International Law Commission,
Draft articles on the responsibility of international organizations
II(2) Yearbook of the International Law Commission (2011)
UN Doc. A/CN.4/SER.A/2011/Add.1 (Part 2)[24]

Article 8 Excess of authority or contravention of instructions

The conduct of an organ or agent of an international organization shall be considered an act of that organization under international law if the

---

22 Reparation for Injuries Suffered in the Service of the United Nations, Advisory Opinion, 1949 ICJ Reps. 174, 177 (International Court of Justice, 11 April 1949).
23 *See* Applicability of Article VI, Section 22, of the Convention on the Privileges and Immunities of the United Nations ["Mazilu case"], Advisory Opinion, 1989 ICJ Reps. 177 (International Court of Justice, 15 December 1989); Difference Relating to Immunity from Legal Process of a Special Rapporteur of the Commission on Human Rights ["Cumaraswamy Case"], Advisory Opinion, 1999 ICJ Reps. 62 (International Court of Justice, 29 April 1999).
24 From the Yearbook of the International Law Commission, by the International Law Commission © 2011 United Nations. Reprinted with the permission of the United Nations.

organ or agent acts in an official capacity and within the overall functions of that organization, even if the conduct exceeds the authority of that organ or agent or contravenes instructions.

This possibility had already been identified by the ICJ in the *Certain Expenses* advisory opinion:[25]

> If it is agreed that the action in question ... has been initiated or carried out in a manner not in conformity with the division of functions among the several organs which the [UN] Charter prescribes, one moves to the internal plane, to the internal structure of the Organization. If the action was taken by the wrong organ, it was irregular as a matter of that internal structure, but this would not necessarily mean that the expense incurred was not an expense of the Organization. Both national and international law contemplate cases in which the body corporate or politic may be bound, as to third parties, by an *ultra vires* act of an agent.

Moving away from organs and agents of the international organization, we next examine organs and agents of states, who may be partially under the control of the international organization. A classic example would be members of the armed forces of a state who are participating in a peacekeeping operation under the control of the UN, but other examples could include domestic officials, judges or other civil servants who are fulfilling the state's obligations to an international organization. Especially for civil servants of states within the EU, a considerable amount of their administrative framework for everything ranging from procurement to customs regulations is governed by EU rules. In all of these cases, the individual remains partly under the command, administrative control, or hierarchical structure of the state (or another international organization), and yet is also partly acting as a *de facto* official of the international organization.

International Law Commission, Draft articles on the responsibility of international organizations II(2) Yearbook of the International Law Commission (2011) UN Doc. A/CN.4/SER.A/2011/Add.1 (Part 2)[26]

Article 7 Conduct of organs of a State or organs or agents of an international organization placed at the disposal of another international organization

---

25 Certain Expenses of the United Nations (Article 17, Paragraph 2, of the Charter), Advisory Opinion, 1962 ICJ Reps. 151, 168 (International Court of Justice, 20 July 1962); Difference Relating to Immunity from Legal Process of a Special Rapporteur of the Commission on Human Rights ["Cumaraswamy Case"], Advisory Opinion, 1999 ICJ Reps. 62, 89, para. 66 (International Court of Justice, 29 April 1999) ("it need hardly be said that all agents of the United Nations, in whatever official capacity they act, must take care not to exceed the scope of their functions, and should so comport themselves as to avoid claims against the United Nations").

26 From the Yearbook of the International Law Commission, by the International Law Commission © 2011 United Nations. Reprinted with the permission of the United Nations.

The conduct of an organ of a State or an organ or agent of an international organization that is placed at the disposal of another international organization shall be considered under international law an act of the latter organization if the organization exercises effective control over that conduct.

The Draft Articles identify the control by the organization as being the determinative test to identify when acts of the individual are attributable or not. Looking at the example of peacekeeping or other military intervention in pursuit of a UN Security Council resolution, consider the *Behrami* case. This case was particularly difficult in that the allegedly wrongful conduct by the states would potentially have violated human rights. The case was litigated against several European states before the European Court of Human Rights:

Behrami and Behrami v France, Application No. 71412/01
Saramati v France, Germany and Norway, Application No. 78166/01
Decision as to the Admissibility
European Court of Human Rights (Grand Chamber), 2 May 2007[27]

2. The conflict between Serbian and Kosovar Albanian forces during 1998 and 1999 is well documented. On 30 January 1999, and following a decision of the North Atlantic Council ("NAC") of the North Atlantic Treaty Organisation ("NATO"), NATO announced air strikes on the territory of the then Federal Republic of Yugoslavia ("FRY") should the FRY not comply with the demands of the international community. Negotiations took place between the parties to the conflict in February and March 1999. The resulting proposed peace agreement was signed by the Kosovar Albanian delegation but not by the Serbian delegation. The NAC decided on, and on 23 March 1999 the Secretary General of NATO announced, the beginning of air strikes against the FRY. The air strikes began on 24 March 1999 and ended on 8 June 1999 when the FRY troops agreed to withdraw from Kosovo. On 9 June 1999 "KFOR", the FRY and the Republic of Serbia signed a "Military Technical Agreement" ("MTA") by which they agreed on FRY withdrawal and the presence of an international security force following an appropriate UN Security Council Resolution ("UNSC Resolution").

3. UNSC Resolution 1244 of 10 June 1999 provided for the establishment of a security presence (KFOR) by "Member States and relevant international institutions", "under UN auspices", with "substantial NATO participation" but under "unified command and control". NATO pre-deployment to The Former Yugoslav Republic of Macedonia allowed deployment of significant forces to Kosovo by 12 June 1999 (in accordance with OPLAN 10413, NATO's operational plan for the UNSC Resolution 1244 mission called "Operation Joint Guardian"). By 20 June FRY withdrawal was complete. KFOR contingents were grouped into four

---

[27] © Council of Europe.

multinational brigades ("MNBs") each of which was responsible for a specific sector of operations with a lead country. They included MNB Northeast (Mitrovica) and MNB Southeast (Prizren), led by France and Germany, respectively. Given the deployment of Russian forces after the arrival of KFOR, a further agreement on 18 June 1999 (between Russia and the United States) allocated various areas and roles to the Russian forces.

4. UNSC Resolution 1244 also decided on the deployment, under UN auspices, of an interim administration for Kosovo (UNMIK) and requested the Secretary General ("SG"), with the assistance of relevant international organisations, to establish it and to appoint a Special Representative to the SG ("SRSG") to control its implementation. UNMIK was to coordinate closely with KFOR. UNMIK comprised four pillars corresponding to the tasks assigned to it. Each pillar was placed under the authority of the SRSG and was headed by a Deputy SRSG. Pillar I (as it was at the relevant time) concerned humanitarian assistance and was led by UNHCR before it was phased out in June 2000. A new Pillar I (police and justice administration) was established in May 2001 and was led directly by the UN, as was Pillar II (civil administration). Pillar III, concerning democratisation and institution building, was led by the Organisation for Security and Co-operation in Europe ("OSCE") and Pillar IV (reconstruction and economic development) was led by the European Union.

II THE CIRCUMSTANCES OF THE BEHRAMI CASE

5. On 11 March 2000 eight boys were playing in the hills in the municipality of Mitrovica. The group included two of Agim Behrami's sons, Gadaf and Bekim Behrami. At around midday, the group came upon a number of undetonated cluster bomb units ("CBUs") which had been dropped during the bombardment by NATO in 1999 and the children began playing with the CBUs. Believing it was safe, one of the children threw a CBU in the air: it detonated and killed Gadaf Behrami. Bekim Behrami was also seriously injured and taken to hospital in Pristina (where he later had eye surgery and was released on 4 April 2000). Medical reports submitted indicate that he underwent two further eye operations (on 7 April and 22 May 2000) in a hospital in Bern, Switzerland. It is not disputed that Bekim Behrami was disfigured and is now blind.

...

III. THE CIRCUMSTANCES OF THE SARAMATI CASE

8. On 24 April 2001 Mr Saramati was arrested by UNMIK police and brought before an investigating judge on suspicion of attempted murder and illegal possession of a weapon. On 25 April 2001 that judge ordered his pre-trial detention and an investigation into those and additional charges. On 23 May 2001 a prosecutor filed an indictment and on 24 May 2001 the District Court ordered his detention to be extended. On 4 June 2001 the Supreme Court allowed Mr Saramati's appeal and he was released.

9. In early July 2001 UNMIK police informed him by telephone that he had to report to the police station to collect his money and belongings. The station was located in Prizren in the sector assigned to MNB Southeast, of which the lead nation was Germany. On 13 July 2001 he so reported and was arrested by UNMIK police officers by order of the

Commander of KFOR ("COMKFOR"), who was a Norwegian officer at the time.

10. On 14 July 2001 detention was extended by COMKFOR for 30 days.

11. On 26 July 2001, and in response to a letter from Mr Saramati's representatives taking issue with the legality of his detention, KFOR Legal Adviser advised that KFOR had the authority to detain under the UNSC Resolution 1244 as it was necessary "to maintain a safe and secure environment" and to protect KFOR troops. KFOR had information concerning Mr Saramati's alleged involvement with armed groups operating in the border region between Kosovo and the Former Yugoslav Republic of Macedonia and was satisfied that Mr Saramati represented a threat to the security of KFOR and to those residing in Kosovo.

...

1. The entity with the mandate to detain and to de-mine

123. The respondent and third party States argued that it made no difference whether it was KFOR or UNMIK which had the mandate to detain (the *Saramati* case) and to de-mine (the *Behrami* case) since both were international structures established by, and answerable to, the UNSC. The applicants maintained that KFOR had the mandate to both detain and de-mine and that the nature and structure of KFOR was sufficiently different to UNMIK as to engage the respondent States individually.

...

127. Accordingly, the Court considers that issuing detention orders fell within the security mandate of KFOR and that the supervision of de-mining fell within UNMIK's mandate.

2. Can the impugned action and inaction be attributed to the UN?

(a) The Chapter VII foundation for KFOR and UNMIK

128. As the first step in the application of Chapter VII, the UNSC Resolution 1244 referred expressly to Chapter VII and made the necessary identification of a "threat to international peace and security" within the meaning of Article 39 of the Charter (paragraph 23 above). The UNSC Resolution 1244, *inter alia*, recalled the UNSC's "primary responsibility" for the "maintenance of international peace and security". Being "determined to resolve the grave humanitarian situation in Kosovo" and to "provide for the safe and free return of all refugees and displaced persons to their homes", it determined that the "situation in the region continues to constitute a threat to international peace and security" and, having expressly noted that it was acting under Chapter VII, it went on to set out the solutions found to the identified threat to peace and security.

129. The solution adopted by UNSC Resolution 1244 to this identified threat was, as noted above, the deployment of an international security force (KFOR) and the establishment of a civil administration (UNMIK).

In particular, that Resolution authorised "Member States and relevant international organisations" to establish the international security presence in Kosovo as set out in point 4 of Annex 2 to the Resolution with all necessary means to fulfil its responsibilities listed in Article 9. Point 4 of Annex 2 added that the security presence would have "substantial [NATO] participation" and had to be deployed under "unified command and control". The UNSC was thereby delegating to willing organisations and members states (see paragraph 43 as regards the meaning of the term "delegation" and paragraph 24 as regards the voluntary nature of this State contribution) the power to establish an international security presence as well as its operational command. Troops in that force would operate therefore on the basis of UN delegated, and not direct, command. In addition, the SG was authorised (Article 10) to establish UNMIK with the assistance of "relevant international organisations" and to appoint, in consultation with the UNSC, a SRSG to control its implementation (Articles 6 and 10 of the UNSC Resolution). The UNSC was thereby delegating civil administration powers to a UN subsidiary organ (UNMIK) established by the SG. Its broad mandate (an interim administration while establishing and overseeing the development of provisional self-government) was outlined in Article 11 of the Resolution.

130. While the Resolution referred to Chapter VII of the Charter, it did not identify the precise Articles of that Chapter under which the UNSC was acting and the Court notes that there are a number of possible bases in Chapter VII for this delegation by the UNSC: the non-exhaustive Article 42 (read in conjunction with the widely formulated Article 48), the non-exhaustive nature of Article 41 under which territorial administrations could be authorised as a necessary instrument for sustainable peace; or implied powers under the Charter for the UNSC to so act in both respects based on an effective interpretation of the Charter. In any event, the Court considers that Chapter VII provided a framework for the above-described delegation of the UNSC's security powers to KFOR and of its civil administration powers to UNMIK (see generally and *inter alia*, White and Ulgen, "*The Security Council and the Decentralised Military Option: Constitutionality and Function*", Netherlands Law Review 44, 1997, 386; Sarooshi, "*The United Nations and the Development of Collective Security: The Delegation by the UN Security Council of its Chapter VII powers*", Oxford University (1999); Chesterman, "*Just War or Just Peace: Humanitarian Intervention and International Law*", (2002) Oxford University Press, pp. 167–169 and 172); Zimmermann and Stahn, cited above; De Wet, "*The Chapter VII Powers of the United Nations Security Council*", 2004, pp. 260–265; Wolfrum "*International Administration in Post-Conflict Situations by the United Nations and other International Actors*", Max Planck UNYB Vol. 9 (2005), pp. 667–672; Friedrich, "*UNMIK in Kosovo: struggling with Uncertainty*", Max Planck UNYB 9 (2005) and the references cited therein; and *Prosecutor v. Duško Tadić*, Decision of 2.10.95, Appeals Chamber of ICTY, §§ 35–36).

131. Whether or not the FRY was a UN member state at the relevant time (following the dissolution of the former Socialist Federal Republic of Yugoslavia), the FRY had agreed in the MTA to these presences. It is true that the MTA was signed by "KFOR" the day before the UNSC Resolution creating that force was adopted. However, the MTA was completed on the express basis of a security presence "under UN auspices" and with UN approval and the Resolution had already been introduced before the UNSC. The Resolution was adopted the following day, annexing the MTA and no

international forces were deployed until the Resolution was adopted.(b) Can the impugned action be attributed to KFOR?

132. While Chapter VII constituted the foundation for the above-described delegation of UNSC security powers, that delegation must be sufficiently limited so as to remain compatible with the degree of centralisation of UNSC collective security constitutionally necessary under the Charter and, more specifically, for the acts of the delegate entity to be attributable to the UN (as well as Chesterman, de Wet, Friedrich, Kolb and Sarooshi all cited above, see Gowlland-Debbas "*The Limits of Unilateral Enforcement of Community Objectives in the Framework of UN Peace Maintenance*" EIL (2000) Vol 11, No. 2 369–370; Niels Blokker, "*Is the authorisation Authorised? Powers and Practice of the UN Security Council to Authorise the Use of Force by 'Coalition of the Able and Willing'*", EJIL (2000), Vol. 11 No. 3; pp. 95–104 and *Meroni v. High Authority* Case 9/56, [1958] ECR 133).

Those limits strike a balance between the central security role of the UNSC and two realities of its implementation. In the first place, the absence of Article 43 agreements which means that the UNSC relies on States (notably its permanent members) and groups of States to provide the necessary military means to fulfil its collective security role. Secondly, the multilateral and complex nature of such security missions renders necessary some delegation of command.

133. The Court considers that the key question is whether the UNSC retained ultimate authority and control so that operational command only was delegated. This delegation model is now an established substitute for the Article 43 agreements never concluded.

134. That the UNSC retained such ultimate authority and control, in delegating its security powers by UNSC Resolution 1244, is borne out by the following factors.

In the first place, and as noted above, Chapter VII allowed the UNSC to delegate to "Member States and relevant international organisations". Secondly, the relevant power was a delegable power. Thirdly, that delegation was neither presumed nor implicit, but rather prior and explicit in the Resolution itself. Fourthly, the Resolution put sufficiently defined limits on the delegation by fixing the mandate with adequate precision as it set out the objectives to be attained, the roles and responsibilities accorded as well as the means to be employed. The broad nature of certain provisions (see the UN submissions, paragraph 118 above) could not be eliminated altogether given the constituent nature of such an instrument whose role was to fix broad objectives and goals and not to describe or interfere with the detail of operational implementation and choices. Fifthly, the leadership of the military presence was required by the Resolution to report to the UNSC so as to allow the UNSC to exercise its overall authority and control (consistently, the UNSC was to remain actively seized of the matter, Article 21 of the Resolution). The requirement that the SG present the KFOR report to the UNSC was an added safeguard since the SG is considered to represent the general interests of the UN.

While the text of Article 19 of UNSC Resolution 1244 meant that a veto by one permanent member of the UNSC could prevent termination of the relevant delegation, the Court does not consider this factor alone sufficient to conclude that the UNSC did not retain ultimate authority and control.

135. Accordingly, UNSC Resolution 1244 gave rise to the following chain of command in the present cases. The UNSC was to retain ultimate authority and control over the security mission and it delegated to NATO (in consultation with non-NATO member states) the power to establish, as well as the operational command of, the international presence, KFOR. NATO fulfilled its command mission *via* a chain of command (from the NAC, to SHAPE, to SACEUR, to CIC South) to COMKFOR, the commander of KFOR. While the MNBs were commanded by an officer from a lead TCN, the latter was under the direct command of COMKFOR. MNB action was to be taken according to an operational plan devised by NATO and operated by COMKFOR in the name of KFOR.

136. This delegation model demonstrates that, contrary to the applicants' argument at paragraph 77 above, direct operational command from the UNSC is not a requirement of Chapter VII collective security missions.

137. However, the applicants made detailed submissions to the effect that the level of TCN control in the present cases was such that it detached troops from the international mandate and undermined the unity of operational command. They relied on various aspects of TCN involvement including that highlighted by the Venice Commission (paragraph 50 above) and noted KFOR's legal personality separate to that of the TCNs.

138. The Court considers it essential to recall at this point that the necessary (see paragraph 24 above) donation of troops by willing TCNs means that, in practice, those TCNs retain some authority over those troops (for reasons, *inter alia*, of safety, discipline and accountability) and certain obligations in their regard (material provision including uniforms and equipment). NATO's command of operational matters was not therefore intended to be exclusive, but the essential question was whether, despite such TCN involvement, it was "effective" (ILC Report cited at paragraph 32 above).

139. The Court is not persuaded that TCN involvement, either actual or structural, was incompatible with the effectiveness (including the unity) of NATO's operational command. The Court does not find any suggestion or evidence of any actual TCN orders concerning, or interference in, the present operational (detention) matter. Equally there is no reason to consider that the TCN structural involvement highlighted by the applicants undermined the effectiveness of NATO's operational control. Since TCN troop contributions are in law voluntary, the continued level of national deployment is equally so. That TCNs provided materially for their troops would have no relevant impact on NATO's operational control. It was not argued that any NATO rules of engagement imposed would not be respected. National command (over own troops or a sector in Kosovo) was under the direct operational authority of COMKFOR. While individual claims might potentially be treated differently depending on which TCN was the source of the alleged problem (national commanders decided on whether immunity was to be waived,

TCNs had exclusive jurisdiction in (at least) disciplinary and criminal matters, certain TCNs had put in place their own TCNCOs and at least one TCN accepted civil jurisdiction (the above-cited *Bici* case)), it has not been explained how this, of itself, could undermine the effectiveness or unity of NATO command in *operational* matters. The Court does not see how the failure to conclude a SOFA between the UN and the host FRY could affect, as the applicants suggested, NATO's operational command. That COMKFOR was charged (the applicants at paragraph 78 above) exclusively with issuing detention orders amounts to a division of labour and not a break in a unified command structure since COMKFOR acted at all times as a KFOR officer answerable to NATO through the above-described chain of command.

140. Accordingly, even if the UN itself would accept that there is room for progress in co-operation and command structures between the UNSC, TCNs and contributing international organisations (see, for example, Supplement to an Agenda for Peace: Position paper of the SG on the Occasion of the 50th Anniversary of the UN, A/50/60–S/1995/1; the *Brahami* report, cited above; UNSC Resolutions 1327 (2000) and 1353 (2001); and Reports of the SG of 1 June and 21 December 2001 on the Implementation of the Recommendations of the Special Committee on Peacekeeping Operations and the Panel on UN Peace Operations (A/55/977, A/56/732)), the Court finds that the UNSC retained ultimate authority and control and that effective command of the relevant operational matters was retained by NATO.

141. In such circumstances, the Court observes that KFOR was exercising lawfully delegated Chapter VII powers of the UNSC so that the impugned action was, in principle, "attributable" to the UN within the meaning of the word outlined at paragraphs 29 and 121 above.

(c) Can the impugned inaction be attributed to UNMIK?

142. In contrast to KFOR, UNMIK was a subsidiary organ of the UN. Whether it was a subsidiary organ of the SG or of the UNSC, whether it had a legal personality separate to the UN, whether the delegation of power by the UNSC to the SG and/or UNMIK also respected the role of the UNSC for which Article 24 of the Charter provided, UNMIK was a subsidiary organ of the UN institutionally directly and fully answerable to the UNSC (see ILC report at paragraph 33 above). While UNMIK comprised four pillars (three of which were at the time led by UNHCR, the OSCE and the EU), each pillar was under the authority of a Deputy SRSG, who reported to the SRSG who in turn reported to the UNSC (Article 20 of UNSC Resolution 1244).

143. Accordingly, the Court notes that UNMIK was a subsidiary organ of the UN created under Chapter VII of the Charter so that the impugned inaction was, in principle, "attributable" to the UN in the same sense.

3. Is the Court competent ratione personae?

144. It is therefore the case that the impugned action and inaction are, in principle, attributable to the UN. It is, moreover, clear that the UN has a legal personality separate from that of its member states (*The Reparations case*, ICJ Reports 1949) and that that organisation is not a Contracting Party to the Convention.

...

146. The question arises in the present case whether the Court is competent *ratione personae* to review the acts of the respondent States carried out on behalf of the UN and, more generally, as to the relationship between the Convention and the UN acting under Chapter VII of its Charter.

...

152. In these circumstances, the Court concludes that the applicants' complaints must be declared incompatible *ratione personae* with the provisions of the Convention.

Notes

- Who acted in this case? Was it the UN, or the states? If they both acted, what were their respective acts? Are their acts relevant? Or is it the results of their acts that are important? Does this mean that attribution is based on cause and effect, or do we use a different test?
- The court observed that there was "effectiveness or unity of [the] operational command [of NATO]" regarding KFOR, but then discussed the legal basis for KFOR's presence and operations in Kosovo being a Security Council resolution. How is the Security Council resolution relevant? Does this mean that responsibility is attributable to the UN because it authorized the actions in Kosovo? Is authorization the legal test?
- However, the court also discussed the notion of control as being critical. The court mentions "operational" control and "ultimate" control. Are those different, and if so, is the difference important? Does "ultimate" seem more or less significant? Are those notions different from "effective" control? Does "effective" suggest *de facto* control versus *de jure* control?
- So what is the test? Is it actions, authorization, or control? And what kind of control do we need? And if it is control, how does factual control interact with authorization?
- Did the armed forces of the states involved ever leave the command structure of their respective states? Surely those states did not give up disciplinary and even criminal jurisdiction over their troops. How does this change our understanding of the kind of control the court expects?

In *Behrami*, the ECHR considered that the acts were attributable to the UN, and not to the states against whom the individuals complained. The reasoning was based on control. When, in comparable situations, would the national authority retain enough control to also attract responsibility? It must be more than merely retaining disciplinary control and criminal jurisdiction. Various courts have considered this question, including the House of Lords in the following case:

R (on the application of Al-Jedda) v Secretary of State for Defence
Judgment
[2007] UKHL 58, [2008] 1 AC 332, [2008] 2 WLR 31
House of Lords, United Kingdom, 12 December 2007[28]

Lord Bingham of Cornhill

My Lords,

1. Since October 2004 the appellant, who is a national of both this country and Iraq, has been held in custody by British troops at detention facilities in Iraq. He complains that his detention infringes his rights under article 5(1) of the European Convention on Human Rights, a Convention right protected by the Human Rights Act 1998, and also founds a good claim in this country under the English common law. These claims were rejected by the Queen's Bench Divisional Court (Moses and Richards JJ: [2005] EWHC 1809 (Admin), HRLR 1355) and also by the Court of Appeal (Brooke, May and Rix LJJ: [2006] EWCA Civ 327, [2007] QB 621. Both courts below delivered lengthy and careful judgments, commensurate with the importance and difficulty of the issues then raised, but a new issue has (by agreement) been raised and argued before the House, as explained below.

2. The appellant has not been charged with any offence, and no charge or trial is in prospect. He was arrested and has since been detained on the ground that his internment is necessary for imperative reasons of security in Iraq. He was suspected of being a member of a terrorist group involved in weapons smuggling and explosive attacks in Iraq. He was believed by the British authorities to have been personally responsible for recruiting terrorists outside Iraq with a view to the commission of atrocities there; for facilitating the travel into Iraq of an identified terrorist explosives expert; for conspiring with that explosives expert to conduct attacks with improvised explosive devices against coalition forces in the areas around Fallujah and Baghdad; and for conspiring with the explosives expert and members of an Islamist terrorist cell in the Gulf to smuggle high tech detonation equipment into Iraq for use in attacks against coalition forces. These allegations are roundly denied by the appellant, and they have not been tested in any proceedings. Nor is their correctness an issue in these proceedings. The House must therefore resolve the legal issues falling for decision on the assumption that the allegations are true, without forming any judgment whether they are or not.

...

The first issue

5. It was common ground between the parties that the governing principle is that expressed by the International Law Commission in article 5 of its draft articles on the Responsibility of International Organizations (adopted in May 2004 and cited by the European Court in *Behrami and Saramati*, para 30): "*Conduct of organs or agents placed at the disposal of an international organization by a state or another international organization ...*

---

[28] Contains Parliamentary information licensed under the Open Parliament Licence v3.0.

6. Practice relating to peacekeeping forces is particularly significant in the present context because of the control that the contributing state retains over disciplinary matters and criminal affairs. This may have consequences with regard to attribution of conduct ... Attribution of conduct to the contributing state is clearly linked with the retention of some powers by that state over its national contingent and thus on the control that the state possesses in the relevant respect.

7. As has been held by several scholars, when an organ or agent is placed at the disposal of an international organization, the decisive question in relation to attribution of a given conduct appears to be who has effective control over the conduct in question."

6. Invited by the ILC to comment on the attribution of the conduct of peacekeeping forces to the UN or to contributing states, the UN Secretariat responded (A/CN.4/545, 25 June 2004, pp 17–18):

> "The question of attribution of the conduct of a peacekeeping force to the United Nations or to contributing states is determined by the legal status of the force, the agreements between the United Nations and contributing states and their opposability to third states.
>
> A United Nations peacekeeping force established by the Security Council or the General Assembly is a subsidiary organ of the United Nations. Members of the military personnel placed by member states under United Nations command although remaining in their national service are, for the duration of their assignment to the force, considered international personnel under the authority of the United Nations and subject to the instructions of the force commander. The functions of the force are exclusively international and members of the force are bound to discharge their functions with the interest of the United Nations only in view. The peacekeeping operation as a whole is subject to the executive direction and control of the Secretary-General, under the overall direction of the Security Council or the General Assembly as the case may be.
>
> As a subsidiary organ of the United Nations, an act of a peacekeeping force is, in principle, imputable to the Organization, and if committed in violation of an international obligation entails the international responsibility of the Organization and its liability in compensation. The fact that any such act may have been performed by members of a national military contingent forming part of the peacekeeping operation does not affect the international responsibility of the United Nations vis-à-vis third states or individuals.
>
> Agreements concluded between the United Nations and states contributing troops to the Organization contain a standard clause on third-party liability delineating the respective responsibilities of the Organization and contributing states for loss, damage, injury or death caused by the personnel or equipment of the contributing state. Article 9 of the Model Memorandum of Understanding between the United Nations and [participating state] contributing resources to [The United Nations Peacekeeping Operation] provides in this regard:
>
>> The United Nations will be responsible for dealing with any claims by

third parties where the loss of or damage to their property, or death or personal injury, was caused by the personnel or equipment provided by the Government in the performance of services or any other activity or operation under this memorandum. However if the loss, damage, death or injury arose from gross negligence or wilful misconduct of the personnel provided by the Government, the Government will be liable for such claims. (A/51/967.annex)

While the agreements between the United Nations and contributing states divide the responsibility in the relationship between them, they are not opposable to third states. Vis-à-vis third states and individuals, therefore, where the international responsibility of the Organization is engaged, liability in compensation is, in the first place, entailed for the United Nations, which may then revert to the contributing state concerned and seek recovery on the basis of the agreement between them.

The principle of attribution of the conduct of a peacekeeping force to the United Nations is premised on the assumption that the operation in question is conducted under United Nations command and control, and thus has the legal status of a United Nations subsidiary organ. In authorized chapter VII operations conducted under national command and control, the conduct of the operation is imputable to the state or states conducting the operation. In joint operations, namely, those conducted by a United Nations peacekeeping operation and an operation conducted under national or regional command and control, international responsibility lies where *effective* command and control is vested and practically exercised (see paras 17–18 of the Secretary-General's report A/51/389)."

The cited paragraphs in the Secretary-General's report A/51/389 (20 September 1996) read:

"17. The international responsibility of the United Nations for combat-related activities of the United Nations forces is premised on the assumption that the operation in question is under the exclusive command and control of the United Nations. Where a Chapter VII-authorized operation is conducted under national command and control, international responsibility for the activities of the force is vested in the state or states conducting the operation. The determination of responsibility becomes particularly difficult, however, in cases where a state or states provide the United Nations with forces in support of a United Nations operation but not necessarily as an integral part thereof, and where operational command and control is unified or coordinated. This was the case in Somalia where the Quick Reaction Force and the US Rangers were provided in support of the United Nations Operation in Somalia (UNOSOM II), and this was also the case in the former Yugoslavia where the Rapid Reaction Force was provided in support of the United Nations Protection Force (UNPROFOR).

18. In joint operations, international responsibility for the conduct of the troops lies where operational command and control is vested according

to the arrangements establishing the modalities of cooperation between the state or states providing the troops and the United Nations. In the absence of formal arrangements between the United Nations and the state or states providing troops, responsibility would be determined in each and every case according to the degree of effective control exercised by either party in the conduct of the operation."

The UN Secretariat was further invited by the ILC to address the following question (see A/CN.4/556, 12 May 2005, p4):

"In the event that a certain conduct, which a member state takes in compliance with a request on the part of an international organization, appears to be in breach of an international obligation both of that state and of that organization, would the organization also be regarded as responsible under international law? Would the answer be the same if the state's wrongful conduct was not requested, but only authorized by the organization?"

The Secretariat's answer was (ibid, p 46):

"As for the third question raised by the commission, we are not aware of any situation where the Organization was held jointly or residually responsible for an unlawful act by a state in the conduct of an activity or operation carried out at the request of the Organization or under its authorization. In the practice of the Organization, however, a measure of accountability was nonetheless introduced in the relationship between the Security Council and member states conducting an operation under Security Council authorization, in the form of periodic reports to the Council on the conduct of the operation. While the submission of these reports provides the Council with an important 'oversight tool', the Council itself or the United Nations as a whole cannot be held responsible for an unlawful act by the state conducting the operation, for the ultimate test of responsibility remains 'effective command and control'."

7. It is necessary to identify the main events occurring between March 2003 and the present before considering the application of these principles to the present case.

8. On 20 March 2003 coalition forces invaded Iraq. ... Major combat operations were declared to be complete on 1 May 2003, although hostilities did not end on that date in all parts of the country. As from that date the US and the UK became occupying powers, within the meaning of Section III of the Hague Regulations on the Laws and Customs of War on land (1907) and the Fourth Geneva Convention on the Protection of Civilian Persons in Time of War (1949) in the areas which they respectively occupied.

9. On 8 May 2003 the Permanent Representatives of the UK and the US at the UN addressed a joint letter to the President of the Security Council. In it they said that the states participating in the coalition would strictly abide by their obligations under international law ... On 13 May 2003 the US Secretary for Defence, Mr Donald Rumsfeld, appointed Mr Paul Bremer to be administrator of the CPA, which was divided into regions, that in the south being under British control. The CPA promptly set about the

business of government. By CPA Regulation No 1, dated 16 May 2003, the CPA assumed "all executive, legislative and judicial authority necessary to achieve its objectives, to be exercised under relevant UN Security Council resolutions, including Resolution 1483 (2003), and the laws and usages of war". ...

10. Resolution 1483 was adopted by the Security Council on 22 May 2003. The resolution opened, as is usual, with a number of recitals, one of which referred to the US and UK Permanent Representatives' letter of 8 May "recognizing the specific authorities, responsibilities, and obligations under applicable international law of these states as occupying powers under unified command ('the Authority')". Then, acting under Chapter VII of the UN Charter, the Council called on the Authority, consistently with the UN Charter and other relevant international law, to promote the welfare of the Iraqi people and work towards the restoration of conditions of stability and security. The Council called upon all concerned to comply fully with their obligations under international law, including in particular the Geneva Conventions of 1949 and the Hague Regulations of 1907. ... The Council decided, as it did consistently thereafter, to remain seised of the matter. In July 2003 an Iraqi Governing Council ("IGC") was established, which the CPA was to consult on all matters concerning the temporary governance of Iraq.

...

12. On 16 October 2003 the Security Council adopted Resolution 1511. Acting under Chapter VII of the UN Charter, the Council looked forward to the assumption of governmental powers by the people of Iraq .... In a new departure, the Council determined "that the provision of security and stability is essential to the successful completion of the political process ... and to the ability of the United Nations to contribute effectively to that process and the implementation of resolution 1483 (2003), and *authorizes* a multinational force ['MNF'] under unified command to take all necessary measures to contribute to the maintenance of security and stability in Iraq ..."

...

17. After this date there were two further resolutions of the Security Council (Resolution 1637 of 8 November 2005 and Resolution 1723 of 28 November 2006), to which, however, little significance was, rightly, attached. Their effect was to maintain the status quo. ... The appellant pointed out that, according to an answer given by the armed forces minister in the House of Commons on 10 November 2004, UK forces in Iraq were operating under UNSCR 1546 and were not engaged on UN operations: Hansard (HC Debates), 10 November 2004, col 720W. A similar view, it was suggested, was taken by the Working Group of the UN's Human Rights Council (A/HRC/4/40/Add.1) which considered the position of Mr Tariq Aziz and, in paragraph 25 of its opinion on the case, stated:

> "The Working Group concludes that until 1 July 2004, Mr Tariq Aziz had been detained under the sole responsibility of the Coalition members as occupying powers or, to be more precise, under the responsibility of the United States Government. Since then and as the Iraqi Criminal Tribunal is a court of the sovereign State of Iraq,

the pre-trial detention of a person charged before the tribunal is within the responsibility of Iraq. In the light of the fact that Mr Aziz is in the physical custody of the United States authorities, any possible conclusion as to the arbitrary nature of his deprivation of liberty may involve the international responsibility of the United States Government."

18. As already indicated, the Secretary of State founds his nonattributability argument on the judgment of the European Court, sitting as a Grand Chamber, in *Behrami and Saramati*, which related to events in Kosovo.

...

22. Against the factual background described above a number of questions must be asked in the present case. Were UK forces placed at the disposal of the UN? Did the UN exercise effective control over the conduct of UK forces? Is the specific conduct of the UK forces in detaining the appellant to be attributed to the UN rather than the UK? Did the UN have effective command and control over the conduct of UK forces when they detained the appellant? Were the UK forces part of a UN peacekeeping force in Iraq? In my opinion the answer to all these questions is in the negative.

23. The UN did not dispatch the coalition forces to Iraq. The CPA was established by the coalition states, notably the US, not the UN. When the coalition states became occupying powers in Iraq they had no UN mandate. Thus when the case of Mr Mousa reached the House as one of those considered in *R (Al-Skeini and others) v Secretary of State for Defence) (The Redress Trust intervening)* [2007] UKHL 26, [2007] 3 WLR 33 the Secretary of State accepted that the UK was liable under the European Convention for any ill-treatment Mr Mousa suffered, while unsuccessfully denying liability under the Human Rights Act 1998. It has not, to my knowledge, been suggested that the treatment of detainees at Abu Ghraib was attributable to the UN rather than the US. Following UNSCR 1483 in May 2003 the role of the UN was a limited one focused on humanitarian relief and reconstruction, a role strengthened but not fundamentally altered by UNSCR 1511 in October 2003. By UNSCR 1511, and again by UNSCR 1546 in June 2004, the UN gave the multinational force express authority to take steps to promote security and stability in Iraq, but (adopting the distinction formulated by the European Court in para 43 of its judgment in *Behrami and Saramati*) the Security Council was not delegating its power by empowering the UK to exercise its function but was authorising the UK to carry out functions it could not perform itself. At no time did the US or the UK disclaim responsibility for the conduct of their forces or the UN accept it. It cannot realistically be said that US and UK forces were under the effective command and control of the UN, or that UK forces were under such command and control when they detained the appellant.

24. The analogy with the situation in Kosovo breaks down, in my opinion, at almost every point. The international security and civil presences in Kosovo were established at the express behest of the UN and operated under its auspices, with UNMIK a subsidiary organ of the UN. The multinational force in Iraq was not established at the behest of the UN, was not mandated to operate under UN

auspices and was not a subsidiary organ of the UN. There was no delegation of UN power in Iraq. It is quite true that duties to report were imposed in Iraq as in Kosovo. But the UN's proper concern for the protection of human rights and observance of humanitarian law called for no less, and it is one thing to receive reports, another to exercise effective command and control. It does not seem to me significant that in each case the UN reserved power to revoke its authority, since it could clearly do so whether or not it reserved power to do so.

25. I would resolve this first issue in favour of the appellant and against the Secretary of State.

...

Lord Brown of Eaton-Under-Heywood

My Lords,

...

Issue One – Attributability

141. I have found this altogether the most difficult of the three issues now before your Lordships. The obvious starting point is the ECtHR's recent decision in *Behrami*.

...

143. Lord Bingham (para 24) concludes that the analogy with Kosovo breaks down at almost every point. I wish I found it so easy. My difficulty is not least with my Lord's view that "there was no delegation of UN power in Iraq." By that I understand him to mean (paras 21 and 23) that, in contrast to the position in Kosovo, the UN in Iraq was merely authorising the USA and the UK to carry out functions which it could not perform itself as opposed to empowering them to exercise its own function. It seems to me, however, that in this respect the situation in Kosovo and Iraq was the same: in neither country could the UN as a matter of fact carry out its central security role so that in both it was necessary to authorise states to perform the role. As the court in *Behrami* explained in paras 132 and 133, that necessarily follows from the absence of article 43 agreements. When the court posed "the key question whether the UNSC retained ultimate authority and control so that operational command only was delegated", it noted (para 133): "This delegation model is now an established substitute for the article 43 agreements never concluded". And this seems to me entirely consistent with para 43 of the court's judgment: the mention there of "functions which it could not itself perform" I understand to refer to functions which the Security Council cannot itself perform as a matter of *law* and which accordingly can only be done by a different body properly authorised under the UN Charter – see Sarooshi, "The United Nations and the Development of Collective Security: The Delegation by the UN Security Council of its Chapter VII powers" (1999).

144. I turn, therefore, to "the key question" and in particular to the five factors which led the court in *Behrami* (para 134) to conclude that the UN in Kosovo had retained ultimate authority and control. The first, that Chapter VII of the Charter allows the UNSC to delegate to member states, applies equally here. So too the second, the power to provide for security being a legally delegable power. The third I shall leave over for the moment. It is difficult to find any relevant distinction with regard to the fourth: UNSCR 1511 (which authorised the formation of the

MNF) fixed its mandate no less precisely than UNSCR 1244 defined KFOR's mandate. Indeed, so far as the power of internment was concerned, resolution 1546 was altogether more specific (see paras 14 and 15 of Lord Bingham's opinion), resolution 1244 having entrusted KFOR merely with such general responsibilities as "ensuring public safety and order". Nor could the fifth factor, the reporting requirements, reasonably lead to a different conclusion about ultimate authority and control here. True, this case lacks the additional safeguard noted in *Behrami* that KFOR's report had to be presented by the UN Secretary General, but that surely is counterbalanced by the fact that the MNF's mandate ceases unless renewed by the SC whereas KFOR's mandate was to continue until the SC decided otherwise (a decision which, at least theoretically, a permanent member could have vetoed).

145. To my mind it follows that any material distinction between the two cases must be found in the third factor, or rather in the very circumstances in which the MNF came to be authorised and mandated in the first place. The delegation to KFOR of the UN's function of maintaining security was, the court observed, "neither presumed nor implicit but rather prior and explicit in the resolution itself". Resolution 1244 decided (para 5) "on the deployment in Kosovo, under United Nations auspices, of international civil and security presences" – the civil presence being UNMIK, recognised by the court in *Behrami* (para 142) as "a subsidiary organ of the UN"; the security presence being KFOR. KFOR was, therefore, expressly formed under UN auspices. Para 7 of the resolution "[a]uthorise[d] member states and relevant international organisations to establish the international security presence in Kosovo as set out in point 4 of Annex 2 ...". Point 4 of Annex 2 stated: "The international security presence with substantial NATO participation must be deployed under unified command and control and authorised to establish a safe environment for all people in Kosovo and to facilitate the safe return to their homes of all displaced persons and refugees."

146. Resolution 1511, by contrast, was adopted on 16 October 2003 during the USA's and UK's post-combat occupation of Iraq and in effect gave recognition to those occupying forces as an existing security presence. Para 13 of the resolution is instructive:

> "*Determines* that the provision of security and stability is essential to the successful completion of the political process as outlined in paragraph 7 above and to the ability of the United Nations to contribute effectively to that process and the implementation of resolution 1483 (2003), and *authorises* a multinational force under unified command to take all necessary measures to contribute to the maintenance of security and stability in Iraq, including for the purpose of ensuring necessary conditions for the implementation of the timetable and programme as well as to contribute to the security of the United Nations Assistance Mission for Iraq ['UNAMI'], the Governing Council of Iraq and other institutions of the Iraqi interim administration, and key humanitarian and economic infrastructure."

147. By resolution 1483, adopted on 22 May 2003, the SC had "[r]esolved

that the United Nations should play a vital role in humanitarian relief, for reconstruction of Iraq, and the restoration and establishment of national and local institutions for representative governance" and, pursuant to it, the Secretary General had established UNAMI, an essentially humanitarian and civil aid mission. As para 13 of resolution 1511 indicated, it was that mission which was the UN's contribution to the situation in Iraq. The MNF under unified command which para13 was authorising was to contribute to the security of, amongst others, UNAMI. Unlike KFOR, however, it was not itself being deployed "under UN auspices". UNAMI alone represented the UN's presence in Iraq.

148. Nor did the position change when resolution 1546 was adopted on 8 June 2004, three weeks before the end of the occupation and the transfer of authority from the CPA to the interim government of Iraq on 28 June 2004. UNAMI was to continue with its work (para 7). So too was the MNF, both of them acting at the request of the incoming interim government of Iraq. Resolution 1546 accordingly reaffirmed the authorisation of the MNF under unified command (this time "in accordance with the letters annexed", described by Lord Bingham at para 14). And, as para 10 noted, consistently with the previous position, the MNF's tasks, including the prevention and deterrence of terrorism, were imposed so that, amongst other things, "the United Nations can fulfil its role in assisting the Iraqi people as outlined in para 7 above" – namely UNAMI's humanitarian and civil aid work. Nothing either in the resolution itself or in the letters annexed suggested for a moment that the MNF had been under or was now being transferred to United Nations authority and control. True, the SC was acting throughout under Chapter VII of the Charter. But it does not follow that the UN is therefore to be regarded as having assumed ultimate authority or control over the force. The precise meaning of the term "ultimate authority and control" I have found somewhat elusive. But it cannot automatically vest or remain in the UN every time there is an authorisation of UN powers under Chapter VII, else much of the analysis in *Behrami* would be mere surplusage.

149. It is essentially upon this basis, therefore, that I regard the present case as materially different from *Behrami* and am led to conclude that the appellant's internment is to be attributed, not to the UN acting through the MNF, but rather directly to the UK forces.

Notes

- What is different in this case compared to *Behrami*? These are both peacekeeping operations, aren't they? So how are they different?
- What kind of control does the House of Lords look for? "Ultimate" control? "Overall" control? "Operational" control? Or "effective" control? Is this approach consistent with the ECHR in *Behrami*?

Other cases have found that sometimes peacekeeping troops are still being controlled by the sending state. In *Nissan v Attorney-General*,[29] the House of Lords also found that the UN was not in control of the UK armed forces participating in the United Nations Peacekeeping Force in Cyprus (UNFICYP). In *Mukeshimana-Ngulinzira v. Belgium*,[30] the Court of First Instance in Brussels similarly found that the Belgian peacekeeping troops operating under the United Nations Assistance Mission for Rwanda (UNAMIR), who failed to protect a refugee camp during the Rwandan genocide, were acting under the orders of the Belgian commander, and not UNAMIR.

Notwithstanding the analysis above, does the EU have a *lex specialis* rule on this issue of control, attribution, and responsibility? We have seen that the EU has slightly different rules on responsibility than the UN. The EU constitutes a mandatory legal regime. While UN acts generally need some act of domestic incorporation, EU acts can be directly applicable.

What if the act of the EU and/or state in such a case violated other rules of international law, for example the European Convention on Human Rights? Being a special case, the EU has significantly more authority to bind the member states than other international organizations might have. In fact, in some situations, the EU legislation is directly applicable in the member states' legal order. Surely, then, when a state is implementing binding EU legislation or when the EU is acting by and through the member state, then the EU would be the responsible party? This approach implies admitting the existence of a special rule on attribution, to the effect that, in the case of a European Union act binding a member state, state authorities would be considered as acting as organs of the EU.

Recall the case of *Kadi*, where the UN Security Council Resolution created a binding obligation for states to comply under international law, but states still needed to adopt domestic legal acts to give effect to the UNSC Resolution. However, the EU Regulation in *Kadi* was directly applicable in the domestic legal orders of the Member States. This dynamic might make it more difficult to identify EU responsibility. For example, a domestic governmental official might implement and apply complementary regulations on agriculture, education, or customs policy from both the domestic governmental authority and the EU simultaneously. Can we separate those policies that have their origin in the EU from those that come from the domestic governmental authority? And if so, can we then attribute responsibility accordingly?

---

29 *See* Nissan v Attorney-General, [1969] UKHL 3, [1970] AC 179 (House of Lords, UK, 11 February 1969).
30 *See* Mukeshimana-Ngulinzira and Others v. Belgium and Others, RG Nos. 04/4807/A and 07/15547/A, Judgment (Court of First Instance of Brussels, Belgium, 8 December 2010).

Bosphorus Hava Yollari Turizm ve Ticaret Anonim Şirketi v. Ireland, Application No. 45036/98
Judgment
European Court of Human Rights (Grand Chamber), 30 June 2005[31]

137. In the present case it is not disputed that the act about which the applicant company complained, the detention of the aircraft leased by it for a period of time, was implemented by the authorities of the respondent State on its territory following a decision made by the Irish Minister for Transport. In such circumstances the applicant company, as the addressee of the impugned act, fell within the "jurisdiction" of the Irish State, with the consequence that its complaint about that act is compatible *ratione loci, personae* and *materiae* with the provisions of the Convention.

...

151. The question is therefore whether, and if so to what extent, that important general interest of compliance with Community obligations can justify the impugned interference by the Irish State with the applicant company's property rights.

...

154. In reconciling both these positions and thereby establishing the extent to which a State's action can be justified by its compliance with obligations flowing from its membership of an international organisation to which it has transferred part of its sovereignty, the Court has recognised that absolving Contracting States completely from their Convention responsibility in the areas covered by such a transfer would be incompatible with the purpose and object of the Convention; the guarantees of the Convention could be limited or excluded at will, thereby depriving it of its peremptory character and undermining the practical and effective nature of its safeguards (see *M. & Co.*, p. 145, and *Waite and Kennedy*, § 67, both cited above). The State is considered to retain Convention liability in respect of treaty commitments subsequent to the entry into force of the Convention (see *mutatis mutandis*, *Matthews*, cited above, §§ 29 and 32–34, and *Prince Hans-Adam II of Liechtenstein v. Germany* [GC], no. 42527/98, § 47, ECHR 2001-VIII).

155. In the Court's view, State action taken in compliance with such legal obligations is justified as long as the relevant organisation is considered to protect fundamental rights, as regards both the substantive guarantees offered and the mechanisms controlling their observance, in a manner which can be considered at least equivalent to that for which the Convention provides (see *M. & Co.*, cited above, p. 145, an approach with which the parties and the European Commission agreed). By "equivalent" the Court means "comparable"; any requirement that the organisation's protection be "identical" could run counter to the interest of international cooperation pursued (see paragraph 150 above). However, any such finding of equivalence could not be final and would be

---

31 © Council of Europe.

susceptible to review in the light of any relevant change in fundamental rights protection.

156. If such equivalent protection is considered to be provided by the organisation, the presumption will be that a State has not departed from the requirements of the Convention when it does no more than implement legal obligations flowing from its membership of the organisation.

However, any such presumption can be rebutted if, in the circumstances of a particular case, it is considered that the protection of Convention rights was manifestly deficient. In such cases, the interest of international cooperation would be outweighed by the Convention's role as a "constitutional instrument of European public order" in the field of human rights (see *Loizidou v. Turkey* (preliminary objections), judgment of 23 March 1995, Series A no. 310, pp. 27–28, § 75).

Notes

- How does the court find the relationship of responsibility between the EU, the Member State, and the ECHR obligations? In terms of the measure at issue, the court considered that it did not fall within the "jurisdiction of the Irish State." Does this finding mean that it was not an act of Ireland? Or does it mean something else?
- What do we mean by "jurisdiction" in a human rights case? What question is the expression "jurisdiction" used to answer? Does it have the same meaning of "jurisdiction" that we normally use in international law, or is its use special here?
- It might be interesting to look at the initial decision in this case on whether the matter was admissible to the court at all. In that decision, the court observed that:

> whether the impugned acts can be considered to fall within the jurisdiction of the Irish State within the meaning of Article 1 of the [European] Convention [on Human Rights], when that State claims that it was obliged to act in furtherance of a directly effective and obligatory [European Community/Union] Regulation.[32]

Is this language different from that used in the judgment on the merits above? Compare the use of the term "jurisdiction" from "directly effective and obligatory." Is that difference important?

---

32 Bosphorus Hava Yollari Turizm ve Ticaret AS v. Ireland, Application No. 45036/98, Decision as to the Admissibility, (European Court of Human Rights (Fourth Section), 13 September 2001).

- Even if the state can retain some responsibility in the face of an obligatory EU regulation, is its responsibility altered from what it would otherwise be under our usual appreciation of responsibility? Said another way, does the existence of the EU regulation compelling this act change how we assess responsibility of the state? Should the EU regulation have this effect?

In another case, *Cooperatieve Producentenorganisatie van de Nederlandse Kokkelvisserij U.A. v. The Netherlands*,[33] the European Court of Human Rights was faced with similar issues, though in a case where a company claimed a violation of its human right to a fair trial. The court first observed that the injured company could not claim that the EU violated rights in the ECHR because the EU was not a party to the European Convention, but that finding did not mean The Netherlands was not responsible anyway. It used language similar to that in *Bosphorus* above, presuming that a state has not violated the European Convention when implementing its EC/EU obligations when the EC/EU offered comparable human rights protections. However, it reaffirmed that:

> A Contracting Party is responsible under Article 1 of the Convention for all acts and omissions of its organs regardless of whether the act or omission in question was a consequence of domestic law or of the necessity to comply with international legal obligations.

Does that passage of time from 1969 for *Kokkelvisserij* to 2005 for *Bosphorus* make a difference? Does it change the presumption that it is in compliance? Can this rule of comparable protection apply to organizations other than the EC/EU? Why not? Surely it would provide a sufficient basis for protections.

Consider the following case, and look for an approach on separating acts of the EC/EU from acts of the state:

Case 50/76, Amsterdam Bulb BV and Producktschap voor Siergewassen (Ornamental Plant Authority)
Judgment
Court of Justice of the European Communities [Union], 2 February 1977[34]

...

JUDGMENT

Facts

...

I – Facts and procedure

[ii] 1. The company Amsterdam Bulb BV exports flower bulbs from the Netherlands solely to its parent company which is established in the United States of America. It considers that the minimum prices fixed by the Netherlands

---

33 Cooperatieve Producentenorganisatie van de Nederlandse Kokkelvisserij U.A. v. the Netherlands, Application No. 13645/05, Decision as to the Admissibility (European Court of Human Rights (Third Section), 20 January 2009).
34 https://eur-lex.europa.eu, © European Union, 1998–2020.

Verordening Exportprijzen Bloembollen Oogst 1975 (Flower-bulb (1975 crop) Export Price Order) are so high as to render importation by the parent company unprofitable.

...

[iii] By letter of 5 August 1975 addressed to the said Chairman, Amsterdam Bulb BV applied for exemption from the minimum export prices fixed for America. By letter of 12 August 1975 the Chairman dismissed the application for exemption. ...

...

2. *The Community regulations in question*

[iv] Having regard to the fact that exports of flowering bulbs to third countries are of considerable economic importance to the Community and that the continuation and development of such exports may be ensured by stabilizing prices in that trade, Article 7 of Regulation (EEC) No 234/68 of the Council on the establishment of a common organization of the market in live trees and other plants, bulbs, roots and the like, cut flowers and ornamental foliage (OJ English Special Edition 1968 (I), p. 26) provided that:

> "For each of the products falling within heading No 06.01 A of the Common Customs Tariff, one or more minimum prices for exports to third countries may be fixed each year in good time before the marketing season ..."

The common organization of the market provides for a system of quality standards and minimum prices, compliance with which must be ensured by the Member States. For flowering bulbs, corms and tubers a corresponding system was adopted by Regulation No 315/68 of the Council (OJ English Special Edition 1968 (I), p. 46), which provides in particular for minimum sizes which are applicable both in intra-Community trade and in trade with third countries.

[v] In trade with third countries, however, the Member States may be authorized to derogate from certain requirements of the quality standards in order to allow exporters to meet the trade requirements of certain third countries (Article 2 (2)). Regulation No 537/70 of the Commission (OJ English Special Edition 1970 (I), p. 157) authorized the Member States to take measures derogating from quality standards in respect of sizing as regards a number of flowering bulbs, corms and tubers.

[vi] In implementation of the basic regulation the Commission drew up Regulation (EEC) No 1767/68 on the system of minimum prices for exports to third countries of flowering corms, bulbs and tubers (OJ English Special Edition 1968 (II), p. 530).

[vii] That regulation provides, in particular, that where no minimum price has been fixed for a particular size of a given product the lowest minimum export price fixed for that product shall apply to the size in question (Article 2 (2)).

[viii] As regards the 1975/76 marketing year minimum prices for exports, in particular for tulip bulbs, were fixed by Regulation No 369/75 of the Commission (OJ 1975, L 41, p. 1).

3. *The provisions of Netherlands law*

[ix] The Netherlands Order, the Verordening Exportprijzen Bloembollen Oogst 1975, restates in guilders the

minimum export prices according to size fixed by Regulation No 369/75 of the Commission.

[x] Nevertheless, the Netherlands Order also includes a certain number of other provisions which are not contained in the Community regulations.

[xi] The provisions in question:

– Impose a minimum export price for flower bulbs of a *smaller size* than those for which Regulation No 369/75 fixes minimum export prices (Article 2 (2));

– Impose a minimum export price in respect of *flower bulbs other* than those for which Regulation No 369/75 fixes minimum export prices (Article 2 (5));

– Grant the Chairman of the Produktschap voor Siergewassen the power in certain cases to allow or to lay down exceptions to the provisions of the Netherlands Order;

– Provide penal sanctions in respect of infringements of the regulation. (Article 7).

...

Law

...

2 The Court is asked to rule whether the provisions of those regulations "'or any other provisions or principles of European law" forbid the adoption by a competent national organization of rules fixing export prices for flower bulbs which, whilst in part in conformity with the Community regulations, contain provisions which do not appear in those regulations and have no legal foundation therein.

...

7 Therefore, the Member States may neither adopt nor allow national organizations having legislative power to adopt any measure which would conceal the Community nature and effects of any legal provision from the persons to whom it applies.

8 From the moment that the Community adopts regulations under Article 40 of the Treaty establishing a common organization of the market in a specific sector the Member States are under a duty not to take any measure which might create exemptions from them or affect them adversely.

9 The compatibility with the Community regulations of the provisions referred to by the national court must be considered in the light not only of the express provisions of the regulations but also of their aims and objectives.

...

12 Article 3 of that regulation provides that the Council may adopt rules governing standards of quality, sizing and packaging of the products covered by the common organization of the market and the scope of such standards.

13 According to the same article, when standards have been adopted, the products to which they apply may not be displayed for sale, offered for sale, sold, delivered or otherwise marketed except in accordance with the said standards.

14 Under Article 7 of the said regulation, minimum prices for exports to third countries of those products may be fixed by the Commission.

15 Regulation (EEC) No 315/68 of the Council of 12 March 1968 fixing quality standards for flowering bulbs, corms and tubers (OJ English Special Edition 1968 (I), p. 46), which was adopted in

implementation of the basic regulation, No 234/68, provides in Article 2 that the standards shall apply both to intra-Community trade and to trade with third countries.

...

20   Article 1 of Regulation (EEC) No 369/75 of the Commission fixing for the relevant marketing year minimum prices for exports to third countries of certain flowering corms, bulbs and tubers, provides that the minimum prices are fixed for each product at the levels indicated in the annex to that regulation.

21   The annex in question shows that minimum export prices are fixed in express terms only for certain of the products listed in the annex to Regulation No 315/68 and for certain sizes larger than the minimum sizes indicated in Regulation No 315/68.

22   However, it is clear from Article 2 of Regulation No 1767/68 that a minimum export price is also applicable to sizes other than those for which Regulation No 369/75 expressly fixed such a price.

23   That minimum export price is equal to the lowest minimum price fixed by Regulation No 369/75 for the product in question.

24   Furthermore, it emerges from the Community rules as a whole that products which are smaller than the minimum sizes fixed in the annex to Regulation No 315/68 of the Council cannot be exported.

25   The answer must therefore be that the lowest minimum export price fixed for the product in question by Regulation No 369/75 is applicable to products which are larger than the minimum size but smaller than the sizes expressly listed in the annex to the said regulation.

26   As regards the fixing by the national authority of minimum prices for exports to third countries of products covered by the common organization of the market but of a genus, species or variety other than those for which the Commission has so far fixed minimum prices, it must be stated that no provision of the Community rules expressly prohibits the fixing of such prices.

27   It is not clear from the regulations adopted from time to time fixing minimum prices why the Commission decided to impose minimum prices at Community level for certain varieties only of the products covered by the common organization of the market.

28   In the light of all the Community regulations on the subject it is not possible to conclude that the Commission wished to imply that other products must be exported at prices decided freely by market forces.

29   On the contrary, it may be inferred from the rules drawn up by the Commission for implementing the system of minimum prices that the Member States may continue to impose minimum export prices until such time as the Commission has decided to impose such prices itself at Community level.

30   The reply to be given to the national court must therefore be that a national provision which fixes minimum prices for exports to third countries of certain varieties of bulbs other than those for which the Commission has fixed minimum prices in Regulation No 369/75, which does not create exemptions from

the Community system, does not limit its scope and seeks to achieve the same aim, that is, the stabilization of prices in trade which third countries, cannot be regarded as incompatible with Community law. ...

Notes

- This case is clearly not about the dramatic acts of peacekeeping or sanctions implementation, yet does it also involve responsibility? What is the alleged wrongful act? Who has been wronged?
- Which entity was in control of the actions at issue: the EU (then European Community) or the state?
- How did the state have the authority to adopt the measure it did? Surely the competence for legislating was delegated to the EC/EU? Did the state have any space to act on its own initiative? What if those measures contradicted the EC/EU measures? Does an EU Member State have any ability to adopt regulations different from the EC/EU?
- And if those measures were in contradiction with EC/EU law, which entity would have been responsible?
- Can we apply this same methodology for separating acts of the EC/EU from acts of state to questions of human rights violations under the European Convention? If the acts in *Amsterdam Bulb* above had violated human rights, would the state still enjoy a presumption of compliance with human rights?

Now consider the next case before the World Trade Organization, again concerning the relation between acts of the EC/EU and those of the state, and the issue of responsibility. The first except is the request for consultations by the US, raising an objection under WTO law. The second excerpt is the decision of the WTO panel on the matter.

European Communities – Protection of Trademarks and Geographical Indications for Agricultural Products and Foodstuffs, WTO Case No.WT/DS174/1/Add.1
Request for Consultations by the United States, Addendum
World Trade Organization, 10 April 2003

As you know, on 9 July 1999, the United States and the European Communities first held consultations concerning the protection of trademarks and geographical indications ("Gis") for agricultural products and foodstuffs in the European Communities pursuant to the request of the United States (WT/DS174/1). My authorities have now instructed me to request additional consultations with the European Communities pursuant to Article 4 of the *Understanding on Rules and Procedures Governing the Settlement of Disputes* ("DSU"), Article 64 of the *Agreement on Trade-Related Aspects of Intellectual Property Rights* ("TRIPS Agreement"), and Article XXII of the *General Agreement on Tariffs and Trade*

1994 ("GATT 1994"), regarding the protection of trademarks and geographical indications for agricultural products and foodstuffs in the European Communities ("EC"). This request supplements and does not replace the request for consultations circulated as WT/DS174/1.

EC Regulation 2081/92, as amended, and its related implementing and enforcement measures (the "EC Regulation"), limits the geographical indications that the EC will protect and limits the access of nationals of other Members to the EC GI procedures and protections provided under the Regulation. For example, the EC limits registration to geographical indications identifying goods originating in a member State of the European Union.

The EC Regulation appears to be inconsistent with the obligations of the EC under the TRIPS Agreement ....

...

The EC Regulation also appears to be inconsistent with the obligations of the EC under the GATT 1994. Articles I and III of the GATT 1994 obligate each Member of the WTO to accord to imported goods of other Members most-favoured-nation and national treatment.

...

We look forward to receiving your reply to the present request and to fixing a mutually convenient date for consultations.

European Communities– Protection of Trademarks and Geographical Indications for Agricultural Products and Foodstuffs, WTO Case No. WT/DS174/R
Report of the Panel
World Trade Organization, Panel, 15 March 2005

...

I. INTRODUCTION

1.1 On 1 June 1999, the United States requested consultations with the European Communities pursuant to Article 4 of the Understanding on Rules and Procedures Governing the Settlement of Disputes ("DSU") and Article 64 of the Agreement on Trade-Related Aspects of Intellectual Property Rights ("TRIPS Agreement") (to the extent that it incorporates by reference Article XXIII of the General Agreement on Tariffs and Trade 1994 ("GATT 1994") regarding EC Council Regulation (EEC) No. 2081/92 of 14 July 1992 on the protection of geographical indications and designations of origin for agricultural products and foodstuffs, as amended. The United States and the European Communities held consultations on 9 July 1999, and thereafter, but these consultations failed to resolve the dispute.

...

1.3 On 18 August 2003, the United States requested the Dispute Settlement Body ("DSB") to establish a panel with standard terms of reference as set out in Article 7.1 of the DSU. [footnote 3 – WT/DS174/1] At its meeting on 2 October 2003, the DSB established a single Panel pursuant to the requests of the United States in document WT/DS174/20 and Australia in document WT/DS290/18, in accordance with Article 9 of the DSU (WT/DSB/M/156). [footnote 4 – Letter from Joseph Papovich to Joao Pacheco, dated 6 June 2001, incorporating 20 questions concerning Regulation 2081/92 (Exhibit US-1); Letter from Joseph Papovich to Joao Pacheco, dated 21 August 2001, attaching additional 15 questions (Exhibit US-2); Letter from Steve Kho to Jean-Jacques Boufflet, dated 19 May 2003, enclosing 36 questions for purposes of the 27 May 2003, consultations, and addressing, among other issues relative to Regulation 2081: national treatment, most favored nation treatment, exclusivity of trademarks, implementing regulations and enforcement, availability of legal means for interested parties to prevent misleading uses of geographical indications, transparency, and definitions of geographical indications (Exhibit US-3). These documents from the consultations are relevant because they show that the EC is not in the dark, as it claims to be, concerning problems with respect to Regulation 2081/92. The claims in this dispute, however, are as set forth in the US panel request.]

...

D. OTHER CLAIMS

1. MFN treatment claims

...

(b) Availability of protection: MFN treatment under GATT 1994

(i) *Main arguments of the parties*

7.710 The United States claims that the Regulation is inconsistent with Article I:1 of GATT 1994 because it applies conditions of *equivalence* and *reciprocity* to the benefits of registration. It reiterates its arguments from its national treatment claim under Article III:4 that the Regulation applies to *like products* and is a measure affecting internal sale etc. and argues that, therefore, it is a *matter referred to in paragraph 4 of Article III* within the meaning of Article I:1 of GATT 1994. It reiterates its arguments concerning less favourable treatment of imported products and argues that these are significant *advantages* granted to products imported from a third country that are not immediately and *unconditionally* accorded to the products of all other Members. [footnote 604 – United States' first written submission, paras. 123–127.]

7.711 The European Communities responds that there is no violation of Article I:1 of GATT 1994. It reiterates its arguments in relation to MFN treatment under TRIPS that it does not, in fact, apply the conditions in Article 12(1) of the Regulation to geographical areas located in WTO Members; and that the conditions in Article 12(1) of the Regulation are the same for all third countries which fall under that provision. [footnote 605 – European Communities' first written submission, paras. 261 and 263. From an abundance of caution, the European Communities also stated its view that the product-specific conditions for the registration of individual GIs are examined for each product individually and do not discriminate according to nationality or product origin. As such, there is no violation of Article I:1 of GATT 1994 and, in the alternative, they are justified under Article XX(d): see its first written submission, paras. 262, 265–266.]

...

(d) Execution of the Regulation by authorities of EC member States

(i) *Main arguments of the parties*

7.722 The United States argues that nationals of EC member States – which are WTO Members in their own right – are accorded more favourable treatment than nationals of WTO Members outside the European Communities. EC member States are not excused from this obligation by the fact that they are acting pursuant to an EC Regulation. Measures of EC member States are within the terms of reference because the request for establishment of a panel specifies not only the Regulation but also "its related implementation and enforcement measures". [footnote omitted]

7.723 The European Communities argues that EC member States do not grant "advantages" within the meaning of the MFN treatment obligation because the Regulation is a Community measure adopted to harmonize Community law and the European Communities is an original Member of the WTO in its own right. The European Communities is the respondent in this Panel proceeding and claims of violations by EC member States cannot be raised. In any event, the United States has not identified any measures of EC member States. [footnote omitted]

(ii) Consideration by the Panel

7.724 The Panel observes that in this claim the United States asserts, in effect, that nationals of EC member States are "nationals of any other country" within the meaning of Article 4 of the TRIPS Agreement, quoted at paragraph 7.697 above. This, in turn, depends on the interpretation that each EC member State constitutes "any other country" within the meaning of Article 4 of the TRIPS Agreement.

7.725 The Panel recalls its finding at paragraph 7.150 as to which persons are the European Communities' own nationals. The Panel also recalls its findings at paragraph 7.98 that it has accepted the European Communities' explanation of what amount to its *sui generis* domestic constitutional arrangements that Community laws are generally not executed through authorities at Community level but rather through recourse to the authorities of its member States which, in such a situation, "act *de facto* as organs of the Community, for which the Community would be responsible under WTO law and international law in general". [footnote 615 – European Communities' second oral statement, para. 148.] Therefore, to the extent that advantages are granted under the Regulation, by the Community and EC member State authorities exercising powers under the Regulation, to the European Communities' own nationals, those advantages are not granted to "the nationals of any other country", within the meaning of Article 4 of the TRIPS Agreement.

7.726 Therefore, the Panel rejects this claim, to the extent that it is based on the execution of the Regulation by the authorities of EC member States.

7.727 The Panel wishes to confirm that it has accepted the European Communities' explanation as to the way in which Community laws are executed not only for this MFN claim but also for the national treatment claims. [footnote omitted] This has repercussions for the European Communities' defences to those other claims, in particular concerning the application and objection procedures, as noted at paragraphs 7.269 and 7.339 of this report. The Panel has applied this explanation of the way in which Community laws are executed in a consistent manner to all relevant claims in this dispute.

7.728 Finally, the Panel notes that the United States has also referred to the Paris Convention (1967), which does not contain a MFN treatment obligation. There is no need to consider this further.

7.729 In summary, with respect to the MFN treatment claims:

...

(b) under Article I:1 of GATT 1994, the Panel exercises judicial economy.

Notes

- What is the claim in this case for responsibility? Which actor is being charged with violating which rule of international law?
- What is the difference between the role of the EC/EU in the WTO and the role of the EC/EU under the European Convention on Human Rights? Does this distinction make a difference?
- The WTO appears to be more dismissive of the nuanced relationship between the EC/EU and its Member States. Why is this the case? Does WTO law have a different standard for applying the distinction between those actors?

Moving away from the EC/EU, we next examine another relationship between actors. In the prior sections, we considered when organs or agents of the state were acting as if they were organs or agents of the international organization. In addition to organs or agents being placed at the disposal or otherwise sharing control with an international organization, the organs and agents of another international organization might be placed in a similar relationship with another organization.

This situation is admittedly unusual, though sometimes organizations do share some operability. For example, the ILC considered the agreement between the WHO and the Pan American Health Organization (PAHO),[35] largely integrating the activities of the PAHO into the WHO, where the acts of the organs and agents of the PAHO would entail the responsibility of the WHO.

Another example is the more recent practice of placing treaty monitoring secretariats within existing international organizations for efficiency and economic reasons. On this basis, the officers of the treaty body are housed within the secretariat of another organization with integrated human resources and other management. Compare this practice with that of creating new treaty monitoring bodies, but legally establishing them as subsidiary bodies of an existing international organization, where the treaty body would be truly an organ of the organization. While it is still debatable whether these treaty bodies are truly international organizations in the sense usually meant, to the degree that these bodies are acting as *de facto*

---

35 *See* Agreement between the World Health Organization and the Pan American Sanitary [Health] Organization concerning the integration of the Pan American Sanitary Organization with the World Health Organization, 24 May 1949, 32 UNTS 387 (PAHO, now serving as Regional Office for the Americas of the WHO).

organizations, the actions of their secretariat officers might implicate the responsibility of the host organization.

After having analyzed whether the acts of an individual, organ or agent can be attributed to the organization, a further consideration is: even if the act is not attributable, has the organization accepted responsibility for the act?

International Law Commission, Draft articles on the responsibility of international organizations II(2) Yearbook of the International Law Commission (2011) UN Doc. A/CN.4/SER.A/2011/Add.1 (Part 2)[36]

Article 9 Conduct acknowledged and adopted by an international organization as its own

Conduct which is not attributable to an international organization under articles 6 to 8 shall nevertheless be considered an act of that organization under international law if and to the extent that the organization acknowledges and adopts the conduct in question as its own.

Notes

- In this case, it would appear that the act is not being attributed, but rather just responsibility, because how can an act be adopted? Yet the Draft Articles discuss the option as an adoption of the act. How are these two views different, and what is the significance of adoption of conduct versus responsibility?
- What if an organization expressly adopts responsibility and refuses to adopt conduct? How would this action be treated under the Draft Articles?

Consider the view of the International Criminal Tribunal for the former Yugoslavia:

Prosecutor v Nikolić, Case No. IT-94-2-PT Decision of Defence Motion Challenging the Exercise of Jurisdiction by the Tribunal International Criminal Tribunal for the former Yugoslavia, Trial Chamber II, 9 October 2002[37]

I. INTRODUCTION

1. Pending before this Trial Chamber of the International Criminal Tribunal for the Prosecution of Persons Responsible for Serious Violations of International Humanitarian Law committed in the Territory of the former Yugoslavia

---

36 From the Yearbook of the International Law Commission, by the International Law Commission © 2011 United Nations. Reprinted with the permission of the United Nations.
37 From the United Nations International Residual Mechanism for Criminal Tribunals, archives of the International Criminal Tribunal for the former Yugoslavia.

since 1991 ("Tribunal") is a Preliminary Motion by the Accused, Dragan Nikolic ("Nikolic" or "Accused"), challenging the legality of his arrest.

2. Mr. Nikolic was originally indicted for 24 counts of crimes against humanity, violations of the laws or customs of war and grave breaches of the Geneva Conventions. [footnote omitted] Following two amendments to the Indictment by the Prosecution, the accused now stands charged with eight counts of crimes against humanity. [footnote omitted]

...

II. BACKGROUND

10. On 4 November 1994, pursuant to Rules 47 and 55 of the Rules, Judge Odio Benito confirmed the Indictment against Nikolic. In accordance with Rules 2(A) and 55 of the Rules, two warrants for his arrest were issued, one addressed to the Federation of Bosnia and Herzegovina and the other to the Bosnian Serb administration in Pale. The arrest warrants were served on the authorities, and various attempts were made by the Prosecution to serve the Indictment on Nikolic and to have them executed.

11. On 15 November 1994, the Registrar of the Tribunal received official notification that the Federation of Bosnia and Herzegovina was unable to execute the arrest warrant. The Federation of Bosnia and Herzegovina claimed that Nikolic was residing in the town of Vlasenica. No response was received from the Bosnian Serb administration in Pale concerning its ability or willingness to execute the arrest warrants against Nikolic.

12. On 16 May 1995, Judge Odio Benito ordered the Prosecution to submit the case to the Trial Chamber for a review of the Indictment pursuant to Rule 61(A) of the Rules. [footnote 17 – *Review of the Indictment Pursuant to Rule 61 of the Rules of Procedure and Evidence*, 20 October 1995, para. 35 ("Rule 61 Proceeding").] On 20 October 1995, the Trial Chamber found that it was satisfied by the evidence presented to it that there were reasonable grounds for believing that Nikolic had committed the crimes charged in the Indictment. Accordingly, an international arrest warrant was issued and transmitted to all States. [footnote 18 – *Ibid.*, para. 36.]

13. The Trial Chamber also found that the failure of the Prosecution to effect service of the Indictment was due wholly to the failure or refusal of the Bosnian Serb administration in Pale to co-operate. In accordance with the procedure of Rule 61(E), the Presiding Judge of the Trial Chamber requested the President of the Tribunal to notify the Security Council of this failure. [footnote 19 – *Ibid.*] The President of the Tribunal complied with this request and sent a letter dated 31 October 1995 to notify the Security Council. [footnote 20 – S/1995/910, 31 October 1995.]

...

15. On or about 20 April 2000, Nikolic was arrested and detained by SFOR [Stabilization Force in Bosnia and Herzegovina] and, thereafter, on 21 April 2000, transferred to the Tribunal. How Nikolic came into the custody of SFOR is not entirely clear. It is alleged that he was kidnapped in Serbia by a number of persons and delivered into the hands of SFOR officers stationed in the Republic of Bosnia and Herzegovina. ...

V. ATTRIBUTION

31. As set out above, the Parties are in agreement that the Accused was

apprehended in the territory of the FRY by individuals not related to SFOR, transferred to Bosnia and Herzegovina and then delivered to SFOR. The Parties disagree, however, as to the question how the relationship between the individuals who apprehended the Accused and SFOR and between SFOR and the Prosecution should be assessed. Related to the nature of this relationship is the question of what the consequent effect of any potentially illegal act committed by such individuals prior to the handing over of the Accused to the Tribunal should be on the exercise of jurisdiction by the Tribunal.

32. The Defence submits that when SFOR personnel took custody of the Accused, they had – actual or constructive – knowledge of the fact that he had been unlawfully apprehended and brought against his will from the territory of the FRY into the territory of Bosnia and Herzegovina. The Defence also submits that SFOR, aware of the illegal character of the arrest, took advantage of the situation by taking the Accused into custody and handing him over to the Prosecution. The Defence sets out that "by not only ignoring the illegality but, by actively taking advantage of the situation and taking into custody the accused, SFOR's exercise of jurisdiction over Nikolic was an adoption of the illegality – of which they were aware – and thus, an extension of the unlawful detention." [footnote omitted]

33. The Prosecution replies that any irregularities committed by the authorities of another State or individuals prior to the delivery of the Accused to the jurisdiction of the Tribunal should not suffice to divest the Tribunal of its jurisdiction over him. Here, SFOR appears to have been merely a fortuitous recipient of the Accused. [footnote omitted]

34. In order to be able to determine the issue at hand, the Trial Chamber first must determine the legal framework within which both SFOR and the Tribunal, in particular the Prosecution, operate.

A. Legal framework

35. The Tribunal was established by the Security Council on 25 May 1993 in resolution 827. The resolution was adopted under Chapter VII of the United Nations Charter. Accordingly, the resolution is binding on all Member States of the UN. Paragraph 4 of the resolution specifies that all States "shall co-operate fully with the International Tribunal and its organs in accordance with the present resolution and the Statute of the International Tribunal" and affirms the "obligation of States to comply with requests for assistance or orders issued by a Trial Chamber under Article 29 of the Statute." Subsequent Security Council resolutions, including those relating to the establishment and functioning of IFOR and SFOR, reaffirm that duty on Member States. [footnote 41 – See for example SC resolution 1031 (1995), para. 4 and SC resolution 1174 (1998), para. 4.]

36. Article 29 (1) of the Statute reiterates that States must co-operate with the Tribunal. Paragraph 2 states further, *inter alia*, that "States shall comply without undue delay with any request for assistance or an order issued by a Trial Chamber, including, but not limited to: (a) the identification and location of persons; (…) (d) the arrest or detention of persons, and (e) the surrender or the transfer of the accused to the International Tribunal."

…

39. On 14 December 1995, the Dayton Peace Agreement (the "Dayton Agreement") was signed in Paris. As part of the Dayton Agreement, the multinational military Implementation Force ("IFOR") was created. The Dayton Agreement was concluded between the governments of Bosnia and Herzegovina, Croatia and the FRY ("the Parties"). Article IX of the General Framework Agreement stipulates that the Parties

> [s]hall cooperate fully with all entities involved in implementation of this peace settlement, as described in the Annexes to this Agreement, or which are otherwise authorized by the United Nations Security Council, pursuant to the obligation of all Parties to cooperate in the investigation and prosecution of war crimes and other violations of international humanitarian law.
>
> ...

46. In May 1996, an agreement was concluded between the Tribunal and the Supreme Headquarters Allied Powers Europe ("SHAPE"). In the *Simic* decision [footnote 46 – *Simic* Decision, ft 7 above [*Prosecutor v. Blagoje Simic, Milan Simic, Miroslav Tadic, Stevan Todorovic, Simo Zaric*, Case No. IT-95-9, Decision on Motion for Judicial Assistance to be Provided by SFOR and Others, 18 October 2000], p. 17.] of 18 October 2000, reference is made to the following pertinent provisions in this agreement:

> ...
>
> ... 3.2 ... *The Tribunal will also defend SHAPE and IFOR for any errors or omissions occurring as a result of the application of Articles 1, 2 and 3 by IFOR personnel acting in good faith during such detentions.* [footnote omitted]

47. In 1996, Security Council resolution 1088 (12 December 1996) authorised the Member States, acting through or in co-operation with the organisation referred to in Annex 1-A of the Dayton Agreement to establish SFOR as the legal successor to IFOR for a period of 18 months. Operative paragraph 7 of this resolution

> Reminds the parties that, in accordance with the Peace Agreement, they have committed themselves to cooperate fully with all entities involved in the implementation of this peace settlement, as described in the Peace Agreement, or which are otherwise authorized by the Security Council, including the International Tribunal for the Former Yugoslavia, as it carries out its responsibilities for dispensing justice impartially, and underlines that full cooperation by States and entities with the International Tribunal includes, *inter alia*, the surrender for trial of all persons indicted by the Tribunal and provision of information to assist in Tribunal investigations;

This mandate of SFOR was subsequently renewed by several Security Council resolutions and remained applicable throughout the period relevant for this decision. [footnote 50 – See Security Council resolutions 1174 (15 June 1998) and 1247 (18 June 1999).]

B. Assessment

48. As the Secretary General of the United Nations confirmed in his report on the establishment of this Tribunal,

> [a]n order by a Trial Chamber for the surrender or transfer of persons to the custody of the International Tribunal

shall be considered to be the application of an enforcement measure under Chapter VII of the Charter of the United Nations. [footnote 51 – Report of the Secretary General Pursuant to Paragraph 2 of Security Council resolution 808 (1993), UN Doc. S/25704 (3 May 1993), paras 125–126.]

49. The question that may arise is whether the duty to co-operate, as laid down in Article 29, applies to States only, or also to other entities or collective enterprises, such as SFOR. Read literally, Article 29 seems to relate to States only. This question had been discussed previously, *inter alia*, by the Trial Chamber in the *Simic* Decision. This Trial Chamber sees no reason to take a different view and refers to the following observations in that Decision:

> In principle, there is no reason why Article 29 should not apply to collective enterprises undertaken by States, in the framework of international organisations and, in particular, their competent organs such as SFOR in the present case. A purposive construction of Article 29 suggests that it is applicable to such collective enterprises as it is to States. ... [footnote 52 – *Simic* Decision, ft 7 above, pp. 18–19.]

...

52. The legal basis for the authority of SFOR to arrest, detain and transfer persons indicted by this Tribunal is, in the view of this Chamber, firmly established. ...

...

54. When applying the legal framework to the assumed facts, the following conclusions can be drawn. The Accused was brought into the hands of SFOR troops in Bosnia and Herzegovina by some unknown individuals who had arrested and transferred him from the territory of the FRY to the territory of Bosnia and Herzegovina. The Accused can therefore be said to have "come into contact with" SFOR. SFOR had the authority to detain him and did so in application of the procedure laid down in the SHAPE Agreement. A representative of the Tribunal was informed and the Accused transferred to The Hague.

55. Might SFOR in fact have acted differently and, for example, released the Accused? In the view of this Chamber, that question can be answered in the negative only. Rule 59 *bis*, paragraph (A) explicitly refers to "an order for the prompt transfer of the accused to the Tribunal in the event that the accused be taken into custody by that authority or international body (...).″ The use of the word "order" in this provision is in itself already indicative of a binding character. As discussed above, Article 29 of the Statute does not apply only to States. Here again, a purposive interpretation of this Article, in combination with Rule 59 *bis*, can lead the Chamber to no other conclusion than that, in the particular circumstances of this case the relevant SFOR forces had no other option than to detain the Accused and to set the standard procedures in motion in order to have the Accused transferred to The Hague.

C. Attribution to SFOR

56. On the basis of the legal framework set out above, the question of whether the alleged illegal acts undertaken by unknown individuals against the Accused can be attributed to SFOR needs to be addressed.

57. According to the assumed facts between the Parties, some unknown individuals arrested the Accused in the territory of the FRY and brought him across the border with Bosnia and Herzegovina and into the custody of SFOR. The mandate of SFOR extends only to the territory of Bosnia and Herzegovina. The Parties agree that these individuals had no connection whatsoever with SFOR and/or the Tribunal. SFOR, as described, acted within the applicable legal framework, detained the Accused and handed him over to a representative of the Office of the Prosecutor. Subsequently, he was brought to the United Nations Detention Unit in The Hague.

58. The Defence does not allege that SFOR participated in the illegal conduct of these unknown individuals. It argues primarily that when SFOR personnel took custody of the accused, "they had knowledge, actual or constructive, that the accused had been unlawfully apprehended and brought from Serbia against his free will, that his freedom of movement had been unlawfully restricted, that he had been unlawfully deprived of his liberty and that he had been, and remains, detained against his will." It argues in addition that "SFOR personnel opted to 'take advantage' of the situation by taking custody of the accused, alerting the International Tribunal of his presence and proceeding with the arrest procedures as agreed with the Tribunal." [footnote omitted]

59. The Prosecution counters these arguments and submits that SFOR was merely a fortuitous recipient of the Accused as a result of the fact that unknown individuals had delivered him to SFOR in Bosnia and Herzegovina. It argues that the Prosecution was not involved in these alleged illegal activities, an argument that is not disputed by the Defence. It also claims that there was no form of adoption or approval of these activities by the Prosecution and that "the mere subsequent *acceptance* by the Prosecution of custody of the Accused cannot in and of itself satisfy the required level of 'collusion' or 'official involvement' on the part of the Prosecution." In short, the Prosecution submits that both SFOR and the Prosecution merely carried out their duties in accordance with the legal framework described above. [footnote omitted]

60. In determining the question as to whether the illegal conduct of the individuals can somehow be attributed to SFOR, the Trial Chamber refers to the principles laid down in the Draft Articles of the International Law Commission ("ILC") on the issue of "Responsibilities of States for Internationally Wrongful Acts". These Draft Articles were adopted by the ILC at its fifty-third session in 2001. [footnote 62 – See: Official Records of the General Assembly, Fifty-sixth session, Supplement No. 10 (A/56/10), chp. IV.E.2.] The Trial Chamber is however aware of the fact that any use of this source should be made with caution. The Draft Articles were prepared by the International Law Commission and are still subject to debate amongst States. They do not have the status of treaty law and are not binding on States. Furthermore, as can be deduced from its title, the Draft Articles are primarily directed at the responsibilities of States and not at those of international organisations or entities. As Draft Article 57 emphasises,

> [t]hese articles are without prejudice to any question of the responsibility under international law of an

international organization, or of any State for the conduct of an international organization.

61. In the present context, the focus should first be on the possible attribution of the acts of the unknown individuals to SFOR. As indicated in Article I of Annex 1-A to the Dayton Agreement, IFOR (SFOR) is a multinational military force. It "may be composed of ground, air and maritime units from NATO and non-NATO nations" and "will operate under the authority and subject to the direction and political control of the North Atlantic Council." For the purposes of deciding upon the motions pending in the present case, the Chamber does not deem it necessary to determine the exact legal status of SFOR under international law. Purely as *general* legal guidance, it will use the principles laid down in the Draft Articles insofar as they may be helpful for determining the issue at hand.

62. Article 11 of the Draft Articles relates to "Conduct acknowledged and adopted by a State as its own" and states the following:

> Conduct which is not attributable to a State under the preceding articles shall nevertheless be considered an act of that State under international law if and to the extent that the State acknowledges and adopts the conduct in question as its own. [footnote 63 – *Ibid.*, [Official Records of the General Assembly, Fifty-sixth session, Supplement No. 10 (A/56/10), chp.IV.E.2.] p. 118

63. The Report of the ILC on the work of its fifty-third session sheds light on the meaning of the Article:

> Article 11 (...) provides for the attribution to a State of conduct that was not or may not have been attributable to it at the time of commission, but which is subsequently acknowledged and adopted by the State as its own. (...), article 11 is based on the principle that purely private conduct cannot as such be attributed to a State. But it recognizes "nevertheless" that conduct is to be considered as an act of State "if and to the extent that the State acknowledges and adopts the conduct in question *as its own.* [footnote 64 – *Ibid.*, [Official Records of the General Assembly, Fifty-sixth session, Supplement No. 10 (A/56/10), chp.IV.E.2.] p. 119 (emphasis added)

Furthermore, in this report a distinction is drawn between concepts such as "acknowledgement" and "adoption" from concepts such as "support" or "endorsement". The ILC argues that

> [a]s a general matter, conduct will not be attributable to a State under article 11 where a State merely acknowledges the factual existence of conduct or expresses its verbal approval of it. In international controversies States often take positions which amount to "approval" or "endorsement" of conduct in some general sense but do not involve any assumption of responsibility. The language of "adoption", on the other hand, carries with it the idea that the conduct is acknowledged by the State *as, in effect, its own conduct.* [footnote 65 – *Ibid.*, [Official Records of the General Assembly, Fifty-sixth session, Supplement No. 10 (A/56/10), chp.IV.E.2.] pp. 121–122 (emphasis added).

64. The Trial Chamber observes that both Parties use the same and similar criteria of "acknowledgement", "adoption", "recognition", "approval" and

"ratification", as used by the ILC. The question is therefore whether on the basis of the assumed facts SFOR can be considered to have "acknowledged *and* adopted" [footnote 66 – These conditions are set out in a conjunctive way in Draft Article 11 and the commentary thereto.] the conduct undertaken by the individuals "as its own". It needs to be re-emphasised in this context that it cannot be deduced from the assumed facts that SFOR was in any way, directly or indirectly, involved in the actual apprehension of the accused in the FRY or in the transfer of the accused into the territory of Bosnia and Herzegovina . Nor has it in any way been argued or suggested that SFOR instructed, directed or controlled such acts. What can be concluded from the assumed facts is merely that the Accused was handed over to an SFOR unit after having been arrested in the FRY by unknown individuals and brought into the territory of Bosnia and Herzegovina. From the perspective of SFOR, the Accused had come into contact with SFOR in the execution of their assigned task. In accordance with their mandate and in light of Article 29 of the Statute and Rule 59 *bis*, they were obliged to inform the Prosecution and to hand him over to its representatives. From these facts, the Trial Chamber can readily conclude that there was no collusion or official involvement by SFOR in the alleged illegal acts.

65. Both SFOR and the Tribunal are involved in a peace mission and are expected to contribute in a positive way to the restoration of peace and security in the area. Any use of methods and practices that would, in themselves, violate fundamental principles of international law and justice would be contrary to the mission of this Tribunal.

66. The question that remains is, whether the fact that SFOR and the Prosecution, in the words of the Prosecution, became the "mere passive beneficiary of his fortuitous (even irregular) rendition to Bosnia" could, as the Defence claims, amount to an "adoption" or "acknowledgement" of the illegal conduct "as their own".

67. The Trial Chamber responds to this question in the negative. Once a person comes "in contact with" SFOR, like in the present case, SFOR is obliged under Article 29 of the Statute and Rule 59 *bis* to arrest/detain the person and have him transferred to the Tribunal. The assumed facts show that SFOR, once confronted with the Accused, detained him, informed the representative of the Prosecution and assisted in his transfer to The Hague. In this way, SFOR did nothing but implement its obligations under the Statute and the Rules of this Tribunal. ...

Notes

- What are SFOR, SHAPE, NATO, and the ICTY? What are the relationships between them?
- What is the legal value of the Draft Articles? Which Draft Articles does the chamber cite?
- Does the ICTY express a view whether it is conduct or responsibility being adopted?
- Why does the chamber decide as it does on the question of responsibility?

9.2.3 Other modes of responsibility

An international organization can be responsible for its acts or omissions, as discussed above, but those acts all contemplated direct commission (or adoption of direct commission) of an internationally wrongful act. An organization might still be responsible for aiding or assisting another actor in a wrongful act,[38] controlling[39] or coercing[40] another actor to commit a wrongful act, or otherwise circumventing its international obligations by acting through states.[41] In addition, where an international organization is a member of another organization, then the comparable rules on states incurring responsibility through their membership acts would apply by analogy.[42]

An often cited example of this kind of working relationship is the cooperation of the United Nations Organization Mission in the Democratic Republic of the Congo (MONUC) with the Armed Forces of the DR Congo (FARDC). The UN Office of Legal Affairs (UNOLA) concluded that, if MONUC has reason to believe that FARDC was violating international law, then MONUC may not cooperate or support that operation. UNOLA stated that these were obligations on the UN and MONUC from international law.[43] What kind of help would rise to the level of aid or assistance for purposes of this article? UNOLA understood this help to be any "logistic or 'service' support to any FARDC operation." Would financial aid be sufficient?

9.2.4 Circumstances precluding wrongfulness

In addition, the Draft Articles provide several bases where a wrongful act is excused or justified, and thus not wrongful. These circumstances would include consent of the state being wronged,[44] self-defense,[45] *force majeure*,[46] distress,[47] and necessity.[48] It

---

[38] International Law Commission, Draft Articles on the Responsibility of International Organizations, II(2) Yearbook of the International Law Commission (2011), UN Doc. A/CN.4/SER.A/2011/Add.1 (Part 2), Article 14 Aid or assistance in the commission of an internationally wrongful act.
[39] *Ibid.*, Article 15 Direction and control exercised over the commission of an internationally wrongful act.
[40] *Ibid.*, Article 16 Coercion of a State or another international organization.
[41] *Ibid.*, Article 17 Circumvention of international obligations through decisions and authorizations addressed to members.
[42] *Ibid.*, Article 18 Responsibility of an international organization member of another international organization.
[43] *See* Patricia O'Brien, UN Legal Counsel and Under-Secretary-General for Legal Affairs, Note to Alain Le Roy, UN Under-Secretary-General for Peacekeeping Operations, MONUC – draft policy on conditionality of support to the FARDC (12 October 2009).
[44] International Law Commission, Draft Articles on the Responsibility of International Organizations, II(2) Yearbook of the International Law Commission (2011), UN Doc. A/CN.4/SER.A/2011/Add.1 (Part 2), Article 20 Consent.
[45] *Ibid.*, Article 21 Self-defence.
[46] *Ibid.*, Article 23 Force majeure.
[47] *Ibid.*, Article 24 Distress.
[48] *Ibid.*, Article 25 Necessity.

would also include wrongful acts undertaken as countermeasures to another actor's wrongful acts,[49] and acts taken in order to comply with *jus cogens* norms.[50]

9.2.5 Consequences of responsibility

The Draft Articles also provide for various remedies and other outcomes when an international organization is responsible. Among these are the obligations of cessation and non-repetition,[51] as well as the obligations of reparation,[52] restitution,[53] compensation,[54] and satisfaction,[55] plus interest.[56] In addition, responsibility does not mean that on-going wrongfulness is excused, because there is also a "continued duty of performance."[57]

9.3 SUBSIDIARY RESPONSIBILITY FOR MEMBER STATES

If an international organization is deemed to be responsible under international law for wrongful acts, its member states might also be held to be responsible under the Draft Articles on State Responsibility. However, in cases where the organization is solely responsible and the member states are not deemed to be responsible, can the responsibility borne by the organization be imputed to the member states? After all, the member states created the organization and control it, and keep it funded. When the organization is responsible and must make restitution or pay other damages, those funds come, ultimately, from the member states. Surely it only makes sense that the member states are, in a sense, responsible for the acts of the international organization?

The difficulty with this line of thinking is that the organization, in order to be an organization, must have some appreciably distinct will separate from the member states. Recall the case *HvdP v. The Netherlands*,[58] discussed in Chapter 3 on the creation of international organizations. The Human Rights Committee, in deciding on the applicability of the International Covenant on Civil and Political Rights, held that the acts of the European Patent Office did not fall within the "jurisdiction" of the state, and thus the state could not be responsible for any acts that may have violated the human rights of the individual under the International Covenant on Civil and Political Rights.

If the acts of the organization were at the direction of the state or states, then the states would be responsible under the normal rules on responsibility:

---

49 *Ibid.*, Article 22 Countermeasures.
50 *Ibid.*, Article 26 Compliance with peremptory norms.
51 *Ibid.*, Article 30.
52 *Ibid.*, Articles 31, 34.
53 *Ibid.*, Article 35
54 *Ibid.*, Article 36.
55 *Ibid.*, Article 37
56 *Ibid.*, Article 38.
57 *Ibid.*, Article 29.
58 HvdP v. The Netherlands, Communication No. 217/1986, Decision on Admissibility, UN Doc. A/42/40 (Human Rights Committee, 28 August 1987).

International Law Commission,
Draft articles on the responsibility of international organizations
II(2) Yearbook of the International Law Commission (2011)
UN Doc. A/CN.4/SER.A/2011/Add.1 (Part 2)[59]

Article 58 Aid or assistance by a State in the commission of an internationally wrongful act by an international organization

1. A State which aids or assists an international organization in the commission of an internationally wrongful act by the latter is internationally responsible for doing so if:
    (a) the State does so with knowledge of the circumstances of the internationally wrongful act; and
    (b) the act would be internationally wrongful if committed by that State.
2. An act by a State member of an international organization done in accordance with the rules of the organization does not as such engage the international responsibility of that State under the terms of this article.

Article 59 Direction and control exercised by a State over the commission of an internationally wrongful act by an international organization

1. A State which directs and controls an international organization in the commission of an internationally wrongful act by the latter is internationally responsible for that act if:
    (a) the State does so with knowledge of the circumstances of the internationally wrongful act; and
    (b) the act would be internationally wrongful if committed by that State.
2. An act by a State member of an international organization done in accordance with the rules of the organization does not as such engage the international responsibility of that State under the terms of this draft article.

Article 60 Coercion of an international organization by a State

A State which coerces an international organization to commit an act is internationally responsible for that act if:
    (a) the act would, but for the coercion, be an internationally wrongful act of the coerced international organization; and
    (b) the coercing State does so with knowledge of the circumstances of the act.

---

[59] From the Yearbook of the International Law Commission, by the International Law Commission © 2011 United Nations. Reprinted with the permission of the United Nations.

Other than these cases, in general, the member states of an organization are not automatically responsible for the wrongful acts of the organization under any theory of subsidiary responsibility. The House of Lords had to address the various possible theories of subsidiary responsibility in the litigation over the winding down of the International Tin Council. This case before the Lords was actually a combination of several actions by various applicants all claiming that the dissolution of the International Tin Council left them with significant damages.

J.H. Rayner (Mincing Lane) Ltd v Department of Trade and Industry and Others, and related appeals; Maclaine Watson & Co Ltd v Department of Trade and Industry; Maclaine Watson & Co Ltd v International Tin Council
Decision on Appeal
[1989] UKHL J1026-1, [1990] 2 AC 418, [1989] 3 WLR 969
House of Lords, United Kingdom, 26 October 1989

[p. 525]

Lord Templeman

My Lords, these appeals raise a short question of construction of the plain words of a statutory instrument. The trial judges (Staughton J ([1987] BCLC 667) and Millett J ([1987] BCLC 707, [1987] 1 All ER 890, [1987] 3 All ER 787, 886)) and the Court of Appeal (Kerr, Nourse and Ralph Gibson LJJ ([1988] 3 All ER 257, [1989] Ch 72)) rightly decided this question in favour of the respondents. Losing the construction argument, the appellants put forward alternative submissions which are unsustainable. Those submissions, if accepted, would involve a breach of the British constitution and an invasion by the judiciary of the functions of the government and of Parliament. The government may negotiate, conclude, construe, observe, breach, repudiate or terminate a treaty. Parliament may alter the laws of the United Kingdom. The courts must enforce those laws; judges have no power to grant specific performance of a treaty or to award damages against a sovereign state for breach of a treaty or to invent laws or misconstrue legislation in order to enforce a treaty.

A treaty is a contract between the governments of two or more sovereign states. International law regulates the relations between sovereign states and determines the validity, the interpretation and the enforcement of treaties. A treaty to which Her Majesty's government is a party does not alter the laws of the United Kingdom. A treaty may be incorporated into and alter the laws of the United Kingdom by means of legislation. Except to the extent that a treaty becomes incorporated into the laws of the United Kingdom by statute, the courts of the United Kingdom have no power to enforce treaty rights and obligations at the behest of a sovereign government or at the behest of a private individual.

[p. 526]

The Sixth International Tin Agreement (New York, 30 April 1982; Misc 13 (1982); Cmnd 8546) was a treaty between the United Kingdom government, 22 other sovereign states and the

European Economic Community (the member states). The Sixth Agreement continued in existence the International Tin Council (the ITC) as an international organisation charged with regulating the worldwide production and marketing of tin in the interests of producers and consumers. By art 16 of the Sixth Agreement the member states agreed that:

"1. The Council shall have legal personality. It shall in particular have the capacity to contract, to acquire and dispose of movable and immovable property and to institute legal proceedings ..."

Pursuant to the provisions of the Sixth Agreement a Headquarters Agreement (London, 9 February 1972; TS 38 (1972); Cmnd 4938) was entered into between the ITC and the United Kingdom in order to define "the status, privileges and immunities of the Council" in the United Kingdom. Article 3 of the Headquarters Agreement provided:

"The Council shall have legal personality. It shall in particular have the capacity to contract and to acquire and dispose of movable and immovable property and to institute legal proceedings."

No part of the Sixth Agreement or the Headquarters Agreement was incorporated into the laws of the United Kingdom but the International Tin Council (Immunity and Privileges) Order 1972, SI 1972/120 (the 1972 order), made under the International Organisations Act 1968, provided in art 5: "The Council shall have the legal capacities of a body corporate."

The ITC entered into contracts with each of the appellants. The appellants claim, and it is not disputed, that the ITC became liable to pay and in breach of contract has not paid to the appellants sums amounting in the aggregate to millions of pounds. In these proceedings the appellants seek to recover the debts owed to them by the ITC from the member states.

The four alternative arguments adduced by the appellants in favour of the view that the member states are responsible for the debts of the ITC were described throughout these appeals as submissions A, B1, B2 and C.

Submission A relies on the fact that the 1972 order did not incorporate the ITC but only conferred on the ITC the legal capacities of a body corporate. Therefore, it is said, under the laws of the United Kingdom the ITC has no separate existence as a legal entity apart from its members; the contracts concluded in the name of the ITC were contracts by the member states.

Submission A reduces the 1972 order to impotence. The appellants argue that the 1972 order was only intended to facilitate the carrying on in the United Kingdom of the activities of 23 sovereign states and the EEC under the collective name of "the International Tin Council". Legislation is not necessary to enable trading to take place under a collective name. The appellants suggested that the 1972 order was intended to enable the member states to hold land in the United Kingdom in the name of a nominee. Legislation is not necessary for that purpose either. The appellants then suggested that the 1972 order was necessary to relieve the member states from a duty to register the collective name of the ITC and from complying with the other provisions of the Registration of Business Names Act 1916. This trivial suggestion was confounded when, at a late stage in the hearing, the 1916 Act (now repealed) was examined and found not to apply to an international organisation established by sovereign states. The 1972 order did not confer on 23 sovereign states and the EEC the rights to trade under a name and to hold land in the name of the ITC. The 1972 order conferred on the ITC the legal capacities of a body corporate. The appellants submitted that, if Parliament had intended to do more than endow 23 sovereign states and the EEC trading in this country with a collective name, then Parliament would have created the ITC a body corporate. But the [p. 527] government of the United Kingdom had by treaty concurred in the establishment of the ITC as an *international* organisation. Consistently with the treaty, the United Kingdom could not convert the ITC into a United Kingdom organisation. In order to clothe the ITC in the *United Kingdom* with legal personality in accordance with the treaty, Parliament conferred on the ITC the legal capacities of a body corporate. The courts of the United Kingdom became bound by the 1972 order to treat the activities of the ITC as if those activities had been carried out by the ITC as a body incorporated under the laws of the United Kingdom. The 1972 order is inconsistent with any intention on the part of Parliament to oblige or allow the courts of the United Kingdom to consider the nature of an international organisation. The 1972 order is inconsistent with any intention on the part of Parliament that creditors and courts should regard the ITC as a partnership between 23 sovereign states and the EEC trading in the United Kingdom like any private partnership. The 1972 order is inconsistent with any intention on the part of Parliament that contracts made by the ITC with metal brokers, bankers, staff, landlords, suppliers of goods and services and others shall be treated by those creditors or by the court of the United Kingdom as contracts entered into by 23 sovereign states and the EEC. The 1972 order conferred on the ITC the legal capacities of a body corporate. Those capacities include the power to contract. The ITC entered into contracts with the appellants.

The appellants submitted that if there had been no 1972 order the courts would have been compelled to deal with the ITC as though it were a collective name for an unincorporated association. But the rights of the creditors of the ITC and the powers of the courts of the United Kingdom must depend on the effect of the 1972 order and that order cannot be construed as if it did not exist. An international organisation might have been treated by the courts of the United Kingdom as an unincorporated association if the 1972 order had not been passed. But the 1972 order was passed. When the ITC exercised the capacities of a body corporate, the effect of that exercise was the same as the effect of the exercise of those capacities by a body corporate. The ITC cannot exercise the capacities of a body corporate and at the same time be treated as if it were an unincorporated association. The 1972 order brought into being an entity which must be recognised by the courts of the United Kingdom as a legal personality distinct in law from its membership and capable of entering into contracts as principal. None of the authorities cited by the appellants were of any assistance in construing the effect of the grant by Parliament of the legal capacities of a body corporate to an international organisation pursuant to a treaty obligation to confer legal personality on that organisation. In my opinion the effect is plain: the ITC is a separate legal personality distinct from its members.

The second argument of the appellants, which is known as submission B1, accepts that the ITC enjoys a separate legal existence apart from its constituent members but contends that a contract by the ITC involves a concurrent direct or guarantee liability on the members jointly and severally. This liability is said to flow from a general principle of law, that traders operating under a collective name incur a liability to third parties which can only be excluded by incorporation; the ITC has not been formally incorporated and therefore, it is said, the member states are liable concurrently. No authority was cited which supported the alleged general principle. On the contrary, there is ample authority for the general proposition that in England no one is liable on a contract except the parties thereto. The only parties to the contracts between the appellants and the ITC were the appellants and the ITC. Members of a body corporate are not liable for the debts of a body corporate because the members are not parties to the corporation's contracts. The member states are not liable for the debts of the ITC because the members were not parties to the contracts of the ITC. It was said on behalf of the appellants that under the laws of Scotland, Germany, France, Puerto Rico and Jordan and elsewhere, recognition is accorded to "mixed entities" as a description of associations which are legal entities but whose engagements, notwithstanding the separate legal personality of the associations, involve some form of liability of the members. Authorities were produced which demonstrate that by custom or by legislation the members of some corporations in some [p. 528] countries are not free from personal liability. But no such custom exists in the United Kingdom as a general rule and s 4 of the Partnership Act 1890 which preserves for a Scottish partnership some of the benefits of incorporation and some of the attributes of an unincorporated association, does not prove the existence of any general custom in any part of the United Kingdom that members of a corporation or of a body analogous to corporations shall be liable for the debts of the corporation. Parliament, of course, may provide that members of a corporation shall bear liability for or shall be bound to contribute directly or indirectly to payment of the debts of the corporation to a limited or to an unlimited extent in accordance with express statutory provisions. The history of the Companies Acts illustrates the power of Parliament, if it pleases, to impose some liability on shareholders as a condition of the grant of incorporation. Parliament could have imposed some liability for the debts of the ITC on the member states. But Parliament passed the 1972 order which imposed no such liability. The 1972 order conferred on the ITC the capacities of a body corporate. Those capacities included the power to enter into contracts. In the absence of express parliamentary provision a contract entered into by the ITC does not involve any liability on any person who was not a party to the contract.

The third argument, described as submission B2, is that a rule of international law imposes on sovereign states, members of an international organisation, joint and several liability for the default of the organisation in the payment of its debts unless the treaty which establishes the international organisation clearly disclaims any liability on the part of the members. No plausible evidence was produced of the existence of such a rule of international law before or at the time of the Sixth Agreement in 1982 or thereafter. The appellants submitted that this House was bound to accept or reject such a rule of international law and should not shrink from inventing such a law and from publishing a precedent which might persuade other states to accept such law.

My Lords, if there existed a rule of international law which implied in a treaty or imposed on sovereign states which enter into a treaty an obligation (in default of a clear disclaimer in the treaty) to discharge the debts of an international organisation established by that treaty, the rule of international law could only be enforced under international law. Treaty rights and obligations conferred or imposed by agreement or by international law cannot be enforced by the courts of the United Kingdom. The appellants concede that the alleged rule of international law must imply and include a right of contribution whereby, if one member state discharged the debts of the ITC, the other member states would be bound to share the burden. The appellants acknowledge that such right of contribution could only be enforced under international law and could not be made the subject of an order by the courts of the United Kingdom. This acknowledgment is inconsistent with the appellants' submission B2. An international law or a domestic law which imposed and enforced joint and several liability on 23 sovereign states without imposing and enforcing contribution between those states would be devoid of logic and justice. If the present appeal succeeded, the only effective remedy of the appellants in this country would be against the United Kingdom. This remedy would be fully effective so that in practice every creditor of the ITC would claim to be paid, and would be paid, by the United Kingdom the full amount and any interest payable to the creditor by the ITC. The United Kingdom government would then be embroiled, as a result of a decision of this House, in negotiations and possibly disagreements with other members states in order to obtain contribution. The causes of the failure of the ITC and liability for its debts are disputed. Some states might continue to deny the existence of any obligation, legal or moral, municipal or international, to pay the debts of the ITC or to contribute to such payment. Some states might be willing to contribute rateably with every other state, each bearing 1/23. A state which under the Sixth Agreement was only liable to contribute 1% of the capital of the ITC might, on the other hand, only be prepared to contribute 1% to the payment of the debts. The producing states which suffered more from the collapse of the ITC than the consuming states might not be willing to contribute as much as the consuming states. Some member states might protest that the Sixth Agreement shows [p. 529] an intention that member states should only be liable to contribute to the activities of the ITC a buffer stock of metal and cash intended to be worth £500m and lost as a result of the fall in tin prices on the metal exchanges which the ITC strove to avoid and which resulted in the collapse of the ITC.

The courts of the United Kingdom have no power to enforce at the behest of any sovereign state or at the behest of any individual citizen of any sovereign state rights granted by treaty or obligations imposed in respect of a treaty by international law. It was argued that the courts of the United Kingdom will construe and enforce rights and obligations resulting from an agreement to which a foreign law applies in accordance with the provisions of that foreign law. For example, an English creditor of a Puerto Rican corporation could sue and recover in the courts of the United Kingdom against the members of the corporation if, by the law of Puerto Rico, the members were liable to pay the debts of the corporation. By analogy, it was submitted, an English creditor of an international organisation should be able to sue in the courts of the United Kingdom the members of the international organisation if by international law the members are liable to pay the debts of the organisation. But there is no analogy between private international law which enables the courts of the United Kingdom to resolve differences between different laws of different states and a rule of public international law which imposes obligations on treaty states. Public international law cannot alter the meaning and effect of United Kingdom legislation. If the suggested rule of public international law existed and imposed on a state any obligation towards the creditors of the ITC, then the 1972 order would be in breach of international law because the order failed to confer rights on creditors against member states. It is impossible to construe the 1972 order as imposing any liability on the member states. The courts of the United Kingdom only have power to enforce rights and obligations which are made enforceable by the order.

The fourth argument, described as submission C, asserts that by the Sixth Agreement the ITC was only authorised to contract as agent for the member states. Even if this assertion were correct, the Sixth Agreement could only be considered by the courts of the United Kingdom for the purpose of resolving any ambiguity in the meaning and effect of the 1972 order. There is no ambiguity. The 1972 order authorised the ITC to contract as principal because the 1972 order conferred on the ITC the legal capacities of a body corporate without limitation. The treaty, the Sixth Agreement, has not been incorporated into the laws of the United Kingdom and the provisions of the Sixth Agreement cannot be employed for the purpose of altering or contradicting the provisions of the 1972 order.

Finally, one of the appellants, Maclaine Watson & Co Ltd, appealed against the refusal of the courts below to appoint a receiver. Maclaine Watson is a judgment creditor of the ITC and seeks the appointment of a receiver by way of equitable execution. The receiver is intended to receive and enforce a chose in action belonging to the ITC. The chose in action is an alleged right vested in the ITC to be indemnified by the member states against the debts payable by the ITC and incurred as a result of carrying out the instructions of the member states contained in the Sixth Agreement. My Lords, in English law the members of a corporation are not liable to indemnify the corporation against debts incurred by the corporation. The 1972 order made no provision for the member states to indemnify the

ITC. No doubt the debts of the ITC were incurred in exercise of powers which by the Sixth Agreement the member states agreed between themselves should be exercisable and which they instructed the ITC to exercise. However, powers contained in the Sixth Agreement are treaty powers and any indemnity obligation expressly or impliedly imposed on the member states by virtue of the Sixth Agreement is a treaty obligation which cannot be enforced by the courts of the United Kingdom by the appointment of a receiver or otherwise because the obligation is not to be found in the 1972 order.

Your Lordships were urged to discern or invent and apply some rule of municipal law or international law which would render the member states liable to discharge the debts of the ITC because, so it was said, the member states have behaved badly. These [p. 530] proceedings cannot, however, be decided by criticism of the conduct of the member states for establishing the ITC, or by attaching blame to the member states for the failure of the ITC to prevent the recurring glut and scarcity of tin metal, or by condemning the management of the ITC by the member states, or by attributing to the operations of the metal exchanges the fall in tin prices which bankrupted the ITC, inflicted a loss of up to £500m on the member states and caused poverty and unemployment to the producing states. The courts possess neither the evidence nor the authority to pronounce judgment on these matters. International diplomacy and national policy will decide whether the debts of the ITC, an international organisation established by treaty, shall be discharged by the member states and, if so, in what manner the burden should be shared. English judges cannot meddle with unincorporated treaties. The result of these appeals follows inexorably from the fact that the appellants contracted with the ITC, which by the 1972 order had been clothed with the legal capacities of a body corporate. In *Salomon v A Salomon & Co Ltd* [1897] AC 22 at 30, [1895–9] All ER Rep 33 at 35 Lord Halsbury LC pointed out:

> ... once the company is legally incorporated it must be treated like any other independent person with its rights and liabilities appropriate to itself, and that the motives of those who took part in the promotion of the company are absolutely irrelevant in discussing what those rights and liabilities are.

Since *Salomon*'s case, traders and creditors have known that they do business with a corporation at their peril if they do not require guarantees from members of the corporation or adequate security. At all times the rights of the appellants, who do not lack legal advice, have been governed in the United Kingdom by the 1972 order, which offers no foundation in law for proceedings against the member states. These appeals must be dismissed.

For the conduct of these appeals, there were locked in battle 24 counsel supported by batteries of solicitors and legal experts, armed with copies of 200 authorities and 14 volumes of extracts, British and foreign, from legislation, books and articles. Ten counsel addressed the Appellate Committee for 26 days. This vast amount of written and oral material tended to obscure three fundamental principles: that the capacities of a body corporate include the capacity to contract, that no one is liable on a contract save the parties to the contract and that treaty rights and obligations are not enforceable in the courts of the United Kingdom unless incorporated into law by statute. In my opinion the length of oral argument permitted in future appeals should be subject to prior limitation by the Appellate Committee.

Notes

- You might wish to compare these statements with the Draft Articles on State Responsibility to see if they correctly restate those articles, contradict them, supplement them, or otherwise diverge.
- Can the opinions of the Lords be narrowed? Lord Templeman concluded: "No plausible evidence was produced of the existence of such a rule of international law." Does this mean that such a rule might exist, but was not satisfactorily proved here?
- Is there any fact that might change this outcome? Surely the member states might accept the responsibility willingly? When the above case was before the Court of Appeal, Lord Gibson held that responsibility could be accepted if that outcome was provided in the constitutive instrument of the organization.[60] Do rules of the organization other than the constitutive instrument accept such responsibility? What would be the reason for demanding that such acceptance be included in the constitutive instrument? But don't states already accept responsibility when they join an organization and pledge to keep it funded in good faith? Or is this acceptance of something different than acceptance of responsibility to third parties for wrongful acts? What if the third party was led to believe that the states would compensate it, based on the obligation to keep the organization funded?
- Why can't the International Tin Council simply be wound down like a corporation? In this respect, consider the International Bank for Reconstruction and Development article IV(9), which limits the liability of the Bank to the unpaid capital share.
- Consider once more the *Behrami* case discussed above. The European Court of Human Rights held that the allegedly wrongful acts could not be attributed to the states, so the organization was potentially responsible. If, however, the states bore some kind of subsidiary or joint responsibility, surely the court would have subjected that responsibility to judicial examination? Or is there a reason why, if the states did bear that subsidiary responsibility, it would still be insulated from review by the European Court of Human Rights?

The Draft Articles adopted the Lords' reasoning to a degree in article 62.

---

60 *See* Maclaine Watson and Co. Ltd. v. Department of Trade and Industry; J. H. Rayner (Mincing Lane) Ltd. v. Department of Trade and Industry and others, and related appeals, Judgment (Court of Appeal, England and Wales, 27 April 1988).

International Law Commission,
Draft articles on the responsibility of international organizations
II(2) Yearbook of the International Law Commission (2011)
UN Doc. A/CN.4/SER.A/2011/Add.1 (Part 2)[61]

Article 62 Responsibility of a State member of an international organization for an internationally wrongful act of that organization

1. A State member of an international organization is responsible for an internationally wrongful act of that organization if:
   (a) it has accepted responsibility for that act towards the injured party; or
   (b) it has led the injured party to rely on its responsibility.
2. Any international responsibility of a State under paragraph 1 is presumed to be subsidiary.

In the next case, and last case of this chapter, the Court of Arbitration at the International Chamber of Commerce had to consider a case similar to the *International Tin* case, yet the outcome was different:

Westland Helicopters Ltd and Arab Organization for Industrialization, United Arab Emirates, Kingdom of Saudi Arabia, State of Qatar, Arab Republic of Egypt and Arab British Helicopter Company
ICC Case No. 3879/AS
Interim Award Regarding Jurisdiction ("Compétence") of the Arbitral Tribunal
80 International Law Reports 595, 600
International Chamber of Commerce, Court of Arbitration, Arbitral Tribunal, 5 March 1984[62]

Grounds

I *Summary of the Facts*

On 29 April 1975, the sovereign States of the United Arab Emirates (Respondent No 2), Saudi Arabia (Respondent No 3), Qatar (Respondent No 4) and the Arab Republic of Egypt, hereinafter ARE (Respondent No 5), hereinafter together called the "four States", concluded an agreement entitled "Agreement for Establishing an Arab Industrialization Organization" (hereinafter called the "Treaty", marked No 1 of the supporting documents annexed to Westland's Request for Arbitration, hereinafter called "Exhibits"). By this Treaty an Organization was established, named

---

61 *Ibid.*
62 © Sir E. Lauterpacht, published by Cambridge University Press. Reproduced with permission of The Licensor through PLSclear.

the "Arab Organization for Industrialization" (hereinafter called "AOI"), the object of which was the development of an arms industry for the benefit of the four States. ...

On 27 February 1978, the AOI and the Claimant, Westland Helicopters Limited, a company subject to English law which manufactures helicopters (also called "Westland"), concluded a contract called the "Shareholders' "Agreement" the aim of which was the creation of a "joint stock company" of which AOI had, in the final stage, 70% of the shares and the Claimant the remaining 30%. The intention of the co-contracting parties was that this company (later called "The Arab British Helicopter Company", Respondent No 6, hereinafter "ABH") should serve as the legal base for the creation of a business which would manufacture, overhaul, carry out quality control on and sell the "Lynx" helicopters developed by the Claimant.

...

On 14 May 1979 (i.e. after the Camp David Agreement and the "entente" between the ARE and Israel), Prince Sultan bin Abdul Aziz published in the "Saudi Arabian News Agency" a statement (Exhibit 5) announcing his nomination as Chairman of the Higher Committee of the AOI by the United Arab Emirates, the Kingdom of Saudi Arabia and Qatar (the second, the third and the fourth Respondents, hereinafter called "the three States"). Referring to the recognition of Israel by the ARE and the decisions taken by the Summit Conference at Baghdad, this announcement gave notice that the three States were putting an end to the existence of the AOI as of 1 July 1979, that a Liquidation Committee would be set up and that all investment in the armaments business in question would be discontinued.

...

1 *Westland's Request for Arbitration*

The Claimant filed a Request for Arbitration ("Request for Arbitration") with the Court of Arbitration of the International Chamber of Commerce (ICC). In its original form the Request sought that:

> (1) The first five Defendants pay under a joint and several liability to the Claimant the sum of £126,000,000 – (one hundred twenty six million pounds sterling) plus interest thereon calculated at the rate of 2% above the National Westminster Bank Limited base rate, calculated as from the 14 May 1979 until full and final payment, less such sum as the Claimant shall be entitled to retain pursuant to an order made in accordance with paragraph (2) below.

III *The competence of the Arbitral Tribunal*

...

2 *Arbitration Clause binding the four States*

...

(B. The supranational status of the AOI)

In the circumstances, the first question to be asked concerns the "legal nature" and the status of the AOI. It is necessary to establish what are the legal rules governing this entity, what was the intention on foundation, in this respect, of the four States which created it, and what is the effect that they intended to achieve by their founding steps.

In order to examine this problem reference must firstly be made to the founding documents, that is to say to the constitutional laws creating the AOI: the Treaty, the Basic Statute and the Resolution of the High Committee of the AOI signed on 17 August 1975 and approving the Basic Statute (Exhibits Nos 1, 3 and 2). From these it is clear that the four States, in drawing them up, intended to define in an exhaustive and exclusive manner all legal aspects pertaining to the AOI, and above all that they wished to exclude the application of any national law. ... The four States did not moreover merely exclude the application to the AOI of any national law but undertook by the Treaty to adapt their domestic legislation to the requirements of the establishment of the AOI ..., thereby making it obvious that the AOI, far from being subject to any domestic legislation, was placed above it.

...

(C. The consequence of the possible attribution of personality to the AOI as regards the liability of the four States)

One may be tempted to reduce the question of whether the four States are bound by the acts of the AOI to one of whether the AOI has legal personality or not. A widespread theory, deriving moreover from Roman law ("*Si quid universitati debetur, singulis non debetur, nec quod debet universitas singuli debent*") Dig. 3,4; 7,1), excludes cumulative liability of a legal person and of the individuals which constitute it, these latter being party to none of the legal relations of the legal person. This notion, which could be deemed "strict", cannot however be applied in the present case. Nowhere is it accepted or given effect without limitation. Even in Switzerland, where more than probably anywhere else it serves as a reference, it is subject to important exceptions: A cooperative ("société coopérative") can be formed with the personal and unlimited liability of its members (Article 868 COS) without its legal personality being challenged; the same is true for the limited partnership with share capital [*société en commandite par actions*] (Articles 764 ff. COS). In addition the cooperative, the prototype of the legal person in the modern sense influenced by the doctrines of Germanic law, did not have at its outset an exclusion of the personal liability of its members who, on the contrary, were jointly liable for all its liabilities (*cf.* Otto Gierke, Geschichte des deutschen Körperschaftsbegriffs, vol. II of "Das deutsche Genossenschaftsrecht", Berlin 1873, p. 384). It is revealing that the old Swiss Federal Code of Obligations dated 1881, Article 688, starts from the principle of the joint and unlimited liability of the members; the exclusion of liability presupposes an express provision within the articles and publication in the Official Swiss Commercial Gazette. In France as in other countries, the general partnership [*société en nom collectif*] is deemed a legal person, even though its members are jointly liable for the obligations of the partnership. These observations show that the designation of an organization as "legal person" and the attribution of an independent existence do not provide any basis for a conclusion as to whether or not those who compose it are bound by obligations undertaken by it. One must therefore disregard any question relating to the personality of the AOI.

The possible liability of the four States must be determined by directly examining the founding documents of the AOI in relation to this problem.

(D. The liability of the four States in the light of the constitution of the AOI)

Neither the Treaty nor the Basic Statute of AOI states the effects, as regards the four States, of obligations undertaken by the AOI *vis-à-vis* third parties. As to the liability of the four States, concurrent with that of the AOI, there are no provisions which either expressly stipulate it or exclude it. The fact that the AOI "has the juridical personality", "enjoys full administrative and financial independence" and "has the right of ownership, disposition and litigation as mentioned in its statute" (Treaty, Article 1; in the same vein, see Basic Statute, Article 5), that is to say the express attribution of legal personality, of administrative independence and of the right to sue in the courts, does not in any respect allow one, as has been shown, to deduce an exclusion of the liability of the four States.

The same is true of the provision which states that AOI has a specified sum of capital (Basic Statute, Article 17); in the absence of any rule restricting liability to such capital, one cannot deduce therefrom any obstacle to an action against the four States. The provisions setting out capital are primarily internal to the AOI, determining the funds which its organs have at their disposal. One could perhaps infer that the four States' liability is secondary, in that they could not be proceeded against so long as the AOI performed its obligations whilst using the funds which had been granted to it; but it does not follow that the four States would have no liability whatsoever for obligations entered into by the AOI.

In the absence of any rule of applicable law ["règle de droit positif"], what is to be deduced from the silence of the founding documents of the AOI as to the liability of the four States? In the absence of any provision expressly or impliedly excluding the liability of the four States, this liability subsists since, as a general rule, those who engage in transactions of an economic nature are deemed liable for the obligations which flow therefrom. In default by the four States of formal exclusion of their liability, third parties which have contracted with the AOI could legitimately count on their liability.

This rule flows from general principles of law and from good faith. It can be supported if one likens the given situation to that which existed during the last century, where commercial organizations were formed without a clear legal basis (whether or not they could be considered as possessing personality). As a general rule, the founding members or the members of such bodies were held liable unless they had excluded their liability in a manner which could not escape third parties' notice which, for example, was the case with the establishment of a joint stock company, the generally known structure of which excluded the liability of shareholders. In the present case, the Basic Statute, despite the fixing of capital, does not classify the AOI as a "*société de capitaux*" such as a limited liability company. The AOI is rather more akin to a general partnership ["*sociétéen nom collectif*"] under French, Swiss or German law or a "partnership" under English or United States law. In this context, the phrase in Article 14 of the Treaty "Any Arab government may join this Agreement" and also that of the Basic Statute at Article 4 "those States which join the agreement" are significant, as are Articles 10(I), 1e and 15 of the Treaty calling the four States "participating countries". The provisions relating to its constitution and to the possible increase in capital of the AOI do not prevent this entity from being much closer to a partnership than to a "*société de capitaux*". This corresponds to the concept of "member" and "membership" which, in the constitution of the AOI, characterizes the position of each of the four States within it. The provisions of Article 3 of the Basic Statute ("The original members of the Organization are the four Arab States ..."), of Article 57 ("member State") and Articles 4 and 9 of the MOU ("the Member States of the AOI") lead one to think that the four States, in forming the AOI, did not intend wholly to disappear behind it, but rather to participate in the AOI as "members with liability" ("membres responsables").

One could equally compare the AOI to a cooperative which, in the absence of contrary provisions in existing legislation or within the articles, would leave subsisting the liability of the members.

(E. Limitation on the scope of the personality of the AOI by its constitution)

a) The foregoing is all the more true given that the personality conferred upon the AOI by the founding States was expressly limited, both by Article I of the Treaty and by Article 5 of the Basic Statute, solely to operational needs, as is provided in the articles of many international organizations.

b) The AOI was designated by its founders as an "organization" and as a "body", as opposed to the "joint-stock company" ABH, and the legal status of such a joint inter-state enterprise ["entreprise commune interétatique"] – to the extent that it can exist at all – cannot be relied upon in order to eliminate the liability of the States which are partners therein.

c) Finally, one must admit that in reality, in the circumstances of this case, the AOI is one with the States. At the same time as establishing the AOI, the Treaty set up the Higher Committee ("joint Ministerial Higher Committee") composed of the competent Ministers of the four States, charged with the responsibility not only to approve the Basic Statute, and to set up a provisional Directorate, but furthermore to direct the general policy of the AOI, and Article 23 of the Basic Statute describes this Committee as the "dominating authority". There could be no clearer demonstration of this identification of the States with the AOI, especially since Article 56 of the Statute specifies that in case of disagreement within the Committee, reference should be made to the Kings, Princes and Presidents of the States.

This Committee thus played a double role, both as organ of the AOI and as a grouping of States ["réunion d'Etats"]. In fact, in its role as organ of the AOI, it had under its control the operations of the AOI and, as a grouping of States ["réunion d'Etats"], it signed the MOU (Exhibit 3). It was in this way that Westland made arrangements to protect itself against the risks involved, through the signature of a series of documents intended to obtain the effective guarantee of the States themselves. First, these States represented *vis-à-vis* the British Government by the Egyptian Minister of War signing in the name of the High Committee, undertook, in this Memorandum, to ensure that the AOI and such companies as it controlled "will properly execute their obligations to all the British companies participating under the provisions of this Memorandum", which undertaking necessarily bound these States and was to Westland's benefit. Secondly, Westland executed with the AOI – indistinguishable from the States – the Shareholders Agreement, in Annex D of which the AOI guaranteed the purchase of 250 helicopters by ABH, and the two parties bound themselves, in Clause 12 of the Shareholders Agreement, to arbitration, the principle of which had been set out within Article 59 of the Statute.

All these precautions testify fully to Westland's desire to be protected by the States' guarantees and the latter could not help but be aware of the implications of their actions. Westland would not have entered into the transaction without them.

If it is true that the four States are bound by the obligations entered into by the AOI, these four States are equally bound by the arbitration clause concluded by the AOI, since the obligations under substantive law cannot be dissociated from those which exist on the procedural level. In making this appraisal, the Arbitral Tribunal does not at this stage intend to rule upon the substance of the Request.

(F. Rejection of the Respondents' arguments)

a) It is to no avail that ABH cites the *Wetco* judgment against the foregoing reasoning. In that case, the legal entity which had signed the arbitration clause (Linoco) was a company incorporated under Libyan national law and, unlike the AOI, did not have the character of a supra-national body. We do not know the details of the position of Linoco, but one can deduce from the grounds of the judgment that the constitutional provisions under which Linoco was established were to be interpreted in the sense that the Libyan Arab Republic wished to create an independent entity, solely responsible for its acts without the founding State being liable for Linoco. From the available information, it may even be deduced that Linoco resembled to a certain degree a legal person governed by private and commercial law, as can be created by States, and which, by its character, is distinct from its founder. These elements are not found in the present circumstances where, as has been shown, neither the Treaty nor the Basic Statute set out the limitation of any such liability.

b) It is also appropriate to reject the argument, raised by the ARE, that it is not authorized by its domestic legislation to undertake the obligations to which it subscribed at the international level. It has been held that no State can avail itself of its domestic laws in order to escape from its international obligations.

(G. Equity; abuse of law)

Finally, mention must be made of the practical reasons and considerations of equity which have motivated the arbitrators in this matter, quite apart from the legal grounds.

It would be wrong if the disagreement which arose between the four States, in May 1979, were to be prejudicial to Westland, rendering all the guarantees worthless. It matters little whether the

AOI had disappeared or not. Whether faced with either an Egyptian company which makes itself out as the successor of an international organization ["société internationale"] – contrary to what had been stipulated – or a liquidation committee, which remains mute, Westland is justified in bringing the four States themselves before the Arbitrators. Were this not the case, there would be a real denial of justice.

Equity, in common with the principles of international law, allows the corporate veil to be lifted, in order to protect third parties against an abuse which would be to their detriment (International Court of Justice, 5 February 1970, *Barcelona Traction*).

For all these reasons, which complement one another, the Tribunal considers that it cannot hold itself incompetent.

Notes

- Does the 1984 *Westland Helicopters* award follow the reasoning of Lord Templeman in the *International Tin Council* case? How about the Gibson opinion at the Court of Appeal regarding the assumption of responsibility in the constitutive instrument? So is the *Westland Helicopters* award in step with the House of Lords in the *International Tin Council* case, or out of step with it?
- The arbitral tribunal addresses the legal personality theory of responsibility. What is that argument, and how does the tribunal deal with that argument? Why is personality not determinative? Is personality determinative in domestic law?
- And what do we make of the equity argument? Does equity apply under international law? Is it possible that *Westland Helicopters* relied on the states? Under equity, reliance can be used as a substitute for acceptance, provided other conditions are met. Does this case comply with our usual understanding of equitable reliance? How does a reliance argument relate to the judgment in the *International Tin Council* case? Surely it calls for the same outcome there?
- How different is this case from the concept of "piercing the corporate veil"? That principle is based on equity too.
- The second arbitral award in the *Westland Helicopters* case was issued in July 1991, and the tribunal based its award on "the trust of third parties contracting with the organization as to its ability to cope with its commitments because of the constant support of the member States."[63] Is this reasoning different from that in the 1984 award discussed above? How does it differ, if it does? Or does this reasoning give us more insight into why the tribunal ruled as it did in 1984?

---

63 Westland Helicopters Ltd and Arab Organization for Industrialization, et al., ICC Case No. 3879/AS, Award, para. 56 (International Chamber of Commerce, Court of Arbitration, Arbitral Tribunal, 21 July 1991).

- Is the number of states party to the AOI relevant? Could we apply the same reasoning in this case to a similar case against a larger organization such as the EU or UN? If the size of the AOI is significant, then what is the legal rule to distinguish those types of cases from those involving the EU or UN? Consider that the Treaty establishing the European Economic Community states in article 300(7) that "Agreements concluded under the conditions set out in this Article shall be binding on the institutions of the Community and on Member States." But the Court of Justice of the EU later determined that this provision only applied to obligations towards other Member States of the EU, not non-member states.[64]

---

64 *See* Case C-327/91, French Republic v. Commission of the European Communities, Judgment, para. 25 (Court of Justice of the European Communities [Union], 9 August 1994).

CHAPTER 10
Conclusion

The structure of this book is naturally organized around thematic chapters. These chapters each approached the study of international organizations from a different angle, but, as students have seen, the chapters all touched on recurring and overlapping issues by necessity.

Following the introductory Chapter 1 with its overview of the topic in international law, the definition, and this textbook, the discussion began with the law of treaties. In Chapter 2, we considered whether the law of treaties had been modified in its application to international organizations. There were three types of treaties at issue. The first type of treaties were those where international organizations were the parties. These treaties could be adopted between two or more international organizations, or between a state or states and international organizations. For these treaties, the rules seemed relatively stable, though we did have to give attention to whether an organization had the capacity to enter into a treaty. This question of capacity in turn involved an analysis of organization's powers. Where an organization has those powers, either expressly or by implication, then it could enter into the treaty, largely following the normal framework of the law of treaties.

The second type was treaties between states, but adopted within the context of an international organization. Under this type, the treaty might enter into force without the traditional signature and ratification, or accession. Instead, where the organization was empowered to do so, consent to the treaty could be derived from acts of the international organization. Here as well, we had to complete a powers analysis, but also a legal effects analysis, to determine whether the organization had both the capacity and ability to produce an act that had the legal effect of substituting for state consent.

The third type of treaties is those that create international organizations. For this type, the usual rules on treaty reservations, invalidity, and interpretation seemed to take on a different character. For reservations, we had to consider whether the organization consented to the reservations, which implicated questions about which competent organ within the organization could make that decision. Invalidity was problematic because the constitutive instrument had created a new international legal person with independence from its member states, so questions of invalidity might be applied as questions of treaty interpretation instead. When we considered treaty interpretation, we found that the particular nature of the underlying treaty being a constitutive instrument seems to shift the balance toward object and purpose when we attempt to interpret the treaty's meaning, although it was challenging to reconcile the text-context-object and purpose interpretation methodology with the express-implied-inherent approach.

Chapter 3 then turned to issues of creation and dissolution. The first difficulty of creation was identifying a consistent definition of international organizations, which was problematic for many of the reasons discussed in Chapter 1. If international legal personality is a part of the definition, rather than being a consequence of the creation, then we have difficulties identifying whether an organization has personality or not. The approach to that question in the *Reparations* case was almost identical to powers analysis, looking for express, implied, or inherent personality. Creation of an organization also required a treaty, so we were reminded of the need to apply the law of treaties to check whether the underlying agreement had created an organization. We also required an organization to have certain objectives, which is not only relevant for its nature as an organization, but also for an analysis of powers, and potentially immunities. One of the more challenging issues with creation is structuring a relationship of meaningful independence between the states and the organization. This issue, in turn, had implications for how we conceived of the organization's responsibility.

Dissolution raised another set of questions. One issue is the power of states to terminate a legal person, yet our analysis of treaty invalidity suggested that having personality, and a degree of meaningful independence, appeared to insulate an organization from the whims of the states. This outcome suggests that the law of treaties continues to apply in normal application, at least in terms of treaty termination, which might contrast with the less strict application of treaty invalidity and treaty interpretation. It also poses the problem of succession to rights and obligations. While we mostly focused on succession to rights, a dissolved organization might be abandoning its international responsibility. This problem would then appear again with the question of whether states should be ultimately responsible when organizations violate international law, although, of course, that would then possibly conflict with the organization's independence.

Because of this on-going issue of the relationship between the member states and the organization, Chapter 4 dealt with issues of membership. First, we saw that the law of treaties on adherence, while still being applied within a liberal interpretation of the Vienna Convention, imposed far higher standards for adhering to a constitutive instrument, i.e. membership in an international organization, than it might for other treaties. Just as organizations could have objective or relative personality in relation to states, it seemed that states might also have relative personality in relation to organizations, largely depending on the terms of the constitutive instrument. This situation, of course, creates the challenge of identifying through which perspective different questions of membership are viewed. In addition, other substantive requirements also had a fairly relative nature when assessment of qualifications was delegated to the member states to determine whether a potential member was peace-loving, oil exporting, or located in Europe. We discovered a similar relativity when it came to state succession to membership. While decisions on membership had to follow certain procedures, which required a law of treaties analysis to discover, we found that it is possible that states are not completely protected from international responsibility when they act on membership applications. Selecting representatives also required a law of treaties analysis, but additionally had to take note of the independence or dependence of the organization on the member states. Termination of membership raises the curious problem of a state being expelled from its membership, and also adherence to the constitutive instrument, by vote of its peers, rather than through the normal mechanism of state consent.

Since many of the chapters had already touched on the question of the international organization's powers, it was then critical to turn to that topic in Chapter 5. We found that the analysis of powers was primarily a question of the law of treaties, although the actual application of the law of treaties appears to be heavily influenced by not only the object and purpose consideration – perhaps operationalized as the express-implied analysis – but also the organization's personality and independence, i.e. using inherent powers theory and subsequent practice of the organization as interpretive aids. These powers were then held in tension with the member states, so that the exercise of certain competences always existed with some overlap. This situation then, in turn, raised the issue of the independence of the organization, with responsibility, and accountability to the member states. Someone must decide whether the organization acts within its powers (*intra vires*) or outside of its powers (*ultra vires*). Assessing this question forced us to consider whether the member states or the organization itself made that decision, and if the decision was negative, whether that decision-maker had the powers to invalidate *ultra vires* acts. This is, of course, partly a matter of treaty interpretation, but also raises quasi-constitutional issues, questions of the proper allocation of competences among the organs of the organization, and the responsibility of the organization should it act beyond its powers.

Following an analysis of the powers of an organization, it is only natural to then look at the effects of the organization's acts in Chapter 6. Again, the legal effect was to a large degree a question of treaty interpretation. But it is not entirely clear that the acts of an organization can be assimilated to treaties, so while we use the law of treaties to determine whether an act has legal effect, the contents of that act could only be interpreted under the law of treaties by analogy. This situation means that the intention of the organ, or organization, and thus its independence, potentially becomes part of the analysis. Recall, for example, efforts to interpret UN Security Council resolutions or judgments of the International Court of Justice. In addition, where acts are non-binding, we still found some residual obligations of the states to the organization. These obligations largely came from the law of treaties, in the sense that states must participate in their international obligations in good faith. Imparting legal effect to an act also has issues of international responsibility, because while the internal validity of an act was largely a quasi-constitutional question, the external effects of an act could violate international law.

The textbook had already referred to the organs of an organization in several instances, and Chapter 7 dealt with them directly. There were two themes. The first theme was the "family" structure of the organization, both hierarchical and in terms of assigning various competences and oversight. The second theme was the function of the organization. While an individual organ might have certain competences, it might be structured to function as either a political, administrative, or judicial body.

In the end, we found that, depending on how the organization was structured and the particular character assigned to those organs, all of which was discovered using the law of treaties, those conclusions would inform our understanding of the powers of the individual organs. In turn, we could apply a powers analysis to the acts of individual organs to determine whether they had acted *ultra vires* within the organization. Of course, whether an organ had acted *ultra vires* was a very different question from whether the organization as a whole had acted *ultra vires*, again distinguishing between the organization's internal and external natures, and thus its relationship with its members.

Chapter 8 dealt with privileges and immunities. The first issue in this chapter was the general analytical framework for determining the scope of immunities, which is based on functional necessity. Once again, this analysis applies the same test of necessity that we apply in powers analysis, i.e. whether a power was implied because it is necessary for the purposes of the organization. Also, the purposes of the organization is one of the fundamental elements for creating an international organization. The particular necessity that underpins immunity is the question of the necessity for independence, raising again the matter of an organization's meaningful independence, and its relationship with its member states. We saw how the rules on immunity were held in tension with obligations of accountability and the need to respect international law, and thus issues of responsibility. It was one of the few chapters where we discussed the activities of international civil servants, although their status appeared again when we considered violations of their employment rights in relation to an organization's personality and responsibility.

Chapter 9, the final substantive chapter, examined the topic of responsibility, which had already appeared numerous times. This chapter dealt with two major issues, among others. The first issue was identifying which rules of international law applied to international organizations. This question touches upon not only an organization's personality, but also its ability to adhere to international agreements under the terms of its constitutive instrument, and thus in turn implicates the law of treaties. The second issue was distinguishing between the acts of the organization itself and the acts of the member states, acting by, through, or on behalf of the organization. Of course, this was a question of the law of treaties, but very few constitutive instruments were very clear about how responsibility was meant to be assessed. Instead, much of our analysis examined the nature of organizations being a distinct person with meaningful independence. Where that act was a result of the organization's independence, then the organization, as a legal person capable of bearing obligations, should bear responsibility. Whether an act fell within an organization's independence could be largely a matter of the powers of the organization and then the legal effects of its acts.

In sum, we see throughout this study that the various issues within the law of international organizations are all layered and connected in a complex web. We do, however, see some common themes arising: issues of a legal person, but with limited competences; strict interpretation with necessary implication; a creation of international law, yet creating new international law; constitutive instruments as both treaties and quasi-constitutions; and the tension between independence and accountability.

CONCLUSION

This textbook ends with a return to the question posed at the outset. Can we study international organizations as a coherent topic? Of course, anything can be studied, so the real question is: does the practice of international organizations make sense, or is it just a collection of wildly diverging situations? And does the study of that practice, as such, contribute to making a student of international law a better student of international law? The view of this author is probably clear, but students are welcome to form their own views on this question. You may want to compare the study of international organizations to your own study of contract law or criminal law. In what ways where those studies the same or different? And what significance would any similarities or differences have? Perhaps a better comparison would be your course on international law, or perhaps a comparative law course. Are those more accurate comparisons? Reflecting on the knowledge and analytical skills you developed through the use of this textbook may help you identify the value, if any, of this study.

While all international organizations have differences in their objectives, staffing, and constitutive instruments, they all have common challenges, whether they are exercising their independence under the oversight of the member states or interpreting their constitutive instruments to identify the scope of their competences. Organizations are, therefore, both incoherent and coherent at the same time, and it is this author's hope to have introduced students to this nuance by studying the knowledge and analysis common to organizations, yet acknowledging their diversity.

Index

accountability 56, 268, 280, 331, 442
adherence instruments 11
adherence to treaties 17–19
adjudicative jurisdiction 308, 338
Administrative Tribunal *see* United Nations Administrative Tribunal
admission to membership 19
advisory opinions 232, 255–258
affiliated entities 232
African Union 89, 128
Ago, Roberto 370
aid provision 420
Amerasinge, C.F. 2–3
Amsterdam Treaty (EU) 39
Arab Organization for Industrialization (AOI) 431–438
archives 338
Armed Forces of the DR Congo (FARDC) 420
Assembly of States Parties (ASP) 41
associate membership 79
asylum claims 376
attribution of internationally wrongful acts 377–419
Austria 20, 53, 180–184
authorizations 231

balance of powers with member states 176–184
bank accounts 51
Bank for International Settlements (BIS) 55
Belarus 76–79, 89, 124
Belgium 55, 110, 127
bilateral relations 66, 180–184
binding effects 202, 208–239
binding obligations 373–377, 400
binding treaties 14–15
Blokker, Niels 2
Bosnia and Herzegovina 109–111
Brexit 128

Carnegie Foundation 281
categories of membership 79, 121
China 89, 124
civil servants 56–63, 148, 382
civil war 124
Cold War 275
comparative approach, benefits of 7
competences: delegated competences 18; implied powers 165, 170–171; legal effects of acts 202, 229, 441, 442; limited competences 265–268; of organs 17, 264–268, 275; sources of power 131–134; *ultra vires* exercises of power 188
conclusion of treaties 18
Conference of States Parties (CSP) 41
Conference of the New Emerging Forces (CONEFO) 129
Conferences of Parties (COP) 41
consensus agreements 64, 79
constitutive instruments: dissolution of international organizations 68; establishment of organs 264–265; grants of personality 39; interpretation of treaties 29–33; law of treaties 12–13, 17–18, 21, 48, 442; legal value of acts 208, 211; and organs 255; powers of international organizations 136–141, 166, 239; qualification for membership 80; responsibility 430, 442; sources of power 147; suspension of membership 128; as treaties 48, 442; violation constituting withdrawal/expulsion 129–130
contracts, power to enter 147
control, operational versus ultimate 390, 399, 407
cooperation, international 141, 195, 322, 411, 420
Council of Europe 166, 268

Court of Appeal, Paris 51
Court of Appeal, UK 430, 437
Court of First Instance, Brussels 400
Court of Justice of the EU *see* EU Court of Justice (ECJ or CJEU)
creation of international organizations 34–68, 440
credentials for membership 124–127
crimes against humanity 231
criteria for membership 80–127
currency movement 338
customary international law 253, 373, 374
Czechoslovakia, former 127

de facto arrangements 54, 229, 382, 390, 411–412
decolonization 108
defense counsel for persons accused of international crimes 362
definitions of international organizations 2–6
delegated competences 18
delegation of powers 202, 208
delegation of sovereign functions 320
delegations and representation of states 124–127
Denmark 20n17, 129
depositary 11
diplomatic protection 147–148, 320, 330, 341
dissolution of international organizations 34, 68–75, 440
dissolution of states 109
Doctors Without Borders 55
domestic law: and immunity 344, 346; and legal personality 35, 38–39, 53–54, 437; responsibility 377, 403
dues payments 127–128

East African Community 68
Egypt 244–247
ejusdem generis 31
employment: implied powers 148, 170; labor rights 280, 323, 330, 331; and legal personality 48; meaningful independence 56–66; organs 280; privileges and immunities 331, 340–351; in treaty bodies 41–42; *see also* civil servants
enforcement jurisdiction 308, 309, 338
estoppel 249
EU Court of Justice (ECJ or CJEU): and the AOI 438; *jus cogens* norms 376; law of treaties 30, 31; legal personality 48; organs 268, 269, 276; powers of international organizations 136–141, 159–162, 163–165, 176–180, 184, 188; powers of review 276
European Charter of Human Rights 166
European Coal and Steel Community 39, 208
European Commission 276, 374
European Communities 18, 39–40, 89, 374; *see also* European Union (EU)
European Community 18, 162, 402, 407; *see also* European Union (EU)
European Convention on Human Rights (EHCR) 400
European Court of Human Rights 21, 323–330, 383–390, 401–407, 430
European Investment Bank (EIB) 346–351
European Parliament 188, 276
European Patent Office (EPO) 64–66, 421
European Road Transport Agreement (ERTA or AETR) 18
European Space Agency (ESA) 68
European Union (EU): attribution of internationally wrongful acts 382; Brexit 128; law of treaties 18, 19; legal personality 39–40, 162; legal value of acts 208–209; mandatory legal regime 400; membership 89, 127; partial withdrawal 129; powers of international organizations 141; powers of organs 276; quasi-organs 255; as regional organization 53; responsibility 371, 400, 402–411, 438; succession of international organizations 68–69; succession of newly independent states 109; suspension of membership 127–128; treaty interpretation 30; and the WTO 80
European Union Satellite Centre 68–69
Europol 323
experts on mission 351–367, 381
express attribution of powers 136–141
express grants of personality 39–40
expulsion of members 29
extinction of state 127

"family" structure 255–303, 441
FARDC *see* Armed Forces of the DR Congo
Faroe Islands 79
favor rei 31
Federal Republic of Yugoslavia (FR Yugoslavia) 108–124
financing 8–9
findings of fact 229
fiscal privileges 338
Food and Agriculture Organization (FAO), UN 68, 89, 309–311, 315–320

force majeure 420
FYROM (former Yugoslav Republic of Macedonia) 104–108

Gaja, Giorgio 2, 3–4
General Agreement on Tariffs and Trade (GATT) 54, 126
Geneva Conventions 18, 56
Genocide Convention 13, 109, 110, 374
Germany 65, 125–126, 188
Ghana 109
Gibson, Lord 430, 437
Global Alliance for Vaccines and Immunization (GAVI) 56
Global Crop Diversity Trust 40
Global Fund to Fight AIDS 56
Grains Trade Convention 55
Greece 104–108
Greenland 129
Greenpeace 55

Hackworth, Justice 167–170, 286
Hague, The 54, 127
headquarters: agreements 18, 48, 56; in non-member states 53; treaty bodies 41
Holy See 55, 80
Hong Kong 79, 89
House of Lords, UK 390–399, 400, 423–430, 437
human rights 74, 165–166, 323–330, 383–390, 402–403, 407
Human Rights Committee 64, 421–422

immunities 18, 148, 308–368, 378, 381, 442
implied personality 39
implied powers 141–171
India 19, 89
Indonesia 129
inherent powers 171–176
institutional balance 268–276
Inter-Governmental Maritime Consultative Organization 19, 192–194; *see also* International Maritime Organization (IMO)
intergovernmental organizations 4–5
International Air Transport Agency (IATA) 56
International Atomic Energy Agency (IAEA) 55
International Chamber of Commerce 431
International Civil Aviation Organization (ICAO) 226–227
International Committee of the Red Cross (ICRC) 55–56

International Court of Justice (ICJ): advisory opinions 255–264; attribution of internationally wrongful acts 381, 382; balance of powers with member states 184; creation of international organizations 47–48, 52–53, 56–57; dissolution of international organizations 69; experts on mission 352–361; implied powers 141–148, 159, 163, 167–171; independent organs 281; judicial review 277–280; law of treaties 12, 30; legal effects of acts 202, 208, 234–239, 250; membership of international organizations 104, 110, 111, 118; non-binding effects 240–244; and organs 269, 280; reservations to treaties 374; *ultra vires* exercises of power 192–193, 286; and the UN General Assembly 231, 232–233; and the UN Security Council 212–227
International Covenant on Civil and Political Rights (ICCPR) 421
International Criminal Court (ICC) 18, 19, 41, 56, 80–89, 100–103, 188, 210, 229–230, 376
International Criminal Tribunal for Rwanda (ICTR) 362–367
International Criminal Tribunal for the former Yugoslavia (ICTY) 56, 172–175, 280, 281, 302, 303, 412–419
International Fund for Agricultural Development (IFAD) 42–47
International Institute of Agriculture 68
International Labour Organization Administrative Tribunal (ILOAT) 41–47, 48, 330
International Labour Organization (ILO): creation of 54; International Labour Conference 16, 125–126; law of treaties 16; sources of power 131–133; succession of international organizations 89
International Law Commission (ILC) 2, 369–370, 375, 411
international legal personality: attribution of internationally wrongful acts 379; constitutive instruments 21; and the creation of international organizations 34–54, 67–68, 440; and the definition of international organizations 5; domestic law 35, 38–39, 53–54, 437; and employment 48; implied powers 147, 162; membership of international organizations 80; of organs 268; privileges and immunities 322; relative legal personality 48–54; responsibility 370,

437, 442; rights and obligations 34–35, 38–39, 40, 47–48; states 34; succession to membership 111
International Maritime Organization (IMO) 79, 194
International Monetary Fund (IMF) 341n19
International Olympics Committee 56
International Refugee Organization 68
International Telecommunications Union (ITU) 55
International Tin Council (ITC) 423–430
International Wheat Agreement 55
internationally wrongful acts 377–419
Interpol 323
interpretation of treaties 29–33, 131–132, 147, 148, 162
invalidity of treaties 20–29
inviolability 309, 338, 351
Ireland 176–180, 401–402
Israel 89, 221–225

Jessup, Judge 248–249
Joint Vienna Institute 55
judicial organs 281–286, 307
judicial review 276–280, 286–303
jure gestionis 318–319, 333
jure imperii 320
jurisdiction 65, 111, 188, 210, 303, 320, 390, 402; adjudicative jurisdiction 308, 338; enforcement jurisdiction 308, 309, 338; nationality jurisdiction 309; prescriptive jurisdiction 308, 309; territorial jurisdiction 308
jus cogens norms 19, 20, 21–29, 184–187, 375, 376, 421

Klaestad, Judge 240–244
Koštunica, Vojislav 110–111
Kyrgyzstan 19

labor rights 280, 323, 330, 331
Lauterpacht, Judge 184–187, 240–244, 311n2, 313n3, 315n4, 320n5, 332n12, 339n18, 341n20, 344n21, 375, 376, 431n62
law of treaties 10–33, 373, 374, 439–443
law-making powers 14
League of Nations 68, 69, 74–75, 213, 264
legal authority 131, 208–209, 231, 390
legal effects of acts: basis for 195–208; legal value 208–253
legal personality *see* international legal personality

lex specialis 372, 400
lex superior 375
liability 430
liberalism 165
Liberia 194
Libya 124, 231
Liechtenstein 95
life cycles of international organizations 34–75
limited liability 430
living constitutions 141
Lockerbie 225–226, 277

Macau 79
Madagascar 128
Major, John 122
mala fides concerns 66
Malaysia 129
mandate system 74, 213
Marrakesh Agreement 18n13, 126
material breaches of treaties 29
meaningful independence 6, 56–66
membership of international organizations 76–130, 440–441; acceding members 7, 19, 165; admission to membership 19; associate membership 79; categories of membership 79, 121; credentials for membership 124–127; criteria for membership 80–127; expulsion of members 29; original members 76–77; permanent membership 38, 79, 104, 124; qualification for membership 80–127; recommendations for membership 100–104; suspension of membership 127–128; temporary membership 79; termination of membership 128–130; types of membership 76–80; universal membership 53, 89; withdrawal of membership 128
Memoranda of Understanding (MOU) 54
micro-states 95
Milošević, Slobodan 110
mission 264, 351–367, 381
Monaco 95
monist legal systems 53–54
Montenegro 110, 113–118, 119
Most-Favored-Nation status 38

Namibia 69, 89, 213–221, 227–229
nationality jurisdiction 309
NATO *see* North Atlantic Treaty Organization (NATO)
natural persons 34, 38
Nazi Germany 126, 248
ne impediatur legatio 340

Nederlandse Taalunie (Dutch Language Union) 55
needs of the community 38
Netherlands, The 18, 55, 65, 281, 376, 377–379, 403–407
neutral states 20
newly-independent states 108–109
Nicaragua 250–253
non-binding effects 208, 213, 231, 239–263, 441
non-cooperation 129
non-governmental organizations (NGOs) 51, 55–56
non-member states 188, 438
non-refoulment 376
non-state bodies 18, 53, 80–89, 127, 141
Nordic Council 54
North Atlantic Treaty Organization (NATO) 108, 110, 255, 275, 379, 390, 419
nuclear weapons 2, 12–13, 15, 124, 255–258, 259–264
Nuremberg Tribunal 248

objectives of international organizations: attribution of internationally wrongful acts 377–378; creation of international organizations 66–68; law of treaties 21–22; legal personality 34; peace objectives 67, 229, 275; and the powers of organs 275; and their powers 141, 162
O'Brien, Patricia 420n43
observer status 80
Office of the UN High Commissioner for Refugees (UNHCR) 68
one state, one vote 104
operational versus ultimate control 390, 399
opinio juris 253
opt-outs 19
organic persons 34
Organisation internationale de la Francophonie 90
Organization for the Prohibition of Chemical Weapons (OPCW) 211
Organization of American States (OAS) 128, 253, 332–338
Organization of Petroleum Exporting Countries (OPEC) 5, 53, 54, 90
organizational immunity 338
organs: attribution of internationally wrongful acts 379–380; definition of organs 254–255; "family" structure 255–303, 441; function of the organ 303–307, 441; independent organs 281–286; powers of organs 159, 255, 268, 275, 280; principal organs 264–280; quasi-organs 255; responsibility 411; subsidiary organs 280–303
original members 76–77
oversight 29, 41, 56, 285

pacta tertiis 48
Palestine 80–89, 221–225
Palestine Liberation Organization (PLO) 80
Pan American Health Organization (PAHO) 411
Panama 194
peace objectives 67, 229, 275
Peace Palace, The Hague 127, 281
peacekeeping 151–159, 378, 383–400, 420n43
Permanent Court of International Justice (PCIJ) 132–133, 148
permanent members of the UN Security Council 38, 79, 104, 124
Philippines, The 89
piercing the corporate veil 437
plenary organs 68
police powers 323
politics: and membership decisions 95; politically binding versus legally binding actions 220; and the powers of organs 275, 280
powers of international organizations: balance of powers with member states 176–184; coercive versus advisory 38; competence of organs 17, 264–268, 275; express attribution of powers 136–141; implied powers 141–171; inherent limitations on 184; inherent powers 171–176; law-making powers 13; and necessity 163, 165; organs versus whole organization 159; overlapping powers 176–180; power of initiative 100; powers of organs 159, 255, 268, 275, 280; sources of 131–187; treaty adherence 17–19; *ultra vires* exercises of power 22, 121, 131, 159, 187–194, 286, 377, 381–382, 441, 442
powers of review 276, 280
prescriptive jurisdiction 308, 309
primary authority 275
principal organs 264–280
principle of speciality 175
privileges 308–368, 442; *see also* immunities
procedural law 99–108, 175–176
public versus private acts 311

quasi-organs 255

ratione materiae 220, 308, 344
ratione personae 220, 308, 341, 344
ratione temporis 308
recognition of other members 89
recommendations for action 208–209, 220, 229
recommendations for membership 100–104
regional organizations 53, 127
registration of treaties 11
relative legal personality 48–54
representation 124–127
res judicata 118, 121
reservations to treaties 19–20, 374
responsibility 187–188, 369–438, 442
Rhine Commission 5
rights and obligations: categories of membership 79, 80, 121; constitutive instruments 13; dissolution of international organizations 74, 440; legal effects of acts 244–247, 250; and legal personality 34–35, 38–39, 40, 47–48; non-parties 48
Russia 19, 121–123; *see also* USSR
Rwanda 400

Schermers, Henry G. 2–3
Scotland 109
Secretariat of the Arms Control Treaty 41
secretariats 41, 411; *see also* treaty bodies
self-defense 420
self-interpretive functions 29–30
Serbia 110, 113–118, 119
shared competences 18
Socialist Federal Republic of Yugoslavia (SFR Yugoslavia) 109–111
South Africa 69–75, 213, 227–229
sovereign equality 309
special responsibilities 371–372
St. Lucia 126
state consent 15, 17
state representatives 338–340
states: balance of powers with member states 176–184; competences 133–134; legal personality 34; responsibility 370, 421–422
statistics on numbers of international organizations 5
sua sponte actions 232
subjects of international law 54–55
subsequent practice approaches 39
subsidiary organs 255, 280–303, 411
subsidiary responsibility for member states 421–438

succession of international organizations 68–69, 108–124, 440
sui generis 111, 118
Sukarno, President 129
supranational organizations 141, 160
Supreme Court of The Netherlands 53–54
Supreme Court, US 202–208
suspension of membership 127–128
Sweden 147–148
Switzerland 53, 55–56, 80

Taiwan 89, 124
taxation 338, 351
temporary membership 79
termination of membership 128–130; *see also* dissolution of international organizations
territorial jurisdiction 308
tobacco advertising 136–141
treaties: adherence to treaties 17–19; binding treaties 14–15; conclusion of treaties 18; depositary 11; invalidity of treaties 20–29; law of treaties 10–33, 373, 374, 439–443; material breaches of treaties 29; reservations to treaties 19–20, 374; treaty bodies 41, 411; treaty interpretation 29–33, 131–132, 147, 148, 162; treaty negotiations 13, 17; violations of 29
Tuberculosis and Malaria (Global Fund) 56
types of membership 76–80

Ukraine 76–79, 89
ultimate control 390, 399, 407
ultra vires exercises of power 22, 121, 131, 159, 187–194, 286, 377, 381–382, 441, 442
UN General Assembly: advisory opinions 255–264; binding effects 213, 227–234; competences 275; implied powers 148, 170–171; membership of international organizations 100, 103–104, 111, 124; non-binding effects 248; powers of organs 269; subsidiary organs 280, 285–286
UN Secretary-General 56–57, 163, 340–341, 361–362, 370
UN Security Council: binding effects 213–227, 229–231; competences 275; and the ICJ 187, 239; judicial review 303; *jus cogens* norms 375–376; legal effects of acts 212; legal personality 38, 63–64; membership of international organizations 79, 100, 103–104, 109, 111, 122, 124, 129; powers of organs 269; powers of review 280;

responsibility 383–390, 400; subsidiary organs 280
unincorporated entities 38
United Arab Republic 127
United Nations (UN): civil servants 148; creation of international organizations by treaty 54; criteria for membership 80, 89; depositary duties 11; headquarters 53; labor rights 330; legal personality 34–41, 53, 147; membership of international organizations 76–77; MONUC (United Nations Organization Mission in the Democratic Republic of the Congo) 420; objectives of international organizations 67–68; observer status organizations 56; Office of Legal Counsel 76, 77–79, 124; peacekeeping 378; powers of international organizations 134–135; responsibility 370; statehood 39; succession from League of Nations 69–75; succession of newly independent states 109; UNAMIR (United Nations Assistance Mission for Rwanda) 400; UNCCD (United Nations Convention to Combat Desertification) 47; UNEP (United Nations Environment Programme) 54; UNESCO (United Nations Educational, Scientific and Cultural Organization) 89, 135, 248; UNFAO (United Nations Food and Agriculture Organization) 68, 89, 309–311, 315–320; UNFICYP (United Nations Peacekeeping Force in Cyprus) 400; UNIDO (United Nations Industrial Development Organization) 54; United Nations Administrative Tribunal 148, 170, 233–234, 280–281, 285–286, 331; UNMIK (UN Interim Administration Mission in Kosovo) 281; UNOLA (UN Office of Legal Affairs) 18, 420; UNRWA (United Nations Relief and Works Agency for Palestine Refugees in the Near East) 54; and the WHO 264; withdrawal of membership 129; working agreement with ICC 19
universal membership 53, 89
Universal Postal Union (UPU) 55
USA 202–208, 250–253, 268
USSR 19, 76–79, 123, 127, 275

Vatican City State 55
Versailles peace treaty 54
veto rights 79, 104, 275
voting rights 79, 104, 108, 125, 127–128

waiver 368
Warsaw Pact 68
Western European Union 68
World Anti-Doping Agency 56
World Bank 68, 330
World Health Organization (WHO) 5, 244–247, 255, 259–264, 341–344, 373n8, 411
World Intellectual Property Organization (WIPO) 5
World Meteorological Organization (WMO) 5, 41
World Tourism Organization (UNWTO) 5
World Trade Organization (WTO) 18, 19, 40, 54–55, 80, 89, 126, 407–411
wrongful acts 377–421
wrongful dismissal 63

Yeltsin, Boris 121, 123–124
Yugoslavia, former 104–124, 127